GLOBE
BIOLOGY

LEONARD BERNSTEIN

GLOBE BOOK COMPANY
Englewood Cliffs, New Jersey

AUTHOR

LEONARD BERNSTEIN
Manhattan Center High School for Science and Mathematics
New York, New York

CONTRIBUTING WRITERS

Deena Cloud
Science Writer
Brooklyn, New York

Jo Anderson Combs
Science Department Chairperson
J. P. Taravella High School
Coral Springs, Florida

James V. Feliciani
Science Instructor
Land O' Lakes Senior High
    School
Land O' Lakes, Florida

Steven W. Gilbert
Assistant Professor of Biology
Ball State University
Muncie, Indiana

Sandra Gottfried
*Assistant Professor of Biology
    and Education*
University of Missouri, St. Louis
St. Louis, Missouri

Dan R. Kunkle
*Biology Teacher/Science
Department Supervisor*
Freedom High School
Bethlehem, Pennsylvania

Mozell P. Lang
Science Consultant
Michigan Department of
    Education
Instructional Specialist Program
Lansing, Michigan

Renee E. Miller
Teacher   Biology, Chemistry
Williamsport High School
Williamsport, Maryland

Karen Ostlund, Ph.D
Associate Professor
*Department of Curriculum and
    Instruction*
Southwest Texas State University
San Marcos, Texas

Cover Photograph

The moose, *Alces alces*, is the largest member of the deer family and native to North America. The moose shown on the cover is wading in a tundra pool in Alaska. Moose often visit ponds and lakes during the summer months to rid themselves of flies and to feed on water plants. In the past, hunters killed almost all of the moose in the eastern United States. Today, however, moose are protected by law and can be found as far south as Massachusetts.

Photo research by Omni-Photo Communications.

 Globe Book Company
A Division of Simon and Schuster Inc.
Englewood Cliffs, New Jersey   07632

10   9   8
ISBN: 1-55675-716-6

ACKNOWLEDGMENTS

CONTENT CONSULTANTS

George C. Brainard, Ph.D
*Assistant Professor of Neurology
and Pharmacology*
Jefferson Medical College
Thomas Jefferson University
Philadelphia, Pennsylvania

Cheryl L. Mason, Ph.D
Assistant Professor
School of Teacher Education,
Science
San Diego State University
San Diego, California

READING CONSULTANT

Louise Vitellaro Tidd
Reading Specialist, Writer, Editor
Elberon, New Jersey

ESL/LDP CONSULTANT

Joseph M. Holloway
ESL Instructor
Baruch College
New York, New York

CONTENT REVIEWERS

John D. Curnow
Science Department Chairman
Richland Center High School
Richland Center, Wisconsin

Jeane J. Dughi, Ph.D
Science Coordinator
Norfolk Public Schools
Norfolk, Virginia

Julia Kron
*President-elect, North Carolina
Association of Educators
Biology Teacher*
Raleigh, North Carolina

David E. LaHart, Ph.D
Principal Instructor
Florida Solar Energy Center
Cape Canaveral, Florida

Sarah Longino
Biology Teacher
Colonial High School
Orlando, Florida

Markley B. Morrill
Science Curriculum Specialist
Santa Ana Unified School District
Santa Ana, California

LaMoine L. Motz
Coordinator, Science Education
Oakland Schools
Pontiac, Michigan

J. J. Olenchalk
Chairman, Science Department
Antioch Senior High School
Antioch, California

Donna Hill Oliver
Associate Professor of Education
1987 National Teacher of the Year
Elon College
Elon College, North Carolina

Carl M. Raab
*Assistant Principal
Supervisor, Biology and General
Science*
Fort Hamilton High School
Brooklyn, New York

Leone Castles Rochelle
Life Science Teacher
Spring Valley High School
Columbia, South Carolina

Hal Robertson
Science Advisor
Los Angeles Unified School
District
Los Angeles, California

CONTENTS

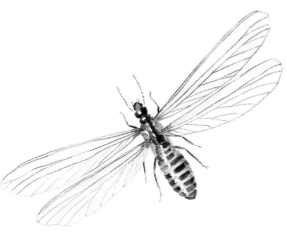
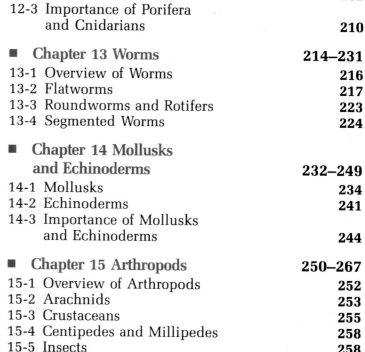

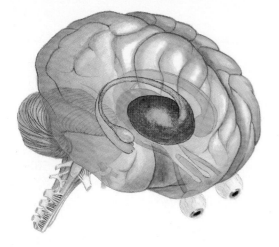

Unit 7
Human Health
454–503

Unit 8
Heredity and Genetics
504–547

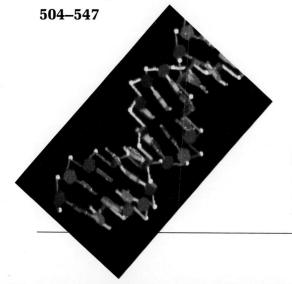

Activities

AIDS virus

Flu virus

Biology, Technology, and Society

Biology and You: Leisure Activity

Biology and You: Consumer Biology

Careers in Biology

Take Charge of Your Studies with Globe Biology

Understand by Previewing

Preview each unit to understand what you will be reading about.
Read the list of chapters that make up each unit.

UNIT 5

Vertebrates

CONTENTS
16 Fishes
17 Amphibians and Reptiles
18 Birds
19 Mammals

Look at the organisms in the drawings and photographs. All of these organisms have vertebrae, or a group of bones that form a backbone. Animals with backbones are called vertebrates. The organisms shown are examples of vertebrates. Vertebrates also have a skeleton inside their bodies.

Most of the organisms that you call animals probably are vertebrates. Yet, vertebrates make up only three percent of the Animal kingdom.

Read the titles of the chapters. The titles are the names of the five main groups of vertebrates. Now look at the photographs and drawings. Match each picture with its chapter. What other animals do you think are classified in each group?

269

268 Vertebrates

Learn Biology and Improve Your Skills!

Look at the illustrations and read the unit introduction.
Do the activity or answer the questions that introduce each unit.

Read the chapter introduction to find out about the chapter contents.

(1) Each chapter is outlined. Use the **Chapter Outline** as a study guide.

(2) The **Objectives** help you understand what you will learn in the chapter.

(3) You will learn two important **Science Process Skills** in each chapter. Look for the symbols to tell you when to practice each skill.

Chapter **13** | Worms

(1)

Chapter Outline

I. Overview of Worms

II. Flatworms
  A. Tapeworms
  B. Flukes
  C. Turbellarians

III. Roundworms and Rotifers
  A. Roundworms
  B. Rotifers

IV. Segmented Worms
  A. Earthworms
  B. Leeches

214

(2)

Objectives

After you have completed this chapter, you will be able to

13-1 **discuss** the general characteristics of worms.
13-1 **name** the four phyla of worms.
13-2 **describe** the characteristics of flatworms.
13-3 **describe** the characteristics of roundworms and rotifers.
13-3 **list** three roundworms that cause disease in people.
13-4 **describe** the characteristics of segmented worms.

Science Process Skills **(3)**

In this chapter, two science skills are highlighted. Symbols show some places where these skills are used.

▶ **Inferring:** When you infer, you form a conclusion based upon facts and not direct observation.

▲ **Organizing:** When you organize information, you put the information in some kind of order.

To many people, a worm is something that is long and soft, wiggles, and lives in the soil. These characteristics describe some worms. However, not all worms are the same. For example, not all worms live in the soil. Some kinds of worms live inside other living things. Other worms live in fresh or salt water.

One group of worms that live in the ocean are the feather-duster worms. Divers sometimes mistake feather-duster worms for underwater flowers. Feather-duster worms live in tubes that they make out of sand. These worms have beautiful feathery structures that extend from the tubes. The feathery structures are used to gather food. Sometimes feather-duster worms pull their feathery structures into their tubes to avoid predators.

Worms **215**

Read the Headings

The headings of each chapter follow the chapter outline.

Topic sentences are used in each paragraph. They tell you the main idea in each paragraph. Use the topic sentences to help you study.

13-2 Flatworms

Have you ever thought of a worm as flat? Flatworms make up the phylum *Platyhelminthes* (plat-ee-HEL-minths). Biologists consider flatworms the least complex worms. Why? Flatworms do not have a space between their three cell layers. That is, they do not have a body cavity. More complex animals have a body cavity.

Because of its flat shape, all of a flatworm's cells are close to its environment. For this reason, flatworms do not need a respiratory or circulatory system. Oxygen and carbon dioxide diffuse directly into and out of its cells.

Flatworms are classified into three groups. Two groups are made up of parasitic worms. In one group, the flatworms are free-living. They move from place to place in search of food.

Tapeworms

Tapeworms are parasitic flatworms. You can observe the structure of a tapeworm in Figure 13-2. Notice that a tapeworm has a flat, ribbonlike body. A tapeworm does not have a digestive system or a mouth. It absorbs nutrients from its host directly through its skin.

The knob-shaped head of the tapeworm's body is called the **scolex.** Suckers and hooks are on the scolex. Behind the scolex are body sections called **proglottids** (proh-GLAHT-ids). Each proglottid has nerves and flame

(4)
Key Points

• Flatworms are the least complex group of worms. They have thin, flat bodies and no body cavity.

• Tapeworms, flukes, and turbellarians are three kinds of flatworms.

(5) ○

Study Hint

After you read Section 13-2, make a chart listing the three kinds of flatworms and the characteristics of each group.

(4) **Key Points** remind you of the important ideas in each section.

(5) Could you use a reminder on how to study a section or get more information? Use the **Study Hints.**

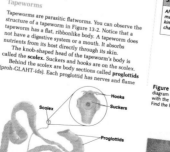

Figure 13-2 Compare the diagram of the scolex (left) with the photograph (right). Find the hooks and suckers.

Hooks
Suckers
Scolex
Proglottids

Worms 217

xiii

Check Your Understanding as You Develop Your Skills

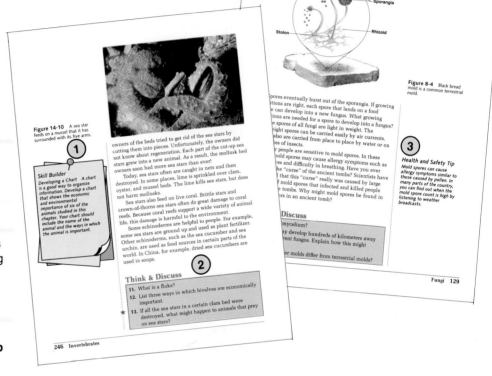

(1) Skill Builders can help you develop skills that lead to success.

(2) Complete **Think & Discuss** to check your understanding of each section. Challenge yourself with the starred question.

(3) Be Safe! Be Healthy! Read each **Health and Safety Tip** to find out how.

Figure 14-10 A sea star feeds on a mussel that it has surrounded with its five arms.

Skill Builder
Developing a Chart   A chart is a good way to organize information. Develop a chart that shows the economic and environmental importance of six of the animals studied in this chapter. Your chart should include the name of the animal and the ways in which the animal is important.

owners of the beds tried to get rid of the sea stars by cutting them into pieces. Unfortunately, the owners did not know about regeneration. Each part of the cut-up sea stars grew into a new animal. As a result, the mollusk bed owners soon had more sea stars than ever!

Today, sea stars often are caught in nets and then destroyed. In some places, lime is sprinkled over clam, oyster, and mussel beds. The lime kills sea stars, but does not harm mollusks.

Sea stars also feed on live coral. Brittle stars and crown-of-thorns sea stars often do great damage to coral reefs. Because coral reefs support a wide variety of animal life, this damage is harmful to the environment.

Some echinoderms are helpful to people. For example, some sea stars are ground up and used as plant fertilizer. Other echinoderms, such as the sea cucumber and sea urchin, are used as food sources in certain parts of the world. In China, for example, dried sea cucumbers are used in soups.

Think & Discuss
11. What is a fluke?
12. List three ways in which bivalves are economically important.
★ 13. If all the sea stars in a certain clam bed were destroyed, what might happen to animals that prey on sea stars?

246   Invertebrates

Figure 8-4 Black bread mold is a common terrestrial mold.

Spores   Sporangia   Stolon   Rhizoid

spores eventually burst out of the sporangia. If growing conditions are right, each spore that lands on a food ... can develop into a new fungus. What growing ... ions are needed for a spore to develop into a fungus? ... e spores of all fungi are light in weight. The ... ight spores can be carried easily by air currents. ... also are carried from place to place by water or on ... es of insects.

... y people are sensitive to mold spores. In these ... old spores may cause allergy symptoms such as ... es and difficulty in breathing. Have you ever ... he "curse" of the ancient tombs? Scientists have ... that this "curse" really was caused by large ... mold spores that infected and killed people ... tombs. Why might mold spores be found in ... rs in an ancient tomb?

Discuss
... mycelium?
... ay develop hundreds of kilometers away ... rent fungus. Explain how this might
... er molds differ from terrestrial molds?

Health and Safety Tip
Mold spores can cause allergy symptoms similar to those caused by pollen. In many parts of the country, you can find out when the mold spore count is high by listening to weather broadcasts.

Fungi   129

Chapter Review
Need a quick review of the chapter? Read the **Chapter Summary** and review the **Vocabulary List.** Check your understanding by answering the questions.

Chapter Review

CHAPTER SUMMARY

5-1 Classification of Living Things
- The large number and wide variety of organisms requires a classification system.
- Taxonomy is the science of classifying living things.

5-2 Modern Taxonomy
- Scientists classify organisms according to evolutionary history, physical similarities, blood proteins, evolutionary history, chromosome structure, and embryology.
- Binomial nomenclature is a system of naming organisms with a two-part scientific name, consisting of a genus name and a species name.

- The seven basic levels of modern classification are (from general to specific): kingdom, phylum or division, class, order, family, genus, and species.

5-3 Five Kingdoms
- The five kingdoms are the Kingdoms Monera, Protista, Fungi, Plantae, and Animalia.
- An autotroph is an organism that makes its own food. All plants and some monerans and protists are autotrophs.
- A heterotroph is an organism that obtains its food from the outside. All animals and fungi are heterotrophs.

VOCABULARY LIST

autotrophs (83)	division (82)	heterotrophs (83)	phylum (82)
binomial nomenclature (80)	family (82)	kingdom (82)	protists (83)
class (82)	fungi (84)	monerans (83)	species (77)
classify (75)	genus (80)	order (82)	taxonomy (76)

VOCABULARY REVIEW

Matching Write the word or term from the Vocabulary List that best matches each description.
1. classification group between phylum and order
2. bacteria
3. organism that makes its own food
4. plant classification group that is equal to phylum
5. to group similar things together
6. smallest of the seven classification groups used by biologists
7. mushrooms
8. group of related species
9. science of classifying living things
10. system used to name living things

Identifying Relationships Identify the word or term in each group that does not belong. Explain why it does not belong with the group.
1. division, phylum, species
2. evolution, Darwin, heterotroph
3. family, virus, order
4. fossils, embryology, remains
5. heterotroph, autotroph, animal
6. Fungi, kingdom, dog
7. chlorophyll, classification, taxonomy
8. multicellular, monerans, single-celled
9. algae, protists, mushrooms
10. binomial nomenclature, autotroph, chlorophyll
11. plants, division, animals
12. protists, bacteria, monerans

86   The Study of Life

CONTENT REVIEW

Completion Write the word or words that best complete each sentence.
1. An organism that cannot make its own food is a _____.
2. In botany, the term _____ is used instead of phylum.
3. Today, most scientists accept the theory that organisms _____ over time.
4. There are _____ major groups in the present-day classification system.
5. Related genera are grouped together in a _____.
6. Aristotle's classification system had _____ major groups.
7. Human beings are members of the class _____.
8. Related phyla are grouped into _____.
9. Binomial nomenclature was developed by _____.

Finding the Main Ideas Use the section number to find the sentence that answers each question. Then, write the sentence.
1. Why are organisms classified? (5-1)
2. What is a taxonomist? (5-1)
3. Why was the work of Linnaeus important to biologists? (5-1)
4. How did Darwin's ideas change taxonomy? (5-2)
5. In addition to appearance, what else is used to classify an organism? (5-2)
6. How are organisms named in the binomial nomenclature system? (5-2)
7. What is the relationship between a family and an order? (5-2)
8. How did the invention of the electron microscope increase the number of kingdoms? (5-3)
9. What is a heterotroph? (5-3)

CONCEPT REVIEW

Writing for Understanding One way to find out if you understand something is to write a brief summary of the information in your own words. Reread Section 5-2, Modern Taxonomy, on pages 79–82, and write a brief summary of the information.

Critical Thinking Answer each of the following in complete sentences.
1. Food is classified in a grocery store. Mail is sorted and classified at the post office. Name two other classification systems used in daily life.
2. How is the system of binomial nomenclature similar to the system for listing names used in a telephone book?
3. If you were to discover a new species, how would you determine its classification?
4. Why is taxonomy an ongoing science?
5. Why is the use of scientific names important for communication among scientists?

EXTENSIONS

1. Use library references to write a brief report describing the contributions of Ernst Haeckel or Robert Whittaker to the science of classification.
△ 2. Research the classifications of five organisms. Make a table listing the classification of each organism at each of the seven main levels.
3. Use library references to find out more about Charles Darwin. Write a description of Darwin's trip on the HMS Beagle.
4. Collect photographs or drawings of organisms from each of the five kingdoms. Use the pictures to make a poster. Label each picture on your poster with its correct kingdom.

Classification   87

Biology in Action!

Do the Activities and read the features to find out how biology is part of everyday life.

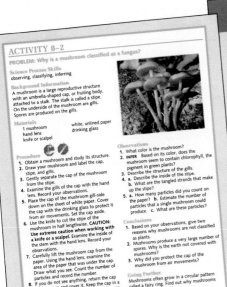

Biology, Technology, and Society Read how biology and technology impact your life.

Learn By Doing Activities! Many **Activities** can be done at home.

Interested in a Career in Biology? Each **Careers in Biology** introduces you to three careers.

Biology and You Discover a new hobby! Read each **Biology and You: Leisure Activity.** Develop everyday skills! Read each **Biology and You: Consumer Biology.**

Have you ever used a magnifying glass to observe something? If so, you have used a simple microscope. You are about to begin a study of life. Microscopes are just one of the many tools that help scientists study living things. Look at the drawings and photographs shown on these two pages. What scientific instruments do you see? What are the instruments being used to study?

In this unit, you will learn about the characteristics of living things and how living things are grouped together. You also will learn how scientists approach problems. Read the title of each chapter in this unit. How do you think each picture is related to the chapters in this unit?

UNIT 1

The Study of Life

CONTENTS

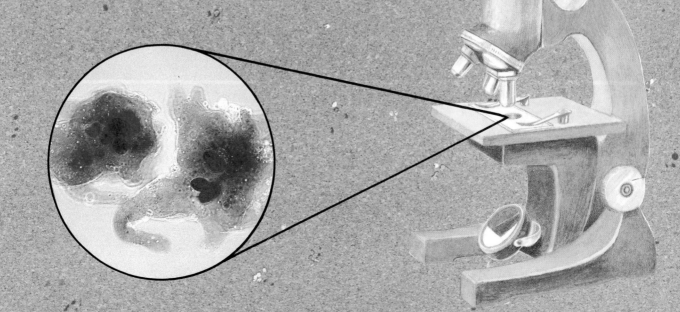

You can use the Chapter Outline as a study guide.

Before you begin each chapter, read the Objectives and review the Vocabulary List at the end of the chapter.

Objectives

After you have completed this chapter, you will be able to

1-1 **list** several branches of biology.

1-1 **identify** three fields that use biotechnology.

1-2 **describe** scientific method.

1-3 **identify** SI units of length, volume, and mass.

1-3 **distinguish** between the Celsius and Kelvin temperature scales.

1-4 **identify** four kinds of microscopes used in biology.

1-4 **recognize** the importance of the computer to scientific research.

Science Process Skills

In this chapter, you will learn about science process skills and how to use them in your study of biology. The science process skills you will use are listed and explained on pages 10–11. You already may be familiar with some of these skills. Throughout this book, symbols will show you places where the skills are used.

What is science? Science is a way of studying the natural world. Scientists are people who are curious about nature. Do you think the diver in the photograph is a scientist? In fact, she is a marine biologist. Marine biologists are scientists who study living things in the oceans. This marine biologist is studying the fishes that live around a coral reef.

Some scientists use the knowledge that they acquire to predict, or state in advance, how and why events will occur. Meteorologists, for example, make predictions about the weather based on their observations of temperature and rainfall. Predicting is just one of the skills that scientists use to solve problems.

Key Points

- Biology is the science that deals with the study of living things.
- Botany, zoology, and ecology are branches of biology.
- Medicine, agriculture, and industry are fields that use biotechnology.

Study Hint

The suffix "-ist" means one who practices in a certain field.

1-1 What is Biology?

The area of science that studies the natural world is called natural science. **Biology** (by-OL-uh-jee) is a natural science. Biology is the science that deals with the study of living things.

Biology and other fields make up the natural sciences. Chemistry is the study of matter and the changes that matter undergoes. Physics is the study of the structure of matter and the forces in the world. Astronomy is the study of stars, planets, and other bodies in space. Geology is the study of the structure and forces of the earth.

As more is learned about the natural world, new fields of science develop. For example, biochemistry combines biology and chemistry to study the matter that makes up living things. Astrophysics uses astronomy and physics to study the chemical and physical makeup of stars and planets. What do you think a biophysicist studies?

Branches of Biology

Earth is home to billions of living things. All of these living things are studied by biologists. One person cannot possibly learn all of biology. For this reason, the field of biology is broken down into many smaller branches.

Two branches of biology are **botany** (BAHT-n-ee) and **zoology** (zoh-AHL-uh-jee). Botany is the study of plants. Zoology is the study of animals. Table 1-1 lists some other branches of biology.

Table 1-1 Branches of Biology		
BRANCH OF BIOLOGY	WHAT IS STUDIED	CAREERS
Anatomy (un-NAT-uh-mee)	Structures that make up living things	Physician, chiropractor
Genetics (juh-NET-iks)	Heredity of living things	Geneticist, plant breeder
Microbiology (my-kroh-by-OL-uh-jee)	Microscopic living things	Microbiologist, bacteriologist, pathologist
Physiology (fiz-ee-OL-uh-jee)	Functions of the structures that make up living things	Physiologist, internist
Taxonomy (tak-SAHN-uh-mee)	Classification of living things	Taxonomist

Most biologists study only one branch of biology. This is called specialization (SPESH-uh-liz-ay-shun). Specialization is needed for good scientific research. What fields can you name other than biology in which people specialize?

Specialized branches of biology often overlap. For example, **ecology** (ee-KAHL-uh-jee) cannot be studied without knowing about plants and animals. Ecology is the study of the relationship between living things and their environments. The environment is everything that surrounds a living thing. Look at Table 1-1. What does a microbial ecologist study?

The number of specialized fields in science grows as more knowledge is gained about the natural world. As a result, many scientists may not know about subjects outside their own fields. For this reason, when someone says "Scientists say . . .," it is important to ask about the qualifications of the scientist.

Biology, Technology, and Society

The use of science to solve everyday problems is called **technology** (tek-NAHL-uh-jee). Technology often is called applied science. Science and technology are not always easily separated. In fact, a person can be both a scientist and a technologist.

Like all sciences, biology can be used to solve everyday problems. The use of biology to solve everyday problems is called **biotechnology.** Medicine, agriculture (AG-rih-kul-choor), and industry are some of the fields that use biotechnology.

Skill Builder

Using Word Parts   Science words often are made up of many word parts. The word "biology," for example, is made up of the root word "bios," meaning "life," and the suffix "-logy," meaning "the study of." Use a dictionary to find the meanings of the following terms:

*pathology   zoologist
chemosynthesis ectoderm
photosynthesis ecology*

Figure 1–2 Artificial limbs have been developed through advances in biotechnology.

Study Hint

Read the Biology, Technology, and Society feature on page 19 to learn about other uses of biotechnology.

Medicine

How is biotechnology used in medicine? Machines, such as X-ray machines, are used to help doctors diagnose illnesses. New materials are being used in artificial organs. For example, artificial skin is being used to treat people with burns.

Biotechnology also is used to make drugs and vaccines. A recent breakthrough in medical technology was the development of the hepatitis B vaccine. Hepatitis is a disease of the liver. In what other ways might biotechnology be used in medicine?

Agriculture

Biotechnology is used in agriculture to keep animals and plants in good health, and to develop more productive animals and plants. Animals that are more productive yield more meat or products such as milk and eggs. More productive plants yield bigger and more nutritious crops. For example, biotechnology has been used to create new kinds of very nutritious corn and wheat. Researchers also are working on ways to create "superplants" that will grow larger and resist disease.

Industry

Living things are used in industry to make or improve products used by society. For example, bacteria are used to break down wastes in sewage treatment plants. As these bacteria break down wastes, they make materials used by people. In fact, more than ten percent of the copper refined in the United States is made by bacteria.

Biotechnology also is used to make food. For example, bacteria are used to make yogurt and sauerkraut. Yeasts are used to make fermented beverages and to make bread rise. In what other ways might biotechnology be used in industry?

Think & Discuss

Check your understanding of the section by answering the Think & Discuss questions.

1. Compare biology and biotechnology.
2. Describe three areas of specialization in biology.
3. How might biotechnology be used in the manufacturing of clothing materials?

1-2 Scientific Methods and Skills

Like all sciences, biology is a learning process. Biologists use many skills and methods in the laboratory and in the field. These skills and methods help biologists learn more about the living world.

What do biologists do with the information they gather about the living world? Like all scientists, biologists might use their information to state a **theory.** A theory is a statement of an idea or principle that has been tested by many scientists over a period of time.

Theories can be large and important ideas. For example, the theory of evolution is an important theory which states that living things have changed over time. Theories also can be small and less well known. The important point is that a theory explains something about the natural world. A theory must be supported by research. If the results of research do not support a theory, the theory must be changed or discarded.

Some theories that have passed many tests are called **laws.** For example, no exceptions to the Law of Gravity have ever been found. Although a law is a well-established theory, a law always can be changed if new evidence is found that does not support the law. For example, some scientists have suggested that there is another natural force in addition to the force of gravity. If experiments show that this new force exists, the Law of Gravity may be changed.

Scientific Method

Most scientists solve problems in a logical and orderly way. How do scientists go about solving problems? Scientists have developed a model, or guide, that they use to approach problems. This model is called **scientific method.**

Scientific method can be broken down into seven parts. Keep in mind that you do not always have to use all the parts of scientific method. It also is not necessary to use the parts of scientific method in the order presented. Every problem is unique and needs to be solved in a different way. As you read about each part, compare the description in the first column with the example in the second column.

Study Hint

The Law of Gravity states that the gravitational force between two objects is directly proportional to the product of their masses and inversely proportional to the square of the distance between them.

Identify and State the Problem

The first step in problem-solving is to identify the problem. When scientists approach a problem, they really are trying to find the answer to a question. For this reason, it is helpful to state a problem as a question.

Suppose you read an article about insects. In the article, the writer states that most insects cannot see red light. You wonder if this is true for a common insect such as a ladybug. Your question is, "Can ladybugs see red light?"

Gather Information

Identifying a problem and gathering information work together. Scientists read and gather information to help define their problems. Gathering known information also helps scientists build upon work that already has been done.

Suppose the information you gather states that insects often move toward or away from light. How can you use this information? You may decide to find out if ladybugs move toward or away from red light.

State a Hypothesis

Before scientists can solve a problem and answer a question, they must state clearly what they expect to find out. This statement is a **hypothesis** (hy-PAHTH-uh-sis). A hypothesis is a suggested solution to a problem based upon known information.

What is a good hypothesis for your ladybug problem? Your hypothesis should state exactly what you expect to find out. Your hypothesis might be, "Ladybugs do not move toward or away from red light."

Design an Experiment

An **experiment** is used to test a hypothesis. Scientists plan their experiments by looking at **variables** (VER-ee-uh-buls). A variable is anything that can affect the results of an experiment. A well-designed experiment tests only one variable at a time. Often scientists compare the experimental results with a **control.** The control is the same as the experiment with the exception of the variable being tested.

In your ladybug experiment, you want to find out if ladybugs move toward or away from red light. The variable you are testing is red light. Your experiment will test the reaction of ladybugs to red light. Your controls will test how ladybugs react to white light and to no light. All other conditions remain the same as in the experiment. Only the variable being tested changes in the two controls. The setup for your ladybug experiment is shown in Figure 1-3 on page 9. Find the controls in this experiment.

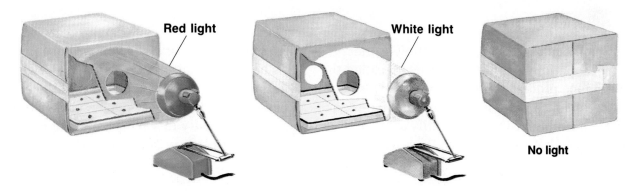

Red light   White light   No light

Figure 1-3

■ Make Observations and Record Data

Scientists keep a record of all the observations they make during an experiment. Observations made during an experiment are called **data** (DAYT-uh). Scientists keep careful records of the data they collect. Often, the data will be in the form of measurements, or numbers.

When you observe, you use your senses to gather information. In your ladybug experiment, you could count the number of ladybugs that moved toward or away from the red and white lights. Then you could compare these two sets of numbers. These numbers are your data.

■ Organize and Analyze Data

The data scientists gather are not very useful until they are organized or put in some kind of order. Scientists often use graphs, charts, tables, and diagrams to organize their data. Once the data are organized, they can be analyzed, or studied, to find out if they support the hypothesis.

In your ladybug experiment, you might decide to organize your data in a diagram that shows the locations of the ladybugs in each setup. You also might list in a table the number of ladybugs that moved in each setup. Then you could study your data to see if the data support your hypothesis.

■ State a Conclusion

After scientists collect, record, organize, and analyze their data, they state a conclusion. A conclusion is a summary that explains the observations and describes how the data relate to the problem. The conclusion also states whether or not the data support the hypothesis. What happens if the data do not support the hypothesis? The scientist must rethink the hypothesis.

Suppose the ladybugs did not move toward or away from the red light. In one control, the ladybugs all moved toward the white light. In the dark control, the ladybugs did not move. What conclusion could you state? You could conclude that ladybugs are attracted to white light, but are not able to see red light. In this case, your data support your hypothesis.

Science Process Skills

Scientists use many skills as they gather information. These skills often are called the science process skills. Throughout this book, two science process skills are highlighted in each chapter. Symbols identify some of the places where you will use these skills.

The science process skills you will use in this book and their symbols are listed in Table 1-2. As you read about each skill, keep in mind that the science process skills are not used only in science. You use many of these skills every day.

Table 1-2 Science Process Skills and Symbols		
👁 Observing	🔺 Organizing	🖻 Hypothesizing
⚗ Measuring	🗀 Classifying	🔺 Modeling
▶ Inferring	❱ Predicting	◤ Analyzing

⚗ Measuring

Process skills symbols identify when a skill is used.

When you measure, you compare an unknown value to a known value. Finding the size of an object, the number of things in a group, or the length of an event all are forms of measurement. Why is measuring important? Measurements make observations more exact.

⚗ Measuring Activity

Work with a partner. Measure the number of times your partner's eyes blink in two minutes. Record the number in your notebook. Switch roles and repeat the activity. Who blinks their eyes more often? What other measurements do you make in your daily life?

▶ Inferring

When you infer, you form a conclusion based upon facts and not direct observation. For example, biologists know that water pollution can kill fish. Suppose untreated sewage was released into a river. A few weeks later, a biologist observes many dead fish in the river. The biologist might infer that the sewage caused the fish to die.

▶ Inferring Activity

Suppose you checked the mailbox one day, and there was no mail. You might infer that the mail had not been delivered. What other inferences could you make to explain why there is no mail in the mailbox?

🗀 Classifying

When you classify, you group things based on similarities. In biology, living things are classified into groups that share certain characteristics.

🗀 Classifying Activity

Fishes are one group of living things. What other groups of living things can you name? Why are these living things grouped together?

❯ Predicting

When you predict, you state in advance how and why something will occur. Scientists make predictions based upon known information. For example, scientists know that the heat released by power plants can cause an increase in water temperature. Using this knowledge, a biologist might predict that certain kinds of fish will die when a power plant is built near a river.

▲ Modeling

Scientific models are used as guides to understanding the real world. When you model, you use a copy or an imitation of an object to help explain or understand something. There are many different kinds of models.

■ Researching and Communicating

When you do research, you gather information about an idea or thing. When you communicate, you share information with others. Scientists often communicate with each other by publishing their work in science journals. Why is communication among scientists important?

❯ Predicting Activity

Weather forecasters predict what the weather will be like during the week. Predict what the weather will be like tomorrow. Then check your prediction to see if it was correct.

Partly cloudy   **Cloudy**   **Snow**

▲ Modeling Activity

A model airplane can be used as a guide to understanding a real airplane. Have you ever made or used a model? What did your model show?

■ Researching Activity

If you go to a library to find information about a person or event, you are doing research. What kinds of library sources do you think you might use to find information about a person or event? How might you communicate this information to others?

Think & Discuss

4. What is scientific method?
5. What is a hypothesis?
6. Why is it important to use a control during an experiment?
7. Is it always necessary to use all parts of scientific method to solve a problem?
★ 8. Choose three science process skills. How do you use these skills every day?

Mini Activity
Suppose you turn on a portable cassette player, and nothing happens. Make a list of the possible problems to investigate. Which of the problems could you investigate? Explain how you would investigate each problem. Which problems would need to be investigated by a repair person?

1-3 Scientific Measurements

Measuring is an important part of science. Scientists use the **Systeme International,** or **SI,** as a standard of measurement. In SI, each unit is ten times smaller or larger than the next unit. This makes division and multiplication as easy as moving a decimal point.

Prefixes are used in SI to indicate the size of the unit you are working with. SI prefixes and their meanings are listed in Table 1-3. What does the prefix "kilo-" mean?

Mass and Weight

Mass and weight sometimes are confused because they are closely related. **Mass** is the amount of matter an object contains. Weight is a measure of the pull of gravity on an object.

An astronaut has the same mass on the earth as on the moon, but not the same weight. As the astronaut moves farther from the earth, the pull of the earth's gravity lessens. Thus, the weight of the astronaut lessens. Since the astronaut is made up of the same matter on the moon as on the earth, the mass of the astronaut does not change.

In SI, the basic unit of mass is the **kilogram** (kg). A kilogram is 1000 grams (g). A gram is a very small unit. It is equal to the mass of one milliliter of pure water. This is about the same as the mass of a one dollar bill. The gram is useful for measuring the masses of small objects. However, the kilogram is a more useful unit for measuring the mass of a large object.

Length

Length is a measure of the distance between two points. In SI, the basic unit of length is the **meter** (m). Length measurements are made with a meterstick. As its name implies, the meterstick is one meter in length.

A meterstick is divided into 100 equal parts, or units, by numbered lines. The distance between each of the numbered lines is 1/100, or 0.01 of a meter. Look at Table 1-3. The prefix that means 0.01 is "centi-" (c). Thus, the distance between one numbered line and the next is one centimeter, or 1 cm.

Key Points

- The meter, liter, and kilogram are the basic SI units.

- The degree Celsius is the metric unit of temperature. The SI unit of temperature is the Kelvin.

Table 1-3	Common SI Prefixes	
PREFIX	SYMBOL	MEANING
kilo-	k	1000
hecto-	h	100
deka-	dk	10
deci-	d	0.1
centi-	c	0.01
milli-	m	0.001

Study Hint

More information about SI is included in Appendix B on page 649.

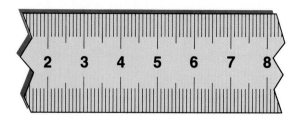

A section of a meterstick is shown in Figure 1-4. Notice that there are ten small spaces between one numbered line of the meterstick and the next numbered line. Each space is 0.001 meter long. The prefix for 0.001 is "milli-" (m), so each small space is one millimeter, or 1 mm in length.

🔺 Place a quarter on Figure 1-4. How many centimeters across is the quarter? How many millimeters? Which direction did the decimal point move as you changed from centimeters to millimeters?

Figure 1–4 A meterstick (left) is used to measure length. Laboratory glassware (right) are used to measure volume.

Volume

The amount of space an object takes up is its **volume.** In SI, the basic unit of volume for liquids and gases is the **liter** (L). A graduated cylinder is used to measure liquid volume. What is the volume of the liquid in the tall graduated cylinder shown in Figure 1-4?

The volume of solids often is measured in **cubic centimeters** (cm³). A cubic centimeter takes up the same space as a cube that is one centimeter long on each side. A cubic centimeter also is equal to one milliliter (mL). What part of a liter is a milliliter? What part of a liter is a cubic centimeter?

Temperature

Temperature is a measure of how hot or cold something is. Temperature rises as a substance absorbs, or takes in, heat energy. Temperature falls when heat energy is lost.

Temperature is measured with a thermometer. In the United States, most thermometers measure temperature on the Fahrenheit (FAHR-un-hyt) scale. In science, temperature usually is measured on the Celsius (SEL-see-us) scale. You will use the Celsius scale in the

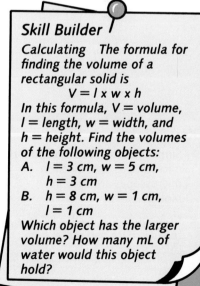

Skill Builder

Calculating   The formula for finding the volume of a rectangular solid is
$$V = l \times w \times h$$
In this formula, V = volume, l = length, w = width, and h = height. Find the volumes of the following objects:
A. $l = 3\ cm$, $w = 5\ cm$, $h = 3\ cm$
B. $h = 8\ cm$, $w = 1\ cm$, $l = 1\ cm$
Which object has the larger volume? How many mL of water would this object hold?

Health and Safety Tip

*Thermometers are very
fragile and may contain
mercury. Mercury is
poisonous if inhaled or
absorbed through the skin.
Never clean up a broken
thermometer with your bare
hands.*

classroom. Each unit on the Celsius scale is a **degree
Celsius** (°C). The degree Celsius is not an SI unit; it is a
metric unit.

Scientists working with very low temperatures use the
Kelvin temperature scale. The Kelvin scale is part of SI.
The Kelvin scale begins at absolute zero, the temperature
at which heat energy is no longer produced. On the
Kelvin scale, absolute zero is 0 K. Look at Table 1-4. What
is the temperature of absolute zero on the Celsius scale?

Table 1-4 Comparing Temperatures on Three Scales			
	KELVIN	CELSIUS	FAHRENHEIT
Absolute zero	0 K	−273 °C	−459 °F
Freezing Point of Pure Water	273 K	0 °C	32 °F
Room Temperature	295 K	22 °C	72 °F
Human Body Temperature	310 K	37 °C	98.6 °F
Boiling Point of Pure Water	373 K	100 °C	212 °F

Think & Discuss

9. What part of a liter is a centiliter?
10. What are the basic units of length, volume, mass,
and temperature in SI?
11. If a kilogram of feathers has the same mass and the
same weight as a kilogram of lead, do these two
objects have the same volume? Explain your
answer.

1-4 Tools of the Biologist

Key Points
- Simple microscopes, compound
microscopes, and electron
microscopes are used in
biology.
- Computers are used in science
to store data and make
calculations.

Biologists use many tools in the laboratory and in the
field. Some of these tools are used for measuring. Others
are used for observation. Several tools of the biologist are
shown in Figure 1-5 on page 15. How many of these tools
do you recognize?

One of the most important tools of the biologist is the
microscope. A microscope is an instrument that makes
things appear larger than they really are. There are several
kinds of microscopes. The microscopes you will use in the
classroom are light microscopes.

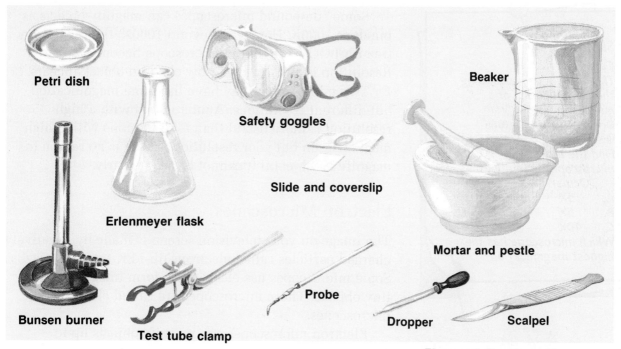

Petri dish

Safety goggles

Beaker

Slide and coverslip

Erlenmeyer flask

Mortar and pestle

Bunsen burner

Probe

Test tube clamp

Dropper

Scalpel

Figure 1-5 You will use many of these tools in the biology laboratory.

Light Microscopes

A light microscope uses lenses to make an object appear larger. A lens is a piece of glass that has been carefully shaped to bend light. Light that passes from an object through a lens is bent so that the object looks either larger or smaller. If the object looks larger, the lens has magnified the object.

A simple microscope is a microscope with only one lens. Have you ever used a magnifying glass? If you have, you have used a simple microscope. Most simple microscopes magnify objects only about ten times (10X). Simple microscopes often are used for studying objects such as the leaves of a plant or the body of an insect.

A compound microscope has two or more lenses. One lens of this microscope, called the ocular lens, is in the eyepiece of the microscope. The other lenses are located on the nosepiece.

The lenses on the nosepiece of a compound microscope are called objective (ub-JEK-tiv) lenses. Most compound microscopes have more than one objective lens. Each objective lens has a different magnification. Magnification refers to the number of times an object appears to be increased in size. The nosepiece of the microscope can be revolved to change the magnification of the microscope.

Figure 1-6 A dissecting microscope produces three-dimensional images of specimens.

Some compound microscopes can magnify objects as much as 1000X. However, beyond 1000X, the **resolution** (rez-uh-LOO-shun) of the microscope becomes poor. Resolution is a measure of how clear an object appears.

Two microscopes may have the same magnification but different resolutions. A microscope with a high resolution is more useful than a microscope with a high magnification but poor resolution. There is no reason to magnify an object if it cannot be seen clearly.

Electron Microscopes

The image on your television screen is made by negatively charged particles called electrons (ih-LEK-trons). Some microscopes use electrons to form images of very tiny objects. These microscopes are called electron microscopes.

Electron microscopes can magnify objects up to 300,000X. The resolution of an electron microscope may be as much as 200,000 times better than the human eye. Unfortunately, electron microscopes are too costly for classroom use.

There are two kinds of electron microscopes. The first kind, called the transmission electron microscope, or TEM, passes electrons through the object being studied. The TEM can magnify an object as much as 200,000X, but it cannot be used to observe living tissue.

◉ The second kind of electron microscope is the scanning electron microscope, or SEM. The SEM reflects electrons from the surface of the object being studied. The SEM produces a three-dimensional, black-and-white image of the object being studied. Computers sometimes are used to add color to the image. Figure 1-7 shows the same bacterium magnified through a TEM and an SEM. Which image was produced using an SEM? How do you know?

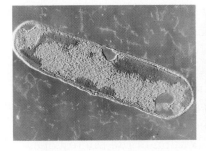

Figure 1-7 One image of the tetanus bacterium was made with a TEM (left); the other was made with an SEM (right).

ACTIVITY 1-1

By doing the activities, you will gain experience in thinking logically.

PROBLEM: How do you use a microscope properly?

Science Process Skills
observing, communicating, comparing

Background Information
The compound microscope has two lenses. The lens at the top of the microscope tube is the ocular lens. The lens in each objective is an objective lens. Some microscopes have three or four objective lenses. An image is magnified by both the ocular and objective lenses.

Materials
compound microscope
prepared slide of the letter "e"

Procedure

1. Carry the microscope upright with one hand firmly grasping the arm and the other hand under the base. Hold the microscope close to your body.
2. Compare your microscope with the one shown in Appendix C, page 650.
3. Turn the nosepiece so that the low-power objective is above the stage.
4. Place the prepared slide on the stage. Use the clips to hold the slide in place.
5. Use the coarse adjustment knob to lower the objective slowly until it is 2 mm above the slide. **CAUTION: Be sure the objective lens does not hit the slide.**
6. Adjust the light source to focus light on the slide.
7. Look through the eyepiece with both eyes open. Use the coarse adjustment knob to raise the objective slowly until you see an image.
8. Use the fine adjustment knob to focus the image clearly.
9. On a sheet of paper, draw a circle to represent the microscope's field of view. Sketch what you see. Calculate the magnification power and include it on your sketch.

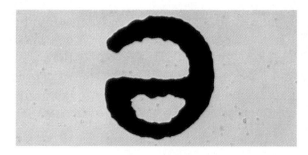

10. Turn the nosepiece until the high-power objective is above the slide. Use only the fine adjustment knob to focus the image clearly.
11. Repeat step 9.
12. On the low-power diagram, circle the part visible with the high-power objective.
13. Before returning the microscope, remove the slide. Put the low-power objective in place, and lower the nosepiece.

Observations

1. **a.** How is your microscope similar to the microscope shown in Appendix C?
   b. How is it different?
2. **a.** When you view an object through the microscope, is the image right-side up or upside down?   **b.** Is the image backward or forward?

Conclusions

1. How should you hold the microscope?
2. **INFER**   Do you think that all compound microscopes are basically the same? Explain your answer.
3. What parts of the microscope are used to focus the image?

Going Further
Use the compound microscope to observe various slides. Sketch what you see with the low-power and high-power objectives. On the low-power sketch, circle the portion of the image visible with the high-power objective.

Computers

Have you ever used a calculator? A calculator is a small computer. A computer is a machine that can store large amounts of data. Scientists often use calculators or computers to solve mathematical problems. A computer can make a calculation much faster and more accurately than a person. In fact, a calculation that might take years to perform by hand can be made in minutes using a computer.

Much of the progress made in science in the last twenty years is due to the computer. Scientists use computers in many ways. Some of these uses are listed in Table 1-5.

Table 1-5   Uses for Computers in Science
• Store data • Make calculations • Run simulations • Take measurements • Add color to pictures • Manipulate laboratory equipment • Keep track of research • Word processing • Make charts, tables, and graphs

Scientists often use computers to run simulations (sim-yuh-LAY-shuns). A simulation is a moving model. Scientists may put data into a computer about a system they think exists in nature. The computer can use this data to make a model.

Think & Discuss

12. What is a compound microscope?

13. What is meant by the term "magnification"?

14. Why is resolution important to the user of a compound microscope?

15. What kind of microscopes might you use in the classroom? Why would you use each?

★ 16. What are the advantages of using a compound microscope rather than an electron microscope?

BIOLOGY, TECHNOLOGY, and SOCIETY
Advances in Medicine

In 1895, the German scientist Wilhelm Roentgen (RENT-gen) discovered that light energy could be used to take photographs through substances such as paper, cloth, and wood. Roentgen also discovered that this invisible form of light energy, called X-rays, could be used to take pictures of structures inside the body.

X-rays have been one of the most useful tools in medicine since the end of the nineteenth century. Why are X-rays so important? X-rays allow doctors to see inside the body without performing surgery.

Bone tissue appears clearly on an X-ray picture. However, blood vessels and soft body tissues do not show up well. In the early 1900s, doctors discovered that dyes could be injected into the body to darken organs and blood vessels. When darkened, organs and blood vessels can be seen clearly on X-ray pictures.

In the mid-1970s, doctors began using CT-scanning machines. A CT-scanner is a large cylinder-shaped machine that can take X-ray pictures. The CT-scanner combines X-rays with computer technology. How does the CT-scanner work?

The patient is placed inside the CT-scanner. As the cylinder of the CT-scanner revolves around the patient's body, many X-rays are taken. The X-rays are then collected and arranged by a computer that displays all of the images as a single picture.

The CT-scanner is helpful for looking at soft body parts, such as the brain. However, the CT-scanner must be used with great care. The strong radiation from X-rays can damage or even kill body cells and tissues.

MRI stands for magnetic resonance (REZ-un-unts) imaging. MRI uses magnets and sound energy to form pictures of the internal organs. The first MRI was used on a human being in 1977. By 1984, MRI machines were being used in hospitals to take pictures inside the body without exposing patients to harmful X-rays.

Unlike X-rays, MRI can pass through bone tissue. The ability of MRI to pass through bone has made this machine very useful for detecting and treating cancer. For example, using MRI, brain surgeons can look through the skull for tumors and damaged blood vessels in the brain. MRI also is used to observe soft tissues of the kidneys, liver, and pancreas.

To Think About
- How are CT-scanning machines an advance over early X-ray machines?
- Why is MRI better than CT-scanning for finding brain tumors?

The Science of Biology 19

Chapter Review

The Chapter Summary is a review of the main ideas in the chapter.

CHAPTER SUMMARY

1-1 What is Biology?

- Biology is the science that studies living things.
- Specialized branches of biology include botany, zoology, ecology, and microbiology, among others.
- Technology is applied science.
- Biotechnology is the use of biology to solve everyday problems. Medicine, industry, and agriculture are fields that use biotechnology.

1-2 Scientific Method

- Scientific method is an organized approach to solving problems.
- It is not necessary to use scientific method or all of the steps of scientific method to solve all problems.

1-3 Scientific Measurements

- The basic unit of length in SI is the meter.
- The liter is used for measuring the volume of liquids and gases. The volume of solids is measured in cubic centimeters.
- The basic unit of mass is the kilogram.
- The degree Celsius is the metric unit of temperature.

1-4 Tools of the Biologist

- Biologists use tools to make measurements and to help make observations.
- Simple microscopes, compound microscopes, dissecting microscopes, and electron microscopes are used in biology.
- Computers are used to store data, run simulations, and solve mathematical problems.

VOCABULARY LIST

biology (4)	degree Celsius (14)	liter (13)	Systeme International (12)
biotechnology (5)	ecology (5)	mass (12)	technology (5)
botany (4)	experiment (8)	meter (12)	theory (7)
control (8)	hypothesis (8)	microscope (14)	variables (8)
cubic centimeters (13)	kilogram (12)	resolution (16)	volume (13)
data (9)	laws (7)	scientific method (7)	zoology (4)

VOCABULARY REVIEW

Check your understanding of the chapter by completing these exercises.

Matching Write the word or term from the Vocabulary List that best matches each description.

1. problem-solving model
2. basic SI unit of mass
3. study of living things
4. test of a hypothesis
5. applied science
6. measuring system of science
7. tool used for observing
8. suggested solution to a problem
9. record of observations made during an experiment
10. amount of space an object occupies

Identifying Relationships Identify the word or term in each group that does not belong. Explain why it does not belong with the group.

1. cubic centimeter, kilogram, liter
2. biotechnology, magnification, resolution
3. botany, zoology, scientific method
4. kilogram, meter, degree Celsius
5. theory, control, variable
6. ecology, experiment, environment
7. mass, kilogram, weight
8. scientific method, theory, law
9. zoology, ecology, technology
10. observation, microscope, liter

Completion Write the word or words that best completes each sentence.

1. An experiment is designed to test a _____.
2. In a well-designed experiment, it is important to test only one _____.
3. A simulation is a _____ of a real system.
4. Biology is a _____ science.
5. The Kelvin temperature scale begins at _____.
6. An electron microscope has higher magnification and better _____ than a light microscope.
7. Ecology is the branch of biology that studies the relationship between living things and their _____.
8. A balance, a thermometer, and a meterstick are tools of _____.
9. A meterstick is divided into 100 smaller units called _____.

Finding the Main Ideas Use the section number to find the sentence that answers each question. Then, write the sentence.

1. What is biochemistry? (1-1)
2. What is biotechnology? (1-1)
3. What is the first step in solving any problem? (1-2)
4. What is the control in an experiment? (1-2)
5. Why is measuring an important science skill? (1-2)
6. How does mass differ from weight? (1-3)
7. Which temperature scale is part of SI? (1-3)
8. What is a microscope? (1-4)
9. What is resolution? (1-4)
10. What kind of image is produced by a scanning electron microscope? (1-4)
11. What is a computer? (1-4)
12. What is a simulation? (1-4)

CONCEPT REVIEW

Writing for Understanding One way to find out if you understand something is to write a brief summary of the information in your own words. Reread Section 1-4, Tools of the Biologist, on pages 14–18, and write a brief summary of the information.

Critical Thinking Answer each of the following in complete sentences.

1. How do measurements make observations more accurate?

2. What is meant by the term "prediction"? Why is prediction important to scientists?
3. Each experimental test is called a trial. Why is it important to perform several trials before stating a conclusion?
4. Give three examples of specimens that you would observe with a simple microscope.
5. Each kelvin has the same value as a degree Celsius. If the freezing point of water is 273 kelvins, what is the boiling point of water in kelvins?

EXTENSIONS

Extensions are different activities that expand a concept related to the chapter.

1. Research the origins of science. Find out when science began as a way of exploring nature, and why it can be said that technology existed before science. Write a report on your findings.
2. Many of the products you use every day use SI measurements. For example, the sizes of automobile engines often are indicated in liters. Find examples of products that use SI measurements. Prepare a poster that displays examples of SI measurements used in daily life.
3. The temperature scales mentioned in this chapter were named for the scientist who developed each scale. Investigate the work of Fahrenheit, Celsius, and Kelvin to find out how they developed their scales. Present your findings in a report.

Chapter 2

The Nature of Living Things

After you have completed this chapter, you will be able to

2-1 **explain** the relationship between organisms and cells.

2-1 **name** six characteristics of all organisms.

2-2 **define** life processes.

2-2 **identify** four life processes.

2-3 **name** five needs of most organisms.

2-3 **explain** the importance of quality living space for plants and animals.

Science Process Skills

In this chapter, two science skills are highlighted. Symbols show some places where these skills are used.

► **Inferring:** When you infer, you form a conclusion based upon facts and not direct observation.

▲ **Organizing:** When you organize information, you put the information in some kind of order.

You probably have heard people talk about nonliving things as if they were alive. For example, people often say that an engine comes "alive." Have you ever heard someone refer to the "life" of a battery? Even hurricanes are given human names.

What is life? Scientists do not have a simple answer to this question. Life is not easy to define. How then do biologists decide what things are alive?

Biologists have discovered that living things have certain characteristics that nonliving things do not have. Using these characteristics, biologists can decide if something is living or nonliving. For example, machines, such as robots, often seem to have a "life" of their own. Robots, however, do not have the characteristics of life.

2-1 Characteristics of Organisms

Key Points

- Unicellular organisms have one cell. Multicellular organisms have more than one cell.

- Organisms are made up of one or more cells, use energy, are adapted to their environments, respond to stimuli, reproduce, grow, and develop.

Study Hint

After you read this section, list examples of the ways in which you meet the six characteristics of life.

Figure 2-1 The redwood tree (left) and the blue whale (center) are among the largest organisms on the earth. Bacteria (right) are among the smallest.

Turn over a rock or rotting log. Look into sidewalk cracks with a hand lens, or study a drop of pond water with a microscope. Almost anywhere you look, you can find some kind of living thing.

Living things are called **organisms** (AWR-guh-nizms). There are many different kinds of organisms. You would grow tired listing the names of all of the known organisms.

Biologists are cautious about defining organisms. Biologists know that a definition of "organism" that is accepted today may be rejected tomorrow. In fact, any scientific definition can be changed as new information is learned.

Organisms do not all look alike. For example, bacteria are so small you need a microscope to see them. Other organisms, such as whales and redwood trees, are huge. The blue whale is the largest animal that lives on Earth. ▲ Organisms differ in what they do, where they live, and how they get energy. Biologists use six characteristics to determine whether something is an organism. The characteristics of life are as follows:

- Organisms are made of one or more cells.
- Organisms use energy.
- Organisms are adapted to their environments.
- Organisms respond to stimuli.
- Organisms produce more organisms of their own kind.
- Organisms grow and develop.

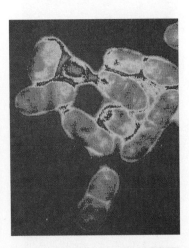

Cells

Only organisms have **cells.** Cells are the basic units of structure and function in living things. For this reason, cells often are called the "building blocks" of life.

Organisms may be made up of one cell or many cells. Some organisms are unicellular, or one-celled. For example, bacteria are unicellular organisms. Yet, bacteria have the six characteristics of life. Other organisms are multicellular. Multicellular organisms are made up of two or more cells. You are a multicellular organism made up of billions of cells.

Energy

Organisms use energy. Energy is the ability to do work. The sun is the major source of energy for most living things. Plants and some bacteria use the energy in sunlight to make food. Animals benefit from the energy in sunlight by eating plants or other animals as shown in Figure 2-2.

Adaptation

Any characteristic of an organism that helps the organism survive, or live successfully in its environment, is called an **adaptation** (ad-uhp-TAY-shun). Adaptations make it possible for one kind of organism to survive in an environment where other kinds of organisms cannot survive. For example, a cactus is a plant that is adapted to life in a very dry environment. A cactus has thick leathery stems and branches that store water. The spines, or leaves, of a cactus are an adaptation that prevent water from being lost by evaporation.

Study Hint

Work is done when an object is moved through a distance.

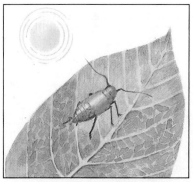

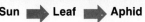
Sun ➡ Leaf ➡ Aphid   Fish ➡ Hawk

Figure 2-2 Plants obtain energy from the sun. How do the aphid (left) and the hawk (right) obtain energy?

Figure 2-3 The hollow white hairs of a polar bear absorb heat energy from the sun.

Study Hint

The plural of "stimulus" is "stimuli" (STIM-yuh-ly).

The thick fur and body fat of a polar bear also are adaptations. Thick fur and layers of fat prevent the loss of body heat from a polar bear. In this way, a polar bear is adapted to life in a very cold environment.

Response and Movement

When the telephone rings, you pick up the receiver. When you inhale pepper, you sneeze. When you hear a loud noise, you jump. Picking up the telephone receiver, sneezing, and jumping are examples of **responses.** A response is a reaction to a change in the environment.

A change in the environment that causes a response is called a **stimulus** (STIM-yoo-lus). The ringing telephone, the pepper, and the loud noise are examples of stimuli. All living things respond to stimuli.

When an earthworm is exposed to bright light, the earthworm burrows quickly into the soil. When you touch a hot plate, you quickly remove your hand. What are the stimuli and responses in these two examples?

▶ The response of a plant to a stimulus is called a **tropism** (TROH-pizm). Farmers do not have to worry about which way to place seeds in the ground. Why not? Because gravity causes the roots of plants to grow downward. The downward growth of roots is an example of a tropism. Many flowers open during the day and close up at night. What stimulus do you think causes this response?

Only certain parts of plants move. When an organism moves its entire body from place to place, the movement is called **locomotion.** Running, swimming, flying, and crawling are some examples of locomotion. Animals use locomotion to find food, shelter, and avoid danger.

Figure 2-4 The leaves of the mimosa plant close when touched (right). What is the stimulus? What is the response?

ACTIVITY 2-1

PROBLEM: How does light affect the pupils of your eyes?

Science Process Skills
observing, inferring, hypothesizing

Background Information
The pupil is the small opening of the eye. Light enters the eye through the pupil. The pupil changes size depending on the amount of light entering the eye. The change in pupil size protects the sensitive area inside the eye from receiving too much light.

    The change in pupil size is an automatic reflex carried out by muscles of the eye. Reflexes do not require any thought and are inborn, or present from birth.

Materials
paper and pencil

Procedure
1. Work with a partner. Have your partner observe while you demonstrate the reflex of the pupil.
2. **HYPOTHESIZE** How does light affect the pupils of your eyes? Write your hypothesis on a sheet of paper. Your hypothesis should answer the question. To test your hypothesis, continue the activity.
3. Have your partner look at the pupils of your eyes in normal light.
4. Close your eyes for one minute.
5. After one minute, open your eyes. Your partner should immediately observe your pupils.
6. Repeat steps 3, 4, and 5 three more times.
7. Reverse roles and repeat the procedure.
8. **ORGANIZE** Gather the results from the other students in the class. Organize the class results in a Data Table.

Observations
1. **a.** Describe the size of your pupils immediately after you opened your eyes.

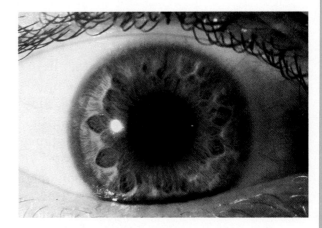

    b. Describe how the size of the pupils changed after opening your eyes.
2. **a.** What was the stimulus in this activity?
    b. What was the response?
3. Did you have to think about changing the size of your pupils?

Conclusions
1. How did the amount of light entering your eyes affect the size of your pupils?
2. Was your hypothesis correct? Use your observations to support your hypothesis.
3. **INFER a.** Did the pupils of all the students in your class react in the same way?
    b. Why might all people have the same reaction?
4. If you are in bright sunlight and walk into a dark room, you cannot see very well for a few seconds. Using the data you gathered, explain why.

Going Further
Hold a piece of clear plastic wrap tightly about 20 cm in front of your face. Have a partner throw a crumpled piece of paper at the clear plastic. Did you blink? Do you think blinking is an automatic reflex? Repeat the action about ten times. Did you blink each time? Could you control your blinking? What is the stimulus? What is the response?

Reproduction

All organisms die. However, before they die, most organisms produce offspring, or more organisms like themselves. Reproduction (ree-pruh-DUK-shun) is the process by which organisms produce offspring.

Until the seventeenth century, many people believed that living things came from nonliving matter. For example, people thought that frogs formed from mud and flies came from spoiled meat. The theory stating that organisms could come from nonliving matter is called **spontaneous generation** (spahn-TAY-nee-us jen-uh-RAY-shun). Why do you think that people once believed in spontaneous generation?

How could you provide evidence that flies do not come from spoiled meat? You might design an experiment like the one Francesco Redi designed. Redi was an Italian doctor of the mid-seventeenth century. He believed that living things could come only from other living things.

Redi placed spoiled meat in several wide-mouthed jars. Some of the jars were left uncovered. Other jars were covered with a thin veil. A third group of jars were sealed tightly with lids. The setup for Redi's experiment is shown in Figure 2-5.

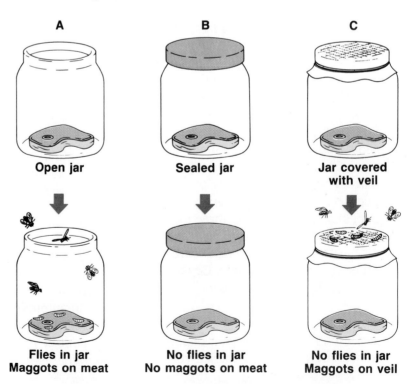

A	B	C
Open jar	Sealed jar	Jar covered with veil
Flies in jar Maggots on meat	No flies in jar No maggots on meat	No flies in jar Maggots on veil

Figure 2-5 Which setup is the control in this experiment?

Observing each group of jars, Redi noticed that newly hatched flies, or maggots, appeared only in the jars that were left uncovered. Today, biologists know that flies often lay eggs on spoiled meat. The spoiled meat serves as food for the maggots that hatch from the fly eggs. Why do you think maggots did not appear in the covered jars?

More evidence was presented to disprove spontaneous generation in the mid-nineteenth century. The French scientist Louis Pasteur conducted an experiment with microorganisms. The results of this experiment showed that even microorganisms do not reproduce by spontaneous generation.

Pasteur poured broth into swan-necked flasks, similar to those shown in Figure 2-6. The broth was made up of water, air, and nutrients. Pasteur reasoned that the bent necks of the flasks would keep microorganisms from entering.

Pasteur boiled the broth in some of the flasks. In these flasks, the broth did not spoil. However, the broth that was not boiled showed signs of spoiling, or the presence of microorganisms. What effect do you think boiling has on the growth of microorganisms? What did the experiments of Redi and Pasteur have in common?

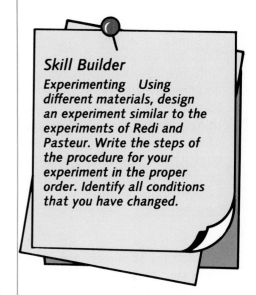

Skill Builder

Experimenting Using different materials, design an experiment similar to the experiments of Redi and Pasteur. Write the steps of the procedure for your experiment in the proper order. Identify all conditions that you have changed.

Experiment   **Control**

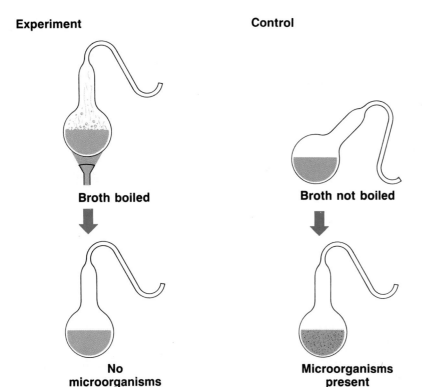

Broth boiled   Broth not boiled

No   Microorganisms
microorganisms   present

Figure 2-6 Pasteur's experiment provided additional evidence that spontaneous generation does not take place.

ACTIVITY 2-2

PROBLEM: Is spontaneous generation possible?

Science Process Skills
observing, comparing, inferring

Background Information
Until the late nineteenth century, most scientists accepted the theory of spontaneous generation. Spontaneous generation is the idea that living things develop from nonliving materials. In 1668, an Italian physician, Francesco Redi, questioned the theory of spontaneous generation. Redi tested his hypothesis. His experiment is described in your text on pages 28–29.

Materials
    3 pieces of raw chopped meat
    3 jars
    piece of cheesecloth
    piece of plastic wrap
    2 rubber bands
    hand lens

Procedure
1. Place some meat in each of the jars.
2. Leave one jar uncovered.
3. Place cheesecloth over the second jar. Place plastic wrap over the third jar. Secure the cheesecloth and plastic wrap tightly with a rubber band.
4. Place all three jars in an open area where flies will be attracted by the odor of the meat.
5. Using the hand lens, observe carefully for the next five days the meat in the uncovered jar and the top of the cheesecloth and plastic wrap on the other jars. Record your daily observations.

Observations
1. Which jars attracted flies?
2. **a.** In which jar did flies come in contact with the meat?   **b.** Which jar contained maggots on the meat?
3. Which jar was the control?

Conclusions
1. **a.** Why were there no maggots in two of the jars?   **b.** Where did the maggots come from?
2. **a.** Use your text as a reference. Were your results the same as Redi's results?   **b.** Why is it important to repeat experiments?
3. Do the results of this experiment disprove the theory of spontaneous generation? Why or why not?

Going Further

Repeat Pasteur's experiment on spontaneous generation. Boil broth for 2 minutes to kill all existing bacteria. **CAUTION: Be careful when heating liquids over an open flame.** Pour some broth into three jars that have been boiled. Leave one jar uncovered, secure cheesecloth around the opening of the second jar, and put aluminum foil tightly over the opening of the third jar. Record your observations each day for one week.

Experiment setup

Asexual Reproduction

Some organisms reproduce by **asexual** (ay-SEK-shoo-wuhl) **reproduction.** Asexual reproduction requires only one parent organism. Offspring are produced when the parent organism splits in two. This process is called fission. Another form of asexual reproduction is budding. Budding is the growth of a new organism from the parent organism. In asexual reproduction, a new organism is an exact copy of its parent. Only some plants and simple organisms produce offspring by asexual reproduction.

Sexual Reproduction

Most organisms reproduce by **sexual** (SEK-shoo-wuhl) **reproduction.** In sexual reproduction, cells from two parents join to form a new organism. Offspring that result from sexual reproduction are not identical to either parent organism. Instead, the offspring have some characteristics of each parent. How is sexual reproduction different from asexual reproduction?

Growth and Development

Think of all the ways you have changed since you were born. You are bigger and stronger. Your movements are more graceful. An organism changes in many ways during its lifetime. All of the changes that take place in an organism over its lifetime are called development.

One way organisms change is by growing, or becoming larger. In unicellular organisms, growth occurs as new materials are added to the cell. The cells of a multicellular organism also grow as new material is added to each cell. However, most growth in multicellular organisms is caused by the formation of new cells.

Life Span

The period of time an organism lives is its life span. Every organism has a life span. Some organisms, such as the bristlecone pine tree, have a life span of more than five thousand years. Other organisms, such as insects, have very short life spans. The mayfly, for example, usually lives for only three or four hours. Look at Table 2-1. What is the life span of a tomato plant?

Table 2-1 Life Spans	
ORGANISM	LIFE SPAN
Tomato plant	7 months
Spider	3 years
Dog	12 years
Horse	30 years
Tortoise	150 years
Bristlecone pine tree	5500 years

Figure 2-7 During its life cycle, a young caterpillar (left) develops into an adult gypsy moth (right).

Life Cycle

The life cycle of an organism is all the changes that the organism goes through during its life span. The life cycle begins when the organism is born and ends when the organism dies. Some organisms, such as dogs and cats, look similar to their parents when they are born. Other organisms, such as frogs and butterflies, go through changes in appearance during their life cycles.

Think & Discuss

1. What is an organism?
2. What are cells?
3. List six characteristics of organisms.
4. What would happen to an organism if it was not adapted to its environment?
★ 5. Explain why a robot is not an organism.

2-2 Life Processes of Organisms

Key Points

- The life processes are all of the things a living thing must do to stay alive.

- Nutrition, respiration, excretion, and transport are four life processes of organisms.

Organisms must carry on certain processes to survive. Together these processes are called the **life processes.** The life processes are also characteristics of organisms.

Being alive means performing all of the life processes. As you read, you will learn about the life processes of many kinds of organisms. You also will learn how the life processes take place in your body.

Nutrition

All organisms need food. Using sunlight and materials from the environment, green plants can make their own food. Animals, however, cannot make their own food. Animals depend on plants and other animals for their food supply.

Think about what you had for breakfast this morning. Maybe you had some fruit or juice. These foods came from plants. Did you have an egg or a glass of milk? These foods came from animals. Whatever you had to eat, you took the food into your body from the outside. Most organisms do this. The process of taking food into the body from the outside is called **ingestion** (in-JES-chun).

Why do organisms need food? Food provides an organism with the **nutrients** (NOO-tree-unts), or materials, needed for growth, energy, and the life processes. Before an organism can use the nutrients in food, the food must be broken down. The process of breaking down food into usable forms is called **digestion** (di-JES-chuhn).

The complete process of ingestion and digestion is called **nutrition** (noo-TRISH-uhn). Proper nutrition provides an organism with energy. Nutrition also provides the materials needed for growth and development.

Photosynthesis

Using water, carbon dioxide, and sunlight, plants are able to make their own food. Plants are called producers because they make, or produce, food. This food-making process is called **photosynthesis** (foht-uh-SIN-thuh-sis). Photosynthesis is a life process of plants.

Photosynthesis usually takes place in the leaves of green plants. The food produced is a simple sugar called glucose. Do you know that your blood contains glucose? In fact, glucose in the body is called "blood sugar." Where do you think the glucose in your blood comes from?

Some of the food made during photosynthesis is used by plants for their growth and development. The rest is stored in the plant. By eating plants, animals obtain energy.

Chemosynthesis

Some organisms use chemicals instead of sunlight to make their food. For example, bacteria that live deep in the ocean do not get sunlight. These bacteria use chemicals

Health and Safety Tip
Eating too much of one nutrient usually is not healthful. For example, people who eat too many fatty foods can become overweight or develop heart disease.

Figure 2-8   The female goldfinch provides food for her young until they are ready to leave the nest.

released by underwater volcanoes to make food. The process in which chemical energy is used to make food is called **chemosynthesis** (kee-moh-SIN-thuh-sis).

Respiration and Excretion

How do organisms obtain energy from food? Organisms obtain energy from food by carrying on **respiration** (res-puh-RAY-shun). Respiration occurs when oxygen is involved in the process of breaking apart food in the cells. The breakdown of food in the cells releases energy. It also produces carbon dioxide and water. A simple formula for respiration is

$$\text{food} + \text{oxygen} \rightarrow \text{carbon dioxide} + \text{water} + \text{energy}$$

The carbon dioxide and water produced by respiration are waste products. The products of digestion that are not used by an organism also are waste products. Organisms must remove waste products from their cells to remain healthy. The removal of waste products from the cells of an organism is called **excretion** (ik-SKREE-shun).

Carbon dioxide, water, and the waste products of nutrition are constantly being produced by animals. Plants also give off carbon dioxide and water as wastes. During photosynthesis, plants give off water and oxygen as waste products.

Transport

Nutrients taken in by one part of an organism usually are needed by other parts of that organism. For example, the roots of a tree take in water and nutrients from the soil. However, water and nutrients also are needed by the leaves of a tree. Water and nutrients are carried through tubelike cells to all the leaves of a tree.

Figure 2-9 Carbon dioxide given off as a waste product by animals is used by plants in photosynthesis. How do animals use oxygen that is given off by plants?

All organisms take in nutrients from the environment. Organisms also release waste products. The life process of moving nutrients throughout an organism and removing waste products is called **transport.**

Most animals take food into their bodies with their mouths. After the food is digested, nutrients are moved throughout the body of the animal. Waste products are removed from the animal. Tubelike cells also move nutrients and waste products through animals.

Microscopic organisms and some plants do not have tubelike cells for transport. However, these organisms are still able to transport nutrients and remove waste products. For example, bacteria and fungi absorb nutrients directly from the environment. In the same way, waste products are released back to the environment.

Figure 2-10 Through what process did the colored water move up this celery stalk?

Think & Discuss

6. Define life processes.
7. Name four life processes.
8. What does transport do for an organism?
9. How are excretion and transport related?
★ 10. Why do you think photosynthesis is necessary for the respiration of animals?

2-3 Needs of Organisms

Organisms get all of the things they need from the environment. The environment is everything that surrounds an organism. What do organisms need to survive? Organisms need water, nutrients, air, a proper temperature, and living space.

Your blood is made mostly of water. Water makes up almost three-quarters of most living things. The life processes of living things depend on water. Plants take in water and nutrients from the soil. Animals obtain water and nutrients by drinking liquids and eating food.

Key Points

- Most organisms need water, nutrients, air, proper temperature, and living space to survive.

- Living space provides plants with sunlight and water. Living space provides animals with food, water, shelter, and a place to reproduce.

Figure 2-11 Animals that live in a dry environment, such as these Burchell's zebras in Kenya, depend upon water holes.

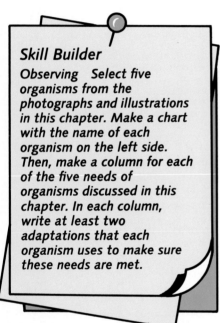

Skill Builder

Observing Select five organisms from the photographs and illustrations in this chapter. Make a chart with the name of each organism on the left side. Then, make a column for each of the five needs of organisms discussed in this chapter. In each column, write at least two adaptations that each organism uses to make sure these needs are met.

Most organisms need air to survive. Plants use carbon dioxide in the air to make food and release oxygen as a waste product. In respiration, animals take in oxygen and release carbon dioxide. What life process do plants and animals perform to obtain energy from food?

Organisms also need a proper temperature to carry out their life processes. When the temperature decreases, the life processes of most organisms slow down. Many organisms are not active in cold weather. For example, in the northern part of the United States, most insects quietly spend the winter under tree bark or rocks. In the spring, when the temperature rises above freezing, these insects surface to continue their life cycles.

Homeostasis (hoh-mee-oh-STAY-sis) is the ability of an organism to keep conditions inside its body constant. Homeostasis allows an organism to keep warm in the winter and cool in the summer. For example, some animals grow thick fur in the fall. Birds lose many of their feathers in the spring.

All organisms need living space. Living space provides plants with enough air, sunlight, water, and nutrients for photosynthesis. Animals need living space for air, food, water, shelter, and reproduction.

The living space in any environment is limited. As a result, organisms must compete with each other for living space. The struggle between organisms for the available living space in an environment is called competition.

Think & Discuss

11. What is homeostasis?

12. Name five needs of living things.

13. What are some ways that an organism would be affected by not having enough living space?

Nature Photography

The photographer has been waiting patiently for nearly an hour. As the sun slips below the horizon, a big, bushy mother raccoon, followed by her three babies, waddles into the campsite. The raccoons tip over the can of food that the photographer has left as bait. Click! The photographer has caught four raccoons in the act of being themselves.

Nature photography is an ideal hobby for someone who enjoys taking pictures and who is interested in plants and animals. Many campers, hikers, and other outdoor enthusiasts also enjoy photographing plants and animals in their natural environments.

All you need to begin taking nature photographs is a camera. Most nature photographers use a 35-mm, single-lens reflex camera. Depending on the kinds of pictures you want to take, you also may need several different lenses. For example, a zoom lens is the best lens for photographing flowers. The best lens for photographing insects is a macro lens. A macro lens "zooms" in on objects, making them appear much larger than they really are. Animals can best be photographed from a distance with a telephoto, wide-angle, or zoom lens.

Because they stay in one place, plants are the easiest subjects to photograph. However, photographing a plant on a windy day can be tricky. Photographing animals is challenging because animals are likely to run away as you get close to them. Insects, which are present in every garden, also make good subjects.

To begin taking pictures of wild animals, you should first learn the habits of the type of animal you wish to photograph. This includes learning where the animal lives, when the animal sleeps, and what the animal eats. The second thing you must do is learn how to move silently through woods, and how to blend in with your surroundings.

Where should you go to take nature photographs? State and national parks, recreation areas, seashores, wildlife preserves, and sanctuaries are all great places for photographing animals. Botanical gardens, meadows, forests, and parks are great places for photographing plants. You can also take nature photographs in your own backyard, especially if you have a bird feeder or an area where you can spread food for small animals such as squirrels.

To Think About

- How is knowledge of biology helpful to a nature photographer?
- Animals have much keener senses than humans. How does this put the nature photographer at a disadvantage?

The Nature of Living Things

Chapter Review

CHAPTER SUMMARY

2-1 Characteristics of Organisms

- Cells are the basic units of structure and function in living things. All organisms are made up of cells.

- Organisms are made up of one or more cells, use energy, are adapted to their environments, respond to stimuli, produce more of their kind, grow and develop.

2-2 Life Processes of Organisms

- The life processes of an organism are all of the things an organism must do to stay alive.

- Nutrition, respiration, excretion, and transport are life processes of all organisms.

2-3 Needs of Organisms

- Organisms need water, nutrients, air, proper temperature, and living space for their survival.

- Living space is needed by plants for air, water, nutrients, and sunlight.

- Living space is needed by animals for air, food, water, shelter, and a place to reproduce.

VOCABULARY LIST

adaptation (25)
asexual reproduction (31)
cells (25)
chemosynthesis (34)
digestion (33)
excretion (34)

homeostasis (36)
ingestion (33)
life processes (32)
locomotion (26)
nutrients (33)

nutrition (33)
organisms (24)
photosynthesis (33)
respiration (34)
response (26)

sexual reproduction (31)
spontaneous generation (28)
stimulus (26)
transport (35)
tropism (26)

VOCABULARY REVIEW

Matching Write the word or term from the Vocabulary List that best matches each description.

1. living things
2. building blocks of life
3. ingestion and digestion
4. breakdown of food into usable forms
5. all of the functions an organism must perform to stay alive
6. useful substances in food
7. theory that organisms could come from nonliving matter
8. characteristic that helps an organism survive in its environment
9. reaction to a stimulus
10. movement of materials within an organism

Finding Word Relationships Pair each numbered word with a word in the box. Explain in complete sentences how the words are related.

chemicals	wastes	energy
tropism	budding	light
balance	eat	parents
movement		

1. excretion
2. ingestion
3. locomotion
4. respiration
5. photosynthesis
6. stimulus
7. asexual reproduction
8. chemosynthesis
9. homeostasis
10. sexual reproduction

True or False   Write true if the statement is true. If the statement is false, change the underlined word or words to make the statement true.

1. The food-making process of plants is called homeostasis.
2. Animals need oxygen for respiration.
3. Bacteria are an example of unicellular organisms.
4. Nutrients often are called the building blocks of life.
5. The experiments of Redi and Pasteur helped support the theory of spontaneous generation.
6. A response is the reaction of an organism to a change in its environment.
7. The response of a plant to a stimulus is called locomotion.
8. Cells from two parents join to produce a new organism during asexual reproduction.

Question and Answer   Rewrite each heading in the Chapter Outline on page 22 as a question. Then, answer each of the questions you have written.

Interpreting a Table   Use the information about the life spans of organisms listed in Table 2-1 (page 31) to answer each of the following.

1. Which has a longer life span, a horse or a tortoise?
2. What is the life span of a spider?
3. How much longer does the average tortoise live than a horse?
4. Which organism in Table 2-1 has the shortest life span?
5. Which organism in Table 2-1 has the longest life span?
6. If you added the life span of humans to the table, where would it be placed?

Writing the Main Ideas   Using the Chapter Outline on page 22, write the main idea for each heading in the outline.

Critical Thinking   Answer each of the following in complete sentences.

1. Why are definitions important to scientists?
2. How do people adapt their environments to meet their needs? Give three examples.

3. How do you think an organism's environment affects its life span?
4. How are the life cycle and life span of an organism related?
5. How are plants important for the respiration of animals? How is respiration of animals important to plants?
6. How is chemosynthesis similar to photosynthesis?

1. Using library books, write a report describing how a tree and a squirrel display the characteristics of life.
2. In a table, list five organisms that live in your neighborhood. Then, describe the adaptations each organism uses to get food.
3. Interview a zookeeper or a veterinarian to find out how much water an elephant drinks in one day. Multiply that amount by 365 to find out how much water an elephant drinks in one year. From your findings, write a report explaining why getting enough water is one of the main problems facing wild elephants.

Chapter 3 | The Chemistry of Life

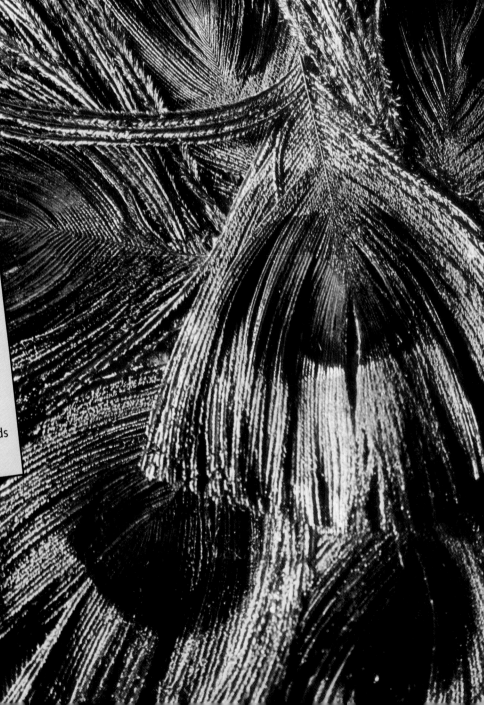

Objectives

After you have completed this chapter, you will be able to

3-1 **distinguish** among the states of matter.

3-2 **define** atom, element, and molecule.

3-2 **compare** mixtures and compounds.

3-3 **recognize** the relationship between chemistry and biology.

3-3 **compare** inorganic and organic compounds.

3-3 **name** six kinds of compounds needed by living things.

Science Process Skills

In this chapter, two science skills are highlighted. Symbols show some places where these skills are used.

Observing: When you observe, you use one or more of your senses to gather information.

Classifying: When you classify, you group things based upon similarities.

Science fiction stories often tell about creatures that are pure energy, but so far these creatures remain fantasies. As far as scientists know, all living things are made up of **matter.** *Matter is anything that has mass and takes up space. Everything that exists is either matter or energy.*

Both matter and energy are important to living things. For example, energy is needed to organize matter and to hold matter together. Matter uses energy to develop into many complex and beautiful forms.

Why should you learn about matter? Your body is made of matter. The life processes that take place in your body are the results of changes in matter. For example, the food you eat can be used to make energy. You can then use this energy to walk, to talk, and to think.

3-1 Matter

Everything you see around you is made of matter. There are many different kinds of matter. You know that air, iron, and your skin are not the same substances. Neither are water, blood, and gasoline. Each of these substances has its own properties, or characteristics.

The characteristics of a substance that you can observe with your senses are its physical properties. For example, shape, volume, color, odor, and texture are physical properties. What are some physical properties of water, air, and iron?

Matter exists in one of three states—solid, liquid, or gas. The state of matter depends mainly upon its temperature. For example, if you place a container of water in a freezer, the water soon changes to ice. Ice exists only below zero degrees Celsius (0 °C). Ice keeps its shape and has a definite volume. Any substance that has a definite shape and a definite volume is a **solid.**

What happens if you remove ice from the freezer and let the ice set upon a counter? As the temperature rises above 0 °C, the ice melts and loses its shape. Its physical properties change, but it is still water. Although the particles of water move around easily, they occupy a definite space. A substance that has a definite volume, but not a definite shape, is a **liquid.** A liquid takes the shape of its container.

Water boils when its temperature rises to 100 °C. At this point, the water is in the process of changing from a liquid to a **gas.** You call this gas steam. A gas has no definite shape or volume.

The physical properties of a substance can change without changing the substance itself. This kind of change is called a **physical change.** A change in state is a physical change. The physical properties of a substance change when its state changes.

Skill Builder

Observing   Obtain several containers of different shapes and sizes. Using a graduated cylinder, measure 20 mL of water. Pour this volume of water into each container. Observe how the same volume of water takes the shape of its container.

Think & Discuss

1. What is matter?
2. Identify and describe three states of matter.
3. How does the state of water limit the way it can be used by living things?

3-2 Elements, Compounds, and Mixtures

Matter is made up of small particles called **atoms.** Different combinations of atoms make up all the different kinds of matter you see around you. So far, chemists have identified about 90 different atoms that exist in nature. Several others can be made in the laboratory.

Atoms and Elements

All atoms have the same basic structure. In the center of the atom is the nucleus (NEW-klee-us). The nucleus of an atom contains particles called protons and neutrons (NOO-trahns). Each proton has an electrical charge of +1. Neutrons do not have an electrical charge.

Particles called electrons are found outside the nucleus of an atom. Each electron has an electrical charge of −1. The number of electrons in an atom is equal to the number of protons in that atom. Thus, an atom does not have an electrical charge. It is neutral.

Electrons move around the nucleus in paths called orbits. Each orbit can hold a certain number of electrons. For example, the orbit closest to the nucleus can hold two electrons. Orbits farther from the nucleus can hold up to eight electrons. Each kind of atom has a different number of electrons moving around its nucleus. However, the number of electrons moving around the nucleus is equal to the number of protons in the nucleus.

Atoms tend to reach a stable state that is similar to homeostasis in living things. A stable atom must have

Key Points

- An element is a substance that cannot be divided into simpler substances. The smallest particle of an element is an atom. A molecule is the smallest particle of a substance.

- A compound is made up of two or more elements that are chemically bonded. A mixture is a combination of substances that are not chemically bonded.

Study Hint

You can imagine electrons moving around the nucleus by comparing the movement of electrons to the movement of bees around a hive.

Figure 3–1 Models are used to represent atoms. Electron orbits can be pictured as a "cloud" (center).

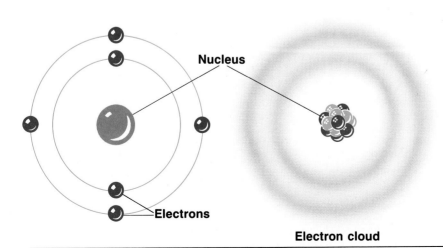

Nucleus

Electrons

Electron cloud

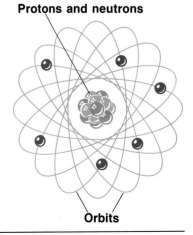

Protons and neutrons

Orbits

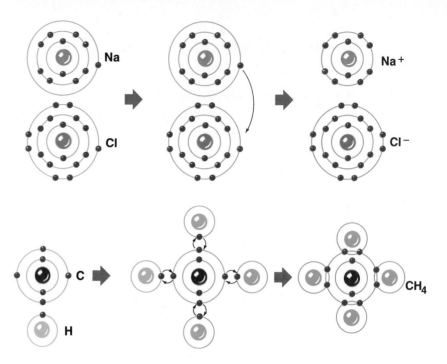

Figure 3–2 When sodium (Na) transfers an electron to chlorine (Cl), the two atoms becomes ions (top). Carbon (C) shares electrons with four hydrogen (H) atoms to form a stable compound (bottom).

eight electrons in its outermost orbit. To become stable, most atoms must give, take, or share electrons with other atoms. An atom that gives or takes electrons becomes an electrically charged atom called an **ion.**

Substances that are made up entirely of atoms of the same kind are called **elements** (EL-uh-munts). Elements cannot be divided into simpler substances by ordinary chemical means.

Look at Table 3-1. Notice that each element has an abbreviation, or symbol. The symbol of an element represents one atom of the element. What is the symbol for hydrogen? The symbol for hydrogen is H. The symbol for iodine is I. What is the symbol for magnesium?

Table 3-1 Some Common Elements Important to Living Things			
ELEMENT	**SYMBOL**	**ELEMENT**	**SYMBOL**
Calcium	Ca	Manganese	Mn
Carbon	C	Nitrogen	N
Chlorine	Cl	Oxygen	O
Copper	Cu	Potassium	K
Fluorine	F	Silicon	Si
Hydrogen	H	Sodium	Na
Iodine	I	Sulfur	S
Iron	Fe	Tin	Sn
Magnesium	Mg	Zinc	Zn

Molecules and Compounds

A **molecule** (MAHL-uh-kyool) is the smallest part of a substance that has all the chemical properties of that substance. Molecules are made up of atoms of the same or different kinds of elements. For example, molecules of gases such as oxygen (O), hydrogen (H), and nitrogen (N) form diatomic molecules. A diatomic molecule is made up of two atoms of the same kind.

When atoms of different elements share electrons, they form a **compound.** A compound is made up of two or more atoms that are chemically combined. Water and carbon dioxide are compounds. Compounds always contain the same elements in the same proportions. For example, a water molecule always has two atoms of hydrogen and one atom of oxygen. Carbon dioxide always has one atom of carbon and two atoms of oxygen. Some common substances are shown in Table 3-2.

Table 3-2 Common Substances	
NAME	MOLECULAR FORMULA
Water	H_2O
Ammonia	NH_3
Oxygen	O_2
Hydrogen	H_2
Carbon dioxide	CO_2
Table salt	$NaCl$
Table sugar (sucrose)	$C_{12}H_{22}O_{11}$

Molecular Formulas

A **molecular** (muh-LEK-yuh-lur) **formula** shows the kind and number of atoms in a molecule. In a molecular formula, subscripts are used to show the number of atoms that make up the molecule. When only one atom of an element is present, a chemist writes the symbol for the element. When more than one atom is present, the chemist writes the number of atoms just below the symbol. That number is called a subscript.

Chemical Change

When atoms join to form a compound, a **chemical change** takes place. A chemical change always uses or gives off energy. Unlike a physical change, a chemical change results in a new substance. The properties of the elements making up the compound also change.

☞ Water is a compound made up of hydrogen and oxygen. However, hydrogen and oxygen are very different from water. Both hydrogen and oxygen are gases. Hydrogen is explosive. Oxygen does not burn, but it is needed for burning to take place. Water is a colorless, odorless, and tasteless liquid. What kind of change do you think takes place when iron rusts?

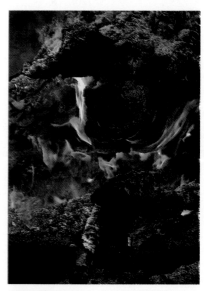

Figure 3–3 A burning log gives off energy in the form of heat and light.

Water molecule   **Sugar molecule**

Figure 3–4 When sugar dissolves in water, a solution is formed.

Figure 3–5 The strength of acids and bases is measured on the pH scale.

Mixtures

When substances combine, but do not change chemically, a **mixture** is formed. You see examples of mixtures every day. For example, tea, mayonnaise, and salad dressing are common mixtures. Most mixtures can be separated easily. How could you separate a mixture of salt and water?

Solutions

A **solution** is a mixture that is formed when the molecules of one substance mix evenly with those of another substance. One substance is called the **solute** (SAHL-yoot). The solute dissolves in the second substance. The substance in which the solute dissolves is called the **solvent.**

Acids and Bases

Water molecules can split into positive hydrogen ions (H^+) and negative hydroxide ions (OH^-). In pure water, the number of H^+ ions is equal to the number of OH^- ions. As a result, pure water is a neutral substance.

A solution that contains more H^+ ions than pure water is called an **acid.** Hydrochloric acid in your stomach helps you digest the food you eat. A solution that contains more OH^- ions than pure water is called a **base.** Ammonium hydroxide is a base that is produced as a waste product by many living things.

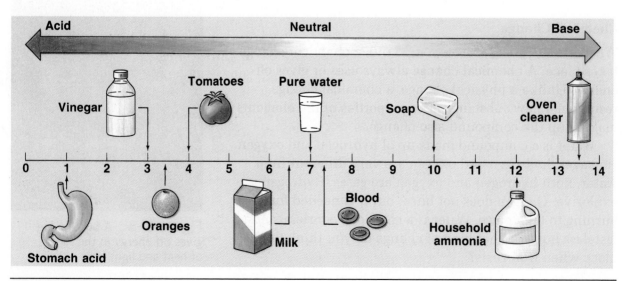

ACTIVITY 3-1

PROBLEM: Are common household substances acidic, basic, or neutral?

Science Process Skills
observing, classifying, predicting, interpreting data

Background Information
The pH scale is a numerical scale that goes from 1 to 14. Any number below 7 represents an acid. Any number above 7 represents a base. The number 7 represents a neutral substance. The pH of a solution can be measured with special paper that changes color at different pH levels. Litmus paper also can be used to identify a base, an acid, or a neutral substance. Red litmus paper turns blue in the presence of a base. Blue litmus paper turns red in the presence of an acid. A neutral substance does not change the color of either blue or red litmus paper.

Materials

dropper	vinegar
red and blue litmus	milk
paper	orange juice
water	ammonia
shampoo	liquid bleach
liquid antacid	dishwashing liquid
lemon juice	

Data Table: Acid, Base, or Neutral?

SUBSTANCE	PREDICTION	ACID	BASE	NEUTRAL
water				
shampoo				
antacid				
lemon juice				
vinegar				
milk				
orange juice				
ammonia				
bleach				
dishwashing liquid				

Procedure

1. Copy the Data Table shown.
2. **PREDICT**   Predict whether you think each substance listed in the table is an acid, a base, or neutral. Write the word "acid," "base," or "neutral" in the Prediction column of your Data Table.
3. Using the dropper, place one drop of water on the red litmus paper and one drop of water on the blue litmus paper. Note any color changes. Place an X in the proper column based on your observations.

4. Repeat step 3 for each substance that you are testing. **CAUTION: Wear your safety goggles and a lab apron. If any substances get on your skin, rinse them off immediately with plenty of water.**
5. Clean your work area. Be sure to dispose of materials properly. Wash your hands thoroughly before leaving your work area.

Observations
1. **a.** Which substances are acids?   **b.** Which are bases?   **c.** Which are neutral?
2. Compare your predictions with your actual results. Were you surprised to find out that certain substances were acidic, basic, or neutral? If so, which ones? If not, why not?

Conclusions
1. Does litmus paper indicate the pH of a substance? Explain your answer.
2. The pH of your skin and hair ranges between a pH of 4.5 to 5.5. Did you test any substances that could be harmful or damaging to your skin or hair? If so, which substances?

Colloids and Suspensions

Sometimes two substances do not mix evenly with each other. Instead, one substance forms fibers, droplets, or particles in the other. If the two substances stay mixed and do not separate, the system is called a colloid (KAHL-oid). Gelatin wiggles because it is partly solid and partly liquid. In your body cells, colloids give the cells a similar fluid firmness. Fog and milk are other colloids.

Unlike the particles in a colloid, the particles or droplets in a suspension are heavy enough to settle out over time. Your blood is a suspension. Red blood cells will settle out of blood fluid if a sample of blood in a container is left undisturbed.

Think & Discuss

4. What is an atom?

5. What is an element?

6. Explain the relationship between molecules and compounds.

7. What is the difference between mixtures and compounds?

★ **8.** Name two chemical changes and two physical changes in matter that you can observe in your environment.

Key Points

- Living things are made up of many kinds of chemicals that can undergo physical or chemical changes.

- Organic compounds contain carbon, while most inorganic compounds do not.

- Compounds needed by living things include water, salts, carbohydrates, lipids, proteins, and nucleic acids.

3-3 Types of Compounds

Chemists divide their field into organic and inorganic chemistry. Organic chemistry is the study of organic compounds. Organic compounds are compounds that contain carbon.

Most inorganic compounds are made from elements other than carbon. One exception is carbon dioxide (CO_2), which is an inorganic compound containing carbon. Your body needs many inorganic compounds, including water.

Water

Many substances will not react with each other unless they are dissolved in water. Water also is an excellent solvent for inorganic molecules. Each water molecule is like a tiny magnet, with a positive end and a negative end. Opposite electrical charges attract each other. Thus, a substance such as an ion, which has either a positive or a negative charge, is attracted to water molecules. This attraction allows ions to dissolve easily in water. Would an ion with a negative charge be attracted to the positive end or negative end of a water molecule? Why?

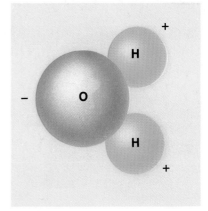

Figure 3–6 The atoms in a water molecule (H_2O) are electrically charged.

Salts

In addition to water, living things also need certain inorganic substances called salts. A **salt** is formed when an acid reacts with a base.

Many salts occur naturally on the earth. You are probably most familiar with sodium chloride (NaCl), or common table salt. In the body, sodium chloride helps your nerves carry messages. If you eat salty foods, you may get very thirsty. You probably would respond by drinking water. This is one example of how chemistry affects your behavior.

Organic Compounds

Most organic compounds contain long chains or rings of carbon. Carbon can bond with itself and with many other elements. Four kinds of organic compounds are important in your body.

Carbohydrates

Compounds made from carbon, hydrogen, and oxygen are called **carbohydrates** (kar-buh-HY-drayts). Sugars and starches are examples of carbohydrates. Sugars are simple carbohydrates that store and transfer energy. Starches are complex carbohydrates made up of long chains of glucose. ☞ Some examples of sugars are sucrose, glucose, and lactose. You are probably most familiar with sucrose, which is table sugar. Glucose is probably the most important sugar needed by your body. Glucose is a simple sugar used by your body for energy. Lactose is milk sugar.

Lipids

Fats, oils, and waxes are examples of **lipids** (LIP-uds). Lipids are made mostly of carbon and hydrogen. Gram for

Figure 3–7 Plants, such as potatoes, store food as starch.

Figure 3–8 A thick layer of fat, or blubber, keeps seals from losing body heat.

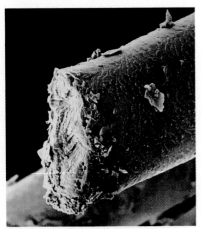

Figure 3–9 Your hair is made of protein. The hair shaft in this SEM has been cut.

gram, lipids store much more energy than other organic compounds.

◑Lipids repel water. The leaves of many plants often have thick, waxy layers. These waxy layers keep the plants from losing water. Animals have oil to protect their fur, feathers, and skin. Oil on the feathers of ducks keeps the feathers from getting waterlogged. Animals also have layers of fat for padding and insulation. How does fat insulate an animal? Fat prevents the body from losing heat, in much the same way that insulation keeps heat in a house. For this reason, a thick layer of fat is very important to animals that live in cold climates.

Proteins

Molecules of carbon, hydrogen, oxygen, and nitrogen are called **proteins** (PRO-teenz). Sulfur is another element that is commonly found in proteins. Proteins are very large molecules. Your body contains thousands of different kinds of proteins. All of these proteins are made up of smaller compounds called amino acids. Do you think amino acids are organic compounds or inorganic compounds?

Nucleic Acids

The making of proteins is controlled by organic compounds called **nucleic** (new-KLEE-ik) **acids.** Nucleic acids control the cell and determine heredity. Heredity is the passing of traits, or characteristics, from parent to offspring.

Think & Discuss

9. Why are amino acids often called the "building blocks" of proteins?
10. What is the difference between organic and inorganic compounds?
11. How are chemistry and biology related?
12. Identify four major groups of organic compounds in living things.
13. Develop a theory to explain why so many different chemicals are needed by living things.

BIOLOGY and YOU
Consumer Biology

Avoiding Excess Salts, Sugars, and Fats in Foods

Many people include too much salt, sugar, and fat in their diets. Excess fat and salt can lead to high blood pressure and heart disease. Sugar promotes tooth decay and gum disease.

Of course, you cannot completely eliminate salt, sugar, or fat from your diet. Your body needs each of these substances to function properly. You should, however, try to limit your intake of these substances.

How can you find out if a food contains a lot of salt, sugar, or fat? One of the best ways to learn what substances foods contain is to read the labels on packaged or prepared foods.

A food label has two parts. The first part indicates the number of calories per serving. It also lists the amounts of fat, protein, carbohydrate, fiber, cholesterol, and sodium contained in the product. The second part of the label lists the U.S. RDA, or percentage of United States Recommended Daily Allowances, for the food. This list contains information about the amounts of vitamins and minerals needed by the body daily.

Most food labels also include a list of ingredients.

This list tells you all the ingredients in the food. It also gives you an idea of how much of an ingredient is in the food. For example, the first ingredient listed is the ingredient used most. The ingredient listed last is the ingredient used least.

Sometimes food labels are deceiving. For example, the words "sugar-free" or "sugarless" often appear on packaged foods. When you see these words, you may think there is no sugar in the food, but this is not necessarily true. The food may contain corn syrup. Corn syrup is another name for sugar. Other names for sugar are dextrose, honey, brown sugar, sucrose, fructose, and natural sweeteners.

"Low Salt" and "Salt-Free" are other phrases found on food labels. These foods may be low in table salt ($NaCl$), but they may still contain sodium. Sodium is the harmful element in salt. Too much sodium can cause your body to retain fluids. Sodium also is believed to be a cause of high blood pressure.

When looking at the fat content listed on a food label, you should look at both saturated and unsaturated fats. Unsaturated fats are not as bad for you as saturated fats. Most unsaturated fats are plant oils. Oils are liquids at room temperature. Corn oil,

olive oil, sunflower oil, and peanut oil all are unsaturated fats.

Saturated fats usually are solid at room temperature. Examples of saturated fats include milk products, butter, shortening, and meat fat. Coconut and palm oils, which are found in most snack foods, also are saturated fats.

To Think About
- Why is it important to understand food labels?
- Why should you know the ingredients of a food item?

The Chemistry of Life 51

Chapter Review

3-1 Matter

- The three common states of matter are solid, liquid, and gas.
- Solids have a definite shape and volume.
- Liquids have a definite volume, but gases do not.

3-2 Elements, Compounds, and Mixtures

- An element is a simple substance that cannot be broken down by ordinary chemical means.
- The smallest particle of an element is an atom.
- A molecule is the smallest part of a compound that has all the properties of that compound.
- A compound is made up of two or more elements that are chemically combined.
- A mixture is a combination of substances that are not chemically bonded.

3-3 Types of Compounds

- Living things are made up of compounds.
- Organic compounds contain carbon; whereas most inorganic compounds do not.
- Compounds needed by living things include water, salts, carbohydrates, lipids, proteins, and nucleic acids.

VOCABULARY LIST

acid (46)	elements (44)	mixture (46)	salt (49)
atoms (43)	gas (42)	molecular formula (45)	solid (42)
base (46)	ion (44)	molecule (45)	solute (46)
carbohydrates (49)	lipids (49)	nucleic acids (50)	solution (46)
chemical change (45)	liquid (42)	physical change (42)	solvent (46)
compound (45)	matter (41)	proteins (50)	

VOCABULARY REVIEW

Matching Write the word or term from the Vocabulary List that best matches each description.

1. solution that has more hydrogen ions than pure water
2. has a definite shape and volume
3. compounds made from carbon, hydrogen, and oxygen
4. formed when two substances combine without chemically reacting
5. anything that has mass and volume
6. smallest particle of a substance
7. fats, oils, and waxes
8. electrically charged atom

Identifying Relationships Identify the word or term in each group that does not belong. Explain why the word does not belong with the group.

1. proteins, base, amino acids
2. gas, liquid, chemical change
3. compound, physical change, molecule
4. nucleic acids, solute, solvent
5. atoms, elements, enzyme
6. molecular formula, atoms, solid
7. proteins, nucleic acid, salt
8. sugars, salts, carbohydrates
9. OH^-, acid, H^+
10. mixture, solution, compound

Completion Write the word or words that best complete each sentence.

1. The science that studies the nature of matter is _____.
2. The nucleus of an atom contains protons and _____.
3. A change in the state of a substance is a _____ change.
4. Fog and milk are examples of _____.
5. An acid that is found in your stomach is _____.
6. When atoms join to form a compound, a _____ change takes place.
7. Molecules made up of carbon, hydrogen, oxygen, and _____ are proteins.
8. The simple sugar used by the body for energy is _____.

Finding the Main Ideas Use the section number to find the sentence that answers each question. Then, write the sentence.

1. What are the three states of matter? (3-1)
2. What are the physical properties of a substance? (3-1)
3. What are the characteristics of a gas? (3-1)
4. What is an ion? (3-2)
5. What is a diatomic molecule? (3-2)
6. How does a chemical change differ from a physical change? (3-2)
7. What is an organic compound? (3-3)
8. What are two examples of carbohydrates? (3-3)
9. What organic compounds control the making of protein? (3-3)
10. How does the body use NaCl? (3-3)

Writing for Understanding One way to find out if you understand something is to write a brief summary of the information in your own words. Reread Section 3-1, Matter, on page 42, and write a brief summary of the information.

Critical Thinking Answer each of the following in complete sentences.

1. If all elements had atoms with a stable number of electrons, what effect would this have on chemical reactions?
2. Bonds are formed when atoms share, give, or take electrons to become more stable. What do you think determines which elements will bond with each other?
3. Based on information in this chapter, describe some of the ways in which matter and energy interact.
4. Why do you think all living things on the earth have the same basic organic compounds?
5. How does the energy released during chemical reactions account for the heat given off from your body?

1. Read about the field of biochemistry as a career. Make a poster that will show your classmates what a biochemist does.
2. Design an experiment to identify important physical characteristics of proteins, lipids, and carbohydrates.
3. Study the effect of dissolved substances on the boiling point or freezing point of water. Determine whether equal amounts of different substances have the same effect.
4. Write a report describing how biochemicals are used in industry.

Chapter 4 | Cells

Objectives

After you have completed this chapter, you will be able to

4-1 **state** the cell theory.

4-1 **explain** how the electron microscope has aided biologists in the study of cells.

4-2 **identify** the main parts of the cell.

4-2 **name** two cell structures found in plant cells but not in animal cells.

4-2 **list** the levels of organization in living things.

4-3 **explain** the importance of respiration and photosynthesis.

4-4 **explain** the difference between mitosis and meiosis.

Science Process Skills

In this chapter, two science skills are highlighted. Symbols show some places where these skills are used.

Observing: When you observe, you use one or more of your senses to gather information.

Inferring: When you infer, you form a conclusion based upon facts and not direct observation.

What are you made of? The ancient Greeks believed that everything was made up of just four substances: earth, air, fire, and water. Around 1609, Galileo used a homemade telescope to observe the night sky. Galileo's discovery of the moons of Jupiter made many people realize that the earth was not the center of the universe.

About 50 years after Galileo, the microscope opened up entire new worlds much smaller than could ever have been imagined. Hundreds of tiny living things could be seen in a single drop of water. Another startling discovery was the existence of cells. One answer to the question "What are you made of?" is cells.

4-1 Cells and Cell Theory

Key Points

- Cell theory states that the cell is the basic unit of living things; that all living things are made up of cells; and that cells come only from other cells.

- The electron microscope creates pictures of cells with better resolution and higher magnifications than the light microscope.

Do you know who the first person was to see a cell? Do you know who named the cell? Take a trip back to the seventeenth century. Imagine that you are the English scientist Robert Hooke. The year is 1665, just after the time of Shakespeare. You have cut a thin slice of cork, and are looking at the cork with a homemade microscope. Look at Figure 4-1 to see what you observe.

Hooke compared what he observed to the cells, or box-like rooms, in which monks slept. For this reason, Hooke named the structures that make up cork "cells." The cork cells observed by Hooke had no structures within them. Hooke saw only the walls of dead plant cells.

Anton van Leeuwenhoek (AN-tun van LAY-vun-hook), a Dutch lens maker, was the first person to observe living cells. Van Leeuwenhoek used a simple microscope he had made to observe such things as blood, rainwater, and teeth scrapings. In 1675, van Leeuwenhoek observed single-celled organisms in a drop of pond water. He called these tiny living things "animalcules." What characteristics of living things do you think led van Leeuwenhoek to conclude that these organisms were "animalcules"?

Cell Theory

Almost 175 years after the discoveries of Hooke and van Leeuwenhoek, two important conclusions were stated about cells. In 1838, Matthias Schleiden (SHLY-dun), a German botanist, concluded that all plants were made up of cells. The next year, Theodor Schwann, a German biologist, concluded that all animals were made up of cells.

In 1855, Rudolph Virchow (FEER-koh), a German physician, stated a third important conclusion about cells. Virchow concluded that cells came only from other living cells. Together, the conclusions of Schleiden, Schwann, Virchow, and other biologists were developed into the cell theory. The cell theory states the following:

- All living things are made up of one or more cells.
- Cells are the basic units of structure and function in living things.
- Cells come only from other living cells.

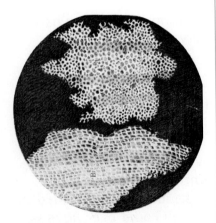

Figure 4-1 This photograph shows what Robert Hooke saw when he first observed cork cells. What was Hooke actually seeing?

Cell Study

Cytologists (sy-TAHL-uh-jists) are biologists who study cells. Today's cytologists agree with the ideas included in the cell theory. Why do cytologists consider these ideas to be part of a theory?

To study most cells, cytologists must use some kind of microscope. Microscopes have been greatly improved since the time of Hooke and van Leeuwenhoek. The instrument that has been most helpful to cytologists in the twentieth century is the electron microscope.

The transmission electron microscope (TEM) was the first electron microscope used by cytologists. The TEM has better resolution than the light microscope. This improved resolution allows objects to be viewed at higher magnifications.

One problem with the TEM was that specimens had to be plated with metal before they could be studied. This metal plating required much time to prepare. It also killed living specimens. In 1981, Gerd Binning of West Germany and Heinrich Rohrer of Switzerland developed the scanning electron microscope, or SEM. The SEM allows cytologists to observe unplated living tissue. Cytologists can then study the cells during the short period before the electrons kill the cells.

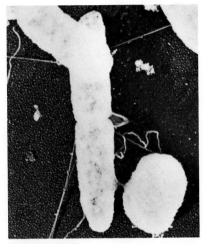

Figure 4-2 This image of bacterial cells was magnified 40,000X by a transmission electron microscope.

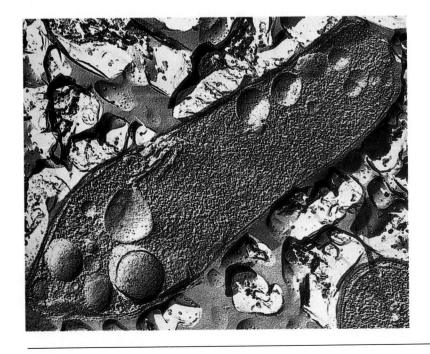

Figure 4-3 The SEM is used to see details in a cell. Notice the details in this SEM image of a bacterial cell.

Study Hint

To find out more about what laboratory technicians do, read the Careers in Biology feature at the end of the chapter.

Cytologists have learned that most cells contain many smaller structures. To observe the structures within cells, the cells must be broken apart. A blender is used to break up the cells and release the cell structures. After the cells have been broken apart, they are prepared for observation under the electron microscope. Much of this work is done by laboratory technicians.

Cytologists also use special laboratory techniques to study cells. For example, laboratory technicians may grow cell cultures, or populations of identical cells. A cytologist may use the cell culture to study cell growth or to observe how cells respond to different substances in the environment.

Think & Discuss

1. What is a cell?
2. Define cytologist.
3. State the cell theory.
4. Describe the difference between the cells observed by Hooke and those observed by van Leeuwenhoek.
5. Why would observing living cells be more important to cytologists than observing dead cells?

4-2 Cell Structure and Function

Key Points

- Three main parts of a cell are the cell membrane, nucleus, and cytoplasm.
- Plant cells have both cell walls and chloroplasts, which are lacking in animal cells.
- Complex living things are organized at different levels, including cells, tissues, organs, and organ systems.

In the cell theory, cells are described as the basic units of structure and function in living things. Do you know why the cell is described in this way? Think of a brick house. What is the basic unit of structure? Just as each brick is the basic unit of structure of the house, a cell is the basic unit of structure of all living things. The house is made up of many bricks. Living things are made up of one or more cells. A cell also is the basic unit of function of living things, because each cell carries out the same life processes as an organism. For example, a cell grows, responds to its surroundings, and reproduces.

👁️ Many different kinds of cells make up your body. Look at the shapes of the human body cells shown in Figure 4-4 on page 59. Notice that a nerve cell has many branches. The branches of a nerve cell are needed to send and

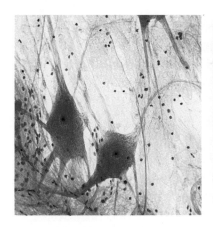
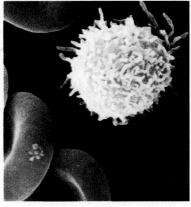

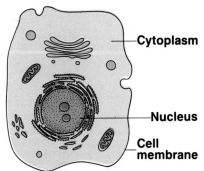

Figure 4-4 Nerve cells (left) and blood cells (right) have different shapes because they perform different functions in the body.

receive messages in many directions at the same time. A nerve cell is adapted to its function. In fact, the shape of every cell in your body is adapted to its function.

Most cells are very small. Plant and animal cells usually are between 10 and 50 micrometers in size. The smallest cells may be 0.2 micrometers in diameter.

► Some cells may be very large. Several nerve cells in your legs are about one meter long. A large cell that is found in many animals is an egg. For example, a single cell that you probably see everyday is a chicken egg. How many cells do you think make up an ostrich egg?

Main Cell Parts

Three cell structures control most of the activities that take place in a cell. Figure 4-5 shows the three main parts of the cell. These structures are common to most cells, including the cells that make up your body.

Cell Membrane

Cells are enclosed by a thin structure called the **cell membrane.** The cell membrane is a living part of the cell made up mostly of lipids and proteins. The cell membrane is sometimes called the plasma (PLAZ-muh) membrane.

The cell membrane has three important jobs, or functions. Its first job is to protect the inside of the cell by separating the cell from its surroundings. The second job is to support the cell and give it shape. The third job of the cell membrane is to control the passage of substances into and out of the cell. This function is very important in maintaining homeostasis, or balance, in the cell.

Figure 4-5 The three basic parts of a cell are the cell membrane, the nucleus, and the cytoplasm.

Cytoplasm

Nucleus

Cell membrane

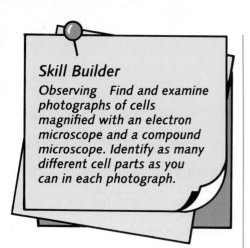
Cell Wall

Some cells, such as plant cells, have a structure surrounding the cell membrane. This structure is the **cell wall.** Unlike the cell membrane, the cell wall is not a living part of the cell.

The cell wall is made mostly of cellulose (SEL-yoo-lohs). Cellulose is a carbohydrate made up of many sugar molecules linked together. Cell walls also contain pectin. Pectin is a starch that is used to thicken jams and jellies.

The cell wall protects a cell and gives it shape. The cell wall also provides the cell with support. Because of the support provided by the cell wall, large plants do not need a skeleton.

Nucleus

If you were to observe a stained cell with a microscope, you would see a dark, round structure near the center of the cell. This structure is the **nucleus** (NEW-klee-us). The nucleus is the "control center" of the cell. The nucleus controls most of the activities that take place in the cell. The nucleus also controls cell reproduction. What would happen to a cell if the nucleus were removed?

▶ The nucleus is separated from the rest of the cell by the **nuclear membrane.** Like the cell membrane, the nuclear membrane has three jobs. What do you think the three jobs of the nuclear membrane are?

◉ Look at Figure 4-5 on page 59. Notice the small round structures inside the nucleus. These structures are called **nucleoli** (new-klee-OHL-y). Cytologists are not completely sure what job the nucleoli perform. However, most cytologists agree that the nucleoli help make proteins.

Structures called **chromosomes** (KROH-muh-sohms) also are located within the nucleus. Chromosomes control heredity (huh-RED-uh-tee). Heredity is the passing of traits from parent to offspring.

Cytoplasm

Have you ever cracked open an egg? The **cytoplasm** (SYT-uh-plaz-um) of most cells resembles the white part of an uncooked egg. Cytoplasm is all the living substance in a cell except the nucleus. Most of a cell is made up of cytoplasm. Most of the life processes take place within the cytoplasm of the cell.

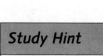

Study Hint

"Cytoplasm" means "cell substance." Cytoplasm is about 80 percent water.

Cell Organelles

A cell can be compared to a factory. A factory has many different machines. Each machine in the factory has a special job to do, but all of the machines must work together to keep the factory running properly.

Think of a cell as a miniature factory. The "machines" of the cell factory are its **organelles.** Organelles are small structures in the cytoplasm that have special jobs to do. The organelles must work together to keep the cell working properly.

Mitochondria

Small rice-shaped structures are also found in the cytoplasm of the cell. These structures are called **mitochondria** (myt-uh-KAHN-dree-uh). Mitochondria can be seen only with an electron microscope.

The mitochondria are often called the "powerhouses" of the cell. Why have the mitochondria been given this name? Mitochondria break down glucose to provide the cell with energy. The energy is used by the cell to carry out its life processes.

Endoplasmic Reticulum

Many different activities take place in a cell. For example, substances constantly move from one cell organelle to another. How is all of the movement managed? Cytologists have discovered a fine network of tubes, or canals, within the cell. This network of tubes is called the **endoplasmic reticulum** (EN-duh-plaz-mic rih-TIK-yuh-lum). The endoplasmic reticulum forms a series of passageways throughout the cytoplasm. It acts as a "highway system" for the cell.

Figure 4-6 Mitochondria (left) are the cell organelles that produce energy. The endoplasmic reticulum (right) appears as a network of tubes within the cytoplasm.

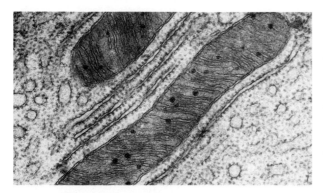
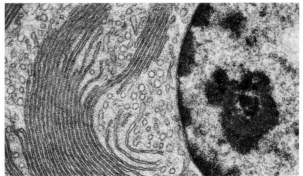

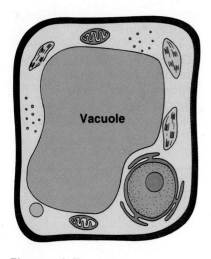

Figure 4-7 The large space in the center of this plant cell is a vacuole.

Vacuoles

Figure 4-7 shows a plant cell. A large liquid-filled space can be seen in the cytoplasm of this cell. This space is called a **vacuole** (VAK-yoo-wohl). Each vacuole is surrounded by a membrane.

Vacuoles are the "storage bins" of the cell. Some vacuoles store substances that will be used by the cell. Other vacuoles store wastes that will be removed from the cell.

Ribosomes

A cell has many small round structures scattered throughout its cytoplasm. These structures are called **ribosomes** (RY-buh-sohms). The job of the ribosomes is to make proteins. For this reason, the ribosomes are often called "protein factories."

Centrioles

Two small rod-shaped organelles are located near the nucleus of an animal cell. These organelles are called **centrioles** (SEN-tree-ohls). The centrioles are involved only in animal cell reproduction.

Plant and Animal Cells

Figure 4-8 shows a plant cell and an animal cell. What differences do you observe between these cells? You may notice that the plant cell has round green structures that the animal cell does not have. These green structures are **chloroplasts** (KLOR-uh-plasts).

Figure 4-8 Compare the structures and organelles in an animal cell (left) and a plant cell (right).

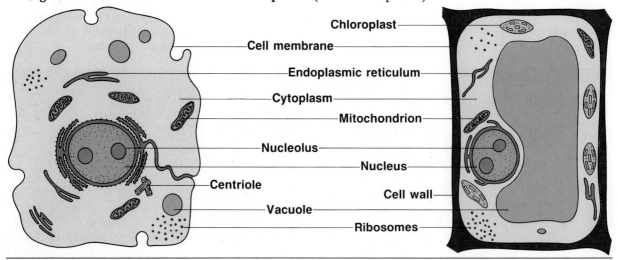

Chloroplast

Cell membrane

Endoplasmic reticulum

Cytoplasm

Mitochondrion

Nucleolus

Nucleus

Centriole

Cell wall

Vacuole

Ribosomes

Chloroplasts contain the green pigment chlorophyll (KLOR-uh-fil). Plants need chlorophyll to carry out photosynthesis. Photosynthesis is the food-making process of green plants. Animal cells do not contain chlorophyll. How do animals obtain their food?

The number and sizes of vacuoles differ from one kind of cell to another. For example, animal cells usually have many small vacuoles in their cytoplasm. A plant cell, however, may contain only one or two large vacuoles.

Two other differences can be observed between most plant and animal cells. One of these differences is the cell wall. Plant cells always have a cell wall. Animal cells do not have a cell wall. Another difference is the centrioles, which are located near the nucleus of an animal cell. Plant cells do not have centrioles.

Organization in Living Things

Some organisms are unicellular. Other organisms, like you, are multicellular. Multicellular organisms may have billions of cells. How do all of these cells work together? What kind of organization do they have? For one thing, complex organisms have cells that specialize. That is, each kind of cell can do one job well.

Complex organisms have several levels of organization. Groups of cells that look the same and do the same job are called **tissues.** You have at least 100 different kinds of cells in your body. Many of these cells are organized into tissues. Your blood, for example, is a tissue made up of several different kinds of cells.

Tissues that work together to do a specific job form an **organ.** Your stomach is an organ. The stomach is made up of different kinds of tissue. For example, the stomach is

Skill Builder

Observing   Examine plant cells from the tip of an Elodea leaf, using the compound microscope. Follow the instructions for mounting and examining the leaf given by your teacher. Sketch one cell and try to identify the location of the vacuole, the chloroplasts, the nucleus, the cell wall, and the cytoplasm.

Figure 4-9   Notice the levels of organization from cells, to tissues, to organs, to organ systems.

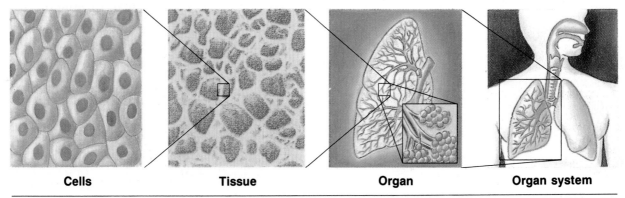

| Cells | Tissue | Organ | Organ system |

made up of nerve tissue, blood tissue, and muscle tissue. Your brain, large intestine, and heart also are organs. Leaves and roots are organs in plants.

Groups of organs that work together to do a certain job form **organ systems.** Your digestive system includes your mouth, stomach, small intestine, and colon, as well as your liver, pancreas, and gallbladder.

Think & Discuss

6. What is cytoplasm?

7. "Organelle" means "little organ." How are organelles similar to organs?

8. List seven important parts of the cell.

9. Which cell parts are found only in plants? Which cell parts are found only in animals?

10. All large organisms have cells with organelles. What advantage do organelles give to the cell?

4-3 Cell Processes

Like all living things, a cell must carry out certain processes and take in needed substances from its surroundings to stay alive. For example, a cell must obtain food. The cell also must be able to break down the food to produce energy. If a cell cannot carry out these processes, it will die.

Diffusion

Place a few drops of ink in a glass filled with water. What happens? The ink quickly begins to spread throughout the water. Why does the ink spread throughout the water? The ink spreads because the molecules that make up the ink are moving. The molecules of all substances are in constant motion.

Most molecules move from areas where they are crowded, or concentrated, to areas where they are less crowded, or less concentrated. The movement of molecules from areas of greater concentration to areas of lesser concentration is called **diffusion** (dih-FYOO-zhun).

Diffusion occurs when substances, such as oxygen and carbon dioxide, move into a cell through the cell membrane. How do substances pass through the cell membrane? The cell membrane has tiny holes, or pores. Substances enter and leave the cell by passing through the pores in the cell membrane.

How does the cell membrane regulate the passage of substances into and out of the cell? The size and concentration of a substance determines what can pass through the cell membrane. If a molecule is too large, it cannot pass through the pores of the cell membrane. Remember that molecules usually move from areas of greater concentration to areas of lesser concentration. Molecules of a substance will move through the cell membrane so that the concentration of that substance is the same on both sides of the membrane.

Osmosis

Many substances dissolve in water before they pass through the cell membrane. The diffusion of water through a membrane is called **osmosis** (ahs-MOH-sis). Osmosis can sometimes be a problem for cells. For example, suppose a cell is placed in pure water. The cytoplasm of a cell is made mostly of water. However, salts and other dissolved substances, called solutes, are also in the cytoplasm. Is the concentration of water molecules higher inside or outside the cell?

Figure 4-10 Molecules of ink spread through a beaker of water until they are evenly distributed. What is this process called?

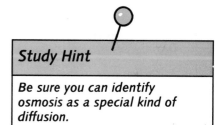

Study Hint

Be sure you can identify osmosis as a special kind of diffusion.

Cells **65**

ACTIVITY 4-1

PROBLEM: Can molecules move through a cell membrane?

Science Process Skills
observing, measuring, inferring

Background Information
The cell membrane separates a cell from other cells and from surrounding fluids. Certain molecules can pass through the cell membrane. The cell membrane is called a selectively permeable membrane because it allows some molecules to pass through, but not others.

Materials

3 eggs	metric ruler
3 250-mL beakers	plastic wrap
vinegar	3 rubber bands
oil	graduated cylinder
water	string

Procedure
1. Copy the Data Table shown.
2. Wrap the string around the middle of the first egg. Measure the length of string that just went around the egg. Record this length in the Data Table.
3. Wrap the string around the ends of the first egg. Measure the length of string that just went around the egg. Record this length in the Data Table.
4. Repeat steps 2 and 3 with the other eggs.
5. Pour 150 mL of vinegar into a 250-mL beaker. Place the first egg in this beaker.

6. Pour 150 mL of oil into a 250-mL beaker. Place the second egg in this beaker.
7. Pour 150 mL of water into a 250-mL beaker. Place the third egg in this beaker.
8. Cover each beaker with plastic wrap and seal the wrap with a rubber band to reduce evaporation.
9. On day 3, remove the first egg from the beaker of vinegar. Repeat steps 2 and 3. Record the amount of vinegar in the beaker after removing the egg.
10. Remove the other eggs from their beakers and repeat steps 2 and 3 for each egg.

Observations
1. **a.** In which beaker did the volume of liquid change? **b.** In which beakers did the volume of liquid stay the same?
2. Which egg changed in size?
3. Describe the differences in appearance and texture of the egg that changed.
4. Which egg is the control?

Conclusions
1. How did the size of the egg change as the volume of the liquid changed?
2. **a.** Which substance's molecules were able to pass through the egg's membranes? **b.** By what process were the molecules able to move through the membranes?

Data Table:	Egg Sizes and Liquid Volumes				
DAY		MEASUREMENT BEFORE SOAKING (CM)	MEASUREMENT AFTER SOAKING IN:		
			VINEGAR	OIL	WATER
1	Egg: Middle				
	Egg: End to end				
	Volume of Liquid				
3	Egg: Middle				
	Egg: End to end				
	Volume of Liquid				

Because there are fewer water molecules inside the cell than outside the cell, water will diffuse into the cell. However, most of the solutes in the cytoplasm cannot diffuse out of the cell. The cell membrane will not let them through. Predict what will happen if water keeps entering the cell and nothing leaves the cell.

Respiration and Photosynthesis

All living things need energy to carry out their life processes. For example, your body uses energy so you can move, think, or speak. Your body cells need a constant supply of energy to stay alive. How do organisms obtain the energy they need? Organisms obtain energy from food. Energy is released when the food molecules are broken down inside the cells.

Cellular Respiration

The process by which food molecules are broken down to provide energy for the cell is called cellular respiration. Cellular respiration takes place in the mitochondria. The chemical equation for respiration is

$$C_6H_{12}O_6 + O_2 \longrightarrow H_2O + CO_2 + energy$$

glucose + oxygen $\longrightarrow$ water + carbon dioxide + energy

During respiration, glucose is broken apart. Carbon dioxide is a waste product. Hydrogen from glucose combines with oxygen from the air to form water.

Photosynthesis

The process by which the sun's energy is converted to the chemical energy of glucose is called photosynthesis. Photosynthesis occurs in plant cells on the membranes of the chloroplasts. The chlorophyll in chloroplasts makes the process of photosynthesis possible.

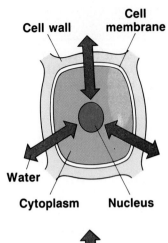
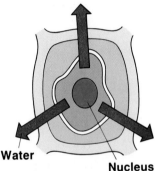

Figure 4-11 Normally, water enters and leaves a plant cell in equal amounts (top). If too much water leaves the cell, the cell will shrink (bottom).

Figure 4-12 Energy from the sun is changed into stored energy by plants through photosynthesis. Animals change stored energy into usable energy through respiration.

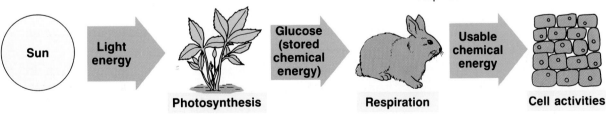

Study Hint

Look back at the equation for respiration. What relationship do you observe between these two equations?

The model of photosynthesis used by biologists begins when chlorophyll splits a water molecule into hydrogen and oxygen. The oxygen from the water is a waste product that is released as a gas. In later stages of photosynthesis, carbon dioxide from the air and hydrogen from the water unite to form glucose. The chemical equation for photosynthesis is

$$CO_2 + H_2O + energy \longrightarrow C_6H_{12}O_6 + O_2$$

carbon dioxide + water + energy $\longrightarrow$ glucose + oxygen

Think & Discuss

11. What is meant by the term "osmosis"?

12. What is diffusion?

13. Explain what would happen if a normal cell were placed in a solution with a very high concentration of solutes.

14. What two factors determine which substances can pass through the cell membrane?

15. Explain the relationship between the processes of osmosis and respiration.

4-4 Cellular Reproduction

Key Points

• Mitosis is the process through which chromosomes are distributed during asexual reproduction.

• Meiosis is the distribution of chromosomes to sex cells, or gametes.

All organisms grow. To make more of their kind, cells also must reproduce. Cells do this by dividing in two. This cell division is called cellular fission. Except in special cases, the cell's cytoplasm is divided almost evenly between the two new cells. The original cell is the parent cell. The new cells are called daughter cells.

Each of your body cells has two sets of 23 chromosomes. Four chromosome sets are shown in Figure 4-13 on page 69. For each chromosome in one set, there is a matching chromosome in the second set. Every time your body cells divide, the daughter cells receive both sets of chromosomes. How many chromosomes are there all together in a human body cell?

Cellular fission is a form of asexual reproduction. In sexual reproduction, a new organism is formed with one set of chromosomes from each parent.

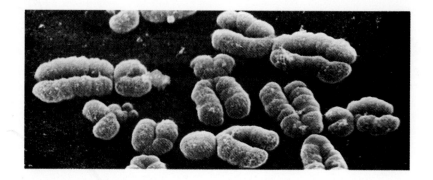

Figure 4-13 How would you describe the shapes of these chromosomes?

Mitosis

The process of distributing the chromosomes during cell division is called **mitosis** (my-TOH-sis). Mitosis is a form of asexual reproduction that results in the formation of identical cells. When a cell is not dividing, the DNA in the nucleus is in thin, uncoiled strands. Just before mitosis begins, the DNA doubles and forms paired chromosomes. Look at Figure 4-14 as you read the description of mitosis.

- By the time a cell is ready to divide, there are two copies of each set of chromosomes. The chromosomes coil, becoming short and thick. The nuclear membrane disappears and the chromosomes float in the cytoplasm. Spindle fibers form in the cytoplasm. The spindle fibers attach to the chromosomes and to both ends of the cell.

- All of the chromosomes line up across the center of the cell.

- The chromosomes separate. One copy of each chromosome is pulled to each end of the cell by the spindle fibers.

- The cell membrane begins to pinch the cell in two to divide the cytoplasm. A new nuclear membrane forms in each daughter cell. The daughter cells are identical to each other because the chromosomes in each cell are the same. The chromosomes uncoil and the cells begin to grow.

Meiosis

Chromosomes must sometimes be exchanged between cells. Otherwise, the offspring of all living things would be exactly like their parents. An exchange of chromosomes

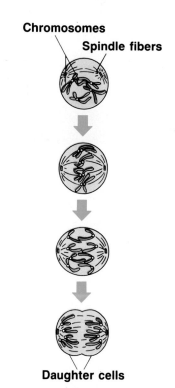

Chromosomes

Spindle fibers

Daughter cells

Figure 4-14 Mitosis results in the formation of two identical daughter cells.

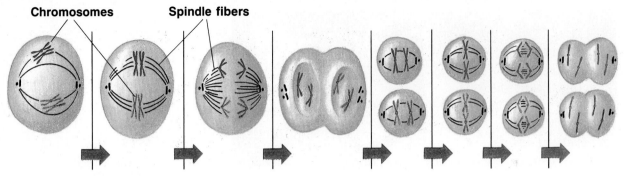

Chromosomes   Spindle fibers

Figure 4-15 Meiosis takes place in special cells in the testes of a male and in the ovaries of a female. The male cells become sperm and the female cells become eggs.

takes place during sexual reproduction. Sex cells, called **gametes** (GAM-eets), are formed. Later, the gametes combine to produce a new individual. The separation of chromosomes during the formation of gametes is called **meiosis** (my-OH-sis). Look at the process of meiosis as shown in Figure 4-15.

- At the beginning of meiosis, the nucleus breaks down and a chromosome from one set pairs up with a similar chromosome from the second set. Spindle fibers form.

- The paired chromosomes line up across the center of the cell.

- The paired chromosomes are pulled to opposite ends of the cell.

- The cell divides into two daughter cells. Each new cell contains one set of chromosomes.

- The new cells almost immediately begin to divide again. The spindle fibers form again.

- The paired chromosomes again line up in the center of the cell.

- One chromosome from each pair goes to each end of the cell.

- A nuclear membrane forms around each set of chromosomes. Four sex cells are formed. Each cell has only one set of chromosomes.

Think & Discuss

16. What are gametes?

17. Distinguish between meiosis and mitosis.

18. Does meiosis take place in body cells?

CAREERS in BIOLOGY

Skin Specialists

What is the first thing you notice when you meet a person? Usually you notice a person's appearance— especially the person's face. Several interesting careers involve improving the appearance of the skin through the use of cosmetics. Other rewarding careers involve treating diseases of the skin, such as skin cancer.

Cosmetologist

"Lights! Camera! Action!" How would you like to work on the set of a major motion picture? You might find yourself there if you decide to become a cosmetologist. A cosmetologist, or make-up artist, is a person who is skilled in applying cosmetics. Cosmetologists may work for a theatrical company, a television station, or in a beauty shop.

Cosmetologists need a steady hand and artistic ability. They also should enjoy working with people. Many high schools offer vocational training in cosmetology. In addition to obtaining a high school diploma, many cosmetologists also take courses in applying cosmetics.

For more information: Write to the National Accrediting Commission of Cosmetology Arts and Sciences, 1990 M St., NW, Suite 650, Washington, DC 20036.

Cosmetician

Cosmeticians sell or make cosmetics. Many cosmeticians also are skilled in applying cosmetics. The person in a department store who gives makeup demonstrations and counsels customers on the right makeup for their skin type is a cosmetician. Someone working in the lab of a cosmetic company also is a cosmetician. Some cosmeticians act as consultants. They visit people in their homes or places of business to sell and demonstrate cosmetics.

To become a cosmetician, you must first graduate from high school. You also must take cosmetics courses at a trade school.

For more information: Write to a cosmetic company or visit the cosmetics department of a major department store.

Skin Cancer Technician

Of all forms of cancer, skin cancer is the most likely to be cured if it is detected early. To detect skin cancer, a doctor specializing in skin diseases takes a sample of skin cells from an area suspected of being cancerous. The sample is sent to a laboratory for analysis. In the laboratory, a skin cancer technician prepares slides of the cells.

Skin cancer technicians work in hospitals, private laboratories, or in the research divisions of medical schools. To become a skin cancer technician, one must complete a formal training program in histologic (his-tuh-LAJ-ik) technology. Histology is the microscopic study of plant and animal tissues.

For more information: Write to the National Society for Histotechnology, 5900 Princess Garden Parkway, Suite 805, Lanham, MD 20706.

Chapter Review

CHAPTER SUMMARY

4-1 Cells and Cell Theory

- The cell theory states that the cell is the basic unit of structure and function in living things; that all living things are made up of one or more cells; and that cells come only from pre-existing cells.
- An electron microscope creates pictures with better resolution than a light microscope.

4-2 Cell Structure and Function

- The three main parts of a cell are the cell membrane, nucleus, and cytoplasm.
- Plant cells have cell walls and chloroplasts; animal cells do not.
- Animal cells have centrioles, which are missing in plant cells.

- Complex living things are organized at different levels, including cells, tissues, organs, and organ systems.

4-3 Cell Processes

- Respiration is the process of making energy from food molecules for use by the cell.
- Photosynthesis is the process through which plants convert sunlight to the chemical energy of glucose.

4-4 Cellular Reproduction

- Mitosis is the process through which chromosomes are distributed during asexual reproduction.
- Meiosis is the distribution of chromosomes to sex cells, or gametes.

VOCABULARY LIST

cell membrane (59)
cell wall (60)
centrioles (62)
chloroplasts (62)
chromosomes (60)
cytoplasm (60)

diffusion (64)
endoplasmic reticulum (61)
gametes (70)
meiosis (70)
mitochondria (61)
mitosis (69)

nuclear membrane (60)
nucleoli (60)
nucleus (60)
organ (63)
organ systems (64)
organelles (61)

osmosis (65)
ribosomes (62)
tissues (63)
vacuole (62)

VOCABULARY REVIEW

Matching   Select the word or term from the Vocabulary List that best matches each description.

1. group of cells that work together to perform a specific job
2. transport organelle
3. group of organs that work together to perform a specific job
4. separates the nucleus from the rest of the cell
5. makes up the largest part of a cell
6. found only in animal cells
7. powerhouses of a cell
8. storage bin of a cell

Applying Definitions   Explain the difference between the words in each pair.

1. diffusion, osmosis
2. mitosis, meiosis
3. cell wall, cell membrane
4. organ, organelle
5. nucleus, nucleolus
6. body cell, gamete
7. chloroplast, chlorophyll
8. ribosome, chromosome

CONTENT REVIEW

True or False   Write true if the statement is true. If the statement is false, change the underlined word or words to make the statement true.

1. A <u>cell</u> is the basic unit of structure and function in living things.
2. The <u>electron</u> microscope is better than a light microscope because it gives biologists a clearer picture of cell structure.
3. <u>Botanists</u> study cells.
4. <u>Ribosomes</u> are the "storage bins" of the cell.
5. The process by which energy is produced for a cell is called cellular <u>respiration</u>.
6. <u>Meiosis</u> results in two cells that have identical chromosomes.
7. The cell <u>membrane</u> is a nonliving part of the cell.
8. Cytologists believe <u>mitochondria</u> help to make proteins in the cell.

Question and Answer   Rewrite each heading in the Chapter Outline on page 54 as a question. Then, answer each of the questions you have written.

Understanding a Diagram   Use the diagram of the plant cell and animal cell shown in Figure 4-8 (page 62) to answer each of the following.

1. What is the outermost structure of a plant cell?
2. What is the outermost structure of an animal cell?
3. Are the vacuoles of plant cells larger or smaller than those of animal cells?
4. What structures do plant cells have that animal cells do not have?
5. What structures do animal cells have that plant cells do not have?
6. Where is the chlorophyll found in a plant cell?

CONCEPT REVIEW

Writing the Main Ideas   Using the Chapter Outline on page 54, write the main idea for each heading in the outline.

Critical Thinking   Answer each of the following in complete sentences.

1. Compare a cell and its parts to the way in which a community such as yours functions. List the processes that have to be carried out for a city, and a cell, to function effectively.
2. Identify the similarities and differences between mitosis and meiosis. Hypothesize a way in which mitosis could have given rise to meiosis at some time in the past.
3. Explain why the organization of parts of the cell into organelles could permit specialization. Discuss the advantages of specialization.
4. Describe the similarities and differences between photosynthesis and respiration.
5. Describe levels of organization in the world around you that are similar to the levels described for living things in the text. How are the two systems of organization similar?

EXTENSIONS

1. Grow bacteria in spoiled broth, or fungi on damp bread. Look at the bacteria and fungi under a compound microscope. Sketch and describe their cellular structure. Prepare a poster of your findings for display.
2. Observe a number of prepared slides of animal tissues. Identify the cells in each tissue. In drawings, identify different tissue groups. Prepare a report that summarizes your observations.

Chapter **5** | Classification

74

Objectives

After you have completed this chapter, you will be able to

5-1 **explain** the need for classifying living things.

5-2 **explain** how the theory of evolution affected classification.

5-2 **list** four things scientists study in order to classify living things.

5-2 **explain** what is meant by the term "binomial nomenclature."

5-2 **list** the seven levels of modern classification.

5-3 **name** the five kingdoms of living things.

Science Process Skills

In this chapter, two science skills are highlighted. Symbols show some places where these skills are used.

➤ **Inferring:** When you infer, you form a conclusion based upon facts and not direct observation.

▲ **Organizing:** When you organize information, you put the information in some kind of order.

Imagine that you are in a supermarket that you have never been in before. You want to buy some apples. You look at the signs hanging above each aisle in the store. The signs list the different foods that are located in each aisle. You locate the aisle containing fresh fruit, and in a short time you are leaving the store with your apples.

The world would be very confusing if people did not **classify** things. To classify is to put things into groups based upon similarities. By classifying things, people organize and communicate information. Scientists use a system of classification to group living things that share common characteristics.

5-1 Classifying Living Things

Key Points
- A system for classifying living things is needed because of the number and variety of organisms.
- Taxonomy is the science of classifying living things.

How many different kinds of organisms do you think live on Earth? Scientists have discovered about 1.5 million different kinds of organisms so far. Many scientists estimate that three times as many organisms have not yet been discovered.

Because there are so many different kinds of organisms, scientists need to classify living things. The science of classifying living things is called **taxonomy** (tak-SAHN-uh-mee). Scientists who classify living things are called taxonomists.

▲ Why do scientists classify living things? Classification is a way of organizing information about different kinds of organisms. Classifying living things also makes it easier to identify unknown organisms. For example, taxonomists can infer, or assume, that organisms with similar characteristics belong to similar groups. Classification also is a way to show relationships among organisms.

One of the first known classification systems was developed more than 2000 years ago. The Greek philosopher and naturalist Aristotle classified organisms into two large groups—plants and animals. Aristotle then classified animals into smaller groups based upon where the animals lived. Aristotle had three groups of animals: land animals, water animals, and air animals.

One of Aristotle's pupils, Theophrastus, classified plants according to their sizes and kinds of stems. Small plants with soft stems were called herbs. Medium-sized plants with many woody stems were called shrubs. Large plants with one woody stem were called trees.

Until the seventeenth century, organisms classified under Aristotle's system also were given common names. The use of common names made it difficult for scientists

Figure 5-1 Aristotle's system of classification lasted from the fourth century B.C. to the seventeenth century A.D.

Aristotle
4th century BC

Middle Ages: Aristotle's system was still widely used.

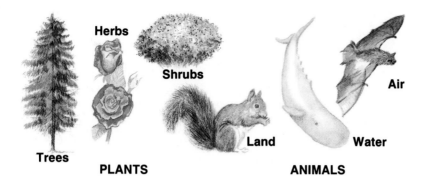

Herbs

Shrubs

Trees

PLANTS

Land

Water

Air

ANIMALS

Figure 5-2   According to Aristotle, sharks and whales both would be water animals. Today, scientists classify sharks as fishes and whales as mammals.

to communicate information about organisms. For example, the mountain lion was called a puma, a cougar, or a panther in different parts of the world. In some cases, different kinds of organisms had the same names.

The number of known organisms increased greatly during the sixteenth and seventeenth centuries. Europeans traveled to faraway places and discovered many organisms they had never seen before. With the invention of the microscope, scientists were discovering tiny organisms that could not be seen with the unaided eye.

How did the discovery of all these organisms affect classification? A new interest in classifying living things developed. Scientists recognized that Aristotle's classification system had problems. For example, using Aristotle's system, bats, birds, and mosquitoes were all grouped together because they fly. Yet, these animals are very different. Scientists recognized the need for an improved classification system.

In the seventeenth century, an English botanist named John Ray identified and classified more than 18,000 plants. His work was used to form modern plant taxonomy. Ray also classified animals, and used the term **species** for each different kind of living thing. Ray defined a species as a group of organisms that looked alike and could reproduce among themselves.

Study Hint

To learn about another system of classification, read the Leisure Activity feature at the end of this chapter.

16th century

Leeuwenhoek's microscope
17th century

Linnaeus
18th century

Darwin
19th century

Electron microscope
20th century

Classification   **77**

ACTIVITY 5-1

PROBLEM: How are books classified in a library?

Science Process Skills
observing, classifying

Background Information
When you classify objects or events, the classification system you use must be useful to other people. Many classification systems are used almost every day. For example, the Dewey Decimal System is used in libraries. The help wanted section of a newspaper has a classification system for jobs. Other classification systems are used in telephone books and in grocery stores.

Materials
library books (optional)
library card catalog (optional)

Procedure
1. In libraries that use the Dewey Decimal System, books are divided into major categories and each category is numbered according to the table shown.
2. Using the Dewey Decimal System, list the call number and category for each of the following:
   a. The experiment on the origins of life performed by Stanley Miller and Harold C. Urey in 1953.
   b. Berger, Melvin. *Disease Detectives.* New York: Harper and Row Publishers, Inc., 1978.
   c. "Red snow," caused by red algae.
   d. Preserving foods with salt and sugar.
   e. Shapiro, Irwin. *Darwin and the Enchanted Isles.* New York: Coward, McCann, and Geoghegan, Inc., 1977.
   f. Laws that have been passed to protect the wild burros in North America.
   g. Types of foods that need to be refrigerated.

Dewey Decimal System

CALL NUMBER	CATEGORY
000–099	general works (bibliographies, encyclopedias, periodicals)
100–199	philosophy, psychology
200–299	religion
300–399	education, government, law, sociology
400–499	language
500–599	pure sciences, mathematics
600–699	technology (medicine, engineering, agriculture, home economics)
700–799	fine arts (painting, architecture, music)
800–899	literature
900–999	history, geography, biography

   h. A biography of the Swedish botanist Linnaeus.
   i. The Greek derivation of science words.

Observations
1. Into how many major groups are books divided in the Dewey Decimal System?
2. What is the entire range of the call numbers in the Dewey Decimal System?

Conclusions
1. Under what call numbers would you find most science books?
2. a. List the call numbers of five other categories in which you might find science books.   b. Give one example of a type of science book that you might find in each of these categories.

Going Further
Choose one topic listed in step 2 of the procedure, or some other topic relating to science. Use the school or public library to research this topic. Write a report on the topic you selected. What is the call number for the book you chose?

In the eighteenth century, a Swedish botanist, Carolus Linnaeus (luh-NAY-us), developed a new way to classify organisms. Linnaeus is credited with being the founder of modern taxonomy. Linnaeus classified organisms according to their physical characteristics. In Linnaeus's system, organisms that looked alike were grouped together.

Think & Discuss

1. What is taxonomy? Why is taxonomy important?
2. How did Linnaeus classify organisms?
★ 3. What are two examples that show how classifying things simplifies your life?

5-2 Modern Taxonomy

Until the late 1800s, most scientists thought that living things did not change. They believed that each species was unchanging and distinct from any other species. By the late 1700s, geologists were finding and studying fossils, or the remains of organisms from long ago. The fossils indicated that living things had changed since they first appeared on the earth. The slow change of living things over time is called evolution.

Some scientists tried unsuccessfully to explain how living things may have evolved, or changed, over time. In 1859, a British scientist named Charles Darwin explained his ideas about evolution. Darwin had spent many years studying different kinds of organisms and how they changed over time. Today, Darwin's theory of evolution is accepted by most scientists.

How did the theory of evolution influence classification? Taxonomists started to classify living things according to their phylogeny (fy-LAJ-uh-nee), or evolutionary history. Today, taxonomists try to develop an evolutionary tree for every species. An evolutionary tree shows the inferred relationships among different species.

How do modern-day taxonomists classify living things? Like Linnaeus, they usually observe the physical appearance of a living thing. Organisms that look the same often are related. However, physical appearance alone is not always a good way to classify organisms.

Key Points

- Scientists classify organisms based upon physical appearance, chromosome structure, blood proteins, embryology, and evolutionary history.

- Binomial nomenclature is a system of naming organisms with a genus and species name.

- The seven levels of modern classification are kingdom, phylum, class, order, family, genus, and species.

Figure 5-3 This fossil wasp looks very much like wasps that are alive today.

Today, taxonomists also study chromosome structure, blood proteins, and the way organisms develop before they are born.

How does the study of chromosomes and blood proteins help taxonomists classify organisms? Taxonomists compare the chromosomes and proteins of different species. If organisms have similar chromosome structure and proteins, scientists infer that the organisms are related.

Organisms in the early stages of development are called embryos. Embryology (em-bree-AL-uh-jee) is the study of a developing embryo. Embryology helps scientists determine evolutionary relationships. If embryos from different species develop in a similar way, scientists infer that the species probably are related.

Binomial Nomenclature

Linnaeus developed a system for naming living things in the mid-1700s. His system is called **binomial nomenclature** (by-NOH-mee-uhl NOH-muhn-klay-chuhr). In the binomial system, each kind of organism is identified by a two-part scientific name. Binomial nomenclature is the system still used today.

What are the two parts of a scientific name? The first part is the name of the **genus** in which the organism is classified. A genus is a group of related species. The second part is the name of the species. For example, *Canis* is the Latin word for dog. All doglike animals belong to the genus *Canis*. Domesticated dogs, such as those kept as pets, belong to the species *Canis familiaris*. Wolves belong to the species *Canis lupus*, and coyotes to the species *Canis latrans*.

Figure 5-4 The domestic dog (left), the wolf (middle), and the coyote (right) all belong to the genus *Canis*. Notice the similarity in appearance.

ACTIVITY 5-2

PROBLEM: How can a classification system be designed?

Science Process Skills
observing, classifying

Background Information
People classify objects, events, and living things according to similarities. For example, animals are classified into related groups in order to understand the characteristics of a group, instead of trying to memorize the characteristics of each animal. Each animal is classified in seven groups. Kingdom is the most general group. Species is the most specific group.

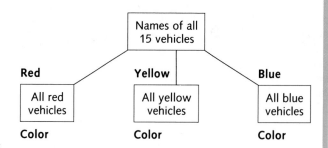

Materials
    15 index cards
    magazines
    scissors
    tape

Procedure

1. Cut out pictures of 15 different types of transportation vehicles. **CAUTION: Always be careful when using scissors.** Tape each picture to the back of an index card.
2. On the lined side of the index card, list the characteristics of each vehicle.
3. Draw a large box at the top center of a sheet of construction paper. Write the names of the 15 transportation vehicles in the box.
4. Choose a general characteristic, such as color. Divide the vehicles into three groups based on three specific characteristics that describe the general characteristic—such as red, yellow, and blue.
5. Write the general characteristic beneath each of the three boxes and the specific characteristic at the top of each box. List the transportation vehicles that have the specific characteristics in the boxes.
6. Divide these three groups into smaller groups. Keep dividing the groups until only

one vehicle is classified in a box. Be sure to label each box with a general and a specific characteristic.

Observations
1. What are some characteristics that you used to classify the vehicles?
2. Which group has the most transportation vehicles?
3. What do you notice about the number of vehicles in each group compared with the group before it?
4. What happens to the number of requirements in each group as you keep classifying the vehicles?

Conclusions
1. How is your classification system similar to the classification system of living things?
2. a. Which group in your classification system is similar to the kingdom level?
   b. Which group is similar to the species level?
3. Why is it useful to use a classification system?

Going Further
Obtain an index card with a transportation vehicle from a classmate, and place the vehicle into your classification system. Does the classification of the vehicle work in your system? If not, revise your classification system to classify the new vehicle.

Today, living things are classified into seven major groups. Some of these groups are the same as those used by Linnaeus in the eighteenth century. Closely related species are grouped in the same genus. Related genera make up a larger group called a **family.** Related families are grouped together in an **order.** Groups of similar orders make up an even larger group called a **class,** and related classes are grouped into a **phylum** (FY-luhm). In botany, the term **division** is used instead of phylum. Related phyla, or divisions, are grouped into a **kingdom.** Which classification group contains the most species of organisms?

Look at Table 5-1. It shows how four different organisms are classified at each of the seven classification levels. How many groups do all the organisms have in common? Which organisms are closely related?

Table 5-1	The Classification of Four Organisms			
CATEGORY	HOUSE CAT	MOUNTAIN LION	DOMESTIC DOG	HUMAN
Kingdom	Animalia	Animalia	Animalia	Animalia
Phylum	Chordata	Chordata	Chordata	Chordata
Class	Mammalia	Mammalia	Mammalia	Mammalia
Order	Carnivora	Carnivora	Carnivora	Primates
Family	Felidae	Felidae	Canidae	Hominidae
Genus	*Felis*	*Felis*	*Canis*	*Homo*
Species	*domesticus*	*concolor*	*familiaris*	*sapiens*

As you move down the seven levels of classification from kingdom to species, the organisms in each classification level are more closely related. For example, members of the same family are more closely related than members of the same order. The more alike organisms are, the more classification levels they share.

Think & Discuss

4. What is binomial nomenclature?
5. How did Darwin's ideas affect classification systems?
6. Why do you think many of the classifications developed by Linnaeus are still used today, even though Linnaeus did not know about evolution?

5-3 Five Kingdoms

At one time, all organisms were classified in either the plant or animal kingdom. When microscopic organisms were discovered, some scientists placed them in a third kingdom. With the invention of the electron microscope, scientists discovered that microscopic organisms are not all alike. For example, some microscopic organisms do not have a nucleus or other organelles. These organisms were placed in a kingdom of their own. When studies showed that fungi and plants were not closely related, scientists placed fungi in a kingdom of their own.

△ Today, most scientists accept the five kingdom classification system. Some scientists, however, would like to create a sixth kingdom for viruses. As new information becomes available, the five kingdom classification system may change. Some taxonomists think that organisms may someday be classified into more than one dozen kingdoms.

- **Kingdom Monera** Monerans are single-celled microscopic organisms. Unlike members of the four other kingdoms, the nucleus of a moneran cell does not have a nuclear membrane. Other cell organelles also lack membranes. Monerans may be either **autotrophs** (AWT-uh-trohfs) or they may be **heterotrophs** (HET-uhr-uh-trohfs). Autotrophs are organisms that can make their own food. Heterotrophs are organisms that cannot make their own food. They must take in food from the outside. Bacteria are examples of monerans.

- **Kingdom Protista** The Kingdom Protista contains many different kinds of organisms. Most **protists** are single-celled organisms. Some protists, however, are simple multicellular organisms. Some protists are

Key Points
- The five kingdoms are the Kingdom Monera, Protista, Fungi, Plantae, and Animalia.

- An autotroph is an organism that makes its own food. A heterotroph is an organism that must take in food from the outside.

Study Hint

After you read Section 5-3, Five Kingdoms, list the major characteristics of the organisms in each kingdom.

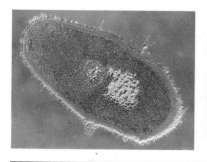 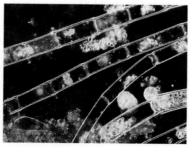

Figure 5-5 The bacterium (left) is classified in the Kingdom Monera. The multicellular green alga *Spirogyra* (right) is classified in the Kingdom Protista.

Classification 83

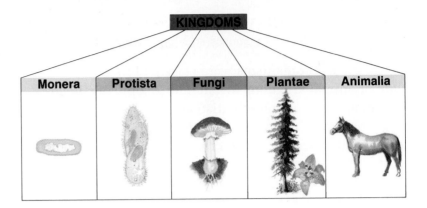

KINGDOMS

| Monera | Protista | Fungi | Plantae | Animalia |

Figure 5-6 All living things are classified in one of the five kingdoms.

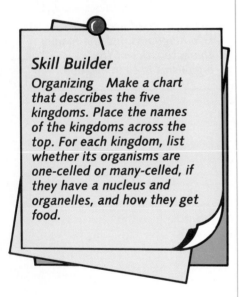

autotrophs. Others are heterotrophs. Algae are members of the protist kingdom.

- **Kingdom Fungi**   The **fungi** you are probably most familiar with are the yeasts, molds, and mushrooms. Most fungi are multicellular organisms, although some are single-celled. The cells of most fungi have cell walls made up of a substance called chitin (KYT-n). Fungi are heterotrophs. They obtain food by absorbing it from the environment, or from plants and animals.

- **Kingdom Plantae**   Plants are autotrophic multicellular organisms. Unlike fungi, the cells of plants have a cell wall made up mostly of cellulose. Plants also have chloroplasts containing chlorophyll and make food by photosynthesis.

- **Kingdom Animalia**   Animals are multicellular organisms. Most animals have organ systems. Unlike plants, the cells of animals do not have cell walls or chloroplasts. Animal cells also lack chlorophyll. Because animals cannot produce their own food, they are heterotrophs.

Think & Discuss

7. How is a heterotrophic organism different from an autotrophic organism?

8. What things seem to be most important for determining which kingdom an organism will be placed in?

9. How has technology affected classification?

Stamp Collecting

"Meet the rugged bighorn sheep, the playful river otter, and 48 other members of America's wild kingdom!" Does this sound like an advertisement for a zoo or a wildlife preserve? It does, but it is actually an advertisement for postage stamps.

In 1987, the United States Postal Service issued a series of 50 wildlife stamps. The American Wildlife Collection contains unique and beautiful stamps that appeal to stamp collectors throughout the world. Stamp collecting, or philately (fih-LAT-uh-lee), has been a popular hobby since the mid-1800s.

Stamp collecting is both a science and an art. It is a science because it involves the systematic study and classification of materials. It is an art because it involves principles of arrangement and expression of individual taste.

How are stamps classified? Stamps are classified in the broadest sense according to function. For example, there are general postage stamps, airmail stamps, special delivery stamps, postage due stamps, and several others. Some philatelists classify their stamps in this way, but most stamp collectors use more specific methods of classification.

Probably the most popular method of classifying stamps is to group them according to their country of origin. The stamps are then placed in order of their dates of issue. Most stamp collecting albums sold in stores are designed to classify stamps according to country and date of issue.

There are many other methods of classification for stamps. For example, stamps may be classified according to subject, or specific periods in history. Stamps also are classified according to the history and development of a particular country.

Many stamps deal with subjects that are related to biology. For example, stamps may have pictures of birds, insects, or other animals. Other stamps may have pictures of flowers or trees. There is even a series of stamps that features shells, such as those you would find on a beach.

There also are stamps that commemorate, or honor, scientists or scientific discoveries. For example, a stamp that honors the discovery of DNA has been issued. There also is a stamp honoring Dr. Jonas Salk for his discovery of a vaccine against polio.

You can begin a stamp collection easily by saving stamps that you receive in the mail and by asking friends and relatives to do the same. You also can visit your local post office and purchase new stamps.

If you want to learn more about stamp collecting, you can obtain a booklet called "The Wonderful World of Stamps" from the United States Postal Service. The postal service also sells kits that include stamps and an album in which to keep them.

To Think About
- How does the classification of stamps differ from the classification system used in biology?
- Airmail stamps are among the most popular with collectors. Can you think of a reason for this?

Chapter Review

CHAPTER SUMMARY

5–1 Classification of Living Things

- The large number and wide variety of organisms requires a classification system.
- Taxonomy is the science of classifying living things.

5–2 Modern Taxonomy

- Scientists classify organisms according to evolutionary history, physical similarities, blood proteins, chromosome structure, and embryology.
- Binomial nomenclature is a system of naming organisms with a two-part scientific name, consisting of a genus name and a species name.

- The seven basic levels of modern classification are (from general to specific): kingdom, phylum or division, class, order, family, genus, and species.

5–3 Five Kingdoms

- The five kingdoms are the Kingdoms Monera, Protista, Fungi, Plantae, and Animalia.
- An autotroph is an organism that makes its own food. All plants and some monerans and protists are autotrophs.
- A heterotroph is an organism that obtains its food from the outside. All animals and fungi are heterotrophs.

VOCABULARY LIST

autotrophs (83)	division (82)	heterotrophs (83)	phylum (82)
binomial nomenclature (80)	family (82)	kingdom (82)	protists (83)
class (82)	fungi (84)	monerans (83)	species (77)
classify (75)	genus (80)	order (82)	taxonomy (76)

VOCABULARY REVIEW

Matching   Write the word or term from the Vocabulary List that best matches each description.

1. classification group between phylum and order
2. bacteria
3. organism that makes its own food
4. plant classification group that is equal to phylum
5. to group similar things together
6. smallest of the seven classification groups used by biologists
7. mushrooms
8. group of related species
9. science of classifying living things
10. system used to name living things

Identifying Relationships   Identify the word or term in each group that does not belong. Explain why it does not belong with the group.

1. division, phylum, species
2. evolution, Darwin, heterotroph
3. family, virus, order
4. fossils, embryology, remains
5. heterotroph, autotroph, animal
6. Fungi, kingdom, dog
7. chlorophyll, classification, taxonomy
8. multicellular, monerans, single-celled
9. algae, protists, mushrooms
10. binomial nomenclature, autotroph, chlorophyll
11. plants, division, animals
12. protists, bacteria, monerans

Completion Write the word or words that best complete each sentence.

1. An organism that cannot make its own food is a _____.
2. In botany, the term _____ is used instead of phylum.
3. Today, most scientists accept the theory that organisms _____ over time.
4. There are _____ major groups in the present-day classification system.
5. Related genera are grouped together in a

   _____.
6. Aristotle's classification system had _____ major groups.
7. Human beings are members of the class

   _____.
8. Related phyla are grouped into _____.
9. Binomial nomenclature was developed by

   _____.

Finding the Main Ideas Use the section number to find the sentence that answers each question. Then, write the sentence.

1. Why are organisms classified? (5-1)
2. What is a taxonomist? (5-1)
3. Why was the work of Linnaeus important to biologists? (5-1)
4. How did Darwin's ideas change taxonomy? (5-2)
5. In addition to appearance, what else is used to classify an organism? (5-2)
6. How are organisms named in the binomial nomenclature system? (5-2)
7. What is the relationship between a family and an order? (5-2)
8. How did the invention of the electron microscope increase the number of kingdoms? (5-3)
9. What is a heterotroph? (5-3)

Writing for Understanding One way to find out if you understand something is to write a brief summary of the information in your own words. Reread Section 5-2, Modern Taxonomy, on pages 79–82, and write a brief summary of the information.

Critical Thinking Answer each of the following in complete sentences.

1. Food is classified in a grocery store. Mail is sorted and classified at the post office. Name two other classification systems used in daily life.
2. How is the system of binomial nomenclature similar to the system for listing names used in a telephone book?
3. If you were to discover a new species, how would you determine its classification?
4. Why is taxonomy an ongoing science?
5. Why is the use of scientific names important for communication among scientists?

1. Use library references to write a brief report describing the contributions of Ernst Haeckel or Robert Whittaker to the science of classification.
2. Research the classifications of five organisms. Make a table listing the classification of each organism at each of the seven main levels.
3. Use library references to find out more about Charles Darwin. Write a description of Darwin's trip on the HMS *Beagle*.
4. Collect photographs or drawings of organisms from each of the five kingdoms. Use the pictures to make a poster. Label each picture on your poster with its correct kingdom.

What do you think of when you hear the term "living thing"? Many people think only of plants and animals. However, many living things are neither plants nor animals. In this unit, you will learn about organisms that make up three of the five kingdoms of organisms— monerans, protists, and fungi. You also will learn about viruses, which are not living cells.

The drawings and photographs shown on these two pages represent the chapters that make up this unit. Which organisms do you recognize? How would you describe the organisms that you do not recognize?

Simple Organisms

CONTENTS

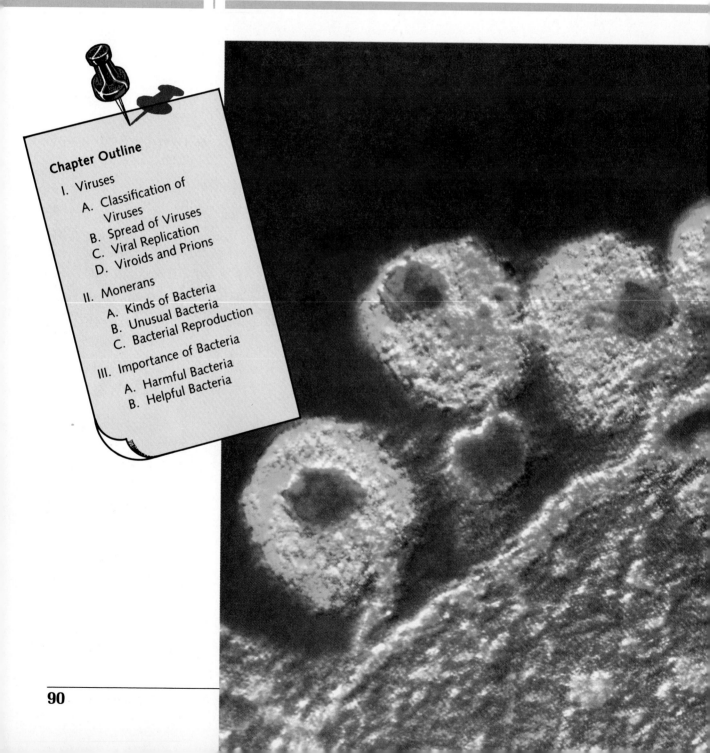

Chapter 6

Viruses and Monerans

Objectives

After you have completed this chapter, you will be able to

6-1 **identify** and **describe** the characteristics of viruses.

6-1 **describe** ways in which viruses are spread.

6-2 **identify** and **describe** the characteristics of monerans.

6-2 **classify** bacteria according to shape.

6-2 **name** and **describe** a group of bacteria that use light for energy.

6-3 **relate** examples of how bacteria are harmful.

6-3 **relate** examples of how bacteria are helpful.

Science Process Skills

In this chapter, two science skills are highlighted. Symbols show some places where these skills are used.

Classifying: When you classify, you group things based upon similarities.

Predicting: When you predict, you state in advance how and why something will occur.

Is the object in the photograph a jellyfish? Is it a strange being from another planet? It is neither of these things. The blue blob in the photograph is a helper T-cell. Helper T-cells are one of many kinds of cells that make up the immune system. The immune system is the body's defense against disease.

Look at the photo again. The helper T-cell is covered with tiny pink dots. These dots are a deadly invader—the AIDS virus. The AIDS virus kills helper T-cells and weakens the body's defenses.

Like all viruses, the AIDS virus can be seen only with an electron microscope. An electron microscope was used to magnify the viruses in this picture. A computer added color to the picture.

6-1 Viruses

The structure of viruses is very different from that of living cells. Viruses do not have any cell parts. A **virus** is just a piece of nucleic acid covered with an "overcoat" of protein. This overcoat is called a **capsid.** The capsid makes up most of the virus.

Capsids give viruses their shapes. Some viruses look like long rods. Others look like soccer balls. Certain viruses have a membrane surrounding the capsid. For example, the capsid of the virus shown in the lower part of Figure 6-1 looks as if it is covered with spikes. Can you find the nucleic acid and capsid of this virus?

Classification of Viruses

Because viruses do not have all the characteristics of living things, they are not classified in the five kingdoms of living things. Instead, most biologists classify viruses according to the host the virus invades. The host is the living organism a virus infects. The three main groups of viruses are bacterial viruses, plant viruses, and animal viruses.

The names of bacterial viruses include a number and the kind of bacteria each virus infects. Plant viruses are named according to the diseases they cause. For example, the virus that causes tobacco mosaic disease is called the tobacco mosaic virus.

Capsid

Nucleic acid

Membrane

Figure 6-1   All viruses have a capsid and nucleic acid. Some viruses also have a membrane.

Figure 6-2   The green and yellow patches on these leaves are caused by the tobacco mosaic virus.

Animal viruses are classified in two ways. One way to classify animal viruses is by the type of nucleic acid the virus contains. An animal virus is either a DNA virus or an RNA virus. Animal viruses also are classified by biologists according to the size of their capsids and the presence of a membrane surrounding the capsid. Animal viruses are divided into groups called families. Each virus within a family also has a common name, such as the mumps virus.

Spread of Viruses

Viruses can cause many serious diseases in plants and animals. The viruses that cause these diseases can be passed from one living thing to another. In humans, viruses can be spread in several ways.

Viruses often are present in the air. The viruses travel on dust particles or on tiny water droplets in the air. The viruses that cause measles and the common cold are spread through the air.

Viruses also can be spread to people by contaminated food or drinking water. For example, the hepatitis virus, which causes a disease of the liver, can be spread in food prepared by a person who has hepatitis.

Animal or insect bites also can spread viruses to people. For example, rabies is spread by the bite of an infected dog or other animal. Biting insects transmit viruses in another way. The insect takes in the virus when it bites an infected host. Then the insect spreads the virus by biting a person. Some types of encephalitis, a disease of the brain and spinal cord, are spread by mosquito bites.

Some insects, such as houseflies, may carry viruses on their bodies. The flies pick up viruses from infected garbage. Then, if a fly walks on uncovered food, it may deposit the virus on the food.

Viral Replication

When a virus enters a cell, it takes over the cell's hereditary material and causes the cell to make new viruses. The new viruses then escape from the cell. The process by which viruses reproduce other viruses is called **viral replication** (rep-luh-KAY-shun).

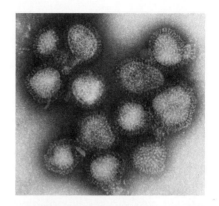

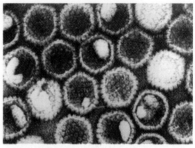

Figure 6-3 The "flu" virus (top) is an RNA virus. The herpesvirus (bottom) is a DNA virus. What are RNA and DNA?

Study Hint

To learn more about viruses that cause the common cold, read the feature "Curing the Common Cold" at the end of this chapter.

ACTIVITY 6–1

PROBLEM: What are the shapes and parts of viruses?

Science Process Skills
generalizing, comparing, modeling, identifying

Background Information
A bacterial virus, or bacteriophage, is a virus that infects only bacteria. The structure of a bacteriophage, the AIDS virus, and a flu virus are shown. Viruses do not have a nucleus, cytoplasm, cell membrane, or organelles. However, viruses have two of the building blocks of life—protein and nucleic acid.

Materials
machine screw, ¼" x 1 ½"
2 acorn nuts to fit screw
pliers
4 pieces of floral wire
2 pipe cleaners
small ball of clay
scissors
small styrofoam ball

Procedure
1. Screw the acorn nuts onto the top of the screw.
2. Twist three pieces of floral wire around the opposite end of the screw. Use the pliers to tighten the wires.
3. Fold down and bend the wires to form the attachment fibers.
4. Coil one pipe cleaner around the screw between the acorn nuts and the end of the screw.

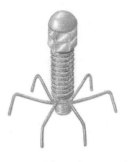

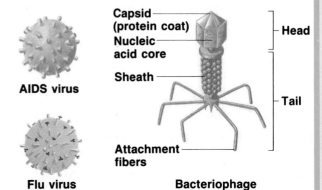

AIDS virus

Flu virus

Capsid (protein coat)
Nucleic acid core
Sheath
Attachment fibers
Head
Tail

Bacteriophage

5. Use the styrofoam ball and a pipe cleaner to construct a model of the AIDS virus shown.
6. Use the clay and floral wire to construct a model of the flu virus shown.
7. Make drawings of each of your models and label the parts of your drawing with the correct viral parts.

Observations
1. **a.** On your bacteriophage model, what part of the model represents the head?
   b. the tail? **c.** the attachment fibers?
   d. the sheath?
2. On your bacteriophage model, which part would contain the nucleic acid?
3. If your bacteriophage model were a real virus, what substance would make up the outside of the acorn nuts?
4. If your AIDS virus and flu virus models were real viruses, what would you find in the center of them?

Conclusions
1. What parts do all viruses have?
2. **a.** Which part of a virus does not enter a cell? **b.** Which part does enter a cell?
3. **GENERALIZE** What general statement can you make about the shapes of viruses?

As you read about viral replication, refer to Figure 6-4.

- A bacterial virus attaches itself to a host cell.
- The virus injects its nucleic acid into the cell. Its capsid is left outside the cell.
- The nucleic acid of the virus directs the cell to make new viral nucleic acids and capsids.
- Viral nucleic acids and capsids combine to make complete viruses.
- New viruses burst out of the host cell, killing it.

A virus can enter a host cell and remain inactive, or dormant. Some viruses, such as the AIDS virus, can remain dormant for many years. However, when activated the virus can cause disease. Have you ever had a cold sore? A cold sore is caused by a virus that may remain dormant in your body for many years. The virus that causes a cold sore often is activated by another virus—the virus that causes the common cold.

Viroids and Prions

Recently discovered agents of infection called **viroids** (VEER-oydz) are much smaller than viruses. Viroids are made up of very short pieces of nucleic acid without a capsid. Scientists have found several viroids that cause diseases in plants.

Other simple agents of infection are called **prions** (PRY-uhnz). Unlike viruses and viroids, prions have no nucleic acid at all. Prions are very small proteins. Scientists are puzzled about how prions replicate. They do know, however, that prions replicate only when inside a living cell. Much research still needs to be done.

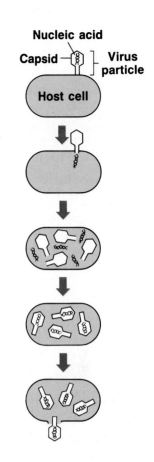

Figure 6-4 Viral replication occurs inside living cells.

Think & Discuss

1. What is the scientific term for viral reproduction?
2. What are the main parts of a virus?
3. List the steps in viral replication.
4. Describe two ways viruses can be spread.
5. Suppose a scientist wanted to stop a virus from infecting a cell. How could this be done?

The Kingdom Monera is one of the five kingdoms of living things. All organisms in this kingdom are **bacteria** (bak-TIR-ee-uh). Bacteria are single-celled organisms with very simple structures. Bacterial cells are very different from the cells of other living things. An important difference is that a bacterial cell does not have a membrane around its nucleic acid. Bacteria, therefore, do not have true nuclei. Bacteria also do not have the organelles found in most other cells.

A single bacterium and groups of bacteria are microscopic. However, under proper growth conditions, bacteria form large masses called colonies. Large colonies of bacteria can be seen with the unaided eye. Each colony may contain billions of bacteria.

Kinds of Bacteria

There are three shapes of bacteria. Spherical or egg-shaped bacteria are called **cocci** (KAK-sy). **Bacilli** (buh-SIL-y) are cylindrical or rod-shaped bacteria. Curved or spiral-shaped bacteria are called **spirilla** (spy-RIL-uh).

Some cocci form pairs. These cocci are called diplococci. Other cocci form chains. They are called streptococci. Have you ever had strep throat? If so, your illness was caused by streptococci. Other cocci form grapelike bunches. These are the staphylococci. Right now, staphylococci are living on your skin. Staphylococci that grow on foods that are not properly refrigerated often cause food poisoning.

Like many cocci, some bacilli also form pairs or chains. Unlike cocci, bacilli do not form bunches. Pairs of bacilli are called diplobacilli. What do you think chains of bacilli are called?

Coccus

Bacillus

Spirillum

Figure 6-5 Bacteria can be classified by their shapes.

Figure 6-6 Notice the grapelike bunches of staphylococci (left) and the pairs of bacilli (right).

Bacilli often are found in the soil or in the air. Many soil bacilli produce **antibiotics** (an-ti-by-AT-iks). Antibiotics are substances that kill harmful bacteria. Penicillin and streptomycin are antibiotics with which you may be familiar. Antibiotics help people fight infection caused by other kinds of bacteria.

❱ Some bacilli are harmful to people. For example, one kind of bacillus causes a type of food poisoning called botulism. The botulism bacillus can grow in improperly canned foods. As the bacillus grows, it produces a deadly poison. One sign of the presence of the botulism bacillus is a bulging can. The bulging is caused by a gas that the bacteria produce. What do you think might happen if food from a can containing the botulism bacillus were eaten?

☞ Unlike cocci and bacilli, spirilla live only as single cells. Spirilla can have three shapes. Some look like tiny commas. Others look wavy. Still others look like corkscrews. These corkscrew-type cells have a special name. They are called **spirochetes** (SPY-ruh-keets).

One of the comma-shaped bacteria causes an intestinal disease called cholera. The cholera organism is spread in water that contains sewage. A spirochete causes syphilis (SIF-uh-lis). Syphilis is a sexually transmitted disease. Symptoms of syphilis include sores and rashes. If left untreated, syphilis also can cause blindness, nervous disorders, and death.

Unusual Bacteria

Bacteria called **blue-green bacteria** use sunlight to make food for energy. This process is called **photosynthesis** (foht-uh-SIN-thuh-sis). During photosynthesis, light energy

Figure 6-7 A spirochete looks something like a corkscrew.

Health and Safety Tip
To avoid botulism food poisoning, never eat food from a bulging can.

Figure 6-8 The beadlike *Anabaena* is a blue-green bacterium.

Health and Safety Tip

When walking in areas with tall grasses, wear long pants, shoes, and socks. This practice will help prevent bites from ticks.

is used to help make food for the organism. In order for photosynthesis to take place, an organism must have the green pigment **chlorophyll** (KLAWR-uh-fil) in its cells. Blue-green bacteria have the same type of chlorophyll as plants.

One group of bacteria called **rickettsia** (ri-KET-see-uh) can live only within a host. Rickettsia are spread by ticks and lice. Rocky Mountain spotted fever is a disease caused by rickettsia. This disease is common in wooded areas of the United States.

Bacterial Reproduction

Bacteria reproduce by **binary fission.** In binary fission, one cell divides into two identical cells. Binary fission is a form of asexual reproduction. Asexual reproduction involves only one parent organism.

A bacterium usually grows to twice its normal size before it divides. During this time, the bacterium makes enough cell material for each new cell. The bacterial cell then splits into two new cells. One complete set of nucleic acid goes to each new cell. A cross wall separates the parent cell into two daughter cells.

Bacteria vary in the time it takes them to divide. Some reproduce every 20 minutes. A few reproduce more quickly. Many take longer. Because bacteria can reproduce rapidly, a population of bacterial cells can grow quickly.

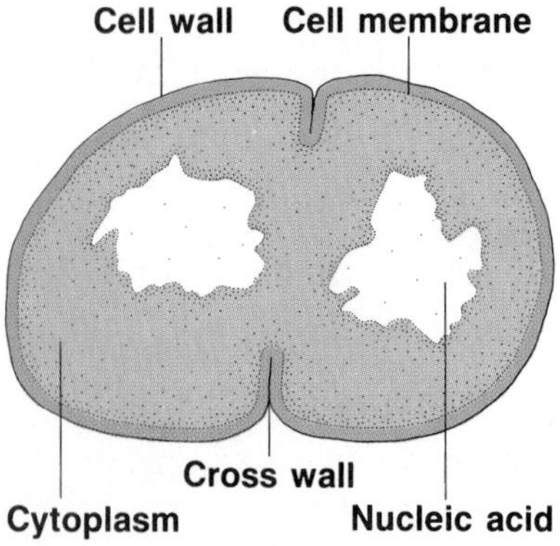

Cell wall
Cell membrane
Cross wall
Cytoplasm
Nucleic acid

Figure 6-9 During binary fission, a bacterium divides into two identical cells.

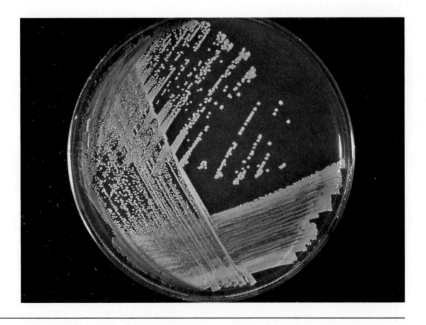

Figure 6-10 Although you need a microscope to see a single bacterium, this colony of staphylococci is large enough to see without a microscope.

ACTIVITY 6–2

PROBLEM: How effective is a mouthwash against bacterial growth?

Science Process Skills
observing, predicting, comparing, analyzing

Background Information
Bacteria are found almost everywhere on your body, including in your mouth. Advertisements for mouthwashes claim to kill bacteria because, they say, the mouthwashes are antiseptic. An antiseptic is a substance that slows or stops the action of microorganisms. You probably have read or heard an advertisement about a mouthwash that claims to be the best one. You can test the effectiveness of a mouthwash against bacterial growth.

Materials

bacterial culture	medicine dropper
5 small jars	250-mL beaker
graduated cylinder	grease pencil
4 different mouthwashes	

Procedure
1. Obtain about 150 mL of bacterial culture. **Note:** The bacterial culture will look cloudy if bacteria are growing in it.
2. Label the five jars 1 to 5 with the grease pencil.
3. Add 20 mL of bacterial culture to each jar.
4. Add 1 dropperful of a different mouthwash to jars 1–4. Do not add any mouthwash to jar 5.
5. Copy the Data Table shown. Fill in the first three columns.

6. Place the jars in the dark for two days.
7. **HYPOTHESIZE** What effect do you think mouthwash will have on bacterial growth? Write your hypothesis below your Data Table. Your hypothesis should answer the question. To test your hypothesis, complete the activity.
8. On the second day, observe each jar and record your observations.

Observations
1. Which jar is your control?
2. **a.** Did the bacteria grow as well in jars 1–4 as in jar 5? **b.** Which jars did not have bacteria in them at the end of the activity?
3. Compare the cloudiness of each of the jars. Rank the jars from most cloudy to least cloudy.

Conclusions
1. How effective were the mouthwashes in controlling bacterial growth?
2. Was your hypothesis correct? Use your observations to support your answer.
3. **ANALYZE** **a.** Which mouthwash seems to be the most effective? **b.** Would you buy this mouthwash? Why or why not?

Going Further
Using the bacterial culture, develop an experiment to test the effectiveness of other antiseptics, such as hydrogen peroxide and rubbing alcohol, on bacterial growth.

Data Table: Bacterial Culture Observations					
JAR	MOUTHWASH NAME	START: CLOUDY OR CLEAR?	BACTERIA PRESENT?	SECOND DAY: CLOUDY OR CLEAR?	BACTERIA PRESENT?
1					
2					
3					
4					
5					

❯ To better understand how a population of bacteria grows, imagine that you had a magic penny. This penny turns into two pennies in 20 minutes. After another 20 minutes, each of these two pennies also doubles. What would happen if each new penny kept doubling every 20 minutes? How many pennies would you have in eight hours? Would you sell your penny for a million dollars?

Bacteria can quickly produce a large population of cells. Imagine what happens in your body if just a few disease-causing bacteria enter and begin to reproduce! Luckily, your body has defenses, such as helper T-cells, to fight this population explosion of bacteria.

Think & Discuss

6. In which kingdom are all bacteria classified?

7. Which group of bacteria obtains energy from sunlight?

8. Describe the three shapes of bacteria and the possible ways that they can form groups.

9. Briefly describe binary fission.

★ 10. Bacteria grow and reproduce very rapidly. If bacteria grow so fast, why is the earth not covered with them?

6-3 Importance of Bacteria

Dinosaurs once roamed the earth. Then, about 65 million years ago, they all died. After the dinosaurs died, what happened to their bodies? The answer lies with organisms known as **decomposers.** Decomposers feed upon the remains of dead organisms. As decomposers feed, they break down their food into simpler substances such as carbon and nitrogen. These substances can then be reused by other living things. Some bacteria are decomposers. These bacteria are some of the first recyclers.

Bacteria are important for many other reasons as well. For example, some bacteria are used to make foods. Bacteria also help some plants survive in nature. Of course, bacteria can also be harmful.

Harmful Bacteria

Like viruses, bacteria can cause disease in animals and people. Only a few types of bacteria, however, cause disease in plants. One group of bacteria causes tumorlike growths in plants.

To cause disease in people, bacteria must first enter the body. Once inside the body, the bacteria begin to multiply. The bacteria may stay in one place, or they may be carried by the blood to other parts of the body.

As they grow, disease-causing bacteria may produce waste products that are poisons. Poisons cause most of the damage to the host. Poisons produced by bacteria may stay in one area of the body, or they may move around and cause damage in widespread areas.

Bacteria also can cause food to spoil. The damage caused by bacteria depends on the kind of food and how it is stored. Foods that are easily spoiled by bacteria include fish, milk, fruits, and vegetables. Foods that are not easily spoiled include flour, nuts, and dried foods.

What makes one food spoil easily while another does not? The key to food spoilage is water. Foods that spoil easily have a high water content. Foods that do not spoil easily have little water. To keep foods from spoiling quickly, they can be dried and salted. Sausages and hams are kept from spoiling in this way.

Food can be kept from spoiling in other ways. Cooling slows the growth of bacteria. Adding large amounts of sugar, as in jams and jellies, also slows bacterial growth. Pickled foods contain acids, which make bacterial growth difficult. Cooking foods thoroughly at high temperatures also kills bacteria. The cooked food can then be sealed in containers. Canned foods are preserved in this way. Finally, chemicals called preservatives can be added to foods such as bread, juice, and dried fruits to slow the growth of bacteria.

Helpful Bacteria

Bacteria are used to make many foods. For example, certain bacteria produce vinegar. In a similar way, other bacteria produce acids that help make yogurt, sauerkraut, and pickles. Many cheeses also are made using bacteria. The next time you have a picnic, you can thank bacteria for some of your food!

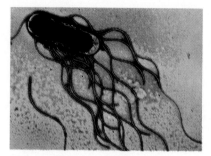

Figure 6-11 *Salmonella* bacteria can cause food poisoning.

Skill Builder

***Researching Data** Chemical preservatives are put in foods to slow spoilage. Some preservatives are sodium or calcium propionate, sorbic acid, and sulfur dioxide. Go to the grocery store and find two foods containing each preservative. Combine your data with your classmates. In which kinds of food is each preservative used?*

Figure 6-12 The small, rounded shapes are nodules of nitrogen-fixing bacteria.

Certain bacteria live within the roots of plants, such as soybeans, clover, string beans, and peas. These bacteria change nitrogen gas into a form that can be used by plants and animals. This process is called **nitrogen fixation.** The plants provide the bacteria with food and protection. In turn, the bacteria supply the plants with nitrogen. When animals eat the plants, the animals get usable nitrogen.

Bacteria also live inside humans and animals. For example, bacteria in your large intestine make vitamin K. Vitamin K helps your blood to clot when you cut yourself. In return, the bacteria feed on food that you cannot digest. In a similar way, bacteria in the digestive tract of cows help the cows digest grass.

Recently, scientists have begun using bacteria in new and exciting ways. Scientists can now insert the nucleic acids of different organisms into bacteria. In this way, the bacteria can be made to produce useful products. For example, human nucleic acid can be inserted into bacteria. If the human nucleic acid contains the instructions for making insulin, the bacteria will become "insulin factories." The body produces insulin to help it use sugar. People with diabetes cannot produce insulin in the amounts their bodies need. Now, using bacteria, scientists can produce insulin and many other chemicals people need.

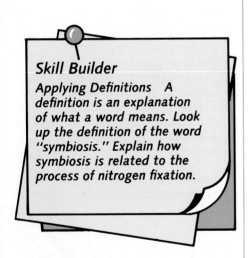

Skill Builder

Applying Definitions   A definition is an explanation of what a word means. Look up the definition of the word "symbiosis." Explain how symbiosis is related to the process of nitrogen fixation.

Think & Discuss

11. What is nitrogen fixation?

12. Describe one way in which humans and bacteria live together for the benefit of both.

13. What growth requirement of bacteria is removed from dried or salted food?

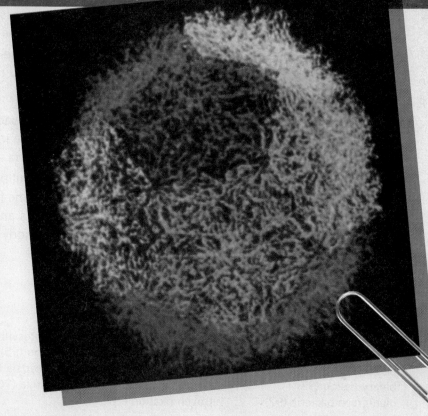

When was the last time you had a cold? If you are like many people, you have probably had several colds in the past year. Like most people, you probably treated your colds with a variety of "cold remedies." Cold remedies relieve some of the symptoms, but they do not cure the cold.

Finding a cure for the common cold has long been a goal of medical researchers. Now, thanks to a drug called WIN 51,711, that goal may be within reach. WIN 51,711 is a new experimental drug that may be able to cure the common cold by attacking the cause of colds.

Colds are caused by viruses. You may recall that a virus has two basic parts: a core of nucleic acid and an outer coat of protein. A virus causes disease by entering a cell and releasing its stored nucleic acid.

Most colds are caused by a particular group of viruses called rhinoviruses. A rhinovirus is shown in the photograph. When a cold-causing rhinovirus attacks a person, it attaches itself to a cell membrane and pushes through the membrane into the cell. Then the virus sheds its protective protein coat and releases its nucleic acid. The nucleic acid begins making new viruses that attack other cells. A full-scale virus infection is underway.

How does WIN 51,711 stop this process of infection? Scientists have discovered that WIN 51,711 stops the rhinovirus from shedding its protein coat. The drug does this by attaching itself to certain points on the surface of the virus in much the same way as one piece of a jigsaw puzzle fits into another. Just why this jigsaw puzzle arrangement works is not yet known, but scientists have an idea. They think that the attachment of the drug may prevent the protein coat from collapsing and falling away from the virus.

Will WIN 51,711 be ready in time for your next cold? Well, probably not. So far, WIN 51,711 has been tested in cell cultures and in animals, but it has not yet been given to people. The results of lab tests are promising, however. Perhaps the day is not too far off when an advertisement for cold medicine will say, "Take WIN 51,711 and see!"

To Think About
- Why do you think scientists have found it so difficult to find a cure for the common cold?

- Why is disease prevented when a rhinovirus cannot shed its protein coat?

Chapter Review

CHAPTER SUMMARY

6-1 Viruses

- Viruses contain a core of nucleic acid covered with a protein capsid.
- Viruses can be spread to humans through the air, by contaminated food and drinking water, by means of animal and insect bites, or on the bodies of insects.
- Viroids and prions are simple agents of infection much smaller than viruses.

6-2 Monerans

- Bacteria are monerans: simple cells that do not have a true nucleus.
- Bacteria have three basic shapes: spherical, or coccus; rod-shaped, or bacillus; and spiral, or spirillum.
- The blue-green bacteria make their own food by photosynthesis.

6-3 Importance of Bacteria

- Some bacteria are harmful and cause disease in plants and in animals. Harmful bacteria also can spoil food.
- Helpful bacteria are used in the production of some foods, provide nitrogen for some plants and animals, play important roles in the body, and produce products people need.

VOCABULARY LIST

antibiotic (97)
bacilli (96)
bacteria (96)
binary fission (98)
blue-green bacteria (97)

capsid (92)
chlorophyll (98)
cocci (96)
decomposers (100)
nitrogen fixation (102)

photosynthesis (97)
prion (95)
rickettsia (98)
spirilla (96)

spirochetes (97)
viral replication (93)
viroid (95)
virus (92)

VOCABULARY REVIEW

Matching   Write the word or term from the Vocabulary List that best matches each description.

1. spiral-shaped bacteria
2. bacterial reproduction
3. change of nitrogen into a form used by plants and animals
4. tiny protein agent of infection
5. reproduction of viruses
6. rod-shaped bacteria
7. use sunlight for energy
8. protein coat of a virus
9. organisms belonging to the Kingdom Monera
10. organisms that feed upon the remains of dead organisms

Finding Word Relationships   Pair each numbered word with a word in the box. Explain in complete sentences how the words are related.

viroid	penicillin	spirilla
cocci	chlorophyll	host
capsid	ticks	bacilli

1. photosynthesis
2. spherical
3. protein
4. nucleic acid
5. spirochetes
6. virus
7. antibiotic
8. rickettsia
9. rod-shaped

CONTENT REVIEW

True or False   Write true if the statement is true. If the statement is false, change the underlined word or words to make the statement true.

1. The shape of a virus is caused by its capsid.
2. The three main groups of viruses are bacterial viruses, plant viruses, and human viruses.
3. Short pieces of nucleic acid that lack protein coats are called prions.
4. Spherical bacteria, or cocci, sometimes form pairs of cells.
5. Large colonies of bacteria cannot be seen with the naked eye.
6. A prefix that means "grapelike bunches" is "strepto-."
7. Blue-green bacteria are bacteria that must live within a host.
8. Bacteria that break down remains of dead organisms are called decomposers.
9. Viral reproduction is called replication.
10. Some disease-causing bacteria produce poisons.

Question and Answer   Rewrite each heading in the Chapter Outline on page 90 as a question. Then, answer each of the questions you have written.

Understanding a Diagram   Use the diagram of binary fission shown in Figure 6-9 (page 98) to answer each of the following.

1. In what part of the cell is the nucleic acid found?
2. What surrounds the cell membrane?
3. What is separating the cell into two daughter cells?

CONCEPT REVIEW

Writing the Main Ideas   Using the Chapter Outline on page 90, write the main idea for each heading in the outline.

Critical Thinking   Answer each of the following in complete sentences.

1. Do viruses and bacteria cause disease in the same way? Explain your answer.
▶ 2. Why would it be unnecessary, and most likely harmful, for a blue-green bacterium to live within a host cell?

3. Why do you think bacteria are classified in their own kingdom and not with plants, animals, protists, or fungi?
4. Do you think that viral infections are hard to treat? Explain why.
5. How do you think people kept food from spoiling before refrigeration and chemical preservatives?
6. Why do you think it is wise to keep houseflies out of your kitchen?

EXTENSIONS

1. List four diseases of the respiratory system. Research these diseases in the library. Prepare a chart that lists the following for each disease: the cause (virus or bacterium), symptoms, and its usual duration.
2. Visit a local sewage treatment plant to learn the role bacteria play in waste water treatment. Prepare a simple diagram showing the steps the plant takes to treat sewage. In what ways is a sewage treatment plant important to public health?
3. Call the health department in your area and ask about careers in microbiology and virology.
4. Interview a local veterinarian. Ask about bacterial and viral animal diseases. Report your findings on one of these diseases to the class.

Chapter 7 | Protists

Objectives

After you have completed this chapter, you will be able to

7-1 **identify** the characteristics of protists.

7-1 **name** three groups of organisms in the Protist kingdom.

7-2 **name** four phyla of protozoans.

7-2 **describe** the method of locomotion for each phylum of protozoa.

7-3 **name** six phyla of algae.

7-3 **explain** how algae are important to humans and other organisms.

7-4 **distinguish** between a plasmodial slime mold and a cellular slime mold.

Science Process Skills

In this chapter, two science skills are highlighted. Symbols show some places where these skills are used.

❯ **Predicting:** When you predict, you state in advance how and why something will occur.

▥ **Hypothesizing:** When you hypothesize, you state a suggested answer to a problem based upon known information.

Imagine that you are standing on the edge of a small pond. What if suddenly you are smaller than a grain of sand and swimming in the pond? What interesting things do you think you might see during your swim? You might see tiny organisms that look like pillboxes. Other organisms look like bells hanging from threadlike stalks.

These microscopic organisms are neither plants nor animals. They are classified as **protists.** The protists are interesting because people usually think of living things as only plants and animals.

7-1 Overview of Protists

Key Points

- Most protists are unicellular organisms that have cells with a true nucleus and organelles.

- Three groups of protists are the protozoans, the algae, and the slime molds.

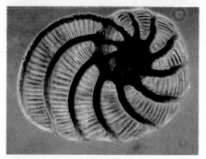

Figure 7–1 Both the dinoflagellate (top) and the foraminiferan (bottom) are one-celled protists.

Look at Figure 7–1. In what ways are the organisms in Figure 7-1 similar? How are they different? Are you surprised to find out that each of these organisms is made up of only one cell?

The organisms shown in Figure 7-1 are protists. They are members of the Protist kingdom. Most protists are unicellular, or made up of one cell. Some protists, however, are multicellular, or made up of more than one cell. The multicellular protists are related to the unicellular protists. Multicellular protists, however, do not have tissues or organs.

More than 50,000 kinds of organisms are classified as protists. The Protist kingdom is divided into three large groups of organisms. The three groups are the protozoans (proht-uh-ZOH-uhns), the algae, and the slime molds.

At one time, biologists classified all microscopic one-celled organisms in the Protist kingdom. The Protist kingdom included the monerans and the protists. Using the electron microscope, however, scientists discovered that there are major differences between monerans and protists. As a result, the protists and monerans were classified in separate kingdoms.

How do protists differ from monerans? Unlike the single cell of a moneran, the single cell of a protist has a nucleus. Also unlike the monerans, protists have organelles that are surrounded by a membrane.

Most protists live in watery environments. They live in lakes, streams, ponds, and in the ocean. However, some protists live in moist soil. Others live in the bodies of animals. Protists that live within animals often cause disease. What name is given to an organism that lives inside another living thing and causes it harm?

Think & Discuss

1. What is a protist?
2. In what ways are protist cells different from moneran cells?
3. Why do you think protists must live in a watery environment?

7-2 Protozoans

One group of protists is made up of unicellular organisms called **protozoans.** They are often called the animal-like protists. Like animals, the protozoans cannot make their own food. Protozoans eat bacteria, algae, and other protozoans. Most protozoans are able to move about freely in search of food. By studying the movement of protozoans, scientists have classified, or grouped, protozoans into four phyla.

Sarcodines

The sarcodines move by using fingerlike projections of their cytoplasm. These fingerlike projections are called **pseudopods** (SOO-duh-pahds). "Pseudopod" means "false foot."

The **amoeba** (uh-MEE-buh) is a common freshwater sarcodine. Under a microscope, an amoeba looks like a blob of cytoplasm that constantly changes shape. Look at the amoeba shown in Figure 7-2. Unlike some types of sarcodines, the amoeba does not have a shell. Sarcodines that have shells move by poking their pseudopods through holes in their shells.

The pseudopods of an amoeba also are used for obtaining food. The pseudopods flow around a bacterium and trap it. After the bacterium is trapped, it is enclosed in a food vacuole. What happens in the food vacuole? The food vacuole contains digestive chemicals that break down the food.

🔖 The amoeba and other freshwater protists also have a contractile vacuole. Find the contractile vacuole of the amoeba shown in Figure 7–2. A contractile vacuole acts as a tiny cell pump. It pumps excess water out of the cell. State a hypothesis about what would happen if excess water were not pumped out of an amoeba.

An amoeba reproduces asexually by binary fission. Binary fission is simple cell division. Bacteria also reproduce by binary fission. During binary fission, the parent cell's hereditary material duplicates. Then the parent cell divides into two daughter cells. Each of the two daughter cells has a complete set of hereditary material from the parent cell.

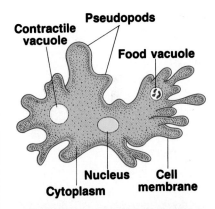

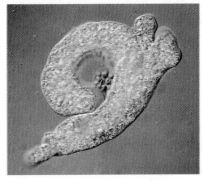

Figure 7–2 The amoeba in the photograph is ingesting food. Where is the food digested?

Ciliates

Protozoans that move by tiny hairlike structures called **cilia** (SIL-ee-uh) are classified as ciliates. The ciliates use their cilia like tiny oars. The cilia beat continuously and rapidly, moving ciliates through the water.

The organism shown in Figure 7-3 is a **paramecium** (par-uh-MEE-see-uhm). A paramecium is a ciliate that lives in fresh water During your imaginary pond swim, you would probably have seen thousands or even millions of paramecia.

Unlike the amoeba, the paramecium has a definite shape. Find the outer edge of the paramecium. What is this outer edge called? The stiff, but flexible, membrane is called the **pellicle** (PEL-i-kal). The pellicle gives the paramecium its slipperlike shape.

A paramecium is like a microscopic food-gathering machine. The paramecium has special parts for capturing and digesting food. As the paramecium moves through the water, the beating cilia push food into the oral groove. The oral groove acts as the mouth of the paramecium. Food is then pushed into the throatlike gullet. At the end of the gullet, the food is enclosed in a food vacuole. Food is digested in the food vacuole.

What happens to undigested material? Undigested material is carried through the paramecium to the anal pore. Like the amoeba, the paramecium also has contractile vacuoles. What is the job of the contractile vacuole?

Do you notice anything unusual about the paramecium shown in Figure 7-3? Count the number of nuclei. The large nucleus is called the macronucleus. It controls most

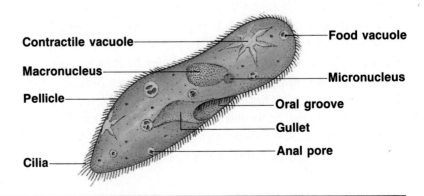

Contractile vacuole — — Food vacuole
Macronucleus — — Micronucleus
Pellicle — — Oral groove
— Gullet
Cilia — — Anal pore

Figure 7–3 How does the paramecium differ from the amoeba shown on page 109?

of the cell's activities. The small nucleus is the micronucleus. The micronucleus controls reproduction.

Paramecia can reproduce asexually and sexually. Paramecia reproduce asexually by binary fission. You may recall that during binary fission an organism simply divides in two. Sexual reproduction in paramecia is called **conjugation** (kan-juh-GAY-shun).

During conjugation, two paramecia join at their oral grooves as shown in Figure 7–4. Each paramecium passes one half of its nucleic acid to the other paramecium. Then, the paramecia separate. Eventually, each paramecium divides. Two new paramecia are produced from each original paramecium. The new paramecia carry some hereditary information from each of the original parent paramecia.

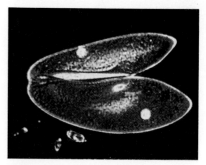

Figure 7–4 What cell materials are exchanged during conjugation?

Flagellates

Flagellates move by means of whiplike structures called **flagella** (fluh-JEL-uh). Small flagellates have only one or two flagella. Large flagellates often have three or more flagella. The movement of flagella pushes or pulls flagellates through the water.

Some flagellates live in fresh or salt water. Most flagellates, however, live within the bodies of animals. Many of these flagellates cause disease. African sleeping sickness is caused by a flagellate called a trypanosome (TRIP-uh-nuh-sohm).

A trypanosome has a complex life cycle that involves two hosts. In Africa, trypanosomes live in the blood of many cattle and antelope. As these infected animals drink from rivers, they are bitten by tsetse flies that breed on the water. When the tsetse (TSEET-see) flies bite the animals, they take in trypanosomes with the blood. The trypanosomes reproduce in the intestines of the flies. Then the trypanosomes move to the flies' salivary glands.

What happens when the flies bite another animal or a person? They inject saliva that contains trypanosomes. Once inside an animal or human host, the trypanosomes travel in the host's bloodstream. Eventually, the trypanosomes infect the nervous system, causing the host to become weak and sleepy. If not treated, the host may go into a coma and die. What are the two hosts of trypanosomes?

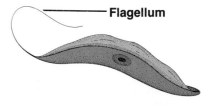

Flagellum

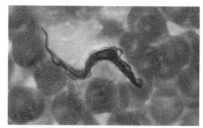

Figure 7–5 The trypanosome that causes African sleeping sickness often is found in the blood.

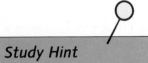

Study Hint

To find out some of the ways you are protected against diseases caused by protists read the Careers in Biology at the end of this chapter.

Sporozoans

Some protozoans cannot move from place to place on their own. They do not have any structures for locomotion. They are called **sporozoans.** Sporozoans are parasites. Sporozoans are transported from place to place within the bodies of the animals they infect.

Like a trypanosome, some sporozoans need two hosts to complete their life cycles. For example, the common sporozoan *Plasmodium* has two hosts. Its hosts are the female *Anopheles* mosquito and a human. In humans, *Plasmodium* cause malaria. *Plasmodium* produce poisons that cause the fever and chills which are characteristic of malaria.

The life cycle of *Plasmodium* can be explained in steps. As you read each step, follow the life cycle of the *Plasmodium* shown in Figure 7-6.

- A mosquito that carries *Plasmodium* injects the sporozoans into the bloodstream of a human.
- The bloodstream carries *Plasmodium* cells to the liver, where they reproduce asexually by cell division.

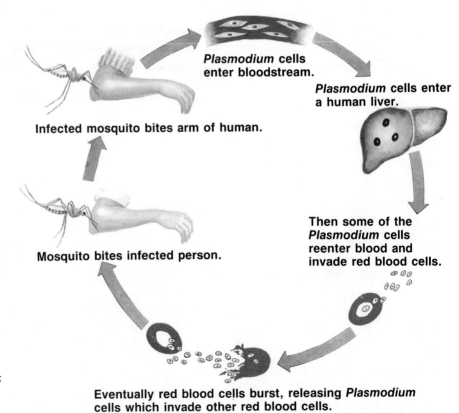

Plasmodium cells enter bloodstream.

Plasmodium cells enter a human liver.

Infected mosquito bites arm of human.

Then some of the Plasmodium cells reenter blood and invade red blood cells.

Mosquito bites infected person.

Eventually red blood cells burst, releasing Plasmodium cells which invade other red blood cells.

Figure 7–6 The *Anopheles* mosquito is a common host of *Plasmodium.*

- Some of the new *Plasmodium* cells reenter the bloodstream and invade red blood cells. Inside the red blood cells the *Plasmodium* continue to reproduce asexually. This causes the red blood cells to enlarge. Some of the *Plasmodium* cells also develop into separate male and female cells. Eventually the red blood cells burst, releasing *Plasmodium* cells back into the bloodstream.

❯ A mosquito bites an infected person, and takes *Plasmodium* cells into its body. The sporozoans enter the stomach of the mosquito where sexual reproduction of *Plasmodium* takes place. Male and female sporozoans unite to produce new *Plasmodium* cells. Then the *Plasmodium* cells move to the salivary glands of the mosquito. Predict what will happen if this mosquito bites a person.

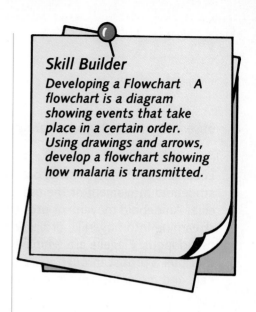

Skill Builder

Developing a Flowchart A flowchart is a diagram showing events that take place in a certain order. Using drawings and arrows, develop a flowchart showing how malaria is transmitted.

Think & Discuss

4. What are pseudopods?
5. Name four phyla of protozoans and describe how organisms in each phylum move.
★ 6. List two similarities in the life cycles of the trypanosome and *Plasmodium*.

7-3 Algae

There are about 22,000 different kinds of **algae.** Some algae exist as single cells or live together as groups of cells. Other algae are large, multicellular organisms that do not have tissues or organs.

All algae contain the green **pigment** chlorophyll. A pigment is a substance that gives an object color. Because algae have chlorophyll, they are photosynthetic. They can make their own food using the sun's energy. Why do you think algae are sometimes called the plantlike protists?

Most algae contain other pigments in addition to chlorophyll. These pigments can mask the green color of chlorophyll. The other pigments give different kinds of algae their characteristic colors. Algae are classified into six phyla according to the pigments they contain.

Key Points

- Fire algae, golden-brown algae, and euglenoids are unicellular algae. Green algae, brown algae, and red algae are multicellular algae.

- Phytoplankton are food for many organisms and also produce oxygen.

ACTIVITY 7–1

PROBLEM: What are the ways in which protists move?

Science Process Skills
observing, classifying, comparing

Background Information
Locomotion in most protists occurs by amoeboid movement or the use of flagella or cilia. Amoeboid movement uses cytoplasm streaming into fingerlike projections, or pseudopods. Flagella are whiplike structures that pull a protist through water. Cilia are like oars and move together in a wavelike motion.

Materials
    hay–grass infusion
    compound microscope
    slides
    cover slips

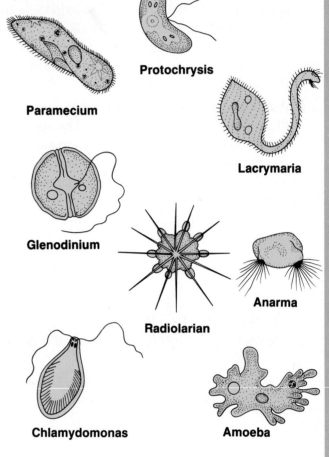

Paramecium

Protochrysis

Lacrymaria

Glenodinium

Radiolarian

Anarma

Chlamydomonas

Amoeba

Procedure
1. Collect 3 water samples from a hay–grass infusion. Take a sample from the top, middle, and bottom of the infusion.
2. Place a drop of water from one of the water samples on a clean glass slide. Place a cover slip over the drop of water.
3. Place the slide on the microscope stage and observe the drop of water under high power. **Note:** Be sure to use the proper procedure for focusing a microscope.
4. Draw outlines of organisms that you can see. Next to each drawing write the method of locomotion each organism uses.
5. Repeat steps 2–4 for the other two water samples.
6. Compare your drawings with the organisms shown. Name any organisms in your drawings that you can.

Observations
1. How many different kinds of protists did you see?
2. Compare the speed of protist movement for each method of locomotion.

Conclusions
1. Which method of locomotion did most protists use?
2. Does one method of locomotion seem to be more efficient than the other two? Explain your answer.
3. What is the method of locomotion for each of the 8 organisms shown in the activity?

Going Further
Make a "World of Protozoans" chart. Find the scientific names of 10 protozoans that cause diseases in humans. In your chart, draw a picture of each protozoan and give its scientific name, the disease it causes, and the body part in which the protozoan lives. Indicate the method of locomotion for each protozoan.

Figure 7–7 Algae often grow on the surface of ponds.

One-Celled Algae

The three phyla of one-celled algae are the fire algae, golden-brown algae, and the euglenoids. These microscopic algae float near the surface of water along with protozoans and tiny animals and plants. Together, all of these organisms are called **plankton.** The microscopic algae and other organisms that contain chlorophyll are called **phytoplankton** (fyt-uh-PLANK-tuhn). One-celled algae make up much of the phytoplankton.

You may be surprised to learn that phytoplankton are important to all life. Phytoplankton are an important food supply to many fishes as well as some kinds of whales. Most importantly, phytoplankton produce about 90 percent of the oxygen in the earth's atmosphere.

Fire Algae

Most fire algae are red in color. Many of these algae also produce light. The cell walls of many fire algae consist of cellulose plates that fit together like the pieces of an armor suit. Many fire algae also have spinelike projections and two flagella. The beating of the two flagella move the algae forward and make the algae spin like a top.

Have you ever seen or heard of a red tide? A red tide occurs when there is a population explosion of fire algae in the ocean. The large number of fire algae give the water a reddish tint.

Skill Builder

Hypothesizing Many kinds of algae can reproduce quickly and in great numbers, producing an algal bloom. As the algae die, they are broken down by bacteria. The bacteria use oxygen when breaking down the algae. What happens to fish as the amount of oxygen in the water decreases?

ACTIVITY 7–2

PROBLEM: Do some pigments mask other pigments in algae?

Science Process Skills
observing, inferring

Background Information
Chromatography is a process by which pigments can be separated from a solution. Paper chromatography uses paper, such as filter paper, to separate the pigments. The result is called a chromatogram. On the chromatogram, you can see the different bands of color and the speed at which separations occur. The closer to the bottom a band of color is, the faster the color separates out of the solution.

Materials

hand lens	tape
algae "pigment" extract	metric ruler
paper towel	scissors
jumbo paper clip	dropper
150-mL beaker	water

Procedure

1. Obtain about 5 mL of "pigment" extract from your teacher.
2. On the paper towel, draw 4 chromatography test strips, like the one shown in Figure A. Your test strip should be the same height as the height of the beaker. Each test strip should be about 3 cm wide.
3. Cut out each chromatography test strip. **CAUTION: Always be careful when using scissors.**
4. Unbend the paper clip so that it is a relatively straight piece of wire.
5. Observe the color of the algae "pigment" extract.
6. Use the dropper to place one drop of extract on each strip in the position shown in Figure A. Let the drop dry. Then place another drop on top of the dried pigment.

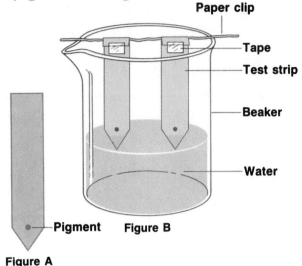

Figure A

Figure B

7. Set up two test strips in the beaker as shown in Figure B.
8. Slowly add water to the beaker until the tip of the chromatography strips are in the water.
9. Wait 10 minutes for the chromatograms to develop.
10. Remove the chromatograms and set them aside to dry. When the strips are dry, examine them with a hand lens.
11. Repeat steps 7–10 for the other two test strips.
12. Draw your chromatograms and label the colors.

Observations
1. What color is the algae "pigment" extract?
2. **a.** How many color bands are there in your chromotograms? **b.** Which color separated out the fastest? **c.** the slowest?

Conclusions
1. Does one pigment mask the other pigments? Explain your answer.
2. **INFER** **a.** If all algae are photosynthetic, why are not all algae green? **b.** How can you explain the different colors of algae?

⟩ A red tide can be dangerous. Fire algae produce a poison that can kill fish and people. Shellfish, such as mussels, are not affected by the poison, but shellfish collect the poison in their bodies. Predict what might happen to a person who eats shellfish contaminated with fire algae poisons.

Golden-Brown Algae

Golden-brown algae have yellow or brown pigments that mask the green color of chlorophyll. The golden-brown algae range in color from yellowish-green to golden-brown. The most well-known group of golden-brown algae are called diatoms.

Diatoms are organisms that look like microscopic pillboxes. Their walls are made up of a hard, glasslike substance called silica. The walls of diatoms have two overlapping halves.

When diatoms die, their shells do not decay, or break down. As a result, large deposits of diatom shells form on the ocean floor. These deposits often are mined from the ocean floor for use in products such as toothpaste, silver polish, and detergents.

Euglenoids

Euglenoids are named for the *Euglena*, the best-known organisms of this group. Most euglenoids are found in fresh water. They grow in large numbers in stagnant, or still, ponds. All euglenoids have one or more flagella.

Euglena contain chlorophyll, and when light is available they can make their own food by photosynthesis. What happens if light is not available? Then *Euglena* can take in food from the outside.

Observe the structure of the *Euglena* in Figure 7–9. Find the organelle called an **eyespot.** Of course, the eyespot is not really an eye, but the eyespot is sensitive to light. A *Euglena* swims toward light when the eyespot senses the light.

Many-Celled Algae

There are three phyla of many-celled algae. These phyla are the green algae, the brown algae, and the red algae. Brown and red algae live in the ocean. Most green algae live in freshwater ponds, puddles, and on tree trunks. Some types of green algae also live in the ocean.

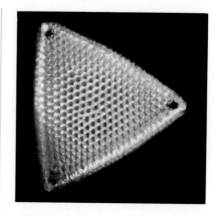

Figure 7–8 Why do you think this diatom is classified as a golden-brown alga?

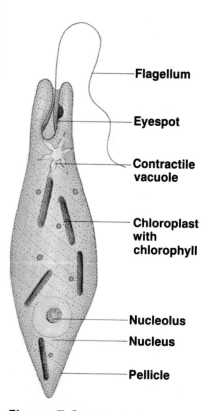

Flagellum

Eyespot

Contractile vacuole

Chloroplast with chlorophyll

Nucleolus

Nucleus

Pellicle

Figure 7-9 The *Euglena* is both animal-like and plantlike.

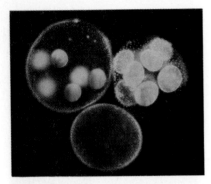

Figure 7–10 How many daughter colonies are shown in these *Volvox*?

Green Algae

Biologists think that green algae are the ancestors of green plants. Unlike other types of algae, green algae contain the same pigments as plants. Chlorophyll is the main pigment in green algae. Green algae also store food as starch and have cellulose in their cell walls.

Freshwater green algae may consist of single cells or groups of cells. An interesting freshwater green alga is *Volvox*. Hundreds to thousands of cells make up one colony of *Volvox*. The cells are held together in a hollow ball by strands of cytoplasm. Each cell in the colony has two flagella. As the flagella beat, they send the colony spinning through the water. Look at the *Volvox* colony in Figure 7-10. You can see tiny daughter colonies within a parent colony. Eventually, the daughter colonies are released to exist on their own.

Brown Algae

Brown algae often are called seaweed or kelp. Brown algae are common along rocky coasts, especially in cold water. You may have seen brown algae washed up on a beach. The brown algae are very large forms of algae. Some brown algae grow to over 100 m long.

If you have ever picked up a piece of seaweed on the beach, you may have noticed small light-colored structures on the seaweed. These structures are called **air bladders.** Air bladders help keep the brown algae floating near the surface of the water. Why do you think it is important that the algae float near the surface of the water?

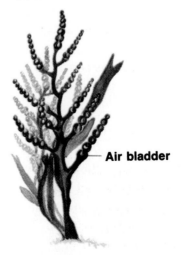

— **Air bladder**

Figure 7–11 Because air bladders are filled with air, these brown algae are light in weight.

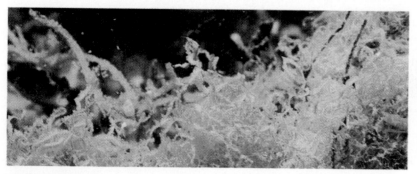

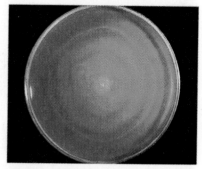

Figure 7–12 Red algae (left) are used to make agar (right).

Red Algae

Like the brown algae, the red algae also are called seaweed. Most red algae grow far below the ocean surface. Red algae can grow far beneath the surface because their red pigments can capture certain light rays that reach deep into the water.

The cell walls of many red algae are coated with a gluelike material. This substance can be removed from the algae and used to make agar. Agar is a substance on which bacteria are grown in the laboratory. Agar also is used to make foods such as puddings thicken. The next time you eat ice cream, cheese, salad dressing, or marshmallows, think of red algae. They probably were used to make these foods.

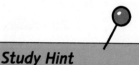

Study Hint

Look at the photographs in Section 7–3, Algae, and see how many kinds of algae you can identify correctly.

Think & Discuss

7. What is plankton?

8. In what ways are algae useful to people?

9. Why are the multicellular algae not classified as plants?

7-4 Slime Molds

If you were walking in the woods, you would find **slime molds** in cool, shady, moist places. Most likely, the slime molds would be living on decaying material, such as rotting logs. Slime molds are unusual protists that at different stages of their lives resemble other organisms. Slime molds have two life stages—a reproductive stage and a feeding stage. Slime molds have reproductive

Key Point

• There are no cell walls or membranes between the cells that form a plasmodial slime mold. Cellular slime molds may group together, but remain as separate cells.

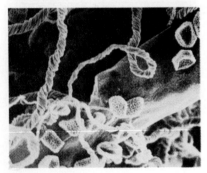

Figure 7–13 The plasmodial slime mold (top) and the cellular slime mold (bottom) grow on decaying logs in forests.

structures much like fungi, so at one time biologists classified slime molds as fungi. However, during their feeding stage, slime molds look and act like amoebas. Therefore, most biologists now classify slime molds with the protists.

Plasmodial Slime Molds

In the feeding stage of its life, a plasmodial slime mold is made up of a large mass of cytoplasm called a **plasmodium** (plaz-MOH-dee-uhm). A plasmodium looks as though it were formed by many cells joined together, but there are no cell walls or membranes between the cells. The nuclei are just scattered throughout the cytoplasm.

What happens to a plasmodial slime mold during its reproductive stage? Small black structures called fruiting bodies grow from the cytoplasm. The fruiting bodies release reproductive cells called spores. The spores develop into amoebalike organisms. When two of the amoebalike organisms unite, they are the beginning of a new plasmodium.

Cellular Slime Molds

Cellular slime molds differ from the plasmodial slime molds in that individual amoebalike cells make up their feeding stage. These cells live in the soil, feeding on bacteria and dead matter. When food becomes scarce, an interesting thing happens. The individual cellular slime molds group together, moving along like a plasmodium. They remain separate cells, however, and do not join into a single mass of cytoplasm. Eventually, fruiting bodies form from this mass of cells. Spores produced by the fruiting bodies give rise to new amoebalike cells.

Think & Discuss

10. What is a plasmodium?
11. Describe the feeding stage of a cellular slime mold.
12. If you were given an unidentified slime mold during its feeding stage to study under a microscope, how would you decide whether it was a plasmodial slime mold or a cellular slime mold?

CAREERS in BIOLOGY
Protecting Against Disease

Are you concerned about water quality when you go swimming? If so, you are probably aware that many diseases are caused by bacteria and other microorganisms. Many rewarding careers involve protecting people against the spread of disease by harmful microorganisms.

Food Service Worker

If you enjoy working in the kitchen and dealing with people, you may want to become a food service worker. Food service workers help prepare and serve meals in restaurants, school cafeterias, hospitals, and other institutions.

Many food service workers receive on-the-job training. The job of a food service worker involves handling food safely and efficiently. One of a food service worker's responsibilities is to make sure that foods such as meat and fish are not left out of the refrigerator too long. If left out too long, these foods will spoil due to microbial growth. Food service workers also should make sure that dishes and cooking utensils are kept clean in order to prevent the growth of bacteria.

For more information: Visit a school or hospital cafeteria and talk to several food service workers.

Sewage Treatment Technician

Sewage and wastewater contain harmful bacteria and other pollutants. This water must be purified. A sewage treatment technician works at a sewage treatment plant, where pollutants are removed from wastewater.

A sewage treatment technician may work for a city or county plant, or for a treatment plant owned by private industry. The duties of a sewage treatment technician include testing water samples and maintaining the equipment used to treat wastewater.

Many sewage treatment technicians are hired with a high school diploma. Those who wish to assume more responsibility may take a special two-year program in wastewater technology.

For more information: Write to the Water Pollution Control Federation, 2626 Pennsylvania Ave., NW, Washington, DC 20037.

Microbiologist

A microbiologist at the Centers for Disease Control in Atlanta, Georgia, peers at a tiny rod-shaped organism. The organism is believed to have caused an illness in hundreds of children in Pennsylvania. The microbiologist knows that the identity of the bacterium must be found in order to treat the illness.

A microbiologist studies microorganisms and their effects on other forms of life. Some microbiologists specialize in the study of particular organisms, such as bacteria or viruses. Other microbiologists specialize in learning how diseases are transmitted to people, animals, and plants.

Microbiologists may work for the government, a university, or a private research laboratory. A person interested in becoming a microbiologist should obtain a college degree with a major in one of the biological sciences.

For more information: Write to the American Society of Microbiology, 1913 I St., NW, Washington, DC 20006.

Chapter Review

CHAPTER SUMMARY

7-1 Overview of Protists

- Most protists are single-celled organisms. Some protists are multicellular, but their cells do not form tissues or organs.
- The cells of protists have a true nucleus and cell organelles.
- Protozoans, algae, and slime molds are the three groups of protists.

7-2 Protozoans

- Protozoans are classified according to their method of locomotion.
- Sarcodines, ciliates, flagellates, and sporozoans are protozoans.

7-3 Algae

- Three phyla of single-celled algae are the fire algae, golden-brown algae, and the euglenoids.

- Microscopic algae, protozoans, and tiny plants and animals form plankton.
- Three phyla of multicellular algae are the green algae, brown algae, and red algae.
- Algae are food for many organisms and produce about 90 percent of the oxygen in the atmosphere.
- Algae are used to make a variety of foods, and in products such as toothpaste and silver polish.

7-4 Slime Molds

- The feeding stage of the plasmodial slime mold is a large mass of cytoplasm.
- There are no cell walls or membranes between the cells that form a plasmodium.
- The feeding stage of a cellular slime mold is made up of individual amoebalike cells.

VOCABULARY LIST

air bladders (118)
algae (113)
amoeba (109)
cilia (110)
conjugation (111)

eyespot (117)
flagella (111)
paramecium (110)
pellicle (110)
phytoplankton (115)

pigment (113)
plankton (115)
plasmodium (120)
protists (107)
protozoans (109)

pseudopods (109)
slime molds (119)
sporozoans (112)

VOCABULARY REVIEW

Matching Write the word or term from the Vocabulary List that best matches each description.

1. fingerlike extensions of cytoplasm
2. substance that gives an object color
3. sexual reproduction in paramecia
4. floating protozoans, algae, tiny plants and animals
5. keep brown algae afloat
6. tiny hairlike structures
7. group of photosynthetic protists
8. feeding stage of one type of slime mold

Identifying Relationships Identify the word or term in each group that does not belong. Explain why it does not belong with the group.

1. amoeba, sporozoan, sarcodine
2. flagella, cilia, eyespot
3. paramecium, algae, pellicle
4. phytoplankton, chlorophyll, pseudopod
5. beavers, protists, microscopic
6. protozoans, multicellular, unicellular
7. slime molds, plasmodia, flagellates
8. air bladders, sporozoans, parasites
9. pigment, conjugation, chlorophyll
10. binary fission, conjugation, slime molds

Completion Write the word or words that best complete each sentence.

1. The walls of diatoms are made up of a glasslike substance called _____.
2. Phytoplankton produce about 90% of the _____ in the earth's atmosphere.
3. Paramecia have _____ kinds of nuclei.
4. Malaria is caused by an organism called the _____.
5. A *Euglena*'s _____ is sensitive to light.
6. The nuclei of a _____ slime mold are scattered throughout the cytoplasm.
7. Protozoans, algae, and slime molds are groups of _____.
8. A poisonous kind of algae is _____.
9. Sarcodines use _____ to move.
10. A contractile vacuole pumps excess out of the amoeba cell.

Finding the Main Ideas Use the section number to find the sentence that answers each question. Then, write the sentence.

1. How can most protists be described? (7-1)
2. What three groups make up the Protist kingdom? (7-1)
3. In what way are protozoans like animals? (7-2)
4. On what basis are protozoans grouped into phyla? (7-2)
5. On what basis are algae grouped into phyla? (7-3)
6. Which algae phyla are unicellular? (7-3)
7. Which algae phyla are multicellular? (7-3)
8. On what kind of matter might you find slime molds? (7-4)
9. How are plasmodial and cellular slime molds different? (7-4)

Writing for Understanding One way to find out if you understand something is to write a brief summary of the information in your own words. Reread Section 7-1, Overview of Protists, on page 108, and write a brief summary of the information.

Critical Thinking Answer each of the following in complete sentences.

1. Choose two different algae and discuss why roots, stems, and leaves are not needed by these organisms.

2. What do you think would happen to the organisms in a pond if there were no algae or water plants in the pond? Give reasons for your answer.
3. Explain why a means of movement is not needed by a sporozoan.
4. Explain the reasoning behind this statement: An effective way of controlling the spread of malaria is to eliminate mosquitos in areas where the disease exists.
5. Why would diatom shells be useful as abrasives in silver polish?

1. Choose three of the following items and copy the ingredients listed on their packages: pudding, ice cream, cheese, salad dressing, marshmallows, toothpaste, silver polish, and detergent. Write to the manufacturers of these products to find out which substances are derived from algae.

2. Using library references, find out how pollution affects protists growing in the ocean. Present your findings to the class.
3. Research how to set up a marine aquarium properly. Write a brief report explaining the role seaweed plays in the maintenance of the aquarium.

Chapter 8 Fungi

Objectives

After you have completed this chapter, you will be able to

8-1 **list** the characteristics of fungi.

8-1 **explain** how fungi are classified.

8-2 **relate** the importance of water molds and terrestrial molds to humans and other organisms.

8-3 **name** three examples of sac fungi and **relate** their importance to humans and other organisms.

8-4 **name** three examples of club fungi and **relate** their importance to humans and other organisms.

8-5 **explain** how imperfect fungi are classified.

8-5 **relate** the importance of imperfect fungi to humans.

Science Process Skills

In this chapter, two science skills are highlighted. Symbols show some places where these skills are used.

▶ **Inferring:** When you infer, you form a conclusion based upon facts and not direct observation.

📁 **Classifying:** When you classify, you group things based upon similarities.

The Kesterson National Wildlife Refuge has a toxic waste problem. Drainage water that passed through the refuge left behind toxic levels of selenium in the soil. Selenium is an element normally found in soil in small amounts. However, a high level of selenium is poisonous to plants and animals.

A fungus living in the soil of the wildlife refuge may help solve the selenium problem. How can a fungus help solve the problem? Fungi break down their food before they ingest it. As the fungus breaks down food in the soil, it changes the selenium into a nontoxic gas. Scientists now are trying to grow more of this fungus with the hope that the fungus will get rid of the extra selenium in the soil.

8-1 Overview of Fungi

Study Hint

Spores are like plant seeds in that they grow into a new organism. In fact, the word "spore" comes from the Greek word meaning "seed."

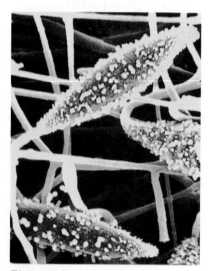

Figure 8-1 Notice the filaments, or hyphae, of this fungus, which causes ringworm.

Do you think that the mushrooms in your salad are related to the lettuce? Many people think that mushrooms are plants. However, mushrooms are not plants. Mushrooms are one of many kinds of organisms in the Fungi kingdom.

For many years, biologists classified fungi as plants. Why were fungi so classified? Fungi have some plant characteristics. For example, fungi often grow in soil or on decaying logs. Most fungi are made up of many cells that are surrounded by cell walls. Fungi, like some plants, reproduce by **spores**. A spore is a cell that can develop into a new organism.

Biologists, however, have discovered that fungi and plants are really not that much alike. Unlike most plants, fungi have the following characteristics:

- Most fungi have cell walls made up mostly of **chitin** (KYT-n). Chitin is the substance that makes up the hard parts of animals such as crabs and insects.

- Fungi often have large cells with many nuclei.

- Fungi grow by producing long, thin filaments called **hyphae** (HY-fay).

- Fungi do not have chlorophyll.

- Fungi digest their food before it is ingested.

- Fungi grow well in dark, warm, moist areas.

The differences between fungi and plants led biologists to rethink how fungi were classified. In 1969, the American ecologist Robert Whittaker suggested that fungi be classified in a separate kingdom.

Most fungi are **saprophytes** (SAP-ruh-fyts). A saprophyte is an organism that feeds upon dead organisms. As fungi feed upon dead organisms, the remains of the organism are broken down into simpler substances. Fungi also are decomposers. A decomposer is an organism that breaks down complex substances into simpler substances. These simpler substances often can be used again by other living things. Name some other decomposers.

Some fungi are parasites. They live on or in plants or animals. In people, parasitic fungi often cause diseases, such as athlete's foot. Fungi also cause the kind of pneumonia that people with AIDS often develop.

Biologists have classified more than 65,000 species of fungi. Most are microscopic. However, many common fungi, such as mushrooms, are visible to the unaided eye.

Fungi are classified according to their structure and the way they produce spores. Like plants, fungi are classified into groups called divisions. Three divisions of fungi include organisms that produce spores sexually. The fourth division of fungi includes fungi that are not known to reproduce sexually.

Think & Discuss

1. What is a saprophyte?
2. What material makes up most of the cell walls of most fungi?
3. Fungi once were called the nongreen plants. Why do you think fungi were described in this way?

8-2 Molds

Fungi that do not have cross walls between the cells that make up their hyphae are called molds. Cross walls are cell walls that separate one cell from another. Without cross walls, the cells that make up mold hyphae are very long and contain many nuclei.

Biologists have identified more than 1100 species of molds. Most molds have been classified as water molds or terrestrial (tuh-RES-tree-uhl) molds. Terrestrial molds are molds that live on land.

Key Points

- Most molds are classified as water molds or terrestrial molds.

- Saprophytic molds break down dead organisms and return useful substances to the environment. Some parasitic molds cause diseases in plants and animals.

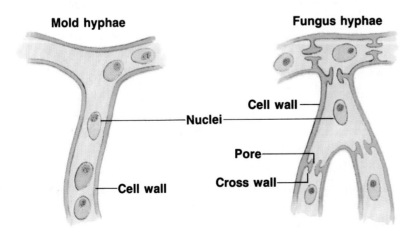

Figure 8-2 What is the difference between the hyphae of molds and those of other fungi?

Water Molds

Water molds differ from other fungi in two ways. First, water molds have cell walls made up mostly of **cellulose** (SEL-yoo-lohs). Cellulose is the nonliving substance that makes up the cell walls of most plants. Second, water molds produce sexual spores from male and female sex cells called **gametes** (GAM-eets). Water molds also produce spores asexually.

Most water molds are saprophytes that live in fresh or salt water. Saprophytes are helpful to the environment. How do you think saprophytes are helpful to the environment?

Some water molds are parasites of fishes and other organisms. A few species of water molds also are parasites of land plants. In the 1840s, the potato crop of Ireland was destroyed by a water mold. Because potatoes were an important part of the people's diet, the loss of the potato crop led to a famine, or lack of food. During the potato famine, many people died of starvation. Others left Ireland in search of food. Many of the people who left Ireland immigrated to the United States.

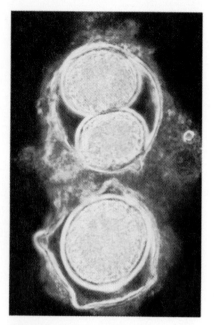

Figure 8-3 The sexual spores of a common water mold develop from gametes.

Terrestrial Molds

Terrestrial molds can be found in almost any area that is dark, warm, and moist. For example, terrestrial molds live in soil, on decaying matter, on leather, and on foods. Have you ever seen grey-black "fuzz" growing on bread? The fuzz that was growing on the bread was the **mycelium** (my-SEE-lee-um) of the mold. A mycelium is a loose, tangled mass of hyphae.

Look at the magnified view of black bread mold shown in Figure 8-4 on page 129. Notice the hyphae, called **rhizoids** (RY-zoyds), extending down into the bread. Rhizoids are rootlike structures that anchor the mold to its food source. Rhizoids also secrete enzymes that digest the food. Nutrients then are absorbed by the rhizoids.

Spores are produced by reproductive hyphae that grow up from the bread. On the ends of these hyphae are structures called **sporangia** (spaw-RAYN-gee-uh). Because the sporangia are filled with spores, they sometimes are called spore cases.

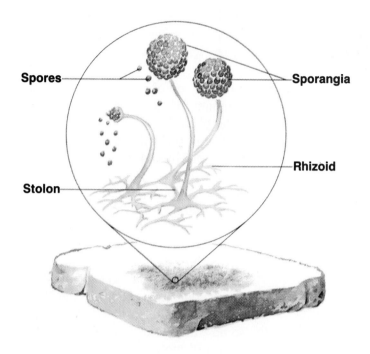

Figure 8-4 Black bread mold is a common terrestrial mold.

Spores eventually burst out of the sporangia. If growing conditions are right, each spore that lands on a food source can develop into a new fungus. What growing conditions are needed for a spore to develop into a fungus?

The spores of all fungi are light in weight. The lightweight spores can be carried easily by air currents. Spores also are carried from place to place by water or on the bodies of insects.

Many people are sensitive to mold spores. In these people, mold spores may cause allergy symptoms such as watery eyes and difficulty in breathing. Have you ever heard of the "curse" of the ancient tombs? Scientists have discovered that this "curse" really was caused by large numbers of mold spores that infected and killed people entering the tombs. Why might mold spores be found in large numbers in an ancient tomb?

Health and Safety Tip
Mold spores can cause allergy symptoms similar to those caused by pollen. In many parts of the country, you can find out when the mold spore count is high by listening to weather broadcasts.

Think & Discuss

4. What is a mycelium?

5. A spore may develop hundreds of kilometers away from its parent fungus. Explain how this might happen.

6. How do water molds differ from terrestrial molds?

ACTIVITY 8–1

PROBLEM: What kind of conditions do molds need to grow?

Science Process Skills
experimenting, predicting, observing

Background Information
Molds are organisms that are classified in the Kingdom Fungi. A mold that is easy to grow is a bread mold. Like most molds, a bread mold is a saprophyte, and lives on dead organic material. The bread is the food supply for the bread mold.

Materials
1 slice of 3-day-old bread
4 small, clear plastic cups
hand lens
aluminum foil

Procedure
1. Label the four small cups 1 through 4.
2. Divide the slice of bread into four equal pieces that will fit into the cups.
3. Place a piece of bread in each cup. Add 5–10 drops of water to cups 1 and 2. **Note:** Do not soak the bread.
4. Leave the cups open for 10 to 15 minutes. While you are waiting, copy the Data Table on a sheet of paper.

5. Cover the top of each cup with a piece of aluminum foil. Seal the foil tightly around the lip of the cup.
6. Place cups 1 and 3 in a dark, warm place. Place cups 2 and 4 in a sunny or light place.
7. **PREDICT** Which piece of bread do you predict will have the most mold growth after 6 days? Continue the activity to find out if your prediction is correct.
8. On the third day, use the hand lens to examine the bread pieces for mold growth. Record your observations in the Data Table. Use the terms "none," "little," "some," and "much" to describe the amount of mold growth.
9. Repeat step 8 each day for three more days.
10. Dispose of all materials properly. Wash your hands with soap and warm water.

Observations
1. What color is the mold growth?
2. **a.** Which piece of bread had the most mold growth? **b.** Which had the least?
3. On which day did mold growth first appear on each piece of bread?
4. What are the two variables in the activity?

Conclusions
1. How does the amount of light affect mold growth?
2. How does moisture affect mold growth?
3. Was your prediction correct? Use your observations to support your answer.
4. What environmental conditions are best for mold growth?

Going Further
Using this activity as a model, develop an experiment to determine how temperature affects mold growth. Write out the steps of the experiment before you perform it.

Data Table: Mold Growth				
CUP	DAYS			
	3RD	4TH	5TH	6TH
1				
2				
3				
4				

8-3 Sac Fungi

Have you ever eaten a truffle or a morel? Truffles and morels are examples of sac fungi. Unlike molds, sac fungi have cross walls in their hyphae. These cross walls have tiny pores in them. The pores allow cytoplasm, and sometimes nuclei, to pass from one cell to another.

The sexual spores of sac fungi are produced in tiny sacs. These sacs give the sac fungi their name. Most of the time, eight spores form in a sac. The formation of the sac and spores begins when reproductive hyphae fuse and join their hereditary material.

Sac fungi also produce asexual spores. The asexual spores of the sac fungi are not enclosed in spore cases. They are formed either singly or in chains at the tips of the hyphae.

Yeasts

Yeasts are single-celled fungi that usually do not form hyphae. Yeasts are classified as fungi because they form filaments under certain conditions.

Unlike most organisms, yeasts obtain their energy through a respiratory process called **fermentation** (fur-mun-TAY-shun). During fermentation, sugars and starches are broken down into alcohol and carbon dioxide gas. At the same time, energy is produced.

If you have ever baked bread, you probably used yeast to make the bread rise. How does yeast make bread rise? As bread dough is baked, yeast in the dough produces carbon dioxide gas. The carbon dioxide gas causes bubbles to form in the bread. As the bubbles form in the bread, the bread rises.

Because they sometimes form sexual spores in tiny sacs, yeasts are classified as sac fungi. However, yeasts most often reproduce by **budding**. Budding occurs when a small part of a cell breaks off to form a new organism. Is budding a sexual or an asexual reproductive process? How do you know?

Yeasts are sometimes used instead of bacteria in medical research. For example, scientists have used yeast cells as models for cancer and AIDS. Yeast also has been used to produce a vaccine against hepatitis B.

Key Points

- Truffles, morels, yeasts, cup fungi, and lichens are examples of sac fungi.

- Sac fungi are used as food by some organisms. Sac fungi also are helpful to the environme .

Skill Builder

Researching Ergot is a parasitic sac fungus of cereal grains, such as rye. Ergot causes more problems to people who eat the rye than to the rye itself. Ergot, however, also can be helpful. Use an encyclopedia or other reference book to find out more about ergot. Prepare a report that tells about the importance of ergot in the Middle Ages and the uses of ergot today.

Figure 8-5 These cup fungi grow in the rain forests of Costa Rica.

Figure 8-6 Lichens, such as this British soldier lichen, grow on rocks and help make soil.

Cup Fungi

Cup fungi are saprophytes that grow in soil. Unlike yeasts, the sexual spores of cup fungi are produced on a fleshy mass called a **fruiting body**. A fruiting body is a tightly packed mass of hyphae. Look at Figure 8-5. The fruiting body of the cup fungus shown is the cuplike structure that gives the fungus its name.

Hyphae line the inside of the fruiting body. These hyphae produce the spore-filled sac of the cup fungus. Spores remain inside the sac until they mature. The sac then bursts open and the spores explode into the air. The spores then are carried by air currents to new locations.

Lichens

One of the most unusual living things is the **lichen** (LY-kuhn). Lichens are really two organisms living together. The two organisms that make up a lichen are a fungus and an alga.

The fungus and the alga that make up a lichen have a symbiotic (sim-by-OT-ik) relationship. In a symbiotic relationship, each organism helps the other organism survive. In a lichen, the alga provides the fungus with nutrients. The fungus, in turn, provides the alga with the water and carbon dioxide needed for photosynthesis. Together, the alga and the fungus can live where neither organism could survive alone.

In most cases, the fungal part of the lichen is a sac fungus, and the alga usually is a green alga. However, not all lichens are made up of a sac fungus and a green alga. For this reason, biologists do not always agree on the classification of lichens. In which classification group do you think lichens belong? Why?

Think & Discuss

7. What is a fruiting body?

8. What is a lichen?

9. How are sac fungi helpful to humans and other organisms?

8-4 Club Fungi

Like the sac fungi, the club fungi are named for the structure that produces their sexual spores. This structure is called a **basidium** (buh-SID-ee-um). The word "basidium" comes from the Greek word meaning "club." The basidia of the club fungi are located on their fruiting bodies.

Most club fungi are saprophytes. Club fungi live in many different environments. All club fungi are made up of a mycelium that develops within a food source. Mushrooms, bracket fungi, puffballs, coral fungi, rusts, and smuts are common examples of club fungi. What are the food sources for the club fungi shown in Figure 8-7?

Mushrooms

Have you ever eaten mushrooms? Mushrooms are examples of club fungi. A mushroom is made up of many hyphae that are packed close together. The umbrella-shaped part of the mushroom's fruiting body is the **cap**.

The life cycle of a mushroom is shown in Figure 8-8. During sexual reproduction, reproductive hyphae fuse and form a new cell. This new cell divides and grows into a mycelium. As a mushroom grows, the mycelium pushes a compact mass of hyphae from the food source. This mass of hyphae grows into a stalk with a cap at the top.

Figure 8-7 These bracket fungi are growing on a dead log on the forest floor.

Figure 8-8 The fruiting body of the mushroom is visible above ground.

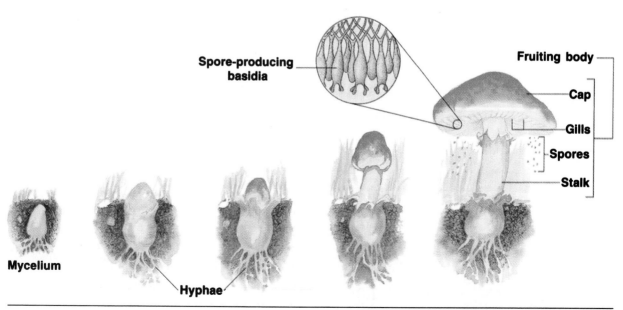

Spore-producing basidia

Fruiting body

Cap

Gills

Spores

Stalk

Mycelium

Hyphae

Figure 8-9 Leaf rust (left) and corn smut (right) can cause severe damage to wheat and corn crops.

The underside of a mushroom cap is lined with structures called **gills**. The basidia of the mushroom are located on the gills. When the spores mature, they drop to the ground. If growing conditions are right, the spores develop into new mushrooms.

Mushrooms are both helpful and harmful. Many mushrooms are eaten by people and other animals. Not all mushrooms, however, can be used as food. Some mushrooms, such as the destroying angel mushroom, are very poisonous.

Rusts and Smuts

Rusts and smuts are parasitic club fungi that often cause severe diseases in plants and can destroy crops. Unlike other club fungi, the rusts and smuts do not form fruiting bodies. They do, however, form sexual spores on basidia.

Smuts appear as dark patches on the leaves, stems, flowers, or fruits of plants. The dark patches on the plant are the powdery spores of the smut. Most rusts look like the orange patch shown on the plant in Figure 8-9.

Think & Discuss

10. What is the name of the structure that produces the sexual spores in the club fungi?

11. Outline the life cycle of a mushroom.

12. Why do you think sac fungi and club fungi often are called the higher fungi?

ACTIVITY 8–2

PROBLEM: Why is a mushroom classified as a fungus?

Science Process Skills
observing, classifying, inferring

Background Information
A mushroom is a large reproductive structure with an umbrella-shaped cap, or fruiting body, attached to a stalk. The stalk is called a stipe. On the underside of the mushroom are gills. Spores are produced on the gills.

Materials

1 mushroom	white, unlined paper
hand lens	drinking glass
knife or scalpel	

Procedure

1. Obtain a mushroom and study its structure.
2. Draw your mushroom and label the cap, stipe, and gills.
3. Gently separate the cap of the mushroom from the stipe.
4. Examine the gills of the cap with the hand lens. Record your observations.
5. Place the cap of the mushroom gill-side down on the sheet of white paper. Cover the cap with the drinking glass to protect it from air movements. Set the cap aside.
6. Use the knife to cut the stipe of the mushroom in half lengthwise. **CAUTION: Use extreme caution when working with a knife or a scalpel.** Examine the inside of the stem with the hand lens. Record your observations.
7. Carefully lift the mushroom cap from the paper. Using the hand lens, examine the area of the paper that was under the cap. Draw what you see. Count the number of particles and record the number.
8. If you do not see anything, return the cap to the paper and cover it. Keep the cap in a place where it will not be disturbed for one day. Then repeat step 7.

Observations

1. What color is the mushroom?
2. **INFER** Based on its color, does the mushroom seem to contain chlorophyll, the pigment in green plants?
3. Describe the structure of the gills.
4. **a.** Describe the inside of the stipe.
   b. What are the tangled strands that make up the stipe?
5. **a.** How many particles did you count on the paper? **b.** Estimate the number of particles that a single mushroom could produce. **c.** What are these particles?

Conclusions

1. Based on your observations, give two reasons why mushrooms are not classified as plants.
2. Mushrooms produce a very large number of spores. Why is the earth not covered with mushrooms?
3. Why did you protect the cap of the mushroom from air movements?

Going Further
Mushrooms often grow in a circular pattern called a fairy ring. Find out why mushrooms often grow in this pattern.

8-5 Imperfect Fungi

- Fungi that are not known to reproduce sexually are classified as imperfect fungi.

- Imperfect fungi often cause diseases in humans. Other imperfect fungi are used to produce antibiotics.

The imperfect fungi could be called the "catchall" group of fungi. Imperfect fungi are fungi for which a sexual, or perfect, stage of the reproductive cycle does not exist or has not been found. If a sexual stage is discovered for an imperfect fungus, the fungus is reclassified into one of the other three divisions of fungi.

In people, imperfect fungi are the cause of diseases such as thrush and ringworm. Thrush is an infection of the mouth and throat. Thrush often is seen in infants and people with AIDS. Ringworm is any fungus infection of the skin, hair, or nails.

The fungus that causes athlete's foot also is an imperfect fungus. This fungus is often spread in public showers. How can you avoid athlete's foot?

Imagine a fungus that is a predator. Some imperfect fungi prey on protists and small animals. Some of these imperfect fungi have knobs growing along their hyphae. The knobs secrete a sticky substance that traps tiny organisms living in soil. Other predatory fungi have rings on their hyphae. When an organism passes through the ring, the ring tightens and traps the organism. The fungus then secretes a poison that kills the prey.

Not all imperfect fungi are harmful. In 1928, Alexander Fleming, a British bacteriologist, discovered a mold that stopped the growth of some bacteria. Today, substances produced by this mold are used to make penicillin. Penicillin is an antibiotic that often is used to treat infections caused by bacteria. You may have seen this greenish mold growing on foods such as breads, oranges, and cheeses.

You learned about the slime molds in Chapter 7. Some biologists classify slime molds as imperfect fungi. Why might slime molds be classified as imperfect fungi?

Figure 8-10 The oyster mushroom is classified as an imperfect fungus.

Think & Discuss

13. What is ringworm?

14. What kind of fungus is used to make penicillin?

15. Why do you think the yeast that causes thrush is classified as an imperfect fungus and not as a yeast?

Fungicides

Fungal infections and diseases affect people, animals, and plants. Chemical preparations called fungicides (FUN-juh-syds) often are used to prevent or cure problems caused by fungi. For example, athlete's foot often is treated with fungicides. Fungal infections also are sometimes treated with medications that can be taken orally, such as sulfa drugs and antibiotics.

Other common fungal disorders include nail infections, a mouth infection called thrush, and scalp diseases in young children. Fungal infections are extremely persistent and hard to get rid of. In fact, the minimum time needed to cure a fungal infection is ten to fourteen days. Some infections take six months to a year to cure. Doctors point out that fungicides often fail to work because people do not use the remedies long enough to achieve a cure.

The old saying "an ounce of prevention is worth a pound of cure" certainly applies to fungal infections. You can guard against some fungal infections by following these guidelines.

To avoid athlete's foot:
- Never share footwear.

- Always dry the skin between the toes after bathing.
- Do not walk barefoot in public showers.
- Change your socks or stockings at least once a day.

To avoid fungal infections of the nails:
- Keep nails clean and dry.
- Wear protective gloves if your hands must be in water for long periods of time.

Fungal diseases of plants are even more difficult to treat than fungal diseases in people. In fact, experts state that most agricultural fungicides are effective only if applied before a fungal disease strikes. For this reason, it is important to treat crops, trees, and garden plants with fungicides as a preventive measure.

Professional farmers often mix their own fungicides. However, it is best for the amateur gardener to buy ready-to-use fungicides that are sold in garden stores and nurseries. A fungicide should be clearly labeled as to the type of plant or tree it is designed to

protect. The fungicide should also be labeled with instructions for application. For example, some fungicides should be used when the seeds are planted. Other fungicides are used in the soil before planting. Still other fungicides are sprayed or dusted over growing plants or trees.

What kinds of plants need to be protected from fungal diseases? Elms, maples, and chestnut trees are common fungal hosts. Apple and peach trees also are commonly destroyed by fungi. Fungi, however, do not attack only trees. Grapes, strawberries, tomatoes, potatoes, bulb plants, and grain crops are other plants commonly infected by fungi. You can get a complete list of fungal diseases in plants from your state department of agriculture.

To Think About
- Why do you think sharing footwear increases the danger of contracting athlete's foot?
- Agricultural fungicides can be highly toxic. Why would some fungicides need to be applied before the plants are planted?

Chapter Review

CHAPTER SUMMARY

8-1 Overview of Fungi

- Fungi are multicellular organisms that have cell walls and reproduce by spores.
- Fungi are classified into four divisions based upon their structure and how they reproduce.

8-2 Molds

- Most molds are classified as water molds or terrestrial molds.
- Some parasitic molds cause diseases in animals and plants.
- Saprophytic molds act as decomposers, and return useful substances to the environment.
- Molds reproduce by spores.

8-3 Sac Fungi

- Truffles, morels, yeasts, cup fungi, and lichens are examples of sac fungi.

- Sac fungi are used as food by some organisms.
- Lichens are helpful to the environment as decomposers and producers of soil.

8-4 Club Fungi

- Mushrooms, bracket fungi, puffballs, coral fungi, rusts, and smuts are club fungi.
- Club fungi are used as food by humans and other organisms.
- Saprophytic club fungi break down decaying matter and return useful substances to the environment.

8-5 Imperfect Fungi

- Fungi that are not known to reproduce sexually are classified as imperfect fungi.
- Most imperfect fungi cause diseases in humans. Others, however, produce disease-fighting antibiotics.

VOCABULARY LIST

basidium (133)	chitin (126)	gills (134)	rhizoids (128)
budding (131)	fermentation (131)	hyphae (126)	saprophytes (126)
cap (133)	fruiting body (132)	lichen (132)	sporangia (128)
cellulose (128)	gametes (128)	mycelium (128)	spores (126)

VOCABULARY REVIEW

Matching   Write the word or term from the Vocabulary List that best matches each description.

1. method of reproduction in yeast cells
2. rootlike hyphae in the black bread mold
3. makes up the cell walls of most fungi
4. made up of a fungus and an alga
5. fleshy mass on which spores are produced
6. where mushroom basidia are located
7. filaments that make up a fungus
8. cells that develop into new fungi
9. loose, tangled mass of hyphae
10. male and female sex cells

Identifying Relationships   Identify the word or term in each group that does not belong. Explain why it does not belong with the group.

1. chitin, cellulose, fungus
2. yeast, fermentation, mold
3. morels, rusts, smuts
4. cup fungi, sac fungi, club fungi
5. producer, saprophyte, parasite
6. gametes, buds, spores
7. yeasts, buds, spores
8. basidium, sporangium, mycelium
9. sac, cap, gills
10. water mold, gametes, mushroom

True or False Write true if the statement is true. If the statement is false, change the underlined word or words to make the statement true.

1. Fungi <u>do not</u> contain chlorophyll.
2. Fungi that get their food from dead matter are called <u>parasites</u>.
3. <u>Yeasts</u> are single-celled fungi.
4. Fungi are classified according to their type of <u>asexual</u> reproduction.
5. The <u>black bread mold</u> does not have cross walls between its cells.
6. Terrestrial molds produce asexual spores in <u>sporangia</u>.
7. Antibiotics kill <u>molds</u>.
8. In the <u>club fungi</u>, basidia produce spores.
9. Rusts cause severe diseases in <u>plants</u>.
10. Fungi are classified into four groups called <u>phyla</u>.

Question and Answer Rewrite each heading in the Chapter Outline on page 124 as a question. Then, answer each of the questions you have written.

Understanding a Diagram Use the diagram of the mushroom life cycle shown in Figure 8-8 (page 133) to answer each of the following.

1. What is the first stage in the life cycle of a mushroom?
2. What are the two structures that make up the fruiting body of the mushroom?
3. What structures line the underside of the mushroom's cap?
4. What are the spore-producing structures of a mushroom?
5. Where are the spore-producing structures located on the mushroom?
6. What structures form in the gills?

Writing the Main Ideas Using the Chapter Outline on page 124, write the main idea for each heading in the outline.

Critical Thinking Answer each of the following in complete sentences.

1. What growth conditions do you think are required for the athlete's foot fungus?
2. If you wanted to draw pictures of different fungi living in your area, where would you go? Why?

3. Describe one way in which the role of fungi as decomposers is important to the survival of other forms of life.
4. Name one way in which yeasts and fungi with filaments are alike, and one way in which they are different.
5. What survival advantage might a fungus that produces an antibiotic have over a fungus that does not produce an antibiotic? Explain.

1. Prepare a chart that classifies each fungus discussed in this chapter as helpful or harmful. Your chart should include information about the economic, environmental, and medical importance.

2. Some species of *Penicillium* are used to produce blue cheese. *Aspergillus*, a sac fungus, is used to produce soy sauce. Prepare a report that describes the role these molds play in the production of these two foods.

Plants are many-celled organisms that can make their own food. The study of plants is called botany. In this unit, you will study many different kinds of plants and their parts and functions. You also will study how plants reproduce. Some plants reproduce by spores. Can you name the other structure by which plants reproduce? For a hint, read the titles of the chapters that make up this unit.

Study the drawings and photographs shown on these two pages. What plants can you name? What plant parts do you recognize? Can you identify the functions of the structures that you named?

UNIT 3

Plants

CONTENTS

Objectives

After you have completed this chapter, you will be able to

9-1 **identify** four characteristics of all plants.

9-1 **name** the two divisions of the plant kingdom.

9-2 **identify** three classes of bryophytes.

9-2 **describe** alternation of generations.

9-3 **describe** the appearance of horsetails and club mosses.

9-4 **name** the structures of a fern.

9-4 **describe** the gametophyte and sporophyte generations of a fern.

Science Process Skills

In this chapter, two science skills are highlighted. Symbols show some places where these skills are used.

❯ **Predicting:** When you predict, you state in advance how and why something will occur.

▣ **Hypothesizing:** When you hypothesize, you state a suggested answer to a problem based upon known information.

Do you remember the last time you walked through a forest or visited a park? What kinds of plants did you see? Perhaps you saw trees, vines, bushes, or fields of grass. You probably noticed that the plants you saw had green leaves. Plants have green leaves because of a green substance in their cells called **chlorophyll** *(KLAWR-uh-fil). Without chlorophyll, plants would not be able to make food and grow.*

You know from your observations that plants differ from each other in size and shape. For example, some plants are less than one centimeter tall. Other plants may be taller than a building. Compare a towering oak tree to a tiny blade of grass. Believe it or not, both the oak tree and the blade of grass are individual plants.

9-1 Classification of Plants

You probably recognize a plant when you see one. However, some organisms, such as algae, look very much like plants. How can you tell if an organism is a plant? You can find out by answering several questions.

- Does the organism have many cells?
- Are the cells of the organism organized into tissues and organs?
- Do the cells of the organism have cell walls?
- Do the cells of the organism contain chlorophyll?

You would need a microscope to check your answers to these questions. However, if after studying your organism, you answered "yes" to these four questions, your organism definitely is a plant.

Plants use chlorophyll to trap the energy in sunlight. Plants use the energy in sunlight to combine carbon dioxide from the air and water from the soil to make food. This food-making process is called **photosynthesis** (foht-uh-SIN-thuh-sis). Photosynthesis provides plants with the food energy needed for growth and development. Photosynthesis also provides energy to animals that eat the plants.

More than 260,000 organisms have been classified in the Plant kingdom. Botanists (BAHT-n-ists), biologists who study plants, have divided the Plant kingdom into two groups, or **divisions** (duh-VIZH-uns). The divisions of the Plant kingdom are based on how water and dissolved minerals are moved throughout the plant. The two divisions are the **bryophytes** (BRY-uh-fyts) and the **tracheophytes** (TRAY-kee-uh-fyts).

In tracheophytes, water and nutrients move through tubelike cells to all of the plant's structures. These tubelike cells make up **vascular** (VAS-kyuh-luhr) **tissue.** You can compare the vascular tissue of a tracheophyte to the plumbing system of a house. All of the rooms in the house that need water are supplied by pipes.

Most of the plants you are familiar with probably are tracheophytes. Tracheophytes have roots, stems, and leaves. The roots of a tracheophyte anchor the plant in the soil. Roots also take in water and dissolved nutrients from the soil.

Key Points

- Plants are multicellular organisms that have tissues and organs. Plant cells have cell walls and chlorophyll, which is used for photosynthesis.

- The two divisions of the Plant kingdom are the bryophytes and the tracheophytes.

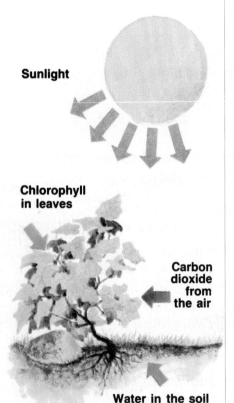

Sunlight

Chlorophyll in leaves

Carbon dioxide from the air

Water in the soil

Figure 9-1 What three things do plants need to carry out photosynthesis?

Figure 9-2 The cypress trees (left) and ferns (right) are tracheophytes. The mosses (right) are bryophytes.

Unlike tracheophytes, bryophytes do not have true roots, stems, and leaves. They do, however, have rootlike and leaflike structures. Bryophytes also lack vascular tissue. In bryophytes, dissolved materials move from one cell to the next by diffusion. Diffusion is a very slow process of transport.

Bryophytes are land plants, but they need water to reproduce. For this reason, botanists believe that bryophytes originally lived in water. In fact, fossil evidence shows that bryophytes invaded the land about 500 million years ago.

Tracheophytes have vascular tissue in their roots, stems, and leaves. For this reason, tracheophytes are called vascular plants. Because they have no vascular tissue, bryophytes are called nonvascular plants. How do you think water and nutrients move through the leaflike structures of a bryophyte?

In addition to supplying a plant with nutrients, vascular tissue also helps support a plant. Because they have vascular tissue, tracheophytes can grow much taller than any of the bryophytes. How do you think water and nutrients reach the leaves of a tall tree?

Think & Discuss

1. What is photosynthesis? Why is photosynthesis important to plants?
2. List four characteristics of all plants.
3. What would happen to a plant if it did not receive enough sunlight?

9-2 Mosses, Liverworts, and Hornworts

Have you seen tiny plants growing on rocks beside a stream, in ditches, or at the base of a tall tree? Some of these plants probably are bryophytes. Unlike most of the plants with which you are familiar, bryophytes most often are found growing in shady areas. Why do bryophytes grow well in shade? Growing in shade helps keep a bryophyte from drying out.

Bryophytes live in very damp areas. Because they are nonvascular plants, all of the bryophytes live close to the ground. Here, at ground level, there is enough moisture for bryophytes to live and reproduce.

Throughout the world, there are over 23,000 species of bryophytes. Bryophytes are separated into three classes: the mosses, the liverworts, and the hornworts.

Mosses

Have you ever seen small, velvetlike plants growing on rocks, trees, or in sidewalk cracks? These tiny plants probably were mosses. Draw a line that is 5 cm long. This line is about the height of most mosses. What do you think would be a good research tool to use when studying mosses? What other plant is about the same height as moss?

Moss is useful to gardeners. Gardeners often mix dried peat moss into the soil. Dried peat moss is used by gardeners because its cells store a lot of water. Why would a gardener put peat moss in a flower bed?

Peat moss has other uses, too. In some countries, dried peat moss is burned as fuel. Peat moss also is used to insulate homes. You may be surprised to learn that peat moss contains a germ-killing chemical. In fact, during World War I, peat moss was used on wounds when sterile cotton was not available.

Structure of Mosses

If you look at a moss plant with a magnifying glass, you will observe a short main stalk with flat, green, leaflike structures growing around it. The leaflike structures of moss are only one or two cells thick. These leaflike structures of the moss plant perform photosynthesis.

Key Points
- Mosses, liverworts, and hornworts are three classes of bryophytes.
- Alternation of generations is a reproductive process that involves a sexual and an asexual stage.

Health and Safety Tip

When looking for mosses at the edge of a stream or pond, wear shoes or sneakers that give you good footing.

Figure 9-3 Farmers add peat moss to the soil to help the soil hold water.

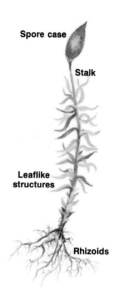

Figure 9-4 Mosses often grow on decaying logs (left). What structures anchor the mosses to the log?

At the base of the stalk are rootlike structures called **rhizoids** (RY-zoids). Rhizoids anchor the moss in the soil. Like the roots of tracheophytes, rhizoids also absorb water and dissolved nutrients from the soil. However, mosses do not have vascular tissue to carry water and nutrients from the rhizoids up to the leaflike structures. Water and nutrients move from one cell to another by diffusion.

You also may see taller stalks sprouting from a moss plant. These stalks have a swollen structure at their tips called a **spore case.** The spore case contains the reproductive cells, or **spores.**

Life Cycle of Mosses

Some organisms go through stages, or generations (jen-uh-RAY-shuns), during their life cycles. For example, a moss plant goes through two alternating generations in its life cycle. One generation is a sexual stage called the **gametophyte** (guh-MEET-uh-fyt). The other generation is an asexual stage called the **sporophyte** (SPAW-ruh-fyt).

The gametophyte of a moss is a leafy green plant with structures that contain sperm and egg cells. Sperm are the male sex cells. Moss sperm cells have whiplike tails that are used to swim to the egg cells. Egg cells are female sex cells.

When a sperm cell unites with an egg cell, **fertilization** (fur-tul-i-ZAY-shun) takes place. Fertilization can take place only when the gametophyte is moist. In fact, sperm cells are not released unless there is enough moisture on the gametophyte.

Spore Plants 147

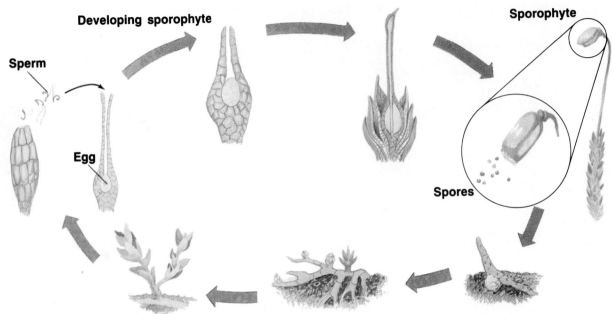

Developing sporophyte

Sporophyte

Sperm

Egg

Spores

Gametophyte plants　　**Developing gametophyte**　　**Germinating spore**

Figure 9-5 Trace the development of a moss plant beginning with the release of mature spores from a sporophyte.

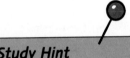

Study Hint

A good way to find out if you understand a new idea is to explain that idea to another person. Explain alternation of generations in mosses to a friend or a member of your family.

The fertilized moss egg develops into the asexual, or sporophyte, generation of the moss. The sporophyte remains attached to the gametophyte. As the sporophyte grows, it makes spores. When the spores are mature, they are released. These spores become new gametophytes. This process is called **alternation** (ol-tuhr-NAY-shun) **of generations.**

In plants that go through alternation of generations, one generation usually is much larger and lives longer than the other generation. For example, in mosses, the gametophyte generation is the larger and longer-living plant. In ferns, however, the sporophyte generation is the larger and longer-living plant.

Liverworts and Hornworts

Liverworts are very small plants. Usually they are between 1 and 2 cm tall. *Marchantia* (mar-KAN-tee-uh) is a liverwort that grows near rivers and lakes. You may even find this liverwort underneath greenhouse tables.

With a magnifying glass, you could observe that the leaflike structures of a liverwort are shaped like the outline of the human liver. These liver-shaped structures are the best way to identify liverworts. Liverworts also feel waxy to the touch. The waxy substance on liverworts prevents them from drying out.

ACTIVITY 9-1

PROBLEM: How does direct sunlight affect moss growth?

Science Process Skills
observing, hypothesizing, comparing

Background Information
Mosses are nonvascular plants. Because mosses do not have vascular tissue, they are not able to grow very large. Most mosses are only a few centimeters tall. Some places where mosses grow are in sidewalk cracks, along the sides of buildings, and at the base of trees in a forest.

Materials

4 clumps of fresh moss	scissors
4 medium-sized paper cups	hand lens
soil	water

Procedure
1. Collect moss specimens from the area where you live. Describe the moss plants.
2. Collect enough soil in which to grow the moss specimens.
3. Cut each of the 4 paper cups in half. **CAUTION: Be careful when using scissors.**
4. Fill the 4 paper cups with the soil and plant a clump of moss in each cup.
5. Label cups 1 and 2 ''Sunlight'' and cups 3 and 4 ''Indirect Sunlight.''
6. Place cups 1 and 2 in an area where the moss plants will receive direct sunlight for most of the day. Place cups 3 and 4 in an area where the moss plants will receive indirect sunlight for part of the day and will be shaded the rest of the day.
7. Water the moss plants each day. Be sure to give the same amount of water to each plant.
8. **HYPOTHESIZE** What effect do you think direct sunlight will have on the growth of moss plants? Write your hypothesis on a sheet of paper. Your hypothesis should

answer the question. To test your hypothesis, continue the activity.
9. After 4–5 days, examine the moss plants with a hand lens. Describe the moss plants in each cup.

Observations
1. What color were the fresh moss plants?
2. **a.** Compare the color of the moss plants grown in direct sunlight with the moss plants grown in indirect sunlight.
   b. Compare your moss plants with the moss plants of some of your classmates.
3. **a.** Why did you give the same amount of water to all of the moss plants? **b.** What is the variable being tested in this activity?

Conclusions
1. Was your hypothesis correct? Use your observations to support your answer.
2. **a.** Which moss plants grew best? **b.** What environmental conditions are best for the growth of moss plants?

Going Further
Make a terrarium in a large bottle using mosses, ferns, and other spore plants. Be sure that your terrarium has the proper growth conditions. Why are mosses and ferns good plants to use in a terrarium?

Figure 9-6 Compare the shape of the liverwort (left) with the hornwort (right).

Hornworts are small plants with flat, round, leaflike structures. Hornworts look a lot like liverworts. However, the sporophyte of a hornwort looks like a long animal horn. Only 100 species of hornworts have been identified and classified. *Anthoceros* (an-THO-sehr-uhs) is a species of hornwort that you might see near a lake or along the edge of a river.

Think & Discuss

4. What are rhizoids?
5. What is the name of the spore-producing stage in moss?
6. Describe the life cycle of moss.
7. How does the moss sperm travel to the egg?
8. Explain why bryophytes often grow at the base of trees.

9-3 Horsetails and Club Mosses

Horsetails and club mosses were among the first tracheophytes to appear on earth. Because they have vascular tissue, horsetails and club mosses can grow much taller than bryophytes. Prehistoric horsetails and club mosses grew much taller than those living today. Prehistoric horsetails grew to a height of about 15 m. Club mosses were even taller; some were over 30 m tall. The remains of prehistoric horsetails and club mosses make up much of the coal deposits in the United States.

Like bryophytes, horsetails and club mosses grow well in damp areas. The stems of horsetails and club mosses grow below ground. These underground stems are called **rhizomes** (RY-zohms). Rhizomes anchor the plants and absorb water and nutrients from the soil. New stems and branches also grow from the rhizomes.

Horsetails have tiny leaves that surround their upright stems. Together, the stems and leaves look like the tail of a horse. Because the leaves of horsetails are so tiny, most photosynthesis takes place in the stems.

The upright stem of a horsetail has a spore case on top. You can see the spore case of a horsetail in the top photograph of Figure 9–7. When the spore case is mature, it breaks apart, releasing hundreds of spores. The spores released by a horsetail can develop into a new plant very quickly. In fact, each spore that lands in soil may germinate, or grow, into a new gametophyte in less than three hours.

❯ The American colonists called field horsetails "scouring rushes" because they were excellent for cleaning, or scouring, pots and pans. Horsetails deposit silica from the soil into their cell walls. Silica is a compound found in sand. This silica makes the branches and stems of horsetails stiff and gritty. Why would horsetails be good for cleaning dirty pots and pans?

Club mosses often are found living in forests with many pine trees. Many people call club mosses ground pines because they look like tiny pine trees. A common club moss is called *Lycopodium* (ly-kuh-POH-dee-uhm). *Lycopodium* is found in damp, shady forests. The tiny leaves of *Lycopodium* remain green all year.

Some club mosses have leaves that form bushy masses that look like the tail of a fox on top. Other club mosses have leaves that look like a baby-bottle brush. Still others have thin, wiry leaves or vinelike stems.

Figure 9-7 Horsetails (top) and club mosses (bottom) are among the simplest tracheophytes.

Think & Discuss

9. What is the underground stem of a club moss called?

10. Why are horsetails called scouring rushes?

★ 11. How are club mosses and horsetails similar to bryophytes?

9-4 Ferns

There are about 12,000 different kinds of ferns. Like the horsetails and club mosses, all species of ferns are vascular plants. As vascular plants, ferns can grow very large. Some ferns are treelike, and grow to be more than 25 m tall. Other ferns are very small, only about 3 cm tall.

Most ferns grow in warm tropical climates. Ferns, however, are adapted to most climates in the world. You even can find some ferns growing in very cold climates.

Of all the spore plants, ferns probably are the kind with which you are most familiar. Because of their large, attractive leaves, ferns are popular houseplants. Two ferns that are grown as houseplants are the Boston fern and the maidenhair fern.

❯ Ferns grow well indoors because they do not need much sunlight. In fact, ferns cannot grow in direct sunlight. Outdoors, you can find ferns growing in moist woods or in the shade of large trees. Where do you think a fern would grow best in your home?

Structure of a Fern

Like the horsetails and club mosses, ferns also have rhizomes. The roots of the fern grow downward from the rhizome. The roots absorb materials from the soil and also anchor the plant. The large leaves of a fern, called **fronds,** grow upward from the rhizome.

Look at the underside of the fern frond in the photograph on the right in Figure 9-8. Notice the brown spots. These brown spots are the spore cases. Hundreds of spores are contained within each spore case.

Figure 9-8 Compare the diagram (left) of the fern to the photographs. What structures are shown on the underside of the fern (far right)?

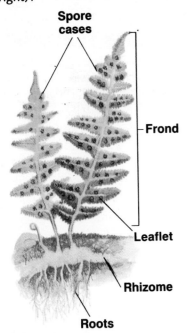

Spore cases

Frond

Leaflet

Rhizome

Roots

ACTIVITY 9-2

PROBLEM: What is the structure of a fern frond?

Science Process Skills
observing, inferring, comparing

Background Information
Ferns are green plants that grow in fields, forests, and wetlands. The stem of a fern, or rhizome, is underground. The leaves of a fern are called fronds. Each frond is made up of blades. On the underside of the blades, spore cases develop. If environmental conditions are right, each spore in the spore case can grow into a new fern plant.

Materials

fern frond	paper, white
hand lens	

Procedure

1. Obtain a fern frond.
2. Using the hand lens, examine the frond. Sketch the frond and label its main stalk, or stipe, and the blades.
3. Using the hand lens, examine the upper sides of several blades. Then examine the lower sides of several blades. Draw what you see on the upper side and lower side of the blades. Label the spore cases.
4. Estimate the number of spore cases on the entire frond.
5. Using your fingernail, scrape spore cases onto a sheet of white paper. Gently crush the spore cases by rolling your pencil over the cases.
6. Using the hand lens, examine the spores. Estimate the number of spores in one spore case.

Observations
1. Where are the youngest blades on the frond?
2. Do the blades of the fern have veins, or tubes, to carry water and food?

3. **ESTIMATE** **a.** About how many spore cases are on your frond? **b.** About how many spores are in each spore case? **c.** About how many spores would the entire frond have?

Conclusions
1. **INFER**   Based on your observation of the fern blades, is the fern a vascular or nonvascular plant? Explain your answer.
2. Is the frond part of the gametophyte or sporophyte generation of a fern? How do you know?
3. **a.** Why is it important for a fern to produce so many spores? **b.** If a fern produces so many spores, why are the floors of forests not completely covered with ferns?

Going Further
Use the spores from your fern to try to grow several ferns. Keep a record of the growth of your ferns.

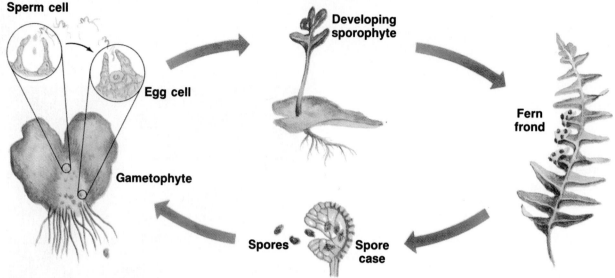

Sperm cell

Egg cell

Gametophyte

Developing sporophyte

Fern frond

Spores

Spore case

Figure 9-9 Compare the life cycle of the fern with the life cycle of the moss on page 148.

Compare the life cycle of the fern with the life cycle of the moss on page 148.

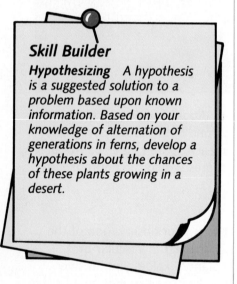

Skill Builder

Hypothesizing *A hypothesis is a suggested solution to a problem based upon known information. Based on your knowledge of alternation of generations in ferns, develop a hypothesis about the chances of these plants growing in a desert.*

Life Cycle of a Fern

The life cycle of a fern involves alternation of generations. During its life cycle, a fern spore develops into a gametophyte. The gametophyte of the fern is a small, heart-shaped plant that grows on soil, tree bark, or rocks. ▪ Sperm and egg cells are made on the underside of the gametophyte. Fertilization takes place when a sperm cell swims across the plant and unites with one of the egg cells. Do you think fertilization would take place if the gametophyte were dry?

The sporophyte develops from the fertilized egg that is attached to the gametophyte. The gametophyte supplies the growing sporophyte with water and nutrients. However, as the sporophyte matures, it makes its own food. Then, the gametophyte shrivels up and dies.

Think & Discuss

12. What is a frond?

13. What is the name of the structure of a fern that holds the spores?

14. Why is water important for fern reproduction?

15. How does the fern sporophyte differ from the fern gametophyte?

16. How is the fern gametophyte generation different from the moss gametophyte generation?

CAREERS in BIOLOGY
Working with Plants

Do you grow indoor plants? Do you like the smell of roses and freshly mowed grass? If so, you may enjoy a career working with plants.

Gardener

Gardeners work mostly outdoors. They prune trees, trim hedges, and remove weeds from lawns and gardens. They also plant bulbs, shrubs, and trees. With a high school diploma and on-the-job training, a gardener can become a park superintendent. Some gardeners even open their own companies. Because they do plenty of bending and lifting, gardeners must be healthy.

Gardeners often use tools such as rakes and spades for small jobs. Machines such as power mowers and seed spreaders are used for large jobs. Large jobs would include work on schoolgrounds and ball fields.

For more information: Write to your local parks department or a local botanical garden.

Florist

If you enjoy working with plants and dealing with people, you may want to become a florist. Florists need at least a high school diploma. They also require vocational training in flower arranging, preserving cut flowers, and caring for houseplants. Courses in small business management also may be helpful.

Florists often are asked for advice by their customers. From what florists know about plants, they must be ready to answer such questions as "How often must I water this plant?"

A florist's success often depends on ordering enough cut flowers and houseplants for times of heavy demand. A successful florist always is well-stocked for special occasions.

For more information: Write to the Society of American Florists, 901 North Washington Street, Alexandria, VA 22314.

Landscape Architect

A landscape architect needs a college degree and artistic ability. Using live plants, drawings, and models, landscape architects create indoor and outdoor environments. With their help, a weed-covered lot can be turned into a scenic area with flowering trees, shrubs, and a healthy lawn.

Landscape architects also use plants to design indoor environments. Eye-catching green areas designed by landscape architects can be found in hotel lobbies, office buildings, and shopping malls.

For more information: Read *Design With Nature* by Ian McHarg.

Spore Plants   155

Chapter Review

CHAPTER SUMMARY

9-1 Classification of Plants

- Plants have many cells and are organized into tissues and organs. Their cells contain cell walls and chlorophyll. Plants perform photosynthesis.
- The Plant kingdom is separated into two divisions: the bryophytes and the tracheophytes.
- Tracheophytes have roots, stems, and leaves. All three contain vascular tissues.
- Bryophytes lack vascular tissues and do not have true roots, stems, or leaves.

9-2 Mosses, Liverworts, and Hornworts

- Mosses, liverworts, and hornworts are bryophytes.

- Alternation of generations is a life cycle that involves two stages: a sexual stage, called a gametophyte, and an asexual stage, called a sporophyte.

9-3 Horsetails and Club Mosses

- Horsetails and club mosses are vascular plants that have underground stems called rhizomes.

9-4 Ferns

- Ferns are vascular plants that have roots, rhizomes, fronds, and spore cases.
- Ferns are spore plants that undergo alternation of generations.
- In ferns, a small, heart-shaped gametophyte produces a taller sporophyte.

VOCABULARY LIST

alternation of generations (148)
bryophytes (144)
chlorophyll (143)
divisions (144)

fertilization (147)
fronds (152)
gametophyte (147)
photosynthesis (144)

rhizoids (147)
rhizomes (151)
spores (147)
spore case (147)

sporophyte (147)
tracheophytes (144)
vascular tissue (144)

VOCABULARY REVIEW

Matching   Write the word or term from the Vocabulary List that best matches each description.

1. brown spot underneath fern fronds
2. union of a sperm cell and an egg cell
3. underground stems of a fern
4. process that plants use to make their own food
5. tubelike cells of tracheophytes
6. generation of a spore plant that makes eggs and sperm
7. leaves of a fern
8. rootlike structures of a moss
9. green substance in plant cells
10. reproductive cycle of spore plant

Identifying Relationships   Identify the word in each group that does not belong. Explain why it does not belong with the group.

1. tracheophytes, mosses, bryophytes
2. spores, sporophyte, photosynthesis
3. sporophyte, sexual, asexual
4. spore case, reproduction, rhizoids
5. silica, photosynthesis, chlorophyll
6. stem, frond, rhizome
7. gametophyte, asexual, fertilization
8. fronds, leaves, silica
9. rhizoids, spore case, roots
10. vascular tissue, bryophytes, tracheophytes
11. moss, liverwort, fern
12. gametophyte, frond, spore case

Completion   Write the word or words that best complete each sentence.

1. The roots, stems, and leaves of tracheophytes contain _____ tissue.
2. Gardeners use _____ to increase the water-absorbing ability of the soil.
3. A green substance found in all plant cells is _____.
4. The _____ generation of a hornwort looks like an animal horn.
5. The Plant kingdom is divided into bryophytes and _____.
6. The moss gametophyte produces both sperm and _____ cells.
7. The complete life cycle of a spore plant is called _____.
8. The cells of bryophytes receive nourishment by _____.
9. Horsetails contain _____, which makes them a good scouring material.
10. Botanists are _____ who study plants.

Finding the Main Ideas   Use the section number to find the sentence that answers each question. Then, write the sentence.

1. Why is photosynthesis important to plants? (9-1)
2. What are the two divisions of the Plant kingdom? (9-1)
3. What are the classes of bryophytes? (9-1)
4. The moss's life cycle includes a sexual generation and an asexual generation. What is this process called? (9-2)
5. How are present-day horsetails and club mosses different from those of prehistoric time? (9-3)
6. How long does it take for a spore of a horsetail to germinate? (9-3)
7. How is a fern's structure like that of horsetails and club mosses? (9-4)
8. What part of the fern grows upward? (9-4)
9. What does the fern's sexual generation look like? (9-4)

Writing for Understanding   One way to find out if you understand something is to write a brief summary of the information in your own words. Reread Section 9-1, Classification of Plants, on pages 144–145, and write a brief summary of the information.

Critical Thinking   Answer each of the following in complete sentences.

1. How are ferns and mosses alike?

2. What would happen to mosses growing next to a stream if the stream dried up?
3. How is the fern sporophyte different from the moss sporophyte?
4. Suppose you met a person who had never seen a fern. How would you explain the fern's life cycle?
5. Would you be more likely to find ferns growing on a sandy beach or beside a stream in a forest? Explain your answer.

1. A terrarium is a glass container enclosing a garden of small plants. Use your knowledge about the life cycle and needs of mosses to set up a moss terrarium.
2. Mosses often grow in sidewalk cracks, rock outcrops, and on park statues. If you were the groundskeeper of a public park, would you have your employees clean mosses off the statues? Give several reasons to support your answer.
3. People who are interested in birds keep a "life list" of all the birds they have seen. Use a guidebook of spore plants to start a life list of all the species of spore plants you find.

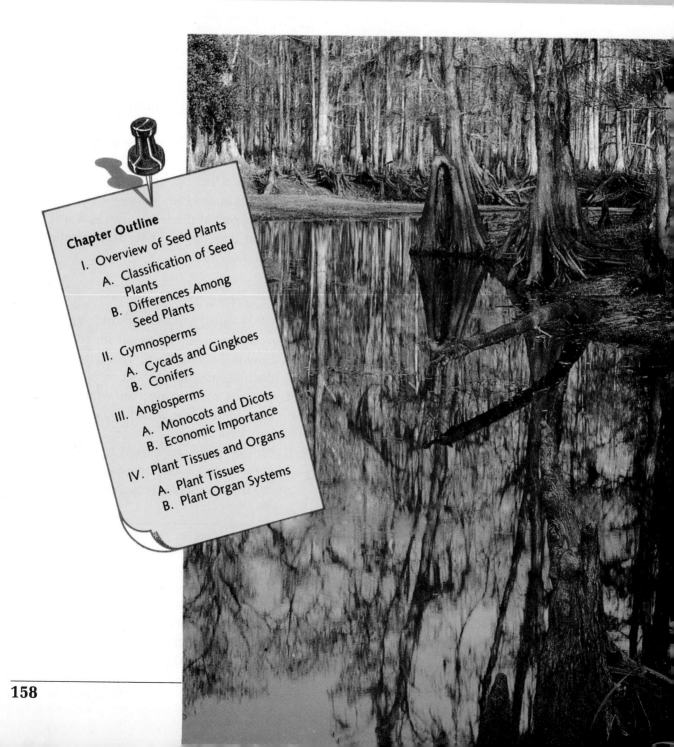

Objectives

After you have completed this chapter, you will be able to

10-1 **distinguish** between angiosperms and gymnosperms.

10-2 **name** three kinds of gymnosperms.

10-2 **discuss** the economic importance of conifers.

10-3 **explain** why flowering plants are a successful group.

10-3 **identify** monocots and dicots as two kinds of angiosperms.

10-4 **name** four kinds of plant tissues.

10-4 **name** and **describe** the functions of the two organ systems of plants.

Science Process Skills

In this chapter, two science skills are highlighted. Symbols show some places where these skills are used.

Classifying: When you classify, you group things based upon similarities.

Analyzing: When you analyze, you break down a complex idea into simpler parts to make it easier to understand.

Imagine you are in a canoe gliding under leafy cypress trees in a Southern swamp. Overhead, a wispy gray-green plant called Spanish moss hangs from the cypress branches. What do you think the tall cypress trees and the Spanish moss have in common? Although they do not look alike, both the cypress tree and the Spanish moss are seed plants.

You do not have to visit a swamp to find seed plants. In fact, you probably see many kinds of seed plants every day. Look at some of the plants growing outside your home or school. Grasses, dandelions, rose bushes, as well as maple and oak trees all are seed plants.

10-1 Overview of Seed Plants

Key Points

- Angiosperms are seed plants. Most angiosperms have broad leaves and flowers.

- Gymnosperms are seed plants. Most gymnosperms have needlelike leaves and cones.

Figure 10-1 If soaked in water, the seed coat will slip off a lima bean.

Study Hint

If plants can make their own food, why do they sometimes need "plant food"? To find out, read the feature at the end of this chapter.

All you have to do is walk outdoors to discover that seed plants are among the most successful organisms on the earth. In fact, seed plants grow throughout the world, including the icy tundras of Canada and steamy swamps of Central America. Why are seed plants so successful? You may find the reason by thinking of a seed as a "packaged" plant.

In Figure 10–1, you see that a seed has an outer covering, called a **seed coat.** The hard seed coat protects the developing plant, or **embryo** (EM-bree-oh), from drying out or freezing. In fact, an embryo can remain inactive for many months inside its seed coat. For example, many seeds are not active during very cold or dry periods of the year. When conditions improve, however, many of these seeds will germinate, or grow.

Seeds also contain food for the plant embryo. The food stored inside a seed provides an embryo with enough energy to grow. Stored food is used by the plant embryo for growth until its leaves can carry out photosynthesis.

Classification of Seed Plants

Biologists classify seed plants into two groups, based upon the appearance of their seeds. One group of seed plants is the **gymnosperms** (JIM-nuh-spurms). Gymnosperms have uncovered seeds. The other group of seed plants is the **angiosperms** (AN-jee-uh-spurms). Angiosperms have covered seeds.

You probably are familiar with the cones of a gymnosperm. You call these pine cones. The seeds of gymnosperms lie uncovered on the flat scales of the cone. Unlike the seeds of gymnosperms, the seeds of angiosperms develop inside a covering, called a **fruit.** Many angiosperms have sweet, fleshy fruits. Each fruit contains one or many seeds. Do you think a cherry tree is an angiosperm or gymnosperm? Why?

The fossil record indicates that gymnosperms were growing at the time of the dinosaurs. Angiosperms, however, do not appear in the fossil record until 150 million years after the dinosaurs. Today, there are many more species of angiosperms than of gymnosperms.

Differences Among Seed Plants

Angiosperms and gymnosperms differ from each other in several ways. One important way that angiosperms differ from gymnosperms is that angiosperms produce **flowers.** In fact, angiosperms commonly are called the flowering plants. You may be familiar with the colorful flowers of angiosperms, such as roses, tulips, and petunias. Flowers are the reproductive parts of an angiosperm.

◤The leaves and stems of angiosperms and gymnosperms also differ. For example, most angiosperms have broad leaves. Most gymnosperms, however, have needlelike leaves. Look at Figure 10-2. Compare the leaf of the Norway maple with the leaves of the Scotch pine.

Have you ever pulled a dandelion from the soil? If so, you may have noticed that the stem of the dandelion was soft and green. This kind of stem is called a **herbaceous** (huhr-BAY-shus) **stem.** Herbaceous stems are a common characteristic of many angiosperms. For example, lilies, thistles, carnations, and all species of grasses have herbaceous stems.

Gymnosperms have **woody stems.** For example, woody shrubs, such as juniper and yew, are gymnosperms. Gymnosperms also include tall trees, such as pine, spruce, and fir. Woody stems are nongreen stems that are harder and thicker than herbaceous stems.

Some angiosperms also have woody stems. Many woody angiosperms shed all their leaves each fall. These woody angiosperms are called deciduous plants. Oak and

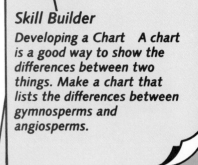

Figure 10-2 The leaves of a Norway maple tree (left) are broad and flat. The leaves of a Scotch pine tree (right) are needlelike.

Figure 10-3 This series of photographs shows the changes in a deciduous tree from season to season. Identify the season for each photograph.

maple trees are deciduous plants. Unlike angiosperms, most of the gymnosperms, such as pine, spruce, and fir trees grow leaves throughout the year. For this reason, many gymnosperms commonly are called evergreen trees. Homeowners often plant evergreens in front of their houses to have some greenery to look at during the winter months. Why would you not expect to see a maple tree with leaves in winter?

Think & Discuss

1. What is the main difference between a gymnosperm and an angiosperm?

2. Which group of seed plants is a relative "newcomer" in the earth's history?

3. Why is an oak tree classified as a deciduous plant?

10-2 Gymnosperms

There are about 700 species of gymnosperms. You can recognize most gymnosperms by their cones. Some gymnosperm cones are very large, such as the cones of the Southern pine tree. Other cones are small, such as those of the swamp cypress. In Figure 10-4, you see the cones of three different gymnosperms.

The seeds of some gymnosperms look like the fruits of angiosperms. For example, the seeds of a juniper tree look like small blueberries. The seeds of a yew have red fleshy seeds that look like tiny cherries.

Cycads and Gingkoes

Imprints of seed ferns are among the fossils found in coal deposits. Seed ferns are now extinct. However, many scientists believe that the seed ferns are relatives of the gymnosperms. Two gymnosperms also have been found among these fossils. These very old gymnosperms are the cycads (SY-kads) and gingkoes (GIN-kohs).

Today, most cycads grow in tropical areas. Cycads look like small palm trees. Cycads often are used as garden plants in Florida and California. If you do not live in these states, you may see cycads in a flower shop or a botanical garden.

Unlike conifers, cycads produce male and female sex cells on separate plants. After fertilization takes place, a female cycad produces a very large conelike structure. This conelike structure grows from the center of a cycad.

Study Hint

Use the index to find the page number of the geologic time scale. Turn to the geologic time scale to find out when the first seed plants appeared.

Figure 10-4 Gymnosperm cones vary greatly in size and shape.

Figure 10-5 The cycad (left) and the gingko (center) are living fossils. The unusual fruit of the gingko (right) can irritate the skin of some people.

The gingko tree grows wild only in China. In fact, gingkoes are among the rarest of all plants. The gingko tree is the only species of its kind that still survives from the Age of Dinosaurs.

For centuries, gingkoes were planted in Chinese temple gardens. Today, gingkoes often are planted in cities in the United States. There are several reasons why gingkoes are popular city trees. First, the fan-shaped leaves of gingkoes create cooling shade during the summer months. Second, gingkoes are not bothered by insects. Finally, gingkoes can grow in polluted air.

You may have seen gingkoes growing in your city or town. You also may have smelled them. Gingko trees, like cycads, are either male or female. The female gingko produces fleshy seeds that look like large apricots. These fleshy seeds have a very bad odor. For this reason, male trees are most often planted on city streets.

Conifers

Most of the 700 species of gymnosperms are **conifers,** or "cone-bearing" seed plants. As you walk around your neighborhood, keep in mind the two main features of a conifer. Look for a tree with needlelike leaves and cones scattered among its branches.

Conifers are very old trees. The fossil record indicates that conifers were living about 200 million years ago. Today, there are more kinds of conifers than any other kind of gymnosperm.

Conifers can live in many different environments. Some conifers grow in rocky and sandy soil. Other conifers grow in swamps, bogs, and around the edges of lakes. For example, spruce, fir, and pine trees grow in the cold environments of Siberia and Canada. Cypress trees can survive in the hot and humid bayous (BY-oos) of the southern United States.

Conifers grow larger and live longer than all other trees. For example, the giant redwood trees of northern California and the bristlecone pine trees are the tallest and oldest organisms on the earth. Some redwood trees grow to heights of more than 100 m. Some bristlecone pine trees have been alive for more than 5000 years.

Figure 10-6 Bristlecone pines have short, fat needles that stay on the tree for 17 years.

Reproduction in Conifers

A conifer produces two kinds of cones on the same tree. If you look closely at a conifer, you can easily identify the two different kinds of cones. Male cones are called **pollen cones.** The yellow or red colored pollen cones often grow in clusters at the ends of branches. Female cones are called **seed cones.** Seed cones grow singly and are larger than the pollen cones. Seed cones also are woodier than pollen cones.

Egg cells form on the scales of the seed cones. Grains of **pollen** form within the scales of the pollen cones. Pollen are small yellow grains that contain sperm cells. When pollen grains are released into the air, some of them land on the seed cones. The transfer of pollen from the male reproductive organ to the female reproductive organ is called **pollination** (pahl-ih-NAY-shun). Look at the seed

Figure 10-7 How does the seed cone (left) differ from the pollen cone (right)?

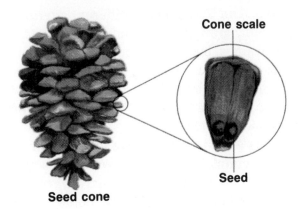

Cone scale

Seed

Seed cone

Figure 10-8 Fertilization takes place on the scale of a seed cone.

cone in Figure 10-8. Seed cones produce a sticky sap that traps the pollen grain. When a grain of pollen lands on the scale of a seed cone, fertilization takes place.

Economic Importance of Conifers

Did you know that some areas of the United States were first explored to harvest trees? In the nineteenth century, American pioneers found a rich source of lumber in the cypress swamps of Florida and redwood forests of California. Today, conifers provide people with wood, paper, and other useful products, such as varnishes and turpentine.

Conifers often are planted on hillsides to prevent flooding after heavy rain. Instead of flooding areas where people live and work, rainwater is absorbed by the roots of conifers. Farmers also plant a row of conifers at the edges of their fields to keep topsoil from blowing away. How do you think conifers prevent topsoil from being blown away?

Think & Discuss

4. What is an evergreen?
5. What is the difference between a pollen cone and a seed cone?
6. What are the three kinds of gymnosperms?
7. Why are conifers important resources for people?
8. Why are the gingkoes and cycads called "living fossils"?

10-3 Angiosperms

Biologists have classified more than 275,000 species of angiosperms. Some angiosperms, such as oak trees and dandelions, are supported by strong stems that help them stay erect as they grow. Others, such as poison ivy and grapevines, climb or creep with flexible stems. Some angiosperms, such as waterlilies, even float on the surface of water.

Most angiosperms produce a lot of seeds. Have you ever counted the number of seeds in an apple? The seeds in the apple were produced in one growing season. The seeds of angiosperms are protected by a covering, or fruit. In fact, the production of fruits with many seeds is one reason the angiosperms are so successful.

Monocots and Dicots

The first leaf of an angiosperm is called the **cotyledon** (kaht-LEED-on). Because a cotyledon develops inside a seed a cotyledon commonly is called a "seed leaf." The number of cotyledons inside a seed determines how an angiosperm is classified.

Biologists classify angiosperms into two classes. One group of angiosperms is called the **monocots.** The seeds of monocots have only one cotyledon. The other group is called the **dicots.** The seeds of dicots have two cotyledons. Have you ever looked carefully at the leaves of an angiosperm? Angiosperms are vascular plants. The leaves of all vascular plants have veins, or tubes, that transport food and water throughout the leaf. The leaves of a monocot plant have parallel veins. The leaves of a dicot

Key Points

- Because they produce many covered seeds, angiosperms are a successful group of plants.

- Monocots and dicots are two kinds of angiosperms.

Skill Builder

Making a Diagram   A diagram can be used to illustrate the parts that make up an object. Obtain a lima bean. Break open the seed and make a sketch of the two seed halves. Locate the seed leaves, the embryo plant, and the seed coat. Using Figure 10-9 as a model, label the parts of the seed on your diagram.

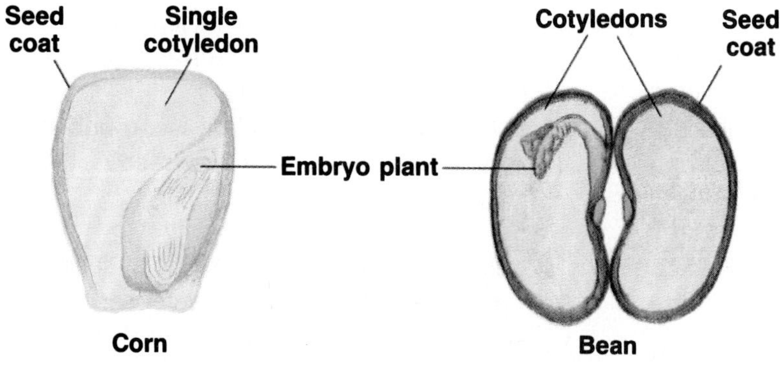

Seed coat   Single cotyledon   Cotyledons   Seed coat

Embryo plant

Corn   Bean

Figure 10-9   Where does a cotyledon develop?

ACTIVITY 10-1

PROBLEM: How can a germinating seed indicate if a plant is a monocot or a dicot?

Science Process Skills
observing, classifying, predicting

Background Information
As a seed begins to germinate, or grow, the first seed leaf or leaves can be seen. Monocots have one seed leaf. Dicots have two seed leaves.

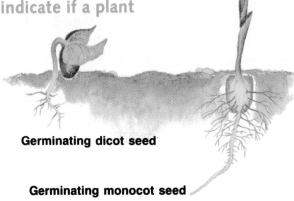

Germinating dicot seed

Germinating monocot seed

Materials
3 lima bean seeds	3 lentil seeds
5 grass seeds	several paper towels
3 corn seeds	aluminum foil
3 kidney bean seeds	hand lens

Procedure
1. Examine the seeds with the hand lens.
2. Copy the Data Table onto a sheet of paper.

Data Table: Monocot or Dicot Seeds?		
Seeds	**Prediction**	**Actual**
Lima Beans		
Grass		
Corn		
Kidney Beans		
Lentils		

3. **PREDICT** Which seeds are from monocots? Which are from dicots? Write the word "monocot" or "dicot" in the "Prediction" column of your Data Table. To find out if your predictions are accurate, continue the activity.
4. Make 5 small, 15 cm x 15 cm trays out of the aluminum foil.
5. Wet the paper towels thoroughly. Place one wet towel in each aluminum tray.
6. Place all of one kind of seed in each tray.
7. Place a damp paper towel over each tray of seeds. Be sure to keep the paper towels moist for the two-week observation period.
8. Using the hand lens, observe the seeds as they germinate. Record your observations each day in a daily log. Include a sketch of the germinating seeds for each day.
9. After two weeks, indicate whether each seed is from a dicot or monocot plant. Record your results in the "Actual" column of your Data Table.

Observations
1. Which seeds were the first to begin germinating?
2. Did all the seeds germinate the same way? Use the data in your daily log to support your answer.

Conclusions
1. a. Which seeds were from dicot plants?
   b. Which seeds were from monocot plants?
2. a. Were your predictions accurate?
   b. Explain why you made the predictions that you did.
3. How can you tell if a plant is a monocot or a dicot from its germinating seed?

Going Further
Try this activity using other kinds of seeds, such as fresh pea seeds and flower seeds. Classify the plants as monocots or dicots.

plant have branched, or netlike veins. Look at the structure of the veins in the leaves shown in Figure 10-10. Classify each leaf shown as a monocot or a dicot.

By counting the number of **petals** of a flower, you also can tell whether the plant is a monocot or dicot. Petals are the colorful parts of a flower. On the flowers of monocot plants, petals grow in groups of three. Lilies and tulips are monocots. Petals in groups of four or five grow on the flowers of dicot plants. The petals of a familiar monocot and dicot are shown in Figure 10-11.

Economic Importance

Angiosperms supply many of the foods that people eat every day. Do you know that when you eat rice, wheat, or oat cereal, you are eating the seeds of grasses? Angiosperms also are the sources of fruits and vegetables. For example, there are salad vegetables, such as lettuce, carrots, and cucumbers. For dessert or snacks, you may enjoy eating the fleshy fruit of apple, pear, peach, and cherry trees. Some juices that you drink for breakfast also come from the fruits of trees.

You probably have eaten the flowers of angiosperms. For example, broccoli and cauliflower are edible flowers. Many people also use angiosperms for decoration. For example, arrangements of roses, tulips, and carnations often are used as decorations at school graduations, weddings, and other special events.

Figure 10-10 A monocot leaf (top) has parallel veins. A dicot leaf (bottom) has branched veins.

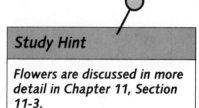

Study Hint

Flowers are discussed in more detail in Chapter 11, Section 11-3.

Figure 10-11 In which of these photographs is a monocot shown? How do you know?

The tough fibers of some angiosperms are used by people to make clothing and other materials. For example, many garments that you wear are made from fibers of the cotton plant. Strong rope is made out of fibers of the hemp plant.

Drugs and medicines also are made from angiosperms. The nightshade plant, or belladonna (bel-uh-DAHN-uh), for example, is the source of a drug that relieves muscle spasms. The foxglove plant contains a substance that helps heart attack victims. Aspirin was first made from the bark of willow trees.

Think & Discuss

9. What is a cotyledon?
10. What class of angiosperm has petals in groups of three?
11. What are two features you can use to distinguish between monocots and dicots?
12. How does the production of many seeds help to make angiosperms a successful group of plants?
13. How would planting conifers on a hillside prevent flooding?

10-4 Plant Tissues and Organs

Seed plants are multicellular organisms. The cells of seed plants are organized into tissues. Tissues are groups of cells that look alike and do the same job. The tissues of seed plants also are organized into organs. Organs are made up of several tissues that work together to do a specific job. For example, leaves, stems, and roots are organs in a plant.

Plant Tissues

There are four main kinds of plant tissue. The thin outer layer of cells that covers a plant is called the **epidermis.** Just as your skin covers your body, the epidermis covers the body of a plant. The leaves, stems, and roots of all plants are covered by epidermis. The main job of the epidermis is to prevent seed plants from drying out.

Key Points

- The four kinds of tissues that make up seed plants are epidermis, meristem, ground, and vascular.

- Seed plants have a shoot system above the ground and a root system below the ground.

Most of a plant is made up of **ground tissue.** Ground tissue stores food and provides support for the plant. Several different kinds of cells make up ground tissue. For example, the ground tissue in a leaf is made up of **parenchyma** (puh-REN-ky-muh) **cells.** The parenchyma cells in a leaf make food for all the other organs of a plant.

In seed plants, water is carried up to the leaves and food is carried down to the roots by vascular tissue. Vascular tissue is made up of two kinds of tissue. One kind of tissue is called **xylem** (ZY-luhm). The woody stems of plants are made up of xylem. Xylem carries water up from the roots to the leaves. The other kind of tissue is **phloem** (FLOH-em). Phloem carries food made in the leaves to all other parts of the plant.

Some plant tissue grows very rapidly. This kind of plant tissue is called **meristem** (MER-uh-stem). Meristem tissue is found at the tops of plant stems and in the lower tips of roots. Meristem tissue also is found as a layer inside stems or branches. Rapid division of the cells in the meristem causes plants to grow up, out, and down.

Plant Organ Systems

Roots, stems, leaves, and flowers contain all four kinds of plant tissue. However, the same tissues may perform different jobs in each organ. For example, ground tissue in a root stores food and water for the plant. Ground tissue in a stem provides support for the plant. Vascular tissue in a root transports water to the stem. What job do you think vascular tissue in a stem performs?

Like other complex organisms, plant organs form organ systems. The stem, leaves, and flowers make up the shoot system. The shoot system is the part of the plant that grows above ground. The root system grows below ground.

Think & Discuss

14. What two kinds of tissue make up vascular tissue?

15. What are the functions of the root system and the shoot system of a plant?

★ **16.** What do you think would happen if all the leaves of a plant were removed? Explain.

ACTIVITY 10–2

PROBLEM: What is the importance of a vascular system in a plant?

Science Process Skills
observing, inferring, predicting

Background Information
The vascular system of a plant is the system of tubes that carry water and minerals throughout the plant. The vascular system is made up of two tissues. One tissue, called xylem, carries water and minerals. The other tissue, called phloem, carries food.

Materials

celery stalk	clear plastic drinking cup
food coloring	hand lens
water	knife

Procedure

1. Fill the plastic cup halfway with water. Add several drops of food coloring.
2. Using the knife, cut off about 1 cm of the base of the celery stalk. **CAUTION: Be careful when you cut the celery.**
3. Place the celery into the food-coloring solution with the freshly cut base in the solution.
4. Copy the Data Table shown.

Data Table: Water Movement in Celery	
TIME	HEIGHT (MM)
5 MIN	
10 MIN	
15 MIN	
20 MIN	
24 HR	

5. After 5 minutes, measure the height (in mm) of the food coloring in the celery. Record the height in the Data Table.

6. Measure the height of the food coloring in the celery after 10, 15, and 20 minutes. Record each measurement in the Data Table.
7. **PREDICT** What do you predict will happen to the food coloring in the celery after 24 hours? Write your prediction on a sheet of paper. Continue the activity to find out if your prediction is correct.
8. Let the celery stalk remain in the food coloring for 24 hours.
9. After 24 hours, measure and record the height of the food coloring in the celery.
10. Cut off a thin slice of the celery. Examine the slice with a hand lens. Draw what you see.

Observations

1. What happens to the food coloring in the celery stalk?
2. a. What tissue transports the food coloring? b. In your model, what would the food coloring represent if the celery were growing?
3. Does the vascular system of the celery stalk extend its entire length? How do you know?
4. Does the movement of the liquid seem to occur quickly? Use your data to support your answer.

Conclusions

1. Was your prediction correct? Use your data to support your answer.
2. a. What life process does this activity show? b. Why is a plant's vascular system important?
3. **INFER** Carnations are the flowers of a vascular plant. If you placed a white carnation in blue-colored water, would the flower eventually have blue coloring in it? Explain your answer.

Plant Foods

The idea of plant food may sound odd. After all, plants make their own food. Plants, however, cannot always get enough materials from the soil to carry on their food-making processes. When this happens, supplements called plant food must be added to the soil in which a plant grows.

A scientific term for plant food is fertilizer. Fertilizers can be either organic or inorganic. Organic fertilizers come directly from living things. The most commonly used organic fertilizer is manure. Inorganic fertilizers are chemical mixtures made by people.

Plants must take three substances from the soil to adequately nourish themselves. These substances are nitrogen, phosphoric acid, and a phosphorus-containing compound called potash. All commercial fertilizers contain these three substances. However, the amounts of nitrogen, phosphoric acid, and potash needed by the plant vary according to the kind of plant and the type of soil to which the fertilizer will be added.

A person buying fertilizer should look for a brand with a guaranteed formula on the label. "Guaranteed" means that the formula has been tested by an agricultural experiment station. Experts in agriculture caution against buying high-priced fertilizers that have no formula. These products may be useless or much too expensive for what they offer.

How does one know which fertilizer to buy? An important skill is knowing how to read the formula on a fertilizer bag. The formula consists of three numbers, such as 4-8-4. Throughout the United States, these numbers always have the same meaning. The first number in the formula indicates the percentage of nitrogen in the fertilizer. The second number indicates the percentage of phosphoric acid, and the third number indicates the percentage of potash. Thus, a bag of fertilizer labeled 4-8-4 contains 4% nitrogen, 8% phosphoric acid, and 4% potash. The remaining 84% of the fertilizer will consist of soil, sand, or other filler materials.

Different types of plants require fertilizers with different formulas. For example, most garden flowers, including roses, do best with a 4-12-4 or a 5-10-5 fertilizer. Vegetables grow best with a 5-8-7 or a 4-8-4 fertilizer.

In addition to knowing which fertilizer to buy, it is important to know how much to buy. A general rule of thumb is two to three pounds of fertilizer per 100 square feet of garden area. This is about the same as one cup of fertilizer per plant.

To Think About
- What are the contents of a fertilizer labeled 5-12-5?
- How might air pollution such as acid rain interfere with plant nourishment?

Chapter Review

CHAPTER SUMMARY

10-1 Overview of the Seed Plants

- Most angiosperms can be identified by their broad leaves and flowers.
- Seeds of an angiosperm develop inside a covering, called a fruit.
- Most gymnosperms can be identified by cones and needlelike leaves.
- Seeds of a gymnosperm lie uncovered on the scale of a cone.

10-2 Gymnosperms

- Conifers, cycads, and gingkoes are all gymnosperms.
- Conifers are economically important plants. The wood of conifers supplies people with products, such as furniture and paper. Varnish and turpentine are other products that come from conifers.

10-3 Angiosperms

- Because most angiosperms produce many seeds each year, the angiosperms are a successful group of plants.
- Monocots and dicots are two kinds of angiosperms. Monocots have only one seed leaf, while dicots have two seed leaves.

10-4 Plant Tissues and Organs

- Plant tissues provide protection (epidermis), and support (ground tissue), make growth possible (meristem), and transport food (vascular tissue).
- The root system takes in water and minerals.
- The shoot system carries water and minerals to the leaves.

VOCABULARY LIST

angiosperm (160)
conifer (164)
cotyledon (167)
dicot (167)
embryo (160)
epidermis (170)

flower (161)
fruit (160)
ground tissue (171)
gymnosperm (160)
herbaceous stems (161)
meristem (171)

monocot (167)
parenchyma cells (171)
petals (169)
phloem (171)
pollen (165)
pollen cone (165)

pollination (165)
seed coat (160)
seed cone (165)
woody stems (161)
xylem (171)

VOCABULARY REVIEW

Matching Write the word or term from the Vocabulary List that best matches each description.

1. a developing plant
2. reproductive organ of an angiosperm
3. outer layer of cells that covers a plant
4. cells that make up ground tissue
5. gymnosperm with cones
6. rapidly growing plant tissue
7. grains that contain sperm cells
8. colorful part of flowers

Applying Definitions Explain the difference between the words in each pair.

1. angiosperm, gymnosperm
2. monocot, dicot
3. seed cone, pollen cone
4. xylem, phloem
5. ground tissue, meristem tissue
6. fruit, cone
7. cotyledon, seed coat
8. herbaceous stems, woody stems
9. pollination, fertilization

True or False Write true if the statement is true. If the statement is false, change the underlined word or words to make the statement true.

1. All <u>gymnosperms</u> produce flowers.
2. Gymnosperms produce their seeds in <u>fruits</u>.
3. The <u>cycad</u> is a gymnosperm that has male and female plants.
4. Most paper is made from the wood of <u>gingko</u> trees.
5. In gymnosperms, brightly colored <u>seed cones</u> grow in clusters.
6. <u>Monocot</u> plants have two cotyledons.
7. A tomato plant is an <u>angiosperm</u> because it produces covered seeds.
8. <u>Ground</u> tissue grows rapidly.
9. <u>Vascular</u> tissue consists of xylem and phloem.

Question and Answer Rewrite each heading in the Chapter Outline on page 158 as a question. Then, answer each of the questions you have written.

Interpreting a Diagram Use the diagram of monocotyledon and dicotyledon seeds shown in Figure 10-9 (page 167) to answer each of the following.

1. In what class of angiosperm does corn belong?
2. Is a bean plant a monocotyledon or a dicotyledon?
3. Where does the embryo of a cotyledon develop?
4. What is the outer covering of a cotyledon called?
5. How does a monocotyledon differ from a dicotyledon?

Writing the Main Ideas Using the Chapter Outline on page 158, write the main idea for each heading in the outline.

Critical Thinking Answer each of the following in complete sentences.

1. Why is a gingko considered a link between plants with naked seeds and plants with covered seeds?
2. Why could a seed be called a packaged plant?

3. Why would planting conifers near a shoreline help to prevent the erosion, or wearing away, of the sand?
4. Explain how a seed cone can be identified by its size, structure, and location on a conifer.
5. How could you tell if a plant was a monocot or dicot by observing its leaves?
6. Identify three examples of angiosperms with woody stems and three with herbaceous stems.

1. Use a field guide to classify the trees on your street as angiosperms or gymnosperms.
2. Draw an outline map of the United States. On your map, show where all the seed plants mentioned in this chapter are found.

3. The tropical rain forests contain many types of seed plants. Why else are these forests considered to be of great importance? Research this topic and present an oral report to the class.

11 | Plant Structure and Function

Objectives

After you have completed this chapter, you will be able to

11-1 **describe** the functions of roots and stems.

11-1 **explain** the difference between herbaceous and woody stems.

11-2 **describe** the structure and function of a leaf.

11-3 **name** the parts of a flower.

11-4 **explain** the difference between fruits and seeds.

11-5 **name** four growth requirements of plants.

11-5 **describe** three tropisms in plants.

Science Process Skills

In this chapter, two science skills are highlighted. Symbols show some places where these skills are used.

Measuring: When you measure, you compare an unknown value to a known value.

Hypothesizing: When you hypothesize, you state a suggested answer to a problem based upon known information.

People in the United States eat millions of kilograms of fruits and vegetables each year. What is the difference between a fruit and a vegetable? You may be surprised to learn that many of the foods you call vegetables are classified as fruits by botanists.

You probably have eaten every part of a plant. For example, a carrot is a root. Celery is a stem and spinach is a leaf. When you eat broccoli, you are eating a flower. The next time you eat dinner, look carefully at the vegetables on your plate. You probably will be able to identify from which part of the plant each vegetable came.

11-1 Roots and Stems

Key Points

- Roots anchor a plant in soil and take in water and dissolved nutrients.

- Stems support a plant, store food and water for the plant, and transport substances between the roots and leaves.

- Herbaceous stems are soft and green. Woody stems are hard and nongreen.

Have you ever heard someone say that the best place to start is from the ground up? When studying plants, the best place to start usually is with the roots. The roots of most plants grow underground and anchor the plant in the soil. Have you ever pulled weeds and grasses from your lawn or garden? If so, you probably noticed how well the roots held the plants in the soil.

Root Structure and Function

There are two kinds of root systems. One kind of root system is called a **taproot.** In a taproot, one root grows much larger than the other roots. In addition, many smaller roots grow from the large root. A carrot is an example of a taproot. Taproots such as carrots store food. What other plants with taproots can you name?

In the second kind of root system, one root does not grow larger than the others. Instead, the plant has a dense root network made up of many thin, stringlike roots. These stringlike roots are called **fibrous** (FY-bruhs) **roots.** Taproots often grow deep into the soil to absorb water and minerals found deep below the surface. For example, the taproot of a tall oak tree may grow more than 30 m down into the soil. Fibrous roots, however, do not grow as deep in the soil as taproots. Instead, fibrous roots spread out and absorb water and minerals close to the surface of the soil. What kind of root system do you think grass has?

Figure 11–1   The carrot (left) is a taproot. The plantain (right) has fibrous roots.

Root Growth

The first root that grows from a seed is called the primary root. As the primary root grows downward into the soil, smaller roots begin to grow from it. These smaller roots are called secondary roots. Tiny, hairlike structures called root hairs grow from the primary and secondary roots. The root hairs increase the surface area of the roots. With more surface area, the roots can absorb more water and minerals from the soil.

How does a root grow down into the soil? A root grows as new cells are produced by the meristem tissue in the root tip. The tip of the root is covered by the root cap. The root cap protects the tip of the growing root. The root cap also helps the root grow deeper into the soil. A slimy substance produced by the root cap acts like lubricating oil. Because of this slimy substance, the root tip is able to move easily through the soil.

Figure 11–2 Tiny root hairs grow from the secondary roots.

Parts of a Root

A root is made up of several layers. Imagine that you are a drop of water absorbed from the soil by a root hair. The root hairs grow from the epidermis, or outer layer, of the root. From the root hair you would pass into the next cell layer, called the **cortex.** Water and food are stored in the cortex. If you were not stored in the cortex, you would pass into the vascular tissue in the center of the root. You may recall that vascular tissue is made up of xylem and phloem. The phloem carries food made in the leaves to the roots. What do you think the xylem does?

Study Hint

Review the functions of xylem and phloem discussed in Section 10-4, Plant Tissues and Organs.

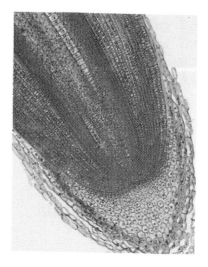

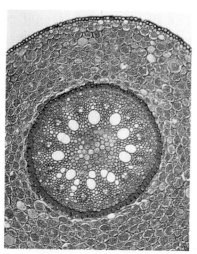

Figure 11–3 Find the meristem tissue in the cross section of the root tip (left). Where is the epidermis in the cross section of the root (right)?

Figure 11–4 How do these prop roots differ from the fibrous roots shown in Figure 11–1 on page 178?

Specialized Roots

Some plants have roots that are adapted for certain functions. For example, some specialized roots can absorb water from the air. This kind of root is called an aerial (AYR-ee-uhl) root. A plant with aerial roots, such as a bromeliad (broh-MEE-lee-ad), is called an air plant. Another kind of specialized root supports the stems and leaves of a plant. These specialized roots are called prop roots. Corn is an example of a plant with prop roots.

Stem Structure and Function

Most of the plants with which you are familiar have stems that grow above ground. Some plants, however, have stems that grow along the surface of the soil. These stems are called runners. Strawberry plants are examples of plants with runners. Other plants have underground stems called tubers. These stems are modified for storing food. A white potato is an example of a tuber. What other stems can you name that store food?

Stems are made up of the same four kinds of tissue that make up roots. For example, the outer cell layer of a stem is made up of epidermal tissue. The epidermis protects the plant and prevents water loss. Inside the epidermis is the cortex. As in roots, stems also have vascular tissue made up of phloem and xylem. In the center of the stem is a layer of tissue, called **pith.** Pith cells store water in a stem.

The stems of many plants are soft, green, and filled with water. These soft, green stems are called herbaceous (huhr-BAY-shus) stems. Plants that do not live for more than one growing season have herbaceous stems. In fact, some plants with herbaceous stems live for only a few weeks. Many flowers, such as lilies and dandelions, have herbaceous stems.

Because herbaceous stems are soft, most plants with this kind of stem do not grow very tall. For example, grasses have herbaceous stems. Daisies also have herbaceous stems. Herbaceous plants do not grow taller than 2 m. What do you think would happen if a herbaceous plant grew taller than 2 m?*

Figure 11–5 Dandelions have herbaceous stems.

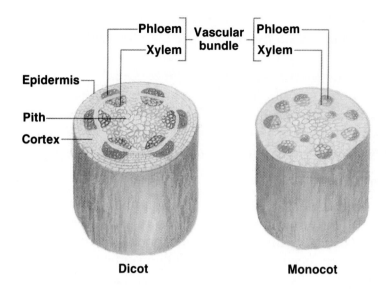

Figure 11–6 What tissues make up the vascular bundles of monocot and dicot stems?

Figure 11-6 shows cross sections of the herbaceous stems of a dicot and a monocot. The bundles of vascular tissue around the cortex are called vascular bundles. The vascular bundles contain xylem and phloem. Notice that the arrangement of vascular bundles is different in dicots and monocots. For example, in a dicot, such as a bean plant, the vascular bundles are arranged in a ring around the cortex. In a monocot, such as a corn plant, the vascular bundles are scattered throughout the cortex.

Woody Stems

All trees have woody stems. Woody stems are nongreen stems that are much thicker and harder than herbaceous stems. Why do you think that plants with woody stems grow much taller than plants with herbaceous stems?

Look at Figure 11–7. The rough outer covering of a woody stem is called the bark. Like the skin, the bark of a tree is the first line of defense against injury and disease. Bark is made up of **cork,** the cortex, and phloem. Cork is a layer of dead cells that protects the stem from insects, bacteria, and fungi. The cork also prevents the inner layers of a stem from drying out.

Beneath the cork layer is the cortex. The cortex of a woody stem functions like the cortex of a root. What is the job of the cortex?

A very thin layer of living meristem tissue is located between the phloem and xylem of a woody stem. This

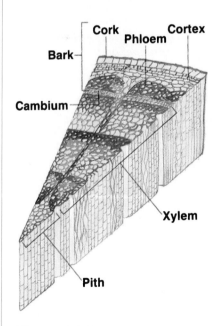

Figure 11–7 What is the name of the layer of tissue between the xylem and the phloem?

Figure 11-8 The ringlike pattern of this stem is formed by the growth of springwood and summerwood.

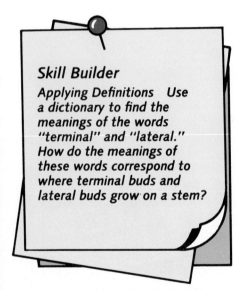

layer is called the **cambium** (KAM-bee-uhm). As the cambium layer of a tree grows, the tree gets wider. Cells on the outer part of the cambium produce new phloem cells. Dead phloem cells become the cork of the tree. Cells on the inner part of the cambium produce new xylem cells. When the xylem cells die, they form the inner woody part of a tree. The largest part of a woody stem is made up of dead xylem cells.

Stem Growth

The xylem of a tree goes through two growth periods each year. In the spring, large xylem cells are produced. This wood is called springwood. In the summer, smaller xylem cells are produced. This wood is called summerwood.

Springwood and summerwood do not look exactly alike. You can see the difference between springwood and summerwood in Figure 11-8. Notice the ringlike pattern. The rings were formed by the growth of the springwood and summerwood.

Botanists have found that the difference in appearance between springwood and summerwood, or **annual rings,** can be used to determine the age of the tree when it is cut down. Each ring represents one year's growth. Thus, a tree with 100 rings is 100 years old. Count the annual rings on the section of tree shown in Figure 11-8. How old was this tree when it was cut down?

How do stems grow in length? At the tip of a stem is a bud called the **terminal** (TUR-muh-nul) **bud.** The stem of a plant gets longer as cells are produced by the meristem tissue in the terminal bud. New branches, leaves, and flowers are produced by **lateral** (LAT-uhr-uhl) **buds.** Lateral buds grow from the sides of the main stem of a plant.

Think and Discuss

1. What is the function of the cortex in a root or woody stem?
2. What are two main differences between herbaceous and woody stems?
3. Many farmers plant grasses to keep soil from being carried away by wind or water. Why are fibrous roots better than taproots in preventing soil erosion?

11-2 Leaves

How would you describe a leaf? Probably, you would say that a leaf is green, flat, and thin. Leaves are green because of the green pigment chlorophyll found in their cells. The chlorophyll absorbs energy from sunlight. This energy is then used by the leaf to make food in the process of photosynthesis. Most of the photosynthesis in a plant takes place in the leaves. Why do you think that most leaves are flat and thin?

Leaf Structure and Function

Most leaves are broad. The broad, flat part of a leaf is called the **blade.** The blade is attached to the stem by a stalk called the **petiole** (PET-ee-ohl). Some plants do not have petioles. The leaves of these plants are attached directly to the stem.

In most leaves, the petiole becomes the main vein of the leaf. The veins in a leaf carry food and water. What kind of tissue do you think the veins in a leaf are made of?

Plants have either simple leaves or compound leaves. A simple leaf has one blade and one petiole. The leaf of an oak tree or a maple tree is an example of a simple leaf. A compound leaf has a blade that is divided into smaller parts, called leaflets.

Leaf Layers

Have you ever seen a plant with shiny leaves? If you rubbed a leaf of this plant between your fingers, the leaf would feel waxy. This is because the upper epidermis of many leaves is protected by a nonliving waxy substance, called the **cuticle** (KYOOT-ih-kuhl). Together, the cuticle and the epidermis of a leaf reduce water loss. The cuticle and the epidermis also protect a leaf from most bacteria, fungi, and insects.

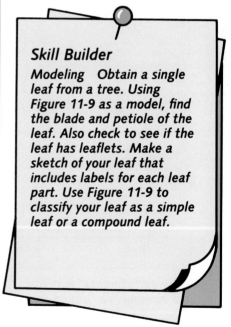

Skill Builder

Modeling   Obtain a single leaf from a tree. Using Figure 11-9 as a model, find the blade and petiole of the leaf. Also check to see if the leaf has leaflets. Make a sketch of your leaf that includes labels for each leaf part. Use Figure 11-9 to classify your leaf as a simple leaf or a compound leaf.

Figure 11-9   Compare the simple leaf (left) with the compound leaf (right). How are the two types of leaves different?

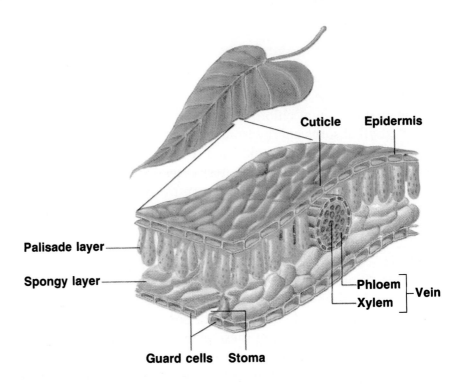

Cuticle   Epidermis

Palisade layer

Spongy layer

Phloem ⎫
Xylem ⎭ Vein

Guard cells   Stoma

Figure 11–10 The cells making up the palisade layer of a leaf contain most of the chlorophyll of the plant.

Study Hint

The word "stomata" is plural. One opening is a "stoma."

Below the epidermis is a layer of tissue, called the **palisade** (pal-uh-SAYD) **layer.** The palisade layer is made up of parenchyma (puh-REN-ki-muh) cells. Most photosynthesis in plants takes place in the palisade layer of the leaves. What substance needed for photosynthesis do you think is found in the parenchyma cells?

Vascular tissue from the roots and stem continue into the leaf and end in the palisade layer. Below the palisade layer is a layer that contains many air spaces. This layer is called the **spongy layer.** The spongy layer is involved in gas exchange.

Gas Exchange

Find the openings that cover the lower surface of the leaf shown in Figure 11-10. These openings are called **stomata** (STOH-muh-tuh). During the day, stomata absorb carbon dioxide from the air and release oxygen and water. The stomata also absorb the oxygen needed by the plant for respiration and release carbon dioxide and water.

Two bean-shaped cells, called **guard cells,** surround each of the stomata. The guard cells control the size of the stomata. When the guard cells swell, the stomata open. When the guard cells shrink, the stomata close.

ACTIVITY 11-1

PROBLEM: What are some ways leaves can be classified?

Science Process Skills
classifying, identifying, measuring, inferring

Background Information
Leaves can be classified as simple or compound. A simple leaf is a leaf that does not have a divided blade. A compound leaf is divided into two or more leaflets, or bladelike parts. If you look at the veins, or tubelike structures, of a leaf, you also can tell if the leaf is from a monocot or a dicot. Monocots usually have veins that are parallel, or run side by side, to each other. Dicot leaves have veins that spread out in a netlike pattern.

Simple   Compound

Materials
    10 leaves from different plants or trees
    hand lens (optional)
    metric ruler

Procedure
1. Choose one of your leaves.
2. Draw the leaf that you chose and label the petiole, blade, and veins. If your leaf has a midrib, label it.
3. Examine each leaf. Then draw a small outline of each of your leaves.
4. Measure the length of each blade from its top to its base. Record the length of each blade next to your drawings.
5. Examine the blades of each leaf. Classify each leaf as simple or compound. Write the word "simple" or "compound" next to each leaf.
6. Examine the vein pattern of each leaf.
7. Draw the veins in your leaf outlines. Write the type of vein pattern each leaf has. Use the word "netlike" or "parallel."
8. Next to each leaf, write whether the plant from which the leaf was taken is a monocot or a dicot.

Observations
1. **INFER** Do all leaves have a petiole?
2. Can you name the plant from which any of the leaves were taken? If so, label the leaves with the plant name.
3. **a.** Which type of leaf—simple or compound—was more common in the leaves you examined? **b.** Which vein pattern was more common?

Conclusions
1. Do leaf blades vary in size? Use your observations to support your answer.
2. Which of the leaves that you examined was the most unusual? Why?
3. **a.** What are two ways leaves can be classified? **b.** From your observations, what other ways can leaves be classified?

Going Further
Take a walk around your neighborhood. Bring along a guide to trees and plants. Identify 15 trees or plants. Then classify their leaves as simple or compound. Classify the vein patterns and identify the tree or plant as a monocot or a dicot.

Water Loss

The surface of a balloon is firm to the touch because of the air inside. The leaf of a plant is filled with water in the same way that a balloon is filled with air. Water fills up the air spaces inside a leaf, making the leaf firm to the touch. What do you think would happen to the leaves of a plant that was not getting enough water?

Plants lose water through the stomata in their leaves in a process called **transpiration** (trans-puh-RAY-shun). Like people, many plants tend to lose a lot of water on hot days. To reduce water loss, the guard cells shrink and close the stomata on hot days. What do you think happens to the guard cells on cool days?

Specialized Leaves

Did you know that the spines of a cactus are really leaves? Because a cactus lives in a very dry environment, such as a desert, the cactus cannot afford to lose much water by transpiration. For this reason, the cactus has spinelike leaves instead of broad leaves. The spines of a cactus are an example of specialized leaves

Plants such as vines often have specialized leaves also. The specialized leaves of vines are called tendrils. Tendrils are wiry structures that wind around objects. For example, vines such as morning glory or poison ivy cling to fence posts and tree limbs with their tendrils.

A few species of plants have specialized leaves that trap insects. Plants that trap insects with their leaves are called carnivorous (kar-NIV-uh-ruhs) plants. When an insect lands on the leaves of a carnivorous plant, the leaves close and trap the insect. The insect then is digested by chemicals inside the plant. The pitcher plant and Venus's-flytrap are examples of carnivorous plants.

Figure 11–11 The Venus's-flytrap catches insects with its leaves.

Think & Discuss

4. What is the process of water loss in a leaf called? How does a leaf prevent too much water loss?

5. What is the difference between a simple leaf and a compound leaf?

6. How does having spines instead of broad flat leaves help a cactus survive in a dry environment?

11-3 Flowers

What do you think of when you hear the word "flower"? Do you think of colorful petals of roses, lilies, or carnations? You may be surprised to learn that some flowers are so small, you would need a magnifying glass to see them. However, all flowers, no matter what their size or color, are the reproductive parts of a plant.

Parts of a Flower

The outer parts of a flower are called **sepals** (SEE-puhls). Sepals are green leaflike structures that surround and protect the petals. Some flowers, such as roses and lilies, are sweet-smelling and have large, colorful petals. Unlike roses and lilies, the flowers of grass plants have very small petals that are not colorful or sweet-smelling. Petals surround the male and female reproductive organs.

The male reproductive organ of a flower is called the **stamen** (STAY-muhn). The stamen is a thin stalk. At the tip of the stamen is a structure called the **anther.** Pollen grains are formed by the anther. Sperm cells are formed inside the pollen grains.

The female reproductive organ of a plant is a tube called the **pistil.** The pistil usually is surrounded by several stamens. The bottom of the pistil is called the **ovary** (OH-vuh-ree). The ovary contains small structures called **ovules.** Egg cells develop inside the ovules.

Pollination and Fertilization

The transfer of a pollen grain from a stamen to a pistil is called pollination (pahl-uh-NAY-shun). In some plants, a pollen grain is carried from the stamen to the pistil of the same flower. This process is called self-pollination. Most plants, however, are pollinated by other flowers of the same species. This process is called cross-pollination.

After landing on the sticky tip of a pistil, a pollen grain develops a tubelike structure called a pollen tube. The pollen tube grows down the entire length of the pistil. Then the sperm cells inside the pollen grain travel down through the pollen tube to the ovary.

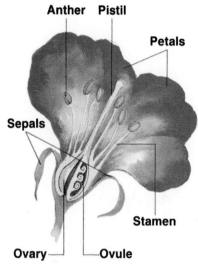

Figure 11–12 A flower that has both male and female reproductive organs is called a perfect flower.

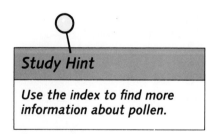

Study Hint

Use the index to find more information about pollen.

Figure 11–13 This honeybee is helping to pollinate the flower.

After traveling down the pollen tube, a sperm cell unites with one of the egg cells in an ovule. This process is called fertilization (fur-tul-ih-ZAY-shun). As a result of fertilization, an embryo plant begins to develop inside the ovule. As the embryo plant grows, the ovary of the flower gets larger.

Think & Discuss

7. What is a stamen?
8. What is the function of a pollen tube?
★ 9. Does pollination alone result in the formation of an embryo plant? Explain.

11-4 Seeds and Fruits

Key Points

- A fertilized ovule is called a seed.
- A fruit is a mature ovary that contains seeds.

A fertilized ovule is called a seed. After fertilization takes place, the ovule begins to grow and change. A seed contains the embryo plant and stored food for the embryo.

The seeds formed by a plant remain inside the ovary. A mature ovary containing seeds is called a fruit. All fruits, therefore, contain seeds. A peach is a fruit. Is a tomato a fruit? Why or why not?

Seed Dispersal

Some plants have fruits that are light and shaped for air travel. The seeds of these plants are scattered, or dispersed, by the wind. For example, the fruit of a maple tree has winglike structures that can carry the fruit hundreds of meters on a windy day. Other plants have fruits that float. The seeds of these plants are dispersed by water. The air-filled pods of a milkweed plant often float down rivers. The fruit of a coconut palm can carry its seed thousand of kilometers on ocean currents.

Some plants have sweet fleshy fruits. The seeds of these plants are dispersed by animals. For example, many animals eat sweet berries. As the animals move from place to place, they eliminate some of the seeds as waste products. Some fruits have hooklike structures that stick to the fur of mammals. These fruits even may stick to your clothing. Have you ever walked through a field or

Figure 11–14 The seeds of this dandelion may be carried great distances by the wind.

ACTIVITY 11-2

PROBLEM: What are some plant parts that are used as food?

Science Process Skills
observing, classifying, organizing

Background Information
Plants are important to people in two ways: plants give off oxygen and many plants are grown as food. Roots, stems, leaves, fruits, and seeds of plants are all used as food. Keep in mind that a fruit is a ripened ovary with one or more seeds. Thus, many plant parts that are called vegetables in the supermarket are really fruits to a biologist.

Materials
    magazines, including food magazines
    scissors
    glue
    index cards

Procedure
1. Look through magazines and find pictures of 25 different vegetables and fruits.
2. Cut out each of the pictures. **CAUTION: Be careful when using scissors.** Glue each picture onto an index card.
3. Label the name of the vegetable or fruit.
4. Exchange your 25 vegetable and fruit pictures with one of your classmates.
5. **ORGANIZE** Develop a table to classify the plant part that you would be eating if you ate each of the 25 vegetables and fruits you have.

Observations
1. Which of the 25 vegetables and fruits do you eat?
2. Which plant parts of these vegetables and fruits do you eat most often?

Conclusions
1. Are all plant parts edible? Explain your answer.
2. Could people survive without eating any plant parts? Explain your answer.
3. Scientifically, why would you classify cucumbers and peppers as fruits?
4. Vegetables are any part of a plant people eat. However, this definition is not scientifically correct. How could you rewrite this definition so that it is scientifically correct?

Going Further
Keep a record of the fruits and vegetables that you eat during one week. Classify the vegetables and fruits according to their plant parts. Which plant part do you eat most often? Which part do you eat the least often?

Cotyledons

Figure 11–15 A seed undergoes many changes as it develops into a new plant.

park and noticed small burrs on your socks and jeans? These small burrs are the fruits of grasses and other nonwoody plants.

Seed Germination

The growth of an embryo plant from a seed is called germination (jur-muh-NAY-shun). If a seed lands in moist, warm soil, it will begin to germinate, or grow. Moisture and warmth are the two main requirements for germination.

Figure 11-15 shows the germination of a dicot seed. The two cotyledons contain the stored food for the embryo plant. As the seed germinates, the cotyledons are pushed above the ground. At the same time, the primary root begins to grow down into the soil. The stem and first leaves begin to grow upward. As the first leaves unfold and begin to carry on photosynthesis, the cotyledons wither and die. Why do you think the cotyledons die after the first leaves open up?

Think & Discuss

10. What is the relationship between a fruit and a seed?
11. What are the two main conditions necessary for germination?
 12. Why are plants dependent on wind, water, and animals to disperse their seeds?

11-5 Growth and Response

What do seedlings need to grow into healthy plants? All plants have certain growth requirements. Basic growth requirements include light, water, minerals, and a proper temperature.

Plants need light to carry on photosynthesis. However, not all plants need the same amount of light. Dandelions require direct sunlight for proper growth. Other plants, such as ferns, grow best in shady areas. Why would the forest floor not be a good place to look for dandelions?

You may have noticed that not all flowers appear at the same time of the year. Some plants, such as the daylily, produce flowers in the summer. Other plants, such as the aster, produce flowers in the fall. Why do different kinds of plants produce flowers at different times of the year?

The amount of sunlight a plant receives determines when it will produce flowers. Different kinds of plants need different amounts of sunlight. Plants that produce flowers in the summer are called long-day plants. Long-day plants need at least 12 hours of sunlight each day to flower. Plants that produce flowers in the fall are called short-day plants. Short-day plants can flower with less than 12 hours of sunlight. Plants that do not depend on the length of the day to produce flowers are called day-neutral plants.

Do you think a cactus needs the same amount of water as a fern? All plants need water to grow. However, different plants require different amounts of water. If you gave a cactus too much water, it would die, just as a fern would die with too little water.

When plants absorb water they also absorb certain minerals. Nitrates and phosphates are two minerals that plants need for proper growth. Usually the minerals a plant needs are found in the soil. Sometimes, however, farmers must add fertilizer to the soil. Fertilizer is a mixture that contains nitrogen, phosphorous, and potassium.

You probably have noticed that many plants do not begin growing until March or April. One of the reasons is that seeds will not germinate unless the soil is warm enough. Most plants grow best at temperatures between 10 °C and 38 °C.

- Plants need light, water, minerals, and a proper temperature to grow.

- The response of a plant to a stimulus is called a tropism.

- Light, gravity, and touch are three stimuli to which plants respond.

Figure 11–16 Farmers often use large equipment to apply fertilizer to their crops.

Any organic chemical that makes an organism grow is called a growth hormone. In plants, the growth of roots and stems is controlled by growth hormones. Growth hormones cause roots to grow deeper and stems to grow taller. In what kind of plant tissue do you think growth hormones are found?

🔖 Growth hormones are located in the root tips, lateral buds, and terminal buds of plants. Most plants are taller than they are wide. This is because the terminal bud of a plant makes a hormone that prevents the lateral buds from growing too fast. What do you think would happen if the terminal bud of a plant were cut off?

Tropisms

Plants do not move from place to place the way animals do. All plants, however, move in response to stimuli. The response of a plant to a stimulus is called a **tropism** (TROH-pizm).

All plants grow toward light. You may have observed that the stems and leaves of your houseplants bend in the direction of sunlight. The response of a plant to sunlight is called phototropism (foh-TAH-troh-piz-uhm).

The roots of all plants grow downward and the stems grow upward. Why do plants grow this way? The direction of the growth of roots and stems is the response of a plant to gravity. The response of a plant to gravity is called geotropism (jee-AH-truh-piz-um).

Some plants respond to touch. The response of a plant to touch, or contact with a solid object, is called thigmotropism (thig-MAH-truh-piz-um). For example, grapevines often coil around fence posts or climb up walls. What structure of the grapevine responds to contact with a fence post or a wall?

Figure 11–17   What stimulus are these sunflower plants responding to?

Think & Discuss

13. What is a tropism? Give one example.
14. List four growth requirements of plants.
★ 15. What would happen to the stem of a potted plant if you placed the plant on its side?

The year is 2020. Your job is to prepare dinner for yourself and the other astronauts aboard the space station *Galaxy*. You pick some big ripe tomatoes from the space station garden, then begin gathering lettuce leaves for a salad.

A garden in space is not as impossible as it sounds. Thanks to a relatively new technology called hydroponics, vegetables and flowers can grow in outer space, in Arctic regions, on rocky mountain slopes, and in barren deserts.

What is hydroponics? Hydroponics is the science of growing plants without soil. From your study of plants, you know that soil is important to plants in two ways. First, soil provides support for the plants. Soil is the medium in which plants grow. Second, soil provides plants with essential nutrients. Plants can live without soil, however, if two basic requirements—support and nourishment—are met.

When plants are grown hydroponically, they are placed in a growing tank. A medium such as sand or gravel is used to support the plants. Then chemicals that match the nutrients found in fertile soil are dissolved in water and fed to the plants. The nutrient solution can be sprayed onto the plants from above, or it can be pumped into the plant bed from below. The second method usually is preferred, because the roots of the plants can grow down into the nutrients. This way the nutrients get to the plant faster.

In order for hydroponics to be successful, plants must receive controlled amounts of carbon dioxide, oxygen, water, nutrients, heat, and light. You can see that growing plants without soil is a real challenge for gardeners!

Although plants have been grown without soil since ancient times, hydroponics has been used commercially for less than 50 years. Some of the advantages of growing plants hydroponically include lack of competition from weeds, freedom from soil-transmitted diseases, and reduced labor costs. A disadvantage is the high cost of the equipment that is needed for hydroponics.

To Think About
- Why might hydroponics be important in light of the world's growing population?
- How might hydroponics improve the quality of flowers and vegetables?

Plant Structure and Function 193

Chapter Review

11-1 Roots and Stems

- Roots anchor a plant in soil and absorb water and dissolved nutrients.
- Stems support a plant and store and transport water and food.
- Herbaceous stems are soft green stems. Woody stems are nongreen stems that are thicker and harder than herbaceous stems.

11-2 Leaves

- Leaves carry out most of the photosynthesis for the plant.
- Plants have either simple leaves or compound leaves.

11-3 Flowers

- Flowers are the reproductive organs of a plant.

- The male reproductive organ of a flower is the stamen. The female reproductive organ is the pistil.

11-4 Seeds and Fruits

- A seed is a fertilized ovule.
- A fruit is a mature ovary with seeds.
- The process by which seeds are moved form one place to another is called seed dispersal. Seeds are dispersed by wind, water, and by animals.

11-5 Growth and Response

- Plants need light, water, minerals, and a proper temperature to grow.
- The response of a plant to a stimulus is called a tropism. Phototropism, geotropism, and thigmotropism are three plant responses.

VOCABULARY LIST

annual rings (182)	cuticle (183)	palisade layer (184)	stamen (187)
anther (187)	fibrous roots (178)	petiole (183)	stomata (184)
blade (183)	guard cells (184)	pistil (187)	taproot (178)
cambium (182)	lateral buds (182)	pith (180)	terminal bud (182)
cork (181)	ovary (187)	sepals (187)	transpiration (186)
cortex (179)	ovules (187)	spongy layer (184)	tropism (192)

VOCABULARY REVIEW

Matching   Write the word or term from the Vocabulary List that best matches each description.

1. where pollen grains are formed
2. female reproductive organ
3. layer between xylem and phloem in a woody stem
4. stores water in a stem
5. layer of cells that stores water and food for a root
6. leaf layer made up of parenchyma cells
7. waxy substance that covers some leaves
8. layer of cells beneath palisade layer
9. produce new branches and leaves

Identifying Relationships   Identify the word or term in each group that does not belong. Explain why it does not belong with the group.

1. sepals, petals, taproot
2. stamen, tropism, ovary
3. transpiration, water, photosynthesis
4. fibrous root, carrot, grass
5. blade, petiole, cork
6. stomata, bark, guard cells
7. seeds, ovules, pollen tube
8. terminal bud, lateral buds, annual rings
9. ovules, sepals, petals
10. stamen, terminal bud, pistil
11. ovary, stamen, anther

Completion   Write the word or words that best complete each sentence.

1. The surface area of roots is increased by _____.

2. Aerial roots absorb _____ from the air.

3. Vascular tissue is made up of xylem and _____ cells.

4. Most photosynthesis takes place in the _____ layer of leaves.

5. Short-day plants need _____ than 12 hours of sunlight to flower.

6. The response of a plant to _____ is called geotropism.

7. A tree's main defense against injury and disease is its _____.

8. Carnivorous plants feed upon _____.

9. Food and water are carried by the _____ of a leaf.

Finding the Main Ideas   Use the section number to find the sentence that answers each question. Then, write the sentence.

1. What is the purpose of roots? (11-1)

2. What is the function of the epidermal layer of a stem? (11-1)

3. How do woody stems differ from herbaceous stems? (11-1)

4. How does chlorophyll affect the appearance of a leaf? (11-2)

5. How does chlorophyll affect the function of a leaf? (11-2)

6. How are all flowers alike? (11-3)

7. What is a seed? (11-4)

8. What is a fruit? (11-4)

9. What are the four growth requirements of plants? (11-5)

10. What causes plants to move? (11-5)

Writing the Main Ideas   Using the Chapter Outline on page 176, write the main idea for each heading in the outline.

Critical Thinking   Answer each of the following in complete sentences.

1. Why is a cuticle especially important for a plant that lives in a dry area?

2. Ordinarily, fruit does not ripen until a seed is mature. Why do you think this is important for the survival of a plant?

3. Why do you think plants absorb carbon dioxide from the air during the day?

4. Would you classify a pumpkin as a fruit or a vegetable? Why?

5. Why do you think xylem cells produced in the stem during the summer are smaller than those produced in winter?

1. Do you think that "plant foods" affect the growth of plants? Design an experiment to test your hypothesis. Your plan should include more than one plant and should involve measurement. Conduct your experiment and report the results to the class.

2. Some flowers have only a stamen; others have only a pistil. Research how cross-pollination takes place in such flowers. Draw one or more diagrams to illustrate this process.

3. The growth of a new plant from a part of a plant is called vegetative propagation. Grafting, layering, budding, and cuttings are methods of vegetative propagation. Find out how plants can be grown using one of these methods. Then, demonstrate the procedure to your class.

4. Collect leaves from a variety of trees. Preserve the leaves by ironing them between 2 sheets of wax paper. Paste each leaf on a poster under the heading "Simple Leaves" or "Compound Leaves." Identify each leaf.

Look at the photographs and drawings on these two pages. How many of the organisms do you recognize? You may be surprised to learn that each of the organisms shown is classified in the Animal kingdom.

The Animal kingdom is divided into two large groups. One group is made up of animals with backbones. The other group is made up of animals without backbones. Animals without backbones are called invertebrates. Most animals are invertebrates. In fact, invertebrates make up 97 percent of all animal species. Each of the animals shown is an invertebrate. Look at the photographs again. What other invertebrates can you name?

UNIT 4

Invertebrates

CONTENTS

After you have completed this chapter, you will be able to

12-1 **describe** the structure of a sponge.

12-1 **identify** two methods of asexual reproduction in sponges.

12-2 **identify** the body forms of a cnidarian.

12-2 **list** four examples of cnidarians.

12-3 **describe** the importance of porifera and cnidarians.

Science Process Skills

In this chapter, two science skills are highlighted. Symbols show some places where these skills are used.

Observing: When you observe, you use one or more of your senses to gather information.

Inferring: When you infer, you form a conclusion based upon facts and not direct observation.

Imagine you are scuba diving off the coast of Florida. What kinds of animals do you think you might see below the ocean's surface? You probably would see many different kinds of fishes. You also might observe crabs, sea stars, shrimps, clams, and conchs. The earth's oceans are home to a variety of organisms.

Now, imagine that you are scuba diving near the reef shown in the photograph. What kinds of animals do you observe? Two kinds of animals shown in the photograph are sponges and corals. Sponges are members of the phylum Porifera (paw-RIF-uhr-uh). Corals belong to the phylum Cnidaria (ni-DER-ee-uh). Sponges and corals are among the simplest of the animals. They also are **invertebrates** *(in-VUR-tuh-brayts), or animals without backbones.*

12-1 Porifera

Key Points

- Sponges are simple animals without backbones.
- Sponges reproduce sexually and asexually.

More than 5000 species of animals make up the phylum Porifera. All porifera are sponges. Most sponges live attached to the ocean floor. A few species, however, live in fresh water.

Have you ever used a sponge to clean up a spill or wash dishes? Most of the sponges used today are synthetic (sin-THET-ik), or made by people. However, this was not always the case. At one time, all of the sponges used by people for cleaning were the skeletons of sponges that once lived in the ocean.

In some ways, synthetic sponges are similar to the natural sponges. Think about the sponges you use for cleaning. What is the most outstanding feature of these sponges? Synthetic sponges have many holes, or **pores,** on their surfaces. Sponges that are animals also have pores. In fact, the phylum name, "Porifera," means "pore-bearer." With its pores, a sponge can take in a large amount of water.

◉ Sponges range in size from less than 1 cm to more than 2 m. Sponges also vary in shape and in color. In fact, some sponges, such as the ones shown in Figure 12-1, can be very colorful. How would you describe the shapes of the sponges shown in Figure 12-1?

Structure of Porifera

A sponge has a hollow body shaped like a sac. At the top of its saclike body, a sponge has a large opening called the **osculum** (AS-kyuh-luhm). What are the many smaller openings on the surface of a sponge called?

The body of a sponge is made up of two layers of cells. The outer layer of body cells is called the **ectoderm** (EK-tuh-durm). The inner layer of cells is called the **endoderm** (EN-duh-durm). Between the two cell layers is a jellylike substance. In this jellylike substance, some sponges have small solid structures called **spicules** (SPIK-yools).

Some sponges have spicules made out of calcium carbonate. Calcium carbonate is a white, powdery compound that is found in chalk, bones, and a rock called limestone. Other sponges have spicules made out of silica. Silica is a mineral that makes up beach sand. In addition,

Figure 12-1 The blue vase sponge (top) and the finger sponge (bottom) are found in warm ocean waters.

some spicules are made out of a rubberlike substance called **spongin** (SPUN-jin). After the sponge dies and decays, its spongin skeleton remains.

The body cavity of a sponge is lined with **collar cells.** In Figure 12-3, notice the small whiplike structures, or **flagella** (fluh-JEL-uh), on the collar cells. The moving flagella help a sponge keep a steady stream of water flowing into its body cavity.

Water moves through a sponge in one direction. For example, water enters a sponge through its pores. The water then exits the sponge through the osculum. As water flows through a sponge, the sponge filters out food, such as bacteria, algae, and other microscopic organisms. Food is digested and oxygen is absorbed by the collar cells. Waste products are removed as water flows out of the osculum.

Cells called **amoebocytes** (uh-MEE-boh-syts) are scattered throughout the jellylike layer of a sponge. Amoebocytes transport digested food to all of the cells of a sponge. Amoebocytes also help a sponge to reproduce.

Reproduction of Porifera

Sponges can reproduce asexually or sexually. Sponges reproduce asexually in two ways. The first way is by budding. During budding, small bulges called **gemmules** (JEM-yoolz) form on the outside of a sponge's body.

Figure 12-2 Spicules give a sponge its shape.

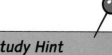

Study Hint

As you read about the reproduction of sponges, classify each method of sponge reproduction as sexual or asexual.

Figure 12-3 The flagella of collar cells keep water moving through the sponge's body cavity.

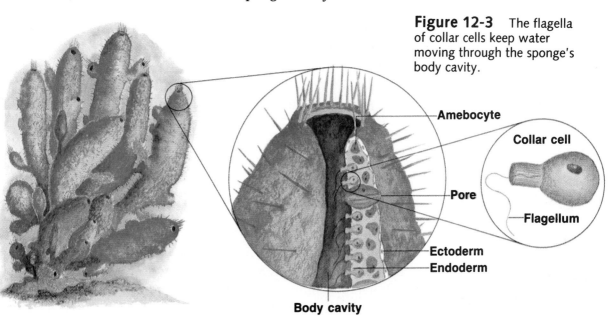

Amebocyte

Collar cell

Pore

Flagellum

Ectoderm

Endoderm

Body cavity

Gemmules contain food, amoebocytes, and spicules. After a while, the gemmules break off and develop into new sponges.

Sometimes, strong waves break off pieces, or fragments, of a sponge. Each piece that breaks free from a sponge can develop into a new sponge. This kind of asexual reproduction is called **regeneration** (ri-jen-uh-RAY-shun). Regeneration is common among many simple animals.

Most sponges are able to produce both male and female sex cells. However, in a single sponge, each kind of sex cell is produced at different times. Male sex cells are sperm cells. Female sex cells are eggs.

During sexual reproduction, a sponge that has produced sperm cells releases the sperm into the water. The sperm cells may then enter another sponge through its collar cells. If this sponge has produced eggs, amoebocytes carry the sperm to the eggs. Fertilization takes place when the sperm and egg join. Why would it be difficult to tell whether a sponge is male or female?

▶ The fertilized egg develops into a free-swimming larva with a flagellum. After a short time, the sponge larva loses its flagellum. Then, the sponge larva attaches itself to a rock or the ocean floor for the rest of its life. Why do you think a sponge larva needs a flagellum, but a developing sponge does not?

Think & Discuss

1. What are amoebocytes? What is their function?

2. What substance makes up the spicules of a sponge used by people for bathing?

★ 3. Until the mid-nineteenth century, most scientists thought that sponges were plants. Why might scientists have considered sponges to be plants?

12-2 Cnidarians

The phylum Cnidaria includes more than 9000 species of animals. Like sponges, all cnidarians live in water. Most live in salt water. Sea anemones, corals, and jellyfish are examples of marine cnidarians. The hydra is an example of a freshwater cnidarian.

Key Points
- Cnidarians live either as a polyp or as a medusa.
- Hydra, corals, sea anemones, and jellyfish are examples of cnidarians.

Body Forms

Cnidarians have either one of two body forms. One body form looks like a cup or vase. The cuplike form of a cnidarian is called a **polyp** (PAL-ip). A polyp lives attached to rocks or other surfaces. The other body form looks like an opened umbrella. The umbrellalike form of a cnidarian is called a **medusa** (muh-DOO-suh). The medusa form is free-swimming.

The easiest way to tell whether a cnidarian is a polyp or a medusa is by the location of its mouth. The mouth of a polyp is in an upward position. A medusa always has its mouth in a downward position. Why would the mouth of a polyp always be in an upward position?

Structure of Cnidarians

The body structure of cnidarians is very similar to the body structure of sponges in some ways. For example, both sponges and cnidarians have bodies made up of two layers of cells separated by a jellylike material. The outer layer of cells is called the ectoderm. What do you think the inner layer of cells is called?

Although they share some characteristics, cnidarians are more complex than sponges. For example, all cnidarians have long armlike structures called **tentacles** (TEN-tuh-kuls). Located on the tentacles are special stinging cells called **cnidocytes** (NY-duh-syts). Cnidarians are named for the cnidocytes found on their tentacles. Cnidarians use their tentacles and cnidocytes to help them catch much larger organisms for food.

➤ Cnidarians may have as few as 6 or as many as 100 tentacles. Look at how the tentacles are arranged around the mouth of the polyp and the medusa shown in Figure 12-4. How do you think this arrangement helps a cnidarian get food?

All cnidarians have tentacles surrounding their mouths. In fact, all the body parts of a cnidarian are arranged around its mouth much as the spokes of a bicycle wheel are arranged around its hub. This arrangement is called **radial symmetry** (RAY-dee-uhl SIM-uh-tree).

The tentacles of cnidarians have **nematocysts** (NEM-uh-toh-sists), or coiled stingers, inside their cnidocytes. When a small fish gets close enough, a

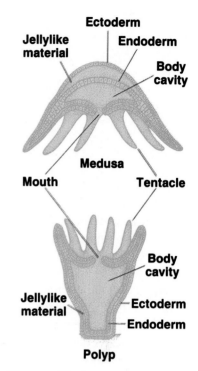

Figure 12-4   How does a medusa differ from a polyp?

ACTIVITY 12-1

PROBLEM: How can you find the symmetry of an organism?

Science Process Skills
analyzing, predicting, inferring

Background Information
The symmetry of an object or an organism is the arrangement of its parts around a point. You can draw a line or lines through an object or an organism to show its symmetry. Organisms without a definite shape are asymmetrical. Organisms that are spheres have spherical symmetry. Some organisms can be divided into two equal and almost identical halves in one place. One half is a mirror image of the other half. These organisms have bilateral symmetry. Other organisms have body parts around a central area. These organisms have radial symmetry.

Materials
ruler	tracing paper
pencil	magazines

Procedure
1. Study the examples of symmetry shown.

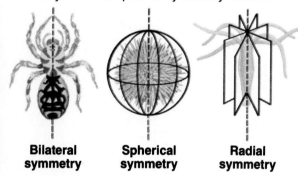

| Bilateral symmetry | Spherical symmetry | Radial symmetry |

2. Using tracing paper, trace the outlines of the 8 organisms shown.
3. Using your ruler and pencil, draw a line or lines through each organism's outline to show its symmetry.
4. Label the symmetry of each organism.

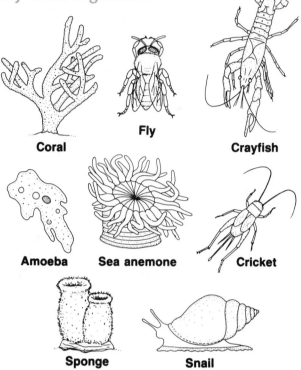

Coral   Fly   Crayfish

Amoeba   Sea anemone   Cricket

Sponge   Snail

5. Find 10 pictures of organisms in a magazine. Trace their outlines. Then repeat steps 3 and 4.

Observations
1. Do all organisms have the same symmetry?
2. Do any of the organisms you traced have more than one type of symmetry?

Conclusions
1. Can symmetry be used to describe different organisms? Explain.
2. What type of symmetry do people have?
3. **INFER** What type of symmetry do you think is most common in higher animals? Why?

Going Further
Use a dictionary to define the following: dorsal, ventral, caudal, cranial, posterior, and anterior. After you define the terms, find a picture of an animal and label the animal using the terms.

cnidarian shoots it with one or more of its nematocysts. Then the tentacles draw the wounded fish into the mouth of the cnidarian.

Food is taken in through the mouth and passes into the body cavity of the cnidarian. Inside the body cavity, food is digested, or broken down into usable forms. After the food is broken down, food particles are absorbed by the cells that line the body cavity. Undigested food is released through the mouth of the cnidarian.

Examples of Cnidarians

The phylum Cnidaria is made up of three classes. The three classes include the hydras and related animals, sea anemones and corals, and the jellyfishes. There are about 3700 species of hydra (HY-druh) and related animals. Sea anemones and corals are classified into about 6100 species. More than 200 species of jellyfish have been classified.

Hydra

Hydras are small cnidarians that live near the surface of freshwater streams and ponds. Most hydras are either white or brown. However, some hydras may look green

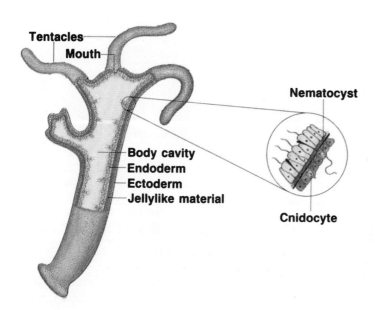

Tentacles
Mouth
Nematocyst
Body cavity
Endoderm
Ectoderm
Jellylike material
Cnidocyte

Figure 12-5 Notice the bud forming on the side of the hydra. The bud will grow into a new hydra.

because of algae living beneath their outer layer of cells. Because hydras live in shallow water, algae living inside the hydra are able to obtain enough sunlight for photosynthesis. Why do you think green hydras would not be found living in caves or under rocks?

Most of the time, hydras live as polyps attached to underwater objects. However, hydras can move from place to place. They move by releasing air bubbles that loosen them from rocks on the pond floor. Once it is free, a hydra moves by floating upside down, sometimes with a somersaulting motion.

Corals and Sea Anemones

Corals and sea anemones are polyps that live attached to rocks on the ocean floor. Because they have brightly colored bodies and waving tentacles, corals and sea anemones often are called flower animals. Many people think that the tentacles of these animals look like flower petals.

Corals and sea anemones are different in several ways. First, sea anemones are much larger than corals. Second, sea anemones do not have an outer skeleton and corals do. Corals have hard, rocklike skeletons. Finally, sea anemones live as individuals, while corals live in huge colonies called coral reefs.

Figure 12-6 The red sea anemone (left) can be found off the coast of Maine. The coral polyps (right) live in the coastal waters of Hawaii.

ACTIVITY 12-2

PROBLEM: How do hydras move about, feed, and reproduce asexually?

Science Process Skills
observing, sequencing, organizing

Background Information
Hydras are simple, stinging-celled animals that can reproduce either sexually or asexually. Most of the time, hydras remain attached to objects. However, hydras can move. They move around to find more favorable environments. Hydras do not move to chase prey.

Materials
paper and pencil

Procedure
1. Study the diagram that shows one of the ways in which a hydra can move.
2. On a sheet of paper, place the drawings for movement in the proper sequence using the letters beneath each drawing.
3. Study the food-getting diagram.
4. Place the drawings in the proper sequence, using the letters beneath each drawing.
5. Study the diagram of asexual reproduction in a hydra. Repeat step 4.

Observations
1. In your own words, explain one way in which a hydra moves.
2. In your own words, explain how a hydra gets its food.
3. In your own words, explain how the hydra reproduces asexually.

Conclusions
1. What are the two ways in which a hydra moves?
2. What structures does a hydra use to move food to its mouth?
3. What type of asexual reproduction takes place in a hydra?
   - **a.** binary fission
   - **c.** budding
   - **b.** regeneration
   - **d.** spore formation

Going Further
Examine a hydra under a microscope or with a hand lens. Draw the hydra and identify its parts. How many tentacles does the hydra have?

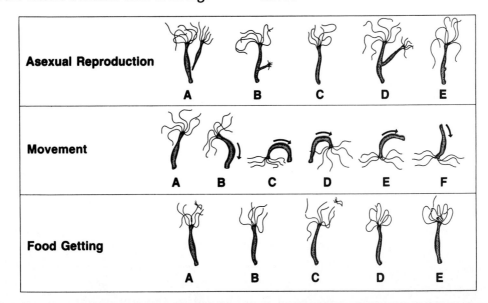

Fringing reef

Barrier reef

Atoll

Figure 12-7 The three kinds of coral reefs are a fringing reef, a barrier reef, and an atoll. The Great Barrier Reef is almost 2000 km long and 80 km wide.

Health and Safety Tip
Jellyfish stings can be dangerous. The poison from the cnidocytes can cause red welts to form on the skin. Never swim in an area where jellyfish warnings have been posted.

A coral reef is made up of billions of skeletons of dead corals that are covered by a layer of living coral polyps. A coral reef may be as much as 1500 m thick. Coral reefs are located in the shallow waters of the southern Pacific Ocean, Caribbean Sea, and Atlantic Ocean. Along the coastline of the United States, coral reefs are found off the coast of Florida.

There are three kinds of coral reefs. Examples of each kind of reef are shown in Figure 12-7. One kind is called a fringing reef. A fringing reef forms close to the shoreline of either an island or a continent. Coral reefs in the Caribbean Sea usually are fringing reefs.

Another kind of coral reef is a barrier reef. The largest barrier reef is the Great Barrier Reef, located off the coast of Australia. Because barrier reefs are formed when coastal areas sink into the sea, barrier reefs are located farther out in the ocean than fringing reefs.

The third kind of reef is called an **atoll** (A-tawl). An atoll is formed when a fringing reef sinks. Sometimes, an atoll forms around the top of a mid-ocean volcano.

Jellyfish

Jellyfish commonly are called cup animals. Some jellyfish have cups only 2 cm across. Other jellyfish may have cups more than 4 m across.

During its life cycle, a jellyfish lives as both a polyp and a medusa. The medusa is the sexual generation of a jellyfish. The polyp is the asexual generation.

You probably have never seen a jellyfish polyp. Few people have, because a jellyfish polyp is short-lived and attached to the ocean floor. A jellyfish lives as a free-swimming medusa during most of its life. The jellyfish medusa swims or floats with a jerky motion. The jerky motion is caused by water being taken in and released. As the water is released, the medusa is pushed forward.

Most people are familiar with the free-swimming medusa form of a jellyfish and its long, stinging tentacles. The stinging tentacles of some jellyfish may be up to 70 m long. A jellyfish medusa usually uses its tentacles to catch small fish. However, people are sometimes stung by jellyfish. For this reason, jellyfish warnings are sometimes posted at beaches during the summer.

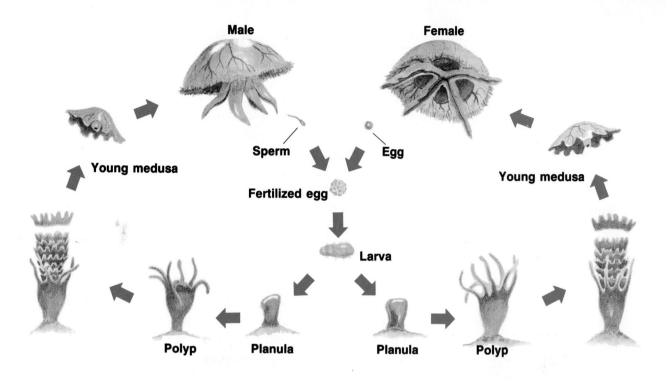

Male   Female

Sperm   Egg

Young medusa   Young medusa

Fertilized egg

Larva

Polyp   Planula   Planula   Polyp

Figure 12-8   During its life cycle, the jellyfish *Aurelia* goes through both polyp and medusa stages.

During sexual reproduction, a male jellyfish medusa releases sperm and a female releases eggs into the water. After the eggs are fertilized, they develop into oval-shaped larvae. The larvae have tiny hairlike cilia covering their bodies. In Figure 12-8, you can see that a jellyfish larva does not look at all like an adult jellyfish.

Once a larva attaches its body to a rock or piece of seaweed, it is called a **planula** (PLAN-yoo-luh). The planula grows a mouth and tentacles. After a planula develops a mouth and tentacles, it is called a polyp. As a jellyfish polyp develops, its body divides into saucerlike structures. These saucerlike structures soon break off, one by one, and swim away as young medusas.

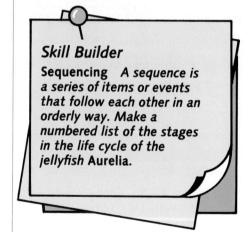

Skill Builder

Sequencing   *A sequence is a series of items or events that follow each other in an orderly way. Make a numbered list of the stages in the life cycle of the jellyfish* **Aurelia.**

Think & Discuss

4. How does a polyp differ from a medusa?

5. What is a cnidocyte?

6. Name four cnidarians.

7. What type of body form does a hydra have? Explain why.

8. Compare the movement of a sea anemone to a jellyfish medusa.

12-3 Importance of Porifera and Cnidarians

- Natural sponges are used by people for cleaning and bathing.
- Coral reefs protect coastal areas and provide marine organisms with food and a place to live.

Figure 12-9 Sponges are still harvested in parts of Florida.

People have used natural sponges for more than 2000 years. For example, the early Greeks used natural sponges for cleaning and bathing. Today, natural sponges are still used for these purposes. For example, hospital patients often are bathed with natural sponges. Sponges also are used by many people to apply and remove cosmetics. Why do you think a natural sponge would be better for bathing than a synthetic sponge?

In some parts of the Gulf of Mexico and the Mediterranean Sea, natural sponges are commercially grown. Sponge farmers use a sponge's ability to regenerate its body parts to grow large sponge beds. Sponges are cut into pieces and spread along the sea bottom in much the same way as a farmer plants seeds in a field.

When the sponges are mature, they are harvested by divers. Sponges also are harvested by dragging the sponge beds with large hooks. Then the sponges are brought to shore and dried. The sponge skeletons that remain are washed, sorted by size, and sent to market.

Coral reefs are valuable to marine organisms. For example, coral reefs are important sources of food and shelter for fish and many other marine organisms. Coral reefs also protect coastal areas from damage caused by large storm waves.

Pollution has become a threat to the survival of many coral reef environments. For example, water pollution from the dumping of sewage and oil spills kills corals that live on top of a reef. After the living corals are killed, waves and currents break apart the coral skeletons that make up the reef. Soon, the coral reef is completely destroyed.

Think & Discuss

9. What is a coral reef?
10. Name two ways that people use natural sponges.
11. What effect do you think the destruction of a coral reef would have on the fish and other marine organisms living near it?

What do oil rigs, old tires, sunken ships, junk cars, and concrete blocks have in common? All of these materials have been used to build artificial reefs.

A reef is a ridge of sand, coral, or other material at or near the surface of water. You may be familiar with coral reefs, which form from the remains of dead sea animals known as corals.

Reefs are important because they attract large numbers of fishes and other water animals. Some of the best fishing spots in the world are located near reefs. For this reason, people thought, "Why not build an artificial reef in an area that is convenient for fishing?" This is exactly what the Japanese have been doing for more than 300 years.

Artificial reefs have been used in America for more than 100 years. The first artificial reef in the United States was built in 1830 off the coast of South Carolina. The reef was made up of logs attached to the ocean floor by rocks.

The idea of building artificial reefs is not new. However, modern research and technology are now being used to improve artificial reefs and to make sure that they do not damage the environment.

One goal of Japanese scientists is to design reefs that will attract certain kinds of fishes. So far, the scientists have classified over 100 kinds of fishes according to the kind of reef that these fishes prefer. By learning about the behaviors of fishes, scientists can design reefs that will attract the kinds of fishes that people use as food.

What makes an artificial reef so attractive to fishes? Scientists are not sure. Some scientists think that fishes use artificial reefs to help them navigate in the ocean. Other scientists feel that reefs provide protection from water currents, strong sunlight, and predators. Most scientists agree that fishes are attracted to the food sources provided by the reefs.

In addition to attracting fishes, artificial reefs are useful in another way. Scientists have discovered that artificial reefs can be used to prevent shoreline and beach erosion. A reef that was built offshore from Palm Beach, Florida, has been very effective in stopping beach erosion without destroying the beauty of the shoreline.

To Think About
- Can an artificial reef have a harmful effect on the environment? Explain.
- How does an artificial reef prevent shoreline and beach erosion?

Chapter Review

CHAPTER SUMMARY

12–1 Porifera

- Sponges are invertebrates that have a hollow body, an osculum, pores, two layers of cells, and spicules.
- Sponges reproduce asexually by budding and regeneration.
- Sponges reproduce sexually by the joining of sperm cells and egg cells.

12–2 Cnidarians

- A cnidarian lives attached to a solid surface as a polyp or swims freely as a medusa.

- Corals, hydras, and sea anemones are cnidarians that live as polyps.
- Jellyfish can live as both a polyp and a medusa.

12–3 Importance of Porifera and Cnidarians

- Natural sponges are used by people for cleaning and bathing.
- Coral reefs provide food for marine organisms and people. They also provide shelter for marine organisms.
- Coral reefs protect coastal areas from damage caused by storms.

VOCABULARY LIST

amoebocytes (201)
atoll (208)
cnidocytes (203)
collar cells (201)
ectoderm (200)

endoderm (200)
flagella (201)
gemmules (201)
invertebrates (199)
medusa (203)

nematocysts (203)
osculum (200)
planula (209)
polyp (203)
pores (200)

radial symmetry (203)
regeneration (202)
spicules (200)
spongin (201)
tentacles (203)

VOCABULARY REVIEW

Matching   Write the word or term from the Vocabulary List that best matches each description.

1. animals without backbones
2. whiplike structures of a collar cell
3. body arrangement of cnidarian
4. jellyfish larva
5. sponge buds
6. free-swimming form of a cnidarian
7. attached form of a cnidarian
8. stinging cells of a cnidarian
9. cells between the endoderm and ectoderm
10. opening at the top of a sponge
11. regrowth of an organism from a body part
12. kind of coral reef
13. inner cell layer

Finding Word Relationships   Pair each numbered word with a word in the box. Explain in complete sentences how the words are related.

nematocysts	endoderm	medusa
spongin	flagella	coral
pores	budding	opening
buds	larva	regrowth

1. Porifera
2. tentacles
3. spicules
4. collar cells
5. regeneration
6. polyp
7. atoll
8. ectoderm
9. osculum
10. planula
11. gemmules
12. asexual reproduction

True or False   Write true if the statement is true. If the statement is false, change the underlined word or words to make the statement true.

1. The surface of a jellyfish is covered with many pores.
2. The outer layer of cells of either a sponge or cnidarian is called the ectoderm.
3. Some sponges have rubberlike spicules made of calcium.
4. Invertebrates are animals that do not have backbones.
5. The flagella of amoebocytes help a sponge keep a steady flow of water coming into its body.
6. The umbrellalike form of a cnidarian is called a polyp.
7. A coral has a rocklike skeleton.
8. Coral reefs that form around mid-ocean volcanoes are called fringing reefs.
9. Undigested food is released through the pores of a cnidarian.
10. The polyp is the asexual generation of a jellyfish.

Question and Answer   Rewrite each heading in the Chapter Outline on page 198 as a question. Then, answer each of the questions you have written.

Understanding a Diagram   Use the diagram of the life cycle of a jellyfish (*Aurelia*) shown in Figure 12–8 (page 209) to answer each of the following.

1. Which jellyfish fertilizes the egg?
2. Name the stage between the fertilized egg and the planula.
3. What body form does the adult jellyfish develop into?
4. How are the planula and the polyp stages different from the young medusa?

Writing the Main Ideas   Using the Chapter Outline on page 198, write the main idea for each heading in the outline.

Critical Thinking   Answer each of the following in complete sentences.

1. Why do you think biologists are interested in the way sponges can grow entire bodies from fragments?
2. Why should swimmers or bathers get out of the water if they see jellyfish close to shore?
3. Compare the way a cnidarian gets food with the way a sponge gets food.
4. Why do sponge farmers cut up sponges and throw them back into the water?
5. What do you think would happen to a cnidarian if it were born without cnidocytes and nematocysts? Explain.

1. Coral reefs are important to people living on some islands in the Pacific Ocean. Using library references, prepare a report about how coral reefs are used by people. Present your report to the class.
2. Natural sponges are used for cleaning. Make a flowchart that shows how natural sponges are cultivated and harvested.
3. Prepare a report on the three main kinds of coral reefs. Include how pollution affects these coral reefs.
4. Cut out pictures from old magazines of sponges, hydras, corals, sea anemones, and jellyfish. Paste each organism on a piece of construction paper under the heading Porifera or Cnidaria.

Chapter 13 | Worms

After you have completed this chapter, you will be able to

13-1 **discuss** the general characteristics of worms.

13-1 **name** the four phyla of worms.

13-2 **describe** the characteristics of flatworms.

13-3 **describe** the characteristics of roundworms and rotifers.

13-3 **list** three roundworms that cause disease in people.

13-4 **describe** the characteristics of segmented worms.

Science Process Skills

In this chapter, two science skills are highlighted. Symbols show some places where these skills are used.

▶ **Inferring:** When you infer, you form a conclusion based upon facts and not direct observation.

▲ **Organizing:** When you organize information, you put the information in some kind of order.

To many people, a worm is something that is long and soft, wiggles, and lives in the soil. These characteristics describe some worms. However, not all worms are the same. For example, not all worms live in the soil. Some kinds of worms live inside other living things. Other worms live in fresh or salt water.

One group of worms that live in the ocean are the feather-duster worms. Divers sometimes mistake feather-duster worms for underwater flowers. Feather-duster worms live in tubes that they make out of sand. These worms have beautiful feathery structures that extend from the tubes. The feathery structures are used to gather food. Sometimes feather-duster worms pull their feathery structures into their tubes to avoid predators.

13-1 Overview of Worms

Key Points

- Worms have bilateral symmetry and a mesoderm.

- The four phyla of worms are flatworms, roundworms, rotifers, and segmented worms.

Study Hint

After you read Section 13-1, list three characteristics of worms.

Worms are more complex than porifera and cnidarians. What are the main characteristics of worms? Unlike porifera and cnidarians, worms have three layers of cells. Worms also have organs and organ systems. The organs develop from the **mesoderm** (MES-uh-durm). The mesoderm is a layer of cells that forms between the ectoderm and the endoderm. Do porifera and cnidarians have a mesoderm?

▶ All worms have **bilateral symmetry** (by-LAT-uhr-uhl SIM-uh-tree). An animal with bilateral symmetry can be divided into similar halves at only one place, as shown in Figure 13-1. Do you have bilateral symmetry?

Like all animals with bilateral symmetry, worms have a head end and a tail end. Most animals with bilateral symmetry have nerve tissue and sense organs at their head ends. Most animals with bilateral symmetry also have a **dorsal,** or upper, side and a **ventral,** or lower, side.

How do biologists classify worms? Most biologists classify worms into four phyla. The four phyla include the flatworms, roundworms, rotifers, and segmented worms.

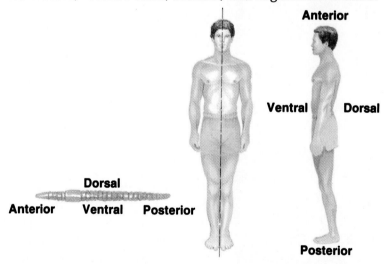

Figure 13-1 What is the front, or head, end of an animal with bilateral symmetry called?

Think & Discuss

1. What is the mesoderm?

2. List the four phyla of worms.

3. How is the adaptation of having sense organs in the head region helpful to organisms?

13-2 Flatworms

Have you ever thought of a worm as flat? Flatworms make up the phylum *Platyhelminthes* (plat-ee-HEL-minths). Biologists consider flatworms the least complex worms. Why? Flatworms do not have a space between their three cell layers. That is, they do not have a body cavity. More complex animals have a body cavity.

Because of its flat shape, all of a flatworm's cells are close to its environment. For this reason, flatworms do not need a respiratory or circulatory system. Oxygen and carbon dioxide diffuse directly into and out of its cells.

Flatworms are classified into three groups. Two groups are made up of parasitic worms. In one group, the flatworms are free-living. They move from place to place in search of food.

Tapeworms

Tapeworms are parasitic flatworms. You can observe the structure of a tapeworm in Figure 13-2. Notice that a tapeworm has a flat, ribbonlike body. A tapeworm does not have a digestive system or a mouth. It absorbs nutrients from its host directly through its skin.

The knob-shaped head of the tapeworm's body is called the **scolex.** Suckers and hooks are on the scolex.

Behind the scolex are body sections called **proglottids** (proh-GLAHT-ids). Each proglottid has nerves and flame

> **Study Hint**
>
> *After you read Section 13-2, make a chart listing the three kinds of flatworms and the characteristics of each group.*

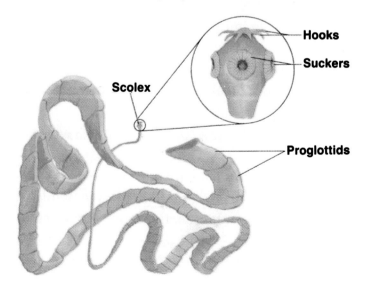

Figure 13-2 Compare the diagram of the scolex (left) with the photograph (right). Find the hooks and suckers.

Hooks

Suckers

Scolex

Proglottids

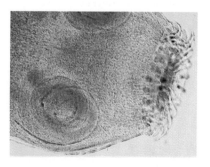

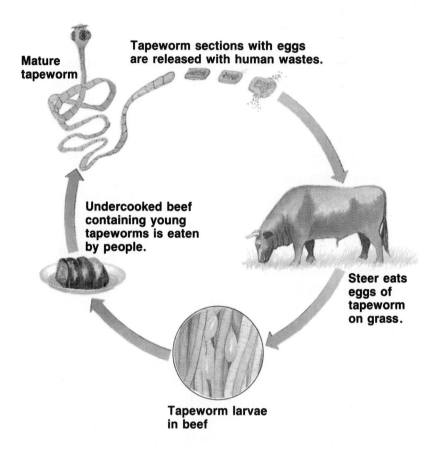

Tapeworm sections with eggs are released with human wastes.

Mature tapeworm

Undercooked beef containing young tapeworms is eaten by people.

Steer eats eggs of tapeworm on grass.

Tapeworm larvae in beef

Figure 13-3 Follow the sequence of steps in the tapeworm's life cycle.

Health and Safety Tip

People can become infected with tapeworms by eating raw or undercooked beef, pork, or fish. Always cook these foods thoroughly.

cells. Each proglottid also is filled with male and female reproductive organs.

⚠ Most tapeworms have a life cycle that involves more than one host. For example, the beef tapeworm spends part of its life cycle in cattle and another part in people. Refer to Figure 13-3 as you read about the life cycle of the beef tapeworm.

- Cattle eat grass containing proglottids and eggs.
- Larvae hatch and enter the bloodstream.
- The larvae then burrow into muscle tissue where they form cysts.
- People become infected when they eat beef that has not been cooked enough to kill the larvae in the cysts.
- Inside the human intestine, the larvae are released from the cysts and develop into adult tapeworms.
- The cycle continues when proglottids and eggs are released with human wastes.

Flukes

Flukes are parasitic flatworms that live inside the bodies of animals. Flukes are very well adapted to a parasitic way of life. For example, some flukes have a **cuticle** (KYOOT-i-kuhl) around their bodies. The cuticle is a nonliving layer produced by the fluke's outer cells. It protects the fluke from being digested by its host. Most flukes also have two suckers that they use to attach themselves to their host.

Most flukes have life cycles that involve more than one host. For example, the blood fluke, called *Schistosoma* (SHIS-tuh-sohm-uh), has two hosts. Its hosts are snails and people. The *Schistosoma* larvae must reach a host snail in a few hours in order to survive. In people, *Schistosoma* causes intestinal and urinary infections.

Schistosoma also causes a disease of the blood. Between 200 and 300 million people suffer from this disease. The disease occurs mostly in Asia, Africa, South America, and the Middle East.

The life cycle of *Schistosoma* can be explained in the following steps.

- Adult flukes develop in the bloodstream of people and produce large numbers of eggs. The eggs pass into a person's intestines and leave the body with wastes.

- The egg-infested wastes may be carried to a body of water as sewage. If the eggs are deposited in the water, they hatch into larvae.

- The larvae burrow into a snail. The larvae then reproduce asexually to form a different kind of larvae.

- The new larvae go back to the water.

- The larvae enter a person through the skin. Once inside, the larvae mature into adults.

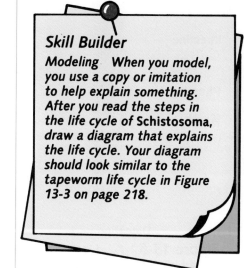

Skill Builder

Modeling When you model, you use a copy or imitation to help explain something. After you read the steps in the life cycle of **Schistosoma**, draw a diagram that explains the life cycle. Your diagram should look similar to the tapeworm life cycle in Figure 13-3 on page 218.

Turbellarians

Free-living flatworms are classified as turbellarians (tur-buh-LER-ee-uns). Most turbellarians live in the ocean. However, some live in fresh water. The planarian is a common, free-living flatworm that lives in fresh water. The planarian often is used as a model for describing all turbellarians.

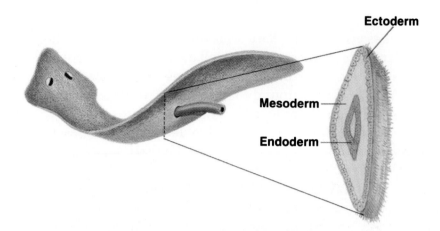

Figure 13-4 The planarian has three body layers. What is the middle layer called?

Look at the cross section of a planarian shown in Figure 13-4. This diagram shows the three layers of the planarian's body—the ectoderm, mesoderm, and endoderm. Notice that there is no space, or body cavity, between the layers. The space in the center of the endoderm is the planarian's digestive cavity.

Digestion and Excretion

Like other flatworms, the planarian has a one-way digestive system. Food enters and solid wastes leave through the same opening. A planarian takes in food by extending a tube called the **pharynx** (FAR-inks) from its mouth. Find the planarian's mouth and pharynx in Figure 13-5. The mouth and pharynx are located on the planarian's ventral surface. Food passes from the pharynx into the intestine, where it is digested and absorbed. Undigested food is excreted through the pharynx and the mouth.

Liquid wastes and excess water are removed from a planarian by a series of branching tubes. These tubes have tiny cells called **flame cells.** Each flame cell has cilia. The beating cilia make the cells look like flames. What do the cilia do? The cilia move liquid wastes into the tubes and out of the pores in the ectoderm.

Nervous Control

The planarian has a simple nervous system. The head region contains cells that are sensitive to touch, smell, and taste. The planarian also has two eyespots that are sensitive to light.

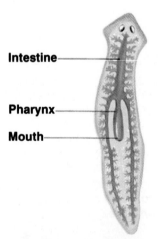

Intestine

Pharynx

Mouth

Digestion

Figure 13-5 Food is sucked into the planarian's mouth and passed into the intestine.

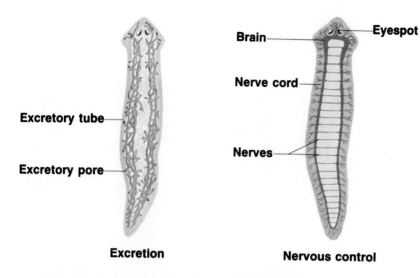

Excretory tube

Excretory pore

Brain

Eyespot

Nerve cord

Nerves

Excretion

Nervous control

Figure 13-6 Planaria have simple systems for excretion (left) and nervous control (right).

Masses of nerve cells called **ganglia** (GAN-glee-uh) are located near the eyespots. The ganglia form a simple brain. Two nerve cords are attached to the brain. The nerve cords are connected to each other by other nerves. You can see the planarian's nervous system in Figure 13-6. What common object does the nervous system look like?

Reproduction

Planaria can reproduce asexually as shown in Figure 13-7. If a planarian is cut into pieces, each piece will grow into a new organism. Freshwater planaria reproduce in this way. A planarian attaches one end of its body to a rock and stretches until it splits in half. Each half then grows into a new planarian.

Planaria also reproduce sexually. Like sponges, planaria produce both male and female sex cells. However, a planarian cannot fertilize itself. Two planaria fertilize each other. Once fertilization occurs, eggs are laid in protective capsules. New planaria hatch from the capsules in about two to three weeks.

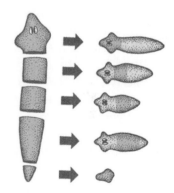

Figure 13-7 Can the tail end of a planarian grow into a new organism?

Think & Discuss

4. How does a planarian eat?
5. What is a fluke's cuticle?
★ 6. Why do you think the digestive system of a fluke is not as developed as the digestive system of a planarian?

ACTIVITY 13-1

PROBLEM: How do planaria respond to light and food substances?

Science Process Skills
observing, hypothesizing, predicting, analyzing

Background Information
Planaria are flatworms that live in fresh water. A planarian has a simple nervous system. It has many nerve cells in its head. All the nerve cells enable the planarian to detect changes in its surroundings. A planarian also has two nerves that extend the length of its body.

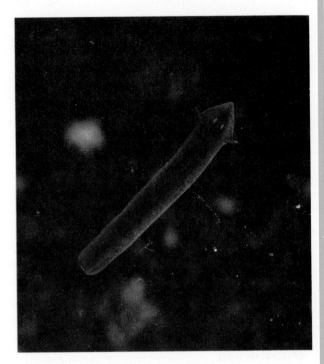

Materials

planaria culture	hand lens
3 small dishes	scissors
dropper	vinegar
liver	small index card

Procedure
1. Place several planaria in the three small dishes. Label the dishes "A," "B," and "C."
2. Using the hand lens, observe the movements of the planaria in each dish. Record your observations.
3. **HYPOTHESIZE** Do you think planaria will move toward or away from light, vinegar, and liver? Write your hypothesis on a sheet of paper. Your hypothesis should answer the question. To test your hypothesis, continue the activity.
4. Using the scissors, remove a very tiny piece of the liver. **CAUTION: Be careful when using scissors.** Place the piece of liver to one side in dish A.
5. Observe the response of the planaria. Record your observations.
6. Using the dropper, place a tiny drop of vinegar to one side in dish B.
7. Observe the response of the planaria. Record your observations.
8. Place dish C under a bright light. Place the index card across the top of the dish so that half of the dish is covered.

9. Observe the response of the planaria. Record your observations.

Observations
1. Describe the behavior of the planaria when they were first placed in the culture dishes.
2. **a.** How did the planaria respond to the liver in dish A? **b.** How did they respond to the vinegar in dish B? **c.** How did they respond to the light in dish C?

Conclusions
1. Do planaria move differently in response to different stimuli? Explain your answer.
2. Was your hypothesis correct? Use your observations to support your hypothesis.

Going Further
How do you think planaria would react to other stimuli? Select a stimulus. Then state a hypothesis. Design an experiment to test this hypothesis.

13-3 Roundworms and Rotifers

Roundworms and rotifers (ROHT-uh-furs) are two separate phyla of worms. However, these two groups of worms share certain characteristics. Both roundworms and rotifers develop a fluid-filled space between the endoderm and the mesoderm. The fluid-filled space helps support the body, and contains body organs.

Both roundworms and rotifers also have a complete digestive system. A complete digestive system has two openings—a mouth and an **anus.** Food enters through the mouth, and wastes leave the body through the anus.

Roundworms

Roundworms have long, slender bodies, which become thinner at the ends. A cuticle covers the outside of the body. Typical roundworms are shown in Figure 13-8.
▲ Roundworms are the most numerous kinds of worms. They live in soil, fresh water, and salt water. Some roundworms even live in hot springs and in the Arctic. Although most roundworms are free-living, some are parasites that do great damage to plants and animals. About 50 species of roundworms are parasites of people. Three kinds of roundworms that harm people are listed in Table 13-1.

TABLE 13-1 Common Roundworm Parasites		
Kind of Roundworm	Hosts Infected	Symptoms
Ascaris	Humans, dogs, cats, pigs, cattle, horses	Intestinal blockage, respiratory illness
Hookworms	Humans, dogs	Anemia
Trichina	Humans, pigs, dogs, cats, rats	Muscular aches, breathing difficulties

One harmful roundworm parasite is called trichina (tri-KY-nuh). At one stage in their life cycle, trichina worms live in the muscles of pigs and other animals. A person can become infected with trichina by eating undercooked pork infected with trichina. An infected person's muscles become inflamed and painful.

Key Points
- Roundworms and rotifers have a fluid-filled body cavity between the endoderm and mesoderm and a complete digestive system.

- Trichina, Ascaris, and hookworms are three roundworms that cause disease in people.

Female   **Male**

Figure 13-8 Notice the difference in size and shape between these male and female roundworms.

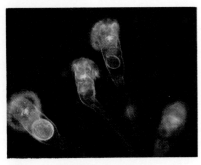

Figure 13-9 Locate the cilia on these rotifers.

Rotifers

Rotifers are microscopic worms that sometimes are mistaken for protozoans. Most rotifers are free-living. They are found in fresh water, salt water, and in moist soil.

Rotifers often are called the "wheel animals." The mouth of a rotifer is surrounded by a circle of cilia. Together, all of the beating cilia look like wheels turning. The beating cilia make a current that moves food into the mouth. The food is broken up by a muscular organ with jawlike structures. Then the food moves to the stomach and intestine. Undigested food passes out of the body through the anus.

Think & Discuss

7. Through what structure do wastes leave a roundworm?

8. What are three roundworms that harm people?

★ 9. Why do you think rotifers are sometimes mistaken for protozoans?

13-4 Segmented Worms

The phylum *Annelida* (AN-ul-id-uh) is made up of segmented worms. The word "annelid" means "little rings." If you look at the body of an annelid, you will see that it is divided into many ringlike sections, or segments. The segments are separated from each other by walls of tissue.

During their development, segmented worms develop a fluid-filled space, or cavity, in the mesoderm. Internal organs develop in this space. The organs are covered by the mesoderm, and are held in place by a membrane that develops from the mesoderm. Segmented worms have more highly developed organ systems than other kinds of worms.

Some segmented worms live in the ocean, and some live in fresh water. Others live in the soil. Earthworms and leeches are two common examples of segmented worms. The feather-duster worms shown in the photograph at the beginning of this chapter also are segmented worms.

Earthworms

You are probably more familiar with the earthworm than with any other kind of worm. Earthworms are a very important group of animals. Why? Earthworms help make soil good for growing plants. As earthworms move through the soil in search of food, they make holes and loosen soil. Water and air can then enter the soil and be used by plants. Also, the wastes of earthworms help fertilize the soil. One earthworm can produce its weight in fertile soil every day.

Have you ever seen an earthworm move? If you rub your finger along the side of an earthworm, you will feel tiny hairlike bristles called **setae** (SEET-ee). Each segment of the earthworm, except the first and last, has four pairs of setae. An earthworm also has two sets of muscles. Figure 13-10 shows how an earthworm moves using its setae and muscles.

Respiration

Have you ever held an earthworm? If so, you know that an earthworm is slimy. An earthworm is slimy because it produces mucus that keeps the skin moist. It is important for an earthworm's body to stay moist because the earthworm does not have a respiratory system. An earthworm takes in oxygen and gives off carbon dioxide directly through its skin.

Nervous Control

An earthworm has a well-developed nervous system. At its front end, the earthworm has a brain that is made up of ganglia. Each segment of an earthworm also contains

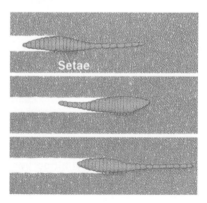

Figure 13-10   The muscles and setae of an earthworm (left) pull and push the worm through the soil (right).

Setae

ganglia. A ventral nerve cord runs from one end of the earthworm to the other. Smaller nerves attach to the ventral nerve cord to connect the brain with other parts of the body. An earthworm does not have eyes or ears, but it does respond to light, touch, temperature, and movement.

Digestion and Excretion

You know that an earthworm burrows in soil. As an earthworm moves through the soil, it sucks in soil using its muscular pharynx. Food moves from the pharynx through the tubelike **esophagus** (ih-SAF-uh-gus) and into the **crop.** The crop stores food temporarily. Then the food goes into the **gizzard.** The gizzard is a muscular organ that grinds food. From the gizzard, food moves into the intestine, where it is digested and passes into the blood. Undigested food and soil are eliminated through the anus.

Earthworms get rid of liquid wastes through tubelike structures called **nephridia** (ne-FRID-ee-uh). Each segment of an earthworm except the first three and the last one has two nephridia. Wastes from the blood pass into the nephridia and then are excreted.

Circulation

The earthworm has a closed circulatory system. In a closed circulatory system, blood moves through the body in tubes. You have a closed circulatory system, too.

In an earthworm, blood is pumped through the body by five pairs of tubes called **aortic arches** (ay-AWR-tic ARCH-es). Blood flows from the head of an earthworm to

Study Hint

As you read about the earthworm's digestive system, list the organs through which food passes in the proper order.

Figure 13-11 Locate the earthworm's nephridia. What is their function?

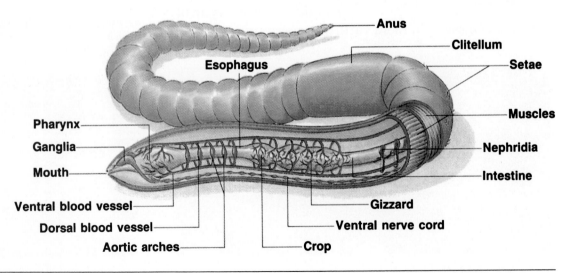

ACTIVITY 13-2

PROBLEM: What adaptations does an earthworm have for burrowing in soil?

Science Process Skills
observing, analyzing, inferring

Background Information
Earthworms are segmented and have bilateral symmetry. Gas exchange occurs through their moist skin. As earthworms burrow through the soil, they ingest the soil and feed on the nutrients in it.

Materials

live earthworm	toothpick
dissecting tray	dropper
hand lens	vinegar
paper towel	

Procedure

1. Wet a paper towel and place the towel in the dissecting tray.
2. Place an earthwom on the wet paper towel.
3. Make a sketch of the earthworm.
4. Use the toothpick to help you count the number of segments on the earthworm. Record the number of segments next to your sketch. **CAUTION: Be sure to keep the earthworm moist. Keep your hands wet when you handle the earthworm.**
5. Examine the ventral (lower) and dorsal (upper) surfaces of the earthworm. Record any differences.
6. Lightly rub your fingers along the earthworm's body. Describe how it feels.
7. Use the hand lens to find the setae. Observe their arrangement on each segment. On your sketch, draw and label the setae on one segment.
8. Use the dropper to place a drop of vinegar in front of the earthworm. Record your observations.

9. Replace the paper towel with a clean towel before continuing.
10. Observe the earthworm as it moves about in the tray. Watch the movement of each segment. Record your observations.
11. Return the earthworm to its environment. Wash your hands thoroughly with soap and water.

Observations

1. Describe the shape and feel of the earthworm.
2. **a.** How many setae are located on each segment of the earthworm? **b.** How are the setae arranged on each segment?
3. How did the earthworm react to the vinegar?

Conclusions

1. Based on your observations, does an earthworm use its setae to aid in movement?
2. What adaptations does the earthworm have for burrowing in soil?
3. Earthworms move away from light, especially sunlight. How does this response help the earthworm survive?

Going Further
Design an experiment to show that earthworms move away from light. Present your experiment and results as a class report.

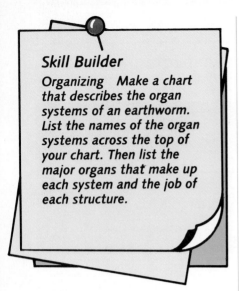
the tail end through the ventral blood vessel. Blood flows from the tail end to the head through the dorsal blood vessel. Blood travels through each segment in tiny tubes.

Reproduction

Earthworms reproduce sexually. Like many other worms, earthworms have both male and female sex organs. The male sex organs are located in the tenth and eleventh segments. The female sex organs are located in the thirteenth segment.

During reproduction, two earthworms come together and exchange sperm. After the worms part, the enlarged part of each earthworm, called the **clitellum** (kly-TEHL-uhm), makes a capsule. Eggs are fertilized in the capsule. Then the capsule is slipped off and left in the soil. After about two weeks, new earthworms hatch.

Earthworms also can reproduce asexually by regeneration. If an earthworm has been cut in two, both halves can grow into complete worms.

Leeches

Leeches are segmented worms that live in ponds and streams. Most leeches are external parasites that feed upon the blood of other animals.

Leeches were once used in medicine. Today, certain chemicals in the leeches' saliva are used to dissolve blood clots. These chemicals may also be helpful in treating heart attack patients.

► How do leeches feed upon the blood of animals? A leech has two suckers that it uses to attach itself to other animals. It also has three razor-sharp teeth for biting. A leech can take in three to five times its body weight in blood in a single feeding. After such a feeding, a leech does not need to feed again for several weeks. Do you think a leech could cause a person to die from loss of blood?

Figure 13-12   Leeches, like this one, are often found among plants in shallow ponds.

Think & Discuss

10. What are nephridia?
11. What is the function of an earthworm's aortic arches?
12. Why do you think earthworms avoid sunlight?

Protecting Your Pet From Worms

Your cat, who always gobbles his food with glee, walks listlessly past his dish. You pick up your cat and observe that he weighs less and that his coat is rough. Why might your cat have these symptoms?

One cause of these symptoms is worms. Other symptoms of worms include nervous behavior and abnormal bowel movements.

Roundworms, whipworms, and hookworms are common parasites of dogs and cats. Most parasitic worms live in the digestive systems of animals. Once inside the digestive system, worms take nourishment from the animals they infect.

If you think your pet has worms, you should take it to a veterinarian. Early treatment of worm infections can save your pet's life. You also can help protect your pet from parasitic worms by knowing how each kind of worm is most likely to infect an animal.

Dogs and cats get roundworms by swallowing roundworm eggs. This can happen if your pet eats an animal that is carrying roundworm eggs or if your pet eats dirt infected with roundworm eggs.

You can protect your pet from roundworms by feeding your pet a regular, balanced diet. This way, the pet probably will not pick up scraps of food from the ground or eat other animals. You also should keep your pet on a leash or confined in your yard.

Whipworms most often infect dogs. Whipworm eggs are passed out of an infected dog in its feces. These eggs will mature into infectious parasites if allowed to lie in soil for several weeks. If a dog then walks on the soil and licks its paws, the whipworms will enter the dog's body.

To prevent whipworm infection, you should encourage your dog to have bowel movements in a gravel- or pavement-covered area. This way, feces can be easily removed. Direct sunlight also helps destroy whipworm eggs, as does sprinkling the area with sodium borate.

Hookworms may be the most harmful parasites of dogs and cats. Hookworms enter an animal through its mouth or by penetrating the animal's skin. Cleanliness is your pet's best protection against hookworms. Pet products also are available for spraying areas that may become infected with hookworms.

Heartworm infection is common in dogs, but rare in cats. Heartworms invade the heart and prevent the dog from getting the oxygen it needs. Heartworms are carried by mosquitoes and enter a dog by way of mosquito bites. Keeping your dog indoors during summer evening hours when mosquitoes are active is one way to prevent heartworm infection. Your veterinarian also can prescribe medications that help prevent heartworm infection.

To Think About

- Why does keeping a dog in a yard help prevent it from getting worms?
- Do you think a pet is more likely to get worms in the winter or in the summer?

Chapter Review

CHAPTER SUMMARY

13-1 Overview of Worms

- Worms have an ectoderm, an endoderm, and a mesoderm.
- Worms have bilateral symmetry.
- Flatworms, roundworms, rotifers, and segmented worms are the four phyla of worms.

13-2 Flatworms

- Flatworms do not have a body cavity.
- Tapeworms, flukes, and turbellarians are three groups of flatworms.
- Tapeworms and flukes are parasitic flatworms.
- Turbellarians are free-living flatworms.

13-3 Roundworms and Rotifers

- Roundworms and rotifers have a cavity between the mesoderm and endoderm and a complete digestive system.
- Trichina, Ascaris, and hookworms are roundworms that harm people.
- Rotifers are microscopic worms.

13-4 Segmented Worms

- Segmented worms have many ringlike sections, or segments, a fluid-filled cavity in the mesoderm, and highly developed organ systems.
- Earthworms and leeches are two groups of segmented worms.

VOCABULARY LIST

anus (223)	cuticle (219)	gizzard (226)	proglottids (217)
aortic arches (226)	dorsal (216)	mesoderm (216)	scolex (217)
bilateral symmetry (216)	esophagus (226)	nephridia (226)	setae (225)
clitellum (228)	flame cells (220)	pharynx (220)	ventral (216)
crop (226)	ganglia (221)		

VOCABULARY REVIEW

Matching Write the word or term from the Vocabulary List that best matches each description.

1. grinds earthworm's food
2. bundles of nerve cells
3. upper side
4. middle cell layer
5. removes liquid wastes from planaria
6. a body with similar halves
7. lower side
8. sections of a tapeworm's body
9. pumps blood in the earthworm
10. nonliving layer

Identifying Relationships Identify the word or term in each group that does not belong. Explain why it does not belong with the group.

1. scolex, parasite, earthworm
2. ganglia, anus, mouth
3. clitellum, scolex, capsule
4. crop, setae, gizzard
5. flatworm, tube, esophagus
6. nephridia, wastes, crop
7. pharynx, cilia, food
8. cuticle, locomotion, setae
9. nervous system, flame cells, excretion
10. cuticle, free-living, flukes

Completion   Write the word or words that best complete each sentence.

1. In worms, organs develop from the cell layer called the _____.
2. The worm's nerve tissues and sense organs are at its _____ end.
3. The four phyla of worms are rotifers, roundworms, segmented worms, and _____.
4. Free-living flatworms live in _____.
5. Planaria can reproduce sexually or _____.
6. Roundworms and rotifers eliminate wastes through the _____.
7. Eating undercooked pork infected with _____ can cause a disease.
8. The bodies of earthworms and leeches are divided into _____.
9. An earthworm's skin must stay _____.
10. Most leeches feed upon the _____ of animals.

Finding the Main Ideas   Use the section number to find the sentence that answers each question. Then, write that sentence.

1. What is the mesoderm? (13-1)
2. Into what four phyla are worms classified? (13-1)
3. Why are *Platyhelminthes* considered the simplest worms? (13-2)
4. One group of flatworms is free-living. How are the others classified? (13-2)
5. What is meant by the term one-way digestive system? (13-2)
6. What is the purpose of the fluid-filled space in roundworms and rotifers? (13-3)
7. How can trichina harm humans? (13-3)
8. Why is ''little rings'' a descriptive term for the phylum *Annelida*? (13-4)
9. How are segmented worms classified? (13-4)
10. How does an earthworm take in oxygen? (13-4)

CONCEPT REVIEW

Writing for Understanding   One way to find out if you understand something is to write a brief summary of the information in your own words. Reread Section 13-1, Overview of Worms, on page 216, and write a brief summary of the information.

Critical Thinking   Answer each of the following in complete sentences.

1. How are earthworms helpful to people?

2. Why are segmented worms considered the most complex worms?
3. A trichina infection can be incurable. Why do you think it is difficult to treat?
4. Why do earthworms move out of the ground during a heavy rain?
5. Why do you think symptoms of tapeworm infection in an animal usually include weight loss and fatigue?

EXTENSIONS

1. Use library references to find out what measures are recommended to control the spread of different parasitic worms. Present your findings to the class.
2. Research the life cycle of a Chinese liver fluke. Then draw a diagram showing its life cycle.

3. Gather information on leeches for medicinal purposes. Write a report on your findings.
4. Use library references to learn about the evolutionary history of the different groups of worms. Write a report on your findings. You may wish to include an evolutionary tree.

Chapter **14** | Mollusks and Echinoderms

Chapter

Objectives

After you have completed this chapter, you will be able to

14-1 **list** the major characteristics of mollusks.

14-1 **name** examples of univalves, bivalves, and cephalopods.

14-2 **identify** two characteristics of echinoderms.

14-2 **describe** the structure of a sea star.

14-2 **list** four examples of echinoderms.

14-3 **discuss** the importance of mollusks to humans and other organisms.

14-3 **discuss** the importance of echinoderms.

Science Process Skills

In this chapter, two science skills are highlighted. Symbols show some places where these skills are used.

▶ **Inferring:** When you infer, you form a conclusion based upon facts and not direct observation.

▲ **Modeling:** When you model, you use a copy or imitation of an object to help explain something.

As you read the menu—clam chowder, oyster stew, linguine with clam sauce—does your mouth begin to water? Do you know what these delicious foods have in common? The clams, oysters, scallops, and mussels displayed in a seafood restaurant all belong to a group of animals called mollusks (MAL-uhsks). Clams and oysters often are used as foods. However, you may be less familiar with other mollusks that are used for food in various parts of the world. Have you ever eaten snails in garlic butter or squid cooked in its own ink? Snails and squids also are mollusks. Mollusks are an excellent source of protein that are low in calories, fat, and cholesterol.

14-1 Mollusks

Key Points

- Mollusks have soft bodies that often are covered by a shell. Mollusks also have three distinct body parts.

- Univalves include snails and slugs; bivalves include clams, oysters, and scallops; cephalopods include squids, octopuses, and the chambered nautilus.

Study Hint

As you read about the body structure of the mollusk, note that the shell is the outer part of the animal, followed by the mantle, and the mantle cavity.

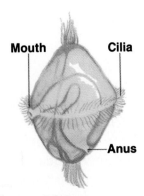

Figure 14-1 A trochophore has cilia to help it move through the water.

Have you ever walked along the beach and picked up shells? If so, you probably have picked up the shells of mollusks. Although some live in fresh water or on land, most mollusks live in the ocean. There are many different kinds of mollusks. Some mollusks that you may have seen in food stores or in photographs are clams, oysters, scallops, squids, and octopuses.

The word "mollusk" comes from the Latin word "mollis," meaning "soft." One characteristic of mollusks is that they have soft, fleshy bodies that often are covered by a hard shell. Mollusks also have three body parts. The three parts of a mollusk are the head, the foot, and the **visceral** (VIS-uhr-uhl) **mass.**

▶ The head of a mollusk contains the mouth. In some mollusks, the mouth is surrounded by one or more pairs of tentacles. What other animals can you name that have tentacles? How do you think a mollusk uses its tentacles?

The foot of a mollusk is muscular. In most mollusks, the foot is used for locomotion. A mollusk also may use its foot to burrow in sand or mud.

The visceral mass, or inside of a mollusk, contains the digestive system, the excretory system, the reproductive organs, and the heart. Covering the visceral mass is a thin membrane called the **mantle** (MAN-tul). The mantle secretes calcium carbonate. Calcium carbonate is the material that forms the mollusk shell.

During their development, mollusks pass through a larval stage. A mollusk larva is called a **trochophore** (TRAHK-uh-fawr). The trochophore is shaped like a top. Look at the trochophore shown in Figure 14-1. The ring of cilia around the middle helps the larva move and obtain food. The mollusk trochophore is very similar to the larval form of the segmented worms. For this reason, biologists think that these animals are closely related.

Univalves

Mollusks with one shell are called **univalves.** Univalves also are known as gastropods (GAS-troh-pods), which means "stomach-foot." There are more than 37,000 species of univalves. Univalves include snails and slugs. These animals live in water and on land.

Snails

Have you ever seen a snail in a pond or in an aquarium? If so, you probably noticed that the snail had a coiled outer shell. The shell is important to a snail because the snail can draw its head and foot into the shell for protection.

▲ Have you ever wondered how the snail got its coiled shell? During the trochophore stage, the snail's visceral mass begins to grow upward. This growth is uneven on the right and left sides of the snail's body. As a result, the snail's body begins to twist. The snail's body rotates so that the back end comes to rest just behind the head. You can imagine this rotation if you have ever watched a gymnast or an acrobat do a back flip. For a few seconds in the air, the acrobat's heels almost touch the head.

Two pairs of tentacles are located on the head of a snail. The longer pair of tentacles has eyes at the ends, and the shorter pair are sensitive to smell. The head also contains a mouth and jaw.

Most snails are plant eaters. They scrape food from plants with a rough tongue called a **radula** (RAJ-oo-luh). The radula is like a file, with hooked, toothlike structures.

The foot of a snail is flat and muscular, and is used for movement. A layer of mucus is secreted by the foot. As the foot muscles contract, the snail moves smoothly over the layer of mucus.

Have you ever heard the expression, "at a snail's pace"? If traffic is moving "at a snail's pace," is the traffic moving quickly or slowly? If you said slowly, you are correct. Snails move very slowly, at a rate of about 5 cm per minute.

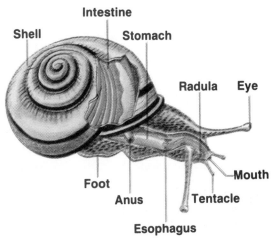

Figure 14-2   Notice the coiled shell of the land snail (left). Study the parts of the snail (right).

Intestine
Shell
Stomach
Radula   Eye
Foot
Mouth
Anus
Tentacle
Esophagus

Figure 14-3 Brightly colored sea slugs live in warm, shallow coastal waters.

Slugs

Most slugs do not have a shell. Some slugs, however, may have a small inner shell. Slugs live in the ocean, in fresh water, and in moist areas on land. Sea slugs are among the most beautifully colored animals in the ocean.

Bivalves

Mollusks that have two shells are called **bivalves.** Clams, oysters, mussels, and scallops are bivalves with which you may be familiar. All bivalves live in the ocean or in fresh water. Bivalves obtain the oxygen they need for respiration with **gills.** Gills are respiratory organs that absorb dissolved oxygen from water. The gills are located between the mantle and the visceral mass.

Clams

The body of a clam is completely enclosed in its two-part shell. A hinge on the back side of the clam joins the shell parts together. Two large muscles hold the shells tightly shut. If you have ever tried to open a clam using only your hands, you know how strong these muscles are.

Clams have a simple system for obtaining oxygen. Water enters the clam through an **incurrent siphon** (in-KUR-unt SY-fuhn), or incoming tube. Cilia push the water through the incurrent siphon and over the gills. The gills absorb oxygen from the water, and release

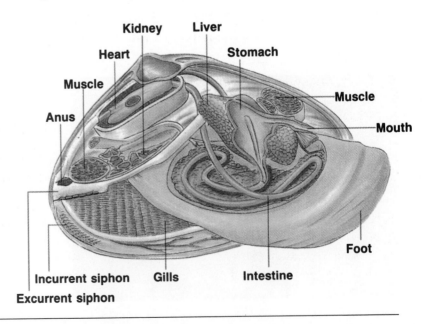

Figure 14-4 Locate the internal organs of the clam. Usually, a clam remains buried in mud with only its two siphons exposed.

ACTIVITY 14-1

PROBLEM: How can you determine the age of a clam?

Science Process Skills
observing, measuring, analyzing

Background Information
Most mollusks, such as clams and mussels, have hard protective shells. Clams grow in size each year. However, they do not shed their old shells and grow new ones. Instead, new layers are added to the shell as the clam grows. Like clams, many other mollusks increase in size by adding a new layer to their shells each year.

Materials
4 clam shells
hand lens
metric ruler
masking tape

Procedure
1. Copy the Data Table shown.

Data Table:	Clam Shell Bands		
SHELL	AVERAGE BAND WIDTH	NUMBER OF BANDS	AGE OF SHELL
A			
B			
C			
D			

2. Obtain 4 clam shells of different sizes. Arrange the shells in order from largest to smallest.
3. Use the masking tape to make labels for the shells. Label the shells A, B, C, and D. (Shell A should be your largest shell.)
4. On shell A, measure the width of 5 different bands in millimeters.
5. Determine the average width of the bands. To find the average width, add the 5 widths together and divide the total by 5. Record the average in the Data Table.

6. Repeat steps 4 and 5 for shells B, C, and D.
7. Use the hand lens to help you see the bands clearly. Count the number of bands on each shell starting with the crown of the shell. Record the number of bands on each shell in the Data Table.
8. Determine the age of each shell. The age of the shell in years is the number of bands counted for the shell. Record the age of each shell in the Data Table.

Observations
1. **ANALYZE** **a.** Was the average width of the bands the same for each shell? **b.** Did larger shells have wider bands?
2. Did the larger shells have more bands than the smaller ones?
3. Which shell is the oldest?

Conclusions
1. How is the age of a clam's shell related to the number of bands of the shell?
2. Which of the following would be the best name for these bands? Explain your answer.
   a. clam rings **b.** shell rings **c.** age rings

Going Further
Could the same method of age determination be used for other mollusks? State a hypothesis. Describe an experiment that would test your hypothesis. List the steps of your experiment.

Figure 14-5 Notice the tiny eyes along the edge of the mantle of the scallop.

carbon dioxide. The water then passes out of the clam through the **excurrent** (ek-SKUR-unt) **siphon,** or outgoing tube.

Because they filter food from ocean water, clams often are called "filter feeders." Mucus in the gills traps microorganisms living in the water. These microorganisms are food for the clam. Cilia move the food-carrying mucus from the gills toward the clam's mouth.

Oysters and Scallops

An oyster has a body structure similar to that of a clam. Like the clam, the oyster is a filter feeder. Unlike the clam and many other bivalves, the oyster does not move from place to place. Instead, an oyster cements one of its shells to an object, such as a rock.

Scallops are bivalves that live on the ocean bottom. The scallop has a row of steel-blue eyes along the outer edge of its mantle. These eyes are able to sense sudden changes in light.

A scallop swims by opening and closing its shells. This opening and closing motion causes a stream of water to shoot out between the shells. The force of the water acts as a jet propulsion system, moving the scallop in the opposite direction.

Cephalopods

The word **cephalopod** (SEF-uh-loh-pahd) has two parts, "cephalo-" and "-pod," which are root words. "Cephalo-"

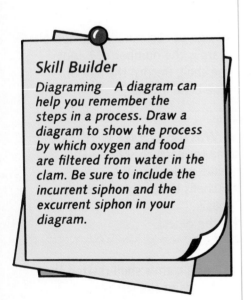

Skill Builder

Diagraming   A diagram can help you remember the steps in a process. Draw a diagram to show the process by which oxygen and food are filtered from water in the clam. Be sure to include the incurrent siphon and the excurrent siphon in your diagram.

ACTIVITY 14-2

PROBLEM: How can you use a model to illustrate the way a squid moves?

Science Process Skills
predicting, observing, modeling, measuring

Background Information
When octopuses and squids need to move about in a hurry, such as in escaping from a predator, they use a type of movement called jet action. This type of movement is achieved by taking in water and then squirting it out through a tubelike structure.

Materials

balloon	heavy string
paper clip	metric ruler
masking tape	

Procedure

1. Take a length of string and stretch it tightly between two chairs that are about 3 m apart. Tie the string securely to the back of each chair.
2. Take a paper clip and bend the inner loop outward so that it makes a right angle to the outer loop. Tape the smaller loop to the middle of an uninflated balloon.
3. Blow up the balloon and hold the end closed with your fingers. Slip the loop of the paper clip over the string and release the balloon. Record the direction that the balloon moves.
4. Inflate the balloon to different sizes and release it. Record the direction and distance for each test.
5. Measure and record the distance in centimeters that the balloon moved.

Observations
1. **a.** Did the balloon travel in the same direction for all of your tests? **b.** In which direction did the balloon travel?
2. How did inflating the balloon to different sizes affect the distance it traveled?

3. **MODEL** Draw the outline of the inflated balloon. If the balloon were a squid, label the mouth, the body, and where the tentacles would be. Use arrows to show the direction of the water and the direction in which the squid would move.

Conclusions
1. How does the movement of the balloon compare to the movement of octopuses and squids?
2. How does inflating the balloon with different amounts of air compare to an octopus or a squid taking in and releasing different amounts of water?
3. Use your observations to explain this statement: "For every action, there is an equal and opposite reaction."

Going Further
The chambered nautilus is an unusual organism. It has the ability to raise and lower itself to different levels in the ocean. Write a report on the way the buoyancy system of the chambered nautilus works.

means head and "-pod" means foot. Another name for the cephalopods is "head-foot" mollusks. Cephalopods include the squid, octopus, and chambered nautilus.

Cephalopods may have an outer shell, an inner shell, or no shell at all. Cephalopods are the most highly specialized of all mollusks because they have a well-developed brain and nervous system. All cephalopods also have tentacles.

Octopuses and Squids

The tentacles of octopuses and squids are used for movement and for capturing prey. Octopuses have eight tentacles. Squids have ten tentacles. One pair of the squid's tentacles is longer than the other four pair. The squid uses these tentacles to grab its prey. The shorter tentacles then hold the prey while the squid bites out chunks with its mouth.

Both octopuses and squids swim by jet propulsion. Water is drawn into the mantle cavity. The water is squirted out through a flexible funnel that is part of the animal's foot. This system of movement also includes a built-in steering mechanism. The octopus or squid can bend the funnel to propel itself in any direction.

Octopuses and squids protect themselves in several ways. First, their jet propulsion system provides a rapid escape. Second, octopuses and squids can change color to blend in with their surroundings. Special cells in an octopus or a squid contain different pigments. The pigment cells can change the color of the animal. Third, an octopus or squid can eject a cloud of purple ink when attacked by a predator. The cloud of ink confuses the attacker and gives the octopus or squid a chance to escape.

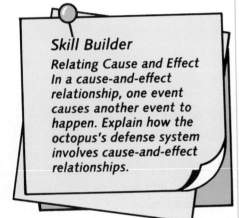

Skill Builder

Relating Cause and Effect
In a cause-and-effect relationship, one event causes another event to happen. Explain how the octopus's defense system involves cause-and-effect relationships.

Figure 14-6 The chambered nautilus (left) and the octopus (right) are cephalopods.

Chambered Nautilus

The chambered nautilus has an outer coiled shell with many chambers, or rooms. By taking in and releasing gas from these chambers, the nautilus can adjust to different water pressures. As a result, the chambered nautilus can live at any depth in the ocean, from sea level to the ocean floor.

Think & Discuss

1. What is a trochophore?
2. What is a radula?
3. List two examples each of univalves, bivalves, and cephalopods.
4. What are the three main body parts of a mollusk?
★ 5. Compare the body structure of a snail and a clam.

14-2 Echinoderms

If you walk along the beach, you may be lucky enough to find a sea star. Sea stars belong to a group of animals called echinoderms (ee-KY-noh-durms). "Echinoderm" means "spiny skin." Echinoderms probably first appeared about 500 million years ago. Today, there are 6000 species of echinoderms. Echinoderms include sea stars, sea cucumbers, sea urchins, and sand dollars.

Echinoderms have an internal skeleton, or **endoskeleton** (en-doh-SKEL-uh-tun). The endoskeleton is made up of spines. The spines are made up of small calcium plates covered by a thin layer of skin.

Echinoderm bodies usually consist of five arms around a central disk. The bodies are radially symmetrical, which means that the body can be divided into many identical parts. An example of radial symmetry is the arrangement of spokes around the hub of a wheel.

Unlike mollusks, echinoderms live only in the ocean. Also unlike mollusks, echinoderms do not have a well-defined head. Circulatory, respiratory, and excretory systems also are missing. Although echinoderms have a nervous system, they do not have a brain.

Key Points

- Echinoderms have radially symmetrical bodies and an internal skeleton.

- The body of a sea star consists of five tapering arms around a central disk.

- Other echinoderms include the sea cucumber, sea urchin, and sand dollar.

Sea Stars

Sea stars commonly are called starfish. Sea stars are not fish, but they are shaped like stars. Sea stars range in size from 1 cm to 1 m in diameter.

The body of a sea star is made up of a central disk surrounded by five tapering rays, or arms. In the central disk are the mouth and stomach. Surrounding the mouth is a nerve ring. The nervous system of a sea star consists of the nerve ring plus nerves that travel out from the ring to each of the five arms.

Like all echinoderms, sea stars have an organ system called the **water-vascular** (VAS-kyuh-luhr) **system.** The water-vascular system is used for movement and for getting food. The major parts of the water-vascular system are shown in Figure 14-7.

▲ Look at the water-vascular system. Find the sieve (SIV) plate. Water enters the sea star through this small opening. Water then moves through the stone canal. Use Figure 14-7 to trace the path of water in the ring canal and into the five radial canals. The ring canal circles the mouth. A radial canal extends down the length of each arm. In Figure 14-7, find the many **tube feet** connected to each radial canal. Tube feet are thin, hollow cylinders that end in suction disks.

Using its hundreds of tube feet, a sea star can move slowly over the ocean floor. Each tube foot acts like a suction cup. Press an eyedropper against your finger and squeeze the bulb. If you try to pull your finger away, you

Figure 14-7 What are two functions of a sea star's water-vascular system?

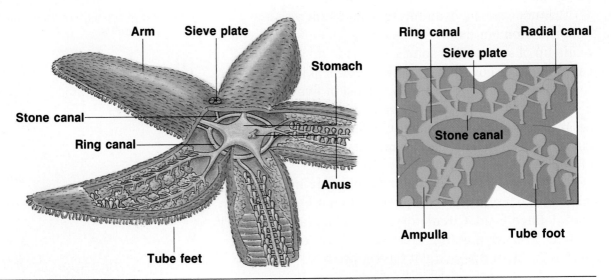

Arm   Sieve plate

Stomach

Stone canal

Ring canal

Anus

Tube feet

Ring canal   Radial canal

Sieve plate

Stone canal

Ampulla   Tube foot

can feel suction. The tube foot of a sea star acts on a rock in the same way.

▶ Sea stars eat mollusks. Remember that clams and other bivalve mollusks are protected by hard shells that are held tightly closed by muscles. The sea star, however, can work long and hard to open a clam shell. With its tube feet, the sea star pushes against the shells of a clam. For a time, the clam's muscles can keep the shells shut. Eventually, however, the clam's muscles tire. The shells open a crack and the sea star is ready to feed.

Sea stars eat clams and other mollusks in an unusual way. The sea star turns its stomach inside out through its mouth. The stomach is then pushed through the opening between the shells. Enzymes secreted by the stomach digest the clam inside its shell. Once the clam has been digested and eaten, the sea star pulls its stomach back in through its mouth and continues on its way.

Sea stars have another unusual property that is common to all echinoderms. This property is regeneration. Regeneration is the development of a whole new animal from one of its parts. If an arm of a sea star is cut off, the arm can regenerate a new sea star. However, the arm must still contain part of the central disk. Why do you think the arm of a sea star must contain part of the central disk in order to regenerate?

Other Echinoderms

The sea cucumber looks very different from the sea star, but the sea cucumber is an echinoderm. The sea cucumber was given its name because it is shaped like a cucumber. At one end of the sea cucumber's body is a

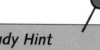

Study Hint

As you read about other echinoderms, make a simple sketch of each animal to help you remember its shape and characteristics.

Figure 14-8 The sea cucumber (left) has ejected its internal organs. Sea urchins are a favorite food of sea otters (right).

mouth surrounded by tentacles. At the other end is an anus.

The sea cucumber has an amazing defense system. When attacked by a predator, such as a crab, the sea cucumber ejects its internal organs. The organs secrete sticky threads around the predator while the sea cucumber escapes. The sea cucumber then regenerates its lost parts.

Sea urchins and sand dollars are echinoderms that do not have arms. Instead, these echinoderms are covered with movable spines. The sea urchins and sand dollars use the spines to move from place to place and to defend themselves. The sea urchin's large spines make the animal look like a prickly burr. Sand dollars are flat and smooth, with very small spines.

Think & Discuss

6. What is an endoskeleton?

7. What are tube feet?

8. Describe the structure of a sea star.

9. Name three echinoderms other than the sea star.

10. How does regeneration help sea stars survive as a species?

14-3 Importance of Mollusks and Echinoderms

Key Points

- Mollusks are important as a food source and for the value of their shells and pearls.

- Echinoderms do significant economic damage by preying on clams, oysters, and mussels.

Mollusks and echinoderms are important in a number of ways. For example, mollusks and echinoderms serve as food for many organisms, including people. Since ancient times, people have used clams, oysters, scallops, and mussels for food. Today, bivalves are more widely used for food than any other invertebrates. Other mollusks that are important food sources include squids, octopuses, and snails.

Univalves and bivalves also are economically important for their shells. In early civilizations, people made cooking utensils out of bivalve shells. These same shells also were used as money. Today, jewelry, buttons,

Figure 14-9 The waters around Japan are a good source of oysters that are harvested for their valuable pearls.

and other ornaments are made from the shells of clams and other bivalves. Shell collectors seek out the valuable shells of rare and beautiful mollusks.

Did you know that oysters produce pearls? Pearls form in an oyster when a piece of foreign matter, such as a grain of sand, becomes trapped between the mantle and the shell. Sand that becomes trapped in an oyster irritates the mantle. As a result, the mantle secretes calcium carbonate around the grain of sand. As more and more calcium carbonate is secreted, a pearl is formed.

Most pearls used in jewelry are found in oysters, but any bivalve can produce a pearl. Valuable pearls are very rare. In fact, you would have to open about 1000 oysters in order to find one usable pearl.

Snails also have economic value. For example, some snails are used as food. However, snails are plant eaters, and they destroy the plants on which they feed. Often these plants are valuable crop plants or garden plants. In some cases, snails also destroy trees, causing damage to forests and orchards.

Snails serve as hosts for disease-causing parasites, such as the fluke. The fluke is a flatworm that has a complicated life cycle involving several hosts. The snail is the host for the fluke's larvae.

You learned earlier that sea stars feed on clams and other bivalves. Each year, valuable clam, oyster, and mussel beds are destroyed by sea stars. At one time, the

Health and Safety Tip
Fishes are one of the fluke's hosts. Fish should always be cooked thoroughly before eating to kill any liver flukes that might be present.

Figure 14-10 A sea star feeds on a mussel that it has surrounded with its five arms.

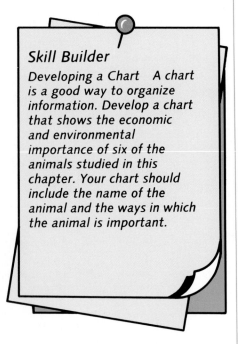

owners of the beds tried to get rid of the sea stars by cutting them into pieces. Unfortunately, the owners did not know about regeneration. Each part of the cut-up sea stars grew into a new animal. As a result, the mollusk bed owners soon had more sea stars than ever!

Today, sea stars often are caught in nets and then destroyed. In some places, lime is sprinkled over clam, oyster, and mussel beds. The lime kills sea stars, but does not harm mollusks.

Sea stars also feed on live coral. Brittle stars and crown-of-thorns sea stars often do great damage to coral reefs. Because coral reefs support a wide variety of animal life, this damage is harmful to the environment.

Some echinoderms are helpful to people. For example, some sea stars are ground up and used as plant fertilizer. Other echinoderms, such as the sea cucumber and sea urchin, are used as food sources in certain parts of the world. In China, for example, dried sea cucumbers are used in soups.

Think & Discuss

11. What is a fluke?

12. List three ways in which bivalves are economically important.

★ 13. If all the sea stars in a certain clam bed were destroyed, what might happen to animals that prey on sea stars?

Collecting Shells

Have you heard that if you hold a conch shell next to your ear, you can hear the ocean? Actually, you can hear the same sound by holding any cup-shaped object, including your hand, over your ear. But many shell collectors like to think that this sound is unique to shells, and that it reflects the ocean's mystery. In other ways, shells do reflect this mystery.

Shell collecting is an easy hobby to begin, especially if you live near the ocean. You can pick up many interesting and beautiful shells while walking along the beach. If a trip to the ocean is not possible you can buy shells from shell dealers, through mail-order catalogues, and from other shell collectors.

Why do people collect shells? Many people collect shells because they remind them of pleasant times spent on the beach or at sea. Other people collect shells because of their beautiful shapes and colors. You may be surprised to learn that some famous artists have been shell collectors. For example, both Leonardo da Vinci and Albrecht Dürer used shells as models for their drawings of spirals and curves.

Shell collecting also can have practical values. For example, shells often are made into jewelry, or used as decorations on boxes, lamps, or other items. Scientists collect shells because they reveal a great deal about the life history and habits of the animals that once lived in them.

Most shell collectors take time to label their shells. Once you begin collecting shells, you probably will want to buy a handbook that identifies and describes the different kinds. One such handbook is *The World of Shells—A Guide for Collectors* by S. Peter Dance.

Serious shell collectors often look for shells that contain living organisms.

The best place to look for live mollusks is in the area of the beach called "middle shore," which lies between the low-tide and high-tide lines. As you might expect, the best time to hunt for mollusks is during low tide. Divers and snorkelers often enjoy looking for shells under water. A good place to find mollusks is along the ledge that separates the shoreline from the ocean floor.

To Think About

- How might water pollution interfere with the hobby of shell collecting?

- How do you feel about capturing and eventually killing a live mollusk in order to obtain its shell?

Chapter Review

CHAPTER SUMMARY

14-1 Mollusks

- Mollusks have soft bodies that usually are covered by a protective shell.
- The three main body parts of a mollusk are the head, foot, and visceral mass.
- Three classes of mollusks are univalves, bivalves, and cephalopods.

14-2 Echinoderms

- Echinoderms have radially symmetrical bodies and an endoskeleton.
- The body of a sea star consists of five arms around a central disk containing the mouth, stomach, and nerve ring.

- Other echinoderms include the sea cucumber, sea urchin, and sand dollar.

14-3 Importance of Mollusks and Echinoderms

- Bivalves are important as a food source and for the value of their shells and pearls.
- Snails can cause damage to plants and are hosts to disease-causing parasites.
- Echinoderms prey on bivalve mollusks and damage coral reefs.
- Some echinoderms are used as food sources in certain parts of the world.

VOCABULARY LIST

bivalves (236)
cephalopod (238)
endoskeleton (241)
excurrent siphon (238)

gills (236)
incurrent siphon (236)
mantle (234)

radula (235)
trochophore (234)
tube feet (242)

univalves (234)
visceral mass (234)
water-vascular system (242)

VOCABULARY REVIEW

Matching   Write the word or term from the Vocabulary List that best matches each description.

1. contains the major internal organs of a mollusk
2. secretes material that forms the mollusk shell
3. organs that absorb dissolved oxygen
4. larval stage of a mollusk
5. one-shelled mollusks
6. rough, food-getting organ
7. mollusks with two shells
8. tube by which water comes into a clam
9. major organ system in sea stars
10. internal skeleton

Finding Word Relationships   Pair each numbered word with a word in the box. Explain in complete sentences how the words are related.

slug	scallop	file
organs	larva	oxygen
outgoing tube	shell	squid
sea star		

1. bivalve
2. tube feet
3. univalve
4. trochophore
5. cephalopod

6. gills
7. mantle
8. radula
9. excurrent siphon
10. visceral mass

True or False Write true if the statement is true. If the statement is false, change the underlined word or words to make the statement true.

1. A membrane called the <u>shell</u> covers the visceral mass of a mollusk.
2. Sea stars, like all echinoderms, have an <u>external</u> skeleton.
3. The development of a whole animal from one of its parts is called <u>regeneration</u>.
4. Snails are hosts for disease-causing flatworms called <u>flukes</u>.
5. Clams take in water through the <u>excurrent</u> siphon.
6. The shell of a mollusk is formed from a material secreted by the <u>visceral mass</u>.
7. The <u>water-vascular</u> system is the major organ system of <u>mollusks</u>.
8. The shell of a mollusk is made up of <u>silica</u>.

Question and Answer Rewrite each heading in the Chapter Outline on page 232 as a question. Then, answer each of the questions you have written.

Understanding a Diagram Use the diagram of the body structure of a clam shown in Figure 14-4 (page 236) to answer each of the following.

1. What organs does a clam use for respiration?
2. Through which organ does a clam take in water?
3. Name three structures located in the clam's visceral mass.
4. What is a second function of the gills?
5. What structure, not shown in Figure 14-4, surrounds the visceral mass?

Writing the Main Ideas Using the Chapter Outline on page 232, write the main idea for each heading in the outline.

Critical Thinking Answer each of the following in complete sentences.

1. Newton's third law of motion states that every action has an equal and opposite reaction. How does this law apply to the movement of squids and octopuses?

2. In what ways are pearls and mollusk shells alike?
3. How is the structure of a chambered nautilus helpful to its survival?
4. Why do you think a sea star would have trouble moving over soft surfaces such as sand or mud?
5. Why should snails used for food be carefully inspected and thoroughly cooked?

1. Many artists have used the spiral shell of the chambered nautilus in their work. Go to a library or art museum and look for examples of art that was inspired by the chambered nautilus. Share your findings with the class in a report, including illustrations.

2. Visit a local seafood store and find out what kinds of mollusks are sold as food. Find out which mollusks are the most popular food choice, where the mollusks come from, and which mollusks tend to be the least and most expensive. Present your findings in a chart.

Chapter **15** | Arthropods

After you have completed this chapter, you will be able to

15-1 **list** the major characteristics of arthropods.

15-2 **describe** the characteristics of arachnids.

15-3 **describe** the characteristics of crustaceans.

15-4 **compare** centipedes and millipedes.

15-5 **describe** the characteristics of insects.

15-5 **describe** ways insects communicate.

Science Process Skills

In this chapter, two science skills are highlighted. Symbols show some places where these skills are used.

Classifying: When you classify, you group things based upon similarities.

Analyzing: When you analyze, you break down a complex idea into simpler parts to make it easier to understand.

Are you afraid of tarantulas? Does the sight of a tarantula give you the "creeps?" Some people think that tarantulas make great pets. Most people, however, do not like to be near them. Tarantulas are just one example of the wide variety of animals called **arthropods** *(ar-thruh-PODS). Arthropods are the jointed-legged animals.*

Arthropods are the most numerous group of animals on Earth. About 1,000,000 species of arthropods have been identified, so far. For example, insects, ticks, spiders, and crabs are all arthropods. Some scientists estimate that as many as 10,000,000 arthropod species may be living on Earth.

15-1 Overview of Arthropods

Key Point

- Arthropods have jointed appendages, segmented bodies, an exoskeleton, and an open circulatory system.

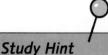

Study Hint

After you read Section 15-1, Overview of Arthropods, list five characteristics of arthropods.

Figure 15-1 A cicada molts its skin five times before it reaches adulthood.

Fossil records indicate that the first arthropods appeared on Earth more than 500 million years ago. However, many species have become extinct. Some ancient arthropods were much different from those that live today. For example, the wingspans of ancient dragonflies were more than half a meter across.

What are the main characteristics of arthropods? For one thing, all of the arthropods have jointed **appendages** (uh-PEN-dij-es). An appendage is any movable extension of an animal's body. Arthropods use their appendages for movement, food-gathering, chewing, and defense.

Like annelids, arthropods have segmented bodies. However, arthropods have fewer segments than annelids. Appendages are attached to the different segments.

Arthropods have a hard, outer covering called an **exoskeleton** (ek-so-SKEL-uh-tun). The exoskeleton is made up mostly of a substance called **chitin** (KYT-n). The exoskeleton protects and supports the body. An arthropod's exoskeleton also is waterproof.

The exoskeleton cannot grow as an arthropod grows. Thus, an arthropod must shed its exoskeleton as it gets bigger. The shedding process is called **molting.** As an arthropod molts its exoskeleton, a new exoskeleton is formed. The new exoskeleton is soft. During the time the new exoskeleton takes to harden, arthropods are not protected from predators. The arthropods also are not protected very well from drying out.

In addition to jointed appendages, segmented bodies, and an exoskeleton, all arthropods have an open circulatory system. In an open circulatory system, blood does not always flow through tubes. Instead, blood flows into cavities in the body and bathes the body organs. You have a closed circulatory system. You have many tubes that lead to and away from your heart.

Think & Discuss

1. What are appendages?
2. Why must an arthropod molt its exoskeleton?
3. Why do you think that many arthropods hide in secluded places when they shed their exoskeletons?

15-2 Arachnids

Did you answer yes to the question, "Are you afraid of tarantulas?" If so, you are afraid of one kind of arachnid (uh-RAK-nid). Arachnids are a class of arthropods that includes spiders, scorpions, and ticks. So far, scientists have identified more than 100,000 species of arachnids. Most arachnids live in warm, dry areas.

Arachnids have two main body parts: the head-chest section and the abdomen. You can observe the structure of a typical arachnid in Figure 15-2. Notice that six pairs of appendages are attached to the head-chest region. The first pair of appendages are used for feeding upon or killing prey. The second pair of appendages have different jobs in different arachnids. They may act as sense organs and be used for touching and smelling. In addition, the second pair of appendages may be used to hold food in place while the arachnid is feeding. The last four pairs of appendages are walking legs. Are any appendages attached to the abdomen?

Most arachnids have simple eyes at the front of their heads. For example, a spider has eight simple eyes arranged in two rows of four. Simple eyes can see only changes in light.

Spiders

You are probably more familiar with spiders than with any other group of arachnids. Spiders have a major role in the environment. By feeding mainly on insects, spiders help control insect populations.

Spider webs are familiar sights. Have you ever wondered how spiders make their webs? Do you know

Key Point
- Arachnids have bodies with two main sections and six pairs of appendages.

Study Hint

After you read Section 15-2, Arachnids, list three kinds of arachnids, and give three characteristics of each organism.

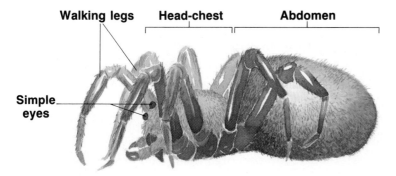

Walking legs   Head-chest   Abdomen

Simple eyes

Figure 15–2   How many body sections does a spider have?

Arthropods   253

Figure 15-3 Spider silk is a protein substance that hardens when it comes in contact with the air.

what spider webs are made of? Spider webs are made up of strands of silk. Spiders spin webs with **spinnerets** (spin-uh-RETS), which are small tubelike structures located near the rear of the abdomen.

Spider silk is not used only for building webs. Some spiders use silk to line their shelters. Others use silk to wrap up insects that the spiders store to eat later. Some baby spiders even use a strand of silk as a balloon to ride away in the wind to new places.

Have you ever seen an insect trapped in a spider's web? Building sticky webs is one way that spiders capture prey. However, not all spiders capture prey in webs. Some spiders actively chase their prey. Once spiders capture an insect, they use their first pair of appendages to kill it. The first pair of appendages are connected to poison glands. All spiders have poison, but only a few spiders are dangerous to people. The black widow spider and brown recluse spider are examples of harmful spiders.

Scorpions and Ticks

Scorpions are found mainly in tropical, subtropical, and desert areas. During the day, scorpions hide under rocks. At night they hunt for insects, spiders, and other scorpions. In the United States, scorpions most often are found living in the desert areas of the Southwest.

Scorpions are the only arthropods to bear live young. After they are born, the young scorpions are carried on their mother's back until they molt for the first time. How do you think this adaptation helps the young?

A scorpion's second pair of appendages have claws at the end. Scorpions capture prey and hold it with their claws. Then, they kill the prey by stinging it with poison. The stinger is found on the abdomen.

Ticks differ from other arachnids in body shape. Look at the tick shown in Figure 15-4. How many body sections do you count? You should notice that the head and abdomen sections of a tick are joined together.

Most ticks are parasites that attach to the outside of plants or animals. The tick bites into its host and feeds on the blood or body fluids of the organism. What other parasites can you name?

When ticks feed upon organisms, the ticks can transmit diseases. Two diseases that ticks transmit to people are

Figure 15-4 Ticks often are found in wooded areas or areas with tall grass.

Rocky Mountain spotted fever and Lyme disease. Rocky Mountain spotted fever is common in the southeastern United States. Lyme disease is common in the northeastern United States.

Think & Discuss

4. What is the function of spinnerets?

5. Why are spiders important to people?

★ **6.** Why do you think ballooning is useful for spiders?

15-3 Crustaceans

Have you ever eaten crabs, lobster, or shrimp? All of these animals belong to the class of arthropods called *Crustacea* (krus-TAY-shuh). Crayfish, barnacles, water fleas, and pill bugs are other kinds of crustaceans.

Most crustaceans live in water. Crustaceans are an important food source for people and other living things. Many fishes eat crustaceans. Tiny crustaceans called krill are one of the main food sources for whales.

Like arachnids, crustaceans have two main body parts, a head-chest part and an abdomen. Can you find the two body parts of the crayfish shown in Figure 15-5? Notice that the head-chest region is covered by a part of the exoskeleton called the **carapace** (KAR-uh-pays).

Figure 15–5 What part of the exoskeleton makes up most of the head-chest region of a crayfish?

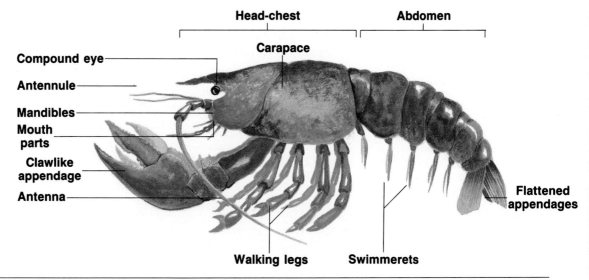

Head-chest

Abdomen

Carapace

Compound eye

Antennule

Mandibles

Mouth parts

Clawlike appendage

Antenna

Flattened appendages

Walking legs

Swimmerets

Arthropods 255

Crustaceans have a pair of appendages attached to each body segment. The first two pairs of appendages are **antennae** (an-TEN-ay). Antennae are sense organs used for taste and touch. Find the smaller pair of antennae in Figure 15-5 on page 255. What are they called?

Behind the antennae are the crayfish's **mandibles** (MAN-duh-bulz), or jaws. The mandibles tear, crush, and chew food. Other appendages around the mouth region are used to hold food. A crayfish also has large clawlike appendages. It uses these appendages for capturing food and for protection.

What other appendages does a crayfish have? Four pairs of walking legs are located behind the clawlike appendages. Attached to the abdomen are appendages used for reproduction and swimming. These are the swimmerets. At the end of the crayfish there are several flattened appendages. They also are used for swimming.

Have you ever seen a lobster or crayfish in an aquarium? If so, you may have noticed two large eyes looking back at you. Some crustaceans, such as the lobster and crayfish, see with compound eyes. Compound eyes are made up of many light-sensitive parts. Compound eyes can detect movement and changes in light.

Barnacles are crustaceans that have a different number of eyes at different stages of their lives. When they are hatched, barnacles have only one eye. In the next stage of life, they develop two more eyes. As adults, however, barnacles have no eyes at all.

A crayfish takes in oxygen through gills. Gills are organs used to absorb oxygen dissolved in water. In a crayfish, the gills are attached to each walking leg.

If a crustacean loses an appendage, it can regenerate a new one. When a crustacean molts, it partially replaces the lost appendage. After molting several times, the lost appendage is completely replaced. What other animals can you name that regenerate new parts?

Figure 15–6 Barnacles do not move from place to place on their own. They often are carried by boats or whales.

Think & Discuss

7. What are antennae used for?

8. How does a crayfish eat?

9. How might a crustacean's ability to regenerate lost appendages help protect it from predators?

ACTIVITY 15–1

PROBLEM: Do isopods prefer moist environments instead of dry ones?

Science Process Skills
predicting, observing, hypothesizing

Background Information
Isopods are members of the class Crustacea. They are commonly called ''pill bugs'' and often are found in gardens and lawns. You often find them under objects, such as logs and blocks used for garden borders.

Materials
> 15 pill bugs
> 2 small sponges
> shoe box with cover
> water
> metric ruler

Procedure

1. Copy the Data Table shown.

Data Table:	Pill Bug Response				
LOCATION	NUMBER OF PILL BUGS				TOTAL
	1	2	3	4	
On or near wet sponge					
On or near dry sponge					
Elsewhere in the shoe box					

2. Draw a band about 5 cm wide across the inside bottom of the shoe box. Draw the band across the center so that it divides the box in half.
3. Take one of the sponges and dampen it with water. Squeeze the sponge out so that it is only damp.
4. Place the damp sponge inside the shoe box at one end. Place the dry sponge at the other end.

5. Place the 15 pill bugs in the center band.
6. Cover the box and leave it undisturbed for 10 minutes.
7. **HYPOTHESIZE** Do you think the pill bugs will move toward the damp sponge, toward the dry sponge, or remain near the center of the shoe box? Write your hypothesis on a sheet of paper. Your hypothesis should answer the question. To test your hypothesis, continue the activity.
8. After 10 minutes, uncover the box. Count the number of pill bugs near or on the damp sponge, near or on the dry sponge, and elsewhere in the shoe box. Record these numbers in the Data Table.
9. Repeat steps 5, 6, and 8 three more times.
10. Total the results of the four trials. Record the totals in your Data Table.

Observations
1. **a.** By which sponge did you find the most pill bugs? **b.** By which sponge did you find the least number of pill bugs?
2. Why was it important to place the pill bugs halfway between the two sponges?

Conclusions
1. Was your hypothesis correct? Use your observations to support your hypothesis.
2. What type of environment do pill bugs prefer? Explain your answer using your data.

15-4 Centipedes and Millipedes

Study Hint

After you read Section 15-4, Centipedes and Millipedes, make a chart comparing centipedes and millipedes.

Centipedes and millipedes look a lot alike. However, they are placed in two separate classes of arthropods. Centipedes have flat bodies with one pair of legs attached to each segment. Poisonous claws are attached to the first segment. In contrast, millipedes have round bodies. Two pairs of legs are attached to each segment, except the first four. Unlike centipedes, a millipede has one pair of legs attached to each of the first four segments.

The things centipedes and millipedes eat also are different. Centipedes are predators that eat insects and worms. How do you think centipedes kill their prey? Millipedes feed on decaying plants. If a millipede is attacked, it rolls itself up into a ball. The millipede also may give off a poisonous and bad-smelling substance in an effort to drive away a predator.

Think & Discuss

10. What do millipedes eat?

11. What are two ways centipedes differ from millipedes?

12. You are given an arthropod that is either a centipede or a millipede. The animal has 40 body segments and 152 legs. Is it a centipede or a millipede? How do you know?

15-5 Insects

Key Points

- Insects have three major body sections: a head, a thorax, and an abdomen.

- Insect behaviors include forming societies, mating rituals, and mechanisms for defense.

Did you know that insects are the single largest group of animals on Earth? Of the one million species of arthropods that have been identified, about 700,000 are species of insects. Insects live in all kinds of environments except the ocean.

Do you know of any ways insects affect people? Some insects are harmful to people. Termites are an example of an insect that can cause a large amount of damage to property. Some insects, such as weevils, destroy crops. Other insects can transmit diseases to plants and animals. For example, some mosquitoes transmit malaria to people.

However, many insects are helpful to people and the environment. For example, bees and butterflies help pollinate many flowering plants. Bees and other insects also produce useful products, such as honey and silk. Insects also serve as food for many other kinds of organisms. In addition, some insects, such as the preying mantis, feed on insect pests.

Like all arthropods, insects have jointed appendages, an exoskeleton, and a segmented body. However, while most arthropods have only two major body sections, insects have three. Insects have a head, an abdomen, and a **thorax** (THOR-aks). The thorax is the middle, or chest, section of an insect.

Anatomy of a Grasshopper

Grasshoppers often are studied as a model for all insects. The structure of a grasshopper is shown in Figure 15-7. Notice that the head of a grasshopper has simple eyes, compound eyes, and two antennae. The grasshopper also has mandibles, which it uses to chew food. Other appendages around the mouth help hold the food.

Look at the abdomen of the grasshopper in Figure 15-7. Can you find the **tympanum** (TIM-puh-num)? The tympanum is used for hearing by the grasshopper. Now look at the **spiracles** (SPIH-ruh-kuls), or small openings, near the bottom of each segment of the abdomen. Insects breathe by contracting and relaxing their bodies. The spiracles are connected to tubes that carry air into and out of an insect's body.

Figure 15–7 How does the number of body sections of a grasshopper differ from that of a crayfish?

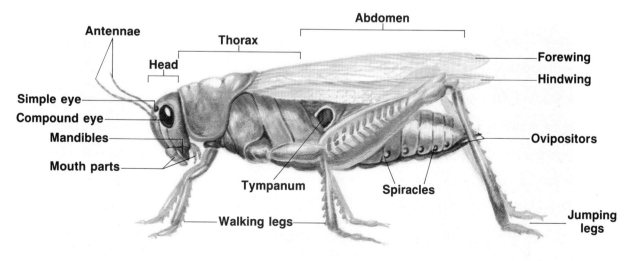

Antennae · Thorax · Abdomen · Head · Forewing · Hindwing · Simple eye · Compound eye · Mandibles · Mouth parts · Ovipositors · Tympanum · Spiracles · Walking legs · Jumping legs

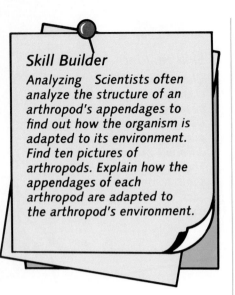
Grasshoppers are common insects. Like all insects, a grasshopper has three pairs of legs. The first two pairs of legs are walking legs. The last pair are large jumping legs. The grasshopper uses its jumping legs to escape predators and to launch into flight.

A grasshopper also has two pair of wings. It uses a pair of hindwings to fly. Covering the hindwings are a pair of leathery forewings. They protect the hindwings when the grasshopper is not flying.

Growth and Development

Just as all arthropods must do, insects shed their exoskeletons as they grow. As an insect develops into an adult, it changes in form and size. An insect goes through stages during its development. The series of changes an insect undergoes as it develops into an adult is called **metamorphosis** (met-uh-MOR-fuh-sis).

Incomplete Metamorphosis

Some insects, such as a grasshopper, undergo incomplete metamorphosis. Incomplete metamorphosis has three stages—egg, nymph, and adult. Figure 15-8 shows the stages of development of a grasshopper.

A female grasshopper has two pointed structures near the end of her abdomen. These structures are used to dig holes in the ground. Then, the female grasshopper lays her eggs in the holes. The eggs hatch into **nymphs** (NIMFS). Nymphs are young grasshoppers. A nymph looks like an adult grasshopper except that the nymph has a large head. A nymph also does not have wings or reproductive structures. After the grasshopper molts several times, the nymph develops into an adult grasshopper.

Complete Metamorphosis

Have you ever seen a caterpillar crawling along a plant? Did you know that caterpillars turn into butterflies? The stages of development of a butterfly are shown in Figure 15-9 on page 261. What do you notice about each stage? At each stage, the developing butterfly looks very different from an adult butterfly.

Some insects, like butterflies and moths, undergo complete metamorphosis. Insects that go through complete

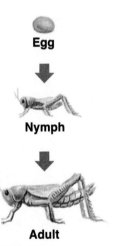

Egg

Nymph

Adult

Figure 15–8 A grasshopper nymph molts five or six times before becoming an adult. This process takes 40 to 60 days.

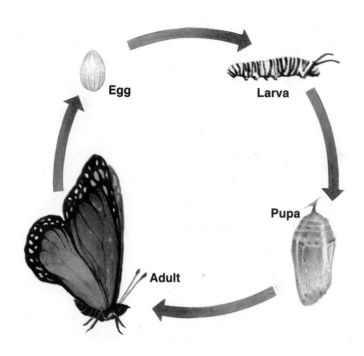

Egg

Larva

Pupa

Adult

Figure 15–9 How does the development of a butterfly differ from that of the grasshopper?

metamorphosis completely change in body form in each stage of their development. There are four stages in complete metamorphosis—egg, larva, pupa, and adult.

An egg from a female butterfly hatches into a wormlike form called a **larva.** A caterpillar is the larval form of a butterfly. Larval insects eat a lot of food. After several molts, the larva becomes a **pupa.** During the pupal stage, the insect does not eat. The pupa spins a protective covering around itself. In moths the covering is called a **cocoon.** While inside the protective covering, the pupa changes into an adult.

Insect Behavior

Insects demonstrate a wide range of behaviors. Behavioral adaptations help insects survive. Insect behaviors include the formation of societies and mating rituals. Many insects also have mechanisms for defense.

Social Insects

Most insects live alone in their environment. However, some insects live in colonies. Have you ever seen a beehive or an anthill? Honeybees and ants are social insects that live in colonies.

Study Hint

To read more about insects, see the Careers Feature at the end of the chapter.

ACTIVITY 15–2

PROBLEM: What type of metamorphosis does a mealworm undergo?

Science Process Skills
observing, hypothesizing, applying concepts

Background Information
Mealworms are actually insects, not worms. Like many insects, mealworms undergo metamorphosis. There are two kinds of metamorphosis. Complete metamorphosis is development in four stages—egg, larva, pupa, and adult. Incomplete metamorphosis is development in only three stages—egg, nymph, and adult. The nymph appears to be a smaller version of the adult.

Mealworm beetles

Materials

20 mealworms	uncooked rice
large glass jar	hand lens
bran cereal	cheese cloth
potato slices	rubber band

Procedure

1. Sprinkle several grains of uncooked rice in the glass jar.
2. Fill the jar about 1/3 full with bran cereal.
3. Place a potato slice on top of the bran. Place the mealworms in the jar.
4. Cover the top of the jar with cheesecloth. Secure the cheesecloth with a rubber band.
5. Use the hand lens to observe the mealworms. Make a sketch of the mealworms, and write any comments you can about the insects.
6. **HYPOTHESIZE** What kind of metamorphosis do mealworms undergo? Write your hypothesis on a sheet of paper. Your hypothesis should answer the question. To test your hypothesis, continue the activity.
7. Observe the mealworms each day for three weeks. Keep a daily log of your observations. If you observe the mealworms in any new stages, be sure to sketch them.

8. Look at the potato slice. If it appears to be dried out, place another one in the jar.

Observations

1. **a.** In what developmental stage were the mealworms when you placed them in the jar? **b.** Did you count the legs? How many were there?
2. **a.** What other stages of development did you observe? **b.** How did these stages differ from one another?
3. **a.** Did you observe mealworms on the potato? **b.** Why do you think the potato slice was necessary?

Conclusions

1. Why do you think the rice was needed?
2. Was each stage of mealworm development completely different from the other stages?
3. **a.** Based on your observations, do mealworms undergo complete or incomplete metamorphosis? **b.** Was your hypothesis correct? Use your observations to support your hypothesis.

Going Further
List the names of 5 insects. Visit the library to find out what type of metamorphosis each insect undergoes. Sketch the stages for each insect.

Look at the honeybees shown in Figure 15-10. In a beehive, each of the honeybees has a special job to do. There are three kinds of bees in a colony—worker bees, drones, and a queen bee.

Worker bees are female bees that protect and build the hive. They also find and gather flower pollen and nectar and feed the larvae, the queen bee, and the drones. Drones are male bees whose only job is to fertilize the queen. When drones are no longer needed, they are either driven from the hive or killed by the workers. The queen's only function is to lay eggs.

Communication

Insects that live in colonies must communicate with other insects in the colony. However, even insects that do not live in colonies must communicate with other members of their species at mating time. Insects communicate by using chemicals, sound, and visual displays.

Some insects give off chemical scents to communicate. The chemicals affect the behavior of other members of the same species. Female moths use chemicals to attract mates. Male moths, as far away as two to three kilometers, can detect the chemical given off by a female moth.

Have you ever seen a moth flying in a zigzag pattern? The male moths fly in a zigzag pattern so that they do not lose the trail of the chemical. The antennae of a male moth are very sensitive to smell. The male moth uses the fine hairs on its antennae to locate the female.

Insects also use sound to communicate. For example, a female mosquito buzzes in order to attract male mosquitoes. Have you ever heard a cricket chirp? A male cricket produces a chirping sound by rubbing one wing against another. The sound is used to attract a mate.

Have you ever seen a firefly lighting up the night? Fireflies use visual displays to communicate. Male fireflies produce light in order to attract females. The light is produced by a chemical reaction. Each species of firefly has its own flashing pattern.

Honeybees have an unusual way of communicating with each other. When worker bees return to the beehive after finding a food source, they communicate the direction and distance of the food source to other bees by doing a dance.

Worker bee

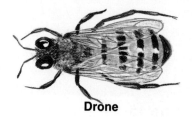

Drone

Queen bee

Figure 15–10   A single colony of honeybees may have as many as 50,000 to 60,000 bees. Only one queen bee lives in a colony.

Health and Safety Tip

Some people are allergic to the sting of a bee or wasp. If you are allergic to either a bee or wasp sting, ask your doctor about precautions you should take if you go camping or are active outdoors.

Figure 15–11 The monarch butterfly (left) is better able to survive in its environment by looking like the viceroy butterfly (right)

Figure 15–12 Camouflage helps the katydid avoid predators.

Defense

Insects have many adaptations for defense. Some insects, like the bombardier beetle and the bee, defend themselves by attacking predators. The bombardier beetle sprays a bad-smelling gas into the mouth of its predator. The bee uses a stinger at the end of its abdomen.

Some insects are avoided by predators because they look like other insects that have a bad taste or can sting. This adaptation is called **mimicry** (MIM-ik-ree). For example, the viceroy butterfly looks very much like the monarch butterfly. The monarch butterfly is distasteful to birds. Birds avoid eating the viceroy butterfly because it looks like the bad-tasting monarch butterfly.

Some insects are able to blend into their surroundings. Their body shapes and colors help them blend in. This adaptation is called **camouflage** (KAM-uh-flahj). Camouflage helps hide an insect from its predators. Would a bird looking for food have trouble finding the insect shown in Figure 15-12?

Think & Discuss

13. What is the function of the tympanum?

14. Define metamorphosis.

15. What are some examples of how insects communicate?

16. What is the function of the queen bee?

17. How does the practice of burying eggs aid in the reproduction of grasshoppers?

Do you think of insects as friends or foes? Many insects, such as bees, are helpful to people. Others, such as termites, are destructive to property. If you find insects and their effects on people interesting, then you may enjoy one of the careers discussed below.

Beekeeper

Many useful products come from bees. Bees produce honey, which is used as a sweetener. Bees also produce beeswax, which is used in making candles, lipsticks, and polishes. A beekeeper is a person who maintains beehives and collects honey and beeswax from them. Beekeepers sell the honey and beeswax they collect from beehives.

Beekeepers construct beehives that consist of wooden boxes with removable frames. Bees build honeycombs on the frames. Most beekeepers maintain hives on their own property, although some beekeepers work for other people who own hives.

A beekeeper should have a high school diploma. Courses in beekeeping, agriculture, and business also are recommended.

For more information: Write to the New Jersey Beekeepers Association, 157 Five Point Road, Colts Neck, NJ 07722.

Exterminator

An exterminator usually uses chemicals to rid buildings of unwanted pests, such as termites and roaches. Some exterminators also combat mice, rats, and other vermin. An exterminator may work for a city or county government, or for a private exterminating service. Some exterminators own their own companies.

Exterminators need a high school diploma. They also need vocational training in pest control methods. High school courses in biology and chemistry are recommended for a person who plans to become an exterminator.

For more information: Contact your local board of health or a private exterminating company.

Insect Control Researcher

Each year, large numbers of crops are destroyed by insects. Insect control researchers study the problem of insect control. Controlling insects that damage crops is a difficult task because many insecticides (in-SEK-tuh-syds), or chemicals that kill insects, also are harmful to people and other living things.

Insect control researchers may work for the government, in a private research laboratory, or in the research division of a university. Insect control researchers need a college degree with a major in biology or environmental science. Many insect control researchers begin their careers as research assistants. They work under the supervision of a scientist in a university or research laboratory.

For more information: Write to the Department of Agriculture in your state.

Chapter Review

CHAPTER SUMMARY

15-1 Overview of Arthropods

- Arthropods have jointed appendages and segmented bodies covered by an exoskeleton.
- Arthropods have an open circulatory system.

15-2 Arachnids

- Arachnids have two main body parts: a head-chest and an abdomen.
- Spiders, scorpions, and ticks are three kinds of arachnids.

15-3 Crustaceans

- Crustaceans have two main body parts: a head-chest and an abdomen.
- Crustaceans have antennae to sense taste and touch, and mandibles for chewing.
- Crustaceans use gills to breathe.

- Crabs, lobsters, shrimp, pill bugs, and barnacles are all crustaceans.

15-4 Centipedes and Millipedes

- Centipedes have flat bodies with one pair of legs attached to each segment.
- Millipedes have round bodies with two pairs of legs attached to each segment, except the first four.

15-5 Insects

- Insects have three main body parts: a head, a thorax, and an abdomen.
- Insects have three pairs of walking legs. Many insects also have one or two pairs of wings.
- Insects communicate with each other by using chemicals, sound, and visual displays.

VOCABULARY LIST

antennae (256)	chitin (252)	metamorphosis (260)	spinnerets (254)
appendages (252)	cocoon (261)	mimicry (264)	spiracles (259)
arthropods (251)	exoskeleton (252)	molting (252)	thorax (259)
camouflage (264)	larva (261)	nymphs (260)	tympanum (259)
carapace (255)	mandibles (256)	pupa (261)	

VOCABULARY REVIEW

Matching Write the word or term from the Vocabulary List that best matches each description.

1. used for hearing
2. used for breathing
3. hard outer covering
4. single largest group of animals
5. appendages used to chew and crush food
6. used by crustaceans to taste and touch
7. protective covering for pupae of moths
8. movable extensions of an arthropod's body

Identifying Relationships Identify the word or term in each group that does not belong. Explain why it does not belong with the group.

1. tympanum, grasshopper, spider
2. camouflage, chitin, mimicry
3. exoskeleton, thorax, molting
4. cocoon, antennae, appendages
5. crustacean, carapace, arachnid
6. nymphs, pupa, spinnerets
7. mandibles, antennae, spiracles
8. thorax, insect, millipede
9. metamorphosis, mimicry, larva
10. chitin, exoskeleton, spiracles

Completion Write the word or words that best complete each sentence.

1. The single largest group of animals are the _____.
2. The circulatory system of an arthropod is a _____ system.
3. Centipedes have _____ of legs on each body segment.
4. A crayfish uses its _____ for swimming and reproduction.
5. Centipedes have _____ attached to their first segment.
6. Arachnids have _____ body segments.
7. Crustaceans use _____ to chew food.
8. Most _____ are parasites that feed off other living organisms.
9. Insects develop through a series of stages called _____.
10. The ability of an insect to blend into its surroundings is called _____.

Finding the Main Ideas Use the section number to find the sentence that answers each question. Then, write the sentence.

1. What is the function of an exoskeleton? (15-1)
2. How does the circulatory system of arthropods differ from the circulatory system of humans? (15-1)
3. What three groups of animals are classified as arachnids? (15-2)
4. What are the body parts of an arachnid? (15-2)
5. In what way do scorpions differ from all other arthropods? (15-2)
6. What diseases do ticks transmit to people? (15-2)
7. How does a crayfish use its claws? (15-3)
8. What do millipedes eat? (15-4)
9. How are insects helpful to people? (15-5)
10. What are some insect behaviors? (15-5)

Writing for Understanding One way to find out if you understand something is to write a brief summary of the information in your own words. Reread Section 15-2, Arachnids, on pages 253-255, and write a brief summary of the information.

Critical Thinking Answer each of the following in complete sentences.

1. Why do you think that many scientists estimate that as many as ten million arthropods may exist on Earth?

2. Scorpions are active at night. How does this adaptation benefit scorpions?
3. Many people think spiders are insects. Explain why spiders are not classified as insects.
4. Why does the pupa of a butterfly surround itself with a covering?
5. Some insects that taste bad to predators have a very bright coloration. These insects do not blend into their environment. Instead, they attract attention. How might this adaptation be helpful to these insects?

1. Make a poster of pictures of insects common to your community. Identify and label each insect.
2. Research the use of natural methods for insect control. Write a report on your findings.

 3. Lyme disease is becoming a serious problem in the northeastern United States. Use science journals and magazines to find out where this disease originated, how the disease affects the body, and what scientists are doing to combat this disease.

Look at the organisms in the drawings and photographs.
All of these organisms have vertebrae, or a group of bones
that form a backbone. Animals with backbones are called
vertebrates. The organisms shown are examples of
vertebrates. Vertebrates also have a skeleton inside their
bodies.

Most of the organisms that you call animals probably
are vertebrates. Yet, vertebrates make up only three
percent of the Animal kingdom.

Read the titles of the chapters. The titles are
the names of the five main groups of vertebrates.
Now look at the photographs and drawings.
Match each picture with its chapter. What
other animals do you think are classified in
each group?

UNIT 5

Vertebrates

CONTENTS

Chapter 16 | Fishes

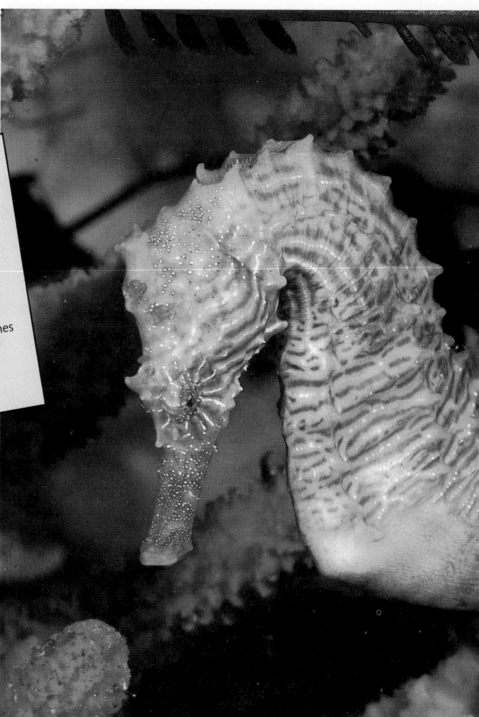

Objectives

After you have finished this chapter, you will be able to

16-1 **list** the characteristics of vertebrates.

16-1 **define** cold-blooded.

16-1 **name** and describe three classes of fishes.

16-2 **identify** two groups of jawless fishes.

16-3 **identify** three groups of cartilaginous fishes.

16-4 **identify** three groups of bony fishes.

16-4 **describe** the anatomy of a bony fish.

Science Process Skills

In this chapter, two science skills are highlighted. Symbols show some places where these skills are used.

👁 **Observing:** When you observe, you use one or more of your senses to gather information.

▣ **Hypothesizing:** When you hypothesize, you state a suggested answer to a problem based upon known information.

What has the head of a horse, the pouch of a kangaroo, and the tail of a monkey? The answer is not some imaginary animal. It is a sea horse. With its tail wrapped around a blade of eelgrass, a sea horse does look like a tiny aquatic horse. Like kangaroos, sea horses carry their young in pouches. However, only the males have pouches, and it is the male sea horse that gives birth!

In spite of their strange appearance and behavior, sea horses are fishes. Do you think sea horses swim in the same way as other fishes, such as sharks? Unlike other fishes, sea horses normally swim in an upright position. Although a sea horse is not a typical fish, it does have many characteristics in common with other fishes.

16-1 Overview of Fishes

Key Points

- Vertebrates are animals with backbones.

- The body temperature of a cold-blooded animal is about the same as the temperature of its surroundings.

- The three major classes of fishes are jawless fishes, cartilaginous fishes, and bony fishes.

Fishes are the most numerous group of **vertebrates** (VUR-tuh-brayts), or animals with backbones. Amphibians, reptiles, birds, and mammals also are vertebrates. In addition to a backbone, all vertebrates have a nerve cord. The nerve cord is protected by small bones called **vertebrae** (VUR-tuh-bray). If you move your hand up and down your back, you can feel your vertebrae. The vertebrae that you feel make up your backbone.

Fishes, like all vertebrates, belong to the phylum *Chordata*. All members of this phylum are called chordates. Chordates are animals that have a **notocord** (NOT-uh-kord) at some time during their lives. A notocord is a strong, flexible support rod just below the nerve cord. In adult vertebrates, the notocord is replaced by the backbone. Do you think you had a notocord at some time during your development?

Your body temperature stays about the same, except when you have a fever. Fishes, however, cannot control their body temperature as you do. Fishes are **cold-blooded.** The body temperature of a cold-blooded animal is about the same as the temperature of its surroundings. Thus, a fish swimming in cold water would feel cold if you touched it. How do you think a fish in warm water would feel if you touched it?

All fishes live in fresh or salt water and take in oxygen with **gills.** Gills are respiratory organs that remove dissolved oxygen from water. A fish has two sets of gills, one on each side of its body.

Fishes live in the deepest, coldest parts of the ocean as well as in shallow freshwater streams and ponds. Each kind of fish is adapted to its own environment. The 31,000 different kinds of fish are divided into three classes.

The three classes of fish are the jawless fishes, the cartilaginous (kart-ul-AJ-uh-nus) fishes, and the bony fishes. Jawless fishes do not have true jaws. These fishes are direct descendents of the oldest fossil fish. Cartilaginous fishes have jaws, and a skeleton made of **cartilage** (KART-ul-ij). Cartilage is a strong, flexible bonelike tissue. You have cartilage in the tip of your nose and in your ears. If you wiggle the tip of your nose with your fingers, you can feel the flexibility of cartilage. Bony

Figure 16-1 The puffer fish (top) and the butterfly fish (bottom) show the great variety among fishes.

fishes have jaws and a skeleton made of bone. Most of your skeleton also is made up of bone. Bone is a much harder, and less flexible, tissue than cartilage.

Think & Discuss

1. What is a cold-blooded animal?
2. List five characteristics of fishes.
★ 3. A fishlike animal called the lancelet is an invertebrate chordate. How can a chordate be an invertebrate?

16-2 Jawless Fishes

The earliest vertebrate fossils are over 500 million years old. These fossils are of a very strange fish called an ostracoderm (AHS-truh-koh-durm). Ostracoderms were covered with heavy bony plates and did not have jaws. Scientists believe that modern jawless fishes probably are descendents of the ostracoderms.

The two groups of jawless fishes are the lampreys and the hagfish. Lampreys and hagfish look very different from their fossil relatives. For example, lampreys and hagfish have soft bodies covered with a slimy skin instead of plates or scales.

Lampreys can live in both fresh and salt water. Most lampreys are **parasites.** Parasites are organisms that live on or in the bodies of other living things. Freshwater lampreys live in the Great Lakes of the United States. Unfortunately, these parasitic fishes have killed many of the other fishes living in the Great Lakes.

◉ The jawless mouth of a lamprey is adapted to the lamprey's life as a parasite. As you can see in Figure 16-2, the mouth looks like a round sucker lined with teeth. The lamprey attaches itself to the body of a fish with its mouth. With its teeth, the lamprey scrapes a hole in the skin of the fish, and sucks out the fish's blood and body fluids.

Unlike lampreys, hagfish are **scavengers.** Scavengers feed on dead or dying animals. The mouth of a hagfish is smaller than the mouth of the lamprey. Instead of a round

Key Points

- The two groups of jawless fishes are the lampreys and hagfish.
- Lampreys are parasites.
- Hagfish are scavengers.

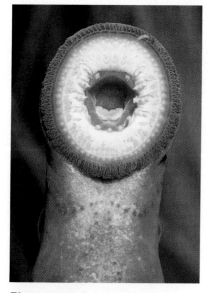

Figure 16-2 Notice the rasping teeth and suckerlike mouth of the lamprey.

sucker, the hagfish's mouth is surrounded by six short, fleshy tentacles. The hagfish, which is blind, uses its tentacles to find food.

Think & Discuss

4. What is an ostracoderm?
5. List three characteristics of jawless fishes.
6. What is the difference between a parasite and a scavenger?

16-3 Cartilaginous Fishes

Key Points

- Sharks, skates, and rays are the three groups of cartilaginous fishes.
- Cartilaginous fishes have hinged jaws and skeletons made up of cartilage.

About 350 million years ago, fishes called placoderms (PLAK-oh-durms) lived in the earth's oceans. These fishes had paired fins and jaws with hinges. Fossil evidence shows that both the cartilaginous and bony fishes are descended from the placoderms. Today, there are three major groups of cartilaginous fishes. These groups are the sharks, skates, and rays.

Sharks

All sharks, except for the bullshark, live in salt water. Sharks range in length from 15 cm to almost 20 m. Like the lamprey and hagfishes, the body of a shark is long and streamlined. However, a shark, unlike the lamprey or hagfish, has paired fins. Its paired fins help the shark change direction as it swims. The shark's strong muscular tail and large tail fin move the shark at great speed through the water.

Figure 16-3 Eugenie Clark (left) studies a live shark. Notice the shark's streamlined shape and muscular tail (right).

ACTIVITY 16–1

PROBLEM: What can you find out about a fish by observing its scales?

Science Process Skills
inferring, comparing, estimating

Background Information
Most fish are covered with scales. Some fish, such as certain eels and catfish, are scaleless. Fish scales grow during the entire life of a fish. When there is a lot of food, the scales grow quickly. When there is less food, the scales grow slowly. Each band on a scale represents growth during one year.

Materials
paper and pencil

Procedure
1. Copy the Data Table shown.

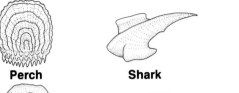
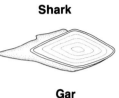

Perch   **Shark**   **Salmon**

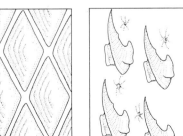

Bass   **Gar**   **Carp**

Figure B: Sample fish scales

Data Table: Ages of Fish		
FISH	NUMBER OF BANDS	AGE OF FISH
Perch		
Shark		
Gar		
Salmon		
Bass		
Carp		

2. Study the drawings of the different kinds of fish scales in Figure A.
3. Notice the bands on some of the scales.
4. Count the number of bands on each scale shown in Figure B. Record the number of bands in the Data Table.

5. Fill in the age of each fish in the proper column in the Data Table. If you cannot determine the age of the fish, write "unknown" in the Data Table.

Observations
1. How many kinds of fish scales are there?
2. **a.** Which fish is the oldest?   **b.** Which fish is the youngest?
3. For which fish could you not determine the age? Explain your answer.
4. **a.** During which year did the perch have less food than in other years?   **b.** During which year did the salmon have a good food supply?

Conclusions
1. What two things can you determine by observing the scales of a fish?
2. How can you determine the age of a fish?
3. A catfish is scaleless. Could you estimate its age? Explain your answer.

Figure A: Kinds of Fish Scales

Figure 16-4 The coloring of the stingray (top) and the manta ray (bottom) provides protection from predators.

Study Hint

Compare the body shape of the rays in Figure 16-4 with that of the shark in Figure 16-3 on page 274.

Most sharks swim constantly in order to take in oxygen for respiration. As a shark swims, water passes into its mouth and over its gills. Oxygen and carbon dioxide are exchanged in the gills. Then the water passes out through gill slits on the sides of the shark's head.

Many sharks are fierce **predators** (PRED-uh-tuhrs). Predators eat other animals, which are called their **prey.** Most sharks are meat-eaters that feed on squid, crustaceans, and other fishes. To locate their prey, sharks rely on a good sense of smell. In fact, a shark can sense a tiny amount of blood in the water from an injured animal, even if the animal is hundreds of meters away. A shark also can sense movement in the water by means of a series of pits in its sides. These pits are called the **lateral line.** Why do you think sharks sometimes are attracted to swimmers near a beach?

Rays and Skates

Rays and skates have flat, wide bodies and long, thin tails. The flat body of rays and skates is an adaptation to life on the bottom of the ocean. The huge **pectoral** (PEK-tuhr-uhl) **fins** on their sides look like wings. In fact, rays and skates swim by slowly beating their pectoral fins as if they were wings.

Like sharks, rays and skates obtain oxygen by moving water over their gills. Because the mouth is located on the underside of the body, a ray or skate cannot take in water through its mouth. Instead, rays and skates take in water through a pair of openings called **spiracles** (SPIH-ruh-kuls) just behind the eyes. The water is pumped over their gills and out through external gill slits.

Rays and skates are generally harmless. However, some species have sharp, poisonous tail spines for defense. Some species can stun small fishes with an electrical shock. Stepping on or touching one of these rays or skates while wading or swimming could be quite dangerous.

Think & Discuss

7. What are spiracles?

8. How do sharks locate their prey?

9. How does the body shape and coloring of rays and skates help protect them from predators?

16-4 Bony Fishes

Most of the fishes living in lakes, ponds, or oceans are bony fishes. There are more than 20,000 species of bony fishes. Bony fishes live in both fresh and salt water, and feed on nearly every kind of food. Like the cartilaginous fishes, bony fishes have an upper and a lower jaw. However, the skeleton of bony fishes is made of bone, not cartilage. The bony fishes are divided into three groups.

Groups of Bony Fishes

The first group of bony fishes are the lobe-finned fishes. Lobe-finned fishes were thought to be extinct for millions of years. Then, in 1938, a lobe-finned fish called a coelacanth (SEE-luh-kanth) was caught off the coast of South Africa. Coelacanths have fleshy fins that resemble paddles.

The lungfishes are the second group of bony fishes. Unlike most fishes, lungfishes have both lungs and gills. Because lungfishes have both lungs and gills, they can take oxygen from the air and from the water.

Lungfishes live in shallow ponds. When a pond dries up in summer, some lungfishes burrow into the mud and secrete a cocoon. Inside its cocoon, the lungfish can breathe with its lungs until the next rainy season.

Most of the fishes with which you are familiar are ray-finned fishes. The ray-finned fishes are the third group of bony fishes. Most food fishes such as trout, perch, herring, and tuna are ray-finned fishes. Unusual fishes such as eels and sea horses also are ray-finned fishes.

Anatomy of a Bony Fish

Bony fishes live in both freshwater and saltwater environments, and have a variety of lifestyles. For this reason, they have many different body shapes and adaptations. However, all bony fishes have some characteristics in common. The perch often is used as a model for all bony fishes.

Perch live in the Great Lakes and other freshwater lakes. Perch are popular food and sport fishes. They have long bodies and may grow to a length of 46 cm. The scales of a perch are small and tough.

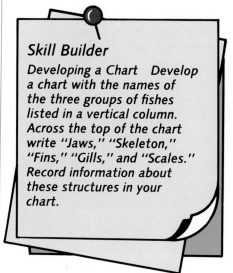

Skill Builder

Developing a Chart Develop a chart with the names of the three groups of fishes listed in a vertical column. Across the top of the chart write "Jaws," "Skeleton," "Fins," "Gills," and "Scales." Record information about these structures in your chart.

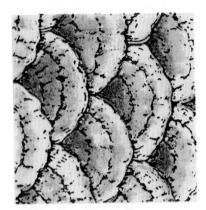

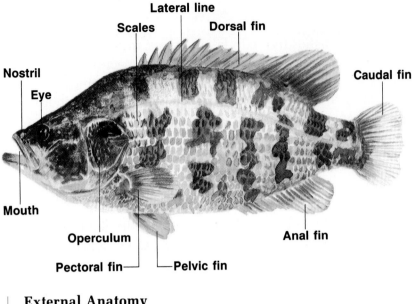

Figure 16-5 Notice the overlapping scales (above) of the perch (right).

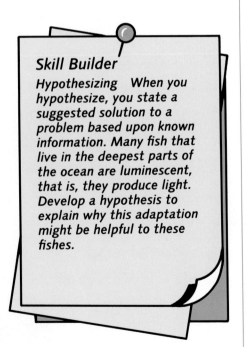

Skill Builder

Hypothesizing When you hypothesize, you state a suggested solution to a problem based upon known information. Many fish that live in the deepest parts of the ocean are luminescent, that is, they produce light. Develop a hypothesis to explain why this adaptation might be helpful to these fishes.

External Anatomy

The perch has a head, trunk, and tail. The mouth, eyes, and nostrils are found on the head. Look at Figure 16-5 and find the **operculum** (oh-PUR-kyoo-luhm), or gill cover. The operculum protects the gills beneath it.
◑Look at the different kinds of fins on the perch. On the trunk are the paired **pelvic fins** and pectoral fins. **Dorsal fins** are on the top of the trunk. The **anal fin** is near the opening of the anus. The anal fin marks the end of the trunk. At the end of the trunk is the tail. The muscular tail helps push the fish through the water. A stiff **caudal fin,** or tail fin, acts as a paddle for swimming.

The body of a bony fish is covered with overlapping scales. The fish secretes a slimy mucus. This mucus lubricates the scales and helps the fish flex its body while swimming. Like sharks, bony fishes have a lateral line. The lateral line is a sense organ that runs from the head to the tail between the rows of scales.

Internal Anatomy

Look at the internal structure of the perch shown in Figure 16-6 on page 279. Bony fishes have an endoskeleton, or internal skeleton. Small vertebrae form a backbone that protects the spinal cord. Because the backbone is not a solid rod, the fish can move its trunk and tail easily as it swims. The muscles in the fish's tail move the tail from side to side and push the fish through the water.

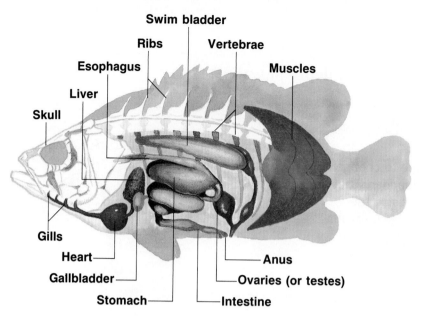

Skull · Liver · Esophagus · Ribs · Swim bladder · Vertebrae · Muscles · Gills · Heart · Gallbladder · Stomach · Intestine · Ovaries (or testes) · Anus

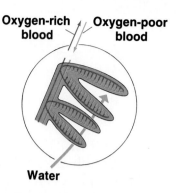

Oxygen-rich blood · Oxygen-poor blood · Water

Figure 16-6 Locate the gills in the diagram (left), and trace the flow of blood through the gill filaments (above).

Respiration takes place in the gills. The gills are made up of flat, feathery gill filaments surrounded by tiny blood vessels. Oxygen and carbon dioxide are exchanged across the gill filaments. What do you think happens to the oxygen and carbon dioxide that are exchanged?

Bony fishes reproduce sexually. The male fish produces sperm in its testes. The female fish produces eggs in ovaries. After the female fish deposits her eggs, the male spreads **milt** over the eggs. Milt is a milky fluid containing sperm. Most bony fishes breed, or **spawn,** once or twice a year, usually in the spring.

Unlike the cartilaginous fishes, bony fishes have a **swim bladder.** The swim bladder acts and looks something like a balloon. The fish can control the amount of gas in the swim bladder to equal the pressure of the water. As a result, the fish can remain at any level in the water without rising or sinking.

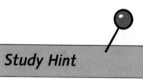

Study Hint

Compare the breathing methods of sharks and rays with that of bony fishes.

Think & Discuss

10. What is the function of the operculum?
11. What is a swim bladder?
12. Name three groups of bony fishes.
13. Name five kinds of fins found on most bony fishes.
★ 14. Why are bony fishes found in so many different environments?

ACTIVITY 16–2

PROBLEM: How can a fish change its depth in water?

Science Process Skills
modeling, observing, relating concepts

Background Information
A bony fish, such as a perch, is able to change its depth in water using its swim bladder. The swim bladder is a gas-filled organ inside the fish. The swim bladder removes oxygen, carbon dioxide, and nitrogen from the blood of a fish. The gases are pumped into or out of the swim bladder as the fish changes depth. Therefore, as a fish changes depth, the swim bladder is inflated or deflated. The response is automatic.

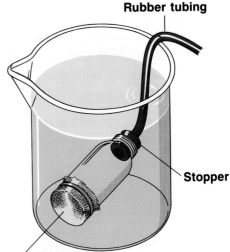

Rubber tubing

Stopper

Plastic bottle with top covered by gauze

Materials

small plastic bottle	gauze pad
500 mL beaker	scissors
rubber tubing	clay
one-holed rubber stopper to fit bottle	knife
	rubber band

Procedure

1. Carefully cut off the bottom of the plastic bottle. **CAUTION: Be careful when using a knife.**
2. Carefully, cut a circle from the gauze pad. The gauze pad needs to be larger than the cut end of the bottle so that you can keep the pad in place with a rubber band. **CAUTION: Be careful when using scissors.**
3. Secure the gauze pad in place with the rubber band.
4. Push the rubber tubing into the hole of the rubber stopper.
5. Use some clay to seal around the area where the rubber tubing enters the stopper.
6. Insert the stopper into the top of the bottle.
7. Sink the bottle into a beaker of water.
8. Slowly blow into the rubber tubing. Record your observations.

9. Stop blowing into the rubber tubing. Record your observations.
10. Try to make the plastic bottle stay in the middle of the water.

Observations
1. What happens to the plastic bottle as you blow air into the tubing?
2. What happens to the plastic bottle when you stop blowing into the tubing?
3. **a.** Could you keep the plastic bottle in the middle of the water? **b.** If so, what did you have to do to keep the bottle at about the same depth?

Conclusions
1. On your model, what does the plastic bottle represent in a fish?
2. On your model, what does your exhaled breath represent in a fish?
3. If a fish's swim bladder is inflating, would the fish be rising or sinking in the water?
4. **MODEL** Use your model to explain how a swim bladder works in a fish.

Fish—The Healthful Alternative

How often do you eat red meat? How often do you eat fish? Many people eat red meat almost every night for dinner. Red meat contains many needed vitamins and minerals. Red meat also contains saturated fat and cholesterol (kuh-LES-tuh-rohl).

Cardiologists, doctors who study the heart, have done research to find out how substances in food affect the heart. The results of this research show that too much saturated fat and cholesterol may cause heart disease. Does this mean you should never eat red meat again? No, but you should try to cut back. By eating less red meat, you will lower your intake of fat and cholesterol.

Foods such as fish and chicken are alternatives to red meat. People have always included fish as a food item, but it is only recently that the benefits of eating fish have been learned.

Studies have shown that people who eat a lot of fish have less heart disease than people who do not include fish as part of their diets. These studies also showed that people who eat a lot of fish live longer and healthier lives than people who eat a lot of meat.

Why do fish eaters have less heart disease and live longer and healthier lives? Researchers have discovered that fish contain an oil called Omega 3. Omega 3 is an unsaturated fat that lowers the blood cholesterol level. This helps prevent cholesterol buildup in your arteries and veins.

All fish contain the fatty oil Omega 3. Some fish, however, contain higher amounts of Omega 3 than others. Fish with high levels of Omega 3 are tuna, bluefish, salmon, cod, mackerel, and trout.

Fish may be eaten either raw or cooked. While raw fish, or sushi, is healthful, you must be careful where you buy the fish. Raw fish can sometimes contain the eggs of tapeworms. These eggs can develop into adult tapeworms inside your intestines. As fish is cooked, tapeworms, or other parasites in the fish, are destroyed. When cooking fish, steam, bake, or broil the fish rather than frying it. Frying fish in oil or butter adds fat and calories.

Have you seen fish oil capsules advertised in health food stores? These capsules are made from fish oil. Fish oil capsules contain Omega 3, but they also contain a large amount of cholesterol. Thus, fresh fish is a better source of Omega 3 than fish oil capsules.

Cutting back on your red meat intake and substituting fish or chicken at least twice a week may reduce your chance of heart disease and stroke. By developing healthful eating habits now, you may be able to avoid serious health problems in the future.

To Think About

- Why is eating fresh fish better for you than taking a fish oil capsule?
- Besides fish, what are some other types of food you can substitute for red meat?

Chapter Review

16-1 Overview of Fishes

- Vertebrates are animals with a backbone that supports and protects the nerve cord.
- Fishes are cold-blooded vertebrates that belong to the phylum *Chordata*.
- The three major classes of fishes are the jawless fishes, the cartilaginous fishes, and the bony fishes.

16-2 Jawless Fishes

- Lampreys and hagfish are the only modern descendents of the ancient jawless fishes, or ostracoderms.
- Lampreys are parasites that use their round suckerlike mouths to attach to host fishes and suck out their blood and body fluids.

- Hagfish are scavengers that feed on dead and dying fishes.

16-3 Cartilaginous Fishes

- The cartilaginous fishes have skeletons made up of cartilage and hinged jaws.
- Sharks, skates, and rays are the three major groups of modern cartilaginous fishes.

16-4 Bony Fishes

- Bony fishes are the largest and most varied group of fishes living today.
- Bony fishes have upper and lower jaws and a skeleton made of bone.
- Lobe-finned fishes, lungfishes, and ray-finned fishes are the three groups of bony fishes.

VOCABULARY LIST

anal fin (278)
cartilage (272)
caudal fin (278)
cold-blooded (272)
dorsal fins (278)
gills (272)

lateral line (276)
milt (279)
notocord (272)
operculum (278)
parasites (273)
pectoral fins (276)

pelvic fins (278)
predators (276)
prey (276)
scavengers (273)
spawn (279)
spiracles (276)

swim bladder (279)
vertebrae (272)
vertebrates (272)

VOCABULARY REVIEW

Matching Write the word or term from the Vocabulary List that best matches each description.

1. flexible support rod below the nerve cord
2. animal with a body temperature controlled by its surroundings
3. organ system that senses movement
4. organ that allows bony fishes to adjust to water pressure
5. sperm-containing fluid
6. openings by which skates breathe
7. fins closest to the head of a fish
8. to breed

Applying Definitions Explain the difference between the words in each pair.

1. predators, prey
2. pelvic fins, dorsal fins
3. cartilage, bone
4. chordate, vertebrates
5. parasites, scavengers
6. vertebrae, backbone
7. gills, lungs
8. caudal fin, anal fin
9. operculum, scales
10. vertebrate, invertebrate

CONTENT REVIEW

True or False   Write true if the statement is true. If the statement is false, change the underlined word or words to make the statement true.

1. The bones that protect the nerve cord of bony fishes are called spiracles.
2. Jawless fishes have a bony skeleton.
3. Most sharks are predators.
4. Sharks, rays, and skates are jawless fishes.
5. The gill cover of bony fishes is called the operculum.
6. Most food fishes are lobe-finned fishes.
7. All bony fishes have gills, fins, and scales.
8. Hagfishes are parasites.
9. Rays and skates take in water through openings called spiracles.
10. Fishes that can take oxygen from the air are called lungfishes.

Question and Answer   Rewrite each heading in the Chapter Outline on page 270 as a question. Then, answer each of the questions you have written.

Interpreting a Diagram   Use the diagram of the external anatomy of a bony fish shown in Figure 16-5 (page 278) to answer each of the following.

1. How many pairs of fins do most bony fishes have?
2. Which fins of a bony fish do not exist as pairs?
3. Where is the lateral line of a bony fish located?
4. Through which organs does a bony fish take in water?
5. Where are the dorsal fins of a bony fish located?

CONCEPT REVIEW

Writing the Main Ideas   Using the Chapter Outline on page 270, write the main idea for each heading in the outline.

Critical Thinking   Answer each of the following in complete sentences.

1. How does a predator differ from a parasite? Compare the lifestyles of sharks and lampreys.
2. What is the difference between a jaw and a mouth?

3. If fishes are cold-blooded, how can they survive the coldest winters and even live in Antarctica?
4. Why are the spiracles of skates and rays an important adaptation for these fishes?
5. Observe the structure of a bony fish. Then explain the advantage of a backbone made up of many small vertebrae rather than one solid rod. Relate your answer to swimming in bony fishes.

EXTENSIONS

1. Halibuts and flounders are bony fishes with flat bodies that are sand-colored on the top side and white on the bottom side. Both fishes also have two eyes on the top side of their bodies and no eyes on the bottom side. State a hypothesis about how the characteristics of halibuts and flounders serve as adaptations for life on the ocean floor.

2. Survey a seafood market to find out what kinds of fish people use as food.
3. Use the library to research South American knifefish and African mormyrids. These fishes use electrical organs to sense their prey and to communicate with each other. Draw a diagram of one of these fishes. Label the organ that produces electricity and describe its function.

Chapter

Objectives

After you have completed this chapter, you will be able to

17-1 **identify** the major characteristics of amphibians.

17-1 **list** examples from each of the three orders of amphibians.

17-2 **describe** the external and internal anatomy of a frog.

17-2 **describe** metamorphosis in frogs.

17-3 **list** structural characteristics of reptiles that are adaptations to life on land.

17-3 **describe** the structure and function of the amniote egg.

17-3 **list** examples from each of the four orders of modern reptiles.

Science Process Skills

In this chapter, two science skills are highlighted. Symbols show some places where these skills are used.

☞ **Classifying:** When you classify, you group things based upon similarities.

❯ **Predicting:** When you predict, you state in advance how and why something will occur.

Although they look alike, salamanders and lizards are not the same kind of animal. Salamanders are amphibians. Lizards are reptiles. Because amphibians and reptiles often are seen in the same kind of environment, many people think that amphibians and reptiles are the same kind of animal. Reptiles and amphibians may be found in the same areas, but they are really quite different animals.

Today's amphibians are the descendants of the first vertebrates that were able to live on land. Their adaptations allow amphibians to live in water and on land. The reptiles are adapted to live on land.

17-1 Overview of Amphibians

Key Points

- Amphibians are cold-blooded vertebrates that go through metamorphosis.

- The three orders of amphibians are amphibians without legs, amphibians with tails, and amphibians without tails.

Skill Builder

Predicting *When you predict, you state in advance how and why something will occur. Biologists use information to make predictions about animals. Suppose the temperature of the earth's climate increased. Write a paragraph predicting how this might affect amphibians and their environment.*

Imagine what the earth was like 350 million years ago. Tall ferns cover the land. Swamps spread over many lowland areas. Small invertebrates live among the plants, and giant flying insects fill the air. Many different kinds of fishes live in the oceans.

How do biologists know what life on Earth was like 350 million years ago? Biologists make inferences about the earth's history by studying fossils. Fossils are the remains or traces of plants and animals that lived millions of years ago. Have you ever seen dinosaur fossils in a natural history museum?

Biologists have found fossils of fishes called lobe-finned fishes. From these fossils biologists infer that the lobe-finned fishes were able to crawl out of the water and onto the land. The lobe-finned fishes were not adapted to breathe air, so they could stay out of the water for only short periods of time. However, descendants of the lobe-finned fishes could stay out of the water for long periods of time. These descendants were the first amphibians. An amphibian is an animal that lives part of its life in the water and part on land. In fact, the word "amphibian" means "double life."

Characteristics of Amphibians

What are some characteristics of the "double-life" animals? Amphibians are cold-blooded vertebrates. Like other cold-blooded animals, amphibians cannot control their body temperature. The temperature of an amphibian stays about the same as its surroundings. What other group of cold-blooded animals can you name?

Figure 17–1 The coelancanth (SEE-luh-kanth) looks like one of the extinct lobe-finned fishes.

During its life cycle, an amphibian changes its appearance and its way of life. For example, in the early stages of development, amphibians live in the water. They breathe with gills. As an adult, an amphibian lives on land and uses lungs to breathe. The process by which a young amphibian changes into an adult is called **metamorphosis** (met-uh-MOR-fuh-sis).

Other characteristics of amphibians are as follows:

- Amphibians have smooth, moist skin.
- Amphibians have webbed feet.
- Amphibians use gills, lungs, and skin for respiration.
- Amphibians reproduce sexually and usually fertilize eggs outside the body.
- Amphibian eggs do not have shells and usually are deposited in water.

Classification of Amphibians

Today there are about 2500 species of amphibians. All amphibians are classified in the phylum *Chordata*. Biologists classify amphibians into three orders based on body structure. Look at the three amphibians shown in Figure 17-2. What differences in structure do you see?

Amphibians Without Legs

Caecilians (see-SIL-ee-uhns) are amphibians without legs. These amphibians have long, slender bodies and look very much like earthworms. Like earthworms, caecilians burrow into soft soil looking for food.

Most caecilians are about 30 cm long. Caecilians are considered blind, but some have very small eyes. How do you think caecilians find their prey if they cannot see? A caecilian has two tentacles near its nostrils. The caecilian uses these tentacles to sense its prey.

Figure 17–2 The caecilian (left), the cave salamander (middle), and the frog (right) are three kinds of amphibians.

Figure 17–3 Notice the feathery gills behind the head of the mud puppy.

Amphibians With Tails

Salamanders are an example of amphibians with tails. Some small salamanders that live mainly in water are called newts. Most salamanders are about 10 to 15 cm long. However, the Japanese hellbender grows to a length of 130 cm.

Salamander eggs are fertilized inside the body of the female. The male salamander deposits a packet of sperm on a leaf or twig. The female picks up the packet of sperm to fertilize the eggs. Female newts deposit the fertilized eggs in water. Other salamanders lay their eggs on damp ground or under logs.

Like all amphibians, young salamanders have gills. Most salamanders develop lungs when they become adults. However, some species of salamanders, such as the mud puppy, have gills throughout their lives.

Amphibians Without Tails

Frogs and toads are amphibians without tails. There are more species of tailless amphibians than any other kind of amphibian. Most frogs spend their lives in water, although some live in trees. Unlike frogs, all toads live on land. Frogs and toads range in size from 1.5 cm to more than 40 cm in length.

☞ Frogs and toads are very similar in appearance. Both have short bodies with strong, muscular hind legs. How can you tell the difference between a frog and a toad? One way to tell the difference between these two animals is by looking at the skin. Frogs have smooth, moist skin. The skin of a toad is rough and bumpy. Can you get warts by touching a toad? No, warts are caused by a virus.

Figure 17–4 The American toad can grow up to 25 cm in length.

Think & Discuss

1. What does the name "amphibian" mean?
2. How does an amphibian change as a result of metamorphosis?
3. List the three orders of amphibians and give an example of each.
4. List the major characteristics of amphibians.
5. Why do more amphibians live in tropical regions than anywhere else on Earth?

17-2 Anatomy of a Frog

Have you ever seen or heard frogs near a lake or pond? Frogs are the most common amphibians alive today. Frogs are easy to recognize and to find. For this reason, the frog is often used as a model for all amphibians.

External Anatomy

The external structures of a frog are adapted to the frog's double life in water and on land. Look at the frog in Figure 17-5. Notice the frog's bulging eyes on top of its head. How do you think the location of the eyes helps the frog?

❯ Each of the frog's eyes is covered with a third eyelid called a **nictitating** (NIK-tuh-tayt-ing) **membrane.** The nictitating membranes are transparent so the frog can see through them. The nictitating membranes protect the eyes and keep them moist. What would happen to a frog's eyes if its nictitating membranes were damaged?

Frogs do not have external ears as you do. Instead, just behind each eye is a round structure called a **tympanum** (TIM-puh-nuhm). The tympanum is the frog's eardrum. The tympanum allows a frog to hear well in both air and water. Hearing is important during the mating season because male frogs use sound to attract females. Some male frogs have vocal sacs. These vocal sacs fill with air when the male frog calls a mate.

❯ All frogs have smooth, moist skin. Because a frog uses its skin for respiration, the skin must be kept moist. When a frog is in the water, the skin is moist. However, when the frog leaves the water, its skin must be kept from drying out. **Mucus** (MYOO-kus) **glands** scattered over the frog's skin secrete a slimy fluid that helps keep the skin moist. What do you think would happen to a frog if its mucus glands stopped functioning?

Frogs are adapted for movement on land or in the water. For example, the powerful hind legs of a frog allow the frog to leap as far as 5 m. Have you ever worn swim fins when you were swimming? What do the swim fins do? Most frogs have webbed feet that help them swim. How do swim fins compare to a frog's feet? Tree frogs have suction pads on their feet. How are suction pads an adaptation to the tree frog's way of life?

Key Points

- The external and internal structures of a frog are adapted to life in water and on land.

- Frogs begin their development as tadpoles with gills and gradually change into adults with lungs.

Figure 17–5 The frog's eyes and nostrils are located on top of the frog's head.

Internal Anatomy

Frogs have an internal skeleton that provides support. The skeleton also protects the frog's internal organs. The organ systems of a frog are adapted to life in water and on land.

Support and Movement

The skeleton of a frog is shown in Figure 17-6. The frog's skeleton is an adaptation to life on land. Unlike a fish's skeleton, a frog's skeleton must support the frog's weight and allow the frog to move on land.

Frogs have two sets of limbs. The front limbs are attached to the skeleton by the **pectoral** (PEK-tuh-ruhl) **girdle.** The hind limbs are attached by the **pelvic girdle.** The hind limbs are strong and muscular, and allow the frog to move around on land.

Circulation and Respiration

Unlike the two-chambered heart of a fish, a frog's heart has three chambers. A three-chambered heart circulates

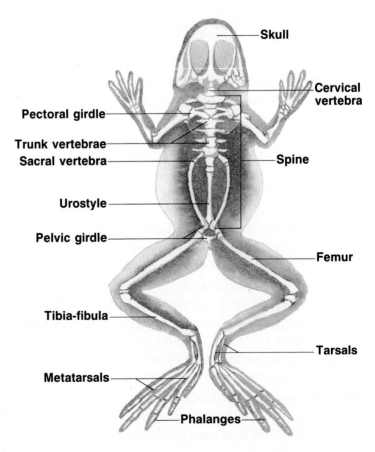

Figure 17–6 The front and hind limbs of the frog are a major adaptation to life on land.

blood more efficiently than a two-chambered heart. This added efficiency is an adaptation to life on land. Why do you think animals that live on land need more energy than animals that live in water?

The three chambers of a frog's heart are the left atrium, the right atrium, and the ventricle. Figure 17-7 shows how blood circulates through the three chambers of the frog's heart. Oxygen-rich blood from the lungs enters the left atrium. Oxygen-poor blood from the body enters the right atrium. Blood from both the left and right atrium empties into the ventricle. The ventricle pumps some of this mixed blood to the lungs and some to the body.

Adult frogs take in oxygen through the lungs, mouth, and skin. When a frog lowers the floor of its mouth, air enters the nostrils. The frog then raises the floor of its mouth and closes the nostrils. Air is forced through the **glottis** and into the lungs. The glottis is the tube between the throat and the lungs.

Some oxygen is absorbed by the moist lining of the frog's mouth. This process is called mouth breathing. Mouth breathing provides only a small amount of oxygen for the frog.

When a frog is underwater, it can take in oxygen through its skin alone. During the winter, frogs often remain buried in mud for months. Respiration through the skin keeps the frog alive during this time.

Regulation

Frogs do not have a lateral line as fishes do. Instead, frogs rely on their senses of sight, smell, and hearing. Nerves connect the frog's sense organs to its brain. The sense organs collect information from the environment.

Digestion and Excretion

Have you ever seen a frog catch a fly? The frog uses its long sticky tongue to catch its prey and bring the prey back into its mouth. Small teeth line the upper edge of the mouth. Two other teeth are on the roof of the mouth. The frog's teeth help it hold its prey.

When the frog swallows, the food enters the esophagus. From the esophagus, the food moves into the stomach. Enzymes in the stomach digest the food. The digested food leaves the stomach and enters the small intestine.

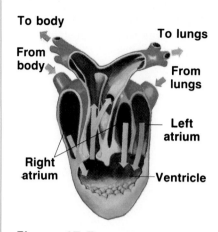

Figure 17-7   Unlike your heart, a frog's heart has only one ventricle.

Study Hint

Look at the diagram of the frog heart. Trace the possible paths the frog's blood can take through the three chambers of the heart.

Figure 17–8 The frog's digestive system is adapted for eating large amounts of small prey such as insects.

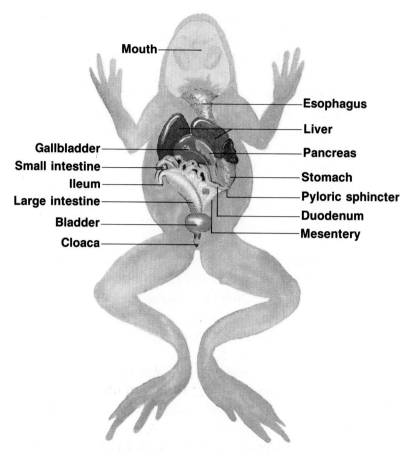

Mouth

Esophagus

Liver

Gallbladder

Pancreas

Small intestine

Ileum

Stomach

Large intestine

Pyloric sphincter

Duodenum

Bladder

Mesentery

Cloaca

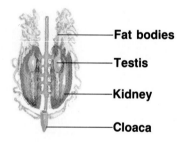

Fat bodies

Testis

Kidney

Cloaca

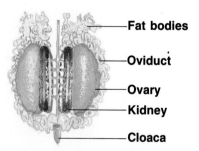

Fat bodies

Oviduct

Ovary

Kidney

Cloaca

Figure 17–9 The male (top) and female (bottom) reproductive organs of frogs are found inside the body cavity.

Nutrients are absorbed in the small intestine. Waste material then moves into the large intestine, where water is absorbed. The remaining waste material leaves the frog's body through the cloaca (kloh-AY-kuh). Trace the path of food through the frog's digestive system shown in Figure 17–8.

The kidneys are the main organs of excretion in the frog. Wastes and excess water are removed from the blood by the kidneys. Together, the waste materials and water form urine. The urine is collected in tubes that lead from the kidneys into the urinary bladder. Urine leaves the frog's body through the cloaca.

Reproduction and Development

Frogs reproduce sexually. Figure 17-9 shows the male and female reproductive organs of the frog. Notice the **fat bodies** on the male testes and the female ovaries. The fat bodies help nourish the developing sperm and eggs.

The female frog produces eggs in two ovaries. When the eggs are mature, they break through the thin walls of

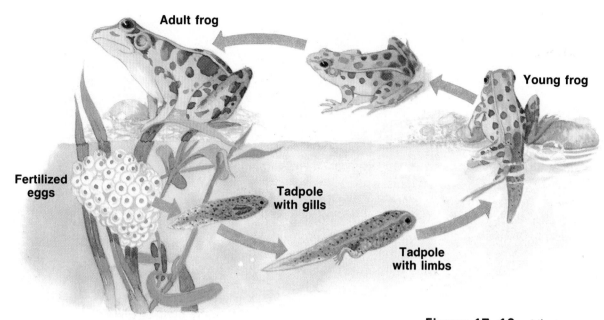

Adult frog

Young frog

Fertilized eggs

Tadpole with gills

Tadpole with limbs

Figure 17–10 Like insects, frogs go through several stages of metamorphosis as they develop into adults.

the ovaries. The eggs pass into tubes called oviducts. As the eggs move through the oviducts, the eggs are covered with a jellylike material. The male frog produces sperm in two testes. The sperm move through tubes into storage organs, where they remain until mating.

Like most amphibians, female frogs lay their eggs in water. Fertilization takes place outside the body. During mating, the male frog clasps the female from behind and fertilizes the eggs as they are released.

If you look carefully around the edges of a pond in late spring, you may see clumps of frog's eggs clinging to water plants. About 12 days after fertilization, the eggs hatch into **tadpoles.** Tadpoles are the larvae of frogs. Like fishes, tadpoles have gills and a two-chambered heart. Tadpoles change into adult frogs through metamorphosis. Figure 17-10 shows the stages in the metamorphosis of a tadpole.

Think & Discuss

6. What is the function of a frog's mucus glands?
7. What is a frog's third eyelid called? What is its function?
8. Trace the flow of blood through a frog's heart.
9. List the stages in the metamorphosis of a tadpole.
10. How is a frog's heart adapted to life on land?

ACTIVITY 17–1

PROBLEM: How long does it take a bullfrog to become an adult?

Science Process Skills
observing, sequencing, interpreting data

Background Information
A female bullfrog may lay up to 20,000 eggs in water. The eggs hatch in 5 to 20 days. The tadpoles that hatch from the eggs are the larval form of bullfrogs. During their development, the larvae must remain in the water. The larvae eat algae. After a period of growth, the tadpoles grow limbs and lose their tails. The time that it takes a bullfrog tadpole to develop into an adult bullfrog varies according to the temperature. In cold areas, the length of development time is longer.

Materials
paper and pencil

Procedure
1. Study the drawings of the development of a tadpole in Figure A.
2. Place the drawings of the development of the tadpole in the correct order.
3. Study the graph that shows the development of a bullfrog.

Observations
1. **a.** Write the correct order of the letters to show the development of the tadpole.
   b. Describe the most obvious changes that take place in each stage.

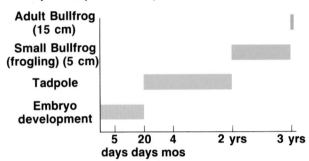

Graph: Tadpole Development in Northern States

2. What is a small bullfrog called?
3. How long may bullfrogs live as tadpoles?

Conclusions
1. How many years does it take a bullfrog to go from embryo to adult?
2. How many years does it take for the small bullfrog to grow to 15 cm?
3. **INFER** What do you think would happen to the length of time it takes a bullfrog to develop if the bullfrog lived in a Southern state?

Going Further
Dianne Seale is a biologist who did research to find out how nutrients in a pond affect the development of a tadpole. Visit the library and find out about Dianne Seale's work. Report your findings to the class in the form of a scientific article.

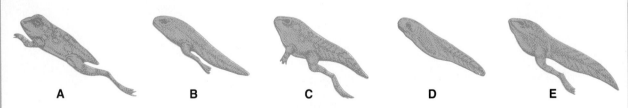

Figure A: Tadpole Development

17-3 Overview of Reptiles

The first reptiles appeared on the earth about 310 million years ago. Biologists infer that these early reptiles were descendants of amphibians. Unlike amphibians, early reptiles did not have to return to the water to keep their skin moist and to lay their eggs. The reptiles could live entirely on land. Because they had no competition for food or living space, the reptiles increased in number and variety.

For millions of years, reptiles ruled the earth. Reptiles were the dominant land animals from 225 million to 65 million years ago. This period of time is called the Age of Reptiles. It also could be called the Age of Dinosaurs, after the most famous of the early reptiles.

Have you ever seen the skeleton of an *Apatosaurus* (uh-pah-tuh-SOR-uhs)? The *Apatosaurus* was one of the largest dinosaurs that ever lived. It lived in swamps and ate plants. Some other dinosaurs included the meat-eating *Tyrannosaurus* (ti-RAN-uh-sor-uhs) rex and the flying pterodactyl (ter-uh-DAK-tul).

Scientists have many theories, but no one knows for sure why the dinosaurs became extinct. Some evidence indicates that a giant meteor may have crashed into the earth and caused the death of the dinosaurs. Today, the closest living relatives of the dinosaurs are the birds.

Key Points

- Reptiles have several characteristics that allowed them to adapt to life on land.

- The amniote egg contains four membranes.

- The four orders of reptiles include tuataras, turtles and tortoises, alligators and crocodiles, snakes and lizards.

Study Hint

Some scientists think that a collision of a meteor with Earth filled the sky with dust and blocked out sunlight. Make a list of possible ways this event might have affected the dinosaurs.

Figure 17–11 Dinosaurs were the dominant animals on Earth for millions of years.

Characteristics of Reptiles

Like the amphibians, reptiles are cold-blooded vertebrates. Because they are cold-blooded, most reptiles live in warm, tropical environments. Reptiles were the first vertebrates to become completely adapted to life on land.

Reptiles have many adaptations that allow them to live away from the water. For example, reptiles have dry skin that is covered with scales. This thick skin prevents the loss of water from the reptile's body. The reptile's method of reproduction also is an adaptation to life on land. Unlike amphibians, fertilization of reptiles takes place inside the body of the female. Because the eggs are fertilized internally, sperm do not need to swim through water to reach the egg cells.

One of the major characteristics of reptiles is a hard-shelled **amniote** (AM-nee-oht) **egg.** The amniote egg also is an adaptation to life on land. Unlike the uncovered eggs of amphibians, the amniote egg provides a self-contained environment for the embryo. Look at Figure 17-12 as you read about the structure of the amniote egg.

An amniote egg surrounds the developing embryo with four membranes covered by a shell. The four membranes in an amniote egg are the amnion, the yolk sac, the allantois (uh-LAN-tuh-wis), and the chorion (KAWR-ee-ahn). The fluid-filled amnion holds the embryo. The fluid in the amnion supports and cushions the embryo. The yolk sac provides stored food for the embryo. Wastes produced by the embryo are collected and kept separate from the embryo in the allantois. The chorion lines the inside of the shell. Both the chorion and the allantois control the exchange of oxygen and carbon dioxide through the shell.

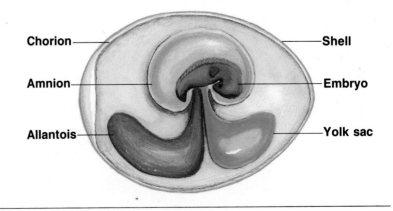

Figure 17-12 Reptiles were the first land animals with an embryo protected by an amniote egg.

Some other characteristics of reptiles include the following:

- Most reptiles have two pairs of legs.
- Reptiles with legs have feet with claws.
- Reptiles use lungs for respiration.
- Reptiles have either a three-chambered or a four-chambered heart.

Classification of Reptiles

About 6500 species of reptiles are living today. Biologists classify reptiles into four orders. The four orders of reptiles are the tuatara (too-uh-TA-ruh), turtles and tortoises, crocodiles and alligators, and snakes and lizards.

Tuatara

Tuataras are sometimes called "living fossils" because they have some of the characteristics of the ancient reptiles. In fact, tuataras have changed very little since they first appeared over 200 million years ago. Tuataras grow to about 60 cm in length and resemble lizards.

One of the most unusual features of the tuatara is a third eye, called a **parietal** (puh-RY-uh-tul) **eye.** The parietal eye is found on top of the tuatara's head. Scientists know that tuataras do not use the parietal eye for seeing, but they are not sure what its function really is.

Turtles and Tortoises

Turtles and tortoises belong to the same order of reptiles. Turtles live mainly in the water. Turtles are found in both fresh water and salt water. Tortoises live mainly on land. There are about 150 species of turtles and tortoises alive today.

Have you ever picked up a turtle? What did the turtle do? You probably noticed that the turtle withdrew its head and legs into its shell for protection. The most obvious feature of turtles and tortoises is a shell. The shell is made up of two separate halves. The shell is covered with modified scales called **scutes** (SKYOOTS). Turtles usually have a flat, streamlined shell. Tortoises have a high, domed shell. Turtles and tortoises cannot leave their shells.

Figure 17–13 Tuataras live only in New Zealand. They are an endangered species.

Figure 17–14 Compare the flat shell of the painted turtle (top) with the domed shell of the Galapagos tortoise (bottom).

Alligators and Crocodiles

Have you ever heard of a caiman (KAY-muhn) or a gavial (GAY-vee-uhl)? Caimans and gavials are related to alligators and crocodiles. These four kinds of animals make up the third order of reptiles. Caimans from Central and South America look very much like alligators. In fact, caimans often are sold in pet stores as baby alligators. Gavials are found in India. They are very similar to crocodiles in appearance. Alligators and crocodiles have thick skin covered with hard scales. They live mainly in water and can grow up to 4.5 m long.

☞ Do you know how to tell the difference between an alligator and a crocodile? Look at Figure 17-15. The main difference between an alligator and a crocodile is the shape of the head. The head of an alligator is broad and rounded, while the head of a crocodile is more triangular. Both alligators and crocodiles have eyes and nostrils on top of their heads. How does this adaptation help the animals?

Snakes and Lizards

Snakes and lizards are classified in the largest order of reptiles. There are about 4500 species of snakes and lizards in this order. A major difference between snakes and lizards is that snakes do not have legs. Snakes are long and slender. They have more vertebrae and ribs than any other animal. The muscles attached to these bones allow snakes to move gracefully over the ground.

Snakes have poor vision and hearing. To gather information about its environment, a snake relies on its senses of taste and smell. Have you ever seen a snake's forked tongue darting from its mouth? A snake senses odors by using its tongue. After sampling the surrounding air, the snake places its tongue in an organ on the roof of its mouth. This organ is called **Jacobson's organ.** It can

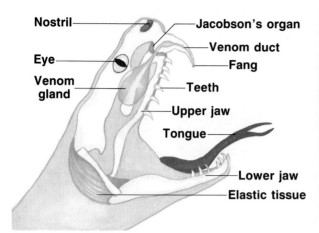

Labels on diagram: Nostril, Eye, Venom gland, Jacobson's organ, Venom duct, Fang, Teeth, Upper jaw, Tongue, Lower jaw, Elastic tissue

Figure 17–16 The water moccasin (right) is a poisonous snake. Find the venom gland in the diagram (left).

detect odors in the air. Snakes can use Jacobson's organ to help them find their prey.

Most snakes are nonpoisonous. Some snakes, however, are poisonous. Three poisonous snakes found in North America are water moccasins, rattlesnakes, and copperheads. They have special hollow teeth called fangs. The fangs are filled with poison, or **venom.** Snakes with fangs inject poison into their prey. Once the prey has been poisoned, the snake swallows its prey whole. Snakes can unhinge their jaws to allow them to swallow their prey whole. A snake's teeth curve backward. These teeth hold the snake's prey and help move it backward.

One of the most interesting characteristics of lizards is **regeneration** (ri-jen-uh-RAY-shun). Regeneration is the ability of an organism to replace lost body parts. A skink, for example, can shed its tail when chased by a predator. The predator is distracted by the wiggling tail. The skink escapes and grows a new tail. What other kind of animal can regenerate body parts?

Health and Safety Tip
A snakebite victim should immediately be taken to the nearest hospital. Never try to treat a snakebite yourself.

Think & Discuss

11. What is regeneration? How does regeneration help lizards survive?

12. What is the function of Jacobson's organ?

13. Give an example of each of the four orders of reptiles.

14. How did the amniote egg get its name?

★ 15. How is the reptile egg an advance over the amphibian egg?

ACTIVITY 17–2

PROBLEM: What are some of the characteristics of the snakes of North America?

Science Process Skills
classifying, interpreting data, comparing

Background Information
Some snakes are poisonous and some are nonpoisonous. Snakes vary in coloration and length. Each snake has a range in length. In data tables or charts, the minimum length to the maximum length usually is given for each kind of snake.

Materials
paper and pencil

Procedure
1. Study the graph of different snakes in North America.

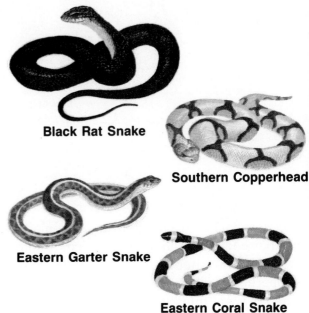

Black Rat Snake

Southern Copperhead

Eastern Garter Snake

Eastern Coral Snake

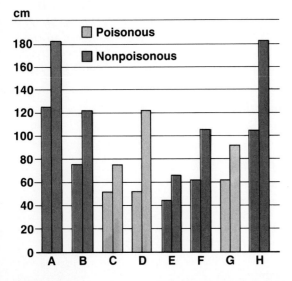

cm	
□ Poisonous	
■ Nonpoisonous	

A Bull snake
B Corn snake
C Eastern coral snake
D Eastern cottonmouth
E Eastern garter snake
F Northern water snake
G Southern copperhead
H Black rat snake

2. List the poisonous snakes and the nonpoisonous snakes.
3. Next to each snake list its shortest and its longest length. These two numbers will give you the range in size for each snake.

Observations
1. **a.** Which snakes are the longest? **b.** Which snake is the shortest?
2. **a.** How many nonpoisonous snakes are shown? **b.** How many poisonous snakes are shown?
3. **a.** Which nonpoisonous snake is the shortest? **b.** Which is the longest?
4. **a.** Which poisonous snake is the longest? **b.** Which is the shortest?

Conclusions
1. **INFER** If the snakes of North America given in the graph represent the total number of types of snakes on the earth, are there more poisonous or nonpoisonous snakes in the world?
2. What is the range in length for all the snakes shown in the graph?
3. **a.** In nature, could you find a garter snake that was 50 cm long? Why or why not? **b.** In nature, could you find an Eastern coral snake that was 160 cm long? Why or why not?

If you have ever owned a pet, you know that animals can be a lot of fun—and very special companions. Do you enjoy caring for animals and think of yourself as an "animal lover"? If the answer is yes, then you may enjoy a career working with animals.

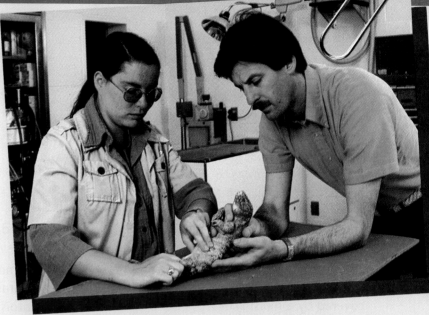

Pet Shop Owner

A pet shop owner stocks the supplies that people need to care for their pets. Many pet shop owners also sell pets—cats, dogs, birds, fish, hamsters, and even snakes. Some pet shop owners provide grooming services, and still others have kennels in which pets can be boarded while their owners are away.

Since pet shop owners are often asked for advice, they need to learn as much as possible about animals. Vocational courses in animal care, grooming, training, and basic medicine will benefit a future pet shop owner. Courses in business also are helpful.

Many pet shop owners begin their careers by working in a pet shop.

For more information: Try to obtain a part-time or summer job working in a pet shop.

Veterinarian

Caring for sick or injured animals is the job of a veterinarian. Veterinarians diagnose medical conditions and prescribe and administer medicines. They also perform surgery on animals.

Most veterinarians are in private practice. Others are employed by government agencies, pharmaceutical or animal food companies, farms, research laboratories, and medical schools.

A veterinarian must obtain a license in the state in which he or she wishes to practice. To qualify for a license, a person must complete a six-year college degree program in veterinary medicine, then pass written and oral examinations.

Animal Technician

Animal technicians assist veterinarians in treating sick animals. The duties of an animal technician include record keeping, specimen collection, laboratory work, and the dressing of wounds. Animal technicians also assist veterinarians with equipment and animals during surgery.

In addition to obtaining a high school diploma, an animal technician must complete a two-year animal technology program. This program provides an animal technician with training in laboratory work and animal research. A high school student who plans to be a veterinarian or animal technician should concentrate on doing very well in science courses. Summer or part-time job experience working with animals also is helpful.

For more information: Write to the American Veterinary Medical Association, 930 North Meacham Road, Schaumburg, IL 60196, about veterinary medicine careers.

Chapter Review

17-1 Overview of Amphibians

- Amphibians breathe with gills during their larval stage and with lungs as adults.
- Amphibians undergo metamorphosis, reproduce sexually, and lay eggs without shells in water.
- Body appearance determines which order an amphibian belongs to. The three orders of amphibians include amphibians without legs, amphibians with tails, and amphibians without tails.

17-2 Anatomy of the Frog

- Frogs have two pairs of legs and are covered by a moist skin.
- Frogs have a three-chambered heart, which circulates their blood.
- Adult frogs have lungs.

- During metamorphosis, a frog egg hatches into a tadpole with external gills. The gills gradually move inside the tadpole and develop into lungs. The tadpole develops legs and loses its tail. The adult frog has legs, lungs, and no tail.

17-3 Overview of Reptiles

- Reptiles reproduce sexually and fertilize their eggs internally.
- Reptiles lay amniote eggs that develop on dry land. When the reptile hatches, it is fully developed.
- The amniote egg contains four membranes: the amnion, the yolk sac, the allantois, and the chorion.
- The four orders of reptiles include tuataras, turtles and tortoises, alligators and crocodiles, and snakes and lizards.

VOCABULARY LIST

amniote egg (296)
fat bodies (292)
glottis (291)
Jacobson's organ (298)

metamorphosis (287)
mucus glands (289)
nictitating membrane (289)
parietal eye (297)

pectoral girdle (290)
pelvic girdle (290)
regeneration (299)
scutes (297)

tadpoles (293)
tympanum (289)
venom (299)

VOCABULARY REVIEW

Matching   Write the word or term from the Vocabulary List that best matches each description.

1. the clear, third eyelid of a frog
2. used by snakes to smell
3. nourish the developing eggs and sperm of a frog
4. hearing organ of a frog
5. larval stage of a frog
6. poison found in some snakes
7. hard, modified scales
8. process of development in amphibians
9. keep the skin of an amphibian moist

Identifying Relationships   Identify the word or term in each group that does not belong. Explain why it does not belong with the group.

1. tadpole, regeneration, adult frog
2. Jacobson's organ, tongue, fangs
3. third eyelid, nictitating membrane, tympanum
4. cloaca, glottis, lungs
6. pectoral girdle, frog's skeleton, allantois
6. parietal eye, tuatara, ventricle
7. metamorphosis, amphibian, reptile
8. amniote egg, amphibian, chorion
9. frog's hind legs, salamander, pelvic girdle

Completion   Write the word or words that best complete each sentence.

1. Modified scales on a turtle's back are _____.
2. The frog uses its _____ to hear.
3. The frog's developing sperm and eggs are nourished by _____.
4. A young amphibian's change into adulthood is called _____.
5. An _____ surrounds a reptile's developing embryo.
6. The frog's _____ secrete a slimy fluid that keeps its skin moist.
7. The unusual structure on top of a tuatara's head is called a _____.
8. Poisonous snakes have hollow teeth called _____ that hold venom.
9. The _____ attaches the frog's front limbs to its skeleton.

Finding the Main Ideas   Use the section number to find the sentence that answers each question. Then, write the sentence.

1. What is an amphibian? (17-1)
2. When do amphibians live in water? (17-1)
3. When do amphibians live on land? (17-1)
4. How are amphibians classified? (17-1)
5. How is a frog's skin kept moist when it is out of water? (17-2)
6. Why is a frog's skeleton different from the skeleton of a fish? (17-2)
7. By what process do tadpoles become adult frogs? (17-2)
8. How is a reptile's skin adapted to life on land? (17-3)
9. What protects the reptile embryo as it develops? (17-3)
10. How do alligators differ from crocodiles? (17-3)

CONCEPT REVIEW

Writing for Understanding   One way to find out if you understand something is to write a brief summary of the information in your own words. Reread Section 17-3, Overview of Reptiles, on pages 295–299, and write a brief summary of the information.

Critical Thinking   Answer each of the following in complete sentences.

1. Caecilians are wormlike in appearance but are not really wormlike in structure. How do caecilians differ from worms?
2. Predict what would happen to a frog if it could not get back to its pond and was stranded on land.
3. When an amphibian uses more energy, it needs more oxygen. How does the respiratory system of an amphibian meet this need?
4. How is the heart of a reptile an improvement over the heart of an amphibian?
5. How might the use of poison be an adaptation to a snake?

EXTENSIONS

1. Marine iguanas are lizards that have adapted to life in the sea. Present an oral report about marine iguanas to your class. In the report, compare the egg-laying of the iguana with that of marine turtles.
2. *Latimeria* is another "living fossil." It is a descendant of the lobe-finned fishes that gave rise to amphibians. Investigate this fish in the library and write a report giving some possible reasons why it is still alive today.

Amphibians and Reptiles   303

Chapter 18 | Birds

After you have completed this chapter, you will be able to

18-1 **list** the major characteristics of birds.

18-1 **explain** how beaks and feet are adaptations.

18-2 **describe** the function of feathers.

18-2 **describe** the general anatomy of a bird.

18-2 **explain** how birds are adapted for flight.

18-3 **identify** three behaviors of birds that are related to reproduction.

18-3 **define** migration.

Science Process Skills

In this chapter, two science skills are highlighted. Symbols show some places where these skills are used.

▶ **Inferring:** When you infer, you form a conclusion based upon facts and not direct observation.

📁 **Classifying:** When you classify, you group things based upon similarities.

When you think of a bird, you probably imagine an animal like a robin, a pigeon, or a sparrow. However, in the swamps of South America there is a bird so strange-looking that some biologists have described it as a punk-rock chicken. This bird, the hoatzin (hoh-AT-sin), smells so bad that local people call it the "stink bird." The hoatzin acts strangely, too. It feeds almost completely on leaves. Its young use special claws on their wings to climb around in trees, and they jump into rivers when something scares them.

There are about 8600 species of birds alive today. Some, such as the harpy eagle, are big enough to catch deer. Others, such as hummingbirds, are so small they can become stuck in spider webs. Despite their differences, all birds share certain features that make them related.

18-1 Overview of Birds

The earliest birds lived at the time of the dinosaurs, more than 100 million years ago. The oldest-known bird fossil is called *Archaeopteryx* (ahr-kee-AHP-tur-iks), which means "ancient wing." *Archaeopteryx* had heavy bones and teeth like a reptile, but also had feathers like a modern bird.

You may be surprised to learn that birds are closely related to reptiles. For example, both birds and reptiles have **amniote** (AM-nee-oht) **eggs.** Amniote eggs have a porous shell and a fluid-filled sac. Birds and reptiles also have claws and scales. Birds, however, have scales only on their legs and feet. Where do reptiles have scales?

Characteristics of Birds

You are **warm-blooded.** Birds also are warm-blooded. The body temperature of a warm-blooded animal usually remains about the same. It does not change as the temperature of the organism's environment changes. How does the body temperature of birds differ from the body temperature of reptiles?

What image comes to mind when you think of a bird? You probably think of a flying animal covered with feathers. Birds are the only animals with feathers. In fact, the presence of feathers is enough to identify an animal as a bird. All birds also have the following characteristics.

- Birds have two pairs of limbs—wings and legs.
- Birds have lightweight bones.
- Birds have a toothless beak.
- Birds reproduce sexually and have amniote eggs.
- A bird's body is divided into a head, neck, trunk, and tail.
- Birds have a backbone.

Classification of Birds

Like fishes, amphibians, and reptiles, birds are classified in the phylum *Chordata*. In addition, all birds belong to the class *Aves*. Birds can be classified into five groups according to their body structures. The groups are listed

Key Points

- Birds are warm-blooded vertebrates that have feathers covering their bodies.
- Bird groups include swimmers, waders, birds of prey, perching birds, and nonperching land birds.
- The shape of a bird's beak and feet are adapted to the bird's way of life.

Figure 18-1 *Archaeopteryx* fossils show an animal with birdlike and reptilian features.

Table 18-1 The Five Groups of Birds				
SWIMMING BIRDS	WADING BIRDS	BIRDS OF PREY	PERCHING BIRDS	NONPERCHING LAND BIRDS
Ducks Geese Swans Loons Gulls	Herons Egrets Flamingos Sandpipers Cranes	Hawks Owls Eagles Vultures Falcons	Cardinals Sparrows Crows Chickadees Blackbirds	Woodpeckers Hummingbirds Grouse Turkeys Whippoorwills

in Table 18-1. The body structures that determine which group a bird will be classified in are the beak and feet. The shape of the beaks and feet of birds enable different kinds of birds to live in different environments.

👉 The structures of the beaks and feet of each group of birds are shown in Figure 18-2. How does the shape of the feet of the swimming birds differ from the waders? Swimming birds, such as ducks, usually have webbed feet. Webbed feet allow a swimmer to push itself through the water. Unlike swimmers, waders have long toes so they do not sink into mud or sand.

Nonperching land birds use their feet for scratching, running, or clinging. However, perching birds have toes that wrap around small branches. Perching birds, such as robins, finches, and sparrows, often feed upon seeds and small insects. Look at Figure 18-2. How is the shape of a perching bird's beak adapted to the kinds of food it eats?

Skill Builder

Classifying   When you classify, you group things based upon similarities. Use a field guide or encyclopedia to find the names of ten kinds of birds that live in your area. Then classify each bird you have identified into one of the five groups discussed in this chapter.

Birds of Prey
Hawk
Tearing
Grasping

Wading Birds
Spearing fish
Heron
Wading

Swimming Birds
Duck
Straining
Swimming

Perching Birds
Cardinal
Cracking seeds
Perching

Nonperching Land Birds
Woodpecker
Chiseling
Clinging

Figure 18-2   The beaks and feet of birds are adaptations.

▶ Birds of prey are predators, or animals that catch and eat other animals. Birds of prey have sharp, curved claws that are used to catch and kill prey. Birds of prey also have strong, sharp beaks. Why do you think birds of prey need strong, sharp beaks?

Think & Discuss

1. How does a warm-blooded animal differ from a cold-blooded animal?

2. List the five major groups of birds.

3. A hawk is a bird of prey. How do you think a hawk's beak and feet are adapted to its way of life?

18-2 Anatomy of a Bird

Have you ever wondered why birds can fly? The body of a bird is adapted for flight. For example, the bird's body is streamlined to reduce air resistance. Its wings fan the air and can be used to soar or glide. The tail is used for steering and balance. Birds also have lightweight bodies covered with feathers. In most birds, feathers also aid in flight.

Feathers

Feathers grow out of a bird's skin in much the same way as scales grow from a reptile's skin. Feathers help keep a bird warm. They also cover and protect the skin.

Two main kinds of feathers on a bird's body are **contour feathers** and **down feathers.** Contour feathers cover the body and give the bird its shape. The flight feathers on the wings and tail also are contour feathers. Down feathers are small fluffy feathers that are close to a bird's skin. You may have seen down feathers on a young bird. People use down feathers in a variety of products.

Molting

Contour feathers often become worn and damaged. They are replaced at least once a year in a process called **molting.** During molting, old feathers fall out and new

Key Points

- Feathers keep a bird warm, protect its skin, and aid in flight.
- Low body weight and high energy efficiency are adaptations for flight in birds.

Contour feather

Down feather

Figure 18-3 Notice the difference in size and texture of the two kinds of feathers.

ones grow in their place. Molting occurs gradually. Only a few feathers are lost at a time. This is why you never see a bird without feathers.

Preening

Birds take good care of their feathers. A common activity among birds is **preening.** During preening, a bird uses its beak to take oil from a gland at the base of its tail and apply the oil to its feathers.

Preening keeps a bird's feathers from drying out and breaking. It also makes the feathers waterproof. Which groups of birds do you think need to be waterproof? Why?

Support and Movement

Look at the bird skeleton in Figure 18-4. Many of the bones are hollow, which reduces their weight. Notice the large **sternum,** or breastbone. Why do you suppose this bone is so large? The sternum is large because it is where the large, powerful flight muscles are attached. These muscles move the wing bones in the flapping motion that produces flight.

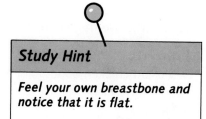

Study Hint

Feel your own breastbone and notice that it is flat.

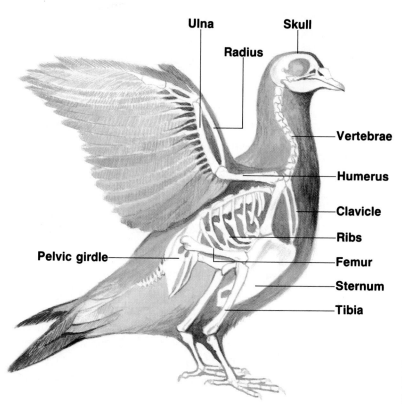

Ulna

Radius

Skull

Vertebrae

Humerus

Clavicle

Ribs

Femur

Sternum

Tibia

Pelvic girdle

Figure 18-4 Can you find the wishbone? What is it called?

ACTIVITY 18–1

PROBLEM: How are a bird's bones adapted for flight?

Science Process Skills
comparing, analyzing, measuring

Background Information
The structure of bones, the way in which bones are connected to each other, and the way in which the bones are connected to muscles are adaptations to different functions, or purposes. For example, the leg bones of an elephant are very dense and are strong enough to support the animal's weight on land. The bones of birds have a structure that enables birds to fly.

Materials
5 clean chicken bones,   hand lens
   all different   scalpel
balance

Procedure
1. Copy the Data Table shown.

Data Table:	Bird Bones		
BONE NAME	LOCATION	FUNCTION	MASS (g)
1.			
2.			
3.			
4.			
5.			

2. **INFER** What characteristics of a bone do you think would aid in flight? Write your inference on a sheet of paper. Your inference should answer the question. To find out if your inference is accurate, continue the activity.
3. Compare each clean chicken bone to the bird skeleton in Figure 18–4 on page 309 of your text. Determine the name and location of each bone.

4. Record the name of each bone, its location, and its function in the Data Table.
5. Use the balance to find the mass of each bone. Record the mass of each bone in grams.
6. Total and record the mass of all the bones.
7. Using the scalpel, carefully cut one of the long bones in half. **CAUTION: Use extreme care when using the scalpel.** Study the cross section with the hand lens. Describe the inside of the bone.
8. Try breaking one of the bones in half with your hands.

Observations
1. **a.** Were the bones easy to cut? **b.** Were the bones strong or very weak?
2. **a.** Would you describe the inside of the bone as porous or dense? **b.** Were the bones heavy or light in weight? **c.** Do the insides of the bones have a large or small hollow space?

Conclusions
1. Did all of the bones seem to have the same characteristics?
2. How are the bones of a bird suited for flight?
3. Was your inference accurate? Use your observations to support your answer.
4. **INFER**   Do you think that flightless birds, such as ostriches, have similar types of bones? Explain your answer.

Going Further
Like birds, bats can fly. They also have an internal skeleton. Do you think that the bones of bats have similar characteristics to those of birds? Visit the library and find out about the bone structure of a bat. Compare the skeletons of a bird and a bat.

Digestion and Excretion

The digestive system of birds works rapidly. The rapid burning of food in the body cells produces large amounts of energy. Much of this energy is used for flight. As you read about the digestive system of a bird, look at Figure 18-5. Notice the **crop.** The crop is an organ that stores food. The bird eats quickly until its crop is full. Then the bird moves to a safe place to digest the food.

Food moves from the crop to the two-part stomach. The second part of the stomach is called the **gizzard.** The gizzard is a strong, muscular grinding organ. Because birds do not have teeth, the gizzard grinds the food. Birds swallow small stones or grit to help crush the food in the gizzard. Digested food is then absorbed by the intestine.

► The excretory system of birds consists of two kidneys that filter uric acid from the blood. Uric acid is a waste product. Very little water is removed as waste and birds do not form liquid urine. Instead, the uric acid from the kidneys is combined with solid wastes from the digestive system. Solid and liquid wastes are excreted together from an opening called the cloaca. Wastes are not stored for long periods of time in birds. Why do you think this helps birds fly?

Skill Builder
Comparing *When you compare, you are looking at how things are alike and how they are different. Compare the functions of the crop and the gizzard of the bird with those of the crop and the gizzard of the earthworm.*

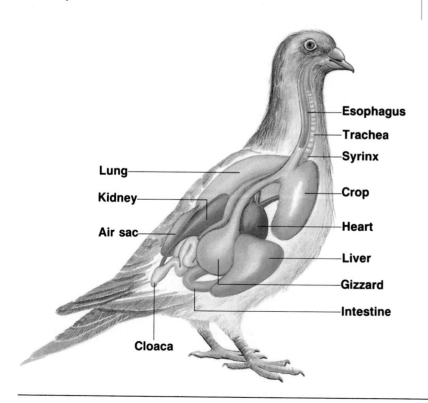

Lung
Kidney
Air sac
Cloaca

Esophagus
Trachea
Syrinx
Crop
Heart
Liver
Gizzard
Intestine

Figure 18-5 Trace the path of a seed through the bird's digestive system.

Study Hint

Refer to Figure 18-5 on page 311 to locate the lungs, air sacs, syrinx, and trachea, of a bird.

Skill Builder

Comparing When you compare two things, you are trying to see how the things are similar. Compare the hearts of fish, amphibians, reptiles, and birds. Explain why the bird heart is the most efficient.

Circulation and Respiration

A bird's circulatory system is adapted for a high-energy life. The four-chambered heart of a bird is the most efficient type of heart found in animals. A bird's heart pumps blood rapidly. The blood carries food and oxygen to all body cells to provide energy for the bird's activities.

Birds must take in a lot of oxygen to produce energy. The respiratory system in birds is very efficient. In addition to lungs, a bird's respiratory system also has **air sacs** connected to the lungs. Air sacs help supply the large amounts of oxygen needed by a flying bird. Air sacs also help regulate the body temperature of a bird by absorbing excess heat. This heat is excreted along with carbon dioxide when the bird exhales.

Do you enjoy hearing a bird sing? Birds can sing because of a structure called the **syrinx** (SIR-inks), or song box. The syrinx is located at the base of the trachea, or windpipe. The syrinx produces the songs and calls of birds.

Regulation

There are three large parts to a bird's brain. The cerebrum (suh-REE-bruhm) is the center for muscle control and behavior. The cerebellum (ser-uh-BEL-uhm) is the center for balance and coordination, which are important to bird flight. Avoiding predators, capturing prey, building nests, and caring for young also require good balance and coordination.

In addition, birds have large optic lobes. Large optic lobes indicate that birds have good vision. In fact, hawks can see as well as a person looking through binoculars. In addition, most birds also have color vision as people do.

Think & Discuss

4. What structure produces songs and calls of birds?
5. Explain the difference between contour feathers and down feathers.
6. Identify two ways that birds are adapted for flight.
7. How are air sacs important in helping birds absorb oxygen?
★ 8. Why does molting occur gradually?

18-3 Reproduction, Development, and Behavior

Birds have some very interesting habits. Most of these habits involve reproductive behavior. Reproductive behavior includes activities such as attracting mates, mating, nesting, and caring for young. These activities have been studied in many bird species. However, there are still many mysteries about bird behavior.

Reproduction and Development

Did you have eggs for breakfast this morning? The eggs you eat come from birds. You may be surprised to learn that besides chicken eggs, the eggs of other birds also can be eaten. Eggs vary greatly in size depending upon the species of the bird. However, all bird eggs are only one cell. The egg is the reproductive cell of a bird.

Reproduction

When birds mate, sperm are transferred from the male's cloaca to the female's cloaca. Once in the cloaca of the female, the sperm move up the oviduct that connects the single ovary of the female to the cloaca.

In the oviduct, a sperm cell unites with an egg cell produced in the female's ovary. This fertilized egg cell then passes through the oviduct where other structures are added around it to form the finished egg that the bird lays. Formation of a finished egg takes about two days. A fertilized bird egg includes an embryo, a food supply, membranes, and a hard outer shell.

The Egg and Hatching

Every bird egg is an amniote egg. An amniote egg has a shell and several membranes that protect the embryo. All birds reproduce with amniote eggs. After an egg is laid, the bird embryo develops quickly. The embryo is supplied with food by the yolk and **albumen** (al-BYOO-mun), or egg white.

A complete group of eggs laid by one female bird is called a **clutch.** A clutch of eggs usually hatches from two to four weeks after the eggs are laid. Hatching is aided by

Key Points
- Singing, defending territories, and display of plumage are bird behaviors related to reproduction.
- Many birds migrate to warmer climates in winter to find food.

Health and Safety Tip
Eggs sometimes contain Salmonella *bacteria. These bacteria are easily destroyed when the eggs are cooked. Food poisoning could result from eating raw eggs.*

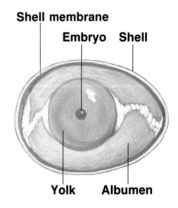

Shell membrane

Embryo Shell

Yolk Albumen

Figure 18-6 A bird's egg is an amniote egg. The shell is porous.

ACTIVITY 18–2

PROBLEM: What are the parts of a bird egg?

Science Process Skills
observing, classifying, comparing

Background Information
Bird eggs are amniote eggs. An amniote egg is a hard-shelled egg with an amnion. The amnion is a fluid filled sac in which a baby bird develops. The amnion surrounds and protects the developing bird and its food supply.

Materials

chicken egg	hand lens
small dish	metric ruler

Procedure
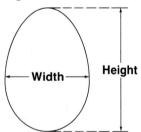

1. Examine the shell of the chicken egg with the hand lens. Describe the shell.
2. Stand the egg on one end and measure the height in centimeters. Record the height. Measure the width at the center. Record the width.
3. Draw an outline of your egg. Your outline should be the same size as the egg. Label the height and width measurements as shown in Figure A.

Figure A: Egg outline

4. Carefully crack open the egg into the dish.
5. Examine the inside of the shell. Find the shell membrane and the air space. Draw and label the shell membrane and air space on your egg outline.
6. Observe the egg in the dish. Sketch the inside of the egg and label the parts of the egg.

7. Using the hand lens, find two twisted white cords, or chalaza, in the egg. Draw and label them on your drawing.
8. Using the hand lens, find a small white speck on the yolk. The white speck is the living part of the egg. Draw and label it on your drawing.
9. **CALCULATE**   Obtain the heights and widths of eggs from 9 other classmates. Find the average egg size among their eggs and your own. To find the average height, add the 10 heights together. Divide the total by 10. Repeat the procedure for widths.

Observations
1. **a.** What color is the egg shell?   **b.** Is the shell smooth or slightly bumpy?
2. **a.** What color is the egg white, or albumen? **b.** What color is the yolk?
3. Does the yolk have a surrounding membrane?
4. What is the average egg size among your 9 classmates' eggs and yours? Give both average height and width.

Conclusions
1. What two parts make up most of a bird egg?
2. **a.** What is the function of the shell? **b.** What is the function of the albumen? **c.** What is the function of the yolk?
3. **INFER**   What is the function of the chalaza?
4. The chicken egg you looked at could never have developed into a chick. Why not?

a sharp, tiny structure on the tip of the beak called the **egg tooth.** The baby bird uses the egg tooth to break the shell and free itself. The egg tooth disappears soon after hatching. Many birds are blind, featherless, and completely helpless when they hatch.

Behavior

Many bird behaviors are related to reproducing and caring for offspring. Think of a way that you have seen a bird behave. Do you think the bird was attracting a mate, building a nest, feeding young birds, or performing some other behavior?

Mating Behavior

Have you ever wondered why birds sing? Singing is just one interesting behavior of birds. In order to attract a mate, most male birds must first claim an area called a territory. A territory is defended from other males of the same species. Male birds sing to announce possession of their territories. Singing also helps attract mates.

Have you ever noticed the bright colors of the feathers of some birds? Female birds often have feathers of very dull colors. Many male birds, however, have colorful plumage, or feather coverings. Male birds often perform certain dances to strut and show off their colorful plumage. This behavior is another way to attract female birds.

Nesting

Many bird species build nests in which the eggs are laid and incubated, or kept warm. Building nests is an innate

Figure 18-7 What kind of behavior is the male peacock performing?

Figure 18-8 The nests of the yellow-rumped cacique (left) and the barn swallow (right) are very different.

Figure 18-9 Cardinals (top) do not migrate. Canada geese (bottom) migrate south for the winter.

(ih-NAYT) behavior of birds. Innate behaviors do not have to be learned. Animals are born knowing how to carry out these behaviors. Bird nests range from depressions scraped out on the ground to the huge stick nest of the bald eagle. Nests may also be built on cliffs, in tree holes, and even in ground burrows.

Migration

Have you ever seen a flock of birds flying to warmer climates in the fall? Have you wondered where they are going, or how they find their way? Perhaps no other behavior in nature is more fascinating and mysterious than **migration** (my-GRAY-shuhn). Migration is the regular movement of a group of animals from one place to another and back again. Birds are not the only animals that migrate, but more birds migrate long distances than any other kind of animal. Birds that migrate usually move between a summer nesting ground and a winter feeding ground.

Birds seem to begin migrating mainly in response to the changing number of daylight hours of the seasons. Cold weather, storms, or lack of food also may stimulate migration. However, most birds leave their breeding grounds and move to warmer climates when the weather is still warm and food is available. Why do you think they leave at this time?

Birds seem to find their way using clues such as the sun and stars, landmarks like mountains or coastlines, and perhaps even the earth's magnetic field. Many questions about migration and other bird behaviors are still unanswered by the scientists who are studying them. Perhaps you could be a part of that discovery.

Think & Discuss

9. What two parts of the egg supply food to the embryo?

10. What is a clutch?

11. List two reasons male birds sing.

12. Why do birds migrate to warmer climates in the winter?

13. The single ovary of the female bird is an adaptation for flight. Explain.

Birding

Bird-watching, or birding, is a hobby for many people. Would you travel one thousand miles to see a rare hawk, sparrow, or warbler? If your answer is yes, you may find birding an interesting and fun-filled hobby.

Each year birders spend millions of dollars on supplies, equipment, and travel. However, all you really need to begin birding is a pair of binoculars and a good field guide. *A Field Guide to the Birds of Eastern and Central North America* by Roger Tory Peterson may be helpful.

Of course, you also will need a yard or nearby park where you can look for birds. Even a large city can be a good place to begin birding. For example, many people take guided bird walks through Central Park in New York City. These bird walks usually are scheduled during the warm months. Does your town or city have guided bird walks?

All birders keep a "life list," or record, of birds they have seen at least once. The record for the most species seen in a lifetime is 777. You can begin your own life list by identifying birds around your home or school.

As a new birder, you should first become familiar with birds commonly found in your neighborhood. You can become familiar with these birds by getting to know their colors, songs, and favorite feeding places. Learning the characteristics and behaviors of most local birds will make rare species easier to spot.

Most birders enjoy watching the graceful flight and beautiful colors of birds. Others may find bird songs relaxing to hear. But birding can be more than a relaxing and enjoyable hobby. Birding also can lead to active support for the conservation of wild birds.

Many birds that were once common in the United States are now extinct. The passenger pigeon, Carolina parakeet, and dusky seaside sparrow are examples of birds that were once found in large numbers in this country. Now, none of these birds are left.

Today, the California condor and peregrine falcon are threatened with extinction. However, their numbers are increasing with the help of conservationists. Many of these conservationists also are birders.

To Think About

- When are the two best times of the year to see many different species of birds? Explain your answer.

- How would learning about the behaviors of birds be helpful to a birder?

Chapter Review

CHAPTER SUMMARY

18-1 Overview of Birds

- Feathers are the most distinguishing characteristic of birds.
- Other characteristics of birds are wings and legs, lightweight bones, a toothless beak, amniote eggs, a backbone, and a body divided into a head, neck, trunk, and tail.
- Five groups of birds are swimmers, waders, birds of prey, perching birds, and nonperching land birds.
- Bird beaks and feet are adapted to the bird's way of life and way of getting food.

18-2 Anatomy of a Bird

- Feathers cover and protect the skin, provide insulation, aid in flight, and give the bird its color.

- The low body weight and streamlined body of a bird are adaptations for flight.
- Birds have efficient digestive, circulatory, and respiratory systems.
- The systems of the bird's body are adapted for flight by lowering weight or increasing the energy efficiency of the bird.

18-3 Reproduction, Development, and Behavior

- Singing, defending territory, nest building, incubation of eggs, and caring for young all are bird behaviors important in reproduction.
- Many birds migrate from summer nesting regions to warmer climates to find a food supply for the winter.

VOCABULARY LIST

air sacs (312)	contour feathers (308)	gizzard (311)	sternum (309)
albumen (313)	crop (311)	migration (316)	syrinx (312)
amniote egg (306)	down feathers (308)	molting (308)	warm-blooded (306)
clutch (313)	egg tooth (315)	preening (309)	

VOCABULARY REVIEW

Matching Write the word or term from the Vocabulary List that best matches each description.

1. feathers lost during molting
2. structure used to hatch from egg
3. movement of birds to warmer climate
4. egg with a porous shell and fluid-filled sac
5. stores food
6. animal with constant body temperature
7. organs that aid respiration
8. organ that stores food
9. organ that grinds food

Finding Word Relationships Pair each numbered word with a word in the box. Explain in complete sentences how the words are related.

insulation	stomach	oil
breastbone	singing	egg
siblings	shed	

1. sternum
2. gizzard
3. molt
4. clutch
5. syrinx
6. preening
7. down feathers
8. amniote

CONTENT REVIEW

True or False   Write true if the statement is true. If the statement is false, change the underlined word or words to make the statement true.

1. Claws, scales, and eggs are characteristics shared by both birds and <u>reptiles</u>.
2. The most distinguishing characteristic of birds is <u>flight</u>.
3. A hooked beak and sharp, curved claws are characteristics of <u>wading birds</u>.
4. Hollow bones, a four-chambered heart and rapid digestion are all considered adaptations for <u>flight</u> in birds.
5. The <u>collarbone</u> of a bird is large for anchoring the bird's flight muscles.
6. The <u>air sacs</u> of a bird produce the songs and calls of birds.
7. The large <u>optic lobes</u> of birds give them good vision.

Question and Answer   Rewrite each heading in the Chapter Outline on page 304 as a question. Then, answer each of the questions you have written.

Understanding a Diagram   Use the diagram of the bird skeleton, shown in Figure 18-4 (page 309) to answer each of the following.

1. What bone makes up the upper part of a bird's leg?
2. What two bones are located in a bird's wing?
3. What is the sternum?
4. What small bones connect the head of a bird with its clavicle?
5. What is the name for the bones that make up the bird's head?
6. Which bones are located between the clavicle and the sternum?

CONCEPT REVIEW

Writing the Main Ideas   Using the Chapter Outline on page 304, write the main idea for each heading in the outline.

Critical Thinking   Answer each of the following in complete sentences.

1. Compare the following features of reptiles and birds: skeleton, body covering, mouth, method of reproduction, and care of eggs and young.
2. Why is preening important to a duck?

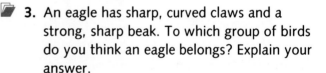

3. An eagle has sharp, curved claws and a strong, sharp beak. To which group of birds do you think an eagle belongs? Explain your answer.
4. Explain how each of the following parts of a bird is adapted for flight: skin, skeleton, muscles, brain, digestive, circulatory, respiratory, excretory, reproductive systems.
5. How do the activities of a cold-blooded reptile differ from those of a warm-blooded bird?

EXTENSIONS

1. The Audubon Society is concerned with the conservation of wildlife. Write to a local chapter of the Audubon Society to obtain information about the work they are doing in your state. Present your findings to the class in an oral report.
2. Build a bird feeder. Observe the feeder and list the number and kinds of birds you can identify at the feeder. Identify birds in the area that do not use the feeder and try to determine why they do not.
3. Visit a zoo and observe the birds there. Notice the beak and feet adaptations. Try to determine the way of life and feeding habits of each bird in the wild, based upon these adaptations.

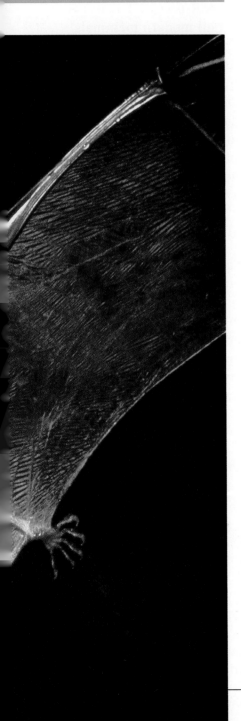

Objectives

After you have completed this chapter, you will be able to

19-1 **list** the major characteristics of mammals.

19-1 **identify** the three main groups of mammals.

19-2 **compare** monotremes and marsupials.

19-3 **identify** the main characteristic of placental mammals.

19-4 **identify** four kinds of mammalian behavior.

Science Process Skills

In this chapter, two science skills are highlighted. Symbols show some places where these skills are used.

▶ **Inferring:** When you infer, you form a conclusion based upon facts and not direct observation.

🗀 **Classifying:** When you classify, you group things based upon similarities.

In a horror movie, you may have seen Count Dracula escape by changing himself into a bat. Of course, people cannot change into bats. However, people and bats do have something in common. Both people and bats are classified as mammals.

The animals with which you are most familiar probably are mammals. Do you have a house pet? The chances are that your pet is a mammal. Cats and dogs are two examples of mammals that are commonly kept as pets. Guinea pigs, gerbils, hamsters, and mice also are mammals. Many people keep horses for riding. Some mammals, such as chimpanzees, even help elderly or handicapped people do household chores.

Imagine finding a fossil of an animal that lived 280 million years ago. Paleontologists (pay-lee-on-TOL-uh-jists), scientists who study fossils, did just that. The fossil they discovered was of a very strange animal. This animal was a reptile, but it also had some mammal-like characteristics. The animal is called a therapsid (THER-up-sid). Fossil evidence led biologists to infer that all modern mammals are descendants of the therapsids.

At the time that the therapsids lived, reptiles were the dominant form of life. During the Age of Reptiles, the dinosaurs were the dominant animals on the earth. There were only a few kinds of small mammals. However, the dinosaurs died out about 65 million years ago. With no competition for food and living space, early mammals were able to survive and reproduce. Today, mammals are one of the most successful groups of animals on the earth.

Characteristics of Mammals

Why do you think mammals are a successful group of animals? Mammals have certain characteristics that allow them to live and reproduce in many different environments. For example, mammals are warm-blooded vertebrates. Because they are warm-blooded, mammals can live in both hot and cold areas of the earth. Mammals also are active during both the day and night.

Other characteristics of mammals include the following:

- Mammals have body hair.
- Mammals nurse their young with milk from mammary glands.
- Mammals have a four-chambered heart.
- Most mammals have a large, well-developed brain.

All of these characteristics helped the mammals to survive and be successful. For example, a covering of body hair can help a mammal stay warm. An efficient, four-chambered heart also helps mammals maintain a constant body temperature.

Young mammals depend on their mothers for food. Some young mammals are dependent for a long time.

Key Points

- Mammals are warm-blooded vertebrates that are covered with hair and nurse their young with milk.
- Monotremes, marsupials, and placentals are the three main groups of mammals.

Figure 19–1 The therapsid had teeth, skull, and limbs similar to those of mammals.

Skill Builder

Classifying When you classify, you group things based upon similarities. Fishes, amphibians, reptiles, birds, and mammals make up the five classes of vertebrates. Cut out five pictures of animals from each class (25 pictures total). Use your pictures to make a poster that indicates the class in which each animal belongs. Include the name of each class above each group of pictures.

Figure 19-2 What characteristics of mammals are shown by this bear and her cubs?

During this time, the young mammals learn to survive on their own. Mammals also have well-developed brains that allow them to learn the behavior patterns necessary for survival.

Classification of Mammals

About 4500 species of mammals live on the earth today. All mammals belong to the class *Mammalia*. Biologists classify mammals into three major groups based upon the way in which the young develop.

The **monotremes** (MAHN-uh-treems) are mammals that lay eggs covered with hard, leathery shells. The eggs of monotremes are very similar to the eggs of reptiles. Young monotremes develop inside the eggs. The platypus is an example of a monotreme.

The **marsupials** (mahr-SOO-pee-uls) are mammals that have a pouch in which the young develop. Unlike most mammals, a young marsupial is not fully developed when it is born. Kangaroos are examples of marsupial mammals.

Mammals that give birth to young that develop inside the mother's body are called **placentals** (pluh-SEN-tuls). Why are these mammals called placentals? The young of placental mammals develop within a saclike organ called the **placenta**. The placenta provides the developing mammal with nourishment. Wastes are also excreted through the placenta.

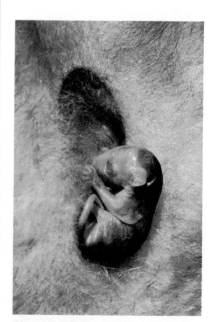

Figure 19-3 This baby opossum will live in its mother's pouch until it is fully developed.

Placental mammals are fully developed at birth. However, like all young mammals, placentals are protected and nursed by their mothers after birth until they are ready to live on their own. Elephants, mice, and bats are examples of placental mammals. What kind of mammal is a human?

Think & Discuss

1. What is a placenta?
2. Name the three major groups of mammals and give an example of each.
3. How might parental care after birth be a survival adaptation for mammals?

19-2 Monotremes and Marsupials

Key Points

- Monotremes are mammals that lay eggs.
- Marsupials are mammals that have pouches in which the young develop after birth.

Only two kinds of monotremes are living today. They are the duck-billed platypus and the spiny anteater. The platypus lives only in Australia. The spiny anteater lives in Australia and New Guinea.

Most marsupials, such as kangaroos and koalas, live in Australia. A few marsupials live in South America. The opossum is the only marsupial found in North America.

Monotremes

Monotremes are similar to reptiles in some ways. Look at the platypus shown in Figure 19-4. Notice that its legs are attached to the sides of its body. The legs of reptiles also

Figure 19-4 The platypus (left) looks very different from the spiny anteater (right), but they are both monotremes.

are attached to the sides of their bodies. Like reptiles, monotremes lay eggs. Both reptiles and monotremes also have a cloaca. The cloaca is used for reproduction and to remove wastes.

If monotremes have so many characteristics of reptiles, why are they classified as mammals? Monotremes have three important characteristics of mammals. First, the bodies of monotremes are covered with hair. Second, monotremes are warm-blooded. However, their body temperature is not as stable as that of other mammals. Third, monotremes have mammary glands.

The platypus and spiny anteater develop in different ways. A female platypus builds a nest in which she lays two or three eggs. When the eggs hatch, the young do not nurse directly from mammary glands as do the young of other mammals. Instead, the female platypus has many mammary glands that secrete milk into her fur. The young lap up the milk from the mother's fur.

The female spiny anteater lays only one egg at a time. The egg is kept in a pouch on the female's abdomen. When the egg hatches, the young anteater nurses from a mammary gland located within the pouch.

Marsupials

Young marsupials develop differently from any other mammals. The young develop inside the mother's body for only a short time. At birth, a young marsupial is weak, blind, and hairless. It crawls through the mother's fur until it reaches the pouch. Like spiny anteaters, the mammary glands of marsupials are inside the female's pouch. Once inside the pouch, a young marsupial attaches itself to a nipple. It remains in the pouch and nurses until it is fully developed.

Study Hint

The word "monotreme" means "one opening" and refers to the cloaca, which is used for both waste removal and reproduction.

Figure 19-5 A baby kangaroo is called a joey.

Think & Discuss

4. How are monotremes similar to reptiles?
5. How are monotremes and marsupials alike? How are they different?
6. Why do you think the single egg produced by the spiny anteater might have a better chance of developing into young than the eggs of a platypus?

19-3 Placental Mammals

Over 95 percent of all mammals are placental mammals. Elephants, mice, and bats are examples of placental mammals. Dogs, horses, and monkeys also are placental mammals. All of these animals look very different from one another. Yet all of these animals have characteristics that make them placental mammals.

Characteristics of Placentals

Unlike a monotreme or a marsupial, a placental mammal develops entirely within the body of its mother. Soon after an embryo begins to develop, it enters the female reproductive organ. This organ is called the **uterus** (YOOT-ur-us). The embryo remains in the uterus until it is fully developed.

The wall of the uterus contains many blood vessels. These blood vessels supply the embryo with food. How do you think food gets to the embryo? The embryo causes a placenta to form. Like the uterus, the placenta has many blood vessels. The placenta attaches to the wall of the uterus. Blood vessels in the placenta come very close to blood vessels in the wall of the uterus. As a result, food can leave the mother's blood and enter the embryo's blood. Wastes also are removed from the blood of the embryo by the placenta. The mother's blood never comes in contact with the embryo.

The length of time during which an embryo develops in the uterus is the **gestation** (jes-TAY-shun) **period.** The gestation period is different for each kind of mammal. For example, the gestation period of a dog is nine weeks. The gestation period for a human however, is nine months.

Major Orders of Placentals

Biologists classify placental mammals into orders according to the adaptations that help the animals live in their environments. For example, some placental mammals are adapted for walking or running. Some are adapted for climbing, and others for swimming. One order of placentals even includes mammals that are adapted for flying. Do you know which mammals belong to this order?

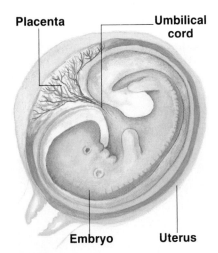

Placenta Umbilical cord

Embryo Uterus

Figure 19-6 All placental mammals develop within the uterus of the mother.

Figure 19-7 A mole spends much of its life in the tunnels it digs in the ground. What adaptation do moles have for digging?

Insect-Eating Mammals

Moles and shrews are the only insect-eating mammals that live in North America. These animals are small and very active. Because they are so active, they must eat a lot of food to supply the energy they need. In fact, some shrews eat twice their body weight in food each day. How much food would you have to eat every day if you ate as much as a shrew?

Moles and shrews have strong limbs. They also have well-developed claws. The claws are adapted for digging. Moles have poor eyesight. However, a mole's nose is very sensitive to touch. Moles rely on their sense of touch to find food. Moles feed mainly on worms. Shrews eat insects and other small invertebrates.

Flying Mammals

Bats are the only true flying mammals. A bat's wing is made up of skin stretched over very long finger bones. Bats do not glide. They fly by flapping their wings as birds do.

Bats are active at night. Do you know how bats find their prey in the dark? Some bats are able to give off high-pitched sounds. The sounds bounce off the bat's prey and are heard by the bats. The bat can tell by the sounds how far away the prey is located. This method of finding prey is called **echolocation.** Can you think of other reasons why bats use echolocation?

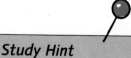

Study Hint

Have you ever heard an echo of your voice in a large, empty room? An echo is a sound that is reflected from, or bounced off, an object or a surface.

Figure 19-8 Armadillos are either six-banded or nine-banded. How many bands does this armadillo have?

Toothless Mammals

Armadillos, sloths, and anteaters belong to the order of toothless mammals. Although all three of these mammals are called "toothless," only the anteaters do not have teeth. Anteaters and armadillos feed mainly on insects. Their long, sticky tongues are adapted to catch insects. Sloths feed on plants. Their teeth are adapted for grinding leaves.

▶ The armadillo is the only toothless mammal that lives in the United States. Like all mammals, the armadillo has hair. It also has armor made up of hardened skin that resembles the shell of a turtle. How do you think an armadillo's armor is helpful to the animal?

Gnawing Mammals

Gnawing mammals are called **rodents.** About 40 percent of all mammals are rodents. Rodents live on every continent and can be found in almost every kind of environment. Some examples of rodents are mice, rats, squirrels, beavers, and porcupines.

The name "rodent" comes from a Latin word that means "to gnaw." Rodents have teeth adapted for gnawing. Look at the rodent shown in Figure 19-9. Notice the two pairs of large front teeth. These teeth are called **incisors** (in-SY-zorz). A rodent's incisors continue to grow throughout its life. Gnawing wears down the incisors and keeps them sharp.

Figure 19-9 The teeth of the beaver are well-adapted for gnawing twigs and small branches.

ACTIVITY 19–1

PROBLEM: How are the teeth of mammals adapted to their diets?

Science Process Skills
classifying, comparing, inferring

Background Information
The teeth of a mammal are adapted to its diet. Most mammals are either carnivores or herbivores. Carnivores eat meat. Herbivores eat plants. Some mammals are omnivores. Omnivores eat both meat and plants.

Materials
paper and pencil

Procedure
1. On a sheet of paper, list the names of each mammal shown below. Next to each name, classify the mammal in its order.
2. Study the teeth of the mammals shown below.

3. Compare the different teeth in the mammals shown. Compare the size of the teeth.

Observations
1. Which mammals shown have large canine teeth for tearing?
2. Which mammals shown have small peglike teeth?
3. Which mammals shown have a lot of flat teeth for grinding?

Conclusions
1. **a.** Which mammals shown are carnivores?
   b. How are the teeth of carnivores adapted for eating meat?
2. **a.** Which mammals shown are herbivores?
   b. How are the teeth of herbivores adapted for eating plants?
3. **INFER** How would you classify humans? Explain your answer.

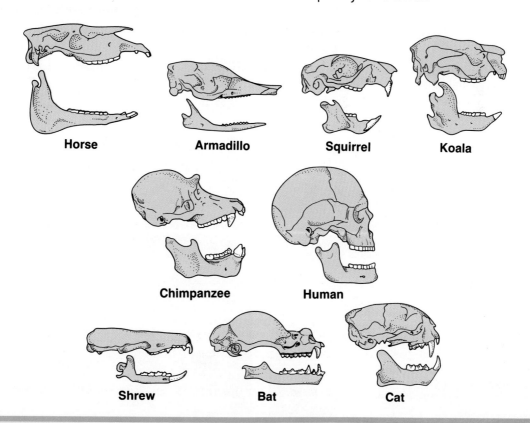

Horse   Armadillo   Squirrel   Koala

Chimpanzee   Human

Shrew   Bat   Cat

Figure 19-10 The large feet and muscular hind legs of this black-tailed jackrabbit are used to quickly escape predators.

Rodentlike Mammals

Rabbits, hares, and pikas all were once classified as rodents. Today, biologists classify these animals in a separate order. Unlike rodents, which have two upper incisors, the rodentlike mammals have four upper incisors. These teeth are adapted for eating plants.

Aquatic Mammals

There are two orders of aquatic mammals. Whales, dolphins, and porpoises belong to one order. Sea cows make up the second order of aquatic mammals. The aquatic mammals spend their entire lives in the water. ▶ Unlike fishes, which have gills, aquatic mammals use lungs to breathe air as you do. Whales take in air through a blowhole located on top of the head. How does the location of the blowhole help the whales?

Whales are divided into two groups based on how they catch their prey. Some whales have teeth. The toothed whales feed on fishes, squids, and seals. Baleen whales do not have teeth. Instead, these whales have rows of a fingernail-like material called **baleen** hanging from the roof of the mouth. Baleen is like a giant strainer. As a baleen whale swims, it gulps water. The baleen strains shrimp and other small invertebrates from the water.

Sea cows include manatees and dugongs. Like whales, sea cows have flippers instead of front legs and flat tails. Sea cows live in warm tropical waters and eat only plants.

Figure 19-11 Why do you think the dolphin (left) and the manatee (right) are classified in separate orders?

Figure 19-12 At one time, elephants were hunted for the ivory in their tusks. For this reason, elephants are an endangered species.

Trunk-Nosed Mammals

The main feature of all the animals in this order is a long trunk. The trunk is a modified nose and upper lip. Only two species of trunk-nosed mammals are living today. Do you know what these animals are? They are the African elephant and the Asian elephant.

Carnivorous Mammals

Dogs and bears look very different from each other, but they are related. How are dogs related to bears? Both dogs and bears are **carnivores** (KAR-nuh-vawrs). Carnivores are animals that eat other animals. The word "carnivore" means "meat eater." However, some carnivores, such as bears, also eat plants.

Carnivores have many adaptations for catching prey. For example, lions have sharp claws for grabbing and holding prey. Most carnivores also have strong jaws and long, sharp **canine** (KAY-nyn) teeth. The canine teeth are used for grabbing, holding, and tearing. People also have canine teeth. Can you locate your canine teeth?

Figure 19-13 Sea lions live in warm waters, such as those off the coast of California.

Seals and walruses are carnivorous mammals that are adapted for life in the water. They have flippers and webbed feet to help them swim. Seals have streamlined bodies to help them chase prey. Walruses are not as streamlined as seals and do not chase their prey. Walruses usually gather mollusks from the mud on the sea floor.

Hoofed Mammals

The hoofed mammal you are probably most familiar with is the horse. Like all hoofed mammals, the weight of a horse is supported only by its toes. To support their weight, horses and other hoofed mammals have toes that end in a hard covering called a hoof.

Almost all of the hoofed mammals are **herbivores** (HUR-buh-vawrs). Herbivores are animals that eat only plants. Many hoofed mammals have stomachs with several chambers. Bacteria in the chambers help the animals digest the plant materials they eat.

Figure 19-14 The feet of camels have two toes. Each toe is covered by a hoof.

Primates

Lemurs, monkeys, apes, and humans all are classified as **primates.** With the exception of gorillas, baboons, and humans, most primates live in trees. Primates have many adaptations for living in trees. For example, all primates have well-developed hands that can be used to grasp and manipulate objects. Most primates have four fingers and an opposable thumb. The thumb is said to be opposable because it works opposite of the fingers. Most primates also have an opposable first toe. What familiar primate can you name that does not have opposable first toes?

The eyes of primates are on the front of the head. This location allows both eyes to focus on an object at the same

Figure 19-15 The mountain gorilla is a primate that eats only plants.

time. Using both eyes at once helps primates judge distance and depth. Try this experiment. Close one eye and try to pick up an object from the floor. Why do you think having eyes on the front of the head might be an adaptation for living in trees?

The diet of primates varies from species to species. Some primates eat only plants. However, primates such as humans eat both plants and animals. Animals that eat both plants and other animals are called **omnivores** (AHM-nuh-vawrs). Can you name another mammal that is an omnivore?

Think & Discuss

7. Why is the gestation period important for placental mammals?

8. What is the function of baleen in a whale?

9. Name three orders of placental mammals and give an example of each.

10. How do rodents differ from rodentlike mammals?

11. How do herbivores, carnivores, and omnivores differ from one another?

ACTIVITY 19-2

PROBLEM: How are humans classified by biologists?

Science Process Skills
observing, classifying, researching

Background Information
Biologists classify all living things from kingdom to species. Even humans are placed into the classification system. By carefully observing people, doing some research, and using your general knowledge, you can classify humans into their classification groupings.

Materials
paper and pencil
reference books (optional)

Procedure
1. Write the classification groupings on a sheet of paper.
2. Beginning with kingdom, choose the kingdom in which humans are classified. Give three reasons for your choice.
3. Choose the phylum in which you think humans are classified. Use these choices: *Arthropoda, Vertebrata, Chordata, Echinodermata.* Give one reason for your choice.
4. Write the class in which you think humans are classified. Give three reasons for your choice.
5. Copy Data Table A. Place a check mark in the "yes" column if the characteristic is a human characteristic. If the characteristic is not a human characteristic, place a check mark in the "no" column.
6. Use your data in Data Table A to help you choose the order in which humans are classified. Give reasons for your choice.
7. Copy Data Table B. Place a checkmark in the proper column. The checklist will help you discover why humans are classified in the family *Hominidae.*
8. Write the genus and species name for humans. Find out what the terms mean.

Data Table A: Human Characteristics		
CHARACTERISTICS	HUMAN CHARACTERISTIC	
	Yes	No
Claws		
Nails		
Opposable thumbs		
Color vision		
Eyes face forward		
Opposable big toes		
Grasping hands		
Tails		

Data Table B: Identifying Hominidae Characteristics		
CHARACTERISTIC	DO HUMANS HAVE?	
	Yes	No
Walk on 4 limbs		
Walk upright		
Large canine teeth		
Small canine teeth		
Small brain case		
Large brain case		
Arms longer than legs		
Legs longer than arms		
Tail		

Observations
1. **CLASSIFY** What characteristics are used to classify humans in their class grouping?
2. **a.** What does the genus name for humans mean? **b.** What does the species name for humans mean?

Conclusions
1. What characteristics are used to classify humans in the family *Hominidae?*
2. What prefix is common to both the family name and genus name of humans?
3. **a.** What characteristics do humans share with other members of their order, such as apes and monkeys? **b.** How are humans different?

19-4 Behavior in Mammals

"Behavior" describes how an animal responds to its environment. There are two kinds of behavior. Learned behavior is a response that must be taught. Training a dog to respond to its name is an example of learned behavior. Innate behavior is a response that does not have to be taught. The way a mammal cares for and protects its young is an example of innate behavior. Mammals are born with many innate behaviors.

Territoriality

All animals need space in which to live, reproduce, and find food. This space is called the animal's territory. Many mammals claim a territory as their own. They defend their territories from other members of the same species.

Some mammals make substances in special scent glands. A mammal rubs against trees and bushes to spread its scent and mark its territory. By scent-marking its territory, a mammal warns others of its species to keep away. Thus, the mammal often can avoid fighting to defend its territory.

Migration

Do you remember that some birds migrate from cold areas to warmer areas to find food in winter? Some mammals also migrate. Caribou (KAR-uh-boo) are deerlike animals that live in the Arctic. In winter, large caribou herds travel hundreds of kilometers to find food.

Key Point

- Behavior patterns in mammals include territoriality, migration, hibernation, and communication.

Figure 19-16 The male white-tailed deer marks its territory by rubbing its antlers against trees.

Figure 19-17 These African antelope called gnu, or wildebeest, migrate to find food and water during the dry summer season.

Some mammals migrate to breed. Pacific gray whales migrate to the coast of California and Mexico to breed. The gray whales feed in the Arctic Ocean during the summer. In September, the whales begin to migrate south. The female whales arrive in the warm waters off the coast of Mexico by January. Here, the females give birth to their young. After a month or two, the whales begin their return migration to the Arctic Ocean.

Hibernation

While some mammals migrate to find food during the winter, others stay in their home territory. How do these mammals survive the cold and lack of food? Some of these mammals can slow down their body functions. The mammals enter a sleeplike state called **hibernation** (HY-buhr-nay-shun).

During hibernation, the mammal usually does not eat or drink. Instead, the hibernating mammal relies on food that was stored as body fat. Some mammals, such as squirrels, are true hibernators. These mammals never wake from their hibernation during the winter months. Other mammals, such as bears, wake from time to time. The bears may leave their dens to find food and water.

Communication

Communication is the process of sharing information among animals. Mammals communicate with one another in many different ways. For example, scent-marking a territory is one form of communication. Wolves use visual displays to establish their position in the group, or pack.

Mammals also can use sounds to communicate. In addition to their visual displays, wolves also may growl, whine, or howl. Humpback whales "sing" long, complicated messages to other whales.

Study Hint

The word "hibernation" comes from a Latin word meaning "to pass the winter."

Figure 19-18 This chipmunk is a true hibernator and will sleep all winter.

Think & Discuss

12. What is hibernation? Why is it important to a mammal's survival?

13. List four kinds of behavior in mammals.

14. When mammals migrate to different areas, how might the animals living in these areas be affected?

Have you ever gone to a supermarket meat department and found a product labeled "Leanest Ground Beef"? At the dairy counter, you might find jumbo eggs that are twice the size of medium eggs. Chances are, at least one of these products was made possible through animal breeding.

Animal breeding is used to develop animals with characteristics that are desirable to people. One of the most important methods of animal breeding is selective breeding. In selective breeding, two animals are crossed to produce offspring with the best characteristics of each animal.

Selective breeding can be used to produce animals that are larger in size or that are resistant to certain diseases. Selective breeding can also produce "thin" cows, the source of the "leanest ground beef" you see in the supermarket meat counter.

Two techniques are important in selective breeding: hybridization and inbreeding. Hybridization is the crossing of two genetically different but related species of animals. The result is an offspring called a "hybrid." A hybrid has the traits of both parents. Scientists have found that hybrids are often better and stronger than either parent.

Inbreeding is the opposite of hybridization. Inbreeding is a breeding technique in which animals with the same or very similar sets of genes are crossed. Inbreeding is used to keep various breeds of animals, such as cocker spaniels, pure.

One problem with inbreeding is that it produces organisms with genetic similarity. This lack of genetic difference may cause inbred animals to be susceptible to certain diseases and unable to adapt to environmental changes.

A new and very interesting technique of animal breeding is transgenesis. In transgenesis, genes from one species are introduced into the genes of another species. As a result, animals that are unable to mate in nature can produce offspring. For example, genes from goats and sheep can be combined to produce an animal that has the coat of a sheep and the horns of a goat. What is the animal called? Why, a "Geep," of course!

To Think About

- Which animal species would be most likely to become extinct: one that is bred by hybridization, one that is inbred, or one that is produced by transgenesis? Why?

- Which technique of animal breeding may be used to produce a show dog? Why?

Chapter Review

CHAPTER SUMMARY

19-1 Overview of Mammals

- Mammals are warm-blooded vertebrates that have body hair, mammary glands, a four-chambered heart, and a large brain.
- The main groups of mammals are the monotremes, marsupials, and placentals.

19-2 Monotremes and Marsupials

- Monotremes are mammals that lay eggs similar to the eggs of reptiles.
- Marsupials are mammals that have pouches in which their young develop.

19-3 Placental Mammals

- Placental mammals give birth to fully developed young.
- The ten orders of placental mammals include insect-eating, flying, toothless, gnawing, rodentlike, aquatic, trunk-nosed, carnivorous, hoofed, and primates.

19-4 Behavior in Mammals

- Territoriality, migration, hibernation, and communication are behavior patterns of mammals.

VOCABULARY LIST

baleen (330)
canine (331)
carnivores (331)
echolocation (327)

gestation period (326)
herbivores (332)
hibernation (336)
incisors (328)

marsupials (323)
monotremes (323)
omnivores (333)
placenta (323)

placentals (323)
primates (332)
rodents (328)
uterus (326)

VOCABULARY REVIEW

Matching   Write the word or term from the Vocabulary List that best matches each description.

1. period of development in placental mammals
2. order of mammals to which spiny anteaters belong
3. used by bats for finding prey
4. gnawing mammals
5. mammals whose young develop in pouches after they are born
6. develop completely within mother's body
7. female reproductive organ
8. front teeth of gnawing mammals
9. used by some whales to strain food from water

Identifying Relationships   Identify the word or term in each group that does not belong. Explain why it does not belong with the group.

1. monotreme, marsupial, elephant
2. kangaroo, platypus, koala
3. pouch, uterus, placenta
4. carnivores, plants, herbivores
5. incisor, flipper, canine
6. dolphins, whales, sharks
7. carnivore, rabbit, wolf
8. deer, monkeys, primates
9. caribou, wildebeest, bears
10. hibernation, communication, songs
11. omnivores, humans, rabbits
12. whale, shark, baleen

CONTENT REVIEW

Completion   Write the word or words that best complete each sentence.

1. All mammals nurse their young with mammary glands that produce _____.
2. The three main groups of mammals are monotremes, _____, and placentals.
3. Mammals that lay eggs covered with leathery shells are _____.
4. Kangaroos, koalas, and opossums belong to the group of mammals called _____.
5. The _____ is the organ that nourishes the developing embryo.
6. Moles belong to the order of _____ mammals.
7. Mammals with two pairs of front teeth adapted for gnawing are called _____.
8. Herbivores are mammals that eat only _____.
9. Carnivores have long, pointed canine teeth for tearing _____.
10. Chambered stomachs are a characteristic of the _____ mammals.

Finding the Main Ideas   Use the section number to find the sentence that answers each question. Then, write the sentence.

1. How did the disappearance of the reptiles help the mammals become dominant? (19-1)
2. What are the three major orders of mammals? (19-1)
3. What are the two kinds of monotremes that are living today? (19-2)
4. Why are monotremes classified as mammals? (19-2)
5. How are wastes removed from the embryo of a placental mammal? (19-3)
6. How do bats fly? (19-3)
7. How do baleen whales catch their prey? (19-3)
8. How are the hands and feet of primates adapted for living in trees? (19-3)
9. What is meant by "behavior"? (19-4)
10. How do humpback whales use sound to communicate? (19-4)

CONCEPT REVIEW

Writing for Understanding   One way to find out if you understand something is to write a brief summary of the information in your own words. Reread Section 19-2, Monotremes and Marsupials, on pages 324–325, and write a brief summary of the information.

Critical Thinking   Answer each of the following in complete sentences.

1. In what ways might moles be beneficial to gardeners?
2. How are the teeth of a rodent adapted to its lifestyle?
3. An elephant often uses its tusks to strip bark from trees. How might this be harmful to the environment?
4. Classify each of the following in its correct order: bat, rat, dolphin, rabbit, dog, and monkey.
5. Mammals that mark their territories with scent must mark them often. Why do you think they must do this?

EXTENSIONS

1. Many recordings have been made of the songs of humpback whales. Find one of these recordings in your local library and play it for the class.
2. Read *Gorillas in the Mist* by Dian Fossey or *Almost Human* by Shirley Strum. Write a book report on one of these books about primate behavior patterns.

Mammals   **339**

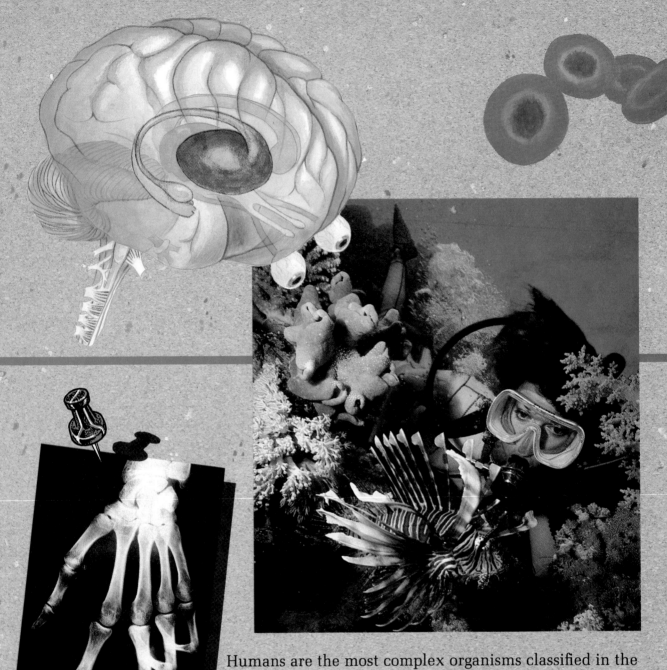

Humans are the most complex organisms classified in the Animal kingdom. Human biology deals with the study of the human body. The human body is made up of ten organ systems. Together, the ten organ systems work to keep the body functioning properly.

Look at the list of chapters that make up this unit. Read the title of each chapter. The chapter titles tell you the functions of the organ systems that make up the human body. Now look at each drawing and photograph and identify what is shown. Each drawing and photograph represents one of the chapters in this unit. Try to match each drawing and photograph with its chapter.

Human Biology

CONTENTS

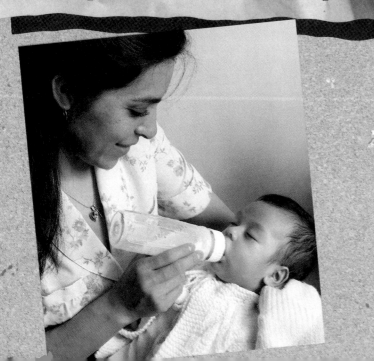

Objectives

After you have completed this chapter, you will be able to

20-1 **describe** the structure and function of the skeletal system.

20-2 **describe** the process of bone development.

20-2 **identify** some problems of the skeletal system.

20-3 **describe** the structure and function of the muscular system.

20-3 **explain** how muscles work.

20-3 **identify** some problems of the muscular system.

20-4 **describe** the structure and function of the skin.

Science Process Skills

In this chapter, two science skills are highlighted. Symbols show some places where these skills are used.

▱ **Classifying:** When you classify, you group things based on similarities.

▲ **Modeling:** When you model, you use a copy or imitation of an object to help explain something.

Have you ever seen a house or a skyscraper being built? If so, you probably noticed that the builder put up a wood frame for the house or an iron girder frame for the skyscraper. Do you know what the frame of a building does? It supports the walls and roof of the building.

You have a frame, too. Your frame is your skeletal system. Just as the frame of a building is inside the building, your skeleton is inside your body. An internal skeleton is called an **endoskeleton.** *What organisms can you name that have an exoskeleton?*

20-1 The Skeletal System

Key Point

- Bones and cartilage protect and support the body, and work with muscles for movement.

Your skeletal system is made up mostly of bone. Bone is a very hard tissue, which is also a little flexible. Your skeleton also contains **cartilage** (KART-ul-ij). Cartilage is a tough, flexible tissue. Your ears and the end of your nose contain cartilage. If you move your ears with your hand, you can feel how tough, but elastic, cartilage is. The ends of some bones also contain cartilage. The cartilage protects the ends of bones from rubbing against each other. If you want to see cartilage on the end of bones, look at the ends of a chicken bone.

Figure 20-1 Scientific names of the parts of the skeletal system are in parentheses.

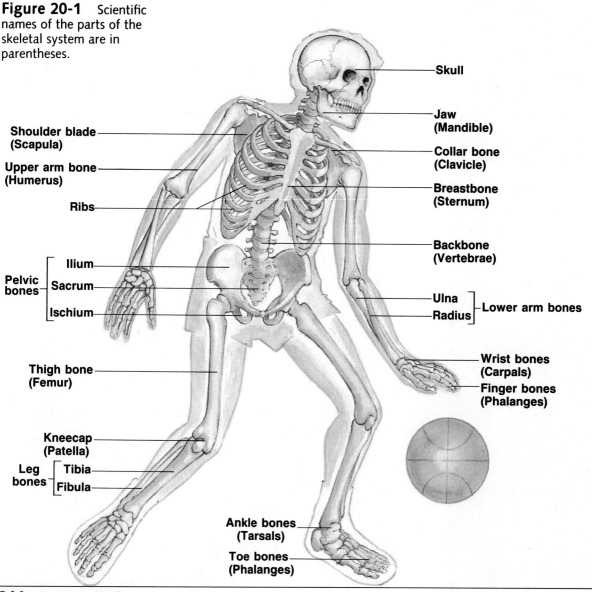

Skull

Jaw (Mandible)

Collar bone (Clavicle)

Breastbone (Sternum)

Backbone (Vertebrae)

Shoulder blade (Scapula)

Upper arm bone (Humerus)

Ribs

Pelvic bones
- Ilium
- Sacrum
- Ischium

Thigh bone (Femur)

Kneecap (Patella)

Leg bones
- Tibia
- Fibula

Ulna
Radius — Lower arm bones

Wrist bones (Carpals)

Finger bones (Phalanges)

Ankle bones (Tarsals)

Toe bones (Phalanges)

▲ The human skeleton is divided into two main parts. In Figure 20-1, find the skull, rib cage, and backbone. The skull, rib cage, and backbone make up the **axial** (AX-see-uhl) **skeleton.** Notice that the backbone is made up of small bones called vertebrae (VUR-tuh-bray). Run your hand along your backbone. Each bump you feel is a vertebra. Now find the bones of the shoulder, hip, pelvis, and arms and legs. All of these bones make up the **appendicular** (ap-uhn-DIK-yuh-luhr) **skeleton.** Look up the word "appendage" in the Glossary to find out how this part of the skeleton gets its name.

What are the functions of your skeletal system? The skeletal system has several important jobs.

- The skeleton supports your body and gives it shape.
- The skeleton covers and protects certain body organs. For example, your skull protects your brain.
- Many bones of the skeleton work with muscles to make movement possible.
- Some bones make blood cells.
- The bones store minerals such as calcium and phosphorous that the body needs.

Study Hint

Refer to Figure 20-1 on page 344 as you read about the axial and appendicular skeletons.

Think & Discuss

1. What bones make up the axial skeleton?
2. What are three functions of the skeletal system?
★ 3. Discs of cartilage are found between the vertebrae. What function do you think the discs serve?

20-2 Bones

If you counted the bones that make up your skeleton, you would count 206 bones. Some of your bones are like long tubes. Other bones are short and flat. Some bones, such as the three bones in your ear that help you hear, are very small. These three bones are the smallest bones in your body. Other bones, such as your femur, or thigh bone, are quite large. In fact, the femur is the largest bone in your body.

Key Points
- Bone replaces cartilage during bone formation.
- Arthritis and scoliosis are two problems of the skeletal system.

Structure of Bones

Although bones have different shapes, they all have a similar structure. Bones are unusual because they are made up of both living and nonliving material. Look at Figure 20-2 as you read about the structure of a bone.

A bone is covered with a thin, tough membrane called the **periosteum** (per-i-AS-tee-um). The periosteum has many blood vessels that supply bone cells with blood. What does the blood do? It supplies living bone cells with food and oxygen.

The hardest part of a bone is under the periosteum. This dense part of a bone is called **compact bone.** Compact bone is made up of living bone cells, tough protein fibers, and mineral deposits. Calcium is the mineral that makes bone hard and gives bone its strength. Calcium in your diet helps keep your bones strong and hard. To get enough calcium in your diet, you should eat calcium-rich foods such as milk and cheese.

The ends of bones are made up of **spongy bone.** You can see that spongy bone has many spaces, like a sponge. The structure of spongy bone adds strength to bone without adding much weight. Strong, lightweight bones are important because your bones need to be strong enough to support your body weight, but light enough so that you can move easily.

▲ The spaces in spongy bone are filled with bone **marrow.** Bone marrow is a soft tissue that is either red or yellow in color. Spongy bone contains red marrow. Why is red marrow important? New blood cells are made in red marrow. The center, or shaft, of long bones contains yellow marrow. Yellow marrow is made up mostly of fat cells. If you break a chicken bone in half, you can see the yellow marrow inside the bone.

Figure 20-2 Compact bone (left) is made up of living bone cells. Find the compact bone in the diagram (right).

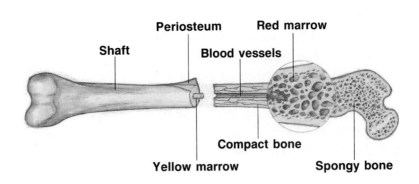

ACTIVITY 20–1

PROBLEM: Is the bone structure of one mammal similar to another mammal?

Science Process Skills
observing, hypothesizing, comparing

Background Information
Bones differ in size, shape, and function. All bones, however, are made up of living tissue and nonliving materials.

Materials

beef bone	small dish
dilute hydrochloric acid	hand lens
chalk	dropper

Procedure

1. Obtain a piece of chalk. **CAUTION: Put on your goggles and lab apron.**
2. Chalk is made up of calcium carbonate. To observe the effect of hydrochloric acid on calcium, place a piece of chalk in a small dish. Use the dropper to place several drops of acid on the chalk. Record your observations. **CAUTION: Work carefully to avoid spilling acid on your skin or clothing. If you do spill acid, rinse the area with plenty of water. Call your teacher.**
3. Obtain a beef bone that has been cut in half along its length and its width.
4. Place several drops of acid on the outer layer of the beef bone. Record your observations.
5. Rinse the acid off the beef bone with plenty of water.
6. Make a simple sketch of the bone to show its shape. Try to identify the name of the bone.
7. Try to scrape away some of the bone in different areas with your fingernail. Record the texture and hardness of the bone in each area.
8. Use the hand lens to observe the inside of the bone. Sketch what you see. Compare the structure of the beef bone to the human bone in Figure 20–2 on page 346 of your text.

Observations

1. **a.** What observations that you recorded show calcium is present? **b.** Does the beef bone contain calcium?
2. How does the inside and outside of the beef bone compare to the inside and outside of a human bone?
3. Does the beef bone have the same texture and hardness in all places that you scraped?

Conclusions

1. **INFER** Do you think all mammal bones contain calcium? Explain your answer.
2. **a.** Is the bone structure of the two mammals you compared similar? **b.** What bone structures are the same in both bones?

Going Further
Test the skeletons of other animals for calcium. You may want to try a shrimp shell, chicken bone, lobster shell, a natural sponge, and so on. Make a data table to show your observations.

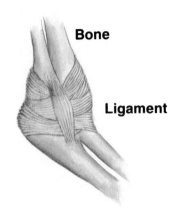

Bone

Ligament

Figure 20-3 This femur (left) is broken above the joint. Ligaments (right) join bones together.

Study Hint

After you read about the joints, make a table listing the three kinds of joints, and examples of each.

Joints

If you have ever broken a bone, you know that bones do not bend. How then, does the skeleton make movement possible? Movement can occur only where bones meet. The place where two or more bones meet is called a **joint.**

You may be wondering what holds your bones together. Some of your bones are connected directly to each other. However, most bones are connected to each other by bands of tough tissue. These bands are called **ligaments** (LIG-uh-muhnts). When bones move at joints, your ligaments are stretched. Have you ever had a sprained ankle? You sprain your ankle when the ligaments connecting the bones of the ankle are stretched too far. What do you think happens when a ligament is torn?

☞ The human skeleton has fixed joints, partially movable joints, and movable joints. Fixed joints do not move at all.

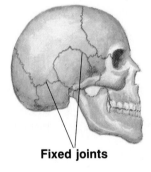

Fixed joints

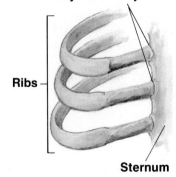

Partially movable joints

Ribs

Sternum

Figure 20-4 Fixed joints connect the bones of the skull. Partially movable joints connect the ribs to the sternum.

They are found in bones that are joined together. For example, the joints in your skull are fixed joints. Partially movable joints allow only a little movement. The joints where your ribs join your sternum, or breastbone, move a little when you breathe in and out. Movable joints permit movement in one or more directions. There are several kinds of movable joints.

Hinge Joints

Bend your arm at the elbow or your leg at the knee. In both of these places of your body, you have a hinge joint. A hinge joint allows bones to move backward and forward in only one direction. How is a hinge joint similar to the hinge on a door?

Ball-and-Socket Joints

Think about a baseball pitcher winding up for a pitch. The pitcher's movements show the wide range of movement that a ball-and-socket joint permits. Ball-and-socket joints connect your upper arm to your shoulder and your upper leg to your pelvis. The ball-and-socket joints in these places permit movement in all directions. Ball-and-socket joints allow the widest range of movement of any kind of joint.

Figure 20-5 Locate the four kinds of movable joints in the pitcher's body.

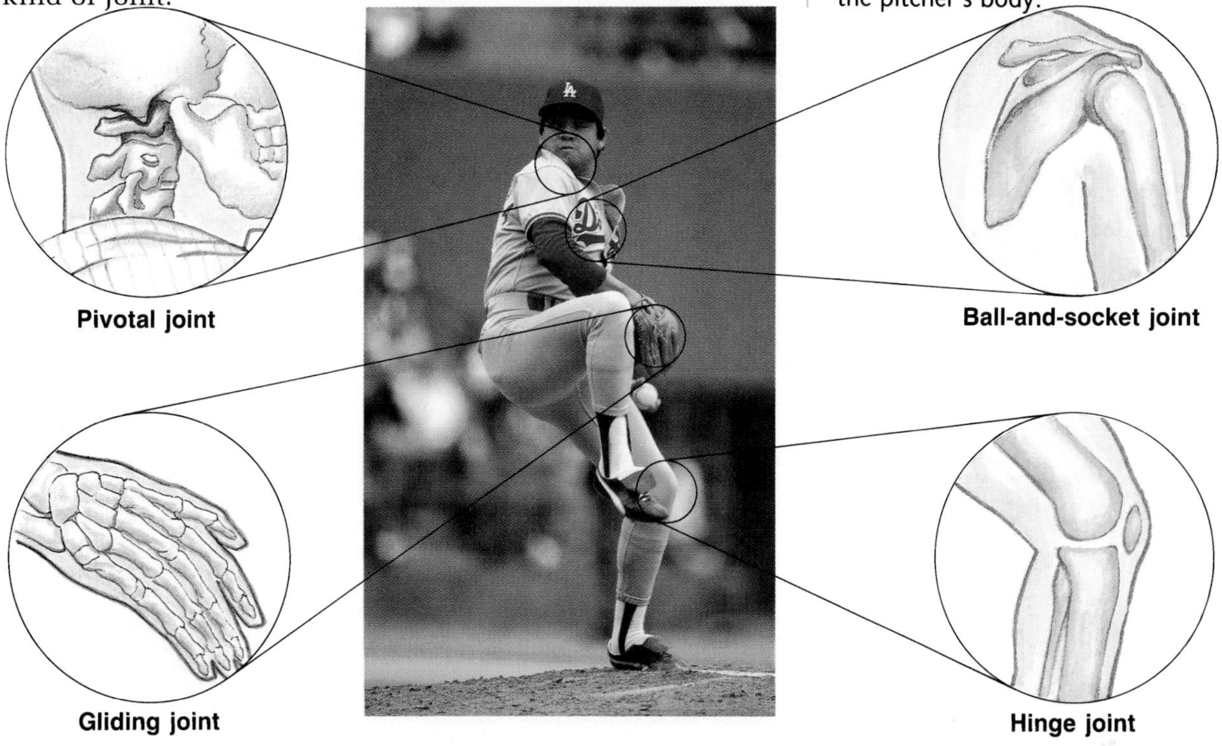

Pivotal joint

Ball-and-socket joint

Gliding joint

Hinge joint

Pivotal Joints

Nod your head. Turn your head from side to side. The place where the skull joins the first vertebra of your backbone is a pivotal joint. A pivotal joint allows both side-to-side and up-and-down movements.

Gliding Joints

Try moving your wrist in as many ways as you can. The gliding joint in your wrist allows some movement in all directions. In a gliding joint, the bones slide along each other. What other parts of your body can you name that have gliding joints?

Formation of Bones

Do you think that you always had a skeleton made of bone? As a developing baby, your skeleton was made up mostly of cartilage. However, during the second and third months of development, your bones began to form. During this process, bone cells replaced cartilage and calcium compounds were deposited. Eventually, most of the cartilage was replaced by bone.

How tall were you when you were three years old? How tall are you now? Even if you do not know the exact heights, you know that you have grown since you were a small child. This growth took place because new bone tissue was produced in the rounded ends of your bones.

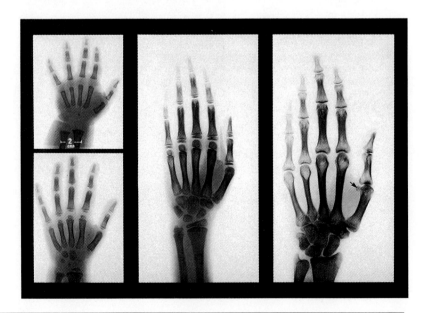

Figure 20-6 Notice the difference in the hand bones of a child (left), teenager (middle), and adult (right).

The rounded end of a bone is an area of cartilage that produces new bone tissue. Bone growth continues until the cartilage is replaced by bone.

The replacement of cartilage with bone is a slow process that will not be complete until you are about 20 years old. Even as an adult, all of your cartilage will not be replaced by bone. What are some parts of your body that remain cartilage?

Skeletal Problems

Have you ever fractured a bone? A fracture is a break in a bone, which may be partial or complete. You can see the different kinds of fractures in Figure 20-7. Why do you think a compound fracture is the most serious?

Fractures are common skeletal problems that usually result from injury. However, not all skeletal problems are due to injury. Some problems of the skeletal system are present at birth. Others develop as a result of disease. In some cases, the cause of the problem is unknown.

Do you know anyone who has arthritis (ar-THRYT-is)? Arthritis is a term used to describe a number of joint problems. People with arthritis have inflamed joints. The joints are painful and movement is limited in the affected joints. In the most common form of arthritis, the cartilage between bones is destroyed and replaced with bone deposits. People with severe cases of arthritis must have surgery so that their joints can be replaced.

Scoliosis (skoh-lee-OH-sis) is a disorder of the backbone. People with scoliosis have unusual curves in their backbones. Some children are born with scoliosis. They usually wear a brace to correct the problem or they have corrective surgery. Scoliosis also can be caused by disease or injury.

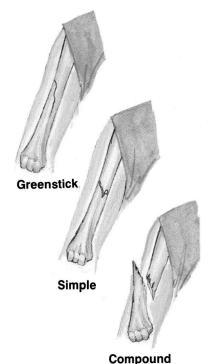

Greenstick

Simple

Compound

Figure 20-7 Compare the breaks in a greenstick, simple, and compound fracture.

Think & Discuss

4. What is the function of red bone marrow?
5. What type of movement does a hinge joint allow?
6. When does the process of forming bones begin?
7. What are some symptoms of arthritis?
8. What kind of joints are found in your fingers?

20-3 The Muscular System

- The human body has three different kinds of muscle tissue, which are needed for all types of movement.

- Muscles move bone when they contract. Muscles work in pairs to cause movement.

- Muscular dystrophy is a serious disease of the muscles.

Study Hint

After you read Section 20-3, The Muscular System, list the three types of muscle tissue and their characteristics.

You have learned that your bones can move at joints. However, without muscles your bones could not be used for movement. Your body is made up of more than 600 muscles. Your muscles help you walk, run, play baseball, and breathe. Without muscles, your heart would not beat, and blood would not flow throughout your body. You could not even digest your food without muscles.

Types of Muscles

The human body has three different kinds of muscle tissue. Each kind of muscle tissue looks different and has a different job in the body. You can see the three kinds of muscle tissue in Figure 20-8.

Look at the **skeletal muscle** in Figure 20-8. Skeletal muscles are attached to the bones, and make movement possible. At movable joints, skeletal muscles are attached to bones by **tendons.** Tendons are tough elastic bands of tissue.

You can make skeletal muscles move whenever you want. Because you can control the movement of skeletal muscles, skeletal muscles also are called **voluntary muscles.** What part of your body has muscles that are not under your voluntary control?

Look at the **smooth muscle** in Figure 20-8. Smooth muscle is found in the walls of blood vessels, the stomach, and other organs. Smooth muscles are **involuntary muscles.** An involuntary muscle is a muscle that you cannot control. For example, you cannot make your stomach muscles work harder to digest food.

Did you know that your heart is a muscle? The walls of the heart are made up of **cardiac muscle.** Cardiac

Figure 20-8 Compare the appearance of skeletal (left), smooth (middle), and cardiac muscle tissues (right).

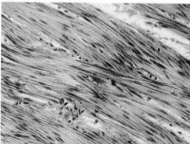

muscles pump blood through the heart and the rest of the body. The cells that make up cardiac muscle seem to branch and weave together. Is cardiac muscle voluntary or involuntary muscle? How do you know?

Muscle Actions

How do muscles work? Muscle cells can change their lengths. When a muscle does its job, the cells in the muscle contract, or shorten. When a skeletal muscle contracts, the muscle pulls on the bone to which it is attached. Movement of the bone causes the body part to move.

Because skeletal muscles move bones when they contract, muscles can only pull bones. Muscles cannot push. For example, the contraction of one muscle can bend your arm. However, this same muscle cannot straighten your arm. A different muscle is needed to straighten your arm. For this reason, muscles always work in pairs.

The teamwork of muscle pairs can be seen in the muscles of the upper arm. The two muscles in the upper arm, the biceps and the triceps, are shown in Figure 20-9. The biceps is in the front of the arm. Bend your arm at the elbow. You should feel the biceps contract. The job of the biceps is to bend the arm at the elbow. You probably have heard people say, "Flex your muscles." A muscle that bends a joint is called a **flexor.** The triceps is in the back of the arm. The triceps' job is to straighten the arm. A muscle that straightens a joint is called an **extensor.**

In Figure 20-9, you should notice that the biceps and triceps are attached to opposite sides of the same bone. When one of the muscles contracts, the other muscle must relax so that movement can occur. What kind of joint allows the arm to bend at the elbow?

Muscle Problems

Have you ever had a charley horse or a muscle cramp? Do your muscles ever get sore after you exercise? A charley horse is caused by a bruise and tears in a muscle, which cause bleeding from small blood vessels. A muscle cramp occurs when muscles contract suddenly and strongly. Sore muscles are caused by small tears in muscles. Usually,

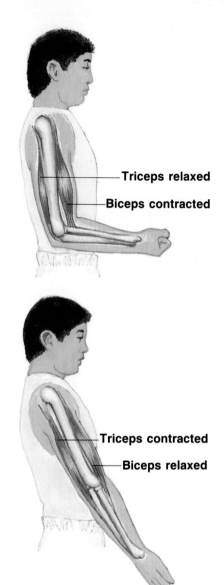

Triceps relaxed

Biceps contracted

Triceps contracted

Biceps relaxed

Figure 20-9   The biceps and triceps muscles work together to move your arm.

Health and Safety Tip
When lifting heavy objects, you should squat and use your leg muscles, not your back muscles.

ACTIVITY 20–2

PROBLEM: How do muscles work in pairs?

Science Process Skills
modeling, observing, relating cause and effect

Background Information
A skeletal muscle that bends a joint is called a flexor. A skeletal muscle that straightens a joint is called an extensor. All muscles work only by contracting. A model can be used to show how movement of skeletal muscle causes bones to move.

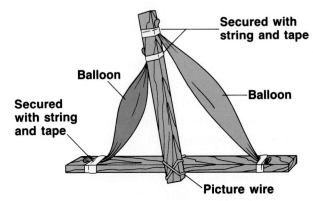

Materials
> 2 pieces of wood, 25 cm × 2.5 cm
> 10 cm length of picture wire
> 2 long balloons
> masking tape
> string
> scissors

Procedure
1. Work with a partner to construct a model of your arm.
2. Join the pieces of wood together by winding the picture wire around the crossed ends of the wood pieces as shown in the figure.
3. To secure the picture wire, wrap some masking tape around the wire and wood. Be sure the two pieces of wood can still move up and down.
4. Blow up the two balloons with 2 or 3 bursts of air. The balloons should be less than half-filled with air.
5. Attach one balloon to the pieces of wood as shown in the figure. Use the string to tie the balloon securely in place. Use the masking tape to further secure the balloon.
6. Attach the other balloon to the pieces of wood as shown in the figure. Secure this balloon the same way as the first balloon.
7. Hold your model at both ends of one stick. Have your partner move the other stick up and down. Observe the shape and size of the balloons.

Observations
1. **a.** On your model, what do the pieces of wood represent? **b.** What do the balloons represent?
2. What type of joint is represented?
3. Draw a sketch of your model and label the parts represented in your arm.
4. What happens to each balloon as you move your model?

Conclusions
1. **a.** When your arm is straight, which muscle is contracted? **b.** When your arm is bent, which muscle is contracted?
2. **a.** Which muscle is the extensor? **b.** Which muscle is the flexor? **c.** How do muscles work in pairs?

you get sore muscles after you use muscles that have not been exercised for awhile. How can you avoid sore, strained muscles or muscle cramps during strenuous exercise? You should always remember to do warm-up exercises before you begin.

Muscular dystrophy (DIS-truh-fee) is a disease of the skeletal muscles in which the muscles gradually are destroyed. The skeletal muscle loses its ability to contract, which may cause the arms and legs to become useless. Some forms of muscular dystrophy are inherited, or passed from parent to child. The cause of muscular dystrophy is not known.

Think & Discuss

9. What is the function of tendons?
10. What does an extensor muscle do?
11. How do skeletal muscles move bones?
12. What causes sore muscles?
★ 13. Why do you think cardiac muscle has a large number of mitochondria?

20-4 The Skin

Did you know that the skin is the largest organ of the human body? You know that the outside of your body is covered by skin. However, skin also covers most of the organs inside your body.

The Outer Layer

Rub your hands together. You just wiped hundreds, or perhaps thousands, of dead skin cells from your hands! These dead skin cells form the outer layer of the skin. This layer of skin is called the **epidermis** (ep-uh-DUR-mis).

The main function of the skin is to support and protect the body. The dead skin cells of the epidermis form a waterproof shield for the body. The epidermis also protects the body from invading germs. Each day, you lose millions of cells from the epidermis. Dead skin cells are constantly replaced by the living cells beneath them.

Key Points

- Skin is made up of two layers called the dermis and epidermis.

- The epidermis protects the body from germs and helps control water loss.

- The dermis contains nerves, blood vessels, hair follicles, oil glands, and sweat glands.

Health and Safety Tip

Skin cancer can result from being in the sun too long. You should avoid too much exposure to the sun.

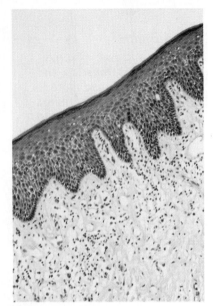

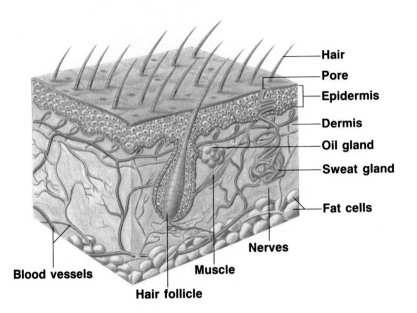

Figure 20-10 Compare the two layers of skin (left) with the diagram (right).

Hair
Pore
Epidermis
Dermis
Oil gland
Sweat gland
Fat cells
Nerves
Muscle
Blood vessels
Hair follicle

The Inner Layer

The living cells beneath the epidermis make up the second layer of the skin. This layer is called the **dermis.** Figure 20-10 shows the two layers that make up the skin. You will notice that the dermis is the thicker skin layer. The dermis contains many different kinds of nerve endings and blood vessels.

Several other structures also are found in the dermis. One of these structures is the **hair follicle.** Your skin contains millions of hair follicles. Each hair that grows on your body grows from a follicle.

The skin also contains oil glands. Oil glands usually are found near the hair follicles. Oil glands secrete a substance that helps soften the skin and keep it waterproof.

Another structure in the dermis is the sweat gland. The dermis contains more than two million sweat glands. Sweat glands are used for excretion. What do you think is excreted by the skin?

Think & Discuss

14. What is the function of the epidermis?

15. What is the function of oil glands?

16. Skin also is a sense organ. What sensations does the skin detect?

The human body is an amazing machine. Bones, muscles, and nerves work together when you walk, run, sit, and stand. If you are fascinated by the structure and movement of the human body, you may enjoy a career as an X-ray technician, physical therapist, or chiropractor.

X-Ray Technician

Have you ever had an X-ray taken? If you have, you may recall that proper positioning of the X-ray machine and you, the patient, was important. Because radiation can harm living things, it also is important to carefully regulate the amount of radiation used in the X-ray procedure. An X-ray technician operates X-ray equipment and prepares patients for X-rays.

To become an X-ray technician, you must first graduate from high school. An X-ray technician also must complete a two-year X-ray technician program.

X-ray technicians work in hospitals, doctors' and dentists' offices, health clinics, and laboratories. An X-ray technician should be in good health and have moderate strength and stamina. X-ray technicians also must be understanding and compassionate because they often work with patients who are ill or injured.

For more information: Write to the Department of Allied Health Education and Accreditation, American Medical Association, 535 N. Dearborn St., Chicago, IL 60601.

Physical Therapist

Physical therapists plan and treat people who have suffered disabling accidents or who have permanent physical disabilities. The purpose of the treatment is to restore movement, relieve pain, and limit permanent disability.

Physical therapists work mostly in hospitals, doctors' offices, and rehabilitation centers. Physical therapists must be patient, kind, and compassionate, since they must help patients deal with disablements.

Physical therapists must complete a college-degree program in physical therapy and pass a state licensing examination. High school students interested in entering this field should take courses in health, biology, chemistry, social science, mathematics, and physics.

For more information: Work as a volunteer in a hospital physical therapy department, or write to the American Physical Therapy Association, 111 North Fairfax St., Alexandria, VA 22314.

Chiropractor

Chiropractic medicine is a system of treatment based on the principle that a person's health is determined largely by the nervous system. Thus, interference with the nervous system damages normal functions and lowers a person's resistance to disease.

A chiropractor must have two years of college and complete a four-year chiropractic program. A chiropractor treats patients mainly by applying pressure to the spine and other body parts. Chiropractors also may prescribe diet, exercise, and rest. Chiropractors do not prescribe drugs or perform surgery.

For more information: Write to the American Chiropractic Association, 1916 Wilson Blvd., Arlington, VA 22201.

Chapter Review

CHAPTER SUMMARY

20-1 The Skeletal System

- The skeletal system is made up mostly of bone.
- The skeletal system also contains cartilage.
- Bones support the body, protect internal organs, store minerals, produce blood cells, and along with the muscles allow movement.

20-2 Bones

- Bones begin to replace cartilage during the second and third months of development.
- Arthritis is a joint disorder. Scoliosis is an abnormal curve of the backbone.

20-3 The Muscular System

- Muscles are needed for all types of movement.

- Skeletal muscle is voluntary muscle that moves bones.
- Smooth muscle is involuntary muscle found in the stomach, the intestines, and the blood vessels.
- Cardiac muscle is found only in the heart.
- Muscles pull on bones when they contract.
- Muscles work in pairs to move bones.
- Muscle tears, muscle cramps, and muscular dystrophy are three problems of the muscular system.

20-4 The Skin

- The skin protects the body.
- The epidermis is the outer layer of skin.
- Nerves, blood vessels, hair follicles, and oil and sweat glands are found in the dermis.

VOCABULARY LIST

appendicular skeleton (345)
axial skeleton (345)
cardiac muscle (352)
cartilage (344)
compact bone (346)
dermis (356)

endoskeleton (343)
epidermis (355)
extensor (353)
flexor (353)
hair follicle (356)

involuntary muscles (352)
joint (348)
ligaments (348)
marrow (346)
periosteum (346)

skeletal muscle (352)
smooth muscle (352)
spongy bone (346)
tendons (352)
voluntary muscles (352)

VOCABULARY REVIEW

Matching   Write the word or term from the Vocabulary List that best matches each description.

1. skull, backbone, and ribs
2. membrane that covers a bone
3. place where bones meet
4. muscle that straightens a joint
5. skeleton found inside
6. produces blood cells
7. muscles you control
8. hair grows from this

Applying Definitions   Explain the difference between the words in each pair.

1. epidermis, dermis
2. flexor, extensor
3. ligaments, tendons
4. bone, cartilage
5. skeletal muscle, involuntary muscle
6. axial skeleton, appendicular skeleton
7. spongy bone, compact bone
8. smooth muscle, cardiac muscle
9. endoskeleton, exoskeleton

True or False Write true if the statement is true. If the statement is false, change the underlined word or words to make the statement true.

1. The spaces in spongy bone are filled with <u>yellow</u> bone marrow.
2. Fixed joints are found in the <u>skull</u>.
3. The bones of the arms and legs are part of the <u>appendicular</u> skeleton.
4. You have over 600 <u>bones</u>.
5. Bones get their strength from <u>calcium</u>.
6. Your upper arm is connected to your shoulder by a <u>hinge</u> joint.
7. The tip of your nose is made up of <u>ligaments</u>.
8. Skeletal muscles only can <u>pull</u> bones.
9. Your skin is made up of <u>two</u> layers.
10. Inflamed joints are the main symptom of <u>muscular dystrophy</u>.

Question and Answer Rewrite each heading in the Chapter Outline on page 342 as a question. Then, answer each of the questions you have written.

Understanding a Diagram Use the diagram of the skeletal system shown in Figure 20–1 (page 344) to answer each of the following.

1. What is the scientific name for your collarbone?
2. What two bones make up your lower arm?
3. What are two bones of the head?
4. What is the largest bone of the body?

Writing the Main Ideas Using the Chapter Outline on page 342, write the main idea for each heading in the outline.

Critical Thinking Answer each of the following in complete sentences.

1. How would you walk if both muscles that control leg movements contracted at the same time?
2. What do the ribs and the sternum protect?
3. Put your hands on your rib cage and take a deep breath. What happens to your ribs when you breathe in? What do you think happens to the cartilage that attaches the ribs to the breastbone when you breathe?
4. Why are cartilage, tendons, and ligaments important parts of the skeletal system?
5. What might happen to your internal organs and muscles if your skin was not sensitive to pressure or pain?

1. Experiments have shown that exposing broken bones to an electric current can help them to heal more quickly. Using library references, find out about this technique. Then write a report on your findings.
2. Parkinson's disease, myasthenia gravis, and multiple sclerosis are diseases that affect the muscular system. Look up each of these diseases in an encyclopedia. Then prepare a table listing the causes and effects of each disease.
3. Use a first-aid manual to prepare a chart on disorders that often are sports injuries. List the symptom and first-aid treatment for each disorder. Include fractures, strains, sprains, tendonitis, and dislocations. Identify each disorder as a skeletal disorder or a muscular disorder.
4. Obtain a long beef bone from a butcher. Have the butcher cut the bone in half lengthwise. Try to find every part of the bone that you have studied.

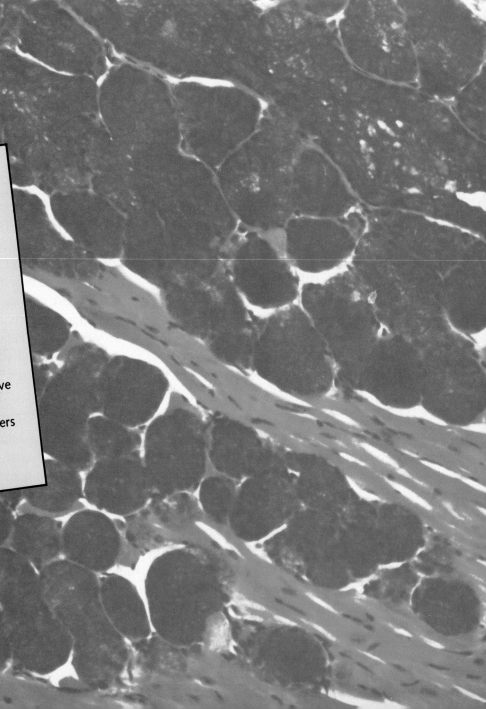

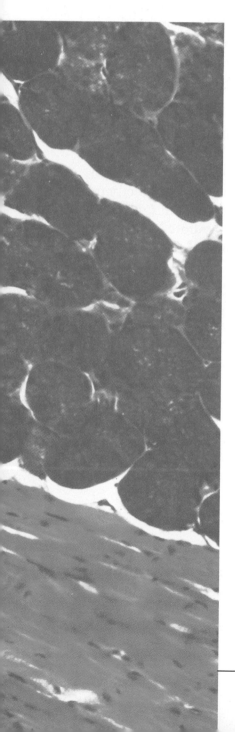

Objectives

After you have completed this chapter, you will be able to

21-1 **compare** mechanical and chemical digestion.
21-1 **describe** the function of enzymes in chemical digestion.
21-2 **identify** the organs of the digestive system.
21-2 **state** what happens to food in the small intestine.
21-3 **identify** some problems of the digestive system.

Science Process Skills

In this chapter, two science skills are highlighted. Symbols show some places where these skills are used.

▲ **Organizing:** When you organize information, you put the information in some kind of order.

▣ **Hypothesizing:** When you hypothesize, you state a suggested answer to a problem based upon known information.

*Nutrients are chemical substances your body needs to function properly. You get the nutrients your body needs from food. However, the food you eat is not in a form your body can use. The large food molecules must be broken down into usable forms. The process of breaking down food into forms the body can use is called **digestion** (dy-JES-chun).*

*Even before you put food into your mouth, your body is getting ready for digestion. When you are hungry and smell food, your brain stimulates the production of **saliva.** You may be familiar with the expression "my mouth is watering" to describe the production of saliva. Saliva is made by the salivary glands. A cross-section of a salivary gland is shown in the photograph. The salivary glands are just one part of the digestive system.*

21-1 The Digestive Process

Key Points

- Mechanical digestion breaks down food into small pieces. Chemical digestion breaks down large molecules into small ones.

- Enzymes are proteins that control chemical reactions in the body.

Study Hint

Turn to Chapter 3 to review proteins, carbohydrates, and fats.

During digestion, food is broken down into forms the body can use. This breaking down process involves both physical and chemical changes in the food. A physical change is a change in the physical properties of a substance. Some examples of physical properties are shape, size, color, and odor.

Tear a sheet of paper into many small pieces. You have just caused a physical change. You have changed the paper's size and shape, but it is still paper. Unlike a physical change, a chemical change results in new substances. Think of what happens when wood burns. Wood is changed into new substances, including ash and soot.

All of your food is made up of one or more nutrients. Proteins, vitamins, and minerals are three groups of nutrients. Carbohydrates and fats are other groups of nutrients. Vitamins and minerals can pass directly from the digestive system into the body without undergoing a chemical change. However, carbohydrates, proteins, and fats must be broken down into smaller, usable forms.

Mechanical Digestion

The physical breakdown of food into small pieces is called **mechanical digestion.** Mechanical digestion breaks large pieces of food into smaller ones. However, it does not change the substances in food.

What would happen if you tried to swallow a whole cracker? You probably would choke. What do you do with the cracker? You chew it and break the cracker into smaller and smaller pieces. Chewing and grinding are two ways that food is mechanically digested.

Chemical Digestion

The process by which large food molecules are broken down into smaller molecules is called **chemical digestion.** For example, a cracker is made up mostly of starch. Starch is a carbohydrate that is made up of many glucose molecules joined together. Glucose is a simple sugar. It is a small molecule that is used by the body for energy. Before your body can use the starch in crackers, the starch must be broken down into simple sugars by chemical digestion. Look at Table 21-1. What small molecules are fats broken down into during chemical digestion?

Table 21–1 Chemical Digestion of Nutrients		
Carbohydrates ⟶	change to ⟶	simple sugars
Proteins ⟶	change to ⟶	amino acids
Fats ⟶	change to ⟶	fatty acids and glycerol

In the digestive system, important chemicals called **enzymes** (EN-zyms) are released. Enzymes are proteins that control chemical reactions in the body, including the chemical digestion of food. How do enzymes control chemical reactions in the body? Enzymes speed up or slow down chemical reactions. They speed up chemical digestion. Enzymes combine temporarily with the large molecules in food and break them apart into smaller molecules.

Each enzyme can break down only one specific kind of food molecule. For example, enzymes that break down fats have no effect on carbohydrates and proteins. In the digestive system, enzymes are produced in liquids called digestive juices.

Think & Discuss

1. What is the function of enzymes?
2. What is the difference between mechanical digestion and chemical digestion?
3. Why must food undergo chemical digestion before it can be used by the body?

21-2 The Digestive System

Digestion is a process in which many organs work together. Some organs that make up the digestive system form a long tubelike structure called the **alimentary** (al-uh-MEN-tuhr-ee) **canal.** Other digestive organs, such as the liver, pancreas, and gallbladder, are not part of the alimentary canal. However, these organs do help with digestion.

Key Points
- The digestive system is made up of organs located in the alimentary canal and other organs that aid in digestion.

- Absorption takes place in the small intestine.

Study Hint

After you read Section 21–2, list the digestive actions that occur in each organ of the alimentary canal.

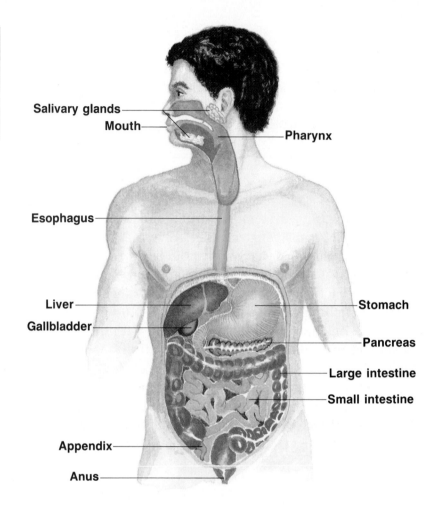

Salivary glands

Mouth

Pharynx

Esophagus

Liver

Gallbladder

Stomach

Pancreas

Large intestine

Small intestine

Appendix

Anus

Figure 21-1 Food does not pass through the salivary glands, liver, gallbladder, pancreas, or appendix on its way through the digestive system. Through which organs does food pass?

Study Hint

You can learn more about caring for your teeth by reading the Biology, Technology, and Society feature at the end of the chapter.

You can see the digestive system in Figure 21-1. Notice that the digestive system begins at the mouth and ends at the anus. In Figure 21-1, you can trace the path food takes on its trip through the digestive system.

The Mouth

Food enters the digestive system through the mouth. In the mouth, the teeth begin the mechanical digestion of food. How do the teeth carry out mechanical digestion? The teeth cut, tear, grind, and crush large pieces of food into smaller pieces. Figure 21-2 on page 365 shows the teeth of an adult. How many teeth do adults have?

People have four different kinds of teeth. Each kind of tooth has a different function. The incisors and canines cut and tear food. The premolars and molars grind and crush food. Look at Figure 21-2 again. How are the shapes of the teeth adapted to their functions?

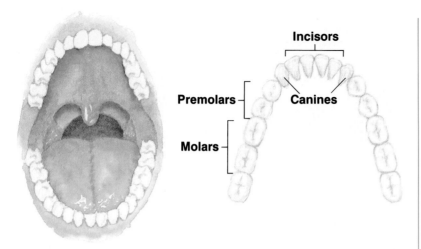

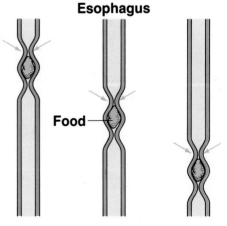

Figure 21-2 You probably have only 28 teeth. The third set of molars, called wisdom teeth, usually grow in during your twenties.

Do you think your tongue helps with chewing? Your tongue is used to move food around in the mouth and keep food where it can be chewed by the teeth. The tongue also helps mix food with saliva and moves food to the back of the mouth when you swallow.

What does saliva do? As food is broken down into smaller pieces by the teeth and tongue, it also is mixed with saliva. Saliva softens and moistens food. Saliva also begins the chemical digestion of food. Saliva contains an enzyme that starts to break down starch into simpler forms. Why do you think it is important for food to be softened and moistened?

Saliva is made by three pairs of salivary glands. Saliva passes from salivary glands through tiny tubes into the mouth.

The Pharynx and Esophagus

When food is swallowed, it enters the **pharynx** (FAR-inks), or throat. The pharynx is a passageway for both food and air. Air goes from the pharynx into the windpipe. Where does food go? It passes into the **esophagus** (i-SAF-uh-gus). The esophagus is a long, muscular tube that connects the mouth to the stomach.

The walls of the esophagus are lined with cells that secrete mucus. The esophagus walls also are made up of two layers of muscles. Mucus helps food move easily through the esophagus. A wave of contractions of the muscles forces the food downward to the stomach. The wavelike movement that moves food through the digestive system is called **peristalsis** (per-uh-STAWL-sis). Gravity

Figure 21-3 Food moves through the esophagus by peristalsis.

Digestion **365**

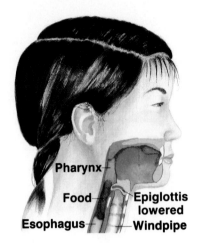

Figure 21-4 Does the epiglottis raise or lower when you breathe?

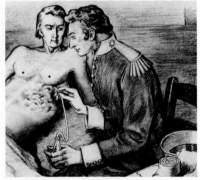

Figure 21-5 Dr. William Beaumont studied digestion by observing a hunter who had a gunshot wound in his stomach.

helps to move food toward the stomach, but gravity is not necessary. Even when astronauts eat in space, where there is no gravity, food reaches their stomachs.

You may be wondering what prevents food from entering the windpipe. When you swallow, a flap of tissue called the **epiglottis** (ep-uh-GLAT-is) covers the opening to the windpipe. The epiglottis blocks off the windpipe so that all your food enters the esophagus.

The Stomach

The stomach is a large, J-shaped, baglike organ that acts as a storage place for food. The stomach also breaks down food. In fact, both mechanical and chemical digestion take place in the stomach.

How does the stomach aid in mechanical digestion? The stomach wall has three layers of muscles. Each layer contracts in a different direction, causing the stomach to twist and churn its contents. These actions help break up food into smaller pieces. The churning action of the stomach tends to begin at usual mealtimes. When you say your stomach is "growling," you are referring to contractions of the stomach muscles.

The strong churning action of the stomach also mixes food with gastric juice. Gastric juice is the digestive juice made by the stomach. Gastric juice contains three substances: mucus, **pepsin** (PEP-sin), and hydrochloric (hy-druh-KLAWR-ik) acid. Pepsin is an enzyme that begins the chemical digestion of proteins. Hydrochloric acid is a strong acid. It is needed for pepsin to work because pepsin can only work in an acid environment.

Hydrochloric acid also kills bacteria in the stomach and helps to break up food. Mucus protects the lining of the stomach from both hydrochloric acid and pepsin.

By the time food leaves the stomach, it is in the form of a thick liquid. This liquid is called **chyme** (KYM). Chyme is gradually released from the stomach, and into the small intestine.

The Small Intestine

The small intestine is a narrow, coiled tube that is about 6.5 m long and 2.5 cm wide. The walls of the small intestine, like those of the esophagus and stomach, are muscular. Food moves through the small intestine by peristalsis.

What happens to food in the small intestine? You already know that some chemical digestion takes place in the mouth and stomach. However, most of the chemical digestion of food takes place in the small intestine.

Digestion in the Small Intestine

Food entering the small intestine is mixed with a variety of digestive juices. The first digestive juices that act on the food are produced by the **pancreas** (PAN-kree-us) and the liver. The pancreas and liver are part of the digestive system. However, they are not part of the alimentary canal.

▲ The small intestine also produces a digestive juice. The digestive juice made by the small intestine contains enzymes that complete the digestion of starches, proteins,

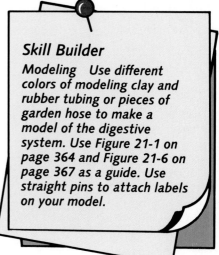

Skill Builder

Modeling Use different colors of modeling clay and rubber tubing or pieces of garden hose to make a model of the digestive system. Use Figure 21-1 on page 364 and Figure 21-6 on page 367 as a guide. Use straight pins to attach labels on your model.

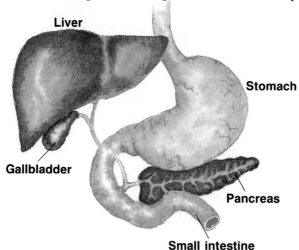

Liver

Stomach

Gallbladder

Pancreas

Small intestine

Figure 21-6 Each of these organs is involved in the process of digestion.

Table 21–2 Summary of Digestion		
NUTRIENT	DIGESTION BEGINS	DIGESTION COMPLETED
Proteins	Stomach	Small Intestine
Carbohydrates	Mouth	Small Intestine
Fats	Small Intestine	Small Intestine

and fats. You can see a summary of chemical digestion in Table 21-2. Where does the digestion of protein begin? Where does it end?

The Job of the Pancreas

The pancreas is a small organ located below the stomach. When food first enters the small intestine, the pancreas releases digestive juices into the small intestine through a small tube. The digestive juice of the pancreas contains a variety of enzymes that change starches, proteins, and fats into simpler forms. Pancreatic juices also neutralize the acidity of the food leaving the stomach.

The Job of the Liver

The liver is the largest organ inside the human body. What is the liver's role in digestion? The liver produces **bile.** Have you ever seen a detergent or soap breaking up grease? Detergents and soap break up grease into small drops that can be carried away in wash water. The action of bile is similar to the action of detergents and soap. Bile is a liquid that breaks down large drops of fat into very tiny droplets. This increases the surface area of fats, making it easier for pancreatic enzymes to act on them.

Bile does not pass directly from the liver to the small intestine. Instead, bile is stored in the **gallbladder.** The gallbladder is a small sac located under the liver. When food enters the small intestine, bile passes from the gallbladder into the small intestine through a small tube.

Absorption from the Small Intestine

After food has been changed into usable forms, it is ready to be absorbed into the bloodstream. The movement of food from the digestive system to the blood takes place in the small intestine. Once inside the blood, digested food is carried to all of your body cells.

Study Hint

The role of the blood and the circulatory system is discussed in Chapter 22.

The absorption (ab-SAWRP-shun) of food into the bloodstream takes place through the wall of the small intestine. The inner lining of the small intestine is folded. The folds have millions of tiny fingerlike projections called **villi.** The many folds and villi give the small intestine a velvety appearance and greatly increase the surface area for absorption.

A single projection is called a villus. You can see the structure of a villus in Figure 21-7. Notice that the villus has many blood vessels. Digested food passes through the absorptive layer of the villus and into the blood vessels. How many cells thick are the villi walls?

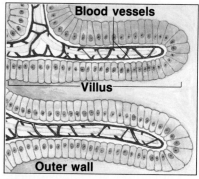

Figure 21-7 When digestion is completed, nutrients are absorbed by the villi of the small intestine.

The Large Intestine

A watery mixture of undigested food moves from the small intestine into the large intestine. The large intestine is the last part of the digestive system. It is a tubelike organ about 2 m long and 7 cm wide. Why do you think it is called the large intestine?

The undigested material that enters the large intestine contains a lot of water and minerals. In the large intestine, water and minerals are absorbed into the blood. The **feces** (FEE-seez), or remaining solid waste materials, move into the lower part of the large intestine called the **rectum.** Wastes are stored temporarily in the rectum until they are eliminated from the body through the anus.

A small, thin sac called the appendix (uh-PEN-diks) is located at the place where the small intestine and large intestine join. Sometimes food gets trapped in the appendix and the appendix becomes infected with bacteria. An infection of the appendix is called appendicitis (uh-pen-duh-SY-tis).

Study Hint

The appendix is a vestigial organ in humans. Use an encyclopedia to find out more about the appendix and what the term "vestigial" means.

Think & Discuss

4. What is peristalsis?
5. What is the function of saliva?
6. Name the four different kinds of teeth and state the function of each.
7. Name the organs of the alimentary canal in order, beginning with the mouth.
8. Is the action of bile mechanical or chemical digestion?

ACTIVITY 21–1

PROBLEM: How do villi help in the absorption of digested food?

Science Process Skills
observing, comparing, relating concepts

Background Information
Digested food is absorbed in the small intestine by fingerlike projections called villi. The process of absorption is increased when the surface area is increased. The larger the surface area, the better is the chance of food molecules being absorbed.

Materials
string
scissors
metric ruler

Procedure
1. To measure the surface area of the villi shown below, place a piece of string along the edge of the villi in the photograph. Be sure that you make the string go up and around each villus. Cut off any extra string. **CAUTION: Be careful when using scissors.**

2. Measure the length of the string in centimeters. Record the length.
3. Measure the length of the photograph in centimeters. Record the length.

Observations
1. **a.** What is the surface area of the villi in the photograph? **b.** What is the length of the photograph?
2. How does the length of the villi compare with the length of the photograph?

Conclusions
1. What effect do villi have on the surface area of the small intestine?
2. How do villi aid in the absorption of digested food?

Going Further
Use a model to show increasing surface area. Obtain a synthetic sponge. Calculate the area of each side. Area = length × width. Add the areas together to get the total surface area. Cut the sponge in half and calculate the surface area.

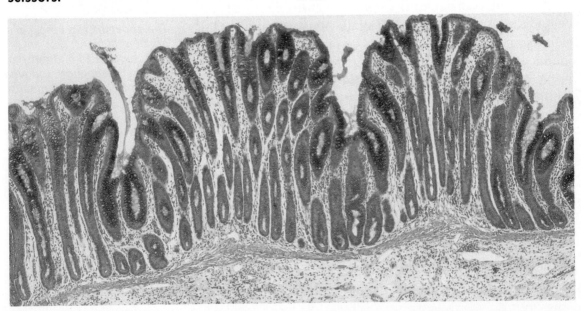

21-3 Problems of the Digestive System

Sometimes the digestive system has problems. Some of the common problems of the digestive system are indigestion, ulcers, diarrhea (dy-uh-REE-uh), and constipation. Can you name any other problems of the digestive system?

▲ Did you name tooth decay as a problem of the digestive system? Have you ever had a cavity? A cavity is a hole in a tooth. A cavity is caused by tooth decay, which is the most common problem of the digestive system. Tooth decay is caused by bacteria that live in the mouth.

Tooth decay begins when a film called **plaque** forms on the teeth. Plaque is made up of saliva, food, and bacteria. The bacteria produce acids that break down the outer covering, or enamel, of the tooth. The structure of a tooth is shown in Figure 21-8. If the decay is left untreated, it spreads to the softer parts of a tooth. If a cavity reaches the tooth pulp, a nerve is exposed. What do you think exposure of the nerve causes? In the final stages of tooth decay, bacteria destroy the tooth pulp.

Indigestion and Ulcers

Have you ever had indigestion? Indigestion is a general term used for pain or discomfort that occurs after eating. Most people have indigestion at one time or another. Usually indigestion is caused by poor eating habits. For example, eating too much, too little, or too fast all can cause indigestion.

Key Point
- Tooth decay, indigestion, and ulcers are problems of the digestive system.

Health and Safety Tip
Flossing your teeth daily helps remove plaque from your teeth. Regular visits to a dentist are important to maintain healthy teeth.

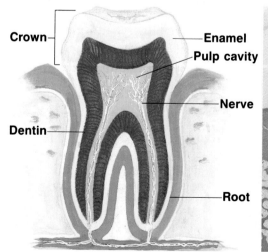
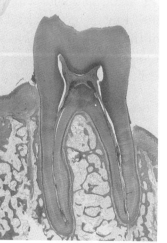

Crown— Enamel
—Pulp cavity
—Nerve
Dentin—
—Root

Figure 21-8 Use the diagram of the tooth (left) to find the nerve in the X-ray of the healthy tooth (right).

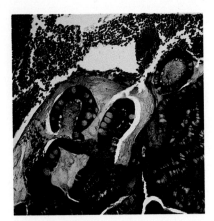

Figure 21-9 An ulcer can begin to bleed if not treated.

Sometimes eating too much causes a burning feeling commonly known as heartburn. Heartburn occurs when acidic juices from the stomach go up into the esophagus. The acid irritates the esophagus and causes a burning sensation. Because the esophagus is located behind the heart, it seems like the pain is coming from the heart.

A more serious problem occurs when stomach acids digest, or "eat" away the lining of the stomach or the small intestine. The sore, or hole, in the lining is called an **ulcer.** Ulcers develop when the mucus that coats the inside of the stomach or small intestine does not protect them from hydrochloric acid and enzymes.

Have you ever heard someone say, "I'm going to get ulcers," when the person was under a lot of stress? How and why ulcers occur is not completely understood. However, stress is known to be a contributing factor in the development of ulcers. Fortunately, most ulcers can be treated or cured with medication.

Diarrhea and Constipation

When the walls of the large intestine fail to absorb water from food wastes, the wastes are very watery. This condition is called diarrhea. Diarrhea results when frequent, strong peristalsis moves wastes through the large intestine too quickly for water to be absorbed.

Diarrhea can be caused by stress and by certain viruses and bacteria. These things cause the lining of the intestine to become irritated. Why do you think it is important for a person suffering from diarrhea to drink plenty of liquids?

What happens when peristalsis in the large intestine is too slow or too weak? The wastes move slowly, and most of the water in the wastes is absorbed. The wastes become more solid than normal, and difficult to eliminate. This condition is called constipation.

Think & Discuss

9. What part of plaque causes tooth decay?

10. What are three reasons people get indigestion?

11. Why do you think diarrhea is a common disorder among visitors to other countries?

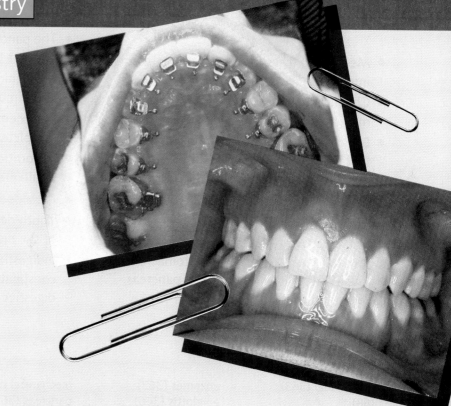

Braces! Have you or a friend ever groaned at the thought of wearing them? Thanks to advances in dental technology, braces may soon be much different from the mouthful of hardware that they once were.

Today, braces are made of either metal wire or clear plastic. The main advantage of metal braces is that they are effective in restraining teeth. However, metal braces have the disadvantage of being visible and sometimes uncomfortable to wear. Plastic braces are less visible than metal braces and are much more comfortable. However, plastic tends to change shape. This means that it cannot exert consistent force on teeth over time. Plastic also can stain and discolor teeth when exposed to substances such as cola and coffee.

The challenge for dental technology has been to create braces that are as effective as metal and as pleasing to look at and comfortable to wear as plastic. One answer to this challenge may be an invention called Starfire Braces. Starfire braces are made of transparent, synthetic sapphires. These colorless sapphires are harder than metal and resistant to stains.

Another new type of braces are called Lingual Braces.

Lingual Braces are designed so that traditional metal braces are attached to the unexposed side of the teeth, as shown in the upper photograph. As a result, the braces are nearly invisible, as shown in the lower photograph.

A third type of braces that may be available in a few years are electric braces. The main appeal of electric braces is that you have to wear them only while you sleep. Electric braces will have a battery attachment that speeds up the alignment of teeth by the use of low-level electricity. In the future, wearers of braces will just have to "hook up" at night in order to achieve the same results that 24-hour wearers of braces achieve now.

An interesting aspect of today's dental technology is the way new products are tested. In the past, dental products intended for people were tested on monkeys. Now the same products are being tested by a robot nicknamed "Motor Mouth." Motor Mouth consists of freshly extracted human teeth mounted in a controlled environmental chamber. Motor Mouth is so efficient that it can simulate one year of chewing in just one day!

To Think About

- Why is Motor Mouth a more efficient way of testing dental products than using monkeys?

- What disadvantages do Lingual Braces have?

Chapter Review

21-1 The Digestive Process

- Mechanical digestion breaks down food into small pieces.
- Chemical digestion breaks down large molecules into smaller ones.
- Enzymes temporarily combine with the large molecules in food and break them apart into smaller molecules.
- Enzymes are specific.

21-2 The Digestive System

- The digestive system is made up of the mouth, pharynx, esophagus, stomach, small intestine, large intestine, pancreas, liver, and gallbladder.

- The pancreas, liver, and gallbladder are not part of the alimentary canal.
- Mechanical and chemical digestion begin in the mouth.
- The chemical digestion of food is completed in the small intestine.
- Absorption takes place through villi in the small intestine.

21-3 Disorders of the Digestive System

- Tooth decay is the most common problem of the digestive system.
- Indigestion, ulcers, diarrhea, and constipation are other problems of the digestive system.

VOCABULARY LIST

alimentary canal (363)	enzymes (363)	mechanical digestion (362)	plaque (371)
bile (368)	epiglottis (366)	pancreas (367)	rectum (369)
chemical digestion (362)	esophagus (365)	pepsin (366)	saliva (361)
chyme (367)	feces (369)	peristalsis (365)	ulcer (372)
digestion (361)	gallbladder (368)	pharynx (365)	villi (369)

VOCABULARY REVIEW

Matching   Write the word or term from the Vocabulary List that best matches each description.

1. digests proteins
2. stores bile
3. solid wastes
4. covers opening to windpipe during swallowing
5. increases surface area of small intestine
6. lower porton of large intestine
7. carries food from the mouth to the stomach
8. common passageway for food and air
9. wavelike motion
10. breakdown of food into smaller pieces

Identifying Relationships   Identify the word or term in each group that does not belong. Explain why it does not belong with the group.

1. alimentary canal, mouth, liver
2. villi, absorption, chyme
3. enzymes, mechanical digestion, chemical digestion
4. bile, cavity, plaque
5. esophagus, peristalsis, digestion
6. pepsin, small intestine, stomach
7. pancreas, mechanical digestion, teeth
8. large intestine, rectum, pharynx
9. ulcer, villi, cavity
10. gallbladder, saliva, mouth

Completion Write the word or words that best complete each sentence.

1. Adults have _____ different kinds of teeth.
2. The _____ moves food to the back of the mouth when swallowing.
3. The stomach wall has three layers of _____.
4. Where the small and large intestines join, there is a small sac called the _____.
5. Saliva, food, and bacteria build up on the teeth in the form of _____.
6. An ulcer is a hole in the lining of the stomach or _____.
7. Chemical reactions in the body are controlled by _____.
8. The passageway for both food and air is the _____.
9. Gastric juice contains pepsin, hydrochloric acid, and _____.

Finding the Main Ideas Use the section number to find the sentence that answers each question. Then, write the sentence.

1. What is a physical change? (21–1)
2. How does mechanical digestion help with the chemical digestion of food? (21–1)
3. What is the pharynx? (21–1)
4. What prevents food from entering the windpipe? (21–2)
5. How does the stomach aid in mechanical digestion? (21–2)
6. What is the liver's role in digestion? (21–2)
7. Where is the appendix located? (21–2)
8. What three things cause plaque to build up on the teeth? (21–3)
9. What are the usual causes of indigestion? (21–3)
10. What causes heartburn? (21–3)
11. What happens when peristalsis in the large intestine is abnormally slow? (21–3)

Writing for Understanding One way to find out if you understand something is to write a brief summary of the information in your own words. Reread Section 21–1, The Digestive Process, on pages 362–363 and write a brief summary of the information.

Critical Thinking Answer each of the following in complete sentences.

1. How would swallowing large chunks of food affect the digestive process?

2. Sometimes doctors must remove part or most of a person's stomach. How would such an operation affect the digestive process?
3. Why is absorption such an important part of the digestive process?
4. Why is the large surface area of the small intestine important?
5. Does any digestion take place in the large intestine?
6. Where does absorption take place?

1. Do library research to find out about Dr. William Beaumont and his patient, Alexis St. Martin. In a brief report, explain how they contributed to an understanding of the digestive system.

2. Using this book as a reference, draw a diagram of the digestive system. Label the parts in the diagram, and include a caption listing the organs through which food passes in the proper order.

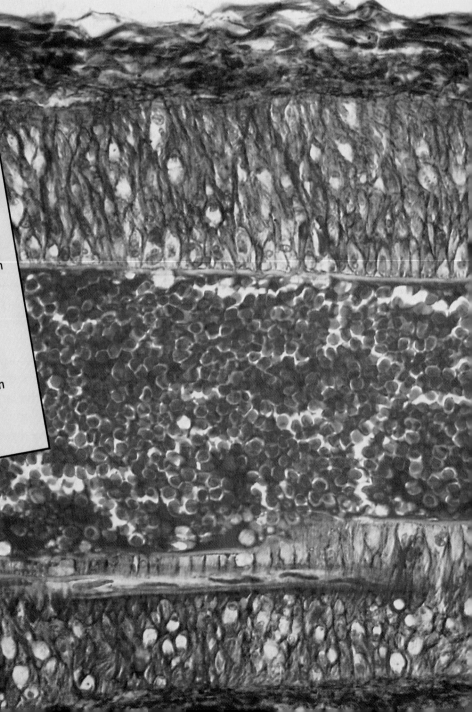

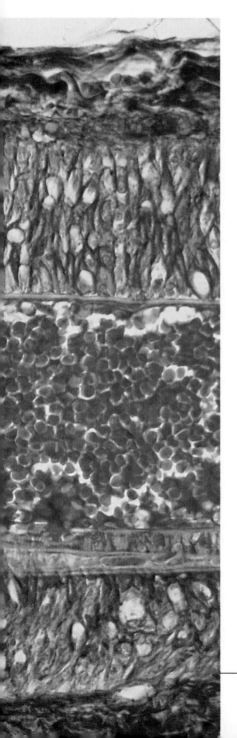

Objectives

After you have completed this chapter, you will be able to

22-1 **describe** the structure and function of the heart.

22-1 **name** and **describe** three kinds of blood vessels.

22-2 **explain** the two subsystems of circulation.

22-3 **compare** red blood cells and white blood cells.

22-3 **identify** the four major blood types.

22-4 **describe** the structure and function of the lymphatic system.

Science Process Skills

In this chapter, two science skills are highlighted. Symbols show some places where these skills are used.

❯ **Predicting:** When you predict, you state in advance how and why something will occur.

❒ **Hypothesizing:** When you hypothesize, you state a suggested answer to a problem based upon known information.

The United States has many roads, railroad tracks, and airline routes that are used to transport food and other items. These pathways make up the transport system of the United States. Trucks, trains, and airplanes carry materials along these pathways.

Your body has a transport system, too. It is called the circulatory system. The circulatory system moves blood throughout your body. What does blood transport? Blood transports many things, including food, oxygen, and waste products. The photograph on the left shows red blood cells moving through a blood vessel. The movement of blood through the body is called **circulation** (sur-kyuh-LAY-shun).

22-1 The Circulatory System

Key Points

- The heart is a four-chambered muscular organ that pumps blood throughout the body.

- Arteries, veins, and capillaries are three kinds of blood vessels.

Your circulatory system is made up of your heart, blood vessels, and blood. Blood vessels are tubes that carry blood through the body. The blood vessels form a closed circulatory system. In a closed circulatory system, blood never leaves the blood vessels. What other organisms can you name that have a closed circulatory system?

The Heart

Have you ever been told to memorize something "by heart"? This expression was first used long ago when people thought that the heart was the center of thinking. Today, however, scientists know that the heart's job is to pump blood throughout the body.

You can think of the heart as a double pump. The right side of your heart pumps blood to your lungs. The left side of your heart pumps blood to all other parts of your body. You can see the structure of the heart in Figure 22-1. Notice that the heart is divided into two sides by a thick wall called the **septum.**

The heart also is divided into four chambers. Each side of your heart has an **atrium** (AY-tree-uhm), or upper chamber, and a **ventricle** (VEN-tri-kuhl), or lower

Skill Builder

Modeling   When you model, you use a copy or an imitation of an object to help explain something. Make a model of the heart using different colors of clay. Label the different parts of the heart. Then display your model in the classroom.

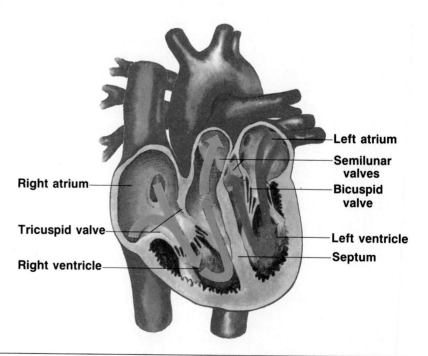

Right atrium

Tricuspid valve

Right ventricle

Left atrium

Semilunar valves

Bicuspid valve

Left ventricle

Septum

Figure 22-1   Your heart is a muscular organ that pumps about 18,175 L of blood throughout your body each day.

378   Human Biology

chamber. The atria are like receiving rooms. They receive blood returning to the heart. The ventricles are like shipping rooms. They pump blood through the rest of the body.

How does blood flow through the heart? As you can see in Figure 22-1, blood flows from the atria to the ventricles. When the atria fill with blood, they contract and blood is pushed into the ventricles. The ventricles then contract and pump blood to other parts of the body.

Heart Valves

Figure 22-2 shows that the heart has valves. Each valve is a thin, strong flap of tissue that acts like a one-way door. The valve between the right atrium and right ventricle is the **tricuspid valve.** The valve between the left atrium and left ventricle is the **bicuspid valve.** The **semilunar valves** are found between the ventricles and blood vessels.

What is the job of the valves? The valves open and close at different times to prevent blood from flowing backwards. Blood can pass freely into the ventricles from the atria. However, when the ventricles are filled, the tricuspid and bicuspid valves snap shut. Blood also flows easily from the ventricles into the blood vessels. When the ventricles relax, the semilunar valves snap shut.

Heartbeat

Your heart is a hardworking muscle that is pumping blood all the time. The pumping rhythm of your heart is called your heartbeat. Have you ever listened to your heartbeat?

If you could listen to your heartbeat through a stethoscope (STETH-uh-skohp), you would hear a lub-dup sound with a steady rhythm. What causes the sound of your heartbeat? The lub-dup sounds you hear are the sounds of the heart valves closing. When the tricuspid and bicuspid valves snap shut, the "lub" sound is heard. When the semilunar valves snap shut, the "dup" sound is heard.

Sometimes, a heart valve is damaged and blood flows backwards. The backward flow of blood causes a swishing sound, called a heart murmur. If a lub-swish-dup sound is heard through a stethoscope, which valves are not closing properly?

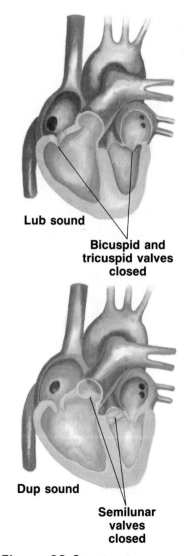

Lub sound

Bicuspid and tricuspid valves closed

Dup sound

Semilunar valves closed

Figure 22-2 The closing of the heart valves causes the lub-dup sounds of a heartbeat.

ACTIVITY 22–1

PROBLEM: How does exercise affect your heart rate?

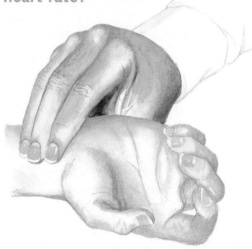

Science Process Skills
hypothesizing, relating concepts, comparing

Background Information
Heartbeat rate can be determined by measuring the pulse rate because the two rates are equal. At rest, pulse rate is about 72 beats per minute. However, pulse rate may vary from person to person.

Materials
clock or watch with second hand

Procedure
1. Copy the Data Table shown.

Data Table: Heartbeat Rate			
PERSON	HEARTBEAT RATE		
	At Rest	Standing	After Exercise	After 2 mins.
You				
Partner				

2. Sit quietly for 1 or 2 minutes.
3. Have your partner locate your pulse by placing the first, second, and third fingers on your wrist along the radial artery, as shown in the diagram.
4. Have your partner count the number of pulses felt in 30 seconds. Multiply this number by 2. Record your pulse rate in the Data Table.
5. Change positions and take your partner's pulse rate.
6. **HYPOTHESIZE** What do you think will happen to your pulse rate when you stand up? When you run in place? Write your hypothesis on a sheet of paper. Your hypothesis should answer the questions. To test your hypothesis, continue the activity.

7. Repeat steps 3–5 while standing.
8. Jog in place for 2 minutes. Then repeat steps 3–5.
9. Sit down and rest for 2 minutes. Then repeat steps 3–5.

Observations
1. Did your pulse rate speed up or slow down after standing up?
2. **a.** Did your pulse rate speed up or slow down after jogging in place? **b.** Did you notice a change in your heartbeat? If so, describe the change.
3. What happened to your pulse rate after you rested for 2 minutes?

Conclusions
1. What effect does exercise have on your heart rate? Remember that pulse rate and heart rate are equal.
2. Was your hypothesis correct? Use your observations to support your hypothesis.

Going Further
Gather pulse rate data for the entire class. Organize the data in a table. Does everyone have the same heart rate at rest, while standing, and after exercise? Compare heart rates after exercise and after 10 minutes of rest.

Blood Vessels

Your circulatory system has three kinds of blood vessels. The **arteries** (ART-uhr-ees) are blood vessels that carry blood away from the heart. The **veins** are blood vessels that carry blood to the heart. Both arteries and veins have many smaller branches. The smallest branches of arteries and veins are connected by **capillaries** (KAP-uh-ler-ees). You can see the relationship among arteries, capillaries, and veins in Figure 22-3.

Arteries

Arteries have thick muscular walls that are both strong and elastic. Why is the structure of arteries important for their job? Think of what happens when you squeeze a tube of toothpaste. When you squeeze the tube, toothpaste moves through the tube under high pressure. As the toothpaste moves through the tube, the tube expands. Each time the heart beats, blood is pushed through the arteries under high pressure. Blood pressure is the force that blood exerts against the walls of a blood vessel. The elastic structure of arteries allows them to stretch as blood flows through. Their strong walls prevent blood pressure from bursting the arteries.

❯ Place your middle and index finger over the inside of your wrist. The beat you feel is your pulse. When you feel your pulse, you are feeling blood pressure against the walls of an artery. The blood pressure in an artery rises and falls with each beat of your heart. Therefore, your pulse rate and heartbeat rate are the same. How do you think strenuous exercise, such as running, would affect your pulse rate?

Veins

As you can see in Figure 22-4, veins have thinner walls than arteries. They also are less muscular. By the time blood reaches the veins, it is under less pressure. Therefore, the veins do not need to be as muscular as arteries. Why do you think you cannot feel your pulse in a vein?

Because the blood in the veins is under low pressure, it does not flow through them as easily as it flows through your arteries. What keeps blood flowing through the veins

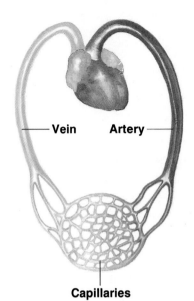

Vein   Artery

Capillaries

Figure 22-3 Arteries and veins are connected by tiny capillaries.

Study Hint

You may find it easy to remember that arteries carry blood away from the heart by associating the two words beginning with the letter "a": "artery" and "away."

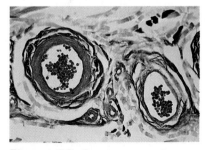

Figure 22-4 Compare the artery (left) with the vein (right).

to the heart? The contraction of skeletal muscles helps move the blood back to the heart. Also, like the heart, some veins have valves that prevent blood from flowing backward. Why do you think the valves in your leg veins are especially important?

Capillaries

Capillaries are microscopic blood vessels with walls that are only one cell thick. Because capillaries are so narrow, red blood cells must move through them in single file. Every substance carried by the blood is exchanged with body cells through the capillary walls. For example, food and oxygen diffuse out of the blood through the capillary wall and into the body cells. Carbon dioxide and other waste products diffuse out of the body cells into the blood through the capillary wall.

Circulatory System Problems

Problems of the circulatory system are among the leading causes of death in the United States. These problems are most common in older people, but the problems often develop gradually over a lifetime. Therefore, it is important for you to know about circulatory system problems and how they might be prevented.

High Blood Pressure

Have you ever had your blood pressure measured? If so, you probably were told that your blood pressure was one number over another number. When your blood pressure is taken, two different measurements are made. The measurements are recorded as a fraction, for example, 120/80. The first number is a measurement of blood pressure in the arteries when the ventricles are contracting. The second number is a measurement of blood pressure in the arteries when the ventricles are relaxed. A blood pressure of 120/80 is normal for humans. A blood pressure reading above 140/90 is considered high. High blood pressure is a serious problem because it increases the risk of serious heart problems.

What causes high blood pressure? In many cases, the cause of high blood pressure is unknown. In other cases, high blood pressure is caused by a narrowing of the

Health and Safety Tip
It is important to have your blood pressure checked at least once a year.

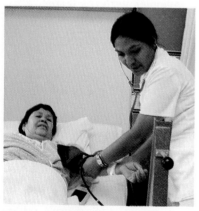

Figure 22-5   Having your blood pressure checked is a simple procedure.

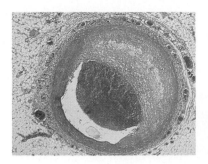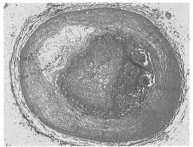

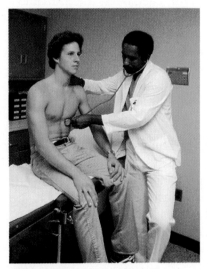

Figure 22-6 Notice the cholesterol buildup on these arteries. The artery on the left is partially blocked. The one on the right is almost completely blocked.

arteries. This is called hardening of the arteries. The arteries become narrow when cholesterol builds up on the walls of the arteries. Cholesterol is a fatty substance found in meats and other foods that come from animals. When the arteries become narrow, there is less room for blood to flow through. As a result, blood exerts a greater pressure on the artery walls.

Heart Attack

Like other body tissues, heart muscle needs a certain amount of blood to stay alive. A narrowed artery blocks the flow of blood to part of the heart. As a result, the part of the heart that does not receive enough blood begins to die. This is called a heart attack. Studies show, however, that lowering blood pressure and cholesterol levels can reduce your risk of a heart attack.

What are some of the signs of a heart attack? Signs of a heart attack include uncomfortable pressure or pain in the center of the chest. This pain sometimes spreads to the left shoulder and arm. Sweating, dizziness, nausea, fainting, or shortness of breath also may occur. Anyone suffering from the signs of a heart attack should be taken to a hospital immediately.

Figure 22-7 A doctor can detect many early signs of circulatory problems.

Think & Discuss

1. What is the function of the bicuspid valve?
2. What is the function of the ventricles?
3. Compare and contrast arteries, veins, and capillaries.
4. What causes a heart attack?
5. Describe the heartbeat sound a doctor would hear if the patient had a defective semilunar valve.

ACTIVITY 22–2

PROBLEM: How does body size affect heart rate?

Science Process Skills
sequencing, graphing, interpreting data, hypothesizing, making generalizations

Background Information
With each beat, the heart moves blood through the body. The longer the path through the body, the longer is the time between heartbeats.

Materials
pencil and paper

Procedure
1. Study the Data Table showing the heartbeat rates of different organisms. List the animals according to heartbeat rate from fastest to slowest.

Data Table:	Heartbeat Rates
ANIMAL	BEATS/MINUTE
Elephant	25
Mouse	1000
Robin	570
Cow	65
Cat	120
Dog	100
Horse	38
Human	72

2. **HYPOTHESIZE**   Do you think that there is a relationship between body size and heartbeat rate? If so, what do you think that relationship is? If not, explain your reason. Write your hypothesis on a sheet of paper. Your hypothesis should answer the questions. To test your hypothesis, continue the activity.

3. Make a bar graph that shows the heart rate of each animal. Place the animal with the fastest heartbeat rate at the far left side of your graph. Place the animal with the slowest heartbeat rate at the far right side of your graph.

Observations
1. **a.** Which animals tend to have the fastest heartbeat rates?   **b.** Are these large or small animals?
2. **a.** Which animals tend to have the slowest heartbeat rates?   **b.** Are these large or small animals?

Conclusions
1. Was your hypothesis correct? Use your observations to support your hypothesis.
2. **GENERALIZE**   What general statement can you make about the relationship between body size and heartbeat rate?

Going Further
Do you think that heartbeat rate varies among humans according to body size? State a hypothesis. Then, design an experiment to test your hypothesis. Prepare your data as a scientific newsletter.

22-2 Circulation

The time is the early seventeenth century. You are working in the office of Dr. William Harvey, an English physician. Dr. Harvey is studying the human circulatory system. He asks you, "If the ventricles of the heart are separated by a wall without any holes and the veins have valves, how could blood travel throughout the body?" How would you answer Dr. Harvey?

🖥 Using his knowledge of the structure of the heart and the function of the valves, Dr. Harvey hypothesized that blood flowed in a circular motion. He was the first scientist to show that the heart and blood vessels form a continuous closed system through which blood circulates. Dr. Harvey came to these conclusions by studying the human heart and the circulatory systems of live animals. From his studies of live animals, Harvey inferred that blood circulates through the human body in a closed system.

Today, biologists divide the circulatory system into two smaller systems of circulation. The pathway of the blood between the heart and the lungs is called **pulmonary** (PUL-muh-ner-ee) **circulation.** The pathway of blood between the heart and all other parts of the body is called **systemic circulation.**

Key Points

- Pulmonary circulation is the movement of blood from the heart to the lungs and then back to the heart.

- Systematic circulation is the movement of blood to all parts of the body, except the lungs.

Figure 22-8 Dr. William Harvey, the English physician, demonstrates his theory of the circulation of the blood to King Charles I.

Study Hint

The term "pulmonary" means related to or associated with the lungs.

Pulmonary Circulation

Your heart has a left side and a right side. Each side of the heart pumps blood to different places. Where does blood go from the right side of your heart? The right side of your heart pumps blood to your lungs. Use Figure 22-9 as a model as your read about pulmonary circulation.

Blood from the body enters the right atrium through veins. What does this blood contain? It carries a lot of carbon dioxide and very little oxygen. From the right atrium, blood passes into the right ventricle. The right ventricle pumps blood through the pulmonary artery. The pulmonary artery has two branches. One branch goes to each lung. In the lungs, the arteries divide many times to form a network of capillaries. In the lungs, the blood picks up oxygen and releases carbon dioxide. Then the blood, with its rich oxygen supply, is carried into the left atrium by the pulmonary veins. Through what blood vessels are oxygen and carbon dioxide exchanged?

Systemic Circulation

Once blood gets a fresh supply of oxygen in the lungs, it is ready to be sent to body cells again. Blood passes from the left atrium into the left ventricle. The left ventricle pumps

Skill Builder

Sequencing One way to organize information is to place events in sequence, or the order in which they take place. Trace the path of blood through the body in sequence, beginning and ending with the blood in the capillaries of the right big toe. Make sure that you mention all the kinds of blood vessels through which the blood passes.

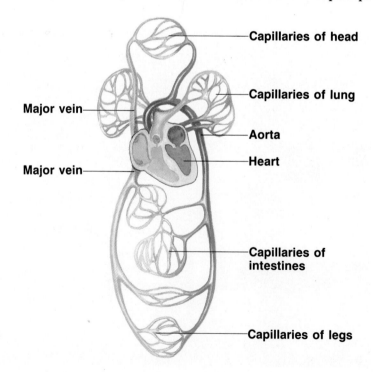

Capillaries of head

Capillaries of lung

Major vein

Aorta

Major vein

Heart

Capillaries of intestines

Capillaries of legs

Figure 22-9 Trace the flow of blood in pulmonary and systemic circulation.

blood into the **aorta** (ay-OWR-tuh), the largest artery in the body. The aorta branches off into arteries, which carry blood to all parts of the body.

The names and functions of some of the main arteries of your body are listed in Table 22-1. Notice that branches from the coronary artery carry blood to the heart itself. After blood carries oxygen and food to your body cells, the blood returns to the heart. Where does the blood enter the heart?

Table 22-1	Major Arteries
ARTERY	CARRIES BLOOD TO:
Carotid artery	Neck and head
Femoral artery	Leg
Brachial artery	Arm
Renal artery	Kidneys
Coronary artery	Heart
Pulmonary artery	Lungs

Think & Discuss

6. What is the function of the aorta? Is the aorta involved in pulmonary circulation or systemic circulation?

7. Where does blood go from the pulmonary artery?

★ 8. What changes take place in the blood as it circulates?

22-3 Blood

Would you classify blood as a tissue? Do you think your blood is only a liquid? Actually, your blood is a tissue that is part liquid and part solid. The liquid part of blood is not made up of living material. However, the solid part of blood is made up of many living cells.

Besides transporting materials, blood also has other jobs. What other jobs does blood have? Blood helps regulate your body temperature. Blood also helps maintain the chemical balance in your body, and protects you against disease.

Parts of the Blood

You have about 5 L of blood in your body. The liquid part of the blood is called **plasma** (PLAZ-muh). Plasma is a straw-colored liquid that is 90 percent water. Plasma carries dissolved vitamins, minerals, digested nutrients, wastes, and different kinds of proteins through the body. The plasma also has substances that are needed to keep the blood working properly. Floating in the plasma are the solid parts of blood.

Key Points

- Red blood cells carry oxygen. White blood cells fight disease.

- The four major blood types are A, B, AB, and O.

Study Hint

After you read Section 22-3, Blood, list the parts of blood and the function of each part.

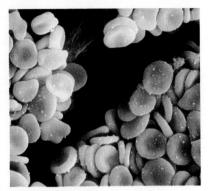

Figure 22-10 Notice the disklike shape of these red blood cells.

Red Blood Cells

Have you ever wondered why your blood is red? Blood gets its color from the 25 trillion **red blood cells** in it. The job of red blood cells is to carry oxygen. Their red color comes from a red, iron-containing molecule called **hemoglobin** (HEE-moh-gloh-bin). Hemoglobin is actually the part of a red blood cell that carries oxygen. Hemoglobin also carries some carbon dioxide away from body cells. Blood that is carrying oxygen is bright red. Blood that is carrying carbon dioxide is dark red. Your blood is never blue.

Look at the red blood cells in Figure 22-10. Do you notice anything unusual about them? Red blood cells do not have a nucleus or any cell parts. When red blood cells first form, they have all cell parts. However, as red blood cells mature, the part of the cell that contains the nucleus breaks apart. Therefore, a mature red blood cell is little more than a sac filled with cytoplasm and hemoglobin.

White Blood Cells

The cells that defend your body against disease are called **white blood cells.** White blood cells are almost colorless and do not have a definite shape. They are larger than red blood cells. You have far fewer white blood cells than red blood cells. In fact, you have only one white blood cell for every 1000 red blood cells.

Have you ever had a cut that became infected? An infection usually is caused by bacteria. The pus that forms around an infected cut is made up of dead white blood cells, bacteria, and tiny pieces of dead tissue.

Why does pus form around an infected cut? The formation of pus shows that your body is fighting the

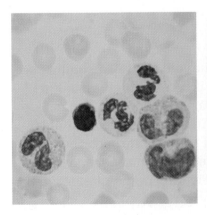
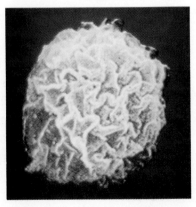

Figure 22-11 Phagocytes (left) and the macrophage (right) are two different kinds of white blood cells.

infection. When you cut yourself, your body goes to work fast. The number of white blood cells in your body increases quickly. White blood cells called phagocytes (FAG-uh-syts) squeeze through capillary walls and move through body tissue to the infected area. The phagocytes then surround bacteria and digest them. After a phagocyte digests many bacteria, the phagocyte dies and becomes part of the pus.

Other white blood cells fight infections by making **antibodies** (AN-ti-bahd-ees). Antibodies are proteins that circulate in plasma and protect the body from **antigens,** or foreign substances. Bacteria and viruses that invade the body are examples of antigens. Antibodies destroy antigens by binding, or joining, to them.

Platelets

Your body has an amazing ability to prevent blood loss as a result of an injury. This ability is called clotting. What controls clotting? Clotting is controlled by **platelets,** which are tiny colorless pieces of cells.

❯ When you are injured and a blood vessel is broken, the injured cells send out chemical signals. The chemicals cause platelets to go to the injured area. The platelets then stick together and form a plug. The platelets also release chemicals, which cause proteins in the plasma to form a mesh over the cut. As you can see in Figure 22-12, platelets and red blood cells get trapped in the mesh, forming a blood clot. The clot acts like a plug, blocking the cut and preventing blood loss. The seal over a cut, or scab, is really a clot on the skin's surface. Predict what would happen if you cut yourself and your blood did not form clots.

Study Hint

The way phagocytes engulf and digest bacteria is similar to the way amoebas eat. Use the Index to find information about the way amoebas get food. Then review the process.

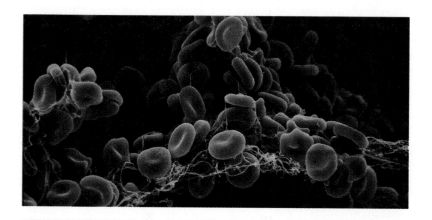

Figure 22-12 A threadlike mesh holds these red blood cells in a clot.

Table 22-2 Blood Types		
BLOOD TYPE	ANTIGEN	ANTIBODY IN BLOOD PLASMA
A	A	Anti-B
B	B	Anti-A
AB	AB	None
O	none	Anti-A and Anti-B

Figure 22-13   Dr. Charles Drew set up the first blood bank in the United States.

Blood Groups

Did you know that not everyone's blood is the same? In 1900, Karl Landsteiner, an American doctor, discovered that people have four main types of blood. The four main blood types are A, B, AB, and O.

How is blood type determined? Blood type depends on the presence or absence of certain proteins on the surface of red blood cells. These proteins are called antigens, because people build up antibodies against blood-type proteins that are not their own. Blood types are summarized in Table 22–2. Notice that type AB blood has no plasma antibodies and type O blood has no antigens.

If you lose a lot of blood, you may need a blood transfusion. It is very important that your doctor know your blood type before giving you a transfusion. Why? If certain blood types are mixed together, the antibodies and antigens join together and form clumps. For example, if type A blood is mixed with type B blood, anti-B forms clumps with antigen B and anti-A forms clumps with antigen A. The clumps can block blood vessels and lead to death.

Blood Disorders

The blood is sometimes referred to as the "river of life." Similar to a river, blood streams through the body performing functions that are essential for life. However, sometimes problems occur in blood. These problems are called blood diseases or blood disorders.

Anemia

The most common blood disorder is called **anemia** (uh-NEE-mee-uh). Anemia is a blood disorder in which the blood cannot carry normal amounts of oxygen to body cells. This causes a person suffering from anemia to be tired, pale, and unable to tolerate cold.

What causes anemia? In some cases, anemia is caused by too few red blood cells. In other cases, enough red blood cells are present in the blood, but the red blood cells do not contain normal amounts of hemoglobin. You may remember that hemoglobin contains iron. People with low amounts of hemoglobin have an iron deficiency. Iron-deficiency anemia is especially common in teenage girls.

Anemia caused by too few red blood cells can be treated with vitamin B-12, which helps make red blood cells. Folic acid is another B vitamin that helps make red blood cells. Foods with a lot of iron, such as liver, lean meat, and leafy green vegetables also can help correct iron-deficiency anemia.

Leukemia

Cancer of the blood, or **leukemia** (loo-KEE-mee-uh), is a disease in which the body produces millions of abnormal immature white blood cells. Because the white blood cells are immature, they cannot carry out their job of fighting infection. These abnormal cells also interfere with the production of red blood cells.

What are the symptoms of leukemia? People with leukemia may have anemia, internal bleeding, and many infections. Why would a person with leukemia be likely to get many different infections?

In many cases, the cause of leukemia is not known. Some cases have been linked to exposure to radiation. Other cases may be caused by viruses. Leukemia often is treated with drugs, radiation therapy, or bone marrow transplants.

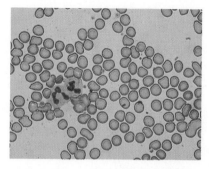

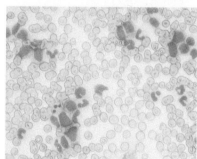

Figure 22-14 A healthy person has fewer white blood cells (top) than a person with leukemia (bottom).

Think & Discuss

9. What is the job of red blood cells?
10. What causes anemia?
11. What are three functions of the blood?
12. How do phagocytes fight disease?
★ 13. Why do you think people with type O blood are referred to as universal blood donors?

22–4 The Lymphatic System

As blood flows through the capillaries, it loses fluid. Why? Pressure from the pumping heart forces plasma through the thin capillary walls. This fluid is called tissue fluid. Tissue fluid fills the spaces between and around all of your body cells.

Key Points
- The lymphatic system is made up of the lymph nodes and lymph vessels.
- Lymph nodes filter and clean lymph.

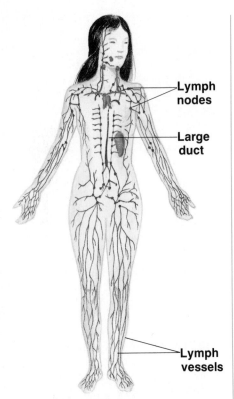

Lymph nodes

Large duct

Lymph vessels

Figure 22-15 Lymph nodes are concentrated in the neck, armpits, and groin.

Study Hint

Use Figure 22-15 to locate the places where lymph nodes are most concentrated.

You may think that tissue fluid is the same as plasma, but it is not. Tissue fluid has a different chemical makeup from plasma because some of the substances in plasma cannot pass through the capillary walls. What substance do you think makes up most of tissue fluid?

Tissue fluid is needed for the exchange of materials between capillaries and cells. Why is tissue fluid important? Most of the substances in body tissues will not pass through a cell membrane unless they are dissolved in a fluid. For example, oxygen, carbon dioxide, nutrients, and wastes must dissolve in tissue fluid to pass between the capillaries and body cells.

Eventually, tissue fluid must be returned to the blood. A separate system of tubes returns tissue fluid to the blood. This system is called the lymphatic (lim-FAT-ik) system. You can see the lymphatic system in Figure 22–15. Once tissue fluid enters the lymphatic system, the fluid is called **lymph** (LIMF). All lymph vessels eventually carry lymph into two large ducts. The ducts empty into large veins in the upper chest.

Scattered along the tubes of the lymphatic system are small bean-shaped structures called **lymph nodes.** Your tonsils are lymph nodes. What is the function of lymph nodes? The lymph nodes clean and filter lymph before it is returned to the blood. The lymph nodes also produce white blood cells that fight disease. When you have an infection, the lymph nodes get bigger because they are producing more white blood cells.

Have you ever had swollen glands? Swollen glands are really enlarged, sore lymph nodes. Lymph nodes get swollen when lymph entering the lymph nodes has more bacteria than the white blood cells can kill. Then, the nodes become infected. If you have had your tonsils removed, it is probably because they became infected often. In addition to the tonsils, lymph tissue also is found in the adenoids, thymus gland, and spleen.

Think & Discuss

14. What is the function of the lymphatic system?

15. What is the function of lymph nodes?

16. What would happen if tissue fluid was not returned to the blood?

Aerobics

What do you think of when you hear the word "aerobics"? Most people think of a room full of people jumping around to loud music. However, aerobics include many other activities besides dance. Aerobic exercise is any activity that increases your heart rate and makes you breathe faster. Other forms of aerobics include jogging, swimming, biking, and even brisk walking.

There are many benefits of aerobic exercise. When you exercise, you burn calories and therefore lose weight. Actually, you are losing body fat. As you lose body fat, your muscle mass increases. Muscle tissue is important to keep your body toned and healthy.

Aerobics also are good for your circulatory system. A regular exercise program increases the strength of your heart. As your heart gets stronger, it forces blood through your arteries and veins faster and more efficiently. Regular exercise also reduces your risk of heart disease.

You may think you need to join a gym or health spa to do aerobic exercises. However, aerobics can be done anywhere. If there is no place to swim or bike near your home, you can walk up and down a flight of stairs. You can also take a brisk walk inside a shopping mall.

To get the most benefit from aerobic exercise, you must do it three to five times a week. However, you should consult your physician before you begin any exercise program. When you start an exercise program, it is important to begin slowly and build up gradually. If you start out too fast, you might get "burnt out" or injured. If you are not doing any exercise now, start by walking around your neighborhood at a slightly quicker than normal pace.

Remember to stretch before and after any aerobic exercise. Stretching prevents your muscles from cramping. If you feel any pain while exercising, do not stop suddenly. Slow down gradually and stretch.

Proper clothing is important when exercising. Loose layers of clothing allow your body to get rid of sweat and body heat. You can also take off layers as you get warm. Footwear is also important. The right footwear can help prevent injuries. A salesperson in an athletic footwear store can best advise you what sneakers or shoes to get for the type of exercise you will be doing.

Now that you know the basics, what are you waiting for? Get up and get moving! You can have fun, feel better, and have a stronger and healthier body just by doing aerobics.

To Think About
- What are some of the benefits of aerobic exercise?
- What does the word "aerobic" mean?

Chapter Review

CHAPTER SUMMARY

22-1 The Circulatory System

- The heart is divided into two sides, each with an atrium and a ventricle.
- The right side of the heart pumps blood to the lungs. The left side pumps blood to all other parts of the body.
- Arteries carry blood away from the heart. Veins carry blood to the heart.
- Capillaries connect arteries to veins.

22-2 Circulation

- In pulmonary circulation, blood from the right ventricle moves through the pulmonary artery to the lungs. Blood is carried back to the heart by pulmonary veins.

- In systemic circulation, blood is pumped from the left ventricle through the aorta to all parts of the body, except the lungs.

22-3 Blood

- Red blood cells carry oxygen to all parts of the body.
- White blood cells are larger than red blood cells, but fewer in number. White blood cells help to defend the body against disease.

22-4 The Lymphatic System

- Lymphatic vessels carry tissue fluid to large veins.
- Lymph nodes filter tissue fluid as it passes through them.

VOCABULARY LIST

anemia (390)
antibodies (389)
antigens (389)
aorta (387)
arteries (381)
atrium (378)

bicuspid valve (379)
capillaries (381)
circulation (377)
hemoglobin (388)
leukemia (391)
lymph (392)

lymph nodes (392)
plasma (387)
platelets (389)
pulmonary circulation (385)
red blood cells (388)
semilunar valves (379)

septum (378)
systemic circulation (385)
tricuspid valve (379)
veins (381)
ventricle (378)
white blood cells (388)

VOCABULARY REVIEW

Matching   Write the word or term from the Vocabulary List that best matches each description.

1. vessels that carry blood to the heart
2. movement of blood throughout the body
3. blood cells needed for clotting
4. separates the right and left sides of the heart
5. vessels that connect arteries and veins
6. filter lymph
7. oxygen-carrying compound of red blood cells
8. located between the ventricles and arteries

Applying Definitions   Explain the difference between the words in each pair.

1. atrium, ventricle
2. red blood cells, white blood cells
3. antibodies, antigens
4. arteries, veins
5. bicuspid valve, tricuspid valve
6. pulmonary circulation, systemic circulation
7. aorta, pulmonary vein
8. anemia, leukemia
9. plasma, lymph
10. pulse, heartbeat

CONTENT REVIEW

True or False   Write true if the statement is true. If the statement is false, change the underlined word or words to make the statement true.

1. The disease in which the body produces large numbers of abnormal white blood cells is <u>leukemia</u>.
2. The smallest blood vessels in the body are <u>arteries</u>.
3. The liquid part of blood is <u>plasma</u>.
4. The <u>tricuspid</u> valve is between the right atrium and the right ventricle.
5. Blood returning from the body enters the right <u>ventricle</u>.
6. The path of blood between the heart and all parts of the body except the lungs is called <u>systemic</u> circulation.
7. Antibodies are produced by <u>red</u> blood cells.
8. Blood returning to the heart carries a lot of <u>oxygen</u>.
9. Fluid that surrounds body cells is called <u>lymph</u>.

Question and Answer   Rewrite each heading in the Chapter Outline on page 376 as a question. Then, answer each of the questions you have written.

Interpreting a Table   Use the information in Table 22–2 to answer each of the following.

1. What antibody is found in the plasma of blood type A?
2. What antigen is found in the plasma of blood type B?
3. Which blood type can give blood to all other blood types?
4. Which blood type can get blood from all other blood types?

CONCEPT REVIEW

Writing the Main Ideas   Using the Chapter Outline on page 376, write the main idea for each heading in the outline.

Critical Thinking   Answer each of the following in complete sentences.

1. Why do you think infants have much higher heartbeat rates than adults?
2. What do you think would happen to a vein if blood entered the vein under the same pressure as blood enters an artery? Explain your answer.
3. Write a hypothesis stating what would happen if type O blood was mixed with type A blood.
4. The circulatory system is a closed system. Is the lymphatic system also a closed system? Explain your answer.
5. Why does untreated high blood pressure strain the heart?

EXTENSIONS

1. Some people suffer damage to their heart valves as a result of disease. Surgeons can replace a damaged valve with an artificial valve. Do research and write a report on heart valve replacement operations.
2. Interview a cardiologist to find out about coronary bypass surgery. Then write your findings in a report.
3. Doctors believe that regular, strenuous exercise over a period of time can increase the efficiency of the heart. Design an experiment that could confirm or disprove this idea. Use the pulse rate before and after exercise as a measure of heart efficiency. Remember to include a control group as part of the experiment.

Chapter **23** | # Respiration and Excretion

After you have completed this chapter, you will be able to

23-1 **identify** organs of the respiratory system.

23-1 **state** the function of the respiratory system.

23-2 **compare** breathing and respiration.

23-3 **identify** some diseases of the respiratory system.

23-4 **state** the function of the excretory system.

23-4 **name** the major organs of the excretory system.

23-5 **identify** some problems of the excretory system.

Science Process Skills

In this chapter, two science skills are highlighted. Symbols show some places where these skills are used.

▶ **Inferring:** When you infer, you form a conclusion based upon facts and not direct observation.

▲ **Modeling:** When you model, you use a copy or imitation of an object to help explain something.

The race is nearly over. You are breathing hard and fast as you approach the finish line. Why do you breathe so much more when you exercise? You breathe more because your body needs energy for all that activity. The energy comes from the "burning," or breakdown, of food in your cells. This process is called **respiration.**

Respiration uses a lot of oxygen. When you breathe in, you take in oxygen-rich air from the outside. Respiration also produces carbon dioxide and water as waste products. You get rid of these waste products when you breathe out. Breathing in and out is part of the respiratory process. Breathing out is also part of the process of **excretion** *(ik-SKREE-shun). Excretion is the process by which waste products are removed from the body.*

Respiration and Excretion   397

23-1 The Respiratory System

Key Points

- The respiratory system consists of the lungs and the tubes and passageways through which air moves.

- The job of the respiratory system is to take oxygen into the body and get rid of carbon dioxide and water.

Study Hint

As you read about the respiratory system, list in the correct order the organs through which air passes.

The human respiratory system is made up of the lungs and the tubes and passageways through which air moves. The lungs are the main organs of the respiratory system. You have two lungs, a left lung and a right lung. Each lung is surrounded by a membrane. This membrane protects the lung and separates it from the chest cavity.

Taking oxygen into the body and removing carbon dioxide and water is the job of the respiratory system. How does oxygen from the air get into the lungs? Air passes through many tubes and passageways before it reaches the lungs.

You can trace the path air takes on its journey through the respiratory system in Figure 23-1. As you trace this pathway, keep in mind that the entire trip takes only a few seconds.

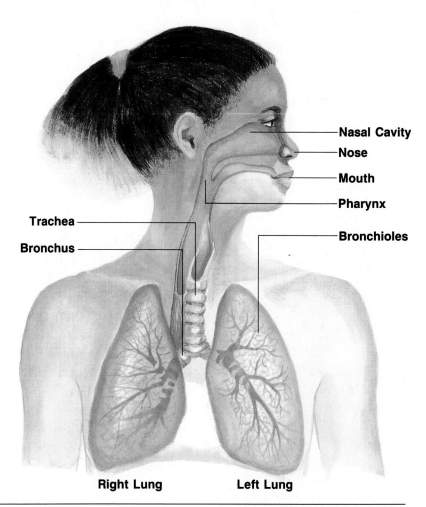

Figure 23-1 Air passes through all parts of your respiratory system every time you take a breath.

The Nose and Mouth

Take a deep breath. When you breathe in, or inhale, air enters your respiratory system. Now breathe out, or exhale. When you exhale, air leaves your respiratory system.

Inhale again. How does air enter your respiratory system? In most cases, air enters the respiratory system through the nose. The nose has two openings called nostrils. The nostrils are lined with short hairs. These hairs filter, or screen, particles of dirt and dust from the air before the air enters the **nasal cavity.** The nasal cavity is a hollow opening between the nose and throat.

Air moving through the nasal cavity is filtered and moistened. How do these activities take place? The nasal cavity is lined with two kinds of cells. Each kind of cell carries out a specific job.

One kind of cell secretes a sticky substance called mucus (MYOO-kus). Mucus traps particles in the air before the air enters the lungs. Mucus also helps keep the respiratory tissues from drying out.

The second kind of cell in the nasal cavity is lined with tiny hairlike structures called cilia (SIL-ee-uh). The cilia move back and forth in a wavelike motion. As the cilia move, mucus is pushed back toward the nostrils.

Mucus that collects in the nostrils can irritate the nose. You respond to this irritation with a forceful burst of air called a sneeze. Sneezing is one way of blowing dirt and dust from the nose.

A fine network of capillaries is located just below the cells that line the nasal cavity. Blood passing through these capillaries warms air passing through the nasal cavity.

Skill Builder

Modeling   Making a model is one way to help you understand an idea. On a sheet of unlined white paper, sketch a drawing of a tree that has a trunk, two large branches, and many twigs. The tubes of the respiratory system are often referred to as the "bronchial tree." Turn your drawing upside-down. Which part of the respiratory system is represented by each part of your tree?

Figure 23-2   Find the cilia in these cells of the nasal cavity.

The Pharynx

Air that has passed through the nose or mouth enters the pharynx (FAR-inks), or throat. The pharynx is a pathway for both food and air. At the end of the pharynx are two tubes. These tubes are like a fork in a road. One tube, called the esophagus, is for food. You may remember that food passes through the esophagus on its way to the stomach. The other tube is the windpipe. The windpipe is a pathway for air.

A flap of tissue called the epiglottis (ep-uh-GLAHT-is) is located at the place where the esophagus and windpipe meet. You may remember that the epiglottis acts as a trapdoor. When you inhale, the epiglottis raises and air moves into the windpipe. When you swallow, the epiglottis lowers and covers the windpipe. Where is food directed when the epiglottis is closed?

Have you ever had food "go down the wrong way"? When this happens, it is a sign that food has gotten past the epiglottis and into the windpipe. Food in the windpipe causes you to choke and cough. Coughing usually forces the food back into the throat. Then, the food can be swallowed.

The Trachea

Gently place your hand on the front of your neck. Can you feel a tubelike structure? This structure is your **trachea** (TRAY-kee-uh), or windpipe. The trachea is a tube about 10 cm long. It is located in front of the esophagus.

At the top of the trachea is an organ called the **larynx** (LAR-inks). It is made of a tough, elastic tissue called cartilage. Place your hand on your neck again. Can you feel a bulge near the top of your trachea? This bulge is your larynx.

▶ The human larynx contains two thin folds of skin called vocal cords. During normal, quiet breathing, the vocal cords are relaxed. However, when you speak, your vocal cords tighten. As you breathe out, air passing over the vocal cords causes them to vibrate and produce sounds. Why do you think that you should not speak while you are eating?

Air that has passed through the larynx enters the trachea. The trachea is made up of rings of cartilage and smooth muscle. The cartilage keeps the trachea open so air can pass through it all the time.

The trachea is lined with two kinds of cells. Like the cells in the nasal cavity, one kind of cell secretes mucus. The other cells have cilia. The mucus traps particles of dirt and dust that were not filtered in the nasal cavity. The cilia push the mucus with its trapped particles back toward the throat. Once the mucus is in the throat, the mucus can be swallowed or expelled from the body.

Study Hint

Refer to Figure 21-4 on page 366 to review the function of the epiglottis.

Health and Safety Tip

The Heimlich maneuver (HYM-lik muh-NYOO-vur) is a first aid procedure that can be used on a choking victim. You can learn how to perform the Heimlich maneuver by consulting a first aid manual.

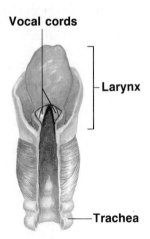

Vocal cords

Larynx

Trachea

Figure 23-3 Place your fingers on your larynx and feel your vocal cords vibrate as you speak.

Mucus that collects in the trachea can cause irritation. Like the nose, the trachea responds to this irritation with bursts of air. These bursts of air are coughs. Coughing gets rid of dirt and dust that is trapped in the trachea.

The Bronchi and Bronchioles

The lower end of the trachea divides into two smaller tubes called **bronchi** (BRAHN-kee). Like the trachea, the walls of the bronchi contain rings of cartilage and smooth muscle. Each bronchus extends into a lung.

Within the lung, the bronchus branches into many smaller tubes called **bronchioles** (BRAHN-kee-ohls). Unlike the bronchi and trachea, the bronchiole walls do not contain cartilage. Their walls are made only of smooth muscle.

► The bronchi and bronchioles are lined with cells that secrete mucus and have cilia. The mucus filters air passing through these organs. What do you think the cilia do?

Air Sacs and Alveoli

Bronchioles end in structures called **air sacs,** or **alveoli** (al-VEE-uh-ly). Alveoli look like bunches of grapes. Each of your lungs contains millions of alveoli.

Study Hint

The plural forms of some words do not end in "s." For example, "bronchi" is the plural form of "bronchus." "Alveoli" is the plural form of "alveolus."

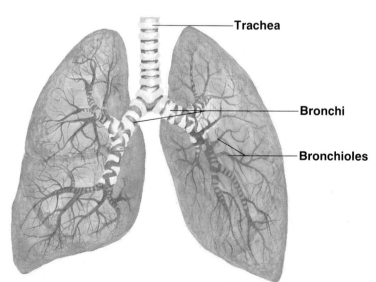

Trachea

Bronchi

Bronchioles

Figure 23-4 The bronchi and bronchioles make up the "bronchial tree."

A network of capillaries surrounds the alveoli, as shown in Figure 23-5. Both the alveoli and the capillaries have walls that are only one cell thick. These thin walls allow oxygen and carbon dioxide to pass easily between the alveoli and the capillaries.

Gas Exchange in the Alveoli

The most important part of the respiratory process is the exchange of the gases oxygen (O_2) and carbon dioxide (CO_2). Within the lungs, these gases are exchanged between the alveoli and the bloodstream. Oxygen moves into the bloodstream. At the same time, carbon dioxide moves into the alveoli. How does this exchange of gases take place?

Air entering the alveoli has a high level of oxygen and a low level of carbon dioxide. Blood in the capillaries surrounding the alveoli is low in oxygen. This blood has a high level of carbon dioxide.

When air enters your lungs, the oxygen from the air dissolves in the mucus within the alveoli. The dissolved oxygen then diffuses out of the alveoli and into the capillaries. At the same time, carbon dioxide in the capillaries diffuses into the alveoli. Figure 23-5 shows the exchange of oxygen and carbon dioxide between the alveoli and the capillaries.

Transport and Gas Exchange

For respiration to occur, every cell of your body must have oxygen. Do you recall the job of red blood cells? Oxygen from the lungs is carried by red blood cells to the

Study Hint

Look up "diffusion" in the index. When diffusion occurs, substances move from areas of greater concentration to areas of lesser concentration.

Figure 23-5 Gas exchange in the lungs takes place between capillaries and alveoli.

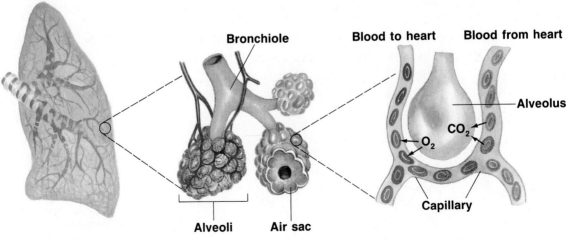

heart. The heart then pumps this oxygen-rich blood to the rest of the body.

When oxygen-rich blood reaches the body cells, the oxygen diffuses out of the blood and into the body cells. At the same time, carbon dioxide produced during respiration diffuses out of the body cells. This carbon dioxide is picked up by the red blood cells. The carbon dioxide is then carried by the blood back to the alveoli in the lungs.

Carbon dioxide cannot be removed from your body until it moves from the capillaries into the alveoli. At the same time, blood in the capillaries picks up fresh oxygen. The carbon dioxide leaves your body when you exhale. What happens to the oxygen that is picked up by the blood?

Study Hint

Look up "red blood cells" in the Glossary to find out their function.

Think & Discuss

1. Define respiration.
2. What is the scientific name for the windpipe?
3. Name and describe three organs of the respiratory system.
4. By what process does carbon dioxide move from body cells to the blood?
★ 5. How do mucus and cilia help the body fight infection?

23-2 Breathing

Breathing and respiration are related, but they are not the same process. Respiration is a chemical process. Breathing is a mechanical process that is only part of the respiratory process. Breathing is the process by which air enters and leaves the body. Together, your lungs can hold between 5 and 6 L of air.

How often do you breathe? You breathe in and out about 18 times each minute. The organs that make breathing possible are the ribs, the rib muscles, and the diaphragm (DY-uh-fram). The diaphragm is a sheetlike muscle located between the chest cavity and the abdomen.

Key Points
- Breathing is the process by which air enters and leaves the body.
- Respiration is the process by which oxygen combines with food to produce energy.

ACTIVITY 23–1

PROBLEM: How does exercise affect your breathing rate?

Science Process Skills
hypothesizing, measuring, recording data, graphing

Background Information
Breathing is the process by which you take oxygen from the air into your body and release carbon dioxide into the air. Normal breathing rates can vary from 12 to 25 times per minute.

Materials
clock or watch with second hand

Procedure
1. Copy the Data Table shown.

Data Table:	Breathing Rates (in Number of Breaths per Minute)	
AT REST	AFTER EXERCISE	
	30 seconds	60 seconds

2. Sit quietly and breathe normally for 1 minute.
3. Continue breathing normally. Have a partner count the number of breaths you take in one minute. Record the number of breaths under "At Rest" in the table.
4. **HYPOTHESIZE** What effect will exercise have on your normal breathing rate? Write your hypothesis on a separate sheet of paper. Your hypothesis should answer the question. To test your hypothesis, continue the activity.
5. Run in place for 30 seconds.
6. Sit down and have your partner count the number of breaths you take in 1 minute. Record this result in your data table.
7. Run in place for 60 seconds.
8. Repeat step 6.
9. Compare your results after 60 seconds of exercise with your results after 30 seconds of exercise.
10. Record your results on a class data table.

Observations
1. **a.** Did your normal breathing rate speed up or slow down after 30 seconds of exercise? Explain your answer. **b.** How did your breathing rate after 60 seconds compare with your rate after 30 seconds? Explain your answer.
2. **a.** Did all the students in your class have the same breathing rate while at rest? **b.** Were all breathing rates the same after 60 seconds of exercise?

Conclusions
1. **a.** How does exercise affect your breathing rate? **b.** Was your hypothesis correct? Use your data to support your answer.
2. Prepare a graph that shows the effect of exercise on breathing rate.
3. Why might people have different breathing rates?

Going Further
How does exercise affect pulse rate? Do you think this effect would be the same for everyone? Explain. Design an experiment to test your hypothesis.

Place your hand on your ribs and take a deep breath. What do you observe? As you take in air, your chest expands, or gets larger. Why?

When you inhale, your rib muscles contract, or tighten. Your ribs move upward and outward. At the same time, your diaphragm contracts and moves downward. The movement of the ribs and diaphragm increases the space, or volume, of the chest cavity.

▲ As the volume of the chest cavity increases, the air pressure within the chest cavity decreases. The air pressure inside the chest cavity becomes much lower than the air pressure outside the body. Air rushes in to fill the lungs, as shown in Figure 23-6. The lungs stop filling with air when the air pressure inside the chest cavity is equal to the air pressure outside the body.

Take a second deep breath. Now, watch your chest as you exhale. What happens? As you exhale, your chest becomes smaller.

When you exhale, your rib muscles relax. Your ribs move inward and downward. Your diaphragm relaxes and moves upward. The movement of the ribs and diaphragm decreases the volume inside the chest cavity.

As the volume of the chest cavity decreases, more air pressure is exerted on the lungs. The air pressure within the chest cavity becomes greater than the air pressure outside the body. The increased air pressure in the chest

Health and Safety Tip
To breathe correctly, you should inhale through your nose and exhale through your mouth.

Study Hint

The amount of force on a unit of area is called pressure. The weight of all the air around you causes pressure. Air moves from areas of high air pressure to areas of low air pressure.

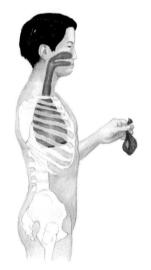
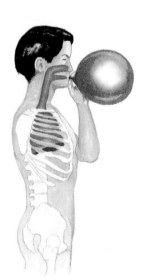

Figure 23-6 Notice the different positions of the diaphragm when you inhale (left) and exhale (right).

forces air out of the lungs. Air stops leaving the lungs when the air pressure inside the chest cavity is equal to the air pressure outside the body.

You do not have to think about breathing to have it happen. Breathing is an involuntary action. What body organ controls breathing? Twenty-four hours a day, every day, your rib muscles and diaphragm contract and relax. In most cases, you do not notice these muscles working. However, sometimes the diaphragm can have a spasm (SPAZ-um). A spasm is a sudden contraction of a muscle. Have you ever had the hiccups? Hiccups are caused by spasms of your diaphragm.

Think & Discuss

6. Define breathing.
7. How are breathing and respiration related?
8. List the organs through which air travels during inhalation and exhalation in the proper order.

23-3 Respiratory Diseases

Key Point

- Pneumonia, bronchitis, and asthma are diseases of the respiratory system.

The job of the respiratory system is to take oxygen into the body and to get rid of carbon dioxide and water. You know that air contains oxygen. Air also contains substances that can be harmful to the body. Some of these substances can cause diseases of the respiratory system. What harmful substances can you name that are found in the air?

Pneumonia

One of the most common diseases of the respiratory system is **pneumonia** (nyoo-MOH-nyuh). Pneumonia is an inflammation (in-fluh-MAY-shun) of the lungs that usually is caused by bacteria. Figure 23-7 shows the bacteria that cause pneumonia.

Viruses can cause pneumonia, too. In both bacterial and viral pneumonia, the disease-causing "germ" invades the lungs. As a result, fluid develops in the alveoli. This fluid prevents the exchange of oxygen and carbon dioxide

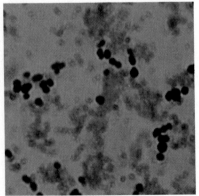

Figure 23-7 The pneumonia bacteria, colored blue in this photograph, are cocci.

between the alveoli and the capillaries. When the exchange of these gases is prevented, the cells of the body do not get enough oxygen.

Pneumonia is a very serious disease. Symptoms of pneumonia include fever and chills, fatigue, coughing, and a tightness in the chest while breathing. A person with pneumonia usually needs to be hospitalized. While in the hospital, the person may be given antibiotics and oxygen.

Bronchitis and Asthma

Particles of dirt and dust are in the air that you breathe. If these particles are not filtered in the nasal cavity and trachea, they can enter the bronchioles. **Bronchitis** (brahn-KYT-us) and **asthma** (AZ-muh) are two diseases of the respiratory system that are caused by dirt and dust in the bronchioles.

Bronchitis is an inflammation of the bronchioles. One symptom of bronchitis is a bad, lasting cough. Bronchitis also can cause difficulty in breathing. If either of these symptoms appear, it is necessary to see a doctor. A doctor can prescribe antibiotics to help fight the infection.

In some people, dirt and dust can cause the muscular walls of the bronchioles to contract. This condition is called asthma. The contraction of the walls of the bronchioles causes the bronchioles to become narrow. As a result, there is less room for air to pass through, and breathing becomes difficult.

Asthma often is treated with medications that cause the muscles in the walls of the bronchioles to relax. When these muscles relax, the breathing passages open wide. Air can then pass through the bronchioles. Doctors are not sure why some people react to dirt and dust in the air more than others. Many doctors, however, think asthma may be a kind of allergy.

Think & Discuss

9. What is pneumonia?
10. Why is breathing difficult for a person with asthma?
11. Explain why a person with pneumonia often is tired.

ACTIVITY 23–2

PROBLEM: Is carbon dioxide present in the air you exhale?

Science Process Skills
measuring, hypothesizing, observing

Background information
The job of the excretory system is to remove wastes from the body. Wastes are made as a result of chemical processes in your cells. The lungs work as both respiratory and excretory organs. In the lungs, oxygen and carbon dioxide are exchanged. The carbon dioxide is released as a waste product when you exhale.

The presence of carbon dioxide can be shown by using an indicator such as bromthymol blue (BTB). An indicator is a chemical substance that reacts in the presence of another substance. A BTB solution changes color from blue to yellow in the presence of carbon dioxide.

Materials
BTB solution
small, clear plastic cup
plastic straw
graduated cylinder
clock or watch with second hand

Procedure
1. **CAUTION: Put on your lab apron and goggles.** Use the graduated cylinder to measure 50 mL of BTB solution.
2. Pour the BTB solution into the plastic cup.
3. **HYPOTHESIZE**   What will happen to the color of the BTB solution when you exhale into it? Why? Write your hypothesis on a sheet of paper. Your hypothesis should answer the questions. To test your hypothesis, continue the activity.
4. Using the plastic straw, exhale normally into the BTB solution, as shown. **CAUTION: Be careful not to inhale the solution into your mouth.**

5. Observe the BTB solution. If no color change occurs after one minute, continue to exhale into the solution until you see a change. Keep a record of the time that it takes the BTB solution to show a change.

Observations
1. What happened to the color of the BTB solution after you exhaled into it?
2. How long did it take for the solution to change color?

Conclusions
1. What gas is present in exhaled air?
2. Was your hypothesis correct? Use your observations to support your answer.

Going Further
What effect does exercise have on the amount of carbon dioxide you exhale? Design an experiment to test your hypothesis.

23-4 The Excretory System

Many chemical changes take place in your cells. As these chemical changes occur, waste products are formed. For example, you have read that carbon dioxide and water are waste products of respiration. Other waste products made by your body cells are salts, nitrogen compounds, and heat.

Waste products can be harmful if they build up and collect in the body. Removing waste products from the body is the job of the excretory system.

You know that the lungs are part of the respiratory system. The lungs also are part of the excretory system. What two waste products do the lungs excrete from the body? The other major organs of the excretory system are the **kidneys** and the skin.

The Kidneys

Humans have two kidneys. Your kidneys are located just above your waistline. One kidney is behind the stomach; the other is behind the liver.

The main job of the kidneys is to remove waste products from the blood. Each minute, about 1 L of blood passes through your kidneys. In a single day, your kidneys remove waste products from over 1400 L of blood.

Millions of tiny tubelike structures called **nephrons** (NEF-ronz) are located inside each of your kidneys. Nephrons are the filtering structures of the kidneys.

As blood flows through the nephrons, excess water, salts, and a nitrogen compound called **urea** (yoo-REE-uh) are filtered from the blood. At the same time, the nephrons also remove nutrients from the blood. Table 23-1 lists the substances that the blood carries into the kidneys. What useful substances are carried by the blood?

Key Points

- The function of the excretory system is to remove waste products from the body.

- The lungs, kidneys, and skin are the main organs of the excretory system.

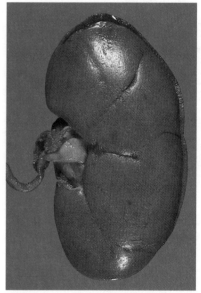

Figure 23-8 Make a fist. Each of your kidneys is about the size of a fist.

Table 23-1 Substances Carried by the Blood	
NUTRIENTS THE BODY NEEDS	WASTE PRODUCTS
Water	Excess water
Sugar	Salts
Minerals	Urea

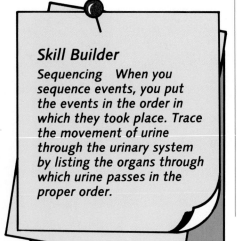

Study Hint

Before you read about how the nephron works, find these structures on Figure 23-9: the cluster of capillaries, the cuplike structure, and the collecting tube.

Skill Builder

Sequencing   When you sequence events, you put the events in the order in which they took place. Trace the movement of urine through the urinary system by listing the organs through which urine passes in the proper order.

The nutrients that are removed by the nephrons are needed by the body. As blood passes through the kidneys, it is filtered a second time. During this second filtering process, the nutrients are separated from the waste products. The nutrients are then returned to the blood before the blood leaves the kidneys.

▲ How do the nephrons filter waste products and nutrients from the blood? How are nutrients returned to the blood? The processes that occur in the nephrons can be explained in steps. As you read each step, look at the nephron in Figure 23-9.

- Blood enters the nephron.
- In the nephron, the blood passes into a cluster of capillaries that are surrounded by a cuplike structure.
- Water, salts, urea, and nutrients are forced out of the capillaries and into the cuplike structure.
- The water, salts, urea, and nutrients leave the cuplike structure and pass into a long tube.
- In the coiled part of the tube, the nutrients pass back into the blood. Excess water, salts, and urea remain in the last part of the tube, called the collecting tube.
- The filtered blood returns to the heart. The water, salts, and urea are carried out of the kidney.

Waste products leave the collecting tube as a liquid. This liquid is called **urine** (YOOR-in). Urine is a liquid waste made up of water, salts, and urea.

Cuplike structure

Figure 23-9 Trace the flow of blood through this enlarged nephron.

Vein   Artery   Collecting tube

Excretion is not complete until the urine is removed from the body. Remember, excretion is the removal of waste products from the body. The job of the urinary (YOOR-uh-ner-ee) system is to remove liquid wastes from the body. This system is part of the excretory system. The urinary system is shown in Figure 23-10.

How is urine removed from the body? Urine leaves each kidney through a tube. This tube is called the **ureter** (YOUR-et-uhr). One ureter from each kidney carries urine to the **urinary bladder.** The urinary bladder is a muscular sac that stores urine until the urine is removed from the body.

The urinary bladder stores urine for only a short period of time. When the urinary bladder is filled, muscles of the bladder contract. Urine is then forced out of the urinary bladder and passes into a tube called the **urethra** (you-REETH-ruh). The urethra carries urine to the outside of the body.

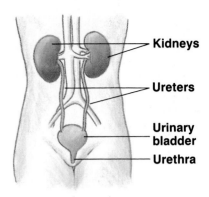

Figure 23-10 The urinary system (shown here) is a subsystem of the excretory system.

The Skin

In the skin are small structures called sweat glands. Sweat glands excrete waste products in the form of perspiration (pur-spuh-RAY-shun). Perspiration is a liquid waste made up of water, salts, and a small amount of urea. What other organs remove water, salts, and urea from the body?

Each sweat gland has a small tube that leads to the surface of the skin. The tiny opening at the surface of the skin is called a **pore.** You have millions of pores in your skin. Sweat produced in the sweat glands leaves your body through these pores.

Sweat that reaches the skin's surface quickly evaporates. The evaporation of sweat cools the body. Excess heat is removed from the body as it is cooled. The removal of excess heat helps to regulate your body temperature. Regulating body temperature also is a function of the skin.

Think & Discuss

12. What is excretion?
13. What is the excretory system?
★ 14. How is the skin like an air-conditioning system?

Key Point
- Kidney stones and acne are problems of the excretory system.

Key Point
- Kidney stones and acne are problems of the excretory system.

Health and Safety Tip

People suffering from severe acne should see a doctor. Medical treatment can help prevent scarring caused by acne.

Table 23-2 Controlling Acne
• Wash your face several times a day with soap and water.
• Apply a drying lotion to the skin after washing.
• Avoid oily cosmetics.
• Remove all cosmetics before going to bed.
• Eat a well-balanced diet.
• Get plenty of rest and exercise.

Calcium compounds and nitrogen wastes that are not excreted by the body can build up and form kidney stones. Small kidney stones can pass through the ureter. However, the passage of these small stones can cause great pain. Larger kidney stones cannot pass through the ureter. In fact, these stones can block the ureter completely. When this happens, urine backs up into the kidney. If urine stays in the kidney, waste products in the urine can quickly destroy kidney cells.

Large kidney stones must be removed to prevent kidney damage. How are these stones removed? Doctors often prescribe medications that cause kidney stones to dissolve or break apart. If the kidney stones break into small enough pieces, they can pass easily through the ureter.

Unfortunately, medications used to break apart kidney stones do not always work. Until recently, kidney stones that could not be dissolved with medications had to be removed surgically. Doctors now have a new way to break kidney stones apart. This new treatment uses sound waves to blast kidney stones apart.

How do doctors use sound to break apart kidney stones? Doctors carefully aim sound waves at the kidney stone. Sound waves strike the particles making up the stone and cause them to vibrate. The kidney stone soon breaks apart. The small pieces of kidney stone can then pass through the ureter with the urine.

Acne is a combination of skin diseases. The symptoms of acne include whiteheads, blackheads, and pimples. Whiteheads and blackheads develop when oil clogs the pores at the surface of your skin. A pimple forms when a blackhead is infected with bacteria. Why would washing your face several times each day help control acne?

Think & Discuss

15. What is a pimple?

16. Name three methods of treatment for kidney stones.

17. How do you think over-the-counter acne medications help control acne?

Preventing Carbon Monoxide Poisoning

Carbon monoxide (CO) is an invisible, odorless gas that is given off when fuels are burned. Wood-burning stoves and fireplaces, oil or gas home heating systems, and furnaces release carbon monoxide. Cigarette smoke also contains carbon monoxide. Most of the carbon monoxide in the air, however, comes from the burning of gasoline. Cars, trucks, and buses all release carbon monoxide in their exhausts.

Carbon monoxide is most dangerous when it is given off in an enclosed area. For example, a garage without proper ventilation can be deadly if carbon monoxide has no way to escape. For the same reason, there may be harmful amounts of carbon monoxide in your home if the fireplace or heating system is not working properly.

As you know, every cell in your body needs oxygen. Oxygen is prevented from reaching body cells, however, if you inhale too much carbon monoxide. The reason for this is that red blood cells pick up carbon monoxide faster and easier than they pick up oxygen. So when you inhale too much carbon monoxide, your cells do not get enough oxygen. As a result, respiration slows down, and body cells begin to die.

What are some symptoms of carbon monoxide poisoning? Symptoms include dizziness, headache, and shortness of breath. The victim may also pass out as more and more body cells die from a lack of oxygen.

Carbon monoxide poisoning can be treated if caught early. The usual treatment involves supplying the victim with oxygen. However, if too many body cells are killed, carbon monoxide poisoning is fatal.

You can lower the risk of carbon monoxide poisoning by following these simple guidelines.

- Do not sit in a parked car with the engine running and the windows closed.

- Never run a car's engine in an enclosed area.

- Check the exhaust system of your car regularly.

- Inspect home heating systems as suggested by the owner's manual.

- Keep fireplaces, wood-burning stoves, and chimneys clean.

- Avoid sitting in poorly ventilated areas filled with cigarette smoke.

Have you ever ridden in a car that leaked exhaust fumes? If you smelled fumes inside the car, the car needed to have its exhaust system fixed. You now know that this repair could save your life.

To Think About
- Why is carbon monoxide poisoning more of a problem in large cities than in small towns?
- Why is carbon monoxide more dangerous in an enclosed area than outdoors?

Respiration and Excretion 413

Chapter Review

CHAPTER SUMMARY

23-1 The Respiratory System

- The respiratory system is made up of the nose, mouth, pharynx, trachea, bronchi, lungs, bronchioles, air sacs, and alveoli.
- The respiratory system takes oxygen into the body and excretes carbon dioxide and water.

23-2 Breathing

- Breathing is the mechanical process by which air enters and leaves the body.
- The organs that make breathing possible are the ribs, rib muscles, and diaphragm.
- Respiration is the chemical process by which oxygen is combined with food to produce energy.

23-3 Respiratory Diseases

- Pneumonia is a respiratory disease that most often is caused by bacteria.
- Bronchitis and asthma are diseases caused by dirt and dust in the lungs.

23-4 The Excretory System

- Excretion is the process by which waste products are removed from the body.
- Removing wastes from the body is the function of the excretory system.

23-5 Excretory Problems

- Kidney stones are a problem of the urinary system.
- Acne is a problem of the skin.

VOCABULARY LIST

air sacs (401)
alveoli (401)
asthma (407)
bronchi (401)
bronchioles (401)

bronchitis (407)
excretion (397)
kidneys (409)
larynx (400)
nasal cavity (399)

nephrons (409)
pneumonia (406)
pore (411)
respiration (397)
trachea (400)

urea (409)
ureter (411)
urethra (411)
urinary bladder (411)
urine (410)

VOCABULARY REVIEW

Matching   Write the word or term from the Vocabulary List that best matches each description.

1. storage sac for urine
2. filtering units of the kidneys
3. carries air from trachea to both lungs
4. energy-producing process of the body
5. inflammation of the bronchi
6. nitrogen waste excreted by skin and kidneys
7. carries urine from kidney to bladder
8. organ used for speaking
9. disease of the lungs caused by bacteria
10. carries urine to the outside of the body

Identifying Relationships   Identify the word or term in each group that does not belong. Explain why it does not belong with the group.

1. kidneys, pore, urine
2. air sacs, alveoli, kidneys
3. bronchioles, asthma, nasal cavity
4. asthma, respiration, excretion
5. respiration, energy, urine
6. pneumonia, trachea, bronchitis
7. cilia, nasal cavity, air sacs
8. bronchioles, trachea, cartilage
9. skin, alveoli, pore
10. excretion, oxygen, nutrients

414   Human Biology

Completion Write the word or words that best complete each sentence.

1. Cells with cilia line the nasal cavity, _____, bronchi, and bronchioles.
2. Respiration is a _____ process.
3. The main organs of the respiratory system are the _____.
4. Nephrons remove salts, _____, water, and nutrients from the blood.
5. Breathing is difficult for a person with asthma because the _____ become narrow.
6. Carbon dioxide and _____ are excreted by the lungs.
7. The ribs, rib muscles, and _____ make breathing possible.
8. The flap of tissue that prevents food from entering the trachea is the _____.
9. The urinary system is responsible for removing _____ waste.

Finding the Main Ideas Use the section number to find the sentence that answers each question. Then, write the sentence.

1. What is the function of the respiratory system? (23-1)
2. Where does respiration take place? (23-1)
3. What happens to your rib muscles and diaphragm when you inhale? (23-2)
4. What causes hiccups? (23-2)
5. What two groups of organisms can cause pneumonia? (23-3)
6. How is asthma often treated? (23-3)
7. What is the main function of the kidneys? (23-4)
8. How is urine removed from the body? (23-4)
9. What are kidney stones? (23-5)
10. What are the symptoms of acne? (23-5)
11. How is sound used to break apart kidney stones? (23-5)

Writing for Understanding One way to find out if you understand something is to write a brief summary of the information in your own words. Reread Section 23-4, The Excretory System, on pages 409-411, and write a brief summary of the information.

Critical Thinking Answer each of the following in complete sentences.

1. Is the air you inhale the same as the air you exhale? Explain your answer.

2. Explain why the human larynx often is called the voice box.
3. What function do the rings of cartilage in the bronchi serve?
4. Urea is poisonous to the body. Predict what would happen if urea was not removed from the blood by the kidneys.
5. When you exercise, your breathing rate increases because your body cells need more oxygen. Explain why exercise also causes your heart rate to increase.

1. Emphysema, black lung disease, and pleurisy are diseases of the respiratory system. Look up each of these diseases in an encyclopedia. Then prepare a table listing the cause and symptoms of each disease.

2. Using this book as a reference, draw a diagram of the urinary system. Label the parts in the diagram. Include a caption that lists the organs through which urine passes in the proper order.

Respiration and Excretion 415

Chapter 24 | Regulation

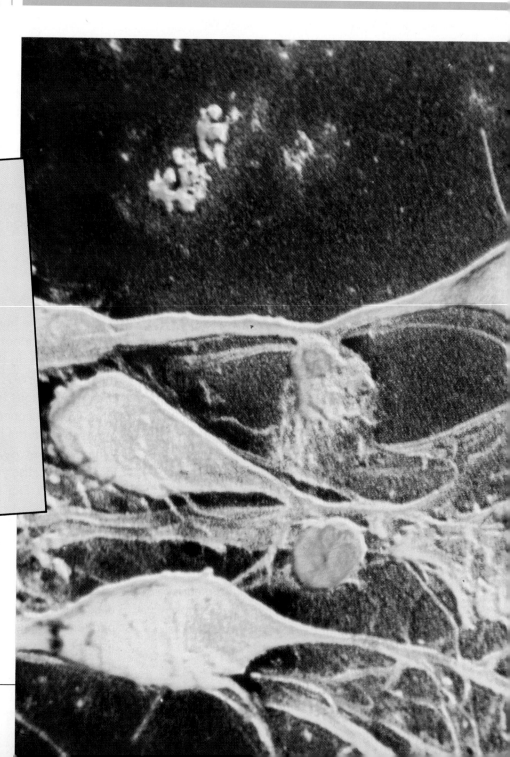

Chapter Outline

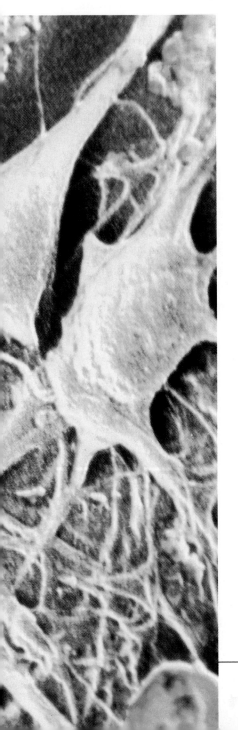

Objectives

After you have completed this chapter, you will be able to

24-1 **describe** the three main parts of a nerve cell.

24-1 **name** and **describe** the functions of the three main parts of the brain.

24-2 **explain** how impulses travel from one neuron to another.

24-2 **describe** a reflex.

24-3 **list** the five senses.

24-4 **describe** the functions of three endocrine glands.

24-5 **compare** innate and learned behaviors.

Science Process Skills

In this chapter, two science skills are highlighted. Symbols show some places where these skills are used.

◉ **Observing:** When you observe, you use one or more of your senses to gather information.

◤ **Analyzing:** When you analyze, you break down a complex idea into simpler parts to make it easier to understand.

You walk into a dark room on a cold, rainy night. A burst of moist air and the rattling of blinds tell you that a window is open. A clap of thunder startles you. You turn on a lamp and sit down. It is only then that you realize your heart is pounding and you are breathing heavily.

Why do you respond to changes around you? Your responses are controlled by your nervous and endocrine systems. In times of stress, the nervous and endocrine systems can throw your body into high gear. Together the nervous and endocrine systems regulate, or control, all of your body's responses.

The nervous system is made up of the brain, the spinal cord, and all of the nerves in your body. Your nervous system detects and responds to changes inside and outside your body. How does the nervous system do all this? First, the nervous system receives information about the environment or other parts of the body. Then it interprets the information. Finally, it responds to the information. For example, consider what happens when you hear the doorbell ring. Nerves in your ear receive information and send it to your brain. Your brain interprets the information as the sound of a ringing doorbell. Then your brain sends a message to your leg and arm muscles. You walk to the door and open it.

Nerve Cells

The nervous system is made up of billions of nerve cells called **neurons** (NOOR-ahns). A neuron is the basic unit of structure and function in the nervous system. The job of neurons is to carry messages.

👁 You can see a typical neuron in Figure 24-1. Notice that a neuron is made up of three parts. The **cell body** contains the nucleus of the neuron and most of the cytoplasm. Short, threadlike **dendrites** (DEN-dryts) branch from the cell body. Dendrites carry messages from other neurons to the cell body.

A long, thin fiber called the **axon** extends from the cell body. What is the job of an axon? It carries messages away from the cell body. The axon often is covered by a fatty membrane that insulates and protects the axon. Bundles of axons are called nerves.

There are three kinds of neurons in your nervous system. Each kind of neuron has a special function. For example, **sensory neurons** carry messages from the sense organs to the spinal cord and brain. **Motor neurons** carry messages from the brain and spinal cord to muscles or glands. **Associative** (uh-SOH-shee-ay-tiv) **neurons** connect sensory neurons to motor neurons.

What kind of messages do neurons carry? In the nervous system, messages called **impulses** are sent from one neuron to another. Impulses are tiny jolts of electrical energy.

Key Points

- A neuron is made up of a cell body, dendrites, and an axon.
- The three main parts of the brain are the cerebrum, cerebellum, and medulla.

Study Hint

Write a description of what happens in the nervous system when a telephone rings.

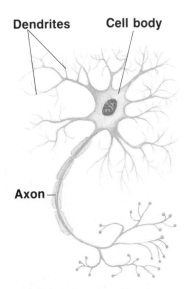

Dendrites   **Cell body**

Axon

Figure 24-1   Neurons are the longest cells in the human body. Some axons may be as much as a meter in length.

Have you ever hit your "funny bone"? A nerve in your arm is well protected except at a spot in the back of the elbow. If you hit that spot you feel a shock, which is an impulse traveling from your arm to your brain.

The Brain

Your brain is the control center of your body. It is made up of three main parts, which you can see in Figure 24-3. The large, upper portion of the brain is called the **cerebrum** (suh-REE-bruhm). The cerebrum controls movement and speech. It also interprets information from sense organs. In addition, the cerebrum controls many functions that are associated with intelligence. For example, the cerebrum allows you to think, reason, and remember.

◉ You may have noticed that the surface of the cerebrum has many folds. These folds increase the surface area of the cerebrum.

The cerebrum is divided into two halves. Each half controls the activities of the opposite side of the body. That is, the left half of the cerebrum controls the right side of the body. The left half of the cerebrum usually is dominant over the right. This explains why most people are right-handed. Which half of the brain do you think is dominant in people who are left-handed?

At the back of your head, beneath the cerebrum, lies the **cerebellum** (ser-uh-BEL-uhm). The cerebellum is much smaller than the cerebrum. Like the cerebrum, the

Figure 24-2 The place where a motor neuron meets a muscle is called a neuromuscular junction.

Figure 24-3 The human brain has three main parts. What part of the brain is shown in the photograph?

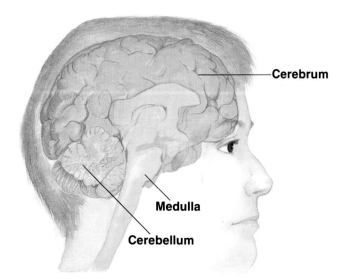

Cerebrum

Medulla

Cerebellum

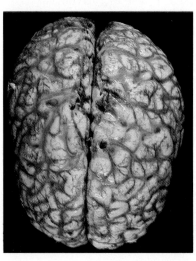

surface area of the cerebellum is increased by folds and wrinkles.

What is the job of the cerebellum? All motor nerve impulses that begin in the cerebrum pass through the cerebellum. The cerebellum adjusts the impulses so that your movements are smooth and graceful. The cerebellum also maintains balance.

Nerves from the cerebrum and cerebellum form a thick stalk called the brain stem at the base of the skull. The lower part of the brain stem is called the **medulla** (mi-DUL-uh). The medulla connects the brain to the spinal cord. The medulla also controls many involuntary actions of the body such as digestion, breathing, blood pressure, and heart rate.

The Spinal Cord

The spinal cord is made up of many nerves that extend from the medulla all the way down the back. All sensory and motor nerves found below the neck pass through the spinal cord on their way to the brain. Run your hand along your backbone. You may remember that the bumps you feel are called vertebrae. The vertebrae protect your spinal cord from injury.

Thirty-one pairs of nerves extend from the spinal cord. These nerves branch many times and go to specific parts of the body. For example, some of your motor neurons connect your skeletal muscles with the spinal cord and brain. You can control these muscles. Other motor neurons go to involuntary muscles and glands, which are not under your control.

Health and Safety Tip

Brain and spinal cord injuries often result from automobile accidents. To help protect your nervous system, always wear your seat belt.

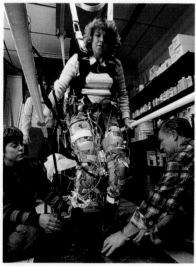

Figure 24-4 Using a computerized walker, Nan Davis is able to overcome a spinal injury which left her paralyzed.

Think & Discuss

1. What is the function of a neuron?
2. What is the function of sensory neurons?
3. What is the main job of the cerebellum?
4. What part of the brain controls heartbeat rate and breathing?
5. A nerve near the stomach is involved in breathing. What do you think happens when a person gets the "wind knocked out"?

24-2 Nerve Pathways

How is an impulse passed from the axon of one neuron to the dendrites of the next neuron? You can see the path an impulse takes in Figure 24-5. Notice that there is a tiny gap called a **synapse** (SIN-aps) between the dendrites of one neuron and the axon of the other.

How does an impulse get across a synapse? When an impulse reaches the end of an axon, the axon releases chemicals into the synapse. The chemicals travel across the synapse and join with molecules in the dendrite. This causes an impulse in the dendrite.

Has a cold breeze ever made you shiver? Shivering is a nervous response. Use Figure 24-6 to follow the pathways of messages involved in a shiver response.

Your skin contains special nerve endings, or receptors, that sense the cold. These nerve endings relay impulses to sensory neurons. The impulses are then passed from one sensory neuron to the next, and travel up the spinal cord to the brain. The brain interprets the message and sends out a "shiver" response. This message travels down the spinal cord along motor neurons to the muscles underneath your cold skin. The message causes these muscles to contract and give off heat.

The shivering response is controlled by the brain. Some responses, however, are not controlled by the brain. Have you ever touched a hot object? If so, you pulled your hand away quickly. When a lot of heat or pressure is applied to any part of your body, you respond

- Impulses travel across synapses.

- A reflex is an automatic response controlled by the spinal cord.

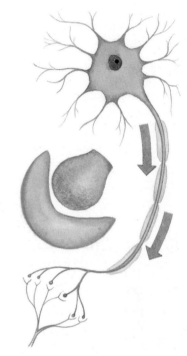

Figure 24-5 Chemicals in the synapse carry messages from one neuron to the next.

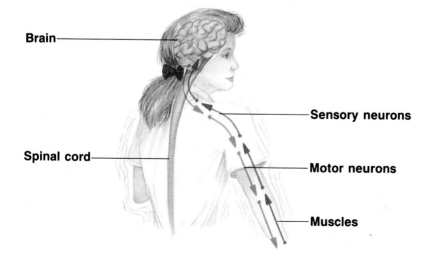

Brain

Spinal cord

Sensory neurons

Motor neurons

Muscles

Figure 24-6 What organ controls the shiver response?

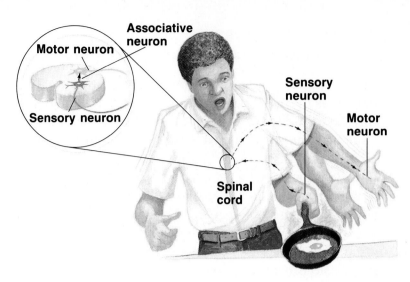

Figure 24-7 Unlike most responses, reflexes are controlled by the spinal cord.

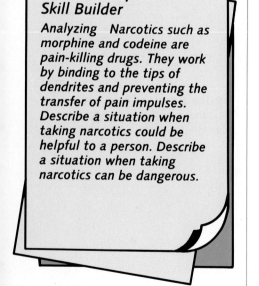

Skill Builder

Analyzing   Narcotics such as morphine and codeine are pain-killing drugs. They work by binding to the tips of dendrites and preventing the transfer of pain impulses. Describe a situation when taking narcotics could be helpful to a person. Describe a situation when taking narcotics can be dangerous.

automatically. The automatic response is called a **reflex.** Reflexes allow your body to react quickly to painful or dangerous situations. By responding rapidly, you decrease the amount of injury to your body.

Unlike most actions of the body, your brain does not control reflexes. Your spinal cord controls reflexes. The path of a reflex is called the reflex arc. Suppose you stuck your finger with a pin. How would your nervous system respond? As you read about this response, follow the path of the reflex arc shown in Figure 24-7.

When you touch the pan, receptors in your skin detect pressure and transfer the impulse to the sensory neurons. The impulses are then sent to the spinal cord. Inside the spinal cord, impulses pass through associative neurons and go directly to motor neurons which carry the impulses to the muscles in your hand. The muscles contract and pull your hand away.

A reflex reaction usually is followed by an "ouch." Why? While impulses are traveling along the reflex arc, the spinal cord sends messages to the brain. Once the brain receives and interprets these messages, it sends messages to pain receptors in your hand. Then, you feel pain.

Think & Discuss

6. What is a reflex?

7. How does an impulse travel across a synapse?

8. Does the spinal cord control the sensation of pain? Explain.

ACTIVITY 24–1

PROBLEM: Do lengths of reaction time vary among individuals?

Science Process Skills
observing, recording data, hypothesizing

Background Information
Your nervous system enables you to respond to changes in your environment. For example, if you are walking down the street and you see a bicyclist coming toward you, you get out of the way. The length of time that passes between seeing a change and reacting to the change is the reaction time.

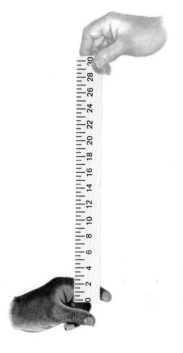

Materials
metric ruler

Procedure
1. Work with a partner. Hold the metric ruler at the 30 cm mark as shown in the diagram. Have your partner position the thumb and forefinger around, but not touching, the zero end of the ruler as shown.
2. Drop the stick at any moment you choose. Your partner must catch the stick as it falls by closing the thumb and forefinger. Your partner's hand must not move.
3. Develop a data table to record the distance in mm from zero that the ruler falls until it is caught.
4. **HYPOTHESIZE** Do you think that your reaction time is the same as your partner's? Why or why not? Write your hypothesis on a sheet of paper. Your hypothesis should answer the questions. To test your hypothesis, continue the activity.
5. Repeat steps 1–4 four more times, then average the five trials. To find an average, add the five trials together, then divide the total by 5.
6. Repeat the activity with you and your partner's roles reversed.
7. **ORGANIZE** Develop a data table to record the average distance for each student in your class.

Observations
1. How did your reaction time compare with that of your partner?
2. How did the reaction times of all the students in your class compare to each other?

Conclusions
1. Was your hypothesis correct? Use your observation to support your hypothesis.
2. Do reaction times vary among individuals? Use your observations to support your answer.

Going Further
Repeat the activity except have your partner say ''Now'' each time the ruler is released. Do you think that this warning will affect your reaction time? Complete the activity and record the results. Does your reaction time change? Explain your answer.

24-3 The Five Senses

Key Point

- The five senses are vision, hearing, touch, taste, and smell.

Observe your surroundings. What do you see? What sounds can you hear? Do you smell any odors? Information about your environment is detected first by your sense organs. Your sense organs include your eyes, ears, skin, tongue, and nose.

How do your sense organs work? Each sense organ has special cells that detect information. These cells are called receptor cells. The receptor cells send nerve impulses to sensory neurons, which carry the impulses to the brain. The brain interprets the impulses as a particular sensation, such as taste or vision.

Vision

Have you ever lit a candle in a dark room? If so, you may recall how bright the room appeared to be. The room appeared bright because your eyes are very sensitive to light. In fact, if you stood on a mountaintop on a clear night, you could see a match being lit 80 km away.

What structures in the eye allow you to see? Light first enters the eye through a clear, curved layer called the **cornea** (KAWR-nee-uh). Behind the cornea is a smooth muscle called the **iris.** The iris is the colored part of the eye. The iris controls the amount of light that enters the eye. The opening in the middle of the iris is called the pupil. In dim light, the iris widens to allow more light to enter the eye. This makes the pupil larger. In bright light, the iris narrows to permit less light to enter. This makes the pupil smaller.

Figure 24-8 Use the illustration of the eye to find the cornea of the eye shown in the photograph.

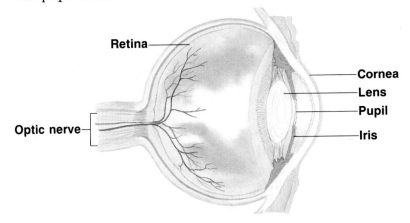

Light that has passed through the pupil enters the lens. Muscles attached to the lens cause the lens to change shape to focus incoming light. Light rays from the lens are then projected onto the **retina** (RET-in-uh) in the back of the eye.

The retina contains two types of light-sensitive receptor cells—rods and cones. Rods are sensitive to dim light. They can detect only black and white. Cones are sensitive to bright light and allow you to see different colors. When light strikes the rods and cones, impulses are produced. The impulses are carried by the optic nerve to the brain where they are interpreted.

Hearing

Whenever someone is talking, or music is playing, sound waves are produced. Special receptors in your ears respond to vibrations made by sound waves. Use Figure 24-9 as a model as you read about your sense of hearing.

The ear is divided into three main parts. You are probably most familiar with the auricle, or ear flap, of the outer ear. The outer ear also is made up of a short canal. Sound waves collected by your auricle travel down the canal and strike the eardrum. The eardrum is a thin membrane separating the ear canal from the middle ear.

When sound waves hit the eardrum, it begins to vibrate. These vibrations are then passed on to three bones in the middle ear. You may remember that the three bones in the middle ear are the smallest bones in your

Health and Safety Tip
Nerve deafness usually is caused by repeated exposure to loud sounds such as those at a rock concert. Brief exposure can cause ringing in the ears. Long-term exposure can cause permanent damage.

Figure 24-9 How are impulses carried from the ear to the brain?

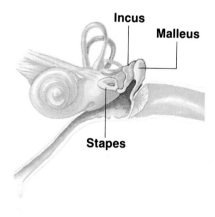

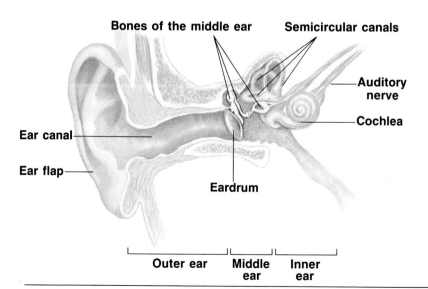

body. Vibrations pass along the middle ear bones to another thin membrane called the oval window. The oval window transfers vibrations to a coiled fluid-filled structure called the **cochlea** (KOK-lee-uh). When the fluid inside the cochlea vibrates, the movement is detected by hairlike receptors in the wall of the cochlea. Nerve impulses are carried to the brain by the auditory nerve. In the brain they are interpreted as sound.

Your ears also help maintain balance. Have you ever felt dizzy after spinning around in a circle? Dizziness is a sensation produced by three looped tubes in your inner ear. These fluid-filled tubes also contain hairlike receptors. Every time you move your head, the fluid inside these tubes moves. The hairlike receptors in each tube sense the change in the position of your head. Sensory neurons carry messages of the exact position of your head to your brain.

Touch

Your skin is the largest sense organ in your body. When you think of feeling in the skin, you probably think of touch. However, touch is only one sensation your skin can detect. Your skin also senses pressure, pain, heat, and cold. Each of these sensations stimulates a different kind of sensory receptor in the skin.

Place your hand lightly on an object. Touch receptors are found near the surface of the skin. They inform the brain of even the lightest touch. However, not all receptors are located near the skin's surface. Pressure and pain receptors are found deep within the skin. These receptors prevent tissue injury and alert the brain to dangerous situations in the environment.

Receptors in the skin are not evenly distributed over your body. For example, you have more touch receptors on your fingertips than on your back. Why do you think this is important?

Taste and Smell

What are some of your favorite foods? Do you like both their tastes and smells? The organs for taste and smell are stimulated by chemicals. What organs do you use for taste and smell?

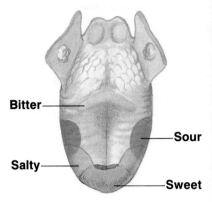

Bitter

Sour

Salty

Sweet

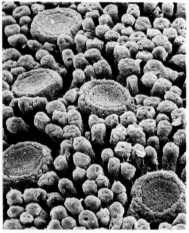

Figure 24-10 Taste buds at the tip of your tongue detect sweetness. Where are the taste buds that detect bitterness located?

Receptors for taste are located on taste buds found on your tongue. When food molecules mix with saliva in your mouth, they activate the receptor cells in taste buds. Nerve impulses then are sent to the brain, where they are interpreted as taste.

You may be surprised to find out that your taste buds can detect only four tastes: sweet, sour, salty, and bitter. Since most foods have a blend of these tastes, food tends to stimulate more than one kind of receptor at the same time. That is one reason foods have many different flavors.

The flavor of food also is detected by the odor receptors in your nose. When your nose is blocked, your odor receptors do not function as well. This is why food often tastes bland when you have a cold. Odor receptors called **olfactory** (ol-FAK-tuhr-ee) **cells** respond to gas molecules. When gas molecules dissolve in the mucus layer inside the nose, the molecules are detected by olfactory cells. Impulses are sent to the brain, where they are interpreted as different odors.

Think & Discuss

9. Where are the receptor cells for taste located?

10. What is the iris? What is its function?

11. What are two functions of your ears?

12. What five kinds of receptors are located in the skin?

★ **13.** What problem would be caused by a lack of cones in the eye? A lack of rods?

ACTIVITY 24–2

PROBLEM: How do the senses of taste and smell work together?

Science Process Skills
identifying tastes, hypothesizing, comparing

Background Information
The tongue is the organ for taste. Your tongue can sense only four basic tastes. These tastes are sweet, salty, sour, and bitter. The nose is the organ for smell. Nerve endings in the nose are sensitive to odors produced by different substances.

Materials
    2 paper plates
    paper towels
    2 plastic spoons
    small pieces of onion, potato, and apple
    1 stick of cinnamon chewing gum
    water
    blindfold
    2 plastic drinking glasses

Procedure
1. Copy the Data Table shown.

Data Table: Tastes and Flavors		
FOOD	NOSE CLOSED	NOSE OPEN
Onion		
Potato		
Apple		
Gum		

2. Work with a partner. Begin by having your partner put on the blindfold.
3. Place a small amount of onion, potato, apple, and a small piece of cinnamon chewing gum on a paper plate.
4. Tell your partner to hold his or her nose closed tightly.

5. Using a plastic spoon, give your partner one of the foods to taste. **Note:** The food should not be swallowed.
6. Ask your partner to describe the taste and name the food. Record your partner's responses.
7. Dispose of the food in a paper towel and have your partner rinse his or her mouth with water.
8. Repeat steps 4–7 for each food sample.
9. **HYPOTHESIZE** Do you think your partner's responses will change if your partner can smell the food? Write your hypothesis on a sheet of paper. To test your hypothesis, continue the activity.
10. Repeat the activity with your partner still blindfolded but with his or her nose open.
11. Switch roles with your partner and repeat the activity.

Observations
1. **a.** Which foods did your partner identify correctly with his or her nose closed?
   b. Which foods were identified correctly with the nose open?
2. What differences did your partner notice in the taste of each food when the nose was closed and when the nose was open?

Conclusion
1. Was your hypothesis correct? Use your observations to support your hypothesis.
2. How do the senses of taste and smell work together?
3. What is the difference between taste and flavor?

Going Further
Test other foods in the same way. In your tests, include sugar and table salt. Can these "pure" substances be identified more easily than foods with "flavors"? Use your observations to support your answer.

24-4 The Endocrine System

Do you know why people grow so rapidly during adolescence? Have you ever heard of a person having "superhuman" strength during an emergency? These responses result from the action of the endocrine (EN-duh-krin) system.

Your endocrine system is made up of a group of glands that secrete **hormones** (HAWR-mohns) into the bloodstream. Hormones are chemical messengers that regulate many of your bodily functions. Along with the nervous system, the endocrine system coordinates all of your body's activities.

Endocrine Glands

You have two kinds of glands in your body. Exocrine (EK-suh-krin) glands secrete, or release, chemicals through ducts, or tubes. The salivary glands are exocrine glands. Endocrine glands, however, do not have ducts. Endocrine glands secrete hormones directly into the bloodstream. The blood then transports the chemicals to where they are needed.

Hormones travel throughout the body and may affect several body systems at once. For example, hormones help regulate metabolism, growth, development, and

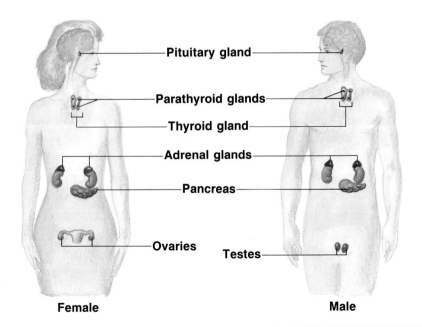

Female   Male

Figure 24-11 The endocrine system of men and women differ slightly. What endocrine glands are found only in women?

- Pituitary gland
- Parathyroid glands
- Thyroid gland
- Adrenal glands
- Pancreas
- Ovaries
- Testes

Table 24-1	The Endocrine System	
ENDOCRINE GLAND	HORMONE	FUNCTION
Pituitary	Growth hormone, other hormones	Controls growth; regulates other glands.
Thyroid	Thyroxine	Regulates growth and metabolism.
Parathyroids	Parathyroid hormone	Regulates calcium use by the body.
Adrenals	Cortisone	Maintains salt–water balance.
	Adrenaline	Regulates body responses to stress.
Pancreas	Insulin	Regulates blood-sugar levels.
Ovaries	Estrogen (female sex hormone)	Controls development of reproductive organs and female characteristics.
Testes	Testosterone (male sex hormone)	Controls development of reproductive organs and male characteristics.

Study Hint

The ovaries and testes also are parts of the human reproductive systems. You will learn more about ovaries and testes in Chapter 25.

reproduction. They also help control the balance of certain substances in the body such as calcium and the sugar glucose. Table 24-1 lists some of the hormones produced by your endocrine glands. What hormones are produced by your adrenal glands? What are their functions?

Pituitary Gland

Your pituitary (pi-TOO-uh-ter-ee) gland is located at the base of the cerebrum. This small, oval gland produces the greatest number of hormones. One hormone produced by the pituitary gland is **growth hormone.** The amount of growth hormone in your body determines how tall you will grow. Other pituitary hormones regulate other endocrine glands.

What controls the release of pituitary hormones? A part of the brain called the hypothalamus sends signals to the pituitary gland. The signals stimulate the release of pituitary hormones.

Thyroid Gland

The two lobes of the thyroid gland are located in the neck just below your voice box. The thyroid gland secretes **thyroxine** (thy-ROK-sin), which regulates metabolism, or the rate at which your cells produce energy. If too little thyroxine is produced, the body metabolism slows down. As a result, a person tends to gain weight and feel tired.

Iodine is needed for the production of thyroxine. The production of too little thyroxine usually results from a lack of iodine in the diet. What do you think happens if too much thyroxine is produced?

Pancreas

The pancreas is located just behind the lower part of the stomach. You may remember that the pancreas is part of the digestive system. The pancreas also is an endocrine gland. It secretes the hormone **insulin** (IN-suh-lin). What is the job of insulin? Insulin reduces the level of glucose in the blood, by allowing glucose to enter body cells.

If too little insulin is produced by the pancreas, an excess of sugar builds up in the blood. This condition is called diabetes mellitus (dy-uh-BEET-is MEL-et-us). Without proper treatment, diabetes can lead to blindness, poor circulation, and even death. Most diabetics must take insulin injections on a regular basis to keep the level of blood sugar normal. Some diabetics, however, can control the disease by carefully maintaining their diets.

Figure 24-12 Gerti Corti was awarded a Nobel Prize in Medicine for her research on insulin.

Feedback

What regulates the endocrine glands? Most endocrine glands are regulated by a feedback mechanism. The feedback mechanism in your body works much like a thermostat. For example, if the temperature in a room drops below the setting on the thermostat, the furnace is turned on. As the furnace continues to run, it heats up the room. When the temperature in the room reaches the setting on the thermostat, the furnace is shut off.

Your hypothalamus regulates the endocrine system in much the same way as a thermostat controls temperature in your home. If the hypothalamus senses the need for a certain substance in you body, it signals the pituitary to "turn on" a gland. The gland secretes a hormone that stimulates production of the substance. Once the

Skill Builder

Diagraming   Draw a diagram to illustrate the feedback mechanism of a thermostat and a furnace. Then, draw a second diagram to illustrate the feedback mechanism that controls the level of sugar in the body.

Study Hint

To learn more about some ways you can control your body's responses, read the Leisure Activity on page 433.

appropriate level of the substance enters the bloodstream and is detected by the hypothalamus, the hypothalamus stops sending signals to the pituitary. Therefore, the pituitary "turns off" the gland and the gland stops secreting the hormone.

Think & Discuss

14. What is the function of thyroxine?
15. What is the difference between an endocrine and an exocrine gland?
16. What would happen if too much insulin were injected into the body?

24-5 Behavior

Key Points

- Innate behaviors are unlearned, inborn behaviors.
- Learned behaviors must be taught.

Everything you do is part of your behavior. There are two main types of behavior. Innate behavior is unlearned behavior that you are born with. Have you ever heard a newborn baby crying? A newborn's crying is an example of innate behavior. The baby did not learn to cry.

Reflex reactions are the simplest form of innate behavior. Coughing, swallowing, sneezing, and blinking are all innate behaviors. Reflexes do not involve any learning or thought.

Another type of behavior is learned behavior. Most human behavior is learned behavior. Learning occurs as a result of all your experiences.

Learning began during the first few days of your life and will continue throughout your whole life. You probably are familiar with the saying "Practice makes perfect." Learned behaviors must be practiced. You learn to do things by doing them over and over. You also can change learned behavior.

Think & Discuss

17. What is an innate behavior?
18. What is a learned behavior?
19. What is the advantage of innate behaviors?

BIOLOGY and YOU

Relaxation and Biofeedback

Did you know that your body reacts to good stress, such as watching an exciting race, and bad stress, such as failing a test, in the same ways? Stress is any demand placed upon the body. Good or bad, too much stress in your life is not healthy.

Relaxation is one of the best ways to control stress. People relax in many ways. These ways include taking a hot bath, using a relaxation technique, practicing yoga, and even exercising.

There are many relaxation techniques. A few examples are progressive relaxation, autogenic (awt-uh-JEN-ik) relaxation, and meditation.

All relaxation techniques start the same way. Find a quiet room and get into a comfortable position. Breathe deeply. Depending on which relaxation technique you choose, you continue in different ways.

In progressive relaxation, you tighten up and then relax each part of your body. For example, start at your feet. Tighten, then relax, your feet. Tighten and relax you calves. Continue through your entire body.

Autogenic relaxation starts the same way as progressive relaxation. However, instead of tightening and relaxing your muscles, you use the power of suggestion. For example, starting at one end of your body, say to yourself, "Warmth is flowing through my head. Warmth is covering my face. Warmth is flowing down my neck," and so forth. Soon your whole body feels warm and relaxed.

Meditation is another method of relaxation. To begin meditation, choose a word. Each time you inhale, say the word. Each time you exhale, repeat the word. During meditation your mind clears as you concentrate only on your chosen word.

Some people do not realize when they are under stress. For these people, a doctor or other trained person can use biofeedback. Biofeedback is used to control high blood pressure and nervousness, which are both signs of stress.

In biofeedback, a machine shows when a person is under stress. A lie detector is an example of a biofeedback machine. A thermometer is another example. When you have a fever, it is an indication that your body is under stress. The cause of this stress is usually illness.

Learning to deal with stress will help keep your body in good health. Whether you choose to deal with stress through relaxation or biofeedback, it is important to find a method you like. Then use the method that you choose regularly.

To Think About
- What can you do to eliminate some of the stress in your life?
- Explain why a lie detector test is an example of biofeedback.

Chapter Review

24-1 The Nervous System

- The three parts of a nerve cell are the cell body, dendrites, and the axon.
- Dendrites carry impulses to the cell body. The axon carries impulses away from the cell body.
- The cerebrum is the body's control center.
- The cerebellum coordinates the movement of the skeletal muscles.
- The medulla controls many involuntary actions such as breathing and heart rate.

24-2 Nerve Pathways

- Impulses travel from dendrites to the cell body, and then down the axon.
- When an impulse reaches the end of an axon, chemicals are released into the synapse.
- A reflex is an automatic response controlled by the spinal cord.

24-3 The Five Senses

- The five senses are vision, hearing, touch, taste, and smell.

24-4 The Endocrine System

- The pituitary gland regulates many other endocrine glands. One of the hormones made by the pituitary gland is growth hormone.
- The thyroid produces thyroxine, which regulates metabolism.
- The pancreas produces insulin, which regulates the amount of sugar in the blood.

24-5 Behavior

- Innate behaviors are unlearned and inborn. Reflexes are innate behaviors.
- Most human behavior is learned behavior. Learned behavior occurs as a result of experience.

VOCABULARY LIST

associative neurons (418)	cornea (424)	iris (424)	retina (425)
axon (418)	dendrites (418)	medulla (420)	sensory neurons (418)
cell body (418)	growth hormone (430)	motor neurons (418)	synapse (421)
cerebellum (419)	hormones (429)	neurons (418)	thyroxine (431)
cerebrum (419)	impulses (418)	olfactory cells (427)	
cochlea (426)	insulin (431)	reflex (422)	

VOCABULARY REVIEW

Matching   Write the word or term from the Vocabulary List that best matches each description.

1. detect gas molecules
2. carry impulses to muscles
3. cytoplasm of neuron
4. hormone secreted by pancreas
5. muscle in the eye
6. automatic response
7. controls thinking

Applying Definitions   Explain the difference between the words in each pair.

1. associative neurons, sensory neurons
2. dendrites, axon
3. cerebellum, medulla
4. hormones, neurons
5. retina, cornea
6. growth hormone, thyroxine
7. synapse, impulses
8. cochlea, olfactory cells

True or False   Write true if the statement is true. If the statement is false, change the underlined word or words to make the statement true.

1. The part of the eye that focuses light is the pupil.
2. Sensory neurons carry impulses to the brain.
3. Reflexes are controlled by the brain.
4. The heart rate is controlled by the cerebellum.
5. Impulses are tiny jolts of electric energy.
6. During emergencies, the level of adrenaline in your body increases.
7. Extending from the spinal cord are 31 pairs of nerves.
8. The cerebrum is the lower part of the brain stem.
9. Taste and smell are both chemical senses.
10. The gland that controls many other endocrine glands is the thyroid.

Question and Answer   Rewrite each heading of the Chapter Outline on page 416 as a question. Then, answer each of the questions you have written.

Understanding a Diagram   Use the diagram of the ear shown in Figure 24-9 (page 425) to answer each of the following.

1. Where is the eardrum located?
2. How many bones are found in the middle ear?
3. What is the shape of the cochlea?
4. What nerve in the ear sends messages to the brain?

Writing the Main Ideas   Using the Chapter Outline on page 416, write the main idea for each heading in the outline.

Critical Thinking   Answer each of the following in complete sentences.

1. The brain and the spinal cord are called the central nervous system. Why do you think the central nervous system is a good name for the brain and spinal cord?
2. Why is the pancreas both an exocrine and an endocrine gland?
3. Taste buds function best within a certain temperature range. Why might food taste bland to chain-smokers?
4. How is the spinal cord like a tree trunk?
5. Suppose you were in the path of a fast-moving car. How would the nervous system and endocrine system work together to protect you from harm?

1. The electricity produced by nerve impulses in your brain can be measured and recorded by an electroencephalograph (EEG). Find out about an EEG. Then write a report explaining how this machine works.
2. The thyroid gland needs iodine to produce thyroxine. Present an oral report explaining which food items contain iodine and how much iodine the body needs.
3. Sound intensity is measured in decibels. Look up the safe decibel range for the human ear in an encyclopedia. Find out what sources of noise produce sound above and below this safe range. Prepare a poster of your findings.
4. Multiple sclerosis is an incurable disease. Find out more about multiple sclerosis. Then write a report on your findings.

Chapter 25

Chapter

Reproduction and Development

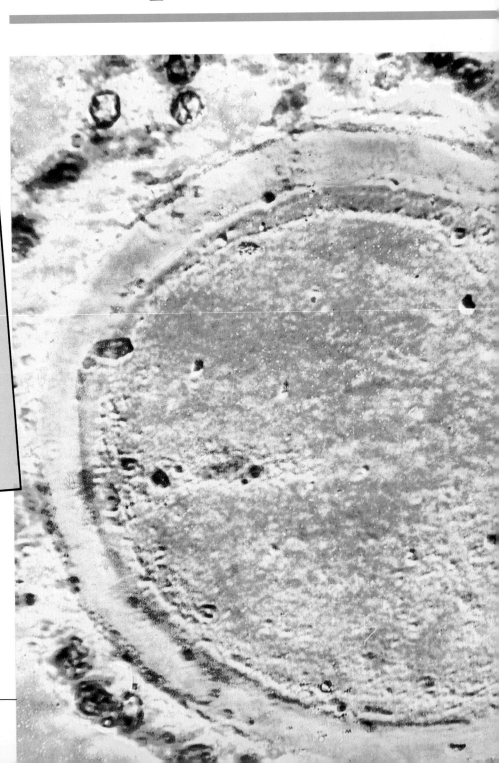

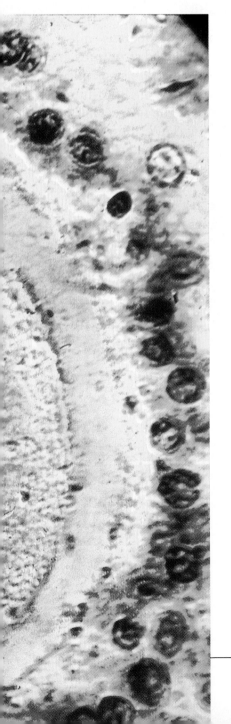

Objectives

After you have completed this chapter, you will be able to

25-1 **identify** the functions of the testes and ovaries.

25-1 **describe** the function of estrogen.

25-2 **describe** how an embryo receives food and oxygen from its mother.

25-2 **compare** a fetus with an embryo.

25-3 **list** the stages in the human life cycle.

25-3 **list** three characteristics of adolescence.

Science Process Skills

In this chapter, two science skills are highlighted. Symbols show some places where these skills are used.

▲ **Organizing:** When you organize information, you put the information in some kind of order.

▣ **Hypothesizing:** When you hypothesize, you state a suggested answer to a problem based upon known information.

What do you see in this picture? The round, yellow structure is a human egg cell. Around the egg are many sperm cells. The sperm have been colored blue in this transmission electron micrograph.

Only one sperm will be able to enter the egg cell. After the sperm cell and egg cell are joined, an embryo begins to develop. The development of the embryo is part of the complex process of human reproduction. About nine months later, the process is completed when a baby is born. During these months, one cell has developed into a complete human being. The newborn will continue to grow and develop from a child into an adult.

25-1 Human Reproduction Systems

The function of the reproductive system is to produce offspring. Unlike most organ systems, the reproductive system differs in men and women. These differences become noticeable as early as six weeks after a baby begins to develop.

The Male Reproductive System

The male reproductive system includes sex organs called the **testes.** (TES-teez). These two egg-shaped structures are located outside the body cavity. The testes are suspended within a pocket of skin called the **scrotum** (SKROH-tum).

Two kinds of cells are found within the testes. One kind of cell produces testosterone (tes-TAWS-tuhr-ohn). Testosterone is a hormone responsible for the onset of **puberty** (PYU-bur-tee). Puberty is the time at which a person develops secondary sex characteristics and becomes sexually mature. In the male, these characteristics include a deeper voice and the growth of body hair. Testosterone also causes a second kind of cell to develop inside the testes. These cells are called **sperm,** or male sex cells.

Sperm are stored in a coiled tube called the **epididymis** (ep-uh-DID-i-mis). Find the epididymis in Figure 25-1.

Key Points

- The testes and the ovaries produce sex cells and secrete hormones.

- Estrogen is a hormone that helps stimulate the onset of puberty, and affects the uterus and pituitary.

Study Hint

As you read Section 25-1, list in order the structures through which sperm and egg cells pass.

Figure 25-1 In males, the urethra is part of both the urinary system and the reproductive system.

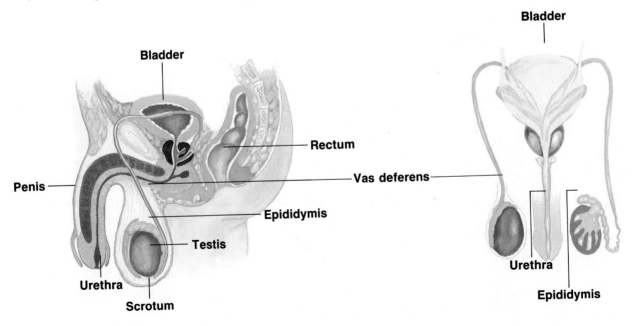

One end of the epididymis connects to the testes. The other end connects to a longer tube called the **vas deferens** (vas DEF-uh-renz). The vas deferens extends upward into the body cavity from the testes.

△ Inside the body cavity, the vas deferens empties into the urethra. The urethra is surrounded and protected by the **penis.** The penis is the male reproductive organ that deposits sperm in the female. Look at Figure 25-1 again. Notice that the epididymis, the vas deferens, and the urethra form a continuous passageway. Sperm enter this passageway from the testes and exit through the penis.

Several glands secrete a special fluid into the passageway. This fluid lubricates the passageway and helps carry the sperm. This combination of fluid and sperm is called semen. Semen is released from the body during the ejaculation (i-jak-yuh-LAY-shuhn), or ejection, process.

The Female Reproductive System

The main sex organs of the female are called the **ovaries** (OH-vuhr-eez). Look closely at Figure 25-3. Compare the shape and location of the female sex organs with the male sex organs in Figure 25-1. Notice that the ovaries are egg-shaped structures much like the testes. The major difference between the ovaries and testes is that the ovaries are located inside the body cavity.

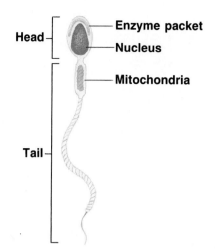

Figure 25-2 A human sperm cell is divided into a head and a tail.

Figure 25-3 All parts of the female reproductive system are inside the body cavity.

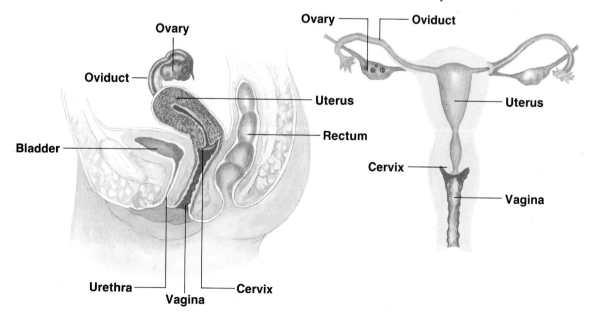

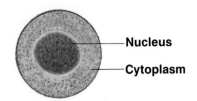

Figure 25-4 An egg cell consists of a nucleus surrounded by cytoplasm.

Like the testes, the ovaries contain two kinds of cells. One kind of cell produces hormones. Two hormones produced by the ovaries are estrogen (ES-truh-juhn) and progesterone (proh-JES-tuhr-ohn). These hormones mainly are responsible for the secondary sex characteristics and the onset of puberty. The other kind of cell in the ovaries produce **eggs.** Eggs are female sex cells.

A long tube called the **oviduct** (OH-vuh-dukt) is located near the ovary. At the end of the oviduct closest to the ovary are fingerlike projections. The opposite end of the oviduct leads into the **uterus** (YU-tur-us), or womb. The uterus is a hollow organ with thick, muscular walls. Look at the diagram of the uterus in Figure 25-3 on page 439. Notice that the lower end of the uterus is narrower than the upper end. The narrow end of the uterus is called the **cervix** (SUR-viks). The cervix extends downward into the **vagina** (vuh-JY-nuh), or birth canal.

Ovulation

The production of egg cells begins before a girl is born. A baby girl is born with all the egg cells she will have in her lifetime. However, these eggs are not mature cells. Egg cells begin to mature, one by one, at the onset of puberty.

Girls usually reach puberty between the ages of 10 and 14. At this time, egg development begins. The eggs in each ovary are enclosed within a tiny capsule. Once a month, a hormone released by the pituitary gland travels through the bloodstream to one of the ovaries. When the hormone reaches the ovary, it causes some of the capsules to grow. One capsule usually grows faster than the others. This capsule becomes swollen with fluid. It begins to move to the surface of the ovary. The capsule continues to grow for 9 to 10 days.

As it grows, the capsule releases estrogen. Estrogen travels to the uterus and to the pituitary. When estrogen

Figure 25-5 Ovulation occurs once every month.

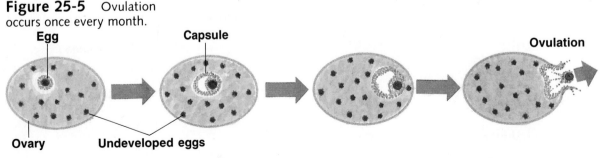

reaches the uterus, the walls of the uterus thicken and the blood supply to the uterus increases. When estrogen reaches the pituitary, the pituitary releases another hormone. This hormone causes the capsule to burst. The egg inside the capsule is then released and moves into the oviduct. The release of the egg occurs about 14 days after the capsule begins to grow. The release of the egg from its capsule is called **ovulation** (oh-vyuh-LAY-shun).

After ovulation, the capsule releases another hormone called progesterone. The progesterone travels to the uterus. Here it stimulates the continued buildup of the uterine wall.

Menstruation

Once the egg is released from the ovary, wavelike motions of the oviduct "fingers" pull the egg inward. The egg is moved through the oviduct by many hairs lining the oviduct. If the egg is not fertilized by a sperm cell, it begins to break down. The capsule also breaks down.

As the capsule breaks down, the amount of progesterone decreases. Without progesterone, the thick tissue lining the uterine wall also breaks down. About 14 days after ovulation, the tissue lining and excess blood leave the uterus through the vagina. This process is called **menstruation** (men-stroo-WAY-shun). Menstruation usually lasts 3 to 5 days.

When the amount of progesterone decreases, the pituitary releases a hormone that stimulates the development of another capsule. Soon a new egg begins to mature. The entire process from the development of a

Figure 25-6 Notice how the hormone levels change during the menstrual cycle.

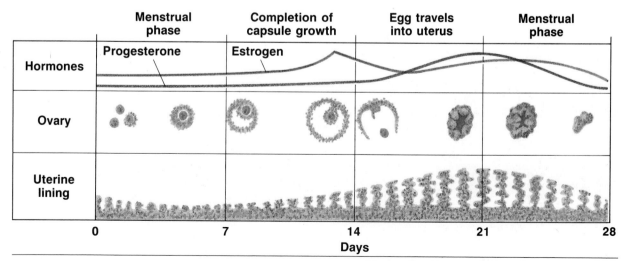

	Menstrual phase	Completion of capsule growth	Egg travels into uterus	Menstrual phase
Hormones	Progesterone	Estrogen		
Ovary				
Uterine lining				

0   7   14   21   28

Days

capsule to menstruation is called the menstrual cycle. The menstrual cycle is repeated every 28 to 32 days.

Think & Discuss

1. What is ovulation?
2. What is the function of the epididymis?
3. Describe the functions of the testes and ovaries.
4. Explain the roles of estrogen and progesterone.
5. Why are the regular changes in the female reproductive system called a cycle?

25-2 Human Reproduction

The process of human reproduction begins when a sperm cell and an egg cell unite inside the oviduct of a woman. Once this union occurs, the egg passes through several stages of growth and development. Many changes also take place inside the woman's body during this period. Her menstrual cycle has stopped. The major job of her body at this point is to maintain the new life she is carrying. Human reproduction is complete when a new human being is born.

Fertilization

After an egg leaves its capsule and enters the oviduct, **fertilization** (fur-tul-i-ZAY-shun) can occur. Fertilization is the union of one sperm and one egg cell. Millions of sperm enter the uterus after ejaculation, but only a few reach the upper oviduct. Of those few, only one sperm is allowed to fertilize the egg.

Look at how many sperm are covering the egg in Figure 25-7. How does a sperm cell enter the egg? What prevents the rest of the sperm from entering?

At the head of each sperm is a packet of enzymes. When the sperm meets the egg, this packet breaks open. The enzymes dissolve a hole in the outer layer of the egg. This hole is big enough for just one sperm. As soon as one sperm has entered, the egg forms a membrane that prevents other sperm from entering the egg.

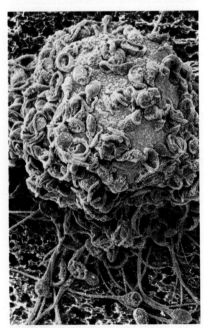

Figure 25-7 Many sperm cover an egg cell in this scanning electron micrograph.

Development of the Embryo

After fertilization has occurred, the **zygote** (ZY-goht), or fertilized egg, travels down the oviduct and enters the uterus. While in the oviduct, the zygote undergoes a series of cell divisions. The single-celled zygote divides to form two cells, then four cells, and so on. Cell division continues until a hollow ball of cells forms. This hollow ball attaches to tissues that line the wall of the uterus.

When the mass is buried deep inside the wall of the uterus, some remarkable events begin to occur. The mass of cells now is called an **embryo** (EM-bree-oh). The tissue surrounding the embryo develops into a thick, flat structure called the **placenta** (pluh-SEN-tuh).

The placenta contains millions of blood vessels. The blood vessels carry blood from the embryo. The blood vessels in the placenta are very close to the blood vessels that line the wall of the uterus. Wastes and carbon dioxide leave the embryo and enter the blood vessels of the placenta by diffusion.

From the placenta, the wastes diffuse into the blood vessels of the uterus. These waste materials leave the woman's body with her own wastes. Food and oxygen from the woman diffuse across the blood vessels of the uterus to the placenta. The blood vessels in the placenta carry these nutrients to the developing embryo.

A thick, ropelike structure called the **umbilical** (um-BIL-ih-kul) **cord** connects the embryo to the placenta.

Health and Safety Tip

The placenta is not a barrier. Everything that enters a pregnant woman eventually will cross the placenta and reach the embryo. Drugs, alcohol, tobacco, and caffeine can cross the placenta and harm the developing embryo.

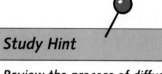

Study Hint

Review the process of diffusion in Chapter 4.

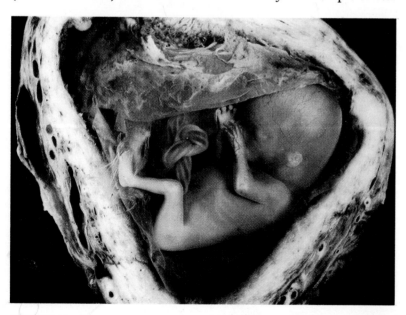

Figure 25-8 Find the umbilical cord in this photo of a ten-week-old fetus.

The umbilical cord contains two large blood vessels. These vessels are the umbilical vein and the umbilical artery. The umbilical vein carries nutrient-rich blood from the placenta to the embryo. The umbilical artery carries wastes from the embryo to the placenta.

A clear, fluid-filled membrane called the **amnion** (AM-nee-on) surrounds the embryo. The amnion prevents the embryo from sticking to the uterine wall. The fluid inside the amnion is called the amniotic (am-nee-AH-tik) fluid. The amniotic fluid cushions and protects the embryo.

Pregnancy

The period of development of an organism inside its mother's body is called the gestation period, or **pregnancy** (PREG-nun-see). Gestation periods vary from one kind of organism to another. In humans, the gestation period is 38 weeks, or about nine months.

Pregnancy brings about many changes in a woman's body. One of the first signs of pregnancy is breast enlargement and periods of nausea. Weight gain usually begins once the placenta, umbilical cord, and amniotic fluid start to develop. Most women gain between 10 and 20 kg during their pregnancy. Some women develop back pain and swollen feet as a result of this extra weight. The most common problem associated with pregnancy is a

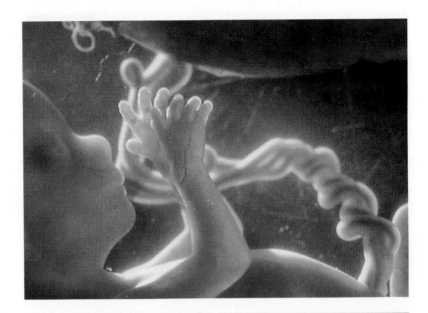

Figure 25-9 This four-month-old fetus is in the second stage of development.

feeling of exhaustion. A woman's body must work harder to meet her own needs as well as those of her baby.

During the first three months of pregnancy, the tiny embryo develops rapidly. The heart, brain, and nerve cord begin to develop. The eyes and ears begin to form. Arm and leg buds with fingers and toes also form. About this time, bone gradually begins to replace cartilage in the embryo's skeleton. After bone replacement is complete, the embryo is called a **fetus.**

During the next three months, the fetus increases in size. Major body systems and organs continue to develop and grow. The arms and legs get longer.

During the last three months of pregnancy, the fetus gains a great deal of weight. Its body grows longer. The fetus also develops a layer of protective fat. At this time, pregnancy is nearing an end. The fetus prepares for birth by turning itself upside down. The fetus remains in this head-down position until birth.

Birth

About nine months after fertilization, hormonal changes begin to occur in the mother. Hormones cause the uterus to tighten, or contract, and then relax. These contractions of the uterus are called labor.

Once labor begins, the force of the contractions pushes the baby's head against the cervix, as shown in Figure 25-10. The cervix stretches to provide an opening of about 10 centimeters. This opening is just big enough for the baby's head to pass through. Labor continues until the

Study Hint

Each three-month period of pregnancy is called a trimester.

Figure 25-10 During labor, the baby is pushed against the cervix (left) and out of the mother's body (right).

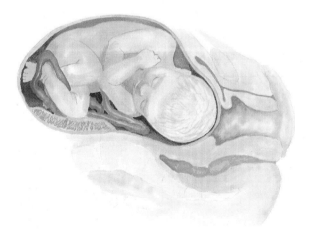
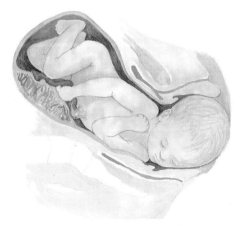

ACTIVITY 25–1

PROBLEM: How does a human baby change during development?

Science Process Skills
observing, comparing, calculating

Background Information
The period of human gestation is about 38 weeks. During this time, a fertilized egg with very small mass develops into a baby. During part of gestation, the developing baby is called an embryo. At about the twelfth week, the developing baby has all individual organs and body systems. At this point, the developing baby is called a fetus.

Materials
paper and pencil
various size paper clips
balance

Procedure
1. Study the diagram of a developing baby and read the data in the Data Table.
2. Use the metric ruler to draw a line 51 cm long.
3. On the line, measure the lengths of a developing baby. Use the data in the Data Table. Mark each length with a dot.
4. Label each dot with the length of the developing baby and the time in weeks.
5. **ESTIMATE**   Determine the number of paper clips you think will have the same mass as an embryo at 5 weeks and 9 weeks. Use the balance to find out if you are correct.

Data Table: Growth of a Developing Baby

TIME (IN WEEKS)	MASS (IN g)	LENGTH (IN cm)
4	–	.5
5	.5	1.3
9	10	5
14	113	18
20	300	24
26	907	38
32	1700	41
38	3180	51

6. Record the number of paper clips that equal the mass of an embryo at 5 and 9 weeks.

Observations
1. **a.** How long is an average baby at birth? **b.** At what time is a developing baby about half its full length at birth?   **c.** At what time is a developing baby about half its full mass at birth?
2. Between which weeks does the developing baby increase in length the most?
3. During which weeks does the developing baby nearly triple in mass?

Conclusions
1. Are the changes in mass and length in a developing baby the same throughout gestation? Use the data to support your answer.
2. Using the diagram, briefly describe the changes in a developing baby from 5 weeks to birth.

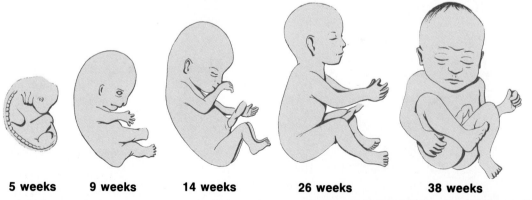

5 weeks   **9 weeks**   **14 weeks**   **26 weeks**   **38 weeks**

baby's body is pushed into the vagina and out of the mother's body. Further contractions push the placenta out of the mother's body.

When the baby leaves the birth canal, it is still connected to its mother by the umbilical cord. The cord first is tied to decrease blood loss and then cut. The small portion of the cord still attached to the baby will dry up and leave a scar. This scar is the navel, or belly button.

Once the umbilical cord is cut, the baby's body must take over all life processes. Shortly after birth, the baby begins to cry. This crying replaces the fluid in the lungs with air and the baby begins to breathe. The baby's circulatory system also changes. The heart starts pumping blood to the baby's lungs. The blood then returns to the heart for circulation to the rest of the body.

Without the umbilical cord, the baby needs a new supply of food. Hormones in the mother cause mammary glands in her breasts to produce milk. Almost all babies are able to start nursing soon after birth.

Think & Discuss

6. What is fertilization? Where does fertilization take place?

7. What is one major difference between an embryo and a fetus?

8. Explain how an embryo receives food and oxygen.

9. What two functions do the contractions of labor serve?

★ 10. What would happen to the fetus if the placenta became detached from the uterine wall? Explain your answer.

25-3 Human Development

Human development occurs in a series of stages that begin at birth and continue through old age. At birth, all of the major body systems and organs are in place. However, it often takes years before all of these systems and organs are fully developed and function efficiently.

Key Points
- The human life cycle includes several stages of development.

- Adolescence is marked by increased height, weight gain, and sexual maturity.

▲ The stages in the development of an organism are described as its life cycle. The stages of the human life cycle include infancy, childhood, adolescence, adulthood, and old age. Certain events that occur at different times in the life cycle make each stage unique.

Early Years

At birth, human newborns are totally helpless. The range of their abilities includes crying, sucking, swallowing, and grasping. Babies usually can see things that are within about 50 cm of them. They usually respond to sudden loud noises or bright lights with a startle reflex. Babies also have other simple reflexes, such as blinking their eyes.

The earliest stage of human life is called infancy. Muscle and nerve development occur rapidly during infancy. By seven months, an infant usually can hold its head up, roll over, and perhaps even crawl. By the time they are one year old, most infants are able to walk and to speak a few words.

Infants between the ages of one and two are very curious about their environment. They place almost everything they pick up in their mouths for a closer inspection. During this period, infants also become aware of the results of their actions. For example, infants realize that certain actions get the attention of adults.

Childhood generally is defined as the period between ages 2 and 12. During this time, children become better

Figure 25-11   An infant (left) begins to notice her surroundings. During childhood (right) coordination increases.

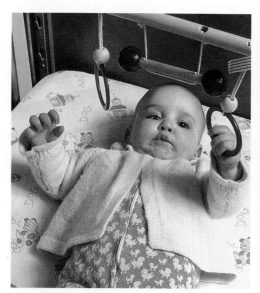

able to express themselves. Their vocabulary and powers of reasoning develop. Increased muscle development allows more complex activities. Children soon are able to feed and dress themselves, and even to ride a bicycle. Most children learn how to read and write during this stage of development. Children at this stage are able to perform activities that require a great deal of coordination, such as playing a sport or a musical instrument.

Between the ages of 11 and 14, most young people go through a period of rapid physical change. This stage is called adolescence. During early adolescence, puberty takes place. At puberty, the testes and ovaries become mature and begin to release high levels of hormones. These hormones largely are responsible for growth spurts. Young people grow taller and gain weight during this time. Boys begin to develop more muscle and body hair. In addition, their voices begin to change. In girls, breast development and a widening of the hips occurs.

Adolescents of both sexes develop the ability to reproduce at this stage in their lives. Boys begin to produce sperm. Girls begin to release mature eggs.

Later Years

Adulthood is the stage at which the physical growth of the human body is complete. The growth process usually is completed between the ages of 18 and 21. Muscle development and coordination reach their peak in early adulthood and remain at that level through the late 20s. Between the ages of 30 and 50, muscle tone and physical strength often decrease. As a result, people find it harder to stay "in shape."

Health and Safety Tip
Long-term use of marijuana affects the production of sex hormones. Men who use marijuana have a lowered sperm count. Women experience disruptions in their menstrual cycles.

Figure 25-12 Regular exercise helps these young adults stay in shape.

Figure 25-13 Many older adults remain active throughout their lives.

Between the ages of 45 and 50, the release of egg cells in women begins to decrease. The menstrual cycle occurs less frequently. By age 50, menstruation has usually stopped completely. However, men do not stop producing sperm. Men continue to produce sperm until they are in their late 80s and early 90s.

Old age, or the beginning of the aging process, occurs at different times in different people. People who have exercised regularly and eaten a balanced diet all of their lives may not show signs of aging until their late 70s or early 80s. On the other hand, people who rarely have exercised and lacked a balanced diet throughout their lives can show signs of aging in their early 60s. What are some of the aging signs?

Your sense organs contain large numbers of sensory receptors. With advancing age, these receptors become less sensitive to stimuli. Older adults usually do not hear or see as well as they once did. They become less able to taste different foods or to smell odors.

Older adults usually notice a loss of muscle strength. They tend to move slowly. Some may even require assistance in moving. Their bones often become soft and even brittle. Bones break more easily and take longer to heal in older adults. Most older adults decrease in height as their bones begin to curve and the cartilage between the bones loses its elastic quality.

Americans are living longer now than at any other period in history. In the 1940s, men usually lived to be 64 and women to be 68. By the 1980s, men were living to age 72 and women to age 78. Many of the factors affecting the aging process are controlled by your genes. However, research has shown that a balanced diet and regular exercise can contribute greatly to the quality of your life as you grow older.

Think & Discuss

11. What is a life cycle? List the stages in the human life cycle.

12. What three major events occur during adolescence?

13. Compare development during infancy with the changes that take place during old age.

Until recently, doctors had no way of diagnosing and treating the medical problems of an unborn baby, or fetus. Then the development of two important medical techniques made the diagnosis and treatment of fetal illnesses possible. These two techniques are amniocentesis and ultrasound.

In amniocentesis, a needle is inserted into the mother's abdomen and a small amount of the fluid in which the fetus floats is removed. The fluid is then analyzed to determine the health of the fetus as well as many of its genetic traits. By using amniocentesis, doctors can tell if a fetus has any genetic disorders.

Ultrasound is a technique in which sound waves are sent through the mother's uterus. The sound waves produce an image of the fetus on a television screen. Ultrasound pictures can be used to diagnose medical problems in fetuses. They also provide a very accurate picture of the fetus's position in the womb.

Scientists have developed a new technique in fetal medicine that may be even more effective than amniocentesis and ultrasound. Using this technique, doctors can treat a fetus by inserting a thin needle into the umbilical cord.

The umbilical cord transports food, oxygen, and wastes back and forth between the fetus and the placenta. The placenta is the organ that receives oxygen and food from the mother. It also transfers wastes from the fetus to the mother's excretory system.

Scientists have discovered that drugs and blood transfusions can be given through the umbilical cord. In one case, a New Jersey woman went to the University of Pennsylvania for a routine ultrasound examination that showed that the fetus had congestive heart failure. The drug that is used to treat heart failure is digitalis. Without the umbilical cord technique, doctors would have had no way of reaching the unborn baby, because digitalis does not pass easily through the placenta.

As it turned out, this story had a happy ending. Within a few days of having digitalis administered through the umbilical cord, the fetus's heartbeat improved. The baby was healthy at birth, and the irregular heartbeats disappeared within a few months.

Perhaps someday you will become a parent. Your chances of having a normal, healthy baby have been greatly increased by advances in fetal medicine.

To Think About
- Birth can be difficult and dangerous when a baby is improperly positioned in the uterus or birth canal. Which of the medical techniques described above would be most useful in diagnosing such a condition? Why?
- Why does treatment through the umbilical cord make it possible to bypass the placenta when administering drugs?

Chapter Review

CHAPTER SUMMARY

25-1 The Human Reproductive Systems

- The testes and ovaries are sex organs that produce sex cells and secrete hormones.
- The hormone estrogen helps stimulate the onset of puberty, causes the uterine wall to thicken, and causes the pituitary to release a hormone that allows the release of an egg from its capsule.

25-2 Human Reproduction

- The period of development of an organism inside its mother's body is called pregnancy.
- In humans, pregnancy lasts for nine months.

- Food and oxygen diffuse across the uterine wall to the placenta and then travel along the umbilical vein to the embryo.
- The embryo is described as a fetus after its skeletal system has changed from cartilage to bone.

25-3 Human Development

- The human life cycle includes infancy, childhood, adolescence, adulthood, and old age.
- Adolescence is characterized by increased height, weight gain, and sexual maturity.
- Adulthood is the stage at which physical growth of the human body is complete.

VOCABULARY LIST

amnion (444)
cervix (440)
eggs (440)
embryo (443)
epididymis (438)
fertilization (442)

fetus (445)
menstruation (441)
ovaries (439)
oviduct (440)
ovulation (441)
penis (439)

placenta (443)
pregnancy (444)
puberty (438)
scrotum (438)
sperm (438)
testes (438)

umbilical cord (443)
uterus (440)
vagina (440)
vas deferens (439)
zygote (443)

VOCABULARY REVIEW

Matching   Write the word or term from the Vocabulary List that best matches each description.

1. female sex organs
2. connects embryo to placenta
3. release of a mature egg
4. time of sexual maturity
5. male sex organs
6. fluid-filled sac that cushions embryo
7. birth canal
8. female sex cell
9. male sex cell
10. womb

Identifying Relationships   Identify the word or term in each group that does not belong. Explain why it does not belong with the group.

1. uterus, cervix, scrotum
2. embryo, placenta, fetus
3. oviduct, vas deferens, penis
4. menstruation, pregnancy, ejaculation
5. egg, zygote, sperm
6. fertilization, zygote, epididymis
7. embryo, fetus, amnion
8. scrotum, uterus, testes
9. amnion, egg, vagina
10. vas deferens, oviduct, epididymis

Completion   Write the word or words that best complete each sentence.

1. The _____ is a tube that can carry sperm or urine.
2. The exchange of material between the embryo and its mother takes place by _____.
3. Brittle or soft bones usually cause problems during _____.
4. _____ is the hormone that causes the uterine wall to thicken.
5. The _____ carries material between the embryo and the placenta.
6. The vas deferens connects the _____ and the urethra.
7. _____ are totally helpless and can perform few functions on their own.
8. The narrow end of the uterus is the _____.
9. _____ is the process by which blood and tissue leave the uterus.

Finding the Main Ideas   Use the section number to find the sentence that answers each question. Then, write the sentence.

1. Where are the testes located? (25-1)
2. What is the function of the sugar found in semen? (25-1)
3. When do girls usually become sexually mature? (25-1)
4. What happens if an egg and a sperm do not meet in the oviduct? (25-1)
5. What happens to the zygote after fertilization has occurred? (25-2)
6. What is the function of the umbilical vein? (25-2)
7. How long is pregnancy in humans? (25-2)
8. What is the earliest stage of human development called? (25-3)
9. When is the growth process usually completed? (25-3)
10. How long do men continue to produce sperm? (25-3)

Writing for Understanding   One way to find out if you understand something is to write a brief summary of the information in your own words. Reread Section 25-1, Human Reproductive Systems, on pages 438–442, and write a brief summary of the information.

Critical Thinking   Answer each of the following in complete sentences.

1. Compare sperm production and egg production.
2. The placenta performs the job of three body systems for the embryo. Identify each system and explain how the placenta does each job.
3. Why does a man produce billions of sperm in his lifetime while a woman produces only a few thousand eggs?
4. Located behind the head of each sperm is a packet of mitochondria followed by a long tail. What function do the mitochondria serve in sperm?
5. How can regular exercise and a balanced diet postpone the aging process?

1. Look up Fetal Alcohol Syndrome in a medical dictionary. Present an oral report explaining the causes and effects of this condition in newborns.
2. Use an encyclopedia to prepare a graph that compares life expectancies of Americans with those of people from other countries. How do the life expectancies compare?

When You've Had Enough, Join

MADD

Mothers Against Drunk Driving

What do you do to take care of your body? Proper nutrition, exercise, and rest all are needed for good health. The avoidance of tobacco, alcohol, and harmful drugs is another good health habit. However, sometimes even a health-conscious person becomes sick. There are many diseases and disorders that affect the body. Preventing and treating different diseases is an area of active scientific research.

Read the titles of the chapters that make up this unit. Then study the drawings and photographs that represent ideas or topics introduced in this unit. How do you think each picture is related to one of the chapters?

UNIT **7**

Human Health

CONTENTS

Chapter 26 | Nutrition

Objectives

After you have completed this chapter, you will be able to

26-1 **explain** why your body needs nutrients.

26-1 **list** five nutrients needed by the body.

26-2 **name** the four food groups and list examples of foods in each.

26-2 **explain** the importance of Calories in your diet.

26-3 **identify** four factors responsible for maintaining good health.

26-4 **recognize** anorexia nervosa and bulimia nervosa as eating disorders.

26-4 **define** deficiency disease.

Science Process Skills

In this chapter, two science skills are highlighted. Symbols show some places where these skills are used.

Measuring: When you measure, you compare an unknown value to a known value.

Classifying: When you classify, you group things based upon similarities.

Think of a car. Gasoline is the fuel that powers a car. A car cannot run on an empty gas tank. The tank must be refilled as the fuel is used. A car also will not run properly on poor-quality fuel.

Now, compare your body to a car. Food provides you with the energy needed to power your body. Like a car, you need to replace the fuel your body uses. You also need the right kinds of fuel to keep your body working properly. The fuels that your body needs are found in food. The study of food and its effect on the body is called **nutrition** (noo-TRISH-uhn).

26-1 Nutrients

Why does your body need food? Every food you eat contains **nutrients** (NOO-tree-unts). Nutrients are chemical substances in food that your body needs. Why does your body need nutrients? Your body uses the nutrients in food to carry out its life processes. For example, your body uses a simple sugar called glucose to carry out respiration. You may recall that respiration is the energy-producing process of the body. Nutrients also are used for the growth and repair of body tissues. There are five kinds of nutrients in food. What do you think the five nutrients are?

Carbohydrates, Fats, and Proteins

Three of the nutrients that your body needs are organic (awr-GAN-ik) nutrients. An organic nutrient contains carbon. **Carbohydrates** (kar-buh-HY-drayts), **fats,** and **proteins** are the three organic nutrients needed by the body.

Carbohydrates are the main source of energy for your body. What is a carbohydrate? A carbohydrate is a compound that is made up of carbon, hydrogen, and oxygen. Carbohydrates are classified into two groups— simple carbohydrates and complex carbohydrates.

Simple carbohydrates are sugars. In your body, carbohydrates are converted into energy and used very quickly. Because they are used up so quickly, carbo- hydrates should make up a large part of your diet. What simple carbohydrate does your body use for respiration?

Complex carbohydrates are starches. Starches take longer to digest than sugar; therefore, they provide energy over a longer period of time. Grains, beans, and bread are good sources of complex carbohydrates.

Fats are compounds made up mostly of carbon and hydrogen. Fats can be either solids or liquids. Solid fats usually come from animal sources, such as meat and dairy products. Liquid fats usually are called oils. Oils come mostly from vegetable sources such as corn. Many of these oils are used in cooking.

Fats fill you up faster and are digested more slowly than carbohydrates. Because fats stay in your body longer,

Study Hint

Nutritionists classify fats as saturated fats and unsaturated fats. Except for palm oil and coconut oil, all saturated fats come from animals.

Figure 26–1 These marathon runners need complex carbohydrates for energy.

you do not need to eat as much fat as carbohydrates. Fats are called the energy-storage nutrients. The stored energy in fats can be used if energy from carbohydrates is used up. Often, the energy in fats is used when you are ill. Fat that is stored in your body is used as insulation to keep the body warm. Fat also is used to protect body organs.

Your body needs proteins to build muscles and for growth. Proteins are nutrients made up of nitrogen compounds called amino acids. Amino acids contain the elements carbon, hydrogen, oxygen, and nitrogen.

Your body uses 20 different amino acids. Twelve of these amino acids are made in the body. The other eight amino acids must be taken into the body from the outside. By combining amino acids in different ways, your body is able to make thousands of different kinds of proteins. This protein-making process is called protein synthesis.

Proteins are classified into two groups, depending on the kinds of amino acids they contain. Animal foods provide complete proteins. Complete proteins contain all eight of the amino acids that the body is unable to make. Milk, cheese, meat, poultry, and fish are foods that contain complete protein. Plant proteins are incomplete proteins, because they do not have all eight essential amino acids. Peas, peanuts, and cereal grains are good sources of plant protein. Why do you think it is important for vegetarians to eat a combination of plant proteins?

Vitamins and Minerals

Organic nutrients that are found naturally in many foods are called **vitamins.** Your body can make two of the vitamins it needs. All others must be obtained from food. The vitamins your body makes are vitamins D and K. Your body uses ultraviolet rays from the sun to make vitamin D. Vitamin K is made in the large intestine.

Vitamins are needed in small amounts for the body to function properly. Most vitamins work as a team with other vitamins or nutrients. For example, some vitamins help change carbohydrates and fats into energy. Others stimulate growth and maintain bones and tissues.

What did you have for breakfast this morning? If you had a glass of orange juice, a glass of fortified milk, and some cereal, you took in some important vitamins. Two of these vitamins are vitamin C and vitamin D. Orange juice

Figure 26–2 What nutrient provides you with insulation against the cold?

ACTIVITY 26–1

PROBLEM: What can you learn about sodium and fat content from food labels?

Science Process Skills
interpreting data, comparing, calculating

Background Information
People who are watching their diets often are concerned about sodium and fat intake. The average person should consume no more than 2000 to 3000 milligrams of sodium per day. No more than 30 percent of your daily calories should come from fat.

Materials
10 food labels from various products

Procedure
1. Copy the Data Table shown. Include numbers 1 through 10. Then, list the foods for which you have labels in the food column.
2. **PREDICT**   Which foods do you think have the highest sodium content? Which do you think have the highest fat content? Place a check mark next to each food that you predict has the highest sodium content and a check mark next to each food that you think has the highest fat content. To check your predictions, continue the activity.
3. Review each food label. In the Data Table, record the serving size, milligrams of sodium per serving, and the grams of fat per serving.
4. **CALCULATE**   To calculate the percentage of calories that come from fat in a product,

multiply the number of grams of fat per serving by 9. (Each gram of fat contains 9 calories.) Then divide that number by the number of calories per serving. Multiply your answer by 100 to get the percentage of calories that come from fat for each product. Record the percentages in the Data Table.

Observations
1. **a.** Which food contains the most sodium per serving?   **b.** the least?
2. **a.** Which food contains the highest percentage of fat-derived calories?   **b.** the lowest?

Conclusions
1. **a.** Were your predictions accurate? **b.** Why did you make the predictions that you did?
2. What can you learn about sodium and fat content from food labels?

Data Table: Sodium and Fats in Food					
FOOD	PREDICTION		SERVING DATA		PERCENTAGE OF FAT
	SODIUM	FAT	SIZE	SODIUM PER SERVING IN MG	FAT PER SERVING IN G	
1. 2.						
10.						

Table 26-1   Vitamins

FAT-SOLUBLE VITAMINS

Vitamin	Needed for:	Best Sources
A (retinol)	Healthy teeth, bones, skin, and eyes	Orange and dark green vegetables, eggs, fruit, liver, milk
D (calciferol)	Strong bones and teeth	Eggs, milk, made by the skin in sunlight
E (trocopherol)	Formation of blood cells; reproduction	Leafy vegetables, vegetable oils
K	Blood clotting	Green vegetables, tomatoes

WATER-SOLUBLE VITAMINS

Vitamin	Needed for:	Best Sources
C (ascorbic acid)	Healthy bones and skin; healing	Citrus fruits, dark green vegetables
B_1 (thiamine)	Use of carbohydrates; healthy heart and nerves	Liver, pork, whole grain foods
B_2 (riboflavin)	Use of nutrients, growth	Eggs, green vegetables, milk
B_3 (niacin)	Use of protein; energy	Beans, chicken, eggs, tuna
B_6 (pyridoxine)	Formation of red blood cells; healthy nervous system	Bananas, fish, spinach, whole grain foods
B_{12} (cobalamin)	Formation of red blood cells; healthy nervous system	Eggs, meat, milk

is a good source of vitamin C. Milk that has been fortified is rich in vitamin D. Many of the vitamins your body needs are listed in Table 26-1.

☞ Notice that the vitamins listed in Table 26-1 are classified into two groups. These groups are fat-soluble vitamins and water-soluble vitamins. All vitamins dissolve either in fat or in water. Fat-soluble vitamins are found in foods that contain fats and oils. These vitamins can be stored in your body cells for several days. Water-soluble vitamins are not stored in the body. If water-soluble vitamins are not used the day they are taken in, they are excreted from the body. Look at Table 26–1. What kind of vitamin is vitamin C?

Study Hint

As you study the vitamin and mineral charts, do not confuse vitamin K with the mineral potassium. Potassium has the chemical symbol K.

Your body needs inorganic nutrients as well as organic nutrients to work properly. Most inorganic substances do not contain carbon. **Minerals** are inorganic nutrients needed by the body. Minerals play an important part in the development of your body. For example, the mineral calcium is needed for the formation of strong bones and teeth. Minerals also aid in the growth of body cells. Minerals either can be used quickly and eliminated, or stored in the body. Minerals are excreted through the skin in perspiration and by the kidneys in urine.

Some minerals are needed in large amounts in the body. Others are needed in very small amounts. Minerals found in large amounts include calcium, phosphorus, and sodium. Why do you think your body uses a lot of calcium? Your body needs only a very small amount of iron, iodine, sulfur, and zinc. Iron is needed for the formation of red blood cells.

Table 26-2 Minerals

MINERAL	NEEDED FOR:	BEST SOURCES
Calcium	Strong bones and teeth; heart and nerve action; blood clotting	Milk and milk products, canned fish, green leafy vegetables
Iodine	Function of the thyroid gland	Seafood, iodized salt
Iron	Formation of red blood cells	Red meats, whole grains, liver, egg yolk, nuts, green leafy vegetables
Magnesium	Strong bones and muscles; nerve action	Nuts, whole grains, green leafy vegetables
Phosphorus	Strong bones and teeth; energy	Red meat, fish, eggs, milk products, poultry
Potassium	Fluid balance in cells; nerve action	Bananas, oranges, meat, bran
Sodium	Water balance; nerve action	Table salt, found naturally in many foods
Sulfur	Formation of body cells	Beans, peanuts, wheat germ, beef
Zinc	Formation of enzymes; proper taste and smell	Meat, eggs, seafood, milk, whole grains

Water

More than two-thirds of your body is made up of water. Although water is not a nutrient, water is needed by your body. For example, water is a basic part of your blood and tissue fluid. Water is needed to carry out the life processes. Water also is needed for every chemical change that takes place in the body. Most chemical reactions only take place in water. When you are hot, water acts as a coolant by evaporating from your skin as perspiration. In digestion, water is used to carry nutrients to your blood. Water also is necessary for the removal of waste products through your kidneys and skin.

Figure 26–3 You could live for about a month without food, but only for a week without water.

Think and Discuss

1. What are nutrients? Why do you need nutrients?
2. What are minerals?
3. Why must you include fat in your diet?
4. Are proteins organic or inorganic nutrients? Why?
★ 5. Why should you avoid low-carbohydrate "liquid diets?"

26-2 The Healthful Diet

Have you ever heard the expression, "You are what you eat"? This is a fairly true statement. The foods you eat help determine how you look and feel.

How do you know how much of a nutrient you need? The Food and Drug Administration has made a list of the U.S. Recommended Daily Allowance, or **U.S. RDA**, for each nutrient. The U.S. RDA is how much of a nutrient a person should consume each day to maintain good health. Most packaged foods contain labels that include the percentage of the U.S. RDA found in that food.

Food Groups

Foods are classified into four groups. A balanced diet consists of foods from each of the food groups. The four food groups are the dairy group, the meat group, the

Key Points
- The four food groups are the dairy group, the meat group, the vegetable-fruit group, and the bread-cereal group.

- Food energy is measured in Calories, or kilocalories.

Table 26-3 Basic Food Groups	
	MAJOR NUTRIENTS EACH GROUP PROVIDES
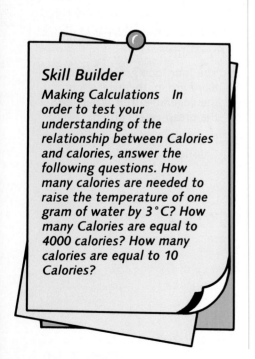	Carbohydrates, Protein, Fat, Vitamins A, D, B_2, and B_{12}, Calcium, Phosphorus, and Zinc
	Protein, Fat, Vitamins B_1 and B_{12}, Iron, Phosphorus, Potassium, and Zinc
	Carbohydrates, Vitamins A, C, and B_2, Calcium, Iron, Potassium, and Magnesium
	Carbohydrates, Vitamins B_1 and B_6, Magnesium, Potassium, Iron, and Zinc

Health and Safety Tip

Milk is essential no matter what your age or weight. Low fat or skim milk has more calcium and less fat than whole milk.

Skill Builder

Making Calculations   In order to test your understanding of the relationship between Calories and calories, answer the following questions. How many calories are needed to raise the temperature of one gram of water by 3°C? How many Calories are equal to 4000 calories? How many calories are equal to 10 Calories?

vegetable-fruit group, and the bread-cereal group. Table 26-3 shows the four basic food groups. Each group is a good source of different nutrients. Which food group is the only source of vitamin C?

A balanced diet provides your body with the nutrients it needs to function properly. You can use the four food groups as a guide in planning well-balanced meals. A diet based on proper servings from the four food groups will provide your body with the nutrients it needs. People who are growing or are very active usually need more servings from the meat group and the vegetable-fruit group. You probably are one of these people.

Calories

Your body must have energy to stay alive. In fact, everything you do requires energy. For example, your heart needs energy to pump blood throughout your body. You use energy to sit, to walk, and to run. Even sleeping requires energy. The faster you grow and the more active you are, the more energy you need. Where do you get this energy?

Food provides you with energy. The energy in food is measured in **kilocalories,** or thousands of calories. Kilocalories is also written as Calories with a capital C. A Calorie is the amount of heat or energy needed to raise one kilogram of water one degree Celsius. How many calories are in a 300-kilocalorie meal?

464   Human Health

ACTIVITY 26–2

PROBLEM: How can you plan a daily balanced diet?

Science Process Skills
classifying, organizing, researching

Background Information
Daily meals should be made up of foods from the basic food groups. Planning a meal takes some time. When you plan a balanced meal, you should be sure that you choose a variety of foods. Balanced meals provide you with the nutrients and calories that your body needs to work properly.

Materials
calorie counters (optional)
reference books

Procedure
1. Classify each of the foods listed in the Data Table into their proper food group.
2. Use the information provided to plan a balanced breakfast, a balanced lunch, and a balanced dinner, using these guidelines:
   a. The total number of calories for each meal must be between 600 and 1000 calories.
   b. One food per meal must be from the milk, meat, and cereal food groups.
   c. Two foods per meal must be from the vegetable-fruit group.
3. Place each meal in a menu plan that gives the name of the food, the food group in which the food is classified, and the number of calories for each food.
4. Add the total number of calories for each meal to get the total calories for the three meals.

Observations
1. **RESEARCH** Find out the main nutrients supplied by each food group. Which nutrients are provided most by the foods that you chose?
2. a. Which foods had the most calories?
   b. Which foods had the fewest calories?

Data Table: Foods and Calories

FOOD	CALORIES	FOOD	CALORIES
Whole milk	160	1 slice of bread	70
Milk (2% Fat)	120	1 egg	80
Pork and beans	330	Orange juice	110
Rice	100	Bologna	40
Cream of potato soup	110	Strawberry jam	18
Raisin bran	110	Baked potato	100
Margarine	100	String beans	20
Egg noodles	110	Spaghetti and meatballs	330
Cauliflower	20	Salad dressing (oil and vinegar)	125
Hamburger	250	Hamburger bun	160
Ham slice	250	Banana	100
Apple	80	Carrots	30
Chicken	180	Fish filet	200
Mayonnaise	70	Lettuce	10
Spinach	25	Tomato slice	6

Conclusions
1. Do you think that it is easy to plan three balanced meals each day? Explain your answer.
2. a. According to your menu, what was your total calorie intake for the day?
   b. Males between 15–18 should have 2800 calories per day. Females between 15–18 should have 2200 calories per day. Compare the total calories of your meals with these numbers.
3. What are four things to consider as you plan a daily balanced diet?

Each nutrient contains a specific amount of energy. The number of kilocalories in a food item depends on the nutrients that are in the particular food. For example, fat produces the greatest amount of energy. For one gram of fat, 9 kilocalories of energy are produced. Proteins and carbohydrates, however, provide only 4 kilocalories per gram. Do you think a baked potato or french-fried potatoes contain more kilocalories? Why?

Think and Discuss

6. What is a Calorie?

7. List the four food groups. Give three examples of foods in each group.

8. Why do foods with high amounts of fat have more calories than foods that are high in protein?

26-3 Maintaining Good Health

A balanced diet is the first step in maintaining good health. However, good nutrition alone will not guarantee good health. You also must watch your weight, exercise regularly, and get enough rest.

Weight control and the foods you eat are closely related. Your weight is influenced by the amount and kinds of food you eat. A proper diet provides the energy you need for daily activities, growth, body maintenance, and **metabolism** (muh-TAB-uh-lizm). Metabolism is the total of all the chemical reactions in your body cells.

Have you ever heard someone talk about their weight in regard to their metabolic rate? Your metabolic rate is the rate at which the body uses energy, or burns calories. The more energy your body uses, the higher your metabolic rate.

The amount of calories you consume each day, and the number of calories you burn up each day, play an important role in weight control. When you eat the same amount of calories as you use up in energy, your weight remains steady. When you use up more energy in calories than what you eat, you will lose weight. What do you think happens if you eat more food than your body needs for energy?

People who are 20 percent over their ideal body weight are considered **obese** (oh-BEES). Anyone who wants to lose weight should see a doctor. A doctor can help you design an eating program that will meet your daily nutritional needs.

Exercise also is important in maintaining good health. By exercising regularly, you will look and feel your best. For example, exercise strengthens your heart. It firms muscle tissue and makes your body stronger. Exercise promotes better posture and improves endurance. For example, you can run longer and swim farther without getting tired.

Exercise also is important for weight control. It "burns up" excess calories and helps you maintain your weight. The best part about exercise is that it can be fun. Walking, running, dancing, swimming, and bicycling all are good ways to exercise.

Rest is as important as exercise in maintaining good health. Sleep is your main source of rest. The amount of sleep a person needs varies from person to person. However, if you get too little rest, your body will become weak and more prone to illness.

Figure 26–4 Swimming is good exercise that can burn 300–700 Calories per hour.

Health and Safety Tip
Muscle tissue weighs more than fat. Therefore, some active, muscular people may exceed their "ideal body weights," without being obese. Consider this when using ideal weight charts.

Think and Discuss

9. What is metabolism?
10. Identify four things that are important for maintaining good health.
★ 11. Why is exercise important in weight control?

26-4 Nutritional Problems

If you do not eat well-balanced meals, you risk serious illnesses or diseases. Eating disorders and **deficiency** (di-FISH-uhn-see) **diseases** are two kinds of illnesses that are associated with poor nutrition. An eating disorder is a serious disturbance in normal eating patterns. Eating disorders usually are caused by emotional problems. A deficiency disease occurs when a particular nutrient is missing from your diet. Table 26-4 on page 468 shows some common deficiency diseases and their causes.

Key Points
- Anorexia nervosa and bulimia nervosa are eating disorders.
- A deficiency disease is caused by a nutrient that is missing from the diet.

Table 26-4   Nutritional Deficiencies

DISEASE	SYMPTOMS	CAUSED BY A DEFICIENCY OF:
Night blindness	Difficulty seeing in dark	Vitamin A
Rickets	Soft bones and teeth	Vitamin D; Calcium
Pellagra	Rough skin; diarrhea	Vitamin B_3
Anemia	Lack of energy	Vitamins B_6, B_{12}, or Iron
Scurvy	Sore gums	Vitamin C
Goiter	Swollen thyroid gland	Iodine

Two eating disorders that seem to be on the rise in the United States are **anorexia nervosa** (an-uh-REK-see-uh nuhr-VOH-suh) and **bulimia** (byoo-LIM-ee-uh) **nervosa.** Anorexia nervosa is an abnormal refusal to eat. Victims of this disease believe they are fat even when they are extremely underweight. Teenage girls and young women make up the largest percentage of anorexics. If not treated in time, anorexia nervosa can lead to death.

Bulimia nervosa is another kind of eating disorder. Bulimia is different from anorexia in that the victim usually is not underweight. A bulimic will go on a food binge and eat everything in sight. After eating so much food, bulimics feel guilty and force themselves to vomit.

A weakened condition that results when your body is not properly nourished is a disorder called **malnutrition** (mal-noo-TRISH-uhn). "Mal" is the prefix meaning "bad." The word "malnutrition" means bad nutrition. Do you think an overweight person could be malnourished? Most people think malnutrition is caused only by a lack of food. However, malnutrition occurs if a person is eating too many foods from one group and not enough from the others. To avoid malnutrition, eat a balanced diet.

Think and Discuss

12. What is a deficiency disease? What are three examples of deficiency diseases?
13. What is the usual cause of eating disorders?
14. What is the difference between anorexia nervosa and bulimia nervosa?

Skill Builder

Researching   Using library references, find out about food additives. Then, write a report describing the benefits and risks of food additives.

Your body needs a constant supply of energy. The fuel that supplies this energy is food. Many interesting careers involve preparing and inspecting food. Other careers involve planning well-balanced diets.

Meat Cutter

Meat cutters prepare meat in supermarkets, wholesale food stores, and meatpacking plants. Meat cutters in grocery stores arrange and display meat products and assist customers with their purchases.

A meat cutter must have good depth perception and good hand-eye coordination. Both of these characteristics are needed for safe handling of sharp objects. A meat cutter also must have physical strength to lift and move heavy pieces of meat.

Most meat cutters receive on-the-job training. Under the guidance of skilled butchers, a meat cutter learns how to use cutting tools and prepare various cuts of meat.

For more information: Write to the United Food and Commercial International Union, 1775 K St., NW, Washington, DC 20006.

Food Inspector

Food inspectors check plant and animal products to make sure that the products are safe to eat. All stages of food processing are checked by food inspectors to make sure that health regulations are followed and that processing facilities are clean. These inspectors also are concerned with the kinds and amounts of additives placed in foods as well as correct product labeling.

Food inspectors need a high school diploma, some college courses, and experience working with animals and meat products. Valuable courses include biology, zoology, agriculture, and chemistry.

For more information: Write to the United States Department of Agriculture, Food Safety and Inspection Service, Room 3438 South, 14th St. and Independence Ave., SW, Washington, DC 20250.

Dietitian

"You are what you eat" is a saying that points out the importance of good nutrition. Dietitians are concerned with the nutrients in food, their use in the body, and the relationship between diet and health. Most dietitians direct large-scale meal planning for schools, hospitals, and other institutions. Dietitians supervise the planning, preparation, and serving of food and establish budgets for food purchases. Dietitians also train food-service workers and other personnel.

A dietitian must have a college degree with a major in food and nutrition. Many dietitians also have degrees in institution management. Dietitians also should have good organizational skills and work well with others. Valuable high school courses for a future dietitian include home economics, biology, health, chemistry, business administration, and mathematics.

For more information: Write to the American Dietetic Association, 430 North Michigan Ave., Chicago, IL 60611.

Chapter Review

CHAPTER SUMMARY

26-1 Nutrients

- Nutrients are chemical substances in food that supply energy, promote growth, and help repair tissue.
- Organic nutrients needed by the body include carbohydrates, fats, proteins, and vitamins.
- Minerals are inorganic nutrients needed by the body.

26-2 The Healthful Diet

- There are four food groups—the dairy group, the meat group, the vegetable-fruit group, and the bread-cereal group.
- By eating the proper amount of food from all four food groups, you will be getting all the necessary nutrients.

- A Calorie is the amount of energy that is needed to raise one kilogram of water one degree Celsius.
- Food energy is measured in kilocalories.

26-3 Maintaining Good Health

- Proper diet, weight control, exercise, and sufficient rest are necessary to maintain good health.
- Metabolism is the total of the chemical processes in the body.

26-4 Nutritional Problems

- A deficiency disease occurs when a particular nutrient is missing from the diet.
- Anorexia nervosa and bulimia nervosa are eating disorders.

VOCABULARY LIST

anorexia nervosa (468)	fats (458)	minerals (462)	proteins (458)
bulimia nervosa (468)	kilocalories (464)	nutrients (458)	U.S. RDA (463)
carbohydrates (458)	malnutrition (468)	nutrition (457)	vitamins (459)
deficiency diseases (467)	metabolism (466)	obese (467)	

VOCABULARY REVIEW

Matching   Write the word or term from the Vocabulary List that best matches each description.

1. total of the chemical reactions in your body
2. the study of nutrients and their effect on the body
3. amount of a nutrient a person should consume each day for good health
4. 20 percent over ideal body weight
5. chemical substances in food that your body needs
6. a disease in which a nutrient is lacking
7. an abnormal refusal to eat

Finding Word Relationships   Pair each word with a word in the box. Explain in complete sentences how the words are related.

insulation	vitamins	minerals
amino acids	eating disorder	kilocalorie
glucose	malnutrition	

1. bulimia nervosa
2. proteins
3. fats
4. carbohydrates
5. niacin
6. inorganic
7. measurement
8. bad nutrition

True or False Write true if the statement is true. If the statement is false, change the underlined word or words to make the statement true.

1. All organic substances contain carbon.
2. Most plant protein is complete.
3. Minerals are organic nutrients.
4. The energy storage nutrients are carbohydrates.
5. The food group that is the best source of protein is the meat group.
6. An excessive buildup of weight is called obesity.
7. Consistently getting too little rest can cause deficiency diseases.
8. "Food binges" are associated with anorexia nervosa.
9. The food group that is the only source of vitamin C is the vegetable-fruit group.
10. Exercise in addition to weight control will help in weight loss.

Question and Answer Rewrite each heading in the Chapter Outline on page 456 as a question. Then, answer each of the questions you have written.

Interpreting a Table Use the table of the vitamins shown in Table 26-1 (page 461) to answer each of the following.

1. What are the fat-soluble vitamins?
2. What are the water-soluble vitamins?
3. What is another name for vitamin B_3?
4. What is another name for vitamin A?
5. What are two sources of vitamin K?

CONCEPT REVIEW

Writing the Main Ideas Using the Chapter Outline on page 456, write the main idea for each heading in the outline.

Critical Thinking Answer each of the following in complete sentences.

1. Bears hibernate in the winter. Why do you think bears eat foods containing a lot of fat prior to hibernating?
2. Do you think you could survive longer without food or water? Explain your answer.
3. Why should an obese person lose weight gradually, rather than quickly? Explain your answer.
4. In order to lose one pound, your body must use up 3500 Calories. If you use 500 more Calories a day than you eat, how long will it take to lose two pounds?
5. A person with anorexia nervosa or bulimia often is treated by both a psychiatrist and a physician. What would each doctor contribute to the person's treatment?

EXTENSIONS

1. List all the foods you eat for three days. Include breakfast, lunch, dinner, and snacks. Name the food group to which each food belongs and the nutrients it contains.
2. Choose a cereal. Prepare a table listing the ingredients on the box. List the percentage of the U.S. RDA for each ingredient.
3. Use the information in this chapter and library resources to plan a well-balanced menu for a one-week period. Your menu should include the kinds and amounts of foods to be served for breakfasts, lunches, and dinners. Be sure to include foods from each of the four food groups.

Chapter 27

Chapter **27** | Diseases and Disorders

Chapter Outline

I. Infectious Diseases
   A. Causes of Disease
   B. Spread of Disease

II. Body Defenses
   A. First Line of Defense
   B. Second Line of Defense
   C. Chemical Defenses
   D. Immunity

III. Chronic Disorders
   A. Allergies
   B. Hepatitis
   C. Cancer

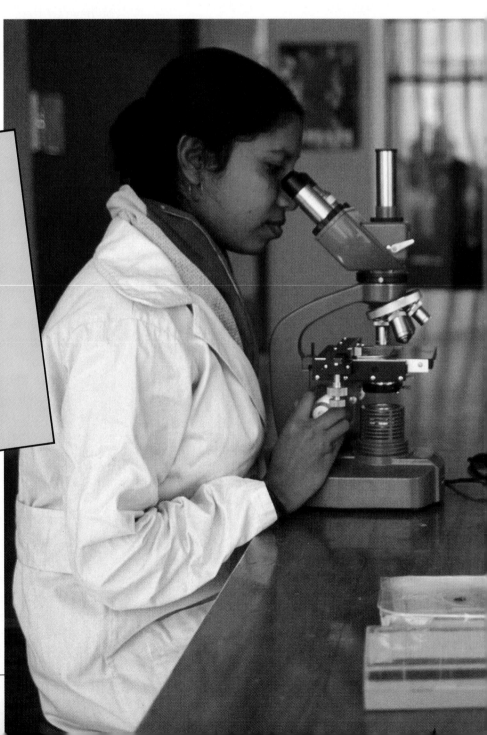

472

After you have completed this chapter, you will be able to

27-1 **name** some causes of infectious disease.

27-1 **list** several ways that infectious diseases are spread.

27-2 **identify** the body's first and second lines of defense against disease.

27-2 **explain** how antibodies fight disease.

27-2 **recognize** the difference between natural and acquired immunity.

27-3 **name** three chronic disorders and their causes.

Science Process Skills

In this chapter, two science skills are highlighted. Symbols show some places where these skills are used.

▲ **Organizing:** When you organize information, you put the information in some kind of order.

▣ **Hypothesizing:** When you hypothesize, you state a suggested answer to a problem based upon known information.

Have you ever heard the expression, "What you don't know can't hurt you"? Don't believe it for a minute. Six hundred years ago, a disease called the Black Plague killed almost one-fourth of the population of Europe. Look around your classroom and imagine that every fourth seat is empty. This is the effect that the Black Plague would have had on your class.

Why was the Black Plague allowed to spread unchecked throughout the population? In the fourteenth century, people did not understand the causes of disease. They did not know how to treat the Black Plague or how to prevent its spread. Today, scientists know that most diseases are caused by **pathogens** *(PATH-uh-juhns). A pathogen is a substance that causes disease.*

Diseases and Disorders   473

27-1 Infectious Diseases

Key Points

- Bacteria, viruses, and fungi can cause infectious diseases.

- Infectious diseases are spread by coughing and sneezing, contaminated food and water, and by contact with an infected person.

How many times have you heard a radio or television commercial state, "Flu season is here"? The "flu," or influenza, is an **infectious** (in-FEK-shus) **disease.** An infectious disease is caused by a pathogen that enters the human body. In the case of flu, the pathogen is a virus. Viruses are the smallest pathogens. People who have the flu often say that they have some kind of virus.

Some infectious diseases can be transmitted, or spread, from one person to another person. An infectious disease that can be transmitted from one person to another person is called a **contagious** (kuhn-TAY-jus) **disease.** Have you ever heard someone with a cold say, "Don't come too close to me, I might be contagious"? The common cold and the flu are examples of contagious diseases.

Causes of Disease

Viruses are not the only kinds of pathogens. Some kinds of bacteria and fungi also cause disease. Some common diseases and the pathogens that cause them are listed in Table 27-1.

Skill Builder

Writing a Biographical Sketch   Use an encyclopedia or other reference book to find out about Typhoid Mary. Write a brief biography about Typhoid Mary that includes information about why she was given this nickname.

Table 27-1 Common Diseases and Their Causes		
DISEASE	PATHOGEN	HOW THE DISEASE IS SPREAD
Athlete's foot	Fungus	Contact with contaminated objects
Botulism	Bacterium	Eating contaminated food
Common cold	More than 100 different viruses	Contact with the mucus or saliva of an infected person
Hepatitis	Virus	Contact with an infected person or eating contaminated foods
Influenza	Virus	Contact with an infected person or with contaminated objects
Malaria	Protozoa	Bite from an infected mosquito
Measles	Virus	Contact with the mucus or saliva of an infected person

How do pathogens cause disease? Most disease-causing bacteria produce **toxins,** or poisons. These toxins interrupt the life processes of cells. Some toxins are released as the bacteria grow. Sometimes, toxins are not released until the bacteria die and break apart.

Some viruses cause disease by destroying cells. Viruses that invade healthy cells change the normal life processes of the cell. As a result, the healthy cells die.

Fungi reproduce in warm, dark, and moist environments. Fungi often grow on, or in, the human body. What parts of the human body do you think that fungi might attack?

Spread of Disease

If you have ever had a contagious disease, there is a chance that the disease was transmitted, or spread to you, by another person. How are diseases spread? Some contagious diseases such as the cold or flu often are transmitted by coughs and sneezes. When an infected person coughs or sneezes, droplets of mucus are sprayed into the air. If you inhale one of these contaminated droplets, you might develop a cold or the flu.

There are several other ways that diseases can be spread. For example, many diseases are spread by taking in water or food that contains a pathogen. Some diseases are spread by contact with a contaminated object. For example, tetanus bacteria often grow on rusty objects. If you step on a rusty nail on which tetanus bacteria are growing, the bacteria can enter your body through the wound.

The bite of an insect also can transmit disease. For example, the bite of an *Anopheles* (a-NOF-uh-leez) mosquito spreads malaria. A kind of protozoan called a *Plasmodium* (plaz-MOH-dee-um) lives in the body of the mosquito. When a person is bitten by an infected mosquito, the *Plasmodium* is injected into the person's blood.

Two contagious diseases spread by contact with another person are gonorrhea (gahn-uh-REE-uh) and syphilis (SIF-uh-lis). The pathogens that cause both gonorrhea and syphilis are transmitted by sexual contact with an infected person. For this reason, gonorrhea and syphilis are classified as sexually transmitted diseases.

Figure 27–1 Polluted water (top) and mosquitoes (bottom) are two ways in which diseases can be spread.

If left untreated, gonorrhea and syphilis can cause serious health problems.

Food Poisoning

Have you or anyone you know ever had food poisoning? Food poisoning is caused by the growth of bacteria in improperly stored or packaged foods. Some of the ways that the growth of bacteria is slowed or stopped in packaged foods are shown in Table 27-2.

Table 27-2 Methods of Preventing Food Spoilage	
CANNING	FREEZING
Foods are cooked at high temperatures and stored in airtight cans or jars.	Foods stored at a temperature of −18 °C or below
DRYING	COLD STORAGE
Most of the water is removed from the food.	Foods stored at temperatures between −1 °C and 10 °C
CURING	IRRADIATION (MEATS ONLY)
Food is cooked or dried. Chemical preservatives, such as salt, sugar, or vinegar are added to the food.	Use of ultraviolet rays or gamma rays

Health and Safety Tip

When buying food, always check the expiration dates printed on food labels. Do not buy food after the expiration date has passed.

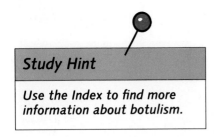

Study Hint

Use the Index to find more information about botulism.

The bacteria that cause botulism (BAHCH-uh-lizm) cannot carry on their life processes if oxygen is present. Botulism is a kind of food poisoning caused by a bacterium that grows in improperly canned foods. Botulism bacteria produce toxins that affect the human nervous system. Death can occur from respiratory or heart failure. One sign of botulism is a bulging can. Why do you suppose that a can with botulism bacteria would bulge?

Another kind of food poisoning is caused by *Salmonella* bacteria. *Salmonella* bacteria grow in foods, such as eggs, ground meat, chicken, and sausages. Usually, food handlers who are contaminated transfer *Salmonella*

ACTIVITY 27-1

PROBLEM: How is bacterial growth slowed or stopped in packaged foods?

Science Process Skills
observing, comparing, analyzing

Background Information
Harmful bacteria grow on and in food because conditions are just right for bacteria to grow and reproduce. To stop bacterial growth, food manufacturers must take away one or more of the conditions bacteria need. The conditions that bacteria need are food, water, darkness, and proper temperature. Most bacteria grow within a range of 27°C to 38°C. Bacteria also need the right pH. A substance cannot be too acidic or too basic. Bacteria also cannot grow if there is too much salt.

Materials
packaging and product labels from 10 different foods

Procedure
1. Copy the Data Table shown.
2. Study the foods shown and the ways they are packaged.
3. Write the name of each food and explain if each food is canned, boxed, in a jar, in a liquid, frozen, and so on. Write as much information as you can that describes how each food is packaged.
4. Place a check mark in the column of the Data Table that indicates which condition

has been removed to control bacterial growth for each food.
5. Repeat steps 3–4 for the 10 different foods for which you have packaging labels.

Observations
1. What bacterial growth condition is removed from boxed foods stored on shelves?
2. What two ways are vegetables packaged to help slow or stop bacterial growth?
3. **ANALYZE** What added ingredient do you find in most canned vegetables that slows or prevents bacterial growth?

Conclusions
1. List several ways bacterial growth is slowed or stopped in packaged foods.
2. When a food is canned, the food first is heated to high temperatures and sealed in airtight cans. How does the canning process prevent bacterial growth?
3. **INFER** Whole milk is pasteurized to kill the bacteria in the milk. Why does bacteria eventually grow in milk and sour it? Where do the new bacteria come from?

Data Table: Packaged Foods and Bacteria						
	GROWTH CONDITION REMOVED					
FOOD	Food supply	Water	Proper temperature	Proper pH level	Amount of salt	Darkness
Sauerkraut						
Cured ham						
Pickles						
Powdered milk						

bacteria to these foods. The symptoms of *Salmonella* food poisoning are vomiting, cramps, and fever. What body system is affected by the *Salmonella* bacteria?

AIDS

Acquired Immune Deficiency Syndrome, or AIDS, is the name of a deadly illness caused by a virus. The virus is HIV. HIV attacks the cells of the **immune system.** The immune system is made up of cells and tissues that help the body fight disease.

Like all disease-causing viruses, HIV causes healthy body cells to produce more of the virus. As the HIV virus takes over the cells of the immune system, it destroys these cells. Therefore, people with AIDS lose their ability to fight disease. For this reason, people with AIDS easily get diseases that most people can fight off.

People with AIDS have the HIV virus in their blood and body fluids. The HIV virus can enter the bloodstream through sexual contact with someone who is infected with the AIDS virus. The HIV virus also can be transmitted by intravenous drug users who use contaminated needles.

Histoplasmosis

Have you ever noticed that there are many pigeons living in large cities? A fungus that grows in the wastes of pigeons causes a respiratory disease in humans called histoplasmosis (his-toh-plaz-MOH-sis). People can get histoplasmosis by inhaling or ingesting spores of the *Histoplasma* fungus. The *Histoplasma* fungus also may be spread by direct contact with the feces of an infected pigeon. Why do you think that many cities have passed laws that prohibit feeding pigeons?

Think and Discuss

1. What is an infectious disease?
2. Name three pathogens.
3. What are three diseases caused by viruses?
4. List three ways that contagious diseases are spread.
5. Why do you think it is unwise to walk barefoot in a park where there are many pigeons?

Health and Safety Tip
AIDS is not transmitted by casual contact.

Figure 27-2 What is dangerous about what this man is doing?

ACTIVITY 27-2

PROBLEM: Is AIDS a worldwide epidemic?

Science Process Skills
classifying, calculating, sequencing

Background Information
Acquired Immune Deficiency Syndrome, or AIDS, first was reported in the United States in 1981. Since 1981, the number of cases of AIDS has increased in the United States and throughout the world.

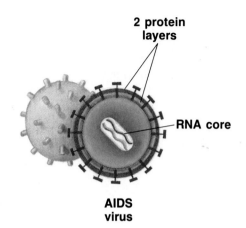

2 protein layers

RNA core

AIDS virus

Materials
paper and pencil
calculator (optional)

Procedure
1. Study the Data Table shown.

Data Table: Countries with Most Reported AIDS Cases*			
AFRICA		**NORTH AMERICA**	
Burundi	1408	Canada	2156
Congo	1250	Haiti	1455
Kenya	2732	Mexico	1502
Malawi	2586	United States	80,996
Rwanda	987		
Tanzania	3055	**EUROPE**	
Uganda	4006	France	4211
Zambia	933	Great Britain	1862
		Italy	2556
SOUTH AMERICA		Netherlands	636
Brazil	3687	Spain	1471
		West Germany	2488
AUSTRALIA	1024		

* Cases as of end of 1988

2. Rank the countries in order from the country with the most reported AIDS cases to the fewest reported AIDS cases.

3. **CALCULATE** Total the number of reported cases in Europe, Africa, South America, North America, and Australia.
4. Rank the 5 continents in order from the continent with the most reported AIDS cases to the fewest reported AIDS cases.
5. **CALCULATE** Total the number of reported AIDS cases in the countries listed in the Data Table.

Observations
1. Which country has the most reported AIDS cases?
2. Which continent has the most reported AIDS cases?
3. What is the total number of reported AIDS cases in all of the countries with the most reported AIDS cases?
4. How many countries have reported cases greater than 3000?

Conclusions
1. Do you think AIDS is a worldwide epidemic? Give reasons for your answer.
2. **INFER** Find the definition of the word "pandemic." Do you think AIDS is pandemic? Give reasons for your answer.

27-2 Body Defenses

- The skin and the mucus and cilia of the respiratory system are the body's first line of defense against disease.

- White blood cells are the body's second line of defense against disease.

- Natural immunity is present from birth. Acquired immunity is developed during the lifetime of a person.

Your body is under constant attack by pathogens. If pathogens are not destroyed or prevented from entering your body, you may become ill or get an infection. Your body, however, has two lines of defense that protect you against most pathogens.

First Line of Defense

Your skin is the body's first line of defense. In fact, if your skin is not broken, it is almost germ-proof. The perspiration, or sweat, made by the skin contains substances that slow or kill bacteria. For example, salts in perspiration help prevent the growth of bacteria on the skin. Oils and waxes produced by the skin also help keep out pathogens.

Body openings, such as your mouth and nose, are places where pathogens can enter your body. However, other first-line defenses prevent pathogens from entering body openings. For example, hairs in your nose filter air and stop many pathogens. Tiny hairlike cilia (SIL-ee-uh) and mucus in your respiratory system trap pathogens before they can enter the lungs. Mucus also contains substances that kill pathogens. Sneezing and coughing help remove pathogens from the body.

Second Line of Defense

What happens when pathogens get through your body's first line of defense? Then, special white blood cells, called **phagocytes** (FAG-uh-syts), go to work. Phagocytes are shapeless cells that move like amoebas. Phagocytes also feed like amoebas. These white blood cells can surround pathogens and destroy them.

▲ Some phagocytes can leave the blood and move to infected areas. These cells are called leucocytes (LOO-koh-syts). If you have ever had an infected cut on your finger, you have seen the work of leucocytes. During an infection, leucocytes kill pathogens at the site of the infection. The finger may feel hot to the touch, look red, and be very sore. Pus forms at the site of the infection. Pus is made out of dead pathogens, dead leucocytes, and

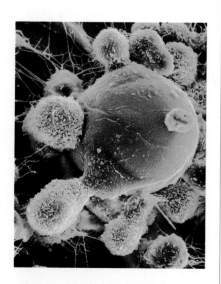

Figure 27–3 This phagocyte is destroying a foreign substance in the blood.

plasma, the liquid part of the blood. How would you know that your leucocytes were working properly if you had an infected cut on your finger?

Chemical Defenses

A chemical defense system also protects your body against disease. The immune system controls the body's chemical defenses. The immune system is made up of cells and tissues that identify and kill pathogens.

Interferon

A chemical called **interferon** (in-tur-FEER-ahn) is made by cells when a virus invades the body. Interferon slows or stops viruses from reproducing. Unlike antibodies, interferon attacks all viruses. However, interferon made by one kind of organism cannot be used by another kind of organism. If you are infected by a virus, only human interferon will help you fight off the disease. Today, scientists use genetic-engineering techniques to make human interferon.

Antibodies and Antigens

What happens when a pathogen enters your body? Your body immediately recognizes that a foreign substance, or **antigen** (AN-tuh-jun), is in the body. For example, an antigen may be the capsid, or protein coat, of a virus. The body responds to the antigen by producing **antibodies.** An antibody is a protein made by your body to fight off a specific antigen.

Antibodies fit a specific antigen like two pieces of a jigsaw puzzle. Once the antibody connects to the antigen, special white blood cells engulf the pathogens.

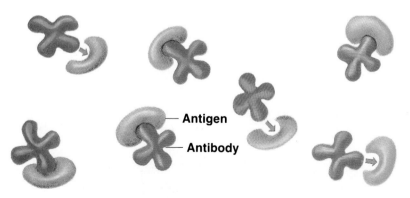

Antigen

Antibody

Figure 27–4 An antigen and an antibody fit together like pieces of a jigsaw puzzle.

Immunity

When a person has resistance to a specific disease, that person has **immunity** (im-MYOON-i-tee). You have two kinds of immunity, natural immunity and **acquired** (uh-KWY-urd) **immunity.** Natural immunity is your body's natural defense against certain diseases. In fact, you are born with natural immunity to many diseases that infect other organisms.

There are several ways of acquiring immunity. You can be injected with a serum. A serum is a substance that contains antibodies against a certain disease. Serums, however, provide only temporary immunity.

One kind of acquired immunity is called **passive immunity.** Passive immunity is acquired when you are injected with antibodies against a certain disease. Passive immunity also can be acquired by a developing baby. The developing baby receives antibodies from its mother. Why do you think that this kind of immunity is not called natural immunity?

Once you have been exposed to some diseases, your body continues to make antibodies against those diseases. This kind of immunity is called **active immunity.** Active immunity usually is permanent. Have you ever had the mumps? If you have, you now have active immunity against the mumps.

Another way to get active immunity is to get a **vaccine.** Most vaccines are made from dead or weakened bacteria or viruses. Vaccines, however, do not cause you to get the disease. When you get a vaccine for measles, your body begins to produce antibodies against the measles virus.

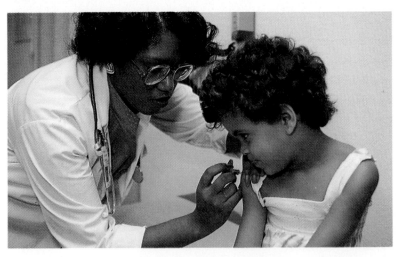

Figure 27–5 A vaccine will help protect this child against the measles virus.

These antibodies remain in the body and protect you from future infections of the measles virus.

Drugs also have been developed to help your body fight pathogens. For example, infections caused by bacteria often are treated with **antibiotics** (an-ti-by-AHT-iks). Antibiotics are chemical substances that kill bacteria or prevent the reproduction of bacteria. Some antibiotics are made from fungi or bacteria. Three widely used antibiotics are penicillin, streptomycin, and tetracycline. Sulfa drugs also are used to fight disease. Doctors often prescribe sulfa drugs to fight bacterial infections of the digestive and urinary systems.

Think and Discuss

6. What is an antigen?
7. How does an antibody fight disease?
8. How does the skin help protect your body against disease?
9. What is the difference between natural and acquired immunity?
★ 10. Why do surgeons wear masks and gloves during operations?

27-3 Chronic Disorders

Some illnesses may last for a long time or can reoccur. These illnesses are called chronic disorders. Allergies, hepatitis (hep-uh-TYT-is), and cancer are examples of chronic disorders.

Key Point
- Cancer, allergies, and hepatitis are three chronic disorders.

Allergies

Do you know someone who sneezes or develops watery eyes if they come in contact with a certain plant or animal? This person probably suffers from an **allergy** (AL-ur-jee). An allergy is an abnormal reaction to a substance in the environment.

Any substance that causes an allergy is called an **allergen** (AL-ur-jun). Common allergens include plant pollen, pet dandruff, and household dust. Hay fever is an

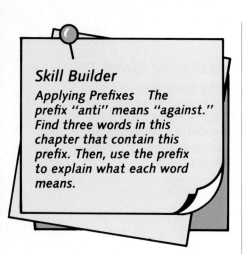
allergy to plant pollen. Why do you suppose many people develop hay fever during the spring and summer?

Sneezing and watery eyes are common symptoms of allergies. The symptoms of an allergy often are called an allergic reaction. Rashes, headaches, and difficulty in breathing are other allergic reactions.

Hepatitis

Hepatitis is caused by a virus that infects the liver. The first symptoms of hepatitis are fatigue, muscle pain, appetite loss, and jaundice (JAWN-dis), or yellowing of the skin. As hepatitis develops, the liver becomes enlarged and tender.

The most common kinds of hepatitis are type A and type B. Hepatitis A, or infectious hepatitis, is spread through contact with a contaminated person. Eating contaminated food or drinking contaminated water also can cause hepatitis A. Hepatitis B, or serum hepatitis, often is spread by the transfusion of contaminated blood or the use of a contaminated needle.

Cancer

You probably have heard the word "cancer" many times. You may have wondered, "What exactly is cancer?" You have learned that normal cells grow and reproduce in an orderly way. Cancer cells, however, reproduce very rapidly in a disorderly way.

As cancer cells grow, they compete with normal body cells for food and oxygen. Because cancer cells grow so rapidly, they use up the available food and oxygen. This destroys normal body cells, tissues, and organs.

▲ Chemicals and radiation can cause cancer. Some kinds of cancer also are caused by viruses. Most forms of cancer, however, are not considered to be contagious. Why do you suppose that cancer victims cannot transmit the disease?

Table 27-3	Seven Warning Signs of Cancer

1. A sore that does not heal
2. Unusual bleeding or discharge
3. Thickening or lump in the breast or elsewhere
4. Continued indigestion or difficulty in swallowing
5. A nagging cough
6. Obvious change in a wart or mole
7. Change in bowel or bladder habits

Think and Discuss

11. Name three chronic disorders.

12. What is hepatitis?

13. How can a drug addict spread hepatitis?

Cancer Detection and Prevention

Cancer is the second leading cause of death in the United States. Scientists are working hard to find cures for cancer. But doctors and scientists agree that the best way to beat cancer is to prevent it from occurring. The next best thing to preventing cancer is to detect it early in its development.

Cancer is the abnormal growth and uncontrolled reproduction of cells. Cancer cells crowd out normal cells by robbing them of food and space. Cancer can occur in just about any part of the body. Some common types of cancer include skin cancer, breast cancer, and lung cancer.

Educating people about cancer prevention and detection has become a major goal of medical scientists. Perhaps you have picked up a favorite magazine and read an article about preventing skin cancer.

Many skin cancers are caused by too much exposure to the sun. Using sunscreens and wearing protective clothing can help to reduce the risk of skin cancer. Skin cancer is the easiest form of cancer to cure if it is detected early. One common sign of skin cancer is a change in a mole or other skin mark. Many magazine articles about skin cancer include photographs that show you how to recognize a mole that may be cancerous.

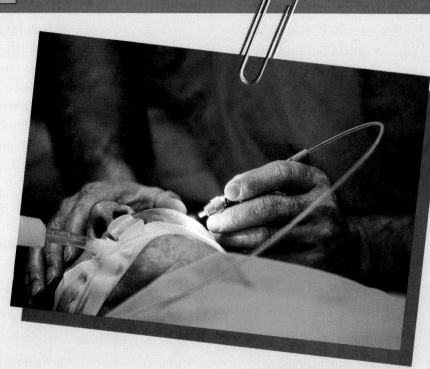

Another type of cancer that has received a lot of attention is breast cancer. Women are encouraged to have breast X-rays, or mammograms, to identify any tiny cancerous tumors that may be present. Women are also encouraged to practice breast self-examination. Diagrams and pamphlets that describe the techniques of breast self-examination are available free of charge from the American Cancer Society.

The prevention of lung cancer has been a major issue since the 1960s, when the Surgeon General's report linked cigarette smoking and lung cancer. Scientists have since discovered other likely causes of lung cancer, such as industrial asbestos and air pollution. However, the best way to prevent lung cancer is to avoid smoking. With lung cancer, an ounce of prevention is certainly worth a pound of cure, because lung cancer is seldom detected early enough to make recovery possible.

To Think About
- Why is a cancer in the early stages much easier to cure than cancer that is more advanced?
- Why do you think skin cancer is one of the easiest cancers to treat?

Chapter Review

CHAPTER SUMMARY

27-1 Infectious Diseases

- Infectious diseases are caused by pathogens.
- Bacteria, viruses, and fungi can be spread by coughing, sneezing, drinking contaminated water, eating contaminated food, or by direct contact with an infected person.

27-2 Body Defenses

- The skin and the cilia and mucus in the respiratory system are the body's first line of defense against disease.
- White blood cells are your body's second line of defense against disease.

- Natural immunity is present in a person at birth.
- Two kinds of acquired immunity that develop during the lifetime of a person are passive immunity and active immunity.
- Antibiotics are drugs that help fight diseases.

27-3 Chronic Disorders

- An allergy is an unusual response to a substance in the environment.
- Hepatitis is a viral infection of the liver.
- Cancer is the rapid, uncontrolled growth of cells.

VOCABULARY LIST

acquired immunity (482)	antibodies (481)	immunity (482)	pathogens (473)
active immunity (482)	antigen (481)	infectious disease (474)	phagocytes (480)
allergen (483)	contagious disease (474)	interferon (481)	toxins (475)
allergy (483)	immune system (478)	passive immunity (482)	vaccine (482)
antibiotics (483)			

VOCABULARY REVIEW

Matching   Write the word or term from the Vocabulary List that best matches each description.

1. a disease caused by a pathogen
2. drugs used to fight bacterial infections
3. proteins made by the body that fight disease
4. immunity acquired when injected with a serum
5. abnormal response to a substance in the environment
6. poisons released by bacteria
7. drugs containing weakened or dead bacteria and viruses
8. infectious disease spread by contact with a victim

9. a pollen grain
10. permanent resistance against disease

Identifying Relationships   Identify the word or term in each group that does not belong. Explain why it does not belong with the group.

1. antibiotics, antibodies, allergen
2. allergy, interferon, hay fever
3. immune system, cancer, hepatitis
4. cilia, mucus, leucocytes
5. immunity, cancer, allergies
6. dust, pollen, lymphocyte
7. pathogens, antibodies, phagocytes
8. antibiotics, sulfa drugs, phagocytes
9. acquired immunity, vaccine, infection
10. macrophage, leucocyte, *Salmonella*

Completion   Write the word or words that best complete each sentence.

1. Athlete's foot and _____ are two kinds of fungus infections.
2. People with AIDS have the HIV virus in their _____ and body fluids.
3. Diseases can be transmitted by taking in _____ or food that contains pathogens.
4. Two requirements for the growth of pathogens are _____ and moisture.
5. Your body's second line of defense against disease is _____.
6. Illnesses that last for a long time are called _____ disorders.
7. Many children get vaccinations for _____, tetanus, and polio before entering school.
8. Three kinds of antibiotics are _____, streptomycin, and tetracycline.
9. The _____ fights pathogens that get past your body's first two lines of defense.

10. Enlargement of the _____ is a symptom of hepatitis.

Finding the Main Ideas   Use the section number to find the sentence that answers each question. Then, write the sentence.

1. What is an infectious disease? (27-1)
2. How do people get histoplasmosis? (27-1)
3. How is *Salmonella* transmitted? (27-1)
4. How are gonorrhea and syphilis transmitted? (27-1)
5. How does perspiration help the body fight disease? (27-2)
6. What kind of acquired immunity does a person get from a serum? (27-2)
7. What chemical is made by the cells when a virus invades the body? (27-2)
8. What is cancer? (27-3)
9. What is an allergy? (27-3)
10. How is hepatitis B transmitted? (27-3)

Writing for Understanding   One way to find out if you understand something is to write a brief summary of the information in your own words. Reread Section 27-2, Body Defenses, on pages 480–483, and write a brief summary of the information.

Critical Thinking   Answer each of the following in complete sentences.

1. Why do dentists wash their hands before examining each patient?

2. Why should you always sneeze or cough into a handkerchief or tissue? Which is better to use? Why?
3. Why do you think your body has several lines of defense?
4. Why do cancer cells travel to other parts of the body?
5. Why must a person infected with AIDS avoid getting a cold or flu?
6. How might hepatitis B be transmitted from one person to another?

1. Pneumonia, typhoid fever, dysentery, and herpes are infectious diseases. Look up each disease in an encyclopedia. Prepare a chart listing the pathogen, symptoms, and method of transmission.

2. Poison ivy, poison oak, and poison sumac are plants that cause allergic reactions in most people. Research and draw a picture of each plant. Under each picture, describe how each plant is harmful.

Chapter 28

Chapter

Drugs, Alcohol, and Tobacco

Objectives

After you have completed this chapter, you will be able to

28-1 **compare** over-the-counter and prescription drugs.

28-1 **name** some commonly abused drugs.

28-1 **identify** some of the dangers of drug abuse.

28-2 **explain** how alcohol affects the body.

28-2 **describe** some of the physical effects of alcoholism.

28-3 **name** three harmful substances in tobacco.

28-3 **list** some tobacco-related illnesses.

Science Process Skills

In this chapter, two science skills are highlighted. Symbols show some places where these skills are used.

▶ **Inferring:** When you infer, you form a conclusion based upon facts and not direct observation.

❯ **Predicting:** When you predict, you state in advance how and why something will occur.

When used properly, drugs serve a useful purpose and can do wonderful things. For example, doctors use drugs to treat and prevent diseases. Each year, drugs used for medical purposes improve or save millions of lives. However, drugs also can be dangerous when used improperly. For this reason, the governments of many countries control the use of some medicinal drugs, and all drugs that do not have an approved medical use. Drugs regulated by the government are called controlled substances.

28-1 Types of Drugs

Key Points

- Prescription drugs can be bought only with a doctor's permission. Over-the-counter drugs can be bought without a prescription.

- Stimulants, depressants, hallucinogens, and narcotics are commonly abused drugs.

- Drug abuse can result in addiction, tolerance, and overdose.

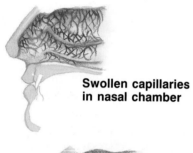

Swollen capillaries in nasal chamber

Nasal spray reduces swelling

Figure 28-1 Decongestants relieve a stuffy nose by reducing swelling in the nasal chamber.

What is a **drug?** A drug is any chemical substance that causes a change in the body. Some drugs cause physical changes in the body. Other drugs change behavior.

Have you ever waited nervously while a doctor prepared to give you a shot? Injection is one way drugs enter the body. Drugs also can be inhaled, swallowed, or placed on the skin.

Drugs for Medical Use

There are two kinds of drugs for medical use. Drugs that can be bought only with a doctor's written permission are called **prescription drugs.** Antibiotics are one group of prescription drugs.

➤ Have you ever received a drug prescription? If so, the prescription was written only for you. Before writing a prescription, a doctor considers your illness, age, medical history, and your size and weight. That is why your prescription should be used only by you in the exact way it was prescribed. What might happen if someone else used your drug prescription?

➤ Medical drugs that can be bought without a doctor's prescription are called **over-the-counter drugs.** Aspirin, decongestants, and antacids are common over-the-counter drugs. Aspirin is used to relieve pain, and to reduce fever and inflammation. Decongestants relieve a stuffy nose caused by colds and allergies. What do antacids do? They neutralize excess stomach acids. You may remember that too much stomach acid can cause heartburn and other stomach problems.

Commonly Abused Drugs

The improper use of a drug is called **drug abuse.** You probably are aware that drug abuse is a major problem in the United States. How are drugs abused? They can be abused in different ways. For example, using too much of a drug or using a drug for the wrong reasons are forms of drug abuse. The use of illegal drugs also is drug abuse. Usually, illegal drugs are the most seriously abused drugs. Why do you think some people abuse drugs?

ACTIVITY 28-1

PROBLEM: What information can you learn from drug labels?

Science Process Skills
comparing, observing, classifying

Background Information
Over-the-counter drugs and medications can be bought without a doctor's prescription. To be safe and effective, these drugs and medications must be used properly. Proper use of a drug includes taking the drug or using the medication for the right reason and taking or using the right amount at the right time. Also, a drug or medication should not be used beyond its "shelf life"—the length of time the drug or medication is effective. You also should follow any special instructions on the label or packaging.

Materials
3 different over-the-counter drug or medication labels or packaging

Procedure
1. Examine one of your drug or medication labels.
2. Write the name of the drug or medication and its use.
3. Find the dosage instructions and record the dosage.
4. Find the expiration date and record it.
5. Record any special warnings or precautions given for the drug or medication.
6. Repeat steps 1–5 for each drug or medication.
7. Get together with 3 classmates. Compare the information you gathered about each drug or medication.
8. **ORGANIZE** In a data table, organize the information for each drug or medication that you and the other 3 members of your class gathered. You should have 9 different drugs or medications.

Observations
1. What two things are given in the dosage instructions for a drug or medication?
2. Do the dosages differ for different age groups? If so, give an example.
3. **a.** Which of the drugs or medications examined would you use to **a.** treat a cold? **b.** relieve pain? **c.** treat a cut? **d.** treat indigestion?
4. **a.** Which of the drugs or medications are to be taken every 3 or 4 hours? **b.** every 6 or 12 hours? **c.** after meals? **d.** What other frequencies for taking the drugs or medications did you find?
5. **a.** Which drugs have expiration dates?
   b. What does the expiration date tell you?

Conclusions
1. **a.** List the types of information that you can obtain from drug or medication labels.
   b. Do all drug labels have this information? Use your observations to support your answer.
2. What general warning statement is found on all drug labels?

Stimulants

Drugs that speed up the activity of the central nervous system are called **stimulants** (STIM-yuh-lunts). You may recall that chemical messengers carry a nerve impulse from one nerve cell to another. Stimulants increase the number of chemical messengers in a synapse. When stimulants enter the body, they increase alertness, pulse rate, and blood pressure. They also decrease the appetite. Some examples of stimulants are caffeine, amphetamines, and cocaine.

Amphetamines (am-FET-uh-meens) also are known as "uppers" or pep pills. In medicine, amphetamines sometimes are used to prevent drowsiness or to treat some nervous-system disorders. When abused, amphetamines can cause violent reactions, convulsions, and even death.

One of the most dangerous illegal stimulants is cocaine. Cocaine comes from the leaves of the coca plant. When taken, cocaine causes a temporary feeling of liveliness, well-being, and confidence. However, when the effects of cocaine wear off, a user feels exhausted, depressed, and fearful.

How does cocaine harm the body? Cocaine often is inhaled through the nose. Inhaling cocaine can damage the membranes in the nose. Cocaine also speeds up respiration and heart rate, and causes a rapid increase in blood pressure. These rapid changes have caused deaths by heart attack and lung failure.

A very dangerous form of cocaine is called crack. Crack is a solid, highly purified form of cocaine, which is smoked. Sometimes, a single use of crack causes coma and death.

Figure 28-2 Cocaine and crack are dangerous drugs. Both drugs come from the leaves of the coca plant.

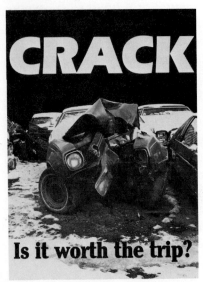

Depressants

Drugs that slow down the activity of the central nervous system are called **depressants** (di-PRES-unts). Depressants decrease the effect of nerve impulses. For example, depressants slow down the heart and lower the breathing rate. How do you think depressants affect blood pressure?

Barbiturates (bar-BICH-uhr-its) and tranquilizers are two groups of depressants. Both kinds of depressants have medical uses. For example, barbiturates often are prescribed as sedatives or sleeping pills. Tranquilizers are prescribed for anxiety and for some emotional disorders.

Hallucinogens

Drugs that distort or alter the senses are called **hallucinogens** (hul-LOO-suh-nuh-jens). The sensory distortions caused by these drugs are called hallucinations (huh-loo-suh-NAY-shuns). People having a hallucination may see or hear things that do not exist.

Hallucinations can cause a person to panic or feel threatened. When abusers of hallucinogens feel this way, they are dangerous to themselves and to others. Hallucinogens also can cause physical changes in the body. For example, hallucinogens can increase heart rate and blood pressure or cause fever, chills, loss of appetite, and nausea.

One of the most dangerous hallucinogens is LSD. Each person's response to LSD is unpredictable. Other hallucinogens include PCP and marijuana.

Marijuana is the most widely abused illegal drug in the United States. Marijuana comes from a plant and usually is smoked. How does marijuana affect the body? Marijuana has mind-altering effects. Marijuana also slows down the activity of the central nervous system. For this reason, marijuana sometimes is classified as a depressant.

Narcotics

Drugs made from the opium poppy are called opiates (OH-pee-uts). Opiates also are called **narcotics** (nar-KOT-iks). In medicine, narcotics are used as painkillers. Codeine and morphine are two opiates used in pain medications. Another opiate, which is made from morphine, is heroin. Heroin is an illegal opiate that has no medical use.

Study Hint

To learn how to store medicine safely, read the Consumer Feature at the end of the chapter.

Figure 28-3 What group of drugs are made from the opium poppy?

Dangers of Drug Abuse

What happens when a person begins to abuse a drug? In some cases, first-time drug abuse may result in death. However, in other cases, little or nothing may happen. The sad story of many drug users is that they began by saying to themselves, "A little bit won't hurt; what's the big deal?"

The "big deal" is that many drugs cause **addiction** (uh-DIK-shun). Addiction is an uncontrollable dependence on a drug. Physical dependence occurs when the body cannot function without a constant supply of a drug. Physical dependence is so strong that a drug-addicted mother will give birth to a drug-addicted baby. Psychological (sy-kuh-LOJ-i-kul) dependence occurs when a person has a strong emotional need for a drug. People who are psychologically dependent on a drug have a mental craving for the drug.

Drug addiction is made worse by drug **tolerance** (TOL-uhr-uhns). Drug tolerance occurs when the body gets used to a drug. Therefore, the body's response to a drug decreases. This means that a person must use more and more of a drug for the drug to produce the same effect. Tolerance can easily lead to a drug **overdose.** An overdose occurs when a person takes so much of a drug that unconsciousness or death results.

Withdrawal is a necessary first step of any treatment program for drug addiction. People who are physically dependent undergo **withdrawal sickness** if they stop taking the drug. Symptoms of withdrawal sickness are vomiting, fever, and chills, and uncontrolled movements of the muscles. Violent behavior and depression also may result from withdrawal sickness. These symptoms may last from a few days to a few weeks.

Think & Discuss

1. What is a drug?
2. How can drugs be abused?
3. What are three commonly abused drugs?
4. How does a stimulant affect the body?
5. Why are opiates usually not prescribed for chronic or long-term pain?

28-2 Alcohol

One of the most widely used and abused drugs is ethyl alcohol. Ethyl alcohol is found in alcoholic drinks. What kind of drug is alcohol? Alcohol is a depressant. Alcohol slows down the action of the central nervous system.

Effects of Alcohol

What happens when someone drinks an alcoholic beverage? Because alcohol is a small molecule, it is quickly absorbed into the bloodstream through the walls of the stomach and small intestine. In fact, alcohol enters the bloodstream about two minutes after it is drunk.

Alcohol enters the bloodstream even more rapidly if the stomach is empty. When food is in the stomach, some alcohol is absorbed by the food. Once alcohol enters the blood, it travels to all body tissues.

When alcohol reaches the brain, it affects the brain's ability to control behavior and body functions. Just a small amount of alcohol affects the cerebrum. You may remember that the cerebrum is the control center of the brain. When alcohol enters the cerebrum, coordination and judgment are impaired and reaction time is slowed.

The amount of alcohol in the bloodstream is called the blood alcohol concentration, or **BAC.** The effects of alcohol on the central nervous system increase as the BAC increases. Table 28-1 describes how alcohol affects the body as the amount of alcohol in the blood increases.

Health and Safety Tip

When alcohol is taken in combination with other drugs, such as tranquilizers, the effects often are greatly increased. Even many over-the-counter drugs, such as aspirin, can change the way alcohol affects a person. To be safe, alcohol never should be mixed with other drugs.

Table 28–1	Blood Alcohol Concentration (BAC) and Its Effects	
DRINKS PER HOUR	**BAC (PERCENT)**	**EFFECTS**
*1	0.02–0.03	Feeling of relaxation
2	0.05–0.06	Slight loss of coordination
3	0.08–0.09	Loss of coordination; trouble talking and thinking
4	0.11–0.12	Slowed reaction time; lack of judgment
7	0.20	Difficulty thinking; loss of motor abilities
14	0.40	Unconsciousness; vomiting may occur
17	0.50	Deep coma; if breathing ceases, death

*1 drink equals 22.1 mL of alcohol

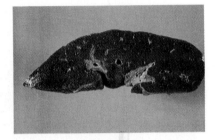

Figure 28-4 Cirrhosis of the liver is common in people who drink heavily. Compare the healthy liver (top) with the diseased liver (bottom).

Alcohol Abuse

People can abuse, or become addicted to, alcohol. **Alcoholism,** or addiction to alcohol, is a major drug-abuse problem in the United States. A person who suffers from alcoholism is called an alcoholic. Alcoholics are physically and psychologically dependent on alcohol. Alcoholism is considered a disease by doctors because it has definite symptoms and causes harmful changes in body organs.

What are the physical effects of alcoholism? Continued abuse of alcohol can cause many serious health problems. For example, alcohol can damage the linings of the esophagus (ih-SAF-uh-gus), stomach, and small intestine. Heavy alcohol use also can damage the kidneys and heart. Alcoholics are more likely to develop high blood pressure and heart disease. In addition, since alcoholics tend to neglect proper nutrition, they often suffer from vitamin and mineral deficiencies.

Heavy drinking also can cause a liver disorder called **cirrhosis** (suh-ROH-sis). Cirrhosis of the liver develops when liver cells are damaged or destroyed by too much alcohol. Gradually, healthy liver cells are replaced by scar tissue, and the liver stops functioning. Therefore, cirrhosis can cause death.

❯ Can alcohol affect an unborn baby? Studies have found that pregnant women who drink have a high risk of giving birth to babies with fetal (FEE-tul) alcohol syndrome. Fetal alcohol syndrome can cause physical and mental disabilities in babies.

Figure 28–5 Why do you think it is unwise to drink and drive?

Alcoholism cannot be cured. However, it can be treated and controlled. Many recovered alcoholics live productive and satisfying lives. What are some sources of help that exist for the alcoholic?

Think & Discuss

6. What is alcoholism?

7. How does alcohol affect the body?

★ **8.** Why are alcoholics more likely to get various diseases and infections?

28-3 Tobacco

Tobacco comes from a plant whose leaves are smoked in cigarettes, pipes, and cigars. Tobacco also can be chewed, or inhaled through the nose in a powdery form called snuff.

▶ When people use tobacco, they are using the drug **nicotine** (NIK-uh-teen). Nicotine is a stimulant that causes both physical and psychological addiction. When tobacco is smoked, nicotine reaches the brain in about seven seconds. How do you think nicotine affects the central nervous system?

Substances in Tobacco

Besides nicotine, scientists have identified 110 different elements and compounds in tobacco. In addition, when tobacco is burned, more than 2000 chemical compounds are produced. These substances have harmful effects on the body.

Carbon monoxide fumes from car exhaust can be deadly. Carbon monoxide also is present in cigarette smoke. Carbon monoxide is a poisonous gas that in small doses can cause dizziness, headaches, and drowsiness. In large doses, carbon monoxide is fatal.

Another substance found in tobacco is tar. What is tar? It is a mixture of chemicals found in cigarette smoke. When inhaled, tar coats the lining of the lungs. Experiments have shown that tar causes cancer in laboratory animals.

Key Points

• Three harmful substances in tobacco are nicotine, tar, and carbon monoxide.

• Tobacco-related illnesses include lung cancer, emphysema, and heart disease.

Health and Safety Tip
Pure nicotine is very poisonous. Each year, many young children die from nicotine poisoning. Always keep cigarettes and ashtrays away from small children.

Study Hint

Use the Index to review the function of cilia in the respiratory system and red blood cells.

Smoking affects both the respiratory and circulatory systems. How does smoking affect the respiratory system? The nicotine and carbon monoxide in tobacco paralyze the cilia that line the respiratory system.

When the cilia do not work properly, a person becomes prone to colds and other respiratory illnesses. Cilia that do not work properly also allow mucus to build up in the air passageways. This build-up of mucus causes the smoker to cough. Tobacco smoke also constricts the air passageways in the respiratory system, making breathing difficult.

The circulatory system is affected by smoking in two ways. First, nicotine causes blood vessels to constrict. This causes an increase in blood pressure and also forces the heart to pump harder. Second, carbon monoxide from cigarette smoke joins with red blood cells. When carbon monoxide joins with red blood cells, they cannot carry oxygen. Therefore, the oxygen supply to vital organs decreases. Over time, this causes damage to the heart, blood vessels, and other organs.

Does smoking have any effect on the health of an unborn baby? Pregnant women who smoke are more likely than nonsmokers to suffer a miscarriage or a stillbirth. They also are at a higher risk of having a baby that is premature or underweight.

Researchers have discovered that cigarette smoke also can affect nonsmokers. For example, children of smokers are twice as likely to have respiratory problems as children of nonsmokers. Because of the dangers of sidestream smoke, which is the smoke from a burning cigarette, smoking is banned in many public places. In addition, many restaurants, offices, airplanes, and trains have special nonsmoking sections.

Skill Builder

Comparing   Write to the Tobacco Institute and request their views on smoking and health-related problems. Then, in a report, compare the Tobacco Institute's views on smoking with the Surgeon General's views.

Figure 28–6   Cigarette smoking is harmful to your health, but sidestream smoke is also harmful to nonsmokers.

ACTIVITY 28-2

PROBLEM: How are advertisements used to convince people not to smoke or to smoke?

Science Process Skills
analyzing, observing, comparing

Background Information
You probably have seen advertisements for cigarettes in magazines and newspapers or on billboards. At one time, cigarette advertisements also were on television. If you read the printed advertisements for cigarettes, you will find that the ads contain warnings about smoking cigarettes. Packages of cigarettes are required to have warnings printed on them. Health groups also advertise about the dangers of cigarette smoking.

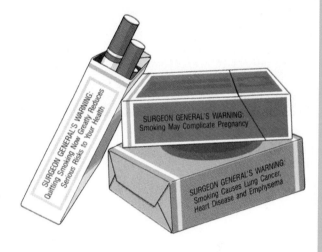

Materials
magazines
newspapers

Procedure
1. Find several advertisements for and against smoking in magazines or in newspapers.
2. Read the advertisements carefully.
3. List the warnings found in the advertisements.
4. Write the message about smoking that the advertisement uses either to get people to smoke or to discourage people from smoking. For example, "Smoking is a dirty habit"; "Smoking is not glamorous"; "Smoking is a refreshing experience"; or "All the beautiful people smoke Brand W."
5. Count the number of cigarette advertisements for smoking and against smoking in one magazine and one newspaper. Record the totals.

Observations
1. How many different warnings did you find in cigarette advertisements?
2. Were there more advertisements for or against smoking cigarettes?

3. Which kind of message was used most often in cigarette advertisements?
4. From whom is the warning on cigarette advertisements?

Conclusions
1. **ANALYZE** Which advertisements for smoking appeal to you the most? Why?
2. How do the advertisements for smoking encourage people to smoke?
3. How do the advertisements against smoking discourage people from smoking?
4. **INFER** Why do you think people smoke even though there are health warnings on the cigarette packages and in advertisements?

Going Further
Using your local daily newspaper, keep a record for 2 weeks of the number of advertisements for cigarettes and the number of anti-smoking advertisements. Also, keep a record of the different brands of cigarettes advertised. Were there more advertisements for or against smoking over the two-week period? What group or groups sponsored the anti-smoking advertisements?

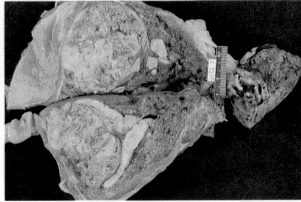

Figure 28-7 The buildup of tar in the lungs prevents the exchange of oxygen and carbon dioxide.

Tobacco-Related Illnesses

Figure 28–7 shows a smoker's lung and a nonsmoker's lung. Notice the deposits of tar on the smoker's lung. How do these deposits affect the lungs?

Cigarette smoking is the leading cause of lung cancer. When cancer occurs in the lungs, cancer cells crowd out healthy lung tissue and the lungs cease to function. Smoking is related to other kinds of cancer, too. For example, cancer of the bladder, kidneys, pancreas, mouth, larynx, and esophagus all have been linked to smoking.

People who smoke pipes or cigars run the risk of developing cancer of the mouth, cheek, lip, and tongue. Chewing tobacco also causes cancer in the mouth. In fact, cancer from chewing tobacco often develops faster than cancers related to other forms of tobacco.

Smoking also causes emphysema (em-fuh-SEE-muh). Emphysema causes the walls of the alveoli to rupture. Therefore, not enough oxygen can get into the lungs and not enough carbon dioxide can be exhaled. The main symptom of emphysema is shortness of breath. A person with emphysema may have to breathe twice as many times per minute as a healthy person in order to get enough oxygen.

Study Hint

The term "emphysema" comes from the Greek word meaning "to inflate."

Think & Discuss

9. What are three harmful substances in tobacco and tobacco smoke?

10. How does smoking affect the circulatory system?

11. Why might it be more difficult for a smoker to exercise than for a nonsmoker?

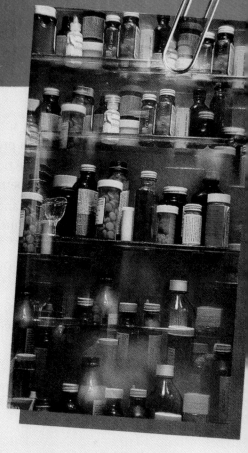

Safe Storage of Medicines

Storing and using medicines properly are important skills. Several factors can act on medicines and cause them to lose their effectiveness or change them into possibly harmful substances. Four of these factors are time, heat, light, and moisture.

Time is probably the greatest enemy of drug effectiveness. Pharmacists claim that a drug begins to lose its effectiveness as soon as the protective seal of the drug is opened. Over-the-counter drugs often last several years under normal conditions. Many prescription drugs, however, have a short shelf life. These medicines should never be used beyond the period of time for which they are prescribed.

Heat, light, and moisture can cause chemical and physical changes in medicines. Heat and light, for example, can cause a drug to decompose. Decomposition breaks the drug down into simpler substances. The breaking down of a drug may render it ineffective. It also may cause the drug to become dangerous.

Moisture can affect a drug in two ways. First, water may react chemically with a drug and change it into a different substance. Second, excess moisture may cause a drug to dissolve.

How do you know when a drug has been in your medicine cabinet too long, or has been acted upon in a harmful way? One thing you can do is look for an expiration date on the medicine. Medicines should never be used beyond their expiration dates. You also should check with your pharmacist, or use a library to find out what signs of spoilage to look for in certain kinds of medicines. For example, one sign that aspirin has spoiled is a strong odor of vinegar. Another sign is that the tablets crumble easily.

Review the guidelines for safe storage of medications. The guidelines will help you store medicines safely. You may find it helpful to copy this list and post it inside your medicine cabinet.

Guidelines for Safe Storage of Medicines

- Store medicines in a cool, dark place away from direct light.
- Make sure all medicines are clearly labeled with the name of the medicine, its expiration date, and its directions for use.
- Never store two different medicines in the same container.
- Throw out prescription drugs as soon as the time of the prescribed dosage has passed.
- Clean out your medicine cabinet regularly. Dispose of all expired or questionable items.
- Ask your pharmacist about special storage instructions, such as keeping a medicine refrigerated.
- ALWAYS KEEP ALL MEDICINES OUT OF THE REACH OF CHILDREN.

To Think About

- Why is a bathroom not a good place to store medicines?
- Why is it unwise to store two different types of pills in the same container?

Chapter Review

CHAPTER SUMMARY

28-1 Drugs

- Over-the-counter drugs, such as aspirin, can be bought without a prescription.
- Prescription drugs can be bought only with a doctor's written permission.
- Stimulants, depressants, and hallucinogens are three kinds of commonly abused drugs.
- Addiction, tolerance, and overdose are three problems caused by drug abuse.

28-2 Alcohol

- Alcohol decreases the activity of the central nervous system.
- When alcohol reaches the cerebrum, judgment is impaired and reaction time is slowed.

- Alcoholism is a progressive disease caused by physical and psychological dependence on alcohol.
- Alcoholics suffer damage to many body organs including the esophagus, stomach, small intestine, heart, kidneys, and liver. Many alcoholics suffer from malnutrition.

28-3 Tobacco

- Nicotine is an addictive drug in tobacco that stimulates the nervous system.
- Tar is a substance in tobacco that builds up on the lungs.
- Carbon monoxide is a poisonous gas that decreases the oxygen supply to the body.
- Tobacco use can cause lung cancer, emphysema, and heart disease.

VOCABULARY LIST

addiction (494)
alcoholism (496)
BAC (495)
cirrhosis (496)

depressants (493)
drug (490)
drug abuse (490)
hallucinogens (493)

narcotics (493)
nicotine (497)
overdose (494)
over-the-counter drugs (490)

prescription drugs (490)
stimulants (492)
tolerance (494)
withdrawal sickness (494)

VOCABULARY REVIEW

Matching Write the word or term from the Vocabulary List that best matches each description.

1. chemical that causes a change in the mind or body
2. symptoms that occur when an addicted person stops using drugs
3. blood alcohol concentration
4. improper use of drugs
5. use of drugs to the point of severe illness or death
6. drug in cigarettes

Applying Definitions Explain the difference between the words in each pair.

1. stimulants, narcotics
2. physical dependence, psychological dependence
3. alcoholism, drug abuse
4. addiction, tolerance
5. prescription drugs, over-the-counter drugs
6. nicotine, tar
7. depressants, hallucinogens
8. fetal alcohol syndrome, cirrhosis

True or False   Write true if the statement is true. If the statement is false, change the underlined word or words to make the statement true.

1. Cocaine, caffeine, and amphetamines are <u>depressants</u>.
2. Alcohol enters the bloodstream more rapidly if the stomach is <u>full</u>.
3. The poisonous gas produced by a burning cigarette is <u>carbon monoxide</u>.
4. <u>Cirrhosis</u> is the major drug abuse problem in the United States.
5. Decongestants are one kind of <u>prescription</u> drugs.
6. <u>Lung cancer</u> is characterized by damaged, inflated alveoli.
7. The ability of the body to become used to a drug is called <u>addiction</u>

8. Aspirin is one kind of <u>over-the-counter</u> drug.
9. Alcohol is a <u>depressant</u> drug.
10. Nicotine causes the heart rate to <u>decrease</u>.

Question and Answer   Rewrite each heading in the Chapter Outline on page 488 as a question. Then, answer each of the questions you have written.

Interpreting a Table   Use the table of Blood Alcohol Concentration (BAC) and Its Effects shown in Table 28-1 on page 495 to answer each of the following.

1. How many drinks per hour result in a BAC of 0.05–0.06?
2. What are the effects of a BAC of 0.05–0.06?
3. How many mL of alcohol are in one drink?
4. What are the effects of a BAC of 0.20?

Writing the Main Ideas   Using the Chapter Outline on page 488, write the main idea for each heading in the outline.

Critical Thinking   Answer each of the following in complete sentences.

1. What factors do you think cause people to become addicted to drugs?
2. How does drug addiction affect a person's life?

3. Why can any drug cause psychological dependence?
4. How would sipping a drink very slowly over several hours help reduce the effect of alcohol on the body?
5. Why is it especially dangerous to drink while taking tranquilizers or barbiturates?
6. Explain why excessive use of alcohol or tobacco can be considered drug abuse.

1. Obtain information about the organizations in your area designed to help alcoholics and their families. Create a classroom display of pamphlets and other sources of information that you have obtained from these organizations.
2. In a written report, explain what you think might happen to a person who occasionally uses drugs.

3. Interview a police officer or a judge in your community to find out about your state's laws with regard to drinking and driving. Then, make a chart of the information to display in the classroom.
4. Prepare a presentation you could give to young children describing why they should never begin smoking. With a classmate, role-play your presentation for the class.

Drugs, Alcohol, and Tobacco   503

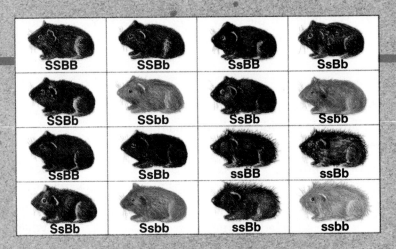

SSBB	SSBb	SsBB	SsBb
SSBb	SSbb	SsBb	Ssbb
SsBB	SsBb	ssBB	ssBb
SsBb	Ssbb	ssBb	ssbb

Have you ever wondered why children look like their parents? Offspring resemble their parents because they inherit certain traits from their parents. Genetics is the study of the inheritance of traits.

Look at the guinea pigs shown on this page. How many are black with short hair? How many are black with long hair? How many are brown with short hair? How many are brown with long hair? These guinea pigs are the offspring of black short-haired guinea pigs. Why do you think some of their offspring are brown and some have long hair? In this unit, you will learn the answer to this question. You also will learn how the other drawings and photographs are related to the field of genetics.

UNIT 8

Heredity and Genetics

CONTENTS

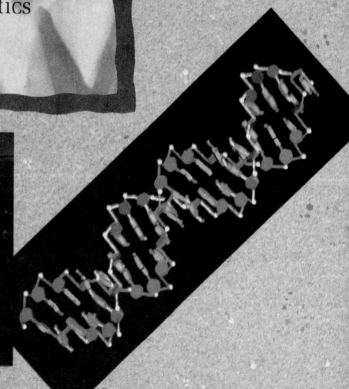

Chapter 29 | Fundamentals of Genetics

Objectives

After you have completed this chapter, you will be able to

29-1 **describe** Mendel's experiments and explain their importance.

29-1 **state** the three principles of genetics.

29-2 **explain** how chance and probability can be applied to genetics.

29-3 **predict** the results of a monohybrid and a dihybrid cross.

Science Process Skills

In this chapter, two science skills are highlighted. Symbols show some places where these skills are used.

❯ **Predicting:** When you predict, you state in advance how and why something will occur.

▣ **Hypothesizing:** When you hypothesize, you state a suggested answer to a problem based upon known information.

Has anyone ever told you that you have your mother's eyes? What did they mean? You know that all organisms produce offspring that are like themselves. For example, pigs produce pigs and horses produce horses. However, there are even closer similarities between parents and offspring.

Children often have some characteristics, such as eye color, that are very similar to their parents' characteristics. For example, if your mother or father has brown eyes, the chances are that you have brown eyes, too. Sometimes a family resemblance can be traced through many generations. How are characteristics passed on from one generation to the next? A nineteenth-century monk named Gregor Mendel tried to find the answer to this question.

29-1 The Work of Mendel

Key Points

- Mendel's experiments showed how genes determine the traits that are passed from one generation to another.

- The three principles of genetics are dominance, segregation, and independent assortment.

Imagine that you are living in Czechoslovakia during the mid-1800s. Next door to you is a monastery with a beautiful garden. One day, you decide to go and talk to the young monk who takes care of the garden. You discover that his name is Gregor Mendel, and that he was born in Austria.

You also discover that Mendel is growing many different kinds of garden peas. You snap open some of the pods and observe that some of the pods contain smooth seeds, while others contain wrinkled seeds. Mendel explains that he is trying to discover how these characteristics are passed on from one generation of plants to the next.

Another name for a characteristic of an organism is **trait.** Stem length, pod color, and seed shape are all traits of pea plants. Other examples of traits include the color of a person's eyes, the length of a cat's whiskers, and the color of a bird's feathers.

The traits that you receive, or inherit, from your parents make up your **heredity** (huh-RED-uh-tee). Heredity, or the inheritance of traits, is studied in the field of biology called **genetics** (juh-NET-iks). Biologists who study heredity are called geneticists (juh-NET-uh-sists).

Mendel's Experiments

Usually, a pea plant reproduces itself by **self-pollination** (PAHL-uh-NAY- shun). A self-pollinating plant has both male and female parts. Mendel found, however, that he could cross different plants by transferring pollen from the male part of one plant to the female part of another plant. This process is called **cross-pollination.**

Mendel began his experiments by studying the stem length of pea plants. For example, Mendel discovered that when he cross-pollinated short plants with other short plants, the offspring produced by these plants also were short. Mendel had expected this result. Mendel was in for a surprise, however, when he cross-pollinated tall plants with other tall plants. Some of the tall plants produced tall offspring. Other tall plants produced both tall and short offspring. Why did this happen?

Figure 29-1 Gregor Mendel often is called the Father of Genetics.

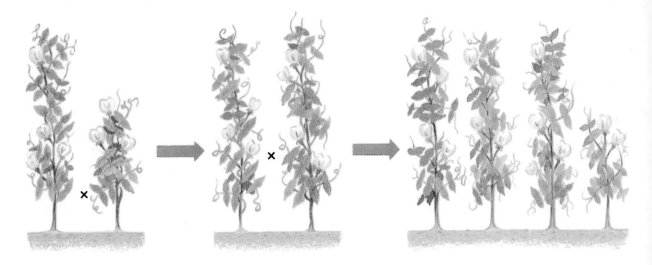

Tall   Short   F₁: All tall   F₂: 3 tall and 1 short

Mendel knew that he had to gather more information. He decided to cross tall plants that had produced only tall offspring with short plants that had produced only short offspring. Mendel called these plants pure-breeding plants. The results of this experiment were very interesting. In the first, or F₁, generation, all the plants were tall. When these tall plants were crossed, however, some of the offspring in the second, or F₂, generation were short. The short trait had reappeared.

Figure 29-2 When Mendel crossed tall and short pea plants, the short plants disappeared in the F₁ generation but reappeared in the F₂.

Dominant and Recessive Traits

After many experiments, Mendel came up with an important hypothesis. He hypothesized that certain "factors" must produce certain traits. He also thought that some of these factors were stronger than others. In Mendel's experiments with tall and short plants, the tall trait often masked the short trait. Mendel concluded that the tall factor must be stronger than the short factor.

Today, biologists refer to Mendel's "factors" as **genes.** An organism receives two genes for each trait. One gene comes from the female reproductive cell, or **gamete** (GAM-eet). The second gene comes from the male gamete. What are the female and male gametes?

▣ The stronger of the two genes is called the **dominant** (DOM-uh-nuhnt) **gene.** The gene that is weaker is called the **recessive** (ri-SES-iv) **gene.** Suppose an organism has one dominant gene and one recessive gene for a particular trait. The organism will have the trait of the dominant gene. The recessive gene will be "hidden" by the dominant gene.

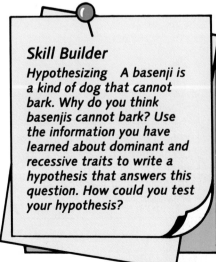

Skill Builder

Hypothesizing   A basenji is a kind of dog that cannot bark. Why do you think basenjis cannot bark? Use the information you have learned about dominant and recessive traits to write a hypothesis that answers this question. How could you test your hypothesis?

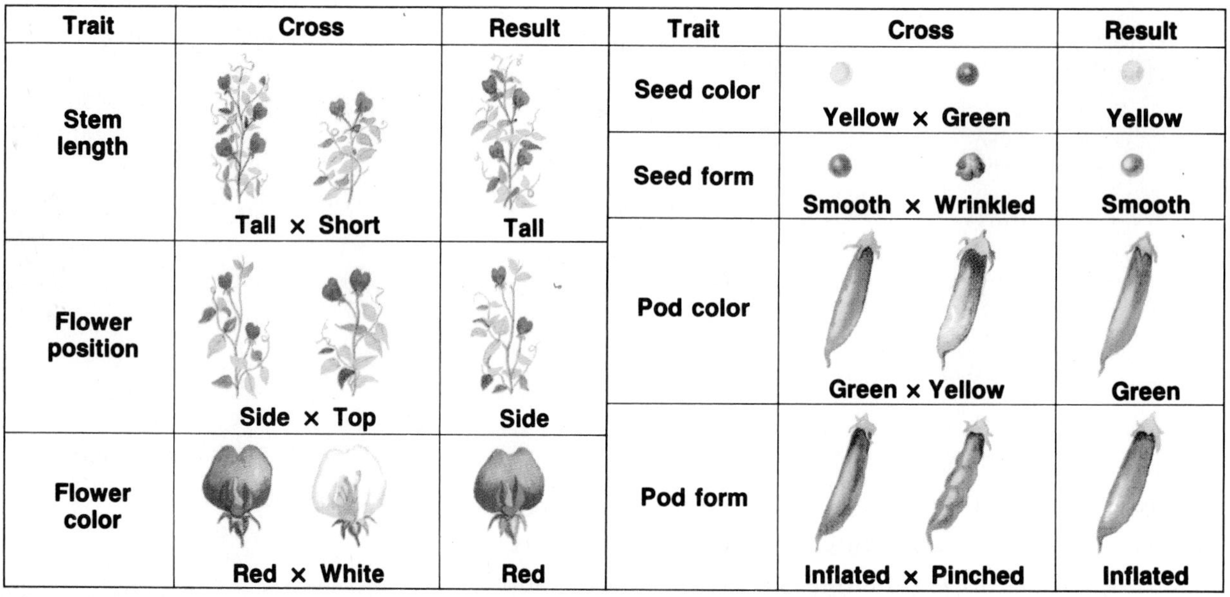

Trait	Cross	Result	Trait	Cross	Result
Stem length	Tall × Short	Tall	Seed color	Yellow × Green	Yellow
			Seed form	Smooth × Wrinkled	Smooth
Flower position	Side × Top	Side	Pod color	Green × Yellow	Green
Flower color	Red × White	Red	Pod form	Inflated × Pinched	Inflated

Figure 29-3 Mendel studied seven pairs of dominant and recessive traits in pea plants.

Mendel studied many other traits of pea plants in addition to stem length. You can see these traits listed in Figure 29-3. What kind of seed would be produced by a plant with one gene for wrinkled seeds and one gene for smooth seeds?

Biologists use symbols to refer to dominant and recessive traits. A capital letter, such as "T" for tall, is always used to represent the dominant trait. The recessive trait is represented by the lower case letter of the dominant trait, for example, "t" for short.

Organisms that have two of the same genes for a particular trait are called **pure.** Pea plants with TT genes or tt genes are pure. Organisms that have two different genes for a particular trait are called **hybrids** (HY-brids). A pea plant with Tt genes is a hybrid. What length stem would a Tt pea plant have? Why?

The visible trait of an organism is called the **phenotype** (FEE-nuh-typ). The combination of genes for a particular trait is called the **genotype** (JEE-nuh-typ). Different genotypes may have the same phenotype. For example, a tall plant may have the genotype TT or Tt.

Incomplete Dominance

If a red four-o'clock flower is crossed with a white four-o'clock flower, the offspring is neither red nor white. Instead, the result is a pink four-o'clock flower. In this case, neither the red gene nor the white gene is dominant.

Study Hint

"Phenotype" comes from a Greek root word meaning "to appear." Phenotype is the appearance of a trait in an organism.

This phenomenon is called **incomplete dominance.** Incomplete dominance results in a blending of the traits carried by two or more different genes.

Principles of Genetics

Three basic principles of genetics have been established as a result of the work of Mendel. These three principles are:

- **The Principle of Dominance**   One "factor," or gene, for a trait may hide the other factor and prevent it from being expressed in the organism.
- **The Principle of Segregation**   The two factors for a trait separate, or segregate, during the formation of gametes.
- **The Principle of Independent Assortment**   Factors for different traits separate independently of one another during the formation of gametes.

Figure 29-4   These white and red impatiens produce plants with pink flowers.

Think & Discuss

1. What is the relationship between heredity and genetics?
2. What is the scientific term for Mendel's "factor"?
3. What did Mendel hypothesize as a result of his experiments?
4. List the three principles of genetics.
5. Why is Mendel called the Father of Genetics?

29-2 Probability and Genetics

In a football game, a coin is tossed to decide which team will kick off. The results of the coin toss are accepted by both teams because people know that a coin toss is fair. A coin can land only one of two ways—heads or tails. Both results are equally likely to occur.

When you toss a coin, you rely on **chance.** Chance is a random, unpredictable event. The likelihood that a chance event will or will not occur is called **probability** (prob-uh-BIL-uh-tee). Probabilities can be expressed as

Key Points
- Probability predicts likely results of repeated chance events.
- Punnett squares are used to predict genetic probabilities.

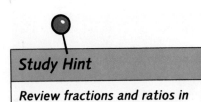

Study Hint

Review fractions and ratios in your mathematics textbook.

fractions or ratios. The probability of a tossed coin landing heads up is one chance out of two, or ½. Another way to express the probability is 1:1

Product Rule

In probability, the results of one chance event do not affect the results of another chance event. The two events occur independently. The probability of two independent events occurring can be found by using the **product rule.** The product rule states that the probability of two independent events both happening is equal to the probability of one event multiplied by the probability of the other event. For example, the probability of one penny landing heads up is ½. The probability of two pennies both landing heads up is ½ x ½, or ¼.

❯ Geneticists use probability to predict possible genotypes and phenotypes. For example, suppose that two hybrid tall (Tt) pea plants are crossed. There is a ½ probability that the female parent will contribute a T gene, and a ½ probability that the female parent will contribute a t gene. The same probability is true for the male parent. The probability that an offspring will have a TT genotype, or a "T" from each parent, is therefore ½ x ½, or ¼. The probability that an offspring will have a tt genotype also is ½ x ½, or ¼. However, the probability that an offspring will have a Tt genotype is (½ x ½) + (½ x ½), or ½.

Punnett Squares

Geneticists use a special chart called a **Punnett square** to show the possible combinations that can result when two organisms are crossed. Suppose, for example, that you want to predict the offspring in a cross between a pure black male guinea pig (BB) and a pure white female guinea pig (bb). Draw a box with four squares, as shown in Figure 29–5. Write the genes contributed by the male parent across the top of the chart. Write the genes contributed by the female parent down the left side of the chart. Now fill in each square with one male gene and one female gene. What you have written in the small squares are the predicted genotypes of the offspring. You can see that all the offspring will be hybrids.

Figure 29-5 In a Punnett square, always identify the symbols used; for example, B = black and b = white.

ACTIVITY 29-1

PROBLEM: How is chance involved with inheritance of genes?

Science Process Skills
predicting, modeling, analyzing

Background Information
Pairs of genes for traits are inherited from parents. Each parent contributes one gene for each trait to the offspring.

Human ears have either unattached or attached ear lobes. Unattached ear lobes sometimes are called free-hanging ear lobes.

Materials
penny   masking tape
nickel   marker

Procedure
1. Place a piece of tape on both sides of the penny and the nickel.
2. Label one side of each coin with an "F" to represent the gene for unattached, or free-hanging, ear lobes and the other side of each coin with an "f" for attached ear lobes.
3. **PREDICT** The Punnett square shows the possible results of an Ff x Ff cross.

	F	f
F	FF	Ff
f	Ff	ff

Each square represents 1/4 of the possible offspring. Therefore, the predicted number of times each gene combination should occur is 1/4, or 25 out of 100 chances. Notice that there are two squares for "Ff." Using this information, fill in the predicted results for 100 tosses of your gene coins.
4. Flip the two coins 100 times each. Record the results of the pairs of flips with slashes on a sheet of paper.

5. After the 100 flips, total the number of slashes and record the totals for each gene pair in the "Actual Results" column of the Data Table.

Data Table: Gene Pairs (100 tosses)

POSSIBLE GENE PAIRS	PREDICTION	ACTUAL RESULTS
FF		
Ff		
ff		

Observations
1. **a.** Which trait is dominant?   **b.** Which trait is recessive?   **c.** How do you know?
2. Do the "gene" coins represent hybrid or pure parents for the trait?
3. How many genes does each parent give to the offspring?
4. **CALCULATE** What is the difference between the predicted results and your actual results for each of the three gene combinations possible? **Hint:** Subtract the smaller from the larger number.

Conclusions
1. **ANALYZE** Are the chance results that can be predicted for the inheritance of these genes good estimates of your actual results? Explain your answer.
2. **a.** What is the chance, or probability, that these parents will have a child with attached ear lobes?   **b.** What is the probability of a child with free-hanging ear lobes? **Hint:** Use the Punnett square for help. Remember both "Ff" and "FF" gene pairs will show free-hanging ear lobes.

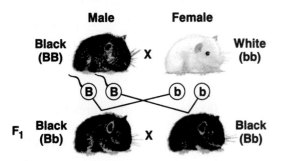

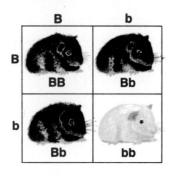

Phenotype:
3 Black
1 White

Genotype:
1 Pure black
2 Hybrid black
1 Pure white

Figure 29-6 When two hybrid black guinea pigs are crossed, the recessive white trait reappears.

Look at Figure 29–6 to see what will happen when two of the hybrids are crossed. According to the Punnett square, the ratio of possible genotypes is 1:2:1, or ¼ BB, ½ Bb, and ¼ bb. The ratio of possible phenotypes is 3:1, or ¾ black and ¼ white.

Think & Discuss

6. What is the difference between chance and probability?

7. How is probability used in genetics?

★ 8. Use a Punnett square to predict the results of a cross between two hybrid green peas (Gg x Gg).

Key Points

- Monohybrid crosses involve one trait.

- Dihybrid crosses involve two traits.

29–3 Predicting the Results of Genetic Crosses

Probability tells you what is likely to happen, but not necessarily what actually will happen. For example, tossing a coin 20 times should result in 10 heads and 10 tails. However, the actual results may be 11 heads and 9 tails. In the same way, the ratios predicted by Punnett squares may be more or less than the results of actual crosses. Still, the Punnett square provides an easy and fairly accurate way to predict genotypes and phenotypes.

Crosses Involving One Trait

A cross involving only one trait is called a **monohybrid** (mon-oh-HY-brid) **cross.** When you cross a parent having a pure dominant trait with a parent having a pure

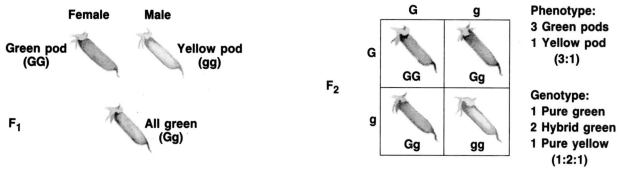

Green pod (GG) Yellow pod (gg)

F₁ All green (Gg)

F₂

	G	g
G	GG	Gg
g	Gg	gg

Phenotype:
3 Green pods
1 Yellow pod
(3:1)

Genotype:
1 Pure green
2 Hybrid green
1 Pure yellow
(1:2:1)

Figure 29-7 In this monohybrid cross, all of the plants in the F₁ generation are hybrids.

recessive trait, all the offspring will be hybrids. In other words, all the offspring will have the phenotype of the dominant parent. When two of the hybrids are crossed, a Punnett square shows that the genotype ratio will be 1:2:1. The phenotype ratio, however, will be 3:1.

Crosses Involving Two Traits

A cross that involves two different sets of traits is called a **dihybrid** (dy-HY-brid) **cross.** For example, you might cross pea plants that have smooth yellow seeds with pea plants that have wrinkled green seeds. Figure 29–8 shows a dihybrid cross. Notice that the Punnett square now has 16 boxes, in order to accommodate the two different gene pairs carried by each parent.

Look at the phenotypes in Figure 29–8. There are 9 smooth yellow peas, 3 smooth green peas, 3 wrinkled yellow peas, and 1 wrinkled green pea. The phenotype ratio is 9:3:3:1.

F₁ All smooth, yellow (SsYy)

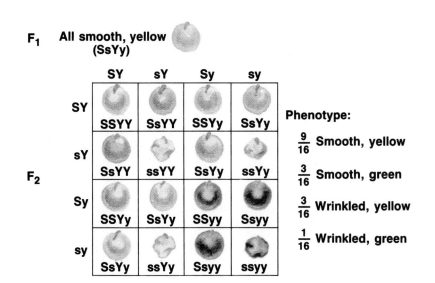

F₂

	SY	sY	Sy	sy
SY	SSYY	SsYY	SSYy	SsYy
sY	SsYY	ssYY	SsYy	ssYy
Sy	SSYy	SsYy	SSyy	Ssyy
sy	SsYy	ssYy	Ssyy	ssyy

Phenotype:

$\frac{9}{16}$ Smooth, yellow

$\frac{3}{16}$ Smooth, green

$\frac{3}{16}$ Wrinkled, yellow

$\frac{1}{16}$ Wrinkled, green

Figure 29-8 This dihybrid cross produces nine different genotypes and four different phenotypes.

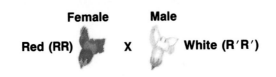

Female   Male

Red (RR)   X   White (R'R')

F₁   All pink (RR')

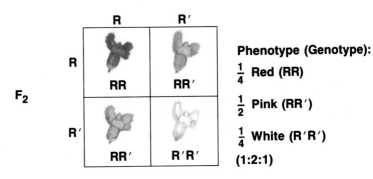

Phenotype (Genotype):

$\frac{1}{4}$ Red (RR)

$\frac{1}{2}$ Pink (RR')

$\frac{1}{4}$ White (R'R')

(1:2:1)

Figure 29-9 When two pink flowers are crossed, the genotype and phenotype ratios are the same (1:2:1).

Crosses Involving Incomplete Dominance

Suppose you cross a white four-o'clock flower with a red four-o'clock flower to get pink four-o'clock flowers. What will happen when you cross two of the pink four-o'clock flowers?

Figure 29–9 shows the results of this cross. Because neither gene is dominant, both red (R) and white (R') are represented by capital letters. According to the Punnett square, what phenotypes result from crossing two pink flowers? What is the phenotype ratio?

Think & Discuss

9. What is the difference between a monohybrid cross and a dihybrid cross?

10. If the hybrid offspring (Pp) of pure dominant (PP) and pure recessive (pp) parents are crossed, what will be the genotype ratio of their offspring?

11. Predict the phenotypes and genotypes that result in the F₁ and F₂ generations when a pure dominant black short-haired guinea pig (BBSS) is crossed with a pure recessive white long-haired guinea pig (bbss).

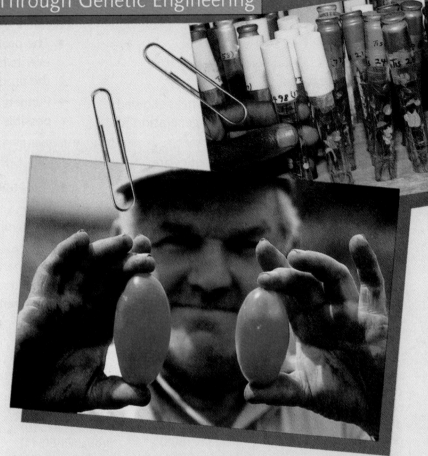

Imagine that you are a farmer and can grow any kind of crop plant that you want. What kind of plant would you choose? What characteristics would you want the plant to have? Would you want a plant that produces very large vegetables or fruit? Would you want a plant that has a long growing season, or one that is resistant to disease? Would you want a plant that cannot be damaged by frost?

Crop plants such as these may sound too good to be true, but by the year 2000, scientists hope that at least some of them will be a reality. The technology that is making these new and useful crop plants possible is called genetic engineering.

Genetic engineering is the process by which genes, or segments of DNA, are transferred from one organism to another. The two pieces of DNA combine to form a new piece of DNA. The new pieces of combined DNA are called recombinant DNA.

The great advantage of genetic engineering is that particular traits carried by the transferred genes are passed on to future generations. For example, suppose that the ability to resist a certain fungus is transferred from the DNA of plant A to the DNA of plant B. From now on, all future generations of plant B will also be resistant to the fungus.

How will genetically engineered crops benefit you, the consumer? Consumers will benefit as improved crop plants produce better foods at lower prices. For example, fruit and vegetable crops are often damaged by disease or insect pests. Thanks to the techniques of genetic engineering, apple trees and potato and tomato plants may soon be strong enough to resist the diseases and insects that threaten them.

Another important crop plant that is being improved by genetic engineering is wheat. Every so often, extreme cold or drought damages wheat crops. As a result, wheat becomes scarce, and the prices of wheat products, such as bread, go up. Today, scientists are working to create wheat plants that are resistant to cold and drought. For you, the consumer, this means lower prices and a more abundant supply of the products that you need.

To Think About
- Why do genetically engineered crops often mean lower food prices?
- How might genetic engineering produce food that is more nutritious?

Chapter Review

CHAPTER SUMMARY

29-1 The Work of Mendel
- Genetics is the field of biology that studies heredity.
- Mendel's experiments with peas showed that traits are passed from generation to generation.
- The three principles of genetics are dominance, segregation, and independent assortment.

29-2 Probability and Genetics
- The results of a chance event cannot be predicted exactly.
- Probability predicts the likely number of times that each possible result will occur.

- The probability of two independent events happening can be found by using the product rule.
- Punnett squares are used to predict the possible results of genetic crosses.

29-3 Predicting the Results of Genetic Crosses
- A monohybrid cross involves only one trait.
- A dihybrid cross involves two traits.
- In a cross involving incomplete dominance, neither trait is dominant; thus, the genotype ratio is the same as the phenotype ratio.

VOCABULARY LIST

chance (511)	genes (509)	incomplete dominance (511)	Punnett square (512)
cross-pollination (508)	genetics (508)	monohybrid cross (514)	pure (510)
dihybrid cross (515)	genotype (510)	phenotype (510)	recessive gene (509)
dominant gene (509)	heredity (508)	probability (511)	self-pollination (508)
gamete (509)	hybrids (510)	product rule (512)	trait (508)

VOCABULARY REVIEW

Matching Write the word or term from the Vocabulary List that best matches each description.

1. combination of genes for a trait
2. likelihood of a chance event
3. the characteristics you inherit
4. the weaker of two genes
5. the appearance of a particular trait
6. characteristic
7. random, unpredictable event
8. the stronger of two genes
9. having two of the same genes for a trait
10. the carriers of traits
11. study of heredity

Identifying Relationships Identify the word or term in each group that does not belong. Explain why it does not belong with the group.

1. product rule, Punnett square, self-pollination
2. cross-pollination, dihybrid cross, self-pollination
3. gamete, genetics, heredity
4. incomplete dominance, recessive, dominant
5. genetics, dominant, heredity
6. hybrid, pure, phenotype
7. monohybrid cross, recessive, dihybrid cross
8. dominant, recessive, pure
9. product rule, probability, trait
10. gamete, phenotype, genotype

Completion   Write the word or words that best complete each sentence.

1. The study of how genes are passed from generation to generation is called _____.
2. Self-pollinating plants have both _____ and _____ parts.
3. Transferring pollen from one plant to another is called _____.
4. Geneticists call Mendel's stronger factors _____.
5. Hybrids carry _____ and _____ genes.
6. For a given trait, each parent contributes _____ gene(s).
7. The masking of a recessive trait by a dominant trait is explained by the principle of _____.
8. The separation of the genes for a particular trait is explained by the principle of _____.
9. The hybrid offspring in a monohybrid cross always have the phenotype of the _____ parent.

Finding the Main Ideas   Use the section number to find the sentence that answers each question. Then, write the sentence.

1. What happened when Mendel crossed short plants with other short plants? (29-1)
2. Describe the offspring produced when Mendel crossed tall plants with other tall plants. (29-1)
3. What type of offspring were produced in the F_1 generation when Mendel crossed pure-breeding tall plants with pure-breeding short plants? (29-1)
4. What did Mendel conclude about the tall and short factors in pea plants? (29-1)
5. How do biologists use symbols to represent dominant and recessive genes? (29-1)
6. What is the result of incomplete dominance? (29-1)
7. What is a Punnett square? (29-2)
8. What is a monohybrid cross? (29-3)
9. What is a dihybrid cross? (29-3)

Writing for Understanding   One way to find out if you understand something is to write a brief summary of the information in your own words. Reread Section 29-2, Probability and Genetics, on pages 511–514, and write a brief summary of the information.

Critical Thinking   Answer each of the following in complete sentences.

1. Biologists of Mendel's time paid no attention to his findings. Why?

2. Why was it necessary for Mendel to study more than one generation of pea plants?
3. Is it possible for a phenotype to change without changing the genotype? How?
4. What do you think would have happened to the science of genetics if Mendel's work had not been rediscovered in 1900?
5. If you were a geneticist, which plant's or animal's genes would you choose to study? Why?

1. Visit a nursery or botanical garden. While you are there, find out which flowers are hybrids and which are pure breeds. Make a list of the varieties of flowers in each category. Take photographs if possible.

2. Make a poster showing Mendel's work. Diagram and illustrate his experiments and the results. Use this poster to decorate your classroom and to help other students learn about the beginnings of scientific genetics.

Chapter 30 | Modern Genetics

After you have completed this chapter, you will be able to

30-1 **state** the chromosome theory.

30-1 **explain** how chromosomes determine the sex of an organism.

30-2 **describe** the structure of the DNA molecule.

30-2 **explain** the process of replication.

30-3 **explain** how some human traits are inherited.

30-4 **name** two human genetic disorders and their effects.

Science Process Skills

In this chapter, two science skills are highlighted. Symbols show some places where these skills are used.

❯ **Predicting:** When you predict, you state in advance how and why something will occur.

◢ **Analyzing:** When you analyze, you break down a complex idea into simpler parts to make it easier to understand.

Have you ever seen identical twins? Perhaps you are a twin yourself. Twins often are common in certain families. Even if there are no identical twins in your family, the members probably look somewhat alike. Why do the members of a family resemble one another? The answer lies in genes. Genes, which code for traits, are passed from one generation to another.

With the exception of identical twins, members of a family usually do not look exactly alike. Children from the same family may have different facial features or different hair color. These differences are also caused by genes. Each person is a unique human being. It is the combination of heredity and environment that makes you who you are.

30–1 Chromosomes

Key Points

- The chromosome theory states that genes are sections of chromosomes.

- Sex chromosomes determine the sex of an organism.

Skill Builder

Building Vocabulary
Knowing the origin of word parts can help you learn new biology terms. The word "chromosome" is made up of two word parts: "chromo" and "some." Use a dictionary to find the meaning of these word parts. Why do you think Flemming called the threadlike particles "chromosomes"?

Gregor Mendel was the first person to suggest that paired factors, or genes, carry inherited traits. Mendel was able to show the inheritance of traits in pea plants. However, Mendel did not know about genes or how they worked.

The first clue that specific parts of a cell might be involved in the inheritance of traits came in 1882. The German biologist Walther Flemming used a compound microscope to observe the nucleus of a cell. Flemming saw dark, threadlike particles in the nucleus. He called these particles **chromosomes** (KROH-muh-sohms).

Chromosome Theory

Imagine being able to see the chromosomes of a grasshopper. In 1902, the American biologist Walter Sutton did just that. In fact, Sutton was able to see the chromosomes move during meiosis. Sutton saw that at the beginning of meiosis, the chromosomes lined up in pairs. Then he saw the chromosome pairs separate. Each chromosome pair seemed to separate independently of the others. One chromosome from each pair went to each gamete. Each gamete therefore had half as many chromosomes as the original cells. When two gametes joined, the fertilized egg had the same number of chromosomes as the original cells.

How were Sutton's observations related to Mendel's experiments? As a result of his observations, Sutton inferred that chromosomes carry the "factors" described by Mendel. Sutton's theory that genes are sections of chromosomes is called the **chromosome theory.**

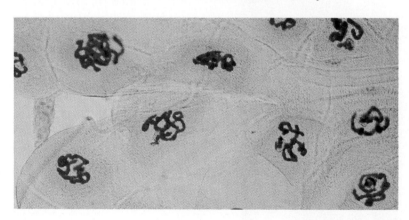

Figure 30–1 Fruit flies often are used in genetics experiments because of their large chromosomes.

Table 30–1	Comparison of the Principles of Genetics with Mendel's and Sutton's Findings	
PRINCIPLES OF GENETICS	GENES ("FACTORS") (MENDEL)	CHROMOSOMES (SUTTON)
Dominance	Genes occur in pairs; one of the pair is dominant.	Chromosomes occur in pairs.
Segregation	Genes of a pair separate.	One chromosome from each pair goes to a gamete.
Independent Assortment	Genes for different traits separate independently.	Each chromosome pair separates independently of other pairs.

Sex Chromosomes

In the early 1900s, an American zoologist, Thomas Hunt Morgan, discovered how chromosomes determine the sex of most organisms. While studying fruit flies, Morgan observed that one pair of chromosomes in the female was different from the corresponding pair in the male. The female had two large chromosomes, or **X chromosomes.** The male had one X chromosome and one smaller chromosome, or **Y chromosome.** After many experiments, Morgan concluded that the X and Y chromosomes determine the sex of organisms such as fruit flies and humans. Morgan called the X and Y chromosomes **sex chromosomes.** All the other chromosomes in an organism are called **autosomes** (AWT-uh-sohms).

How do the X and Y chromosomes determine whether an organism will be male or female? An organism that receives two X chromosomes will be female. An organism that receives one X and one Y chromosome will be male.

Study Hint

Refer to Chapter 29 to review the principles of genetics.

Think & Discuss

1. What are the two sex chromosomes?
2. What is the difference between a sex chromosome and an autosome?
3. State the chromosome theory.
4. How do the sex chromosomes determine the sex of most organisms?
5. How did Sutton's chromosome theory explain the results of Mendel's experiments?

30-2 The Genetic Code

After Sutton and Morgan discovered the function of chromosomes, scientists began to ask more questions about chromosomes. What is a chromosome made of? How can chromosomes carry genetic information? These questions were answered when a chemical called **DNA** was discovered. DNA stands for deoxyribonucleic (dee-oks-ee-ry-boh-noo-KLEE-ik) acid. It is the main substance in chromosomes.

Structure of DNA

By the 1940s, scientists knew that a DNA molecule was made up of four nitrogen bases, sugar, and phosphate. The four nitrogen bases are adenine (AD-uh-neen), guanine (GWAH-neen), thymine (THY-meen), and cytosine (SYT-oh-seen). However, scientists did not yet know the exact structure of the DNA molecule.

■ How is a DNA molecule put together? As scientists continued to study DNA, they found that adenine and thymine always appear in equal amounts. There also are equal amounts of guanine and cytosine. This discovery led scientists to conclude that adenine always pairs with thymine. Guanine always pairs with cytosine in a DNA molecule.

Figure 30–2 shows how the nitrogen base pairs are arranged like rungs on a ladder. The sides of the ladder are made up of sugar molecules and phosphate groups. The structure of DNA was discovered in 1953 by an American biologist, James Watson, and a British scientist, Francis Crick. Their discovery is considered one of the greatest scientific breakthroughs of the twentieth century.

Watson and Crick based their discovery on the work of another British scientist, Rosalind Franklin. Franklin had taken many X-ray photographs of DNA crystals. Based on these photographs, Franklin predicted the shape and composition of a DNA molecule.

The DNA molecule in a single chromosome might have hundreds of thousands of pairs of nitrogen bases. Watson and Crick discovered that the order of the nitrogen base pairs determines the traits of a particular individual. As a result, the order of base pairs is a kind of "genetic code."

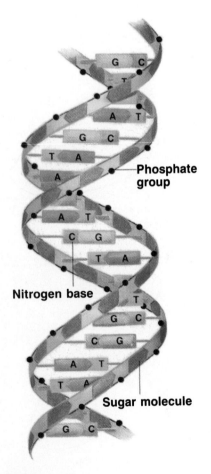

Phosphate group

Nitrogen base

Sugar molecule

Figure 30–2 A molecule of DNA looks like a twisted, or spiral, ladder.

ACTIVITY 30-1

PROBLEM: What is the structure of DNA?

Science Process Skills
modeling, comparing, analyzing

Background Information
A DNA molecule looks like a twisted ladder. A DNA molecule is made up of chains of sugar groups and phosphates connected by pairs of nitrogen bases. The letters A, T, C, and G stand for the four different bases.

Materials
scissors
construction paper in white, black, green, red, blue, and yellow
tracing paper
cellophane tape

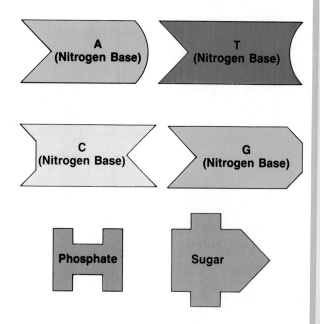

Procedure
1. Trace the DNA parts shown on tracing paper.
2. Cut out the tracings. **CAUTION: Always be careful when using scissors.** The tracings will be used as patterns.
3. Using the tracing patterns, trace and cut out 12 white sugar molecules and 21 black phosphate molecules. Label the molecules.
4. Trace and cut out 12 nitrogen bases as follows: 3 green A's, 3 red T's, 3 yellow C's, and 3 blue G's. Label the bases.
5. Construct the two sides of the DNA molecule with the sugars and phosphates.
6. Complete the molecule of DNA by fitting base pairs along the sides of the molecule.
7. Tape the entire DNA molecule together.

Observations
1. What chemicals make up the sides of the DNA molecule?
2. What chemicals make up the rungs?

3. **a.** Which nitrogen base always pairs up with A? **b.** Which base pairs up with G?

Conclusions
1. **COMPARE** Does your DNA model have the same shape and general pattern as those of your classmates? Explain your answer.
2. Are all the DNA models exactly the same? If not, what are the differences?
3. **MODEL** What do you need to do to your model to make it look like a DNA molecule?

Going Further
Construct a model of a large DNA molecule by tapping all the models in the class together. This large DNA molecule will help you understand better how complex a DNA molecule is. How many nitrogen bases are in this molecule?

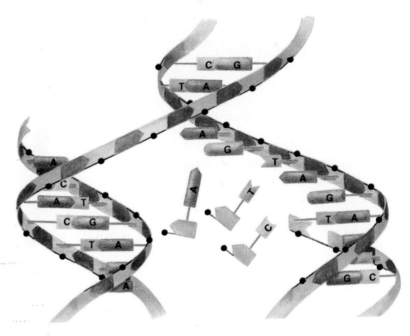

Figure 30-3 During DNA replication, a DNA molecule splits apart and two new molecules are formed.

DNA Replication

You know that your body cells reproduce, or make new cells, by the process of mitosis. Before a cell can divide, the DNA in the nucleus must be duplicated. Why do you think this must happen? The DNA must be duplicated so that each new cell gets the same DNA as the parent cell. As a result of DNA duplication, the new cells have the same genetic code as the parent cell. The DNA in a cell also must be duplicated during meiosis.

The process by which DNA is duplicated is called **replication** (rep-luh-KAY-shun). Look at Figure 30-3 to see how a DNA molecule replicates. The DNA molecule first "unzips," or splits apart, between nitrogen base pairs. Next, nitrogen bases, sugar, and phosphate groups from the cytoplasm move in to take the place of the ones that split off. Replication results in two identical DNA molecules. Each molecule has exactly the same composition as the original DNA molecule.

DNA and RNA

How does the genetic code in DNA control an organism's traits? The traits of all organisms depend on the proteins in their cells. Scientists found that DNA controls the making of proteins. Therefore, the traits of an organism are controlled by its DNA.

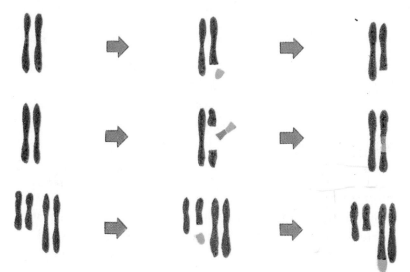

Figure 30–4 In chromosome mutations, a part of a chromosome may be lost, turned around, or attached to a different chromosome.

Proteins are made in the cytoplasm of a cell. DNA is found in the nucleus. How can DNA in the nucleus control the making of proteins in the cytoplasm? Do DNA molecules leave the nucleus? No, a nucleic acid called **RNA** acts as a messenger for DNA. RNA is ribonucleic (ry-boh-noo-KLEE-ik) acid. An RNA molecule is formed according to the genetic code of a DNA molecule in the nucleus and carries the code to the cytoplasm.

Changing the Genetic Code

DNA replication and cell division usually take place without error. Sometimes, however, the DNA does not replicate exactly or the chromosomes do not pair correctly. When either of these mistakes happens, a **mutation** (myoo-TAY-shun) occurs. A mutation is the result of a change in an organism's genetic code.

Anything that causes a mutation is called a **mutagen** (MYOOT-uh-jun). Many drugs and other chemicals are mutagens. X-rays also have been found to be mutagens.

Think & Discuss

6. What is the process of DNA duplication called?
7. Compare a mutation and a mutagen.
8. Name the four nitrogen bases found in DNA.
9. What are the sides of the DNA ladder made up of?
★ 10. Why is DNA duplicated during meiosis?

30–3 Human Genetics

Key Points

- Blood type and skin color are determined by several pairs of genes.

- Sex-linked traits are controlled by the sex chromosomes.

Some organisms have only a few chromosomes. Fruit flies, for example, have only four pairs of chromosomes. Humans, however, have 23 pairs, or 46 chromosomes. About 100,000 different genes are located on these chromosomes.

Human Traits

Some human traits are determined by only one pair of genes. Do you have freckles? Freckles are determined by one gene pair. Other human traits are determined by several pairs of genes.

Blood Types

Blood type is controlled by different genes. The four major blood groups are A, B, AB, and O. Your blood type is determined by the genes you inherit. Genes for group A and group B are dominant over genes for group O. As a result, a person with type A blood may have two A genes (AA) or one A gene and one O gene (AO). A person with type B blood may have two B genes (BB) or one B gene and one O gene (BO). A person with type O blood, however, must have two O genes (OO). What happens if a person inherits one A gene and one B gene?

Skin Color

Skin color is determined by four pairs of genes. This is why human skin color has so many variations. The genes for skin color control the production of melanin

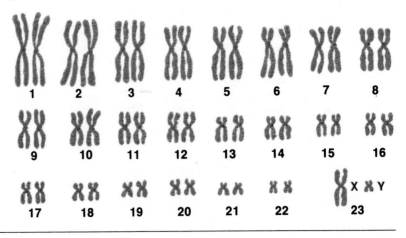

Figure 30–5 All human traits are determined by these 23 pairs of chromosomes.

(MEL-uh-nin), a chemical that adds brown color to the skin. The more melanin produced in a person's skin, the darker the skin color.

Sex Determination

A person's sex is determined at the moment of fertilization. The egg from the mother (XX) must donate an X chromosome. The sperm from the father (XY) can donate either an X chromosome or a Y chromosome. Which parent determines the sex of the child?

Sex-Linked Traits

The sex chromosomes contain genes for several traits. Two of these traits are hemophilia (hee-moh-FIL-ee-uh) and color blindness. Hemophilia is a blood disorder in which the blood does not clot. For a hemophiliac, even a small cut can be fatal. Color blindness is a visual disorder in which people cannot see the difference between certain colors.

Geneticists use a chart called a **pedigree** to trace some genetic traits in families. Look at Figure 30–7. This pedigree shows that Queen Victoria of England carried the gene for hemophilia. As her children and grandchildren married members of other royal families, the disorder spread throughout Europe.

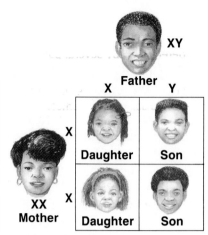

Figure 30–6 A mother donates only X chromosomes, while the father donates either an X or a Y chromosome.

Figure 30–7 Squares on a pedigree chart represent males. Circles represent females.

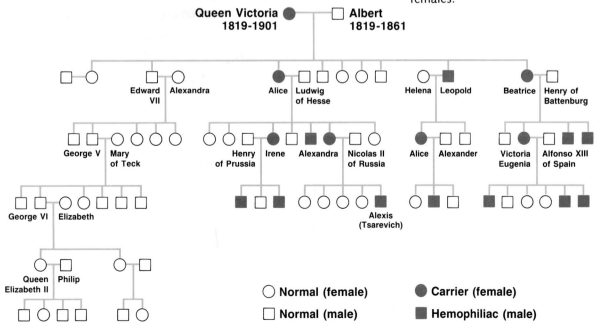

ACTIVITY: 30-2

PROBLEM: How do you read a pedigree chart?

Science Process Skills
classifying, organizing, analyzing

Background Information
A pedigree chart is used to study the passing of a trait through a number of generations. People who raise show animals, such as dogs and cats, often use these charts for their animals so the inheritance of desired traits from generation to generation can be traced. Pedigree charts also are used to study the inheritance of certain diseases or disorders in humans, such as sickle-cell anemia.

Materials
paper and pencil

Procedure
1. Study the key shown for symbols used on a pedigree chart.

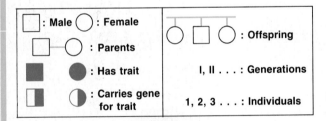

2. Study the pedigree chart shown for sickle-cell anemia.

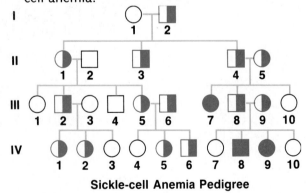

Sickle-cell Anemia Pedigree

3. Study the Data Table shown for deafness in a family. Develop a deafness pedigree chart for the family. Be sure to use the proper symbols.

Data Table: Deafness Pedigree					
GENERATION I		GENERATION II			GENERATION III
Genotype	Sex	Genotype	Sex	Spouse's Genotypes	Grandchildren's Genotypes/Sex
Dd	M	DD	M	Dd	DD/M; Dd/F
		Dd	F	DD	Dd/F
Dd	F	dd	M	Dd	dd/F; Dd/M

D = normal hearing
d = deafness

Observations
1. How many generations are represented in the chart for sickle-cell anemia?
2. How many carriers of the sickle-cell trait are in each generation?
3. How many people in the family were born with sickle-cell anemia?
4. From which parent did the second-generation children inherit the sickle-cell gene?
5. In which generation did sickle-cell anemia first show?

Conclusions
1. **ANALYZE** What can you determine about a family using a pedigree chart?
2. In some pedigree charts, you cannot determine the two genes, or genotype, of each individual. What symbol would not be used in this kind of pedigree chart?

The gene for hemophilia and the gene for normal blood clotting are both carried on the X chromosome. The gene for hemophilia is recessive. For this reason, a woman such as Queen Victoria can have the gene without having the disorder. The only way that a woman can develop hemophilia is to have two of the recessive hemophilia genes. If a man has the gene for hemophilia, however, his Y chromosome does not have a dominant gene to mask the hemophilia gene. The man will develop hemophilia.

Like the hemophilia gene, the gene for color blindness also is recessive. Both the recessive gene and the dominant gene for normal color vision are carried on the X chromosome. Do you think color blindness occurs more frequently in men or in women? Why?

Nondisjunction

Chromosome pairs separate and gametes form during meiosis. Usually a gamete receives one chromosome from each pair. Sometimes, however, the chromosome pairs do not separate correctly. This condition is called **nondisjunction** (non-dis-JUNK-shun).

When nondisjunction occurs, both chromosomes in a pair go to the same gamete. As a result, one gamete has too many chromosomes and the other gamete has too few. If either of these gametes unites with a normal gamete at fertilization, the organism does not develop properly.

There are several conditions that result from nondisjunction. One of these conditions is Down's syndrome. A person with Down's syndrome has three chromosomes in pair 21 instead of two. People with Down's syndrome can lead productive lives, but they usually will have some degree of mental retardation.

20   21   22   23

Figure 30–8 People with Down's syndrome have an extra chromosome in pair 21.

Think & Discuss

11. What is a pedigree?
12. What is nondisjunction?
13. Give an example of a human trait that is controlled by more than one pair of genes.
14. Name one sex-linked trait and describe how it is inherited.
15. How is a pedigree helpful to a geneticist?

30–4 Genetic Disorders

- Sickle-cell anemia and phenylketonuria (PKU) are two human genetic disorders.

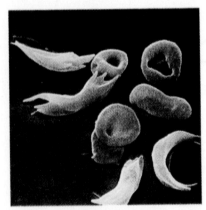

Figure 30–9 Notice the abnormal sickle shape of these red blood cells.

Sometimes a gene contains an error. When this happens, the person who receives the defective gene will have a genetic disorder. Two examples of human genetic disorders are sickle-cell anemia and phenylketonuria (fen-uhl-keet-oh-NOOR-ee-uh), or PKU.

Sickle-cell anemia is most common in people of African descent. The red blood cells of a person with sickle-cell anemia are not shaped normally. The abnormal shape causes the cells to clog blood vessels. The result is severe pain and, in some cases, an early death.

People with PKU are missing an important enzyme that normally is made by the liver. As a result, they cannot break down certain chemicals in food. PKU can cause brain damage and mental retardation.

At the present time, genetic disorders cannot be cured. However, the symptoms of some genetic disorders can be treated if the disorder is detected early in pregnancy or shortly after birth. For example, a simple blood test can detect the presence of PKU in a newborn baby. The child then can be put on a special diet that will enable him or her to live a normal life.

Some genetic tests can be done during pregnancy. One of these tests is amniocentesis. In amniocentesis, a small amount of the amniotic fluid that surrounds the fetus is drawn out of the uterus. The fluid is then analyzed for signs of genetic disorders. In some cases, treatment can begin even before birth.

How can would-be parents determine their chances of having a child with a genetic disorder? The person who could best answer that question is a genetic counselor. A genetic counselor may use family pedigrees or the results of tests to determine if a man or woman carries the gene for a genetic disorder.

Think & Discuss

16. What does a genetic counselor do?

17. Describe two human genetic disorders.

 18. How can an error in a gene cause a disorder such as PKU?

Have you ever seen a square tomato or corn with purple and white kernels? These unusual organisms do exist, thanks to the wonders of modern genetics. If you are interested in how genes affect the characteristics of living things, you might enjoy a career in genetics.

Animal Breeder

A thoroughbred racehorse, a prize steer, a pedigreed cocker spaniel—all these animals are the result of careful breeding. A person who breeds animals to improve their economic and aesthetic (es-THET-ik) value is an animal breeder.

Most animal breeders work with animals in the field. Animal breeders who work directly with animals often are self-employed. Some animal breeders are involved in laboratory research. Breeders who work in a laboratory often work for state and federal governments or for agricultural service companies.

An animal breeder should have a high school diploma. Courses in agriculture and biology also are recommended. It is important for an animal breeder to enjoy working with animals and to be good at handling them.

For more information: Contact your county or state department of agriculture.

Genetics Laboratory Technician

Much of the knowledge people have today about genetics is the result of genetic research. A person who assists a genetic scientist in the laboratory is called a genetics laboratory technician.

To be a genetics laboratory technician, one must complete a formal training program or an associate degree program. Genetics laboratory technicians prepare samples for microscopic study. Technicians also may perform certain microscopic tests and analyze their results.

For more information: Write to the Genetics Society of America, 9650 Rockville Pike, Bethesda, MD 20814.

Genetic Counselor

Some human diseases, such as sickle-cell anemia and Tay-Sachs disease, are inherited. Inherited diseases are passed from parent to offspring. Genetic counselors talk with and advise parents who are concerned about passing on genes to their children.

Most genetic counselors hold a master's degree in genetic counseling, nursing, or social work. Genetic counselors work mainly in medical centers and teaching hospitals. Many genetic counselors also are involved in research.

For more information: Write to the March of Dimes, Birth Defects Foundation, 1275 Mamaroneck Ave., White Plains, NY 10605.

Chapter Review

CHAPTER SUMMARY

30-1 Chromosomes

- The chromosome theory states that genes are found in chromosomes.
- Sex chromosomes determine the sex of an organism.
- Sex chromosomes are called X chromosomes and Y chromosomes.

30-2 The Genetic Code

- The DNA molecule is made up of four nitrogen bases—adenine, thymine, cytosine, and guanine.
- The DNA molecule also contains sugar molecules and phosphate groups.
- DNA replicates by splitting apart between base pairs.
- When a DNA molecule replicates, two new molecules that are identical to the original molecule are formed.

- A mutation results in a change in the genetic code.

30-3 Human Genetics

- Blood type and skin color are human traits that are determined by the combination of several gene pairs.
- The sex chromosomes carry genes for certain traits called sex-linked traits, in addition to determining sex.
- Hemophilia and color blindness are two sex-linked traits.

30-4 Genetic Disorders

- Sickle-cell anemia is a genetic disorder that causes abnormally shaped red blood cells.
- Phenylketonuria (PKU) is a genetic disorder that results in the lack of an enzyme made by the liver.

VOCABULARY LIST

autosomes (523)	mutagen (527)	pedigree (529)	sex chromosomes (523)
chromosomes (522)	mutation (527)	replication (526)	X chromosomes (523)
chromosome theory (522)	nondisjunction (531)	RNA (527)	Y chromosome (523)
DNA (524)			

VOCABULARY REVIEW

Matching   Write the word or term from the Vocabulary List that best matches each description.

1. process by which DNA is duplicated
2. chart showing a family's history for a genetic trait
3. main substance in chromosomes
4. condition when chromosomes do not separate during meiosis
5. genes are carried on chromosomes
6. cause of a mutation

Applying Definitions   Explain the difference between the words in each pair.

1. RNA, DNA
2. sex chromosomes, autosomes
3. mutation, mutagen
4. X chromosome, Y chromosome
5. chromosome, gene
6. replication, nondisjunction
7. gene, trait
8. guanine, cytosine

True or False Write true if the statement is true. If the statement is false, change the underlined word or words to make the statement true.

1. The movement of chromosomes during <u>meiosis</u> proves that Mendel's ideas were correct.
2. <u>Autosomes</u> determine the sex of an organism.
3. A change in the genetic code of an organism results in a <u>mutation</u>.
4. The letters "RNA" stand for <u>ribonucleic</u> acid.
5. Humans have <u>23</u> chromosomes.
6. The four bases in DNA are adenine, <u>thymine</u>, guanine, and cytosine.
7. Females have two <u>Y</u> chromosomes.
8. Blood type is determined by <u>three</u> pairs of genes.
9. Genetic disorders <u>can</u> be cured.
10. Down's syndrome is a condition that results from <u>nondisjunction</u>.

Question and Answer Rewrite each heading in the Chapter Outline on page 520 as a question. Then answer each of the questions you have written.

Understanding a Diagram Use the diagram of sex determination shown in Figure 30–6 (page 529) to answer each of the following.

1. How many different combinations of sex chromosomes are possible?
2. What is the probability of a couple having a son?
3. Which parent determines the sex of the child? Why?

Writing the Main Ideas Using the Chapter Outline on page 520, write the main idea for each heading in the outline.

Critical Thinking Answer each of the following in complete sentences.

1. Why was the development of the microscope important to the science of genetics?
2. Explain the following statement: "The science of genetics is built on the work of many people."
3. Why was the discovery of chromosomes an important breakthrough for genetics?
4. How can an error in only one gene affect future generations?
5. If you knew of a genetic disorder in your family, would you see a genetic counselor before having children? Why or why not?
6. In addition to finding genetic disorders, amniocentesis also indicates whether the fetus is male or female. Should amniocentesis be used for this purpose only? Explain.

1. Read *The Double Helix* by James Watson and write a book report.
2. Make a pedigree of your family for a specific trait, such as tongue rolling, or blood type. Include as many generations and individuals as you can. Your older relatives may be a good source of information.
3. Report to the class on a genetic disorder not mentioned in this chapter. Describe causes and characteristics of the disorder, genetic tests for the disorder, and any treatments available for the disorder. You may want to consult your local March of Dimes for information.

Chapter 31 | Applied Genetics

Chapter Outline

Objectives

After you have completed this chapter, you will be able to

31-1 **describe** the process of mass selection.
31-1 **compare** inbreeding and hybridization.
31-2 **explain** the importance of genetic engineering.
31-3 **explain** what is meant by cloning.
31-3 **explain** what is meant by polyploidy.

Science Process Skills

In this chapter, two science skills are highlighted. Symbols show some places where these skills are used.

▶ **Inferring:** When you infer, you form a conclusion based upon facts and not direct observation.

▣ **Hypothesizing:** When you hypothesize, you state a suggested answer to a problem based upon known information.

Have you ever been to a dog show? If you have, you know how many different kinds of dogs there are. Show dogs are bred to have physical characteristics that meet a certain set of standards. A tail that is too short, or ears that are a little too large, for example, could cause a dog to miss out on a blue ribbon.

People have been selectively breeding animals and plants for thousands of years. In fact, archaeologists (AR-kee-OL-uh-jists) have found that people first domesticated animals about 10,000 years ago. People probably noticed that the offspring of strong animals had the same traits as their parents. The animals with desirable traits could be mated to produce more animals with the same traits. Although they did not know about genes, these early people were using a form of applied genetics.

31-1 Plant and Animal Breeding

Key Points

- Mass selection involves crossing and growing plants with desired traits until the desired traits appear consistently.

- Inbreeding involves crossing genetically similar organisms.

- Hybridization involves crossing genetically different organisms.

Animals and plants are bred to produce organisms with traits that are desirable to people. Dogs may be bred to do certain jobs, such as herding sheep. Beef cattle are bred to provide food. Plants such as wheat and corn are bred to produce hardy and nutritious food crops.

Early people did not know about the science of genetics, but they knew that by planting seeds from productive plants they could grow more productive plants. The process of carefully breeding organisms with certain traits to produce offspring that always have those traits is called **controlled breeding.** Animal and plant breeders use several different techniques when they control the breeding of organisms.

Mass Selection

Imagine that you are a plant grower and that you want to breed plants with colorful flowers. Flowering plants produce many seeds. How can you decide which seeds to grow and which plants to cross?

Plant breeders use a technique called **mass selection.** In mass selection, plants that show the desired traits are crossed. When these plants produce seeds, the seeds are collected and grown. When the plants from these seeds produce offspring, seeds are saved and grown only from the plants that show the desired traits. This process is repeated for several generations. When the plants show the desired traits consistently, a new variety of plant has been developed. For example, over 20,000 new varieties of wheat have been developed. The new varieties of wheat were bred to produce more protein.

Inbreeding

Another breeding technique is **inbreeding.** Inbreeding is the crossing of closely related organisms. Self-pollination in plants is an example of inbreeding. Inbred organisms have genes that are very similar to their parents' genes.

Inbreeding is used to keep certain kinds of animals pure. Purebred animals maintain their desirable traits. For example, thoroughbred racehorses are bred for speed.

Figure 31–1 The American plant breeder Luther Burbank developed new plant varieties by mass selection.

Inbreeding also can be used to strengthen certain traits in plants. One problem with inbreeding is that it produces organisms that are too genetically similar. Because they have few genetic differences, inbred organisms may tend to get certain diseases or may be unable to adapt to environmental changes. How might inbreeding be harmful to a species?

Another problem with inbreeding is that genes for undesirable traits may form pairs during fertilization. As a result, undesirable traits often show up in organisms that have been inbred. For example, inbred dogs may have physical or behavioral problems.

Figure 31-2 The strong muscles of this racehorse are the result of inbreeding.

Hybridization

Have you ever seen a mule? Did you ever hear of a liger? A mule is the offspring of a male donkey and a female horse. A liger is the offspring of a male lion and a female tiger. Mules and ligers are produced by a technique called **hybridization** (hy-brid-ih-ZAY-shun). In hybridization, two different kinds of organisms are crossed. The resulting offspring, called hybrids, have characteristics of both parents. For example, a mule has the traits of two different species—the horse and the donkey.

When two varieties of plants are crossed, the hybrid offspring may show some of the best traits of both varieties. A hybrid called triticale (trit-i-KAY-lee), for example, is produced by crossing wheat and rye. Triticale is more nutritious than either wheat or rye.

Study Hint

Hybridization also can occur naturally in plants and animals.

Figure 31-3 The mule shown with its mother (left) was fathered by a donkey (right).

Hybridization is the opposite of inbreeding. Because the organisms used in hybridization are genetically different, hybrids are likely to be stronger and healthier than inbred organisms. This quality is called **hybrid vigor.**

Think & Discuss

1. What is controlled breeding?
2. What is mass selection?
3. How does inbreeding differ from hybridization?
4. What are two problems with inbreeding?
5. Why might some purebred dogs not be good pets?

31-2 Genetic Engineering

Key Points

- Genetic engineering involves transferring genes from one organism to another.
- Genetic engineering can be used to produce human proteins and better plants.

Have you ever seen a Supermouse? Supermouse is not a character in a cartoon. It is the nickname given to an experimental mouse produced by researchers at the University of Pennsylvania. Supermouse is twice the size of a normal mouse. It is the result of a fascinating new technology called **genetic engineering.** Genetic engineering is a form of applied genetics in which scientists work directly with individual genes.

Recombinant DNA

Pieces of DNA that contain DNA from a different organism are called **recombinant DNA.** Recombinant DNA is made by inserting genes from one organism into an existing strand of DNA. This process is similar to splicing a piece of recording tape. In fact, scientists call this technique **gene splicing.** Gene splicing is the process by which segments of DNA are transferred from the genes of one organism to the genes of another organism. The advantage of gene splicing is that the transferred genes become part of the receiving organism's DNA. As a result, the trait carried by the genes is passed on to future generations.

Look at Figure 31–4 on page 541. Figure 31–4 shows how human genes are inserted into the DNA of *E. coli*, a common bacterium. Part of the DNA of *E. coli* is shaped

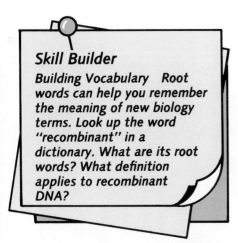

Skill Builder

Building Vocabulary   Root words can help you remember the meaning of new biology terms. Look up the word "recombinant" in a dictionary. What are its root words? What definition applies to recombinant DNA?

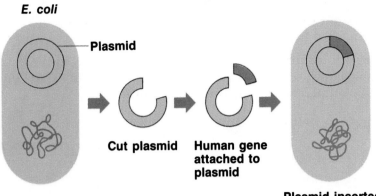

E. coli

Plasmid

Cut plasmid

Human gene attached to plasmid

Plasmid inserted into E. coli

Figure 31-4 Adding a human gene to an *E. coli* plasmid results in a plasmid with both human and bacterial DNA.

like a ring. This ring is called a **plasmid.** Using gene-splicing techniques, scientists snip open the plasmid ring and attach a piece of DNA from a human cell to the cut ends of the plasmid. Then the plasmid ring is closed again. The plasmid now contains a gene that directs the bacterium to produce a human protein.

Products of Recombinant DNA

An important human protein that now is being produced by E. coli bacteria is insulin. Insulin is a hormone that controls the level of sugar in the blood. Insulin is normally secreted by the pancreas. People with diabetes, however, cannot produce insulin. The insulin produced by genetically engineered E. coli can be used by diabetics.

Another useful protein that can be made by bacteria is interferon. Interferon is produced by human body cells for the purpose of fighting viruses. For many years, scientists believed that interferon might be useful in fighting serious diseases such as cancer. There was not enough interferon available, however, to test this hypothesis. As a result of gene splicing, scientists now have enough interferon to carry out their experiments.

A number of vaccines can be produced by genetic engineering. You will recall that a vaccine contains a small amount of a dead or weakened virus. When the vaccine is injected, it causes the body to produce antibodies to the virus. Vaccines can be genetically engineered by inserting viral genes into yeast cells. The yeast cells multiply rapidly, becoming factories for the production of the virus to be used in the vaccine.

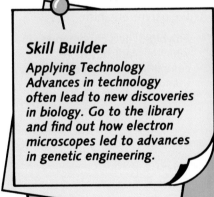

Skill Builder

Applying Technology Advances in technology often lead to new discoveries in biology. Go to the library and find out how electron microscopes led to advances in genetic engineering.

▶ Products of recombinant DNA are becoming very important in agriculture. Plants can be genetically engineered to resist disease, cold, or drought. An interesting example is the development of "ice-minus" bacteria. These bacteria can help slow down the formation of ice on plants. Why is this important?

Think & Discuss

6. What is genetic engineering?
7. Describe the process of gene splicing.
8. How are genetic-engineering techniques used to produce human proteins?
9. How is genetic engineering used in agriculture?
★ 10. How might genetic engineering be harmful?

31-3 Genetic Techniques

In addition to controlled breeding and genetic engineering, scientists can use other methods to change the genetic code of organisms. These techniques have been used for many years to produce unusual plants.

Cloning

Have you ever eaten seedless grapes or a naval orange? Perhaps you have wondered how fruits without seeds are able to reproduce. The answer is **cloning.** Cloning is the production of organisms with identical genes. The plants that produce seedless fruits are **clones.** A clone is an organism that is genetically identical to its parent.
▶ Clones such as seedless grapes are the result of **vegetative propagation** (vej-uh-TAYT-iv   prahp-uh-GAY-shun). Vegetative propagation is a form of asexual reproduction in plants. Do you think a clone could be produced through sexual reproduction? Why or why not?

Have you ever taken a cutting from a plant to grow a new plant? If you put pussywillow branches into water, the branches soon will develop roots. Then the rooted branches can be planted in soil. The pussywillow that grows from the branches will be genetically identical to the original plant from which you took the cuttings.

Key Points

- Cloning produces organisms that are genetically identical to the parent organism.

- Polyploidy is a condition in which a plant has more complete sets of chromosomes than usual.

ACTIVITY 31-1

PROBLEM: How can a model be used to illustrate recombinant DNA technology?

Science Process Skills
modeling, observing, analyzing

Background Information
The common bacterium *Escherichia coli*, or *E. coli*, is used in recombinant DNA technology. Segments of DNA can be spliced into circular forms of DNA, or plasmids. These recombinant DNA organisms then can produce proteins as the organisms grow and reproduce.

Materials

drawing compass   tracing paper
construction paper   tape
scissors

Procedure

1. Using a compass, draw a circle with a diameter of 6 cm on construction paper.
2. Within the circle, draw a smaller circle with a diameter of 2.5 cm so that you have a band of about 1.8 cm around the smaller circle.
3. Cut out the large circle and then cut out the center of the large circle so that you have a ring. **CAUTION: Be careful when using scissors.**
4. Follow steps 1–3 to make two more rings.
5. Using tracing paper, trace the DNA segments shown and label the segments.

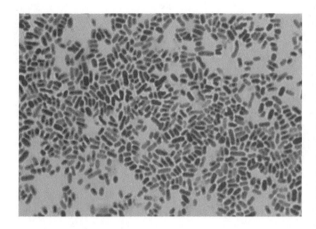

6. Cut out each DNA segment pattern.
7. Use your rings and tracing patterns to make three models of recombinant DNA. Follow the steps that a geneticist would use to form recombinant DNA. Use your text as a reference.

Observations
1. **MODEL**   What do the rings of paper represent on your model?
2. If your model were living, what proteins would each bacterium make?

Conclusions
1. Explain the procedure you used to form your recombinant DNA models.
2. Why can the recombinant DNA models you made be called "protein factories"?

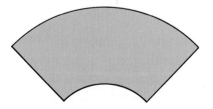

**DNA Segment:
Human Growth Hormone**

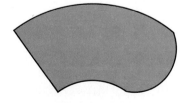

**DNA Segment:
Interferon**

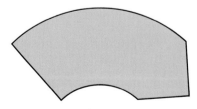

**DNA Segment:
Insulin**

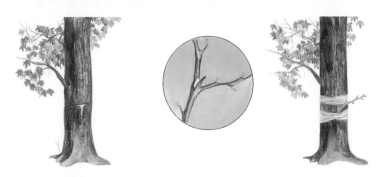

Figure 31-5 In grafting, a branch from one tree is inserted into the trunk of another tree.

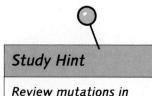

Study Hint

Review mutations in Chapter 30.

Figure 31-6 Notice the difference in size between the polyploid lilies on the left and the day lilies on the right.

The first navel orange tree was the result of a mutation. The orange grower noticed that the seedless oranges were sweeter and jucier than ordinary oranges. The grower then grafted branches from the navel orange tree onto normal orange trees. The grafted branches produced seedless navel oranges.

Recently, scientists have been able to clone entire plants and some animals from a single cell. For example, many banana plants can be grown by taking cells from a single banana plant. Scientists also have used cloning to produce mice that are genetically identical to the mouse from which the original cell was taken.

Polyploidy

Perhaps you have seen vegetables, fruits, or flowers that are much larger than usual. The chances are that some of these fruits, flowers, or vegetables are the result of **polyploidy** (PAHL-i-ploi-dee). Polyploidy is a condition in which a plant has more than two complete sets of chromosomes. Polyploidy occurs when chromosomes do not separate properly during cell division.

Polyploidy can be artificially induced by the chemical colchicine (KOL-chi-seen). Colchicine prevents cells from dividing after the chromosomes are duplicated. This technique is used by plant growers to produce polyploid varieties of plants such as strawberries and marigolds.

Think & Discuss

11. What is cloning? What are two methods of cloning?

12. What is polyploidy?

★ 13. Would a person cloned from a single cell be identical to the person from whom the cell was taken? Explain.

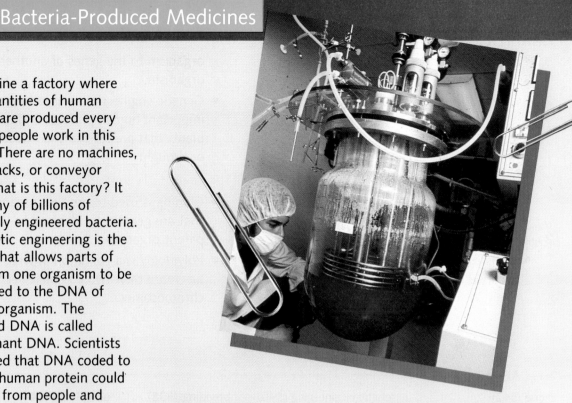

Imagine a factory where huge quantities of human proteins are produced every day. No people work in this factory. There are no machines, smokestacks, or conveyor belts. What is this factory? It is a colony of billions of genetically engineered bacteria.

Genetic engineering is the process that allows parts of DNA from one organism to be transferred to the DNA of another organism. The combined DNA is called recombinant DNA. Scientists discovered that DNA coded to produce human protein could be taken from people and joined with the DNA of simple organisms such as bacteria.

Once a bacterium has the DNA code for a human protein, it will produce that protein. Of course, the amount of protein produced by one tiny bacterium is quite small. When the bacterium reproduces, however, copies of the protein-coded DNA are passed on to the next generation of bacteria. Since bacteria reproduce on the average of once every 20 minutes, it is not long before millions of bacteria are producing the human protein.

Two of the most valuable proteins produced by genetically engineered bacteria are insulin and interferon. Insulin is the hormone that controls the level of sugar in the blood. People who do not produce enough insulin have a disease called diabetes. For the past 60 years, people with diabetes have been treated with insulin produced by animals. The problem with this treatment is that some people are allergic to animal insulin. In addition, animal insulin is expensive and limited in supply. In 1980, the first diabetic was successfully treated with genetically engineered insulin. Scientists predict that soon such insulin will be widely available.

The protein interferon, which is produced by human body cells, helps fight viral diseases. For a long time, scientists have thought that interferon may be effective in treating cancer and other serious diseases. However, there has never been enough interferon available to test this idea. Today, scientists have sufficient amounts of genetically engineered interferon available for use in laboratory experiments. Someday these experiments may lead to the development of an important new drug.

To Think About
- Why would a person allergic to animal insulin not have an allergic reaction to genetically engineered insulin?
- Despite its obvious advantages, genetic engineering is very controversial. Can you think of reasons why people might object to this technology?

Chapter Review

CHAPTER SUMMARY

31-1 Plant and Animal Breeding

- Mass selection involves crossing plants with desired traits for many generations until the offspring show the desired traits consistently.
- Inbreeding is the crossing of closely related organisms.
- Hybridization is the crossing of genetically different organisms.

31-2 Genetic Engineering

- Gene splicing is a form of genetic engineering that involves transferring segments of DNA from the genes of one organism to the genes of another organism.
- Genetic engineering is used to produce important human proteins and to produce plants that are resistant to disease, cold, or drought.

31-3 Genetic Techniques

- Cloning is used to produce organisms that are genetically identical to the parent organism.
- Polyploidy is a condition in which a plant has more than two complete sets of chromosomes.

VOCABULARY LIST

clone (542)	genetic engineering (540)	inbreeding (538)	polyploidy (544)
cloning (542)	hybridization (539)	mass selection (538)	recombinant DNA (540)
controlled breeding (538)	hybrid vigor (540)	plasmid (541)	vegetative propagation (542)
gene splicing (540)			

VOCABULARY REVIEW

Matching   Write the word or term from the Vocabulary List that best matches each description.

1. quality shown by hybrid organisms
2. process by which genes are inserted into a strand of DNA
3. ring of bacterial DNA
4. crossing closely related organisms
5. having more than two complete sets of chromosomes
6. organism that is genetically identical to its parent
7. crossing two different species or varieties
8. pieces of DNA that contain DNA from a different organism
9. breeding organisms to produce offspring with certain traits
10. form of applied genetics involving individual genes

Identifying Relationships   Identify the word or term in each group that does not belong. Explain why it does not belong with the group.

1. gene splicing, genetic engineering, cloning
2. controlled breeding, recombinant DNA, mass selection
3. hybrid vigor, plasmid, gene splicing
4. hybridization, inbreeding, polyploidy
5. vegetative propagation, self-pollination, cross-pollination

Completion   Write the word or words that best complete each sentence.

1. Colchicine is a chemical used to cause _____.
2. The insertion of genes into a strand of DNA is called _____.
3. Rooting a plant cutting is a form of _____.
4. Polyploid plants have _____ chromosomes than normal.
5. Mixed-breed dogs that are stronger than purebred dogs show _____.
6. The breeding technique that is most likely to produce undesirable traits is _____.
7. Mass selection and inbreeding are methods of _____.
8. The DNA in a bacterium such as *E. coli* is in a ring called a _____.
9. Gene splicing is a method of _____.

Finding the Main Idea   Use the section number to find the sentence that answers each question. Then, write the sentence.

1. What is controlled breeding? (31-1)
2. Why are animals and plants bred? (31-1)
3. Why is the process of mass selection repeated for several generations? (31-1)
4. Why are hybrid organisms often stronger and healthier than inbred organisms? (31-1)
5. How is recombinant DNA produced? (31-2)
6. How are human genes inserted into the DNA of *E. coli*? (31-2)
7. What is a human protein that can be made by bacteria? (31-2)
8. What is a clone? (31-3)
9. What is polyploidy? (31-3)
10. How does colchicine cause polyploidy? (31-3)

Writing for Understanding   One way to find out if you understand something is to write a brief summary of the information in your own words. Reread Section 31-3, Genetic Techniques, on pages 542–544, and write a brief summary of the information.

Critical Thinking   Answer each of the following in complete sentences.

1. Do you think that hybridization occurs in nature? Explain.

2. Why do you think some people are opposed to the idea of genetic engineering? Do you agree or disagree with these people? Why?
3. Why are some newly developed kinds of fruits or vegetables more expensive than the original kinds?
4. Would you rather have a mixed-breed dog or a purebred dog? Why?
5. If you were a scientist involved in genetic engineering, which organisms would you use in your research? Why?

1. Find out about different grafting techniques. Describe these procedures to the class. Include diagrams to explain each technique.
2. Choose a breed of dog or horse and write a brief history of the breed. Use library sources to gather your information. How and why

was the breed developed? What different breeds were crossed to produce the breed? How is this breed used today?
3. Read a biography of Luther Burbank and write a report describing his contributions to plant breeding.

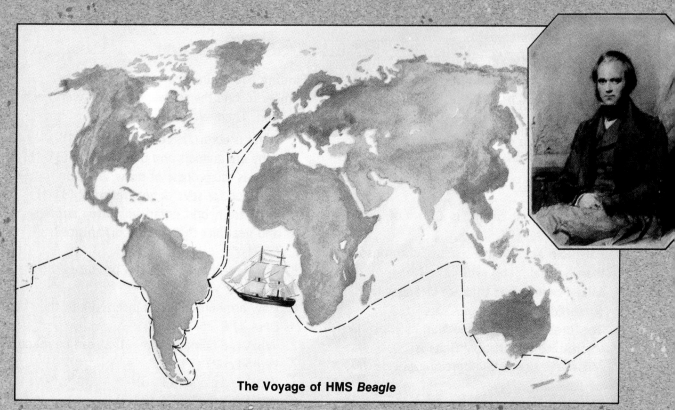

The Voyage of HMS *Beagle*

Evolution is the process by which organisms change through time. In 1859, a scientist named Charles Darwin explained his ideas about evolution. Today, most scientists accept Darwin's ideas.

Darwin took a trip to the Galapagos Islands. You can trace his route on the map shown. While on the Galapagos Islands, Darwin observed many species of birds called finches. Some of the different species of finches are shown here. How are they alike? How are they different?

Now look at the other drawings and photographs that represent chapters in this unit. What organisms do you see here that no longer exist? How do you think these pictures are related to evolution?

Change Through Time

CONTENTS

Theories of Evolution

When you have completed this chapter, you will be able to

32–1 **compare** Lamarck's and Darwin's theories of evolution.

32–1 **explain** the theory of natural selection.

32–2 **identify** four factors that cause changes in the gene pool.

32–2 **explain** how isolation influences evolution.

32–3 **describe** two theories that explain the rate of evolution.

Science Process Skills

In this chapter, two science skills are highlighted. Symbols show some places where these skills are used.

▶ **Inferring**: When you infer, you form a conclusion based upon facts and not direct observation.

▣ **Hypothesizing**: When you hypothesize, you state a suggested answer to a problem based upon known information.

Biologists have classified more than 1,500,000 species of organisms so far. Many scientists estimate that there may be 10 million species of organisms living on the earth.

There are many differences between organisms of two different species. However, there also are differences among organisms of the same species. Biologists call the differences among organisms **variations.** *Notice the variations in the stripe patterns of the zebras in the photograph.*

Have you ever wondered why there are so many variations among organisms? Most biologists conclude that **evolution** *is responsible for the great variety of organisms that exist. Evolution is the process by which organisms change over time.*

Theories of Evolution   551

32-1 Evolution

Until the nineteenth century, most scientists believed that organisms existed as they had first appeared on the earth. By the late 1700s, however, geologists were finding and studying many **fossils.** Fossils are the remains of organisms from long ago. What did the fossils show? The fossils indicated that living things had changed since they first appeared on the earth. For example, geologists were finding fossils of organisms that no longer existed.

Scientists began to wonder how and why living things may have changed. In the 1800s, different theories of evolution were proposed to explain how species, or kinds of organisms, change. One theory was proposed by a French biologist, Jean Baptiste Lamarck. Another theory was proposed by a British biologist, Charles Darwin. Both men believed that organisms change in response to their environment. Their theories of how evolution occurs, however, are different.

Lamarck's Theory

In 1809, Lamarck proposed a way in which evolution could occur. His theory of evolution was based on two hypotheses. One hypothesis stated that organisms develop traits, or characteristics, by the use or disuse of body parts. For example, if a body part is used, it becomes larger and stronger. However, if a body part is not used, it becomes smaller and weaker.

Figure 32–1 By examining the teeth of this fossil, scientists can infer that the animal was a plant eater.

Figure 32-2 What effect will running have on the leg muscles of this deer?

Figure 32-3 Lamarck thought that giraffes developed long necks by stretching to reach the leaves of trees.

Study Hint

Look up the meaning of the word "acquire" in the dictionary.

Lamarck's other hypothesis stated that **acquired characteristics,** or the traits that organisms develop during their lifetimes, are passed on from parents to their offspring. Lamarck believed that evolution takes place as a result of the inheritance of acquired characteristics.

Lamarck used the giraffe as a model for his theory. You can see Lamarck's model in Figure 32–3. Notice that Lamarck assumed that the first giraffes had short necks. What did the short-necked giraffes eat? They fed on grass. Then, due to a change in climate, the grass began to die.

According to Lamarck, giraffes began to eat the leaves of trees in response to their changing environment. As giraffes stretched their necks to reach leaves on high branches, the giraffes' necks grew longer. The acquired trait of a longer neck was passed on to later generations. Thus, after many generations, short-necked giraffes evolved into long-necked giraffes.

You know that when following the scientific method, a scientist must gather evidence to support a hypothesis. Lamarck did not have any observations or evidence to support his theory. Therefore, most scientists did not accept Lamarck's theory. Using what you know about genetics, why do you think that many scientists do not support Lamarck's theory?

Investigations of Charles Darwin

Charles Darwin was born in 1809. As a boy, he was very curious about nature. In 1831, at the age of 22, Darwin went on a voyage with a British ship named the HMS *Beagle*. The HMS *Beagle* went on a mapping and collecting expedition to South America and the South Pacific.

Figure 32-4 Darwin published his ideas about evolution twenty years after his voyage on the HMS *Beagle*.

Darwin served as the ship's chief **naturalist.** What is a naturalist? A naturalist is a person who studies nature by observing plants and animals.

What did Darwin observe during the five-year voyage of the *Beagle*? He observed many interesting things. For example, he saw how earthquakes and other geologic processes could change the land. Darwin began to think that organisms would have to adapt to such changes in their environment.

▶ Darwin observed thousands of species of plants and animals and collected many organisms. In addition, he collected many different kinds of fossils. He also kept careful notes of all his observations. Why do you think it was important that Darwin kept his information organized?

Darwin visited the Galapagos Islands during his time with the HMS *Beagle*. The Galapagos Islands are located about 1000 km off the west coast of South America. While there, Darwin studied many different kinds of plants and animals. He was surprised to find that many of the organisms he observed were similar to those found on the coast of South America. Figure 32–5 shows one of the many interesting species of animals found on the Galapagos Islands.

While on the Galapagos Islands, Darwin observed 13 different species of finches. The different species were similar to each other in many ways. They also were similar to a species of finch found on the mainland of South America.

Darwin observed that the beak of each species of finch had a different shape. Each kind of beak was adapted for eating a certain kind of food. For example, some finches

Figure 32-5 The Spanish word "galápagos" means "turtles." The Galapagos Islands were named for the giant tortoises on the islands.

Fruit eater

Vegetarian tree finch

Insect eater

Woodpecker finch

Cactus eater

Cactus ground finch

Seed eater

Large ground finch

Figure 32-6 Compare the different beak shapes of these four finches.

eat seeds, while others eat insects. You can see four of the species Darwin observed in Figure 32–6. What does the woodpecker finch eat?

Because the finches were similar, Darwin inferred that the finches had a common ancestor, probably one related to the South American finch. He concluded that the 13 species of finches had developed different beaks as a result of evolution.

Darwin's Theory of Evolution

When Darwin returned home, he began to sort out his observations and develop his ideas about evolution. Twenty years after his voyage, he published a book called *On the Origin of Species by Means of Natural Selection.* In his book, Darwin presented a theory explaining how species of organisms may have evolved into new species.

Darwin was influenced by another British scientist, Alfred Russel Wallace. Wallace suggested the same ideas about evolution in 1858. He wrote his ideas in an essay, which he sent to Darwin. Today, Darwin's theory of evolution is accepted by most scientists.

What are Darwin's main ideas about evolution? Darwin's theory of evolution can be summarized in four main ideas:

- **Overproduction.** Each species produces many more organisms than can survive and reproduce. For example, a female codfish produces more than a million eggs each mating season. However, only a few survive to adulthood and reproduce.

- **Competition.** Because of the overproduction of offspring, organisms must compete for limited resources, such as food, water, and a place to live.

Study Hint

After you read about Darwin's theory of evolution, list his four main hypotheses.

Figure 32-7 What similarities can you find between these puppies and their mother?

Study Hint

Study Figure 32-8 as you read about how natural selection affected British peppered moths.

- **Variations.** Variations, or differences among traits, occur among members of the same species. Look at Figure 32–7. Notice that none of the puppies are exactly alike. How are the puppies alike? How are they different?

- **Survival of the Fit.** Organisms with traits that make them well adapted to their environment have a better chance of surviving and reproducing. Darwin used the term **natural selection** to describe the process by which organisms with certain traits have a better chance of surviving and reproducing. What are traits that help organisms survive called?

Organisms that survive and reproduce pass on their traits to their offspring. As the process of natural selection continues through many generations, species change and become better adapted to their environment. As a result, evolution by natural selection occurs.

An example of natural selection took place in England during Darwin's lifetime. As you read about this example of natural selection, keep in mind that the environment does not cause changes in organisms. The environment only determines which variations will be selected.

During the early part of the nineteenth century, most British peppered moths were light gray in color. Some peppered moths were white. There also were a few black peppered moths. The different colored moths were variations of the same species.

The gray peppered moths were the same color as the tree trunks on which the moths would land. Therefore, it was difficult for birds to see the gray moths. However, it

Figure 32-8 Which moth is more fit for its environment? dark moth

was easy for birds to spot the black moths. As a result, many black moths were eaten. Few survived and reproduced.

During the first half of the nineteenth century, many factories were built. The factories gave off large amounts of soot, which began to blacken the trees in England. The environment in which British peppered moths lived changed. Now when a gray peppered moth landed on a blackened tree trunk, the moth could be easily seen and eaten by birds. However, the black moths blended in with their environment. As a result, many black moths survived and reproduced. In a very short period of time, most British peppered moths were black. The color of most British peppered moths had changed due to natural selection.

Skill Builder
Observing   Carefully observe four different organisms. Make a list of as many adaptations as you can for each of the organisms you observe. Then explain how each organism's adaptations help the organism survive.

Think & Discuss

1. What is natural selection?
2. What was Lamarck's theory of evolution?
★ 3. How might a decrease in air pollution affect the color of British peppered moths?

32–2 Evolution and Genetics

You have just learned that an important part of Darwin's theory of evolution is that there are variations among members of the same species. Darwin, however, could not explain the cause of variations, or how they are passed on to offspring. Why do you think Darwin could not explain the cause of variations?

Today, scientists studying evolution examine the variations in a **population.** What is a population? A

Key Point
• Natural selection, mutation, migration, and isolation cause changes in the gene pool.

Figure 32-9   A walrus population is all the walruses that live in the same area.

ACTIVITY 32-1

PROBLEM: How do adaptations help an organism survive in its environment?

Science Process Skills
inferring, observing, organizing

Background Information
An organism lives and reproduces successfully in an environment because the organism is adapted to the environment. An example of an adaptation is protective coloration. Some organisms blend in with their environments. These organisms are less likely to be eaten by predators. An organism that can be seen easily by a predator is more likely to be eaten.

Materials
    3 sheets of black construction
        paper, 11" x 17"
    1 sheet of white construction
        paper, 11" x 17"
    scissors

Procedure
1. Work with a partner.
2. Copy the Data Table shown.

Data Table: Moth Trials		
TRIAL	NUMBER OF MOTHS	
	Black Moths	White Moths
Trial 1		
Trial 2		
Trial 3		
Total		

3. Cut out 15 black squares 3 cm x 3 cm. **CAUTION: Always be careful when using scissors.** These squares will represent black moths.
4. Cut out 15 white squares 3 cm x 3 cm. These squares will represent white moths.

5. Have your partner place 2 large pieces of black construction paper on the floor. The construction paper represents the environment.
6. While you look away, have your partner randomly place the 30 moths on the black construction paper.
7. When your partner says "Ready," turn around and pick up any 12 moths as fast as you can.
8. Count the number of white and black moths that you picked. Record the results for the trial in the Data Table.
9. Repeat step 8 two more times.
10. Find the total number of black moths and the total number of white moths in the three trials.
11. Switch roles with your partner and repeat the activity.
12. Obtain class totals of the black and white moths for the activity.

Observations
1. Did you pick up more white moths or black moths?
2. Which color moth would be more visible to a predator in a dark environment?

Conclusions
1. **a.** Which moths are better adapted to live in a dark environment? **b.** In what way are these moths adapted?
2. Which moths would most likely be eaten by a bird in a dark environment? Explain your answer.
3. Why would finding the class totals be a better sample than you and your partner's samples?
4. **INFER** If the environment were light-colored, how would the results of the activity have been different?

Figure 32-10 How many guinea pigs are shown? What percentage are all black?

population is all the members of the same species that live in the same area. For example, all the striped bass that live in a stream make up a population. All the students in your school make up a population.

When scientists study how populations change, they look at the kind and number of genes in a population. All the genes in a population make up the **gene pool.** The gene pool is a collection of all the genes for all the traits in a population. A gene pool also can be defined by the amounts or percentages of different kinds of genes.

The gene pool for coat color of a population of guinea pigs may contain the dominant gene, B, for black coat and the recessive gene, b, for white coat. In one area, gene B may occur in 10% of the population and gene b may occur in 90%. In another area, gene B may occur in 90% of the population and gene b in 10%. What do you think would happen to the color of guinea pigs if both of these populations moved into the same area?

Evolution can occur only when there is a change in the kinds or percentages of genes in the gene pool of a population. What can cause changes in the gene pool of a population? Four things that can cause changes in the gene pool are natural selection, **mutation** (myoo-TAY-shun), **migration,** and isolation.

Natural Selection

Natural selection is the major cause of changes in the gene pool of a population. How does natural selection change the gene pool of a population? Natural selection allows organisms that are well adapted to their environment to survive and reproduce. Other less-fit

Skill Builder

Organizing   Make a list of some traits found in your classmates, such as eye color and hair color. Which variations of each trait are found most often among your classmates? Using the information you have gathered, describe the gene pool for your class.

organisms have a lower chance of surviving and reproducing. Therefore, well-adapted organisms pass on more of their genes to the next generation. As a result, the frequency of different genes changes from one generation to the next. Frequency is the number of times an action is repeated during a specific period of time. Gene frequency refers to the number of times a gene appears in a population.

Mutation

A mutation is a change in the structure of a gene or chromosome. Today, biologists know that variations in traits are produced through mutations. Mutations are the source of variations that Darwin could not explain. A mutation adds a new gene type to the gene pool. Mutations also may increase the frequency of a gene in a population. Because mutations usually are recessive, a mutated gene may remain in a gene pool for many generations without changing the appearance of a population. A mutation may be either helpful or harmful. Some mutations are neither helpful nor harmful. What do you think is the relationship between mutations and natural selection?

Migration

The movement of members of a species into or out of a population is called migration. When an organism enters a population, the organism adds its genes to the existing gene pool. When an organism leaves a population, its genes are taken out of the gene pool.

Consider a population of white rabbits living in an area. The population has certain genes for different traits. Suppose a group of brown rabbits comes into the area. The brown rabbits will introduce new genes into the gene pool. The brown rabbits also may have different gene frequencies for certain traits. As a result, the gene pool of the original population of rabbits changes.

Isolation

Sometimes, a group of organisms may become isolated from the other members of its population. **Geographic isolation** is a common way for a population to become

Figure 32-11 Albino organisms, such as this bullfrog, lack normal color. Albinism is caused by a mutation.

Figure 32-12 In the Grand Canyon, geographic isolation led to the development of these two squirrel species.

divided. Geographic isolation occurs when a physical barrier separates two populations. Rivers and mountains are two kinds of barriers that can cause geographic isolation. What other kinds of barriers do you think can cause geographic isolation?

▶ Geographic isolation often results in **speciation** (spee-shee-AY-shun), or the development of new species. Why? When a population becomes separated by a barrier, the organisms on either side of the barrier can no longer mate or exchange genes with each other. As a result, variations that occur on one side of a barrier may be different from the variations that occur on the other side of a barrier. What factor would make variations different on each side of a barrier?

What would happen if two populations that have been geographically isolated were reunited? Do you think they could produce offspring? Geographic isolation often results in **reproductive isolation.** Reproductive isolation occurs when organisms in a population can no longer mate and produce offspring. Once reproductive isolation occurs, the two populations cannot produce offspring even if geographic barriers are removed. A new species has evolved.

Study Hint

List four things that cause changes in a gene pool.

Think & Discuss

4. What is speciation?
5. Name four things that can cause changes in a gene pool.
6. How did the gene pool of British peppered moths change as a result of natural selection?

32–3 The Rate of Evolution

Key Point

- The theory of gradualism and the theory of punctuated equilibrium are two theories explaining the rate of evolution.

Study Hint

To see how the front legs of the horse have changed over time, look at Figure 33-4 on page 571.

Most scientists support Darwin's theory of evolution by natural selection. However, not all scientists agree about the rate at which evolution takes place. Like Darwin, many scientists believe that evolution is a slow process in which species change gradually over long periods of time. The gradual change is in response to a slow change in the environment. The process of evolution through slow change is called **gradualism** (GRA-joo-uhl-iz-um).

What evidence supports gradualism? Fossils can support evolution by gradualism. Fossil evidence shows that the structure of the front legs of horses has changed over time. For example, fossils show that as horses became larger, the number of bones in their front legs and toes decreased.

Some scientists have proposed that evolution occurs mostly in a series of rapid changes. In 1972, a theory called **punctuated equilibrium** (PUNK-choo-wayt-ed ee-kwuh-LIB-ree-um) was proposed. The theory of punctuated equilibrium states that species remain unchanged for millions of years. Then, within a short period of time, certain species suddenly die off, while other species suddenly appear.

What evidence supports the theory of punctuated equilibrium? Fossil evidence shows that a group of organisms called the trilobites (TRY-luh-byts) remained unchanged for millions of years. Then the trilobites suddenly died off. Fossil records also show that about 65 million years ago, at the time the dinosaurs died off, many new species of mammals suddenly appeared.

Today, the debate about the rate of evolution continues. Most biologists think that evolution by gradualism takes place. Some biologists, however, think that gradualism has been combined with rapid changes as stated in the theory of punctuated equilibrium.

Think and Discuss

7. What is gradualism?

8. How does the theory of punctuated equilibrium differ from the theory of gradualism?

 9. Why do you think some species die off?

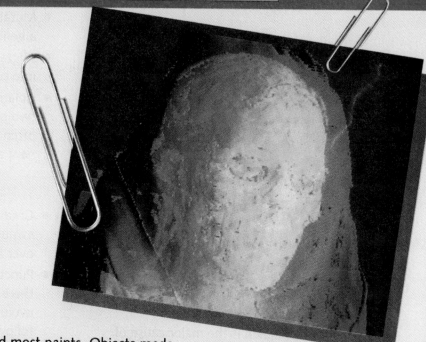

In a laboratory in France, a technician carries out a test called a spectographic analysis. High-energy rays cause the object being analyzed to give off bands of colored light. Does this sound like a nuclear experiment? Actually, the laboratory is located in the Louvre, the famous French museum. The object being analyzed is a bronze Egyptian statue.

Modern technology is often used to study and preserve ancient objects and works of art. For example, spectographic analysis is used to find out what materials an object is made up of. By discovering what objects are made of, scientists can learn about cultures of the past. Scientists also determine what objects are made of so that they can be preserved or protected. Heat, water, light, and chemicals can damage some substances. Art objects also can be damaged by pollutants in the air. Knowing what an object is made of can be used to protect the object from damage by these factors.

Art objects usually are classified into three groups according to the nature of their materials. The first group consists of objects made up of organic materials. Such objects include animal skins, bone, ivory, paper, textiles, wood,

and most paints. Objects made of metals such as gold, silver, copper, bronze, iron, and lead make up the second group. The third group includes objects made up of ceramics, stone, and glass.

Technology often is used to determine the exact composition and structure of an art object. For example, X-ray pictures of furniture can show how the furniture was put together. In electron-probe microanalysis, a beam of electrons is directed at the object being analyzed. The object then gives off X rays that show exactly what elements are present.

Modern technology also is used to preserve objects. For example, objects may be treated with chemicals or paints to protect them from heat and moisture. Objects also

may be placed within a vacuum, or empty space. Not even air is present in a vacuum. Limiting the amount of time an object is exposed to light also can preserve some objects. This is why flash photography is forbidden in some museums. The next time you visit a museum, consider how amazing it is that an object created thousands of years ago has been preserved for you to see.

To Think About

- Many works of art are made of materials from all three groups. How might this make the job of preserving these objects difficult?

- Why would it be helpful to a preserver of art objects to know how a piece of furniture was constructed?

Chapter Review

CHAPTER SUMMARY

32–1 Evolution

- Lamarck believed that organisms develop traits by the use or disuse of body parts.
- The traits an organism develops during its lifetime are called acquired characteristics.
- Lamarck believed evolution occurs by the inheritance of acquired characteristics.
- Darwin's theory of evolution by natural selection states that the environment selects for certain variations.
- Organisms that are well adapted to the environment survive and reproduce.

32–2 Evolution and Genetics

- Natural selection is the major cause of changes in the gene pool.

- Mutation is a change in the structure of a gene or chromosome.
- Migration is the movement of individuals into or out of a population.
- Isolation occurs when barriers separate two populations. Geographic isolation often results in the development of a new species.

32–3 The Rate of Evolution

- Gradualism is the theory that the evolution of new species occurs gradually over long periods of time.
- Punctuated equilibrium is the theory that there are long periods of little evolutionary change. These periods are followed by short periods of time when evolution occurs.

VOCABULARY LIST

acquired characteristics (553)
evolution (551)
fossils (552)
gene pool (559)
geographic isolation (560)

gradualism (562)
migration (559)
mutation (559)
naturalist (554)
natural selection (556)

population (557)
punctuated equilibrium (562)
reproductive isolation (561)
speciation (561)
variations (551)

VOCABULARY REVIEW

Matching   Write the word or term from the Vocabulary List that best matches each description.

1. traits an organism develops
2. the development of a new species
3. evolution of species over a long period of time
4. all the members of the same species in an area
5. movement of individuals into or out of a population
6. a person who studies nature by observing plants and animals

7. change in the structure of a gene or chromosome
8. remains of living things from long ago
9. all the genes in a population
10. process by which well-adapted organisms survive and reproduce

Applying Definitions   Explain the difference between the words in each pair.

1. population, gene pool
2. mutation, variations
3. evolution, punctuated equilibrium
4. geographic isolation, reproductive isolation

True or False Write true if the statement is true. If the statement is false, change the underlined word or words to make the statement true.

1. The theory of evolution by natural selection was proposed by <u>Lamarck</u>.
2. The formation of a new species is called <u>isolation</u>.
3. Variations are produced by <u>mutations</u>.
4. All the frogs in a pond make up a <u>population</u>.
5. On the Galapagos Islands, Darwin observed 13 species of <u>finches</u>.
6. Darwin believed in the theory of <u>punctuated equilibrium</u>.
7. All the <u>genes</u> in a population make up the gene pool.

Question and Answer Rewrite each heading in the Chapter Outline on page 550 as a question. Then, answer each of the questions you have written.

Interpreting a Photograph Use the photograph of the deer in Figure 32–2 (page 552) to answer each of the following.

1. What is the deer doing? running
2. According to Lamarck's theory, what trait is the deer acquiring? strong leg muscles
3. According to Lamarck's theory, why would you expect the deer to have strong leg muscles? because it must run from its predators
4. According to Lamarck's theory of evolution, would the deer's offspring also have strong legs? Explain.

Writing the Main Ideas Using the Chapter Outline on page 550, write the main idea for each heading in the outline.

Critical Thinking Answer each of the following in complete sentences.

1. Compare Lamarck's theory of evolution with Darwin's theory of evolution.
2. How do you think Darwin explained the evolution of 13 species of island finches from a single mainland species?

3. How do you think Darwin's observations of geologic processes influenced his ideas about evolution?
4. An eagle has keen eyesight, which enables it to spot its food. If, as a result of a mutation, an eagle with even keener eyesight arose, what might the effect be?
5. How does the isolation of a small group from the other members of a population favor speciation?

1. Humans, like most other species, have undergone evolution. Using library references, find out about some of the traits in humans that have been selected during evolution. Present your findings to the class.
2. Write a report on one of the following scientists and how he influenced Darwin: Charles Lyell, Thomas Huxley, Joseph Hooker.

3. In recent years, new species of mosquitos have evolved that are resistant to the insecticide DDT. Bacteria that are resistant to penicillin also have evolved. Do research to answer the following questions: **a.** What caused the mosquitos to become resistant to DDT? **b.** Why have penicillin-resistant bacteria become a problem to humans? Write your answers in a report.

Chapter 33 | Evidence for Evolution

Chapter Outline

Objectives

After you have completed this chapter, you will be able to

33–1 **describe** how fossils are formed.

33–1 **explain** two methods of dating fossils.

33–2 **discuss** the importance of the geologic time scale.

33–3 **describe** how evidence from anatomy, embryology, and biochemistry supports the theory of evolution.

Science Process Skills

In this chapter, two science skills are highlighted. Symbols show some places where these skills are used.

Observing: When you observe, you use one or more of your senses to gather information.

Analyzing: When you analyze, you break down a complex idea into simpler parts to make it easier to understand.

Have you ever seen animals such as the ones shown in the picture? These animals are often called horseshoe crabs because their shell is shaped like a horse's hoof. Horseshoe crabs are the only known surviving members of an order of animals that first appeared on the earth over 400 million years ago. Because horseshoe crabs have changed very little over millions of years, scientists refer to them as "living fossils."

Unlike horseshoe crabs, most organisms have evolved, or changed, over long periods of time. For example, the ancestors of modern horses looked very different from the horses of today. Scientists study these changes in organisms to find evidence for evolution.

Evidence for Evolution   567

33–1 Fossil Evidence

- Fossils are the remains or traces of organisms that lived in the past.

- Three kinds of fossils are molds, casts, and imprints.

- Scientists use index fossils and radioactive dating to determine the age of fossils.

Have you ever visited a natural history museum? If you have, you probably saw **fossils** of many different organisms. Fossils are the remains or traces of organisms that lived in the past.

Most fossils are found in layers of **sedimentary** (sed-uh-MEN-tuhr-ee) **rock**. Sedimentary rock is formed from small particles called sediments. Sand, silt, and clay are kinds of sediments. Sediments are carried and deposited by wind and water. Sediments usually build up on the bottom of lakes and ponds.

◉ How is sedimentary rock formed? If you look at a sedimentary rock, such as the one shown in Figure 33–1, you can see the layers of sediment. The layers develop one on top of the other. Over many years, layer upon layer is deposited. The great pressure of all the top layers causes the bottom layers to change to rock. Limestone, sandstone, and shale are three kinds of sedimentary rocks.

◢ How do fossils form in sedimentary rock? Three events must occur before a fossil can form in sedimentary rock. First, an organism must be buried by sediments soon after it dies. Quick burial slows or stops the breaking down of the organism by decomposers such as bacteria. Quick burial also prevents animals from eating the dead organism. Second, the soft parts of the organism decay. Only the bones or other hard parts, such as shells, remain. Third, the layers of sediment surrounding the organism harden into rock. The organism or part of the organism is now a fossil preserved in a layer of sedimentary rock.

Figure 33-1 The walls of the Grand Canyon (left) are made up of layers of sedimentary rock (right).

Figure 33-2 Notice the difference between a fossil cast (top) and mold (bottom).

Kinds of Fossils

The most common fossils are made from the hard parts of animals. These hard parts may form fossil **molds** or fossil **casts**. A fossil mold is a cavity in a rock that has the shape of the buried organism. Sometimes a fossil mold fills with sediments that harden. A fossil cast is then formed. A fossil mold and cast are shown in Figure 33–2.

Have you ever seen a footprint of an animal in the mud? If the mud hardened, the footprint would be preserved. The preserved footprint of an animal is a kind of fossil called an **imprint**. For example, dinosaur footprints have been discovered in sedimentary rock. Whole fish and plant parts, such as leaves and stems, often are preserved as fossil imprints.

Fossils can be formed in other ways as well. Entire insects have been found preserved in amber, or hardened tree sap. Even the insects' thin wings were preserved. Elephantlike animals called mammoths have been found frozen in arctic soil. Have you ever heard of the La Brea tar pits in southern California? The bones of thousands of animals that lived more than 15,000 years ago have been found in these tar pits.

Sometimes organisms are preserved by petrification (peh-tri-fi-KAY-shun). During petrification, water carries away the organic materials in the dead organism. Minerals then replace the lost organic materials. The process of petrification occurs very slowly. In the United States, the petrified logs of conifers can be seen in the Petrified Forest National Park in Arizona.

Study Hint

The word "petrification" comes from the Latin word "petra" meaning "rock." A petrified fossil has turned to rock.

Figure 33-3 These fossil logs have been petrified (turned to stone).

ACTIVITY 33-1

PROBLEM: How do fossils form?

Science Process Skills
modeling, observing, comparing

Background Information
Fossils often form when silt or mud covers an organism or part of an organism. The silt or mud hardens before the organism decays. As the organism decays, a fossil remains. A fossil mold is formed if a cavity is left in rock that has the shape of the organism or part of it. A fossil cast is the filled mold.

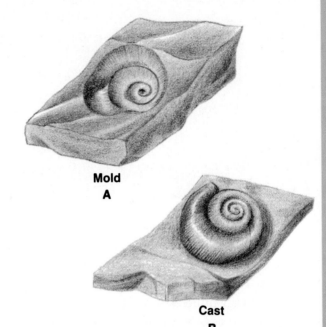

Mold
A

Cast
B

Materials

newspaper	twigs
clay	shells
plaster of Paris	4 small milk cartons
bones	large container
leaves	petroleum jelly

Procedure
1. Cover your work area with newspaper. Wear your laboratory apron to protect your clothing.
2. Choose four parts of organisms, and place the samples on the newspaper.
3. Soften the clay with your hands. Then divide the clay into four parts.
4. Place a layer of clay into the bottom of each milk carton.
5. Coat your samples with petroleum jelly.
6. Carefully press each sample into the clay. Remove two of the samples from the clay. Check the clay to be sure you have left some imprint of the sample in the clay. If not, repeat steps 3–6.
7. In the large container, mix plaster of Paris according to the package instructions.
8. Recoat the two organism samples left in the clay with petroleum jelly. Also coat the imprints in the clay in the other two cartons with petroleum jelly.
9. Pour a layer of plaster of Paris into each milk carton. Let the plaster of Paris dry.
10. After the plaster of Paris has dried, carefully peel away the clay and remove the organism parts. Observe your fossils.
11. Exchange your fossils with a classmate. Identify your exchanged fossils.

Observations
1. **a.** How many mold fossils did you make? **b.** How many cast fossils?
2. Which organism samples formed better fossils? Use your observations to support your answer.
3. **a.** Did you correctly identify your classmate's fossils? **b.** Name your classmate's fossils.

Conclusions
1. How could a mold fossil be formed naturally?
2. How could a cast fossil be formed naturally?
3. **GENERALIZE** What type of organism parts make the best fossils?

Interpreting Fossils

What can scientists learn by studying fossils? By studying fossils, scientists can piece together the history of the earth and its organisms. Fossils can help scientists learn about **extinct** animals and plants. Extinct organisms no longer exist on the earth. Dinosaurs are probably the best-known of the extinct animals. Scientists have learned a lot about dinosaurs by studying their fossils.

Fossils also can show how the environment has changed over time. For example, fossils of ferns have been found in Antarctica. From the fossils of these ferns, scientists can infer that Antarctica once had a very warm climate.

◑ Fossils also show evidence that some species of organisms have changed during the earth's history. For example, Figure 33–4 shows the changes that have taken place in the evolution of the horse. The fossil record of horses is very complete. Many fossils of horses have been found. These fossils indicate that the size of horses has changed over millions of years. Look at the earliest horse shown in Figure 33–4. This horse was about the size of a small dog. What other differences can you see in Figure 33–4? Notice how the number of toes and the structure of the legs have changed.

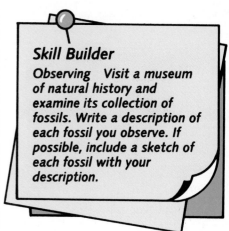

Skill Builder

Observing Visit a museum of natural history and examine its collection of fossils. Write a description of each fossil you observe. If possible, include a sketch of each fossil with your description.

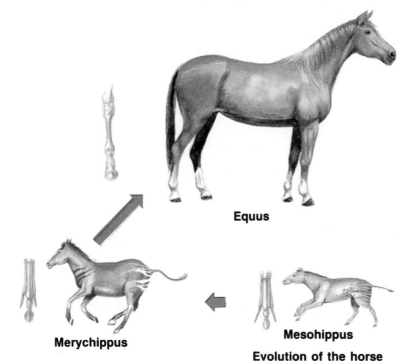

Figure 33-4 The fossil record of horses shows how they have changed over time.

Equus

Merychippus

Mesohippus

Evolution of the horse

Hyracotherium

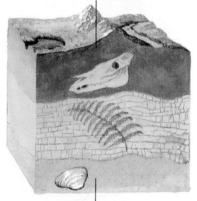

Youngest layer

Oldest layer

Figure 33-5 The relative age of a fossil can be found by noting its position in sedimentary rock layers.

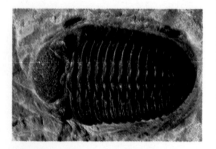

Figure 33-6 This fossil trilobite is an example of an index fossil.

Dating Fossils

Paleontologists (pay-lee-on-TOL-uh-jists) need to know how old fossils are. There are several methods a paleontologist can use to find the age of a fossil. The relative age of a fossil can be found by looking at the fossil's position in sedimentary rock layers. The layers of sediment in sedimentary rock are deposited one at a time. The bottom layers are deposited before the top layers. Therefore, the oldest rock layers are on the bottom and the youngest layers are on the top.

Look at the rock layers shown in Figure 33–5. Each rock layer has fossils in it. The fossils found in the lower layers are older than the fossils found in the upper layers. By comparing the positions of the fossils in the rock layers, you can tell their relative ages. For example, the fossil of the fern is older than the fossil of the horse but younger than the fossil of the clam.

Index Fossils

Some fossils are always found in rock layers of only one age. These fossils are called **index fossils**. Index fossils are useful to paleontologists because they are present in rock layers in many parts of the earth. Index fossils occur in large numbers. They lived only during a relatively short period of the earth's history. An example of an index fossil is the fossil of an animal called a trilobite (TRY-luh-byt). Trilobites lived 500–600 million years ago.

Index fossils can be used to help paleontologists determine the relative age of rock layers in which fossils are found. For example, suppose trilobite fossils are found in rock layers in Africa and in Kansas. Because trilobites lived only between 500 and 600 million years ago, a paleontologist can infer that the two rock layers in which the fossils were found are about the same age. About how old would the rock layers be?

Radioactive Dating

How can paleontologists find the **absolute age**, or actual age, of a fossil? Until the twentieth century, there was no way to find the absolute age of a fossil. In the 1940s, however, scientists discovered that radioactive elements can be used to determine how long ago a fossil organism lived. This length of time is the absolute age of the fossil. The method scientists use to find the absolute age of a fossil is called **radioactive dating**.

Can you name any radioactive elements? Several elements are naturally radioactive. A radioactive element gives off particles and energy as it breaks down, or decays. One radioactive element is called carbon-14. Carbon-14 is a radioactive form of carbon. In 1947, the American scientist W. F. Libby discovered that carbon-14 occurs naturally in the air. While they are alive, organisms take in both carbon-14 and ordinary carbon, or carbon-12, from the air. The ratio of carbon-14 to carbon-12 in the atmosphere is assumed to be constant over time.

How is carbon-14 used in radioactive dating? Carbon-14 acts as a natural clock. When an organism dies, the carbon-14 it contains begins to decay. Like all radioactive elements, carbon-14 decays at a fixed rate that can be measured. As carbon-14 decays, it forms the element nitrogen. The time it takes for one-half of the carbon-14 to decay into nitrogen is called its **half-life**. The half-life of carbon-14 is about 5700 years.

Suppose you want to find out the age of a fossil. You could take a sample of your fossil to a laboratory and compare the ratio of carbon-14 to carbon-12 in the fossil with the ratio of carbon-14 to carbon-12 in the atmosphere. Remember that carbon-14 is continually changing into nonradioactive nitrogen. Suppose that when you compare ratios, you find that half of the carbon-14 in your fossil has changed into nitrogen. How old is your fossil? It is about 5700 years old—the time it takes for half of the carbon-14 to decay.

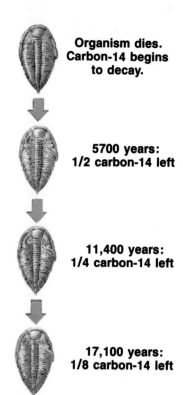

Organism dies. Carbon-14 begins to decay.

5700 years: 1/2 carbon-14 left

11,400 years: 1/4 carbon-14 left

17,100 years: 1/8 carbon-14 left

Figure 33-7 How much carbon-14 is left in the fossil after 17,100 years?

Think & Discuss

1. What is a fossil?
2. What is the difference between a fossil mold and a fossil cast?
3. Why are index fossils useful to paleontologists?
4. How could you find the absolute age of a fossil?
★ 5. Suppose you found two fossils in sedimentary rock. One fossil was in the bottom layer of rock and the other was in an upper layer. Which fossil is older?

ACTIVITY 33-2

PROBLEM: How is the relative age of fossils determined?

Science Process Skills
inferring, interpreting diagrams, comparing

Background Information
Sedimentary rock is formed when sand and silt collect in layers and harden. As time goes on, more layers of sedimentary rock are formed on top of the old layers. Organisms that are trapped in the layers of rock sometimes form fossils.

Materials
paper and pencil

Procedure
1. A side view of a deposit of sedimentary rock is shown in Figure A. Study the rock layers and the fossils in each.
2. Another deposit of sedimentary rock was found near the deposit shown in Figure A. Study the rock layers in Figure B.
3. Compare the two deposits of sedimentary rock.
4. Look at the fossil shown in Figure C.

Identify the fossil. Identify the rock layer in which this fossil probably was found.

Observations
1. **a.** In Figure A, which layer was deposited first? **b.** Which rock layer is the oldest?
2. **a.** Which fossil in Figure A is the oldest? **b.** Which is the youngest?
3. Which layers in Figure A match the layers in Figure B?
4. **a.** What is the fossil in Figure C? **b.** In which rock layer was the fossil probably found?

Conclusions
1. If two fossils are found in the same deposit of sedimentary rock, how can you determine which fossil is older?
2. **INFER** If a fossil of unknown age is found, how can you determine its relative age?
3. **GENERALIZE** What general statement can you make about the age of the rock layers in Figure A?

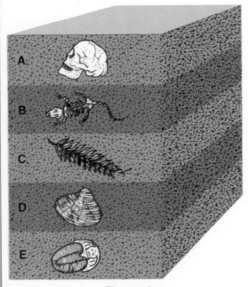

Figure A

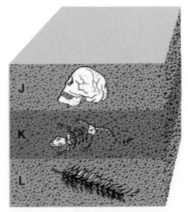

Figure B

Figure C

33–2 Geologic Time

How old do you think the earth is? Evidence from meteors indicates that the earth is about 4.5 billion years old. The earliest fossils are about 3.5 billion years old. By dating fossils and studying layers of sedimentary rock, scientists have been able to put together a geologic time scale of the earth's history.

Table 33–1 shows the geologic time scale. Notice that the geologic time scale is divided into eras, periods, and epochs. Four eras have passed since the fossil record shows life first appeared on the earth.

The geologic time scale shows that living things have become more complex over time. As you can see from Table 33–1, humans first appeared during the Cenozoic (sen-uh-ZOH-ik) Era. Modern humans are still living in this era. During what era did the dinosaurs appear?

Key Point
- The geologic time scale is a record of the earth's history.

Table 33–1 Geologic Time Scale				
ERA	PERIOD	EPOCH	START DATE (MILLIONS OF) YEARS AGO)	ORGANISMS
Cenozoic	Quaternary	Recent	0.025	Modern humans
		Pleistocene	1.75	Mammoths
	Tertiary	Pliocene	14	Large carnivores
		Miocene	26	Many land mammals
		Oligocene	40	Primitive apes
		Eocene	55	Early horses
		Paleocene	65	Primates
Mesozoic	Cretaceous		130	Flowering plants
	Jurassic		180	Dinosaurs, birds
	Triassic		225	Conifers
Paleozoic	Permian		275	Seed Plants
	Carboniferous		345	Reptiles
	Devonian		405	Insects, amphibians
	Silurian		435	Fishes
	Ordovician		480	Algae, fungi
	Cambrian		600	Invertebrates
Precambrian			4.5 billion	Bacteria, blue-green algae

The earliest forms of life were bacteria and blue-green algae. These living things appeared during the Precambrian (pree-KAM-bree-uhn) Era. The Precambrian Era began 4.5 billion years ago and lasted until about 600 million years ago.

About 600 million years ago, the Paleozoic (pay-lee-uh-ZOH-ik) Era began. Paleozoic rocks contain many different kinds of fossils. Some of the animals that first appeared during the Paleozoic Era include trilobites, snails, corals, sharks, amphibians, and reptiles.

Six periods make up the Paleozoic Era. During one of these periods, the Carboniferous (kar-buh-NIF-uhr-uhs), giant tree ferns grew in the swamps. These spore plants eventually formed coal and other fossil fuels. Seed plants appeared during the Permian Period at the end of the era, about 225 million years ago.

The following era, the Mesozoic (mes-uh-ZOH-ik), began 225 million years ago. The Mesozoic was the Age of Dinosaurs. By the end of this era, 65 million years ago, the last of the dinosaurs had disappeared.

The Mesozoic was followed by the Cenozoic Era. The Cenozoic began 65 million years ago and is still going on. Most of the plants and animals alive today first appeared during the Cenozoic Era. Others, such as the mammoths, have become extinct.

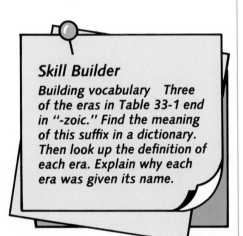

Skill Builder

Building vocabulary *Three of the eras in Table 33-1 end in "-zoic." Find the meaning of this suffix in a dictionary. Then look up the definition of each era. Explain why each era was given its name.*

Think & Discuss

6. What is the geologic time scale?
7. What are the divisions of the geologic time scale?
★ 8. When did the Cenozoic Era begin?

33–3 Evidence from Living Things

Key Point

- Similarities in anatomy, embryology, and biochemistry provide evidence of evolutionary relationships among different organisms.

Fossils provide one kind of evidence that organisms have changed over time. However, scientists also study living things for evidence of evolution. By comparing living organisms to each other, scientists can determine how the organisms are related and how they evolved.

Anatomy

Look at Figure 33–8. The bones in the forelimbs of a whale, a bat, and a human are shown. The forelimbs of these mammals look very different and have different functions. However, notice that the bones are similar in structure. Body parts that have the same basic structure are called **homologous** (hoh-MOL-uh-gus) **structures**. What do homologous structures tell scientists about living things? The presence of homologous structures in different organisms suggests that these organisms are related and have evolved from a common ancestor.

What else do you think scientists can learn by studying the anatomy of living things? Some organisms have organs or structures that seem to have no function. For example, at the end of your spine is a bone called the coccyx (KOK-siks), or tailbone. The tailbone has no function in modern humans. Structures that seem to have no function are called **vestigial** (ves-TIJ-ee-uhl) **structures**.

If vestigial structures have no function, why do they exist? The answer is that these structures probably did have a function at one time. Scientists think that vestigial structures had a function in the ancestors of the organisms that now have them. For example, snakes have vestigial hip bones. The hip is the part of the skeleton to which the legs are attached. The vestigial hip bones of snakes suggest that snakes evolved from an ancestor with legs.

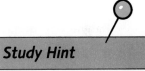

Study Hint

The appendix is a vestigial structure in humans. In rabbits, however, it helps digest plants.

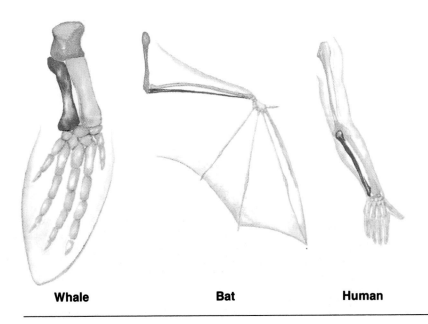

Whale　　　　**Bat**　　　　**Human**

Figure 33-8　Compare the bones in the forelimbs of a whale, a bat, and a human.

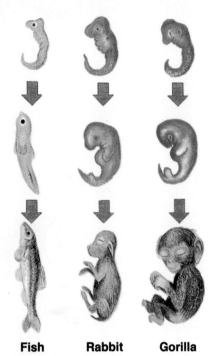

Fish **Rabbit** **Gorilla**

Figure 33-9 Although these three animals look quite different as adults, their embryos are very similar.

Embryology

An organism in the early stages of development is called an embryo. Scientists compare the embryos of different organisms to find similarities among them. Look at Figure 33-9. The early stages in the development of a fish, a rabbit, and a gorilla are shown. Notice how similar these embryos are to one another. Scientists infer that organisms with similar embryos have similar genes and, therefore, probably evolved from a common ancestor.

Biochemistry

Recently, scientists have been able to study the **biochemistry** of living things to find evolutionary relationships. Biochemistry is the study of the molecules that make up living things. For example, many different organisms contain a protein called cytochrome c. Cytochrome c is needed for respiration in these organisms. Scientists infer that these organisms all evolved from a common ancestor that used cytochrome c for respiration.

Scientists compared the structure of cytochrome c in different organisms. They found that the structure of cytochrome c is similar in monkeys and cows, but very different in monkeys and fishes. As a result, scientists infer that monkeys and cows are more closely related than are monkeys and fishes.

Scientists also compared certain proteins that are found in the blood of all animals. Similarities in the structure of these proteins indicate how the different animals are related. Using this evidence, scientists have been able to infer that some species of animals have a more recent common ancestor than do other species. This information helps scientists trace the evolutionary relationships among different species of animals.

Think & Discuss

9. What are homologous structures?
10. What are vestigial structures? Give an example.
11. Explain why biochemical similarities are considered evidence of evolutionary relationships.

Collecting Fossils

Imagine that you have picked up an ordinary-looking rock. As you examine the rock more closely, you notice fine, feathery markings in the shape of a leaf. You have discovered a fossil. A fossil is the remains or evidence of a living thing.

Ninety-nine percent of all fossils are found in sedimentary rock, especially limestone and shale. When you hold a fossil, you are really holding a piece of the earth's history in your hand. Much of what scientists know about the evolution of life on Earth has come from studying fossils. Fossils also provide clues about the earth's past climate and geography.

Collecting fossils can be a fascinating hobby. Where can you find fossils? The best places to find fossils are in areas of exposed rock. For example, quarries and coal and metal mines are excellent places to find fossils. Riverbeds, beaches, and mountain slopes also are good places to find fossils.

A guidebook, such as *Hunting for Fossils* by Marian Murray, can be helpful in locating the best fossil sites in your state. Other sources of information about where to find fossils include geological societies, state geological surveys, hobby magazines, and museums.

As a new fossil collector, you should take time to read about fossils. It also is helpful to visit a museum that has a fossil collection. In this way, you will gain the knowledge needed to recognize different kinds of fossils.

A fossil collector needs several pieces of basic equipment. These include a hand lens, a hammer, a chisel, a notebook, and pens and pencils. Other helpful items include a pocketknife, a sieve, a brush, and plastic bags or tubes.

Because fossils are usually found in rugged outdoor environments, you should have basic outdoor skills. For example, you should know how to recognize poisonous snakes and plants. Dressing for the outdoors and knowing how to protect your feet against rocky terrain also are important.

Although most amateurs collect fossils for their own enjoyment, some have made valuable contributions to the biological and geological sciences. For example, in the 1960s, a fisherman in Illinois discovered fossils of 150 different organisms that had never been known to exist in the area before. Scientists who study fossils urge all collectors to be aware of unusual fossils and bring them to the attention of a museum or other source of expert information. Who knows—someday you may discover a fossil that makes scientific history!

To Think About

- Some states have laws that restrict the collection of fossils. Why do you think these laws exist?

- Suppose you discovered the fossil of a tropical plant on a mountain range in Canada. What might you conclude about the past history of this area?

Chapter Review

CHAPTER SUMMARY

33–1 Fossil Evidence

- Fossils are the remains or traces of organisms that lived in the past.
- Most fossils are found in layers of sedimentary rock.
- Three kinds of fossils are molds, casts, and imprints.
- Index fossils help paleontologists determine the relative age of rock layers.
- Radioactive dating, using carbon-14, can help paleontologists determine the absolute age of fossils.

33–2 Geologic Time

- The geologic time scale shows how organisms have changed during the earth's history.

- The geologic time scale is divided into eras, periods, and epochs.
- The Precambrian, the Paleozoic, the Mesozoic, and the Cenozoic are the four eras of the geologic time scale.

33–3 Evidence from Living Things

- Homologous structures and vestigial structures show how organisms are related or have evolved from a common ancestor.
- The similarity between embryos of some organisms shows that they probably evolved from a common ancestor.
- Biochemical similarities and differences indicate degrees of evolutionary relationships among different organisms.

VOCABULARY LIST

absolute age (572)
biochemistry (578)
casts (569)
extinct (571)

fossils (568)
half-life (573)
homologous structures (577)

imprint (569)
index fossils (572)
molds (569)

radioactive dating (573)
sedimentary rock (568)
vestigial structures (577)

VOCABULARY REVIEW

Matching   Write the word or term from the Vocabulary List that best matches each description.

1. remains of organisms that lived in the past
2. actual age of a fossil
3. no longer living on the earth
4. formed by layers of sediments
5. time needed for half the amount of a radioactive element to decay
6. study of molecules in living things
7. fossils filled with hardened sediments
8. cavities in rock that have the shape of buried organisms
9. preserved footprint

Identifying Relationships   Identify the word or term in each group that does not belong. Explain why it does not belong with the group.

1. index fossils, radioactive dating, absolute age
2. molds, casts, sediments
3. homologous structures, fossils, vestigial structures
4. footprint, imprint, embryo
5. fossils, biochemistry, casts
6. half-life, biochemistry, radioactive dating
7. vestigial structures, fossils, casts
8. index fossils, sedimentary rock, half-life
9. anatomy, fossils, embryology

Completion Write the word or words that best complete each sentence.

1. A bat's wing and a human hand are examples of _____ structures.
2. Similarities in the structure of blood proteins are evidence for evolution based on _____.
3. In sedimentary rock, the oldest fossils would be found in the _____ layer.
4. The impression of a leaf in sedimentary rock is an example of a(an) _____ fossil.
5. Your tailbone is an example of a _____ structure.
6. Scientists estimate that the earth is about _____ years old.
7. A trilobite is an example of a(an) _____ fossil.
8. The upper layers of sedimentary rock are _____ than the bottom layers.

Finding the Main Ideas Use the section number to find the sentence that answers each question. Then, write the sentence.

1. Where are most fossils found? (33–1)
2. What is a fossil mold? (33–1)
3. What can scientists learn by studying fossils? (33–1)
4. How can scientists find the relative age of a fossil? (33–1)
5. What is the half-life of carbon-14? (33–1)
6. What were the earliest forms of life on the earth? (33–2)
7. When did the first humans appear on the earth? (33–2)
8. What do homologous structures tell scientists about living things? (33–3)
9. What can scientists infer about organisms with similar embryos? (33–3)
10. What is biochemistry? (33–3).

CONCEPT REVIEW

Writing for Understanding One way to find out if you understand something is to write a brief summary of the information in your own words. Reread Section 33–2, Geologic Time, on pages 575–576, and write a brief summary of the information.

Critical Thinking Answer each of the following in complete sentences.

1. Why are both homologous structures and vestigial structures considered evidence for evolution?

2. Fossils of the earliest forms of life, such as bacteria and blue-green algae, are rare and hard to find. Explain.
3. How is the study of evolution similar to the study of history?
4. Scientists have found similarities in the blood proteins of horseshoe crabs and spiders. What can you infer about the two organisms based on these similarities?
5. The structure of chlorophyll in plants is similar to that of hemoglobin in the blood of many animals. Is this evidence for evolution?

EXTENSIONS

1. Choose two organisms that you think are closely related. What homologous structures do they have in common? Draw a diagram to show the homologous structures in the two organisms.

2. Find out more about radioactive dating. Report to the class on some radioactive elements used to find absolute age.
3. Read *The Dinosaur Heresies* by Robert Bakker and write a book report.

Chapter 4

Human Change Through Time

Objectives

After you have completed this chapter, you will be able to

34–1 **describe** some characteristics of primates.
34–1 **describe** some unique characteristics of humans.
34–2 **compare** two species of *Australopithecus*.
34–2 **compare** *Homo habilis* with *Homo erectus*.
34–3 **compare** early *Homo sapiens* with modern humans.
34–3 **describe** two theories of human evolution.

Science Process Skills

In this chapter, two science skills are highlighted. Symbols show some places where these skills are used.

△ **Organizing:** When you organize information, you put the information in some kind of order.
◣ **Analyzing:** When you analyze, you break down a complex idea into simpler parts to make it easier to understand.

These beautiful pictures were painted on the walls of caves thousands of years ago by early humans. Cave paintings were first discovered in Spain in 1879. The paintings showed large animals that looked like modern bulls. Scientists studied these paintings to learn about how early humans lived.

What information can cave paintings provide about the people who made them? Very often, the cave paintings show animals that the people hunted for food. Scientists also have found the remains of the tools that people used to hunt the animals and to make clothing from the animal skins. This fossil evidence of the ancestors of modern humans and their tools helps scientists piece together the history of the human species.

34–1 Classification of Humans

Key Points

- Primates have many characteristics that are adaptations to life in the trees.

- Humans have some characteristics that set them apart from the other primates.

Evidence from fossils and biochemistry indicates that humans belong to an order of mammals called **primates.** There are over 200 living species of primates. Living primates include tree shrews, lemurs, monkeys, and apes, in addition to humans.

The earliest known primates lived at the same time as the dinosaurs, over 65 million years ago. These early primates resembled modern shrews and lived in trees. Scientists have inferred that these early primates were probably the ancestors of all modern primates.

Primate Characteristics

Fossil evidence indicates that early primates were adapted to living in trees. Most modern primates also are tree dwellers. Scientists infer that many primate characteristics may have evolved as adaptations to living in trees. For example, all primates have flexible fingers and toes with nails instead of claws. Early primates used their highly movable fingers and toes to grasp branches and cling to tree trunks.

Most primates also have an **opposable thumb.** An opposable thumb can touch all of the other fingers. Some primates also have an opposable big toe. Primates use their opposable thumbs and toes for gripping and grasping.

All primates have eyes in the front of the head, which gives them **frontal vision.** Frontal vision allows primates to focus on an object with both eyes at the same time. Primates also have **stereoscopic** (ster-ee-uh-SKOP-ik) **vision.** With stereoscopic vision, early primates could estimate depth accurately as they moved through the trees.

Figure 34-1   Like humans, this tree shrew is a primate.

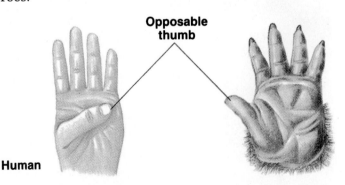

Figure 34-2   Both humans and apes have an opposable thumb.

Human

Opposable thumb

Ape

ACTIVITY 34-1

PROBLEM: How useful is an opposable thumb?

Science Process Skills
experimenting, observing, comparing

Background Information
Humans are classified by biologists in the order Primates. Primates have opposable thumbs. An opposable thumb is long and flexible enough to touch the tips of each finger. An opposable thumb also enables primates to grasp and hold objects in many different ways.

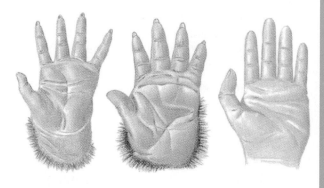

Baboon   **Gorilla**   **Human**

Materials
masking tape
bottle with a screw-on cap
sheet of paper
watch or clock with second hand

Procedure
1. Work with a partner.
2. Copy the Data Table shown.

Data Table:	Activity Times		
ACTIVITY	THUMBS FREE (MINUTES)	THUMBS TAPED (MINUTES)	TIME DIFFERENCE (MINUTES)
A			
B			
G			

3. Have your partner time how long you take to do each of the following activities. Record the time it takes to do each activity in the Data Table.
   a. Write your name.
   b. Fold a piece of paper in half and then in half again.
   c. Remove one shoe and then put it on again.
   d. Unscrew the cap of the bottle.
   e. Open a book and turn to page 25.
   f. Open a door.
   g. Unbutton a button and button it again.
4. Using the masking tape, have your partner tape each of your thumbs to the index finger of each hand.
5. After your thumbs are taped, complete the six activities. Have your partner time you again. Record the time in the Data Table. If any activity takes longer than 5 minutes to do, write "unsuccessful" in the Data Table.
6. Switch positions with your partner and repeat the activity.

Observations
1. How much longer did it take to do each activity with your thumbs taped? List the time differences in the Data Table.
2. a. How many activities could you not do successfully with your thumbs taped?
   b. Did any activities take less time to do with your thumbs taped than with your thumbs free? If so, which ones?

Conclusions
1. Which activities were the most difficult to do with your thumbs taped? Explain why.
2. **INFER** How useful is your opposable thumb?
3. What main function does the thumb serve in each activity?

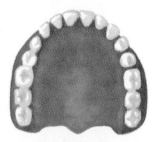

Human teeth

Ape teeth

Figure 34-3 Compare the shape of the jaws and the size of the teeth in a human and an ape.

Figure 34-4 Humans are adapted for walking erect, while apes walk on all fours.

Fossil evidence shows that as primates evolved, their brains got larger. Primates such as monkeys and apes have a large brain in relation to their body size. Although a large brain does not necessarily mean greater intelligence, increased brain size may have helped early primates adapt and survive.

Human Characteristics

Humans have all of the characteristics of the other primates. Humans also have some characteristics that other primates do not have. These characteristics set humans apart from all other primates.

▲ Figure 34–3 shows the difference between the jaws and teeth of a human and an ape. Look at the rows of teeth in an ape's jaw. They form a "U." The human jaw is much more rounded in shape. This difference in shape means that an ape's jaw sticks out from its face while a human jaw does not.

Unlike the other primates, humans are **bipedal** (by-PEED-uhl). Being bipedal means that humans stand upright and walk on two legs instead of four. Look at Figure 34–4 and compare the pelvis of a human with that of an ape. The ape pelvis is adapted for walking on all fours. The broad human pelvis supports the internal organs and allows humans to stand erect and walk on two legs.

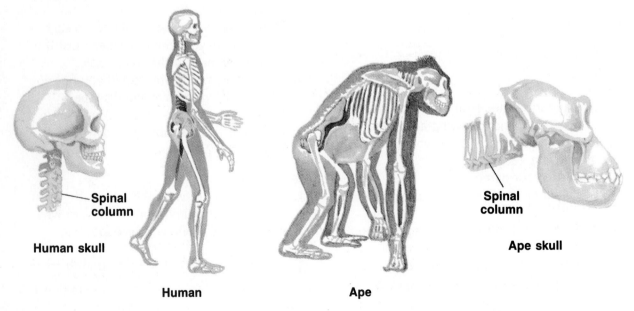

Spinal column

Human skull

Spinal column

Ape skull

Human

Ape

Humans have large brains compared with their body size. The term scientists use for the size of the brain case is **cranial capacity**. The human brain also is more highly developed than the brains of the other primates. The large frontal part of the human brain is responsible for the unique human characteristic of spoken language. Humans are the only animals that use spoken language to communicate with one another.

Think & Discuss

1. What does bipedal mean?
2. Describe three characteristics of primates that are adaptations to life in the trees.
3. How are humans different from all other primates?

34–2 Early Humans

Modern humans and their ancestors are classified in a group of primates called **hominids** (HOM-uh-nids). Scientists study the fossils of early hominids to learn about hominid evolution. Because few hominid fossils have been found, not all scientists agree on how the hominids evolved. Most scientists agree on certain evolutionary trends, however, such as the trend toward increasing brain size, or cranial capacity.

Australopithecus

The earliest fossil hominids were found in South Africa. These hominids are classified in the genus *Australopithecus* (aw-stray-loh-PITH-uh-kus), or "southern ape." Fossils of *Australopithecus* have been found only in southern and eastern Africa.

Australopithecus afarensis

In 1974, Donald Johanson, an American anthropologist, discovered a hominid fossil in the Great Rift Valley of Ethiopia. The shape of the pelvis indicated that the fossil was that of a female. Johanson nicknamed her Lucy. Lucy is about 3 to 3.5 million years old, the oldest hominid

Key Points
- Two early hominids are *Australopithecus afarensis* and *Australopithecus africanus*.
- *Homo habilis* and *Homo erectus* are thought to be direct ancestors of modern humans.

Study Hint

As you read about the discovery of early human fossils, use a map of Africa to locate some of the places where the fossils were found.

fossil found so far. Lucy's skeleton indicates that she was bipedal and about 1.1 meters tall. Scientists named her *Australopithecus afarensis*, or *A. afarensis*. Many other fossil remains similar to Lucy have been found since 1974.

Australopithecus africanus

Lucy was not the first *Australopithecus* fossil to be found. In 1924, an *Australopithecus* fossil was discovered in South Africa. This early hominid was about 2.5 to 3 million years old. Scientists called this fossil *Australopithecus africanus*, or *A. africanus*. *A. africanus* was slightly taller and had a slightly larger brain than *A. afarensis*. Like *A. afarensis*, *A. africanus* also was bipedal.

Two other species of *Australopithecus* have been discovered. These fossils are called *A. robustus* and *A. boisei*. *A. robustus* and *A. boisei* probably evolved after *A. africanus*. Most fossils of the two species are between 1 and 2 million years old.

Homo habilis

In 1959, an important discovery was made in the Olduvai Gorge in Tanzania. The British anthropologists Mary and Louis Leakey found fossils of a new kind of hominid. Because they found stone tools along with the fossils, the Leakeys called their discovery *Homo habilis* (HAB-il-is), or "handy man." Fossils of *H. habilis* are about 1.8 million years old.

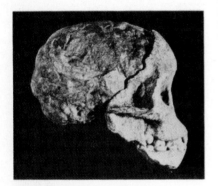

Figure 34-5   Notice the apelike jaw of this *A. africanus* skull.

Figure 34-6   Front and side views of a *H. habilis* skull appear less apelike than the *A. africanus* skull.

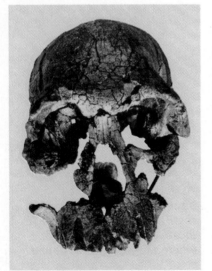

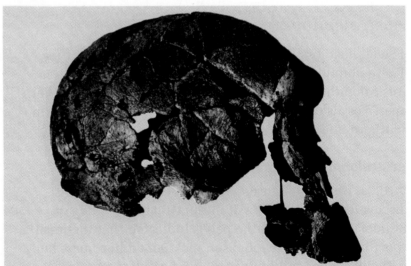

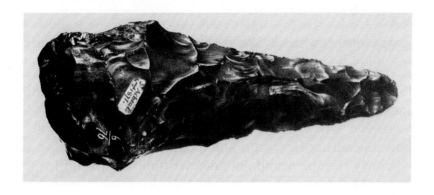

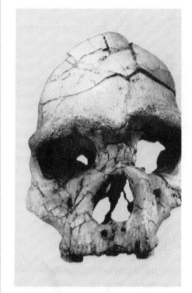

Figure 34-7 Flint tools like this one were used by *H. habilis.*

Homo habilis was a tool user. Simple stone tools found with its remains probably were used to cut meat and to scrape the skin from animals. The brain of *H. habilis* was large and well developed. Based on studies of its skull, some scientists think that *H. habilis* may even have been capable of limited speech.

Homo erectus

In 1891, a hominid skull was discovered near a river on the Pacific island of Java. It was the skull of a species of hominid called *Homo erectus*, or "upright man." *Homo erectus* lived about 0.5 to 1.6 million years ago. Fossils of *H. erectus* also have been found in China and in Kenya.

Fossils indicate that *H. erectus* probably looked somewhat like *H. habilis*. *Homo erectus* had a flat skull with a large jaw and low forehead. Although it resembled earlier hominids, *H. erectus* had a larger and more complex brain.

Homo erectus made their homes in caves. They may have been the first hominids to use fire for cooking and warmth. These hominids used stone tools and hunted animals for food. Most scientists think that *H. erectus* was a direct ancestor of modern humans.

Figure 34-8 The skull of *H. erectus* closely resembles the *H. habilis* skull.

Think & Discuss

4. What are hominids?
5. What does *Homo habilis* mean?
6. How was *A. africanus* different from *A. afarensis*?
7. How was *H. erectus* similar to *H. habilis*?
8. Why do you think *Homo erectus* was given the name "upright man"?

34–3 Modern Humans

Key Points

- Modern humans belong to the species *Homo sapiens.*

- Neanderthals and Cro-Magnons were early humans belonging to the species *Homo sapiens.*

- Scientists have proposed at least two possible pathways for the evolution of modern humans.

Skill Builder

Predicting *The characteristics of modern humans evolved as adaptations to the environment of the past. Which new characteristics do you think humans might develop in response to the environment of the future? Describe what the environment might be like in the future. Then list specific characteristics that might help future humans survive in this environment.*

All modern humans belong to the species *Homo sapiens* (SAY-pee-uhns), meaning "wise human." The fossil record indicates that *H. sapiens* first appeared about 500,000 years ago. Early *H. sapiens* skulls resembled the skulls of both the earlier *H. erectus* and modern humans.

Early *H. sapiens* did not keep written records until about 5000 years ago. Therefore, scientists study bones, tools, and other remains to find out how these people lived.

Homo sapiens

The first fossils of *Homo sapiens* were found in 1856 in the Neander Valley of Germany. These fossils were called **Neanderthals** (nee-AN-dur-thawls). Other Neanderthal fossils have been found in England and France. The Neanderthals lived from 130,000 to 35,000 years ago, during the Ice Age in Europe.

Neanderthals were somewhat shorter than modern humans and walked upright. They had large skulls with sloping foreheads and heavy brow ridges. Their brains were as large as those of modern humans.

Large brains helped Neanderthals adapt to the cold climate of the Ice Age. They lived in caves and used fire to keep warm. The Neanderthals were the first people known to bury their dead. The Neanderthals disappeared from the fossil record about 30,000 years ago.

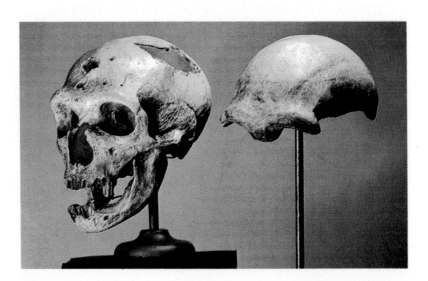

Figure 34-9 Notice the heavy brow ridges on these Neanderthal skulls.

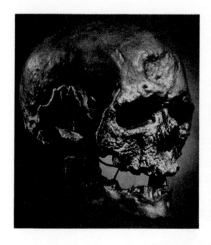

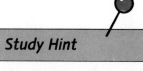

Figure 34-10 The Cro-Magnon skull (left) lacks the brow ridges of the Neanderthal (right). What other difference can you see?

In 1868, railway workers in southwestern France uncovered fossils of modern *H. sapiens*. These fossils were about 35,000 years old. Scientists named these early humans **Cro-Magnons** (kroh-MAG-nuhns). Other Cro-Magnon fossils have been found in Germany, England, and Spain.

Unlike Neanderthals, Cro-Magnons had high foreheads and no brow ridges. The Cro-Magnons looked like modern humans. They were as tall as modern humans. Like modern humans, Cro-Magnons had large brains and rounded skulls.

Most Cro-Magnon remains have been found in caves. However, scientists also have found evidence that Cro-Magnons built rock shelters and huts. The Cro-Magnons probably lived in one place all year instead of following migrating herds of animals.

Scientists have found evidence that Cro-Magnon people had a rich culture. Sculptures and paintings on the walls of their caves have been found. Fossil evidence indicates that Cro-Magnons formed large social groups and buried their dead. The Cro-Magnons were highly skilled hunters and used many kinds of tools including blades, harpoons, and fishhooks.

Human History

Scientists agree that Neanderthals and Cro-Magnons are the nearest direct ancestors of modern humans. However, the fossil record of hominids is incomplete. For this reason, scientists have different theories of how modern *Homo sapiens* evolved from early hominids.

> **Study Hint**
>
> *Cro-Magnons are named after the Cro-Magnon cave in France where the first fossils were found.*

> **Skill Builder**
>
> *Organizing One way to organize information is to place events in a sequence. Make a list of all the ancestors of modern humans mentioned in this chapter. Arrange your list in chronological order, from the oldest to the most recent.*

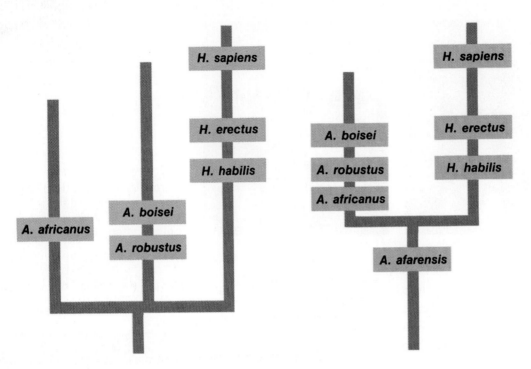

Figure 34-11 Compare the Leakeys' theory of hominid evolution (left) with Donald Johanson's theory (right).

▲ Figure 34–11 shows two possible pathways of human evolution. Donald Johanson, who found the remains of Lucy, thinks that *A. afarensis* was the common ancestor of both the *Australopithecus* species and the line that led to *H. sapiens*. Mary Leakey, who found the first *H. habilis* fossils, and her son Richard Leakey have a different theory. The Leakeys think the *A. afarensis* fossils are not hominids at all. According to the Leakeys, *A. afarensis* died out and did not give rise to later hominids.

The debate between these two theories indicates that science is an ongoing process. Scientists will continue to gather and analyze fossil evidence. In the future, one theory will probably be changed or discarded, based on new evidence. Other theories may be proposed to explain the evidence.

Think & Discuss

9. How were Neanderthals different from Cro-Magnons?

10. Describe two different theories of human evolution.

★ 11. Why do you think Neanderthals disappeared and were replaced by Cro-Magnons about 30,000 years ago?

CAREERS in BIOLOGY
Working in Anthropology

Are you interested in how humans have changed through time? Do you enjoy learning about the cultures of peoples from different parts of the world? If so, you might enjoy a career in anthropology.

Anthropologist

The science that deals with the study of human beings is called anthropology. Anthropology combines the natural sciences with the social sciences. The social sciences are those sciences that study the behaviors of individual people and societies. For example, anthropologists may study the physical, social, or cultural development of humans. They also may study the ways human beings have changed through time.

Most anthropologists are college professors. As professors, they are able to combine teaching with field research. Other anthropologists work in museums.

An anthropologist needs a college degree. Many anthropologists go on to graduate school. Courses in biology, anatomy, chemistry, and physiology are important. Courses in the social sciences also are important.

For more information: Write to the American Association of Physical Anthropologists, 1703 New Hampshire Ave., NW, Washington, DC 20009.

Anthropology Field Worker

A person who assists an anthropologist in the field is called an anthropology field worker. Anthropology field workers may work anywhere in the world. They gather information from the fossil record, the remains of populations, and their observations of nonhuman primates.

An anthropology field worker must be in good health in order to endure physical exertion and adapt to extremes in climate and geography. It is not uncommon, for example, for a team of anthropologists to work in such places as the Sahara Desert.

Educational requirements for anthropology field workers vary according to the situation. However, the minimum requirement is a high school diploma.

For more information: Contact the anthropology department of a college or university in your state.

Fossil Reconstructionist

Have you ever gazed at the skeleton of a prehistoric animal in a natural history museum and wondered how this huge fossil was put together? Chances are, it was put together by a fossil reconstructionist.

Fossil reconstructionists work in museums, educational institutions, and research organizations. They often work with or under the supervision of a paleontologist—a scientist who studies fossils.

A fossil reconstructionist usually has a college degree with a major in geology or anthropology. A person interested in becoming a fossil reconstructionist should have good eye-hand coordination, artistic ability, physical agility, and moderate strength. Fossil reconstructionists also should learn about the type or types of fossils they wish to reconstruct.

For more information: Write to the Museum Reference Center, Smithsonian Institution Libraries, Washington, DC 20560.

Chapter Review

CHAPTER SUMMARY

34–1 Classification of Humans

- Primates have characteristics that evolved as adaptations to life in the trees.
- Primate characteristics include flexible fingers and toes with nails instead of claws, opposable thumbs, opposable big toes, and frontal vision.
- Humans have all the characteristics of primates in addition to some unique characteristics.
- Unique human characteristics include walking upright on two legs, a curved jaw that does not stick out from the face, and a large brain compared with body size.

34–2 Early Humans

- Early hominids include *Australopithecus afarensis*, *A. africanus*, *A. robustus*, and *A. boisei*.
- Members of the genus *Homo*, which are direct ancestors of modern humans, are called *H. habilis* and *H. erectus*.

34–3 Modern Humans

- All modern humans belong to the species *Homo sapiens*.
- Early *H. sapiens* are called Neanderthals and Cro-Magnons.
- Because the fossil record of hominids is incomplete, scientists have proposed different theories of hominid evolution.

VOCABULARY LIST

bipedal (586)
cranial capacity (587)
Cro-Magnons (591)

frontal vision (584)
hominids (587)
Homo sapiens (590)

Neanderthals (590)
opposable thumb (584)

primates (584)
stereoscopic vision (584)

VOCABULARY REVIEW

Matching Write the word or term from the Vocabulary List that best matches each description.

1. able to touch all the other fingers
2. eyes in front of the head
3. walking on two legs
4. ability to estimate depth
5. order of mammals in which humans are classified
6. size of the brain case
7. modern humans and their ancestors
8. modern humans
9. fossils of modern *Homo sapiens*

Applying Definitions Explain the difference between the words in each pair.

1. primates, hominids
2. frontal vision, stereoscopic vision
3. Neanderthals, Cro-Magnons
4. opposable thumb, opposable big toe
5. cranial capacity, brain size
6. *A. africanus*, *A. afarensis*
7. *H. erectus*, *H. sapiens*
8. nails, claws
9. genus, species
10. fossil record, theories

True or False   Write true if the statement is true. If the statement is false, change the underlined word or words to make the statement true.

1. Humans belong to the order of mammals called <u>primates</u>.
2. Apes and humans have <u>claws</u> on their fingers and toes.
3. A characteristic common to humans and apes is an opposable <u>toe</u>.
4. <u>Hominids</u> include modern humans and fossil humans, but not apes.
5. The earliest hominid fossil is of <u>A. africanus</u>.
6. *Homo sapiens* means "<u>wise human</u>."
7. <u>Neanderthal</u> fossils were first found in a cave in France.
8. The fossil called Lucy was discovered by <u>Donald Johanson</u>.
9. The immediate ancestor of modern humans is <u>H. erectus</u>.

Question and Answer   Rewrite each heading in the Chapter Outline on page 582 as a question. Then, answer each of the questions you have written.

Understanding a Diagram   Use the diagram of the human and ape skeletons shown in Figure 34–4 (page 586) to answer each of the following.

1. How does a human foot differ from an ape foot?
2. Why is the position of the ape skull on the spinal column an adaptation for walking on all fours?
3. How is this different from the way the human skull is balanced on the spinal column?
4. Which is the larger, the human skull or the ape skull?
5. What is the difference between the human pelvis and the ape pelvis?

Writing the Main Ideas   Using the Chapter Outline on page 582, write the main idea for each heading in the outline.

Critical Thinking   Answer each of the following in complete sentences.

1. Why are humans considered to be primates?
2. The larynx of apes is not as well developed as that of humans. How might this affect the ape's ability to use spoken language?
3. How might the ability to use fire have affected the development of early humans?
4. What is the place of *A. afarensis* in the two possible pathways to modern humans?
5. Why do scientists consider Cro-Magnons the most immediate ancestors of modern humans?
6. Why is the name *Homo habilis* appropriate for these hominids?

1. Visit a zoo and observe the behavior of primates such as monkeys, chimpanzees, gorillas, and so forth. List several different kinds of behavior, and compare that behavior in each of the primates you observe.
2. Visit a museum of natural history and make sketches of the human fossils on display.
3. Read *Lucy: The Beginnings of Human Kind* by Donald Johanson or *Human Origins* by Richard Leakey. Write a book report on one of these books.

Ecology is a branch of biology that studies the relationships between organisms and their environments. The environment is everything that surrounds an organism. Ecologists are interested in learning how living and nonliving things affect each other. For example, an ecologist might ask, "How does air, the amount of sunlight and rain, and the soil affect the growth of a pine tree?" An ecologist also might ask, "How does the growth of a pine tree affect other organisms?"

Study the photographs and art on these two pages. List the living and nonliving things shown. In what ways do you think the living and nonliving things are interrelated?

Ecology

CONTENTS

Chapter 35 | Ecosystems

Objectives

After you have completed this chapter, you will be able to

35-1 **identify** biotic and abiotic parts of an ecosystem.

35-2 **compare** producers, consumers, and decomposers.

35-2 **explain** how food chains, food webs, and energy pyramids are used as models.

35-3 **recognize** that plants and animals compete for the resources in an ecosystem.

35-3 **identify** four relationships among organisms.

35-4 **define** ecological succession.

35-4 **recognize** the climax community as the final stage in an ecological succession.

Science Process Skills

In this chapter, two science skills are highlighted. Symbols show some places where these skills are used.

➤ **Inferring**: When you infer, you form a conclusion based upon facts and not direct observation.

❯ **Predicting:** When you predict, you state in advance how and why something will occur.

Imagine buying a model. You open the model box and find thousands of parts. However, you cannot find an instruction manual that explains how to put the parts together. Without an instruction manual, there is little hope of understanding how all the parts fit together.

Just as an instruction manual is needed to assemble the parts of a model, an instruction manual also is needed to understand how the organisms on the earth fit together. This chapter is like a manual that tells you how the parts of the earth fit and work together. The branch of biology dealing with the study of the relationships of living things and their environments is called **ecology** *(ee-KOL-uh-jee).*

35-1 Ecology and Ecosystems

What is the **biosphere** (BY-uh-sfir)? You should recognize that "bio" means "life." The biosphere is the thin zone of the earth that supports all life. You may be thinking that living things exist almost everywhere. For example, some fishes and bacteria live in the deepest parts of the oceans. Some spiders live high in the atmosphere. Yet, if you think of the earth as an apple, the biosphere would be just the skin.

The Ecosystem

The biosphere is made up of many smaller units called **ecosystems** (EE-koh-sis-tums). An ecosystem is all the living and nonliving parts of an environment. For example, a pond, a garden, a puddle of rain water, and a riverbank all are examples of ecosystems. Every ecosystem is able to support itself.

Each ecosystem has **biotic** (by-OT-ik) and **abiotic** factors. The biotic factors are the living organisms. The abiotic factors are the nonliving parts of the ecosystem. For example, air, water, sunlight, soil, and rock are abiotic factors. What other abiotic factors might you find in an ecosystem?

Communities and Populations

Each ecosystem is made up of one or more **communities**. What do you think of when you hear the word community? A community is all the people living in a town, city, or area.

▶ In an ecosystem, a community is all the organisms living in a certain area. For example, a pond community may include frogs, fishes, insects, water lilies, and cattails. A forest community may include deer, ferns, mushrooms, and trees. What other organisms do you think might live in a forest community?

Each community is made up of **populations**. A population is all of the organisms of the same species living in the same area. For example, the bullfrogs in a pond are a population. The oak trees in a forest also are a population.

Key Points

- An ecosystem contains biotic and abiotic parts.

- Abiotic substances such as water, carbon dioxide, oxygen, and nitrogen cycle through the biosphere.

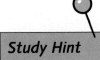

Study Hint

The prefix "a" means "not" or "opposite."

Skill Builder

Comparing   When you make a comparison, you examine two or more things to see how they are alike and how they are different. Compare a population and a community. How are a population and a community alike? How are they different?

ACTIVITY 35-1

PROBLEM: How can you estimate the size of a population of organisms from a sample?

Science Process Skills
estimating, observing, predicting

Background Information
The size of a population of living things can be estimated by sampling. Sampling is a way of finding out about a large number of things. The sample you take is a small part of the larger population.

Materials
paper and pencil

Procedure
1. Look at the grid showing a mouse population.
2. **ESTIMATE** How many mice do you think are in the population? Record your answer on a sheet of paper. Continue the activity to find out how accurate your estimate is.
3. Close your eyes and randomly choose one square in the grid. Count the number of mice in the square you chose.
4. Estimate the total number of mice shown by multiplying the number of mice in the square you chose by the number of squares in the grid. Record your answer.
5. Repeat steps 3–4 two more times.
6. Find the average of your samples by adding the three samples and dividing the total by 3. Record the average.
7. Count the number of mice in the grid.
8. Compare the actual number of mice with each of your samples and with the average of the samples.

Observations
1. How many mice did you predict were in the population?
2. How many mice were in each of your population samples?
3. What was the average of your three population samples?

Conclusions
1. **a.** How did each sample compare with the actual number of mice in the population? **b.** How did the average population size compare with the actual population size? **c.** Were the individual samples or the average of the samples more accurate?
2. Which of the following would best describe your sampling method? Explain your answer. **Hint:** Find out the meanings of any words you do not know.
   a. hit-or-miss method
   b. random-chance method
   c. counting method
   d. biased sample method

Figure 35-1 The habitat of this woodpecker is trees in a forest. Its niche is catching and eating insects.

Habitats and Niches

The place where an organism lives is its **habitat** (HAB-i-tat). The habitat of an organism provides food, water, shelter, and a place to reproduce. For example, the habitat of a squirrel may be a hole in a tree, where the squirrel builds its nest, and other trees in the area from which the squirrel gathers food.

If you describe yourself to someone, you might tell the person that you are a student. Student is your role, or job, in the community. Each organism also has a job, or role in its community. This role is called a **niche** (NICH). A niche is everything an organism does and everything it needs in its habitat.

Cycles in Nature

The abiotic parts of an ecosystem make up the physical environment. Organisms always interact with their physical environments. For example, many substances in the biosphere pass through cycles that allow the substances to be used and reused. These substances pass through both living things and the physical environment as they pass through their cycles.

Three important cycles of abiotic substances are the oxygen-carbon dioxide cycle, the water cycle, and the nitrogen cycle. The oxygen-carbon dioxide cycle is shown in Figure 35–2. Notice how the abiotic substances pass through both living and nonliving parts of the

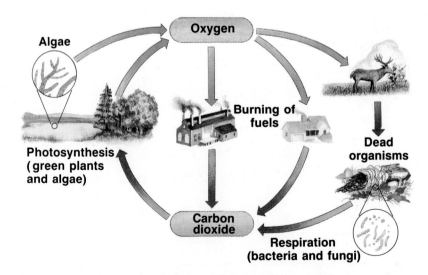

Figure 35-2 The oxygen-carbon dioxide cycle is kept in balance by the processes of photosynthesis and respiration.

environment. What living things are part of the oxygen-carbon dioxide cycle shown in Figure 35–2? What nonliving things are part of this cycle?

You know that green plants and algae use carbon dioxide from the air to make food. In turn, the green plants and algae produce oxygen as a waste product. Some of this oxygen is reused by plants and other organisms for respiration. Look at Figure 35–2. In what two ways do people use oxygen and give off carbon dioxide as a waste product?

❯ The water cycle is shown in Figure 35-3. Most of the water on the earth makes up the oceans. Heat energy from sunlight evaporates water from the oceans into the air. In the air, the water forms clouds. Eventually the water returns to the earth as rain, hail, snow, or sleet. Some of the water that returns to Earth falls in the oceans. What do you think happens to this water?

Water that falls on land may be absorbed from the soil by plants. Some of that water evaporates from the leaves of plants and returns to the air. The rest may be used by the plants to make food. Some of the water in the plants will be passed to animals that eat the plants. That water plus the water the animals drink, is excreted, or released, into the air by breathing out water vapor.

Some water that falls on land runs off into streams and eventually gets back to the ocean. When this water returns to the ocean, it is ready to begin another trip through the water cycle.

Study Hint

Notice that these cycles are not simple circles. Many different routes may be taken as you move through a complete cycle.

Figure 35-3   The water cycle is maintained by evaporation and precipitation.

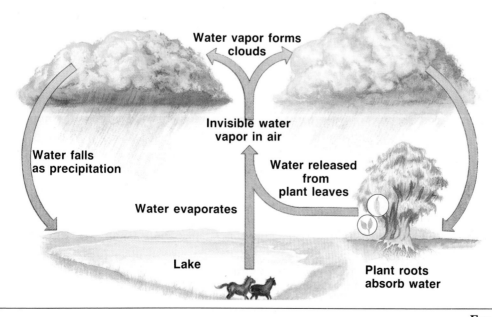

Water vapor forms clouds

Invisible water vapor in air

Water falls as precipitation

Water released from plant leaves

Water evaporates

Lake

Plant roots absorb water

In the nitrogen cycle, nitrogen-fixing bacteria change nitrogen gas into compounds called nitrates and nitrites. Living things use these compounds to make proteins. When plants and animals die, decomposers break down the compounds and release nitrogen gas back into the air.

Think & Discuss

1. What is ecology?
2. What is the biosphere?
3. Name the two parts of an ecosystem that a substance passes through as it cycles.
4. How do a pond community and a pond ecosystem differ?
5. Is it better to study an ecosystem or a community?

35–2 Energy and the Environment

All organisms need energy to stay alive. How do you get energy to run your body? Like all organisms, the energy that powers your body comes from food.

Interaction Among Organisms

You may be surprised to learn that sunlight is the main source of energy in most ecosystems. Why is this so? You have learned that green plants use the energy in sunlight to make food in a process called photosynthesis. During photosynthesis, carbon dioxide and water are combined to form food. The energy from the sun is stored in that food.

Plants use some of the food they make for growth and reproduction. However, extra food is stored in the plants. Animals that eat the plants use stored food in the plants for energy. Ecologists classify organisms into three major groups according to the way they get food.

Producers

Organisms that make, or produce, their own food are classified as **producers**. All green plants are producers. Algae are the producers in water ecosystems. How do algae and green plants make food?

Key Points

- Producers make their own food. Consumers and decomposers feed upon other organisms.

- Food chains and food webs are models that show feeding patterns and energy flow in an ecosystem.

- An energy pyramid shows the energy available at each feeding level in an ecosystem.

Figure 35-4 The brown bear (left) is an omnivore, the tortoise (middle) is a herbivore, and the lion (right) is a carnivore.

Consumers

The second major group of organisms is the **consumers**. Consumers are organisms that obtain their food by eating other organisms. Some consumers, like deer and bison, eat only producers. Consumers that eat only producers are called herbivores (HUR-buh-vawrs). Consumers, such as cougars and wolves, that eat other animals are called carnivores (KAR-nuh-vawrs). Some organisms eat both plants and animals. These organisms are omnivores (AHM-nuh-vawrs). What kind of consumer are you?

▶ Consumers can be grouped into feeding levels according to the foods they eat. Animals that eat plants are in the first feeding level. This level is called the consumer-1, or C_1, level. A second-level consumer, or C_2, is an animal that eats first-level consumers. A third-level consumer, or C_3, eats C_2 consumers, and so on. At what feeding level would a carnivore be classified?

Many organisms feed at more than one level. For example, bears eat berries, mice, and fish. When eating berries, a bear is a C_1. Mice are C_1's, so a bear eating a mouse is then a C_2. For this reason, an omnivore such as a bear may occupy several different feeding levels.

Decomposers

The last major feeding group in an ecosystem is the **decomposers** (dee-kum-POHZ-ers). Decomposers are organisms that feed on dead organisms. In the process of feeding, decomposers break down dead plants and animals and return nutrients to the soil. Bacteria and fungi are the two most important groups of decomposers.

Figure 35-5 These fungi are decomposers that break down dead plants and animals.

Food Chains and Food Webs

You can draw models to show the flow of energy from organism to organism in an ecosystem. The model of the flow of energy through the organisms of an ecosystem is called a **food chain**. This is an example of a food chain:

$$Sun \longrightarrow Grass \longrightarrow Mouse \longrightarrow Hawk$$

The source of energy for the food chain is the sun. The arrows represent the flow of energy through the ecosystem. The arrows always point in the direction energy is flowing. For example, the arrow from the sun points to the grass. Producers are the only organisms that can use sunlight to make food. In the food chain shown, energy flows from the sun to the grass, then to the mouse, and finally to the hawk.

One important fact to remember about food chains is that the energy that flows through the ecosystem is not recycled. Sunlight must continue to flow into the biosphere to supply energy for food chains.

Most plants and animals are involved in many food chains. In ecosystems, many food chains combine and overlap to form a **food web**. A food web includes more information about the flow of energy in an ecosystem than a food chain. For this reason, a food web is a better model of energy flow in an ecosystem than individual food chains. Look at Figure 35–6. Figure 35–6 is a very simple food web. What are some of the individual food chains in the food web?

Skill Builder

Using a Model A food chain is a model that shows the flow of energy through the organisms of an ecosystem. Using this model, you should be able to identify the feeding level of any food-chain organism, even if you do not know what the organism is. Identify the feeding level of each of the imaginary organisms in the following food chain:

$$Sun \longrightarrow Bleep \longrightarrow Zog \longrightarrow Zap \longrightarrow Zonk$$

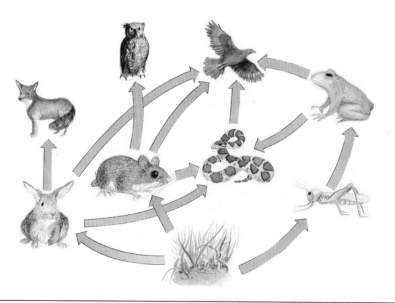

Figure 35-6 A food web is made up of many individual food chains.

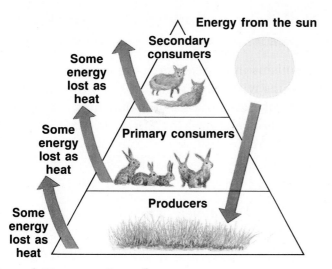

Energy from the sun

Secondary consumers

Primary consumers

Producers

Some energy lost as heat

Some energy lost as heat

Some energy lost as heat

Figure 35-7 An energy pyramid shows how energy moves through a food chain.

Food and Energy Levels

In a food chain, producers capture sunlight energy and store it in food. When a consumer eats a producer, it obtains only a small amount of the energy from that producer. The same is true for each link in the food chain.

Animals gain only a small amount of energy from the food they eat. The rest of the energy is used up or is released as heat energy. A model called an **energy pyramid** shows that the amount of energy decreases at each level of the food chain. As a result, fewer organisms can be supported at each level.

❯ An energy pyramid is shown in Figure 35–7. Notice that there are few predators at the top of the food chain compared with the number of prey organisms. What do you think would happen if the number of predators in an area was greater than the number of prey?

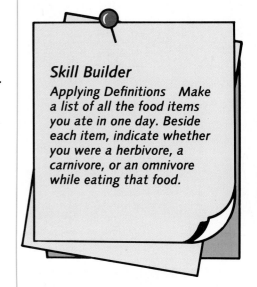

Skill Builder

Applying Definitions *Make a list of all the food items you ate in one day. Beside each item, indicate whether you were a herbivore, a carnivore, or an omnivore while eating that food.*

Think & Discuss

6. What do ecologists call organisms that can make their own food?

7. What kind of diagram shows the amount of energy available at each food level in an ecosystem?

8. Why is a food web a better representation of the flow of energy in an ecosystem than a food chain?

9. How do consumers benefit from photosynthesis?

★ 10. Look at the food web in Figure 35–6. In which two feeding levels does the hawk appear?

- Plants and animals in an ecosystem compete for resources.

- Competition, parasitism, and predation help maintain balance in ecosystems.

- In mutualism, two organisms gain from their relationship.

The organisms in an ecosystem are involved in relationships with other organisms and the physical environment. Some of these relationships help organisms survive. Other relationships, however, make life more difficult for organisms.

Competition

You often hear that athletes are competing in a game. In the science of ecology, competition means organisms striving for the same thing. Competition makes survival more difficult.

Animals compete for resources such as food, water, shelter, territory, and mates. Plant competition is less active than animal competition, but it is just as important. For example, plants compete for sunlight, water, and growing space.

Parasitism and Predation

In some relationships, one kind of organism feeds upon another organism. In **predation** (pri-DAY-shun), one organism kills and eats the other. A relationship in which an organism lives on or in another living organism is called **parasitism** (PAR-uh-syt-izm). A parasite is an organism that takes its nourishment from a living organism called the host.

Ticks, fleas, and leeches are examples of parasites that live outside a host. These parasites feed upon the blood of their hosts. Most parasites, however, live within their hosts. For example, a tapeworm is a parasite that lives in the digestive tract of its host. Many types of worms, fungi, and microorganisms live inside other organisms.

While parasites may eventually weaken or kill their hosts, predators capture and kill their prey before eating it. Wolves feeding upon caribou is an example of predation. It is easy to see that wolves benefit from this relationship because they eat the caribou. What is not easily noticed is that the caribou herd also can benefit from predation.

How do the caribou benefit from predation? Wolves will capture weak or diseased caribou more easily than

Figure 35-8 The kingfisher is a predator that feeds on small fishes.

ACTIVITY 35-2

PROBLEM: What is the relationship between food chains and a food web?

Science Process Skills
relating concepts, classifying, modeling

Background Information
A food chain shows a single feeding pattern in an ecosystem. The chain shows the flow of energy from the sun to a producer, then to a first level consumer (C_1), a second level consumer (C_2), and so on. Food chains usually do not exist alone in nature.

Data Table: Salt Marsh Organisms		
PRODUCERS	C_1	C_2 OR HIGHER
marsh grass water lilies algae cattails lichens ferns	insect larvae mosquitoes snails grasshoppers microscopic animals protozoa insects	small fish medium fish large fish snapping turtle marsh wren blackbird tern snowy egret heron osprey

Materials
3 sheets of construction paper
scissors
yarn
reference books
magazines

Procedure

1. A salt marsh is a thriving ecosystem. Study the list of organisms found in a salt marsh.
2. Use reference books to find out what each organism eats or uses for food. You should be able to infer what some organisms eat. For example, medium fish eat small fish.
3. Cut each sheet of construction paper into 4 rectangles. **CAUTION: Be careful when using scissors.**
4. Construct a food chain with at least four organisms. Draw the sun on one rectangle

of construction paper. Add organisms by writing the name of the organism on each piece of construction paper.
5. Illustrate the organisms in your food chain, if possible. Use pictures from old magazines.
6. Connect the construction paper rectangles with yarn.
7. Choose 3 other classmates and connect your food chain to theirs.

Observations
1. Write your food chain.
2. Write the three other food chains that are connected to yours.
3. **a.** How many producers are in the four food chains? **b.** How many C_1's are in the four food chains?
4. **a.** What is the highest level consumer shown in each of the four food chains? **b.** What animals feed at that level?

Conclusions
1. **MODEL**   When you connect the four food chains, what does the model represent?
2. Where does the energy for each food chain come from?
3. What is the relationship between a food chain and a food web?
4. Why is a food web a better model of energy flow in an ecosystem than a food chain?

strong, healthy ones. Because diseased or less-fit members are removed from the herd, the caribou herd is kept strong and healthy. Predation by wolves also may help prevent overpopulation of the caribou herd.

Mutualism and Commensalism

Some relationships in the environment make survival easier. An example of a helpful relationship is **mutualism** (MYOO-choo-wul-izm). Mutualism is a relationship between two different kinds of organisms that benefits both organisms. For example, when bees obtain food by gathering nectar from flowers, they also pollinate the flowers. Both bees and flowers gain from this interaction. What is the benefit to the bees?

In **commensalism** (kuh-MEN-sul-izm), one organism benefits from the relationship while the other is unaffected. Orchids growing on trees in tropical forests demonstrate commensalism. The orchid grows attached to the tree but does not take nourishment from the tree. The orchid takes everything it needs to grow and survive from the air. The orchid benefits by having a place to grow. The tree is not affected in any way.

Balance in an Ecosystem

All the relationships in an ecosystem help to keep the ecosystem in balance. Natural disasters such as floods or fires may upset the balance in ecosystems. It may take years, but an ecosystem usually will regain its balance after a natural disaster.

Study Hint

Lichens also are an example of mutualism. Refer to Chapter 8 to review lichens.

Figure 35-9 The flower and the hummingbird (left) represent mutualism. The gray whale and barnacles (right) represent commensalism.

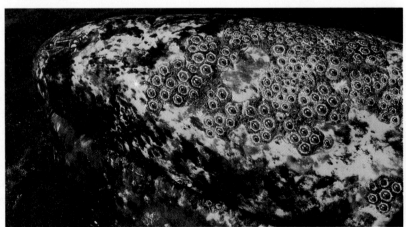

People often change and upset the balance of ecosystems, too. For example, people may remove most of the predators in an ecosystem. This may result in overpopulation of the herbivores upon which they prey. As a result, the herbivores may run out of food and begin to starve. Parasites also can spread more rapidly in the crowded herbivore population.

Most organisms that you consider pests were in balance in ecosystems until people disturbed that balance. For example, by planting huge fields of cotton, farmers created a perfect environment for the boll weevil, which then overproduced and became a pest. Cockroaches and rats were carried in ships to areas where they were not originally found. Cities provided these two organisms with ideal growing conditions, and they have become widespread pests.

Figure 35-10 The boll weevil is a parasite that lives on cotton plants.

Think & Discuss

11. Name the kind of relationship between organisms in which both organisms gain from the relationship.

12. Both predators and parasites get nourishment from other organisms. How are they different?

★ 13. List three ways that people can upset the balance in an ecosystem.

35–4 Ecological Succession

The process by which populations in an ecosystem are gradually replaced by new populations is called **ecological succession** (suhk-SESH-uhn). In succession, changes first occur in the plant populations. As the plant species change, different animal populations replace previous ones. Each community in succession makes the environment better for the next community. One group of organisms prepares the way for another.

Succession can occur when an existing ecosystem is changed. For example, fire, wind, logging, and farming all can change ecosystems. An ecosystem also can change when a new habitat, such as an island, is created.

Key Points

- Ecological succession is a gradual change in the community of organisms.

- The climax community is the final stage of succession.

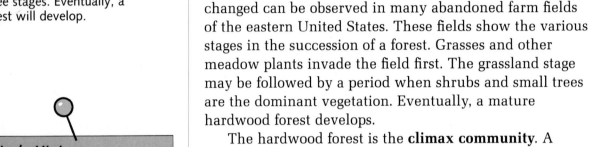

Pond   **Bog**   **Meadow**

Figure 35-11 Pond succession is shown by these three stages. Eventually, a forest will develop.

Study Hint

Hardwoods are deciduous trees like oaks and maples. Refer to Chapter 10 for more information about these types of trees.

Succession can be observed in many places. For example, succession that occurs when an ecosystem is changed can be observed in many abandoned farm fields of the eastern United States. These fields show the various stages in the succession of a forest. Grasses and other meadow plants invade the field first. The grassland stage may be followed by a period when shrubs and small trees are the dominant vegetation. Eventually, a mature hardwood forest develops.

The hardwood forest is the **climax community**. A climax community is a balanced community, which is the end product of succession. The climax community is the one best suited for the existing environment. Physical factors, such as climate and soil types, determine what kinds of plants can exist in a climax community. For example, areas with plenty of rainfall and long summers will support the growth of forest climax communities. Often it takes well over 100 years for a forest climax community to form. Ponds also undergo a natural succession as they fill in and become bogs, then meadows, and finally forests.

Succession is a very slow process. It can be studied by observing areas that are in different stages of the same type of succession. By observing these areas, ecologists can piece together the pattern of succession.

Think & Discuss

14. What is a climax community?
15. Why does succession in different areas result in different types of climax communities?
16. Why are climax communities identified by the plants living in the area instead of the animals?

BIOLOGY and YOU
Leisure Activity

Hiking and Backpacking

It is a sunny July day in New Hampshire. The temperature is in the high 80s as three hikers prepare for their trip up Mount Washington. They each pack a down vest, gloves, a wool hat, and earmuffs. Are the hikers crazy? No, the hikers know that temperatures on a mountaintop can be well below freezing, even in July.

Hiking and backpacking are popular sports in the United States, where areas of unspoiled wilderness offer numerous opportunities for traveling on foot. Hiking and backpacking are similar activities. The main difference between hiking and backpacking is that the hiker's walk is at most a one-day journey, whereas the backpacker carries camping supplies that can extend the walk to a week or more.

You can start hiking close to home, with short walks on any parkland trail. You will need no special equipment at first, but if you plan to take longer hikes on rougher ground, you will need a pair of hiking boots. Hiking boots are designed to provide support and protect your feet against wet, cold, jagged rocks, snakes, and poisonous plants. A sturdy pair of boots also provides protection against mishaps such as twisted ankles and falls due to slipping.

Depending on the type of hiking you plan to do, you also will need a day-pack or a backpack. A day-pack is a small knapsack large enough to hold supplies for one day. These supplies include lunch, a first aid kit, water, and so on. A backpack enables the hiker to carry equipment for nights in the wilderness. The backpack may contain items such as a tent, bedroll, food and water for several days, cooking utensils, and extra clothes. Most experts agree that a person can comfortably carry about one-fifth of his or her own body weight in a well-fitting backpack.

Do you need to be "physically fit" to hike? According to the *Sierra Club Guide to Backpacking*, "Anyone who can climb a few flights of stairs without collapsing can hike." You should be in generally good health, however, and aware of physical problems, such as allergies, that could cause you problems on the trail. You also can build up stamina for longer hikes by engaging regularly in aerobic activities such as swimming, running, and cycling.

If you wish to obtain information about where to hike and backpack, you can contact the National Geological Survey, state and national park services, outdoor stores, and local or regional hiking clubs. If you live in the western United States, an excellent source of information is the Sierra Club. In the eastern United States, you can contact the Appalachian Mountain Club, the oldest hiking club in the United States.

To Think About
- In the Adirondack Mountains of upstate New York, wilderness officials require hikers to sign in at the beginning of a trail, indicating their expected date and time of return. Why do you think this is required?
- Do you think it is best to hike alone or with several other people? Why?

Chapter Review

CHAPTER SUMMARY

35–1 Ecology and Ecosystems

- The biotic factors of an ecosystem are the living organisms. The abiotic factors are the nonliving parts of the ecosystem.
- Water, carbon dioxide, oxygen, and nitrogen cycle through the biosphere.

35–2 Energy and the Environment

- Organisms that make their own food are classified as producers.
- Consumers feed upon other organisms.
- Decomposers feed upon and break down dead organisms.
- Food chains and food webs are models that show feeding patterns and energy flow in an ecosystem.

- An energy pyramid is a model that shows the amount of energy available at each feeding level in an ecosystem.

35–3 Relationships in an Ecosystem

- Plants and animals compete for the resources in an ecosystem.
- Competition, mutualism, parasitism, and predation help maintain balance in ecosystems.

35–4 Ecological Succession

- Ecological succession is a gradual change in an ecosystem that results in a change in the community of organisms.
- The climax community is the final stage of succession.

VOCABULARY LIST

abiotic (600)
biosphere (600)
biotic (600)
climax community (612)
commensalism (610)
communities (600)

consumers (605)
decomposers (605)
ecological succession (611)
ecology (599)
ecosystems (600)

energy pyramid (607)
food chain (606)
food web (606)
habitat (602)
mutualism (610)

niche (602)
parasitism (608)
populations (600)
predation (608)
producers (604)

VOCABULARY REVIEW

Matching Write the word or term from the Vocabulary List that best matches each description.

1. study of living things and their environments
2. model that shows several overlapping food chains
3. model showing the decrease of energy in food chains
4. living organisms
5. relationship in which one organism kills and eats another organism
6. zone of the earth that supports all life

Identifying Relationships Identify the word or term in each group that does not belong. Explain why it does not belong with the group.

1. commensalism, predation, climax community
2. consumers, decomposers, producers
3. ecological succession, climax community, food web
4. communities, niche, populations
5. food chain, niche, habitat
6. food chain, food web, mutualism
7. ecosystems, parasitism, mutualism
8. abiotic, decomposers, water cycle

Completion   Write the word or words that best complete each sentence.

1. An organism that eats only producers is called _____.
2. The gradual replacement of one ecosystem with another is called _____.
3. Organisms are classified according to the way they obtain _____.
4. Plants are producers because they make their own food through the process of _____.
5. The main source of energy in most ecosystems is the _____.
6. In an ecosystem, all of the populations make up a _____.
7. Rocks, water, sand, soil, and air are _____ factors.

Finding the Main Ideas   Use the section number to find the sentence that answers each question. Then, write the sentence.

1. How are communities and populations related? (35–1)
2. What are three important abiotic cycles in the biosphere? (35–1)
3. How do decomposers help an ecosystem? (35–2)
4. What does a food chain explain about an ecosystem? (35–2)
5. In ecology, what is meant by competition? (35–3)
6. Describe a relationship that helps both organisms. (35–3)
7. How does ecological succession benefit the environment? (35–4)

CONCEPT REVIEW

Writing for Understanding   One way to find out if you understand something is to write a brief summary of the information in your own words. Reread Section 35–4, Ecological Succession, on pages 611–612, and write a brief summary of the information.

Critical Thinking   Answer each of the following in complete sentences.

1. Tube worms and some bacteria can make their own food by chemosynthesis. Are these organisms producers?

2. Explain the relationship among food chains, food webs, and energy pyramids.
3. Look at the food web shown in Figure 35–6 on page 606. List the organisms involved in each food chain in the proper order.
4. Barnacles cannot move from one place to another in search of food. How does attaching to a whale or a boat help a barnacle obtain food?
5. What would happen if sunlight could not enter an ecosystem?

EXTENSIONS

1. Use library references to find information about the nitrogen cycle. Draw and label a diagram of this cycle.
2. Plants with nodules on their roots are called legumes. Write a report about how legumes help provide nitrogen to an ecosystem.

3. Make a list of 15 organisms that live in your community. Design a food web that shows how these organisms are related.
4. List five different kinds of animals. Then classify each animal as a herbivore, a carnivore, or an omnivore.

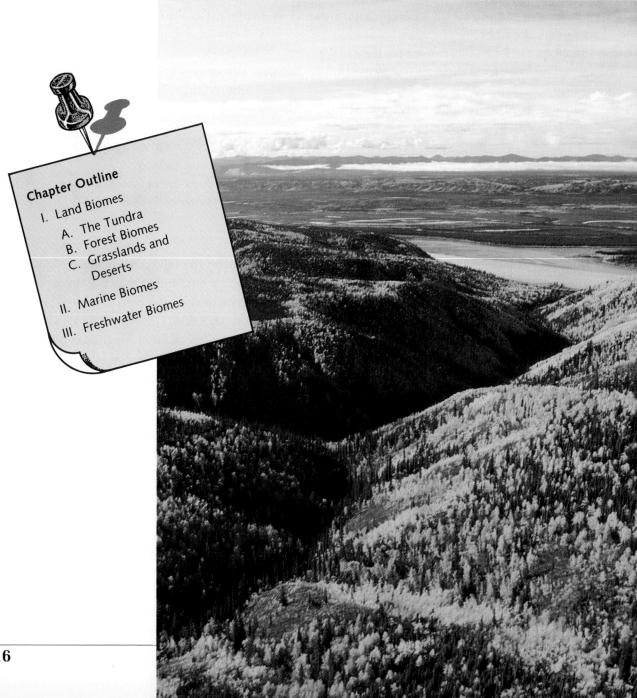

Objectives

After you have completed this chapter, you will be able to

36-1 **identify** two factors that determine a land biome.

36-1 **name** six land biomes.

36-1 **distinguish** among the three kinds of forest biomes.

36-2 **describe** two kinds of water biomes.

36-2 **recognize** the marine biome as the largest biome on Earth.

36-2 **identify** the three areas that make up the marine biome.

36-3 **identify** two kinds of freshwater biomes.

Science Process Skills

In this chapter, two science skills are highlighted. Symbols show some places where these skills are used.

☞ **Classifying**: When you classify, you group things based upon similarities.

▲ **Modeling**: When you model, you use a copy or imitation of an object to help explain something.

Imagine being an explorer in North America before the European settlers arrived. What do you think the United States looked like then? The eastern part of the United States was covered by a huge forest. A squirrel could travel from the Atlantic Ocean to the Mississippi River without touching the ground. The central United States was a rich grassland. You would have found desert areas in the southwestern United States.

Cities, houses, roads, lawns, farms, and shopping centers have replaced much of the natural landscape since that time. What did the land where you live look like before it was changed by people? You may be able to find out by visiting a nearby national or state park.

36-1 Land Biomes

Key Points

- Land biomes are determined by temperature and rainfall.

- Six kinds of land biomes are the tundra, coniferous forest, deciduous forest, tropical rain forest, grassland, and desert.

- Three kinds of forest biomes are coniferous forest, deciduous forest, and tropical rain forest.

A large region of the earth that has characteristic kinds of organisms is called a **biome** (BY-ohm). Biomes are identified by their dominant plant life. Because animals that live in an area depend on the vegetation in the area, each biome also has a distinctive group of animals.

What determines the kinds of organisms that live in a biome? Rainfall and temperature determine the plant life in an area. Therefore, rainfall and temperature determine the kind of land biome in a given area. The average yearly rainfall and temperature range are called the area's **climate.** Table 36-1 shows the average yearly rainfall and temperature range of land biomes.

Table 36-1 Land Biome Climates		
BIOME	AVERAGE YEARLY RAINFALL	AVERAGE YEARLY TEMPERATURE RANGE
Tundra	less than 25 cm	−25 °C– 4 °C
Coniferous forests	35–75 cm	−10 °C–14 °C
Deciduous forests	75–125 cm	6 °C–28 °C
Tropical rain forests	200–450 cm	25 °C–28 °C
Grasslands	25–75 cm	0 °C–25 °C
Deserts	less than 25 cm	24 °C–40 °C

▲ What are the major land biomes? You can observe the location of the major land biomes in Figure 36-1 on page 619. In which biome do you live?

The Tundra

The **tundra** is a treeless biome located near the North Pole. It is a biome with cold temperatures and little rainfall. In the tundra, winters are very long and temperatures stay well below freezing most of the year. During the winter, there is little or no daylight. Summers are cool and short. However, daylight may last 24 hours a day in the summer.

The tundra is covered with snow for about nine months a year. In the summer, only the top meter of soil thaws. The soil below this level remains frozen. The permanently frozen ground is called **permafrost**.

Study Hint

As you read about the different land biomes, refer to Figure 36-1 on page 619 to find their locations.

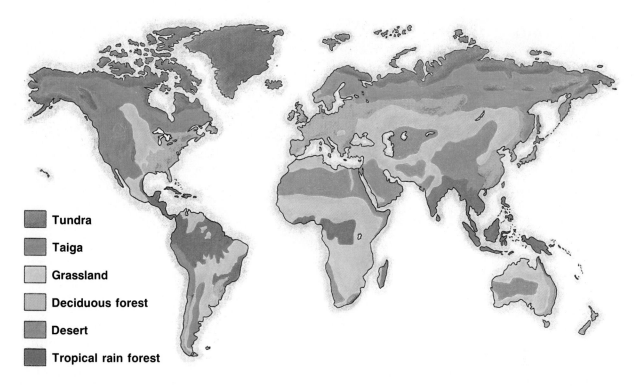

- ■ Tundra
- ■ Taiga
- ■ Grassland
- ■ Deciduous forest
- ■ Desert
- ■ Tropical rain forest

Very few kinds of plants live in the tundra because of the extreme cold, short growing season, and shallow soil. The most common plants are grasses and mosses. Lichens also grow in the tundra. These organisms can grow here because they have shallow roots. Why do you think large trees do not grow in the tundra?

One of the most common animals of the tundra is the caribou. Caribou feed on lichens and mosses. Other large mammals are reindeer and musk oxen. Small animals, such as Arctic hares and wolves, also live here. In the summer, ducks and geese nest in the tundra.

Forest Biomes

Forest biomes cover much of the earth. However, not all forest biomes are alike. Different kinds of forests grow in different areas. In fact, there are three major forest biomes.

Coniferous Forests

Just south of the tundra lies a vast region of **coniferous** (kah-NIF-uhr-uhs) **forests**. Coniferous forests are made up of cone-bearing trees called conifers. Spruce, fir, and pine trees are examples of conifers.

Figure 36-1 What is the largest biome in the United States?

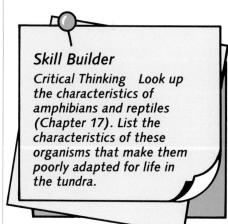

Skill Builder

Critical Thinking   Look up the characteristics of amphibians and reptiles (Chapter 17). List the characteristics of these organisms that make them poorly adapted for life in the tundra.

Figure 36-2 Spruce and fir trees (left) and bull moose (right) are common organisms of the coniferous forest.

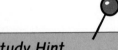

Study Hint

Refer to Chapter 10 to review the characteristics of conifers.

Conifers are well-adapted to long, cold winters and short summers. Conifers have needle-shaped leaves with a waxy coat that protects them against freezing. Many times during the year, there is little rainfall in coniferous forests. During these periods, the leaves of conifers also protect them against water loss.

Ecologists divide the coniferous forests of North America into three areas.

- The **taiga** (TY-guh) is located in northern Canada and Alaska. Winters in the taiga are long, snowy, and cold. Summers are short and warm. Rainfall is between 20 and 60 cm.

- The "spruce-moose" belt is located south of the taiga. This area covers most of Canada and the northern parts of the United States. How do you think this coniferous forest gets its name?

- The southern pine forest covers most of the southeastern United States. Pine forests are located in warmer areas of the United States. Some broad-leaf trees, such as oaks, also grow here.

Many large and small animals live in the coniferous forest biome. Moose, black bears, and deer are some large mammals that live in this biome. Red squirrels and beavers are small mammals. During the summer, geese, ducks, and many small birds migrate to coniferous forests. Where do you think most of the small birds make their nests?

Deciduous Forests

South of the taiga lies the **deciduous** (di-SIJ-oo-wuhs) **forest** biome. In the deciduous forest biome, winters are cold and summers are warm. Rainfall averages more than 50 cm each year. Deciduous forests are the dominant biome in the eastern United States.

The deciduous forest biome is characterized by many kinds of trees that lose their leaves seasonally. Which kinds of trees make up a deciduous forest? Maple, beech, and oak trees are examples of deciduous trees. Deciduous trees are broad-leafed trees. They lose their leaves in the fall and grow new leaves each spring.

The loss of leaves in the fall is an adaptation of deciduous trees. It prevents deciduous trees from losing too much water through their leaves in winter, when the roots cannot absorb water from the frozen ground.

A deciduous forest provides food and shelter to many animals. Squirrels, deer, foxes, raccoons, skunks, rabbits, and black bears are familiar mammals of these forests. Many birds also live in deciduous forests. Reptiles and amphibians, such as snakes, turtles, frogs, and salamanders, are common. Some of the animals living in a deciduous forest migrate to warmer climates or hibernate for the winter.

Figure 36-3 The downy woodpecker is only one of the many species of birds that live in deciduous forests.

Tropical Rain Forests

Figure 36–4 shows three organisms that live in the **tropical rain forest.** The organisms shown are just a few of the millions of species that live in the tropical rain forest. In fact, more than half of all plant and animal species on Earth live in the tropical rain forest.

▲ If you look at Figure 36–1 on page 619, you will see that tropical rain forests are found near the equator. The temperature in a tropical rain forest is warm all year. Rain forests get at least 200 cm of rainfall each year.

Figure 36-4 The gibbon (left), chameleon (center), and parrot (right) are common animals of tropical rain forests.

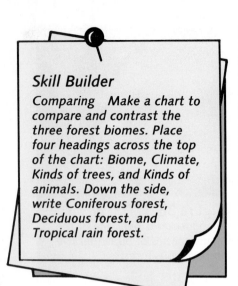
Trees of the rain forest have leaves all year. The tops of the trees in a rain forest make up a dense **canopy** (CAN-uh-pee), or roof, over the forest. Many rain-forest organisms live in the canopy. For example, many birds, insects, amphibians, and reptiles live in the treetops.

Many different plants, such as orchids and vines, grow among the trees. Often, these plants use the tall trees for support. Why do you think that few plants grow on the forest floor?

Grasslands and Deserts

Large areas of the earth do not receive enough rainfall to support the growth of trees. **Grassland** or **desert** biomes are found in these dry areas. In the United States, grasslands cover much of the central part of the country. Deserts are found in the west and southwest.

Grasslands

Have you ever heard the central United States referred to as the "bread basket"? This phrase is used to describe the grasslands of the central United States. In grasslands, rainfall is between 25 and 75 cm per year. Summers are hot and dry, while winters are cold and snowy. The soil is very fertile and ideal for farming. Wheat, oats, barley, and corn are grown in this part of the country.

What animals live in the grasslands? Large populations of grazing animals live here. Bison and antelope are common. Cattle and sheep are raised on farms. Coyotes, jackrabbits, and rattlesnakes also live in the grasslands.

Figure 36-5 Buffalo, or bison, once roamed the grasslands in great numbers. Today, few bison live in the grasslands.

Deserts

Imagine being in a place where rain falls only once every few years. The Sahara Desert, in Africa, is such a place. A desert is a biome where rainfall is less than 25 cm each year. Temperatures range from very hot during the day to very cool at night.

Some deserts are so dry that no plants can grow. Other deserts have plants that are adapted to the dry environment. Cacti, for example, have spines for leaves. The spines and tough covering of the stems help to reduce water loss. The large stems also store water.

Most desert animals are small. They include mice, rabbits, lizards, and birds. Snakes, owls, coyotes, and kit foxes are desert predators. Why do you think desert animals are active mainly at night?

Figure 36-6 Saguaro cactus are common plants of the Arizona desert.

Think & Discuss

1. What is a biome?
2. What is permafrost?
3. Where do the majority of species on the earth live?
4. How do conifers differ from deciduous trees?
★ 5. Which factor causes the differences between deserts and grasslands?

36–2 Marine Biomes

Have you ever heard the earth called the "water planet"? This name is used because more than 75 percent of the earth's surface is covered by water. All of the water on the earth makes up the water biomes.

There are two main water biomes on the earth. Bodies of water with little or no salt, such as lakes and rivers, make up the freshwater biome. The oceans make up the marine biome. The marine biome is the largest biome on earth.

Ecologists divide the marine biome into three areas. These areas are the ocean, the **intertidal zone**, and the **estuary**. An intertidal zone is under water at high tide and exposed at low tide. An estuary is an area where a freshwater river flows into the ocean.

Key Points
- Two water biomes are the saltwater, or marine, biome and the freshwater biome.
- The marine biome is the largest biome on Earth.

ACTIVITY 36-1

PROBLEM: How can the biomes of the United States be determined using climate data?

Science Process Skills
modeling, inferring, generalizing

Background Information
Two factors determine the kind of biome that exists in an area. These factors are average yearly temperature and average yearly rainfall. Using rainfall and temperature data, the location of a particular biome can be predicted.

Materials
tracing paper
colored pencils

Procedure
1. Study the map of North America. The lines on the map indicate areas with the same temperature. Use the key to find out the average yearly rainfall in different places.
2. Trace the United States from the map of North America. Be sure to trace Alaska. Hawaii is a tropical rain forest biome.
3. Study the data in the Data Table showing the annual average temperature and rainfall of different biomes.

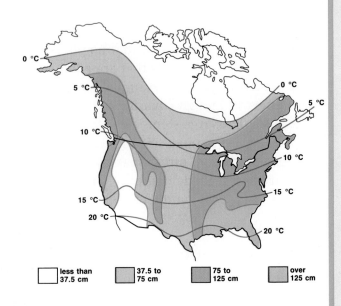

| | less than 37.5 cm | 37.5 to 75 cm | 75 to 125 cm | over 125 cm |

4. Use the data in the Data Table to determine the approximate boundaries of biomes in the United States.
5. Color each biome on your map with a different colored pencil. Be sure to make a map key.

Data Table: Annual Average Temperatures and Rainfall

BIOME	ANNUAL AVERAGE TEMPERATURE	ANNUAL AVERAGE RAINFALL
Tundra	Below 0 °C	0–30 cm
Coniferous forest	5–12 °C	150 cm
Taiga	0–5 °C	25–100 cm
Deciduous forest	5–25 °C	75–150 cm
Grassland	5–25 °C	30–75 cm
Desert	10–25 °C	0–30 cm

Observations
1. How many biomes are in the United States?
2. In which biome do you live?

Conclusions
1. What are the biomes in the United States?
2. In which direction would you travel to find tundra?
3. **GENERALIZE** What happens to the amount of rainfall as you travel from the east coast to the west coast of the United States mainland?

Figure 36-7 The oceans are home to many different kinds of organisms. What kinds of organisms do you recognize in this illustration?

Different parts of the ocean have different characteristics. For example, there are differences in the amount of sunlight and salt. Also, the deeper you go in the ocean, the greater is the water pressure.

The upper level of the oceans receives a lot of sunlight. Many kinds of algae and microscopic organisms live here. Together, these floating organisms are called **plankton**. Many fish, squid, and turtles also live in the upper levels of the ocean.

Organisms in the intertidal zone include clams, oysters, mussels, and crabs. These organisms are adapted to being exposed to the air during part of the day. These animals also must be able to withstand being hit by waves. Crabs burrow into the sand. Mussels, clams, and oysters have hard shells. Mussels also attach themselves to rocks to keep from being washed away by the waves.

Estuaries are important parts of the marine biome. They are rich in nutrients and support many kinds of organisms. Estuaries also are important breeding areas for many fish and other marine organisms.

Study Hint

Remember that most organisms need oxygen to live. In water biomes, the oxygen is dissolved in the water. How do fishes remove dissolved oxygen from the water? Refer to Chapter 16.

Think & Discuss

6. What is an estuary?

7. In what part of the ocean do most plankton live?

★ 8. Explain why a crab would burrow into the sand at low tide.

36-3 Freshwater Biomes

- Freshwater biomes are made up of still-water biomes and running-water biomes.

Freshwater biomes are made up of many small ecosystems. There are two kinds of freshwater biomes. The still-water biomes include lakes and ponds. Rivers and streams are running-water biomes.

The kinds of living things found in lakes and ponds depend mainly on the amount of nutrients available. In rivers and streams, the amount of oxygen dissolved in the water mainly determines what kinds of organisms are found there.

The main producers in lakes and ponds are algae floating in the water. Lakes and ponds also have plankton similar to those in the ocean. Microscopic organisms feed upon the algae and plankton. Fishes and other lake and pond animals depend upon plankton and microorganisms for food. Some plants, such as water lilies, grow rooted in the soil at the bottom of ponds or in the shallow parts of lakes.

Streams are very different from lakes because of the currents, or moving water. In fast-moving streams, water temperatures generally are cool and dissolved oxygen is plentiful. Because rapidly flowing water cannot support a large population of plankton, dead leaves that fall into the stream often are an important food source.

Many insects lay their eggs in fast-moving streams. When the eggs hatch, the larvae use hooks and suckers to cling to rocks and catch food particles that wash by in the current. Trout are common in streams and feed upon the insect larvae.

Slow-moving rivers are similar to lakes and ponds. In slow-moving rivers, plankton are the base of food chains. In fact, the large numbers of plankton make slow-moving rivers appear cloudy. Fishes, similar to those in lakes, also live in slow-moving rivers. Catfish and bass are two kinds of fish that inhabit slow-moving rivers and lakes.

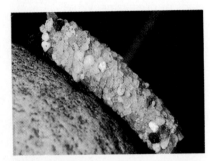

Figure 36-8 Insect larvae, such as this caddis fly larva, serve as food for fishes living in streams.

Health and Safety Tip

Giardia is a single-celled organism found in streams and ponds. It can cause digestive-system disorders in humans. Avoid drinking water from streams and ponds unless it is boiled first.

Think & Discuss

9. What kind of freshwater biome is a lake?

10. What are the primary consumers in a lake or pond?

 11. Why is the water clear in a fast-moving stream?

BIOLOGY, TECHNOLOGY, and SOCIETY

Saving Estuary Systems

If you have ever seen the Golden Gate Bridge rising over San Francisco Bay, you would probably think the water beneath the bridge is clear and deep. But you would be wrong. Like most estuaries in the United States, the San Francisco Bay area is being slowly destroyed by a combination of pollution and natural processes.

An estuary is the zone between a freshwater biome and a saltwater biome. In an estuary, the ocean tide meets a river current. One of the problems with estuaries is that the water flow in these areas is very slow. As a result, sediments pile up, causing the estuary to become more and more shallow. In addition, pollutants from industry, ships, and household wastes collect in an estuary because they are not diluted and carried out to sea.

Estuaries are usually rich in nutrients, which are constantly circulated by the tides. Estuaries also are shallow enough for sunlight to penetrate the water so that photosynthesis can take place at every level. As a result, an estuary supports many kinds of plant and animal life.

Estuaries are of great concern to environmental scientists, because estuaries are important to people in many ways. For example, many of the sea animals that people use for food are found in estuaries. These animals probably include some of your favorite foods—shrimp, oysters, clams, crabs, and many kinds of fish.

Estuaries provide attractive places for people to live and find recreation. Several years ago, a national newsmagazine ran a story about the growing popularity of the Chesapeake Bay area of Virginia and Maryland as a place to live and work. The headline of the story read, "More People, More Pollution." The Chesapeake Bay estuary is in danger of being destroyed as more people and industry come into the area.

What can be done to save the estuary systems? Some solutions include building sewage treatment plants, stopping the use of fertilizers and pesticides, and banning the dumping of industrial wastes. These solutions have not always met with a great deal of support, however, because the economic value of cleaning up estuaries is difficult to measure. Yet the importance of saving estuaries becomes clear if you think of your favorite fish becoming impossible to find at the supermarket, or of the estuary nearest you being destroyed as a place of beauty and recreation.

To Think About

- Why does photosynthesis at all levels allow estuaries to support a wide variety of life forms?

- Is pollution the only problem that threatens estuaries? Explain.

Chapter Review

36–1 Land Biomes

- A biome is a large region of the earth with characteristic kinds of organisms.
- The kind of land biome is determined by the average yearly temperature and amount of rainfall.
- Land biomes include tundra, forests, grasslands, and deserts.
- The three kinds of forest biomes are the coniferous forest, the deciduous forest, and the tropical rain forest.
- The coniferous forest is made up of the taiga, the "spruce-moose" belt, and the southern pine forest.

36–2 Marine Biomes

- The two main water biomes are the saltwater, or marine, biome and the freshwater biome.
- The marine biome is the largest biome on Earth.
- The marine biome includes oceans, intertidal zones, and estuaries.

36–3 Freshwater Biomes

- The freshwater biome is made up of stillwater biomes and running-water biomes.
- Still-water biomes include lakes and ponds.
- Running-water biomes include rivers and streams.

VOCABULARY LIST

biome (618)
canopy (622)
climate (618)
coniferous forests (619)

deciduous forests (621)
desert (622)
estuary (623)
grassland (622)

intertidal zone (623)
permafrost (618)
plankton (625)

taiga (620)
tropical rain forest (621)
tundra (618)

VOCABULARY REVIEW

Matching   Write the word or term from the Vocabulary List that best matches each description.

1. large area with certain kinds of plants and animals
2. permanently frozen layer of ground
3. where fresh water flows into salt water
4. microscopic plants and animals that float in water biomes
5. roof of treetops in a tropical rain forest
6. area of shore that is under water during high tide and exposed during low tide
7. average yearly temperature and rainfall of an area
8. biomes made up of broad-leaf trees that lose their leaves seasonally

Applying Definitions   Explain the difference between the words in each pair.

1. coniferous forest, deciduous forest
2. desert, grassland
3. tundra, taiga
4. tropical rain forest, coniferous forest
5. biome, climate
6. estuary, intertidal zone
7. still-water biome, running-water biome
8. desert, tundra
9. lake, stream
10. marine biome, freshwater biome
11. intertidal zone, ocean
12. taiga, "spruce-moose" belt
13. canopy, permafrost
14. desert, tropical rain forest

True or False Write true if the statement is true. If the statement is false, change the underlined word or words to make the statement true.

1. The climax vegetation of the taiga are <u>deciduous</u> trees.
2. Forest biomes require <u>less</u> rainfall than grassland biomes.
3. Cold temperatures and little rainfall are the dominant characteristics of the <u>tundra</u>.
4. The biome that receives the most rainfall is the <u>deciduous</u> forest.
5. <u>Grasslands</u> support large populations of herbivores.
6. Loss of leaves in the fall is an adaptation of <u>conifers</u>.
7. <u>Deserts</u> receive less than 25 centimeters of rain each year.
8. The <u>shallow</u> ocean supports few organisms.
9. Organisms of the <u>intertidal zone</u> are adapted for surviving in water and for surviving a limited time exposed to the air.
10. Musk oxen, caribou, and reindeer are mammals found in the <u>tropical rain forest</u>.

Question and Answer Rewrite each heading in the Chapter Outline on page 616 as a question. Then, answer each of the questions you have written.

Understanding a Diagram Use the diagram of the world's biomes shown in Figure 36–1 (page 619) to answer each of the following.
1. Where is the largest desert biome?
2. Which kinds of biomes are found in Australia?
3. Are there any tropical rain forests in the United States?

Writing the Main Ideas Using the Chapter Outline on page 616, write the main idea for each heading in the outline.

Critical Thinking Answer each of the following in complete sentences.
1. Why are there few amphibians or reptiles in the tundra?
2. What might happen to the plants of a deciduous forest if the climate suddenly became very dry?
3. How is a deep lake similar to the open ocean?
4. Why are land biomes more affected by climate than water biomes?
5. How does the number and variety of animal species change as you move farther from the equator? Explain.
6. In which of the six major land biomes do you live? Give examples to support your answer.

1. Go to the library and write a research report explaining why the coniferous forest, deciduous forest, and tropical rain forest biomes are important for people.
2. Select one of the earth's land biomes. Then construct a food web for that biome. Include at least ten organisms. Use library books and your textbook to find organisms that live in the biome you select.
3. Choose a land biome and list three reasons why you would like to live in that biome. Then choose another land biome and list three reasons why you would not like to live in that biome.

Chapter 37 | Conservation

Objectives

After you have completed this chapter, you will be able to

37–1 **state** the difference between a renewable and a nonrenewable natural resource.

37–2 **explain** how pollution affects living things.

37–2 **identify** sources of air pollution and water pollution.

37–3 **recognize** the difference between threatened and endangered wildlife.

37–4 **name** four alternative energy sources.

37–4 **identify** four problems related to the use of nuclear energy.

Science Process Skills

In this chapter, two science skills are highlighted. Symbols show some places where these skills are used.

📁 **Classifying**: When you classify, you group objects based upon similarities.

❯ **Predicting**: When you predict, you state in advance how and why something will occur.

About 35,000 years ago, early humans were living in caves and learning how to hunt. At that time fewer than three million people probably lived on the earth. The environment provided everything these early people needed to survive.

About 11,000 years ago, the agricultural revolution led to an increase in the human population. People began to migrate and settle in different areas. Although the population continued to grow, the environment was still able to provide all the air, food, and water that people needed.

Today, the population of the earth is greater than five billion people. In fact, the human population doubles about every 40 years! How long will the earth be able to provide all the resources people need to survive?

37–1 Natural Resources

Key Points

- Renewable resources are renewed or replaced on a regular basis.

- Nonrenewable resources cannot be replaced once they are used up.

The materials and energy in the biosphere that are used by living things are called **natural resources**. Air and water are two natural resources. Most natural resources are needed by all living things to survive.

Natural resources must be used carefully and wisely. The wise use of natural resources is called **conservation** (kon-suhr-VAY-shun). Why do you think conservation of natural resources is important? Conservation is important because natural resources may be used up or permanently damaged.

Renewable Resources

Natural resources that can be reused or replaced are **renewable resources**. Air, water, soil, and living things are examples of renewable resources. What other renewable resources can you name?

Although renewable resources are replaced by the environment, the supply of renewable resources is limited. The rate at which renewable resources are replaced might not be able to keep up with the rate at which they are being used. As a result, people must manage renewable resources carefully.

Nonrenewable Resources

Some natural resources cannot be reused or replaced once they are used. These resources are called **nonrenewable resources**. Oil, coal, natural gas, and minerals are examples of nonrenewable resources. Why are some natural resources considered to be nonrenewable? Nonrenewable resources need millions of years to form. Once existing supplies of these resources are used up, they cannot be replaced.

Conservation of fuels such as coal, oil, and natural gas is important. The wise use of these fuels includes avoiding waste and increasing efficiency, or the amount of work done by the fuels. Cars that get better gas mileage and refrigerators that use less electricity are examples of ways to conserve fuel. What are some ways in which you can conserve fuel?

Skill Builder

Classifying   Make two lists to classify each of the following as renewable or nonrenewable resources: copper, water, soil, nutrients, food, oxygen, wood, coal, fish, marble. Add two more renewable and nonrenewable resources to your lists.

The use of nonrenewable resources also can be managed by **recycling**. Recycling is the process of reusing resources to make new products. For example, minerals used to make products such as steel and aluminum cans can be recycled.

Recycling allows resources to be used many times. Because mining minerals damages the environment, recycling also reduces the damage caused by mining. Some products made from renewable resources also can be recycled. For example, recycling paper helps save forests from being cut down.

Figure 37-1 Recycling aluminum helps conserve the nonrenewable mineral bauxite.

Think & Discuss

1. How do renewable and nonrenewable resources differ?
2. How does recycling help conserve natural resources?
★ 3. Give two reasons why it is important to conserve natural resources.

37–2 Three Renewable Resources

Air, water, soil, and living things are renewable resources. Although these resources can be replaced by natural cycles, they may be threatened by **pollution**. Pollution is anything that harms the environment. Pollution of the environment is a danger to the health of all organisms.

Air

Air is a mixture of gases, including oxygen, carbon dioxide, and nitrogen. Animals take in oxygen from the air when they breathe, and give off carbon dioxide. Plants use carbon dioxide and give off oxygen. This exchange of gases is necessary for all life on the earth.

Air Pollution

Air pollution occurs when harmful substances, or **pollutants** (puh-LOOT-unts), are released into the air. Motor vehicles and industry are the main sources of air

ACTIVITY 37-1

PROBLEM: How can paper be reused to save resources and eliminate waste?

Science Process Skills
observing, describing, relating concepts

Background Information
Recycling can save resources, reduce pollution, and reduce the amount of garbage. In this activity, you will make a recycled paper product from newspaper.

Materials

newspaper	waxed paper
mixing bowl	warm water
food blender (optional)	plastic wrap
fork or egg beater	

Procedure

1. Tear several sheets of newspaper into shreds.
2. Soak the shredded paper in a bowl of warm water overnight. Add just enough water to the bowl to thoroughly soak the shredded paper.
3. After the paper is completely soaked, place it in a food blender. Mix the paper and water until the paper is dissolved. If a blender is not available, use an egg beater, or mash and mix the paper and water with your hands and a fork. **CAUTION: Wear your laboratory apron to keep your clothes from getting splattered.**
4. Cover a work area with waxed paper.
5. Spread the water and newspaper mixture on the waxed paper, forming a 0.5-cm-thick layer.
6. Cover the layer of newspaper mixture with plastic wrap.
7. Place several books on top of the plastic wrap. Squeeze out as much water as possible. Then let the layer of mixture dry overnight.

Observations

1. Describe the texture of the water and newspaper mixture.
2. **a.** After the mixture has dried, describe the paper. **b.** Would you rate the quality of this paper as low, medium, or high? Give a reason for your answer.
3. How many sheets of newspaper did it take to make one sheet of your paper?

Conclusions

1. **INFER** For which of the following do you think your paper would best be used?
   a. an egg carton   **c.** construction paper
   b. writing paper   **d.** cardboard
   Explain your choice.
2. **a.** Why is recycling paper a good idea? **b.** What resources would be conserved by recycling paper?
3. Major cities sometimes have problems disposing of tons of paper. How would recycling paper help solve this problem?
4. What other materials can you name that are easily recycled?

Figure 37-2 Gases in the smoke from factories (left) can cause acid rain, which damages statues (right).

pollution. There are two kinds of air pollutants—**particulates** (pahr-TIK-yuh-luts) and gases. Particulates are tiny pieces of dust or soot that are given off mainly in smoke.

☞ Sulfur dioxide, nitrogen oxide, and carbon monoxide are three gas pollutants. These gases are part of the haze, or smog, that hangs over many large cities. Smog is very dangerous to people with respiratory disorders such as asthma.

Gas pollutants also can affect the environment indirectly. For example, sulfur dioxide and nitrogen oxides combine with water in the air to form acids. These acids fall to the earth as **acid rain**. Acid rain damages stone buildings and statues. Acid rain also is linked to killing living things in lakes and streams, and to slowing the growth of forests. How can damage by acid rain be prevented? The damage caused by acid rain can be stopped by controlling air pollution.

The destruction of the ozone layer is another effect of air pollution. The ozone layer is a layer of ozone gas found high in the atmosphere. The ozone layer protects living things by filtering out the harmful rays of the sun. These rays are the same rays that damage your skin when you get a sunburn. Without the ozone layer, many people might develop skin cancer caused by the sun's harmful rays.

How does air pollution damage the ozone layer? The ozone layer can be destroyed by chemicals called **CFCs**, or chlorofluorocarbons (klawr-uh-floor-uh-KAR-buns). CFCs are gases used mainly in spray cans, air conditioners, and refrigerators.

Health and Safety Tip

In cities with air pollution problems, pollution warnings are sometimes given. You should not exercise outdoors on days when such warnings are posted, because air pollution can damage your lungs.

Figure 37-3 If more people rode bicycles, pollution in cities might be reduced.

Protecting Air Quality

Air pollution is an international problem. Many governments have passed laws to help restore air quality. For example, in the 1970s, the United States passed a law requiring all cars to be equipped with pollution-control devices. Factories were required to install filters on smokestacks. In 1987, 24 nations signed a treaty to cut the production of CFCs in half by 1999, and to stop making them in the future. These steps have helped a great deal. However, many natural areas still are damaged by polluted air.

Air pollution is expensive to control. However, the effects of air pollution are far more expensive and damaging to the environment. Acid rain, for example, causes about five billion dollars in property damage each year. It is impossible to measure the damage caused to natural areas and to people's health in dollars and cents.

❯ One of the least-expensive ways to control air pollution is to conserve fuel. People can conserve fuel by walking, using public transportation, or riding a bicycle instead of driving a car. How do you think the use of public transportation helps reduce air pollution?

Water

Water is one of the most important materials on the earth. Plants and animals need a supply of fresh, clean water to survive. Industry also needs clean water for factories. Farmers depend heavily on rain or irrigation to help their crops grow. People also enjoy swimming, fishing, and boating. These leisure activities require clean water. How many ways do you use water every day?

ACTIVITY 37-2

PROBLEM: Why are some soils and lakes more easily damaged by acid rain than others?

Science Process Skills
modeling, inferring, observing

Background Information
Some soils and bodies of water contain substances that can neutralize acid and help protect against the harmful effects of acid rain. One of the main substances found in soil or dissolved in water that can neutralize acid is calcium carbonate. Soils and bodies of water that contain very little calcium carbonate are damaged easily by acid rain. A soil or water sample can be tested with blue litmus paper to see if it is acidic. If blue litmus paper turns red, the soil or water sample is acidic.

Materials

soil sample	1 lemon
water	blue litmus paper
4 small jars	knife
calcium carbonate	graduated cylinder
tablespoon	

Procedure
1. Label the jars A, B, C, and D.
2. Place 25 mL of water in jars A and B.
   Wear your lab apron for this activity.
3. Dissolve 1 tablespoon of calcium carbonate in jar A.
4. Cut the lemon into 4 equal wedges.
   CAUTION: Be careful when using a knife.
5. Squeeze the juice from 1 lemon wedge into jars A and B. Record your observations.
   Note: Fizzing indicates that an acid is being neutralized by calcium carbonate.
6. Use blue litmus paper to test the acidity of the solutions in the two jars. Record any color changes of the litmus paper.
7. In jar C, place about the same volume of soil as you have water in jar A. Add some water to dampen the soil.
8. Test the soil with litmus paper. Record your observations.
9. Squeeze the juice of 1 lemon wedge into the soil in jar C. Record any observations.
10. In jar D, add another sample of soil. Then add 1 tablespoon of calcium carbonate. Mix the calcium carbonate into the soil.
11. Squeeze the juice from the last lemon wedge into jar D. Record your observations.

Observations
1. Which jar of water showed signs of an acid being neutralized?
2. Did the water in jar A show signs of neutralizing acid? How do you know?
3. What was the acid in this activity?
4. Was the soil sample in jar C acidic? How do you know?
5. Did the soil sample in jar C show signs of neutralizing acid when you squeezed in the lemon juice?
6. Did the soil sample in jar D show signs of neutralizing acid? How do you know?

Conclusions
1. Why were there different results in jars A and B when you added lemon juice?
2. What substance neutralized the acid in the water and soil samples?
3. INFER   If a lake or a farm field were turned acidic by acid rain, how might the damage be fixed?
4. INFER   Would a lake that had calcium carbonate dissolved in its water be damaged more easily by acid rain than a lake with little or no calcium carbonate? Use your observations to support your answer.

Figure 37-4 Polluted water draining into streams reduces the supply of clean water.

Health and Safety Tip

Never drink water from a lake or river. The water may be polluted with toxic chemicals or with harmful bacteria from sewage.

Water Pollution

The supply of fresh, clean water is constantly being replaced by the water cycle. However, people often pollute sources of clean water in the environment. Major sources of water pollution include sewage from cities and towns, and fertilizers and pesticides washed off farm fields by heavy rains. Chemical wastes from factories also pollute water.

Protecting Water Quality

The Clean Water Act is a federal law that protects water quality. This act has helped clean up industrial pollution. It also has provided money for many cities and towns to build sewage-treatment plants. Newer versions of the Clean Water Act attempt to control runoff of fertilizers and pesticides from farms.

Toxic, or poisonous, chemicals are a difficult problem to control. Most toxic waste from industry has been buried in toxic-waste dumps. Many old toxic-waste dumps are leaking into groundwater or streams. Cleaning up these dumps will take a lot of money and a long time. The Superfund law is designed to help clean up these dumps.

Water Conservation

Do you take the water you use for granted? The supply of clean, fresh water is limited. Conservation is as important for water as for all other resources. One way to conserve water is to avoid polluting it. Another conservation method is to use water carefully. For example, bans on washing cars and watering lawns are sometimes used to conserve water during a drought. Can you think of ways in which you can conserve water?

Soil

You probably are surprised to learn that soil is a natural resource. In fact, soil is one of the most important natural resources. Although soil is a renewable resource, the formation of soil is a slow process.

How does soil form? Rocks are slowly broken down into fine particles that become soil. Soil, therefore, is a renewable resource. Because the soil formation process is slow, soil conservation is especially important.

Figure 37-5 Contour plowing (left), strip-cropping (middle), and windbreaks (right) can prevent soil erosion.

Soil Erosion

The loss of soil from the land by wind or running water is called soil **erosion**. A small amount of soil erosion occurs naturally. However, farming practices often increase the rate of erosion. If soil erosion levels are greater than formation levels, soil will be lost. Eventually, heavy erosion could lead to a complete loss of topsoil. As a result, crops could no longer be grown.

Soil Conservation

In order to prevent too much soil erosion, farmers must practice soil conservation. Several farming methods such as contour plowing, planting trees as windbreaks, and strip-cropping have been shown to reduce erosion.

In contour plowing, crops are planted across the slope of a hill instead of up and down the hill. This method of planting helps prevent soil from being carried off by rainwater running down the hill. Windbreaks help prevent soil from being blown away by wind. Strip-cropping is a method of planting rows of grasses in between rows of grain crops. The grasses hold onto soil better than the grains do and prevent soil from being washed away by heavy rain.

Skill Builder

Organizing One way to organize information is in a chart. Make a chart to display information about the following pollutants: acid rain, CFCs, particulates, sewage, toxic waste. Use the following column headings: Pollutant; Causes; Effects; Resource Affected; Controls.

Think & Discuss

4. What is a pollutant?
5. Describe two kinds of air pollutants.
6. Explain why air, water, and soil are considered renewable resources.

37-3 Living Resources

The renewable natural resources you have read about in the first part of this chapter are nonliving parts of the environment. However, living things also are natural resources. Living natural resources replace themselves through reproduction.

Wildlife

The term **wildlife** is used to describe the natural plants and animals living in an area. Wildlife is important to people in many ways. Hiking and camping in natural areas, birding, nature photography, and fishing all are leisure activities that depend on wildlife.

 Many species of wildlife have become **extinct**. All the members of an extinct species are dead and the species will never return. Many other species have declined so much that they are nearly extinct. Any species nearing extinction is considered **endangered**. Some species are declining in number, but are not yet considered endangered. These species are classified as **threatened** species.

Wildlife is declining in many areas of the biosphere. The main threat to wildlife today is loss of habitat. Without its habitat, a species cannot survive. Development of land for roads, shopping centers, housing, and industry destroys wildlife habitats. Many of the habitats being lost are in the tropical rain forest biome. Most of the earth's plants and animals live in these rain forests. As a result,

Figure 37-6 In Brazil, large areas of the Amazon rain forest have been destroyed to build highways.

many species are becoming extinct before scientists even have a chance to discover and study them.

❯ Pollution and pesticides are threats to wildlife. Illegal hunting also threatens some animals such as the rhinoceros and the elephant. How might an increase in pollution affect the wildlife in an area?

Wildlife Conservation

There are many reasons to conserve wildlife. If too many species are destroyed, biologists suspect that entire ecosystems may collapse. For example, many medicines are made from plants and fungi. Some commercial products, such as natural rubber and coffee, come from plants. All these benefits are lost when a species becomes extinct. The opportunity to appreciate the beauty of wildlife and of natural wilderness areas also is lost.

In the past, many people thought that there would always be plenty of wildlife. Animals were killed and forests cut without concern for conservation. By the late 1800s, however, many kinds of wildlife were disappearing. As the bison, alligators, and many other forms of wildlife began to disappear, people recognized the need for conservation.

Hunting and fishing laws were the first steps aimed at conserving wildlife. Refuges, parks, and other public lands were set aside as habitats for wildlife. More recently, laws to prevent habitat destruction and to stop pollution also have helped the cause of wildlife conservation. For example, the Endangered Species Act of 1973 protects endangered species and helps restore healthy populations of these organisms to the environment.

Figure 37-7 Wildlife refuges provide one way of protecting endangered animals.

Think & Discuss

7. What is wildlife?

8. What is an extinct species?

9. Explain the difference between an endangered species and a threatened species.

10. What is the single greatest threat to wildlife?

★ 11. Describe three ways in which humans benefit from wildlife.

Key Points

- Alternative sources of energy include nuclear, solar, geothermal, wind, and water.
- There are several problems involved in using nuclear energy.

Energy resources are very important natural resources. For example, people use energy to cook their food and to heat their homes. Energy also is used for transportation and for lighting. In what other ways do people use energy?

Fossil Fuels

The energy resources people depend on most are **fossil fuels**. Fossil fuels were formed from the remains of plants and animals that lived long ago. Fossil fuels are still forming, but it will take millions of years to replace the fuels that people are using today. Fossil fuels, therefore, are considered nonrenewable energy resources.

Oil, coal, and natural gas are three different kinds of fossil fuels. Oil is used mainly as fuel for transportation. Most coal is burned to produce electricity or heat for industries such as steel-making. Natural gas also is used mostly by industry. All three fuels also are used by people for heating.

Because fossil fuels are being used up much faster than they are being made, it is necessary to find other sources of energy. Burning fossil fuels also causes most of the air pollution. The environment also is damaged by mining or drilling for fossil fuels.

Figure 37-8 Coal is one common fossil fuel. What are two others?

Alternative Energy Resources

Energy sources that are not fossil fuels are called alternative energy resources. Some alternative energy resources, such as wind, have been used for a long time. Others, such as **nuclear** (NOO-klee-uhr) **energy**, were developed using modern technology. Nuclear energy is energy that is released when atoms are split. Today, these alternatives account for between 10 and 20 percent of the energy used in the United States.

Nuclear Energy

In the United States, most nuclear energy uses uranium as a fuel. As a uranium atom is split apart, energy is given off in the form of heat. This heat is used to produce steam. The steam turns large turbines that produce electricity.

Figure 37-9 Nuclear energy (left) and solar energy (right) are two alternatives to fossil fuels.

Nuclear energy does not pollute the air. For this reason, some people consider nuclear energy to be the energy resource of the future. However, there are some problems with nuclear energy. First, the cost of building nuclear power plants is very high. Second, uranium is radioactive. A nuclear accident could release large amounts of radiation that could harm the environment. Third, nuclear power plants produce dangerous radioactive wastes that must be stored safely for thousands of years. Finally, uranium is a nonrenewable mineral.

Solar Energy

You have learned that the sun is the energy source for most ecosystems. The sun also is used to supply energy to homes and offices. The energy supplied by the sun is called **solar** (SOH-lur) **energy**.

Solar energy is used to provide heat and electricity. Sunlight trapped by structures called solar collectors can be used to heat a home or to heat the water used in the home. Solar cells are devices that produce electricity from sunlight. They do not cause any pollution. Solar cells were first invented for use on satellites and spaceships.

Sunlight is a renewable, nonpolluting energy source. However, the uses of solar energy are limited. A major problem with solar energy is storing it for use at night or on cloudy days. Solar energy systems also are expensive to install, even though the fuel is free. Table 37–1 shows world energy use for different energy sources.

Table 37–1	World Energy Use
ENERGY SOURCE	PERCENTAGE OF TOTAL ENERGY USE
Oil	35%
Coal	27%
Solar/Other alternatives	18%
Natural gas	17%
Nuclear	3%

Other Energy Resources

Energy also can be supplied by the products of living organisms. These products are called **biomass fuels**. Wood is a biomass fuel that is produced by trees. Wood is used

Figure 37-10 The Grand Coulee Dam is the greatest source of water power in the United States.

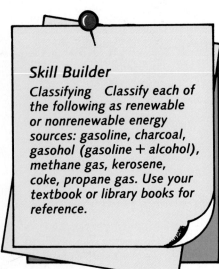

for energy all over the world. In the United States, wood supplies more energy than nuclear power.

Two other biomass fuels are methane and alcohol. Methane is a gas that is made from sewage or animal wastes. Alcohol is a liquid fuel that is made from plant materials. Biomass fuels can supply solids, liquids, and gases that are similar to coal, oil, and natural gas.

Wind and water have been used for many years to produce electricity. In the past, large dams, such as the Grand Coulee Dam in Washington State, were built and used for energy production. New methods are being developed to use water power without building large dams. Equipment that can produce electricity at small dams or rivers is being improved. Wind power has been used for centuries to pump water from wells. Today windmills are being used to make electricity for homes.

Another alternative energy resource in use today is **geothermal** (jee-oh-THUR-muhl) **energy**. Geothermal energy is heat produced inside the earth. This heat from the earth's interior causes volcanoes and geysers such as Old Faithful. In places where this heat is found near the surface of the earth, geothermal energy can be used to heat homes or to produce electricity. A geothermal power plant operates in California. Iceland uses water from hot springs to heat homes. Because of the large supply of heat in the earth, geothermal energy is a renewable energy resource.

Scientists always are looking for new ways to obtain energy. Nuclear fusion, the energy source of the sun, is being researched. Hydrogen gas is being investigated as a fuel for cars. Can you think of a resource that could be used to provide energy?

Think & Discuss

12. Why are oil, coal, and natural gas called fossil fuels?
13. What are biomass fuels?
14. How is nuclear energy produced?
15. What are wind and water used to produce?
16. Why are nuclear and solar energy better for the environment than fossil fuels?

How would you like to spend most of your time at sea? Many fascinating and rewarding careers involve working on or near the ocean.

Fishers

Fishing is one of the oldest occupations. Ever since people have lived near water, they have fished. Today, fishers rely on technological devices such as sonar, radar, and scientific satellites to improve fishing methods and increase their catches.

Fishers spend much of their time on boats at sea. The weather can be harsh, and the hard work of fishing requires good health and a lot of stamina.

For more information: Tour a fishing boat, go on a fishing expedition, and talk to people who are fishers.

Fish Breeder

Fish breeders work in fish hatcheries or on fish farms. Like animal breeders, fish breeders work to develop the genetic strains that will produce the most desirable fish. Fish breeders breed catfish, salmon, trout, bass, and other kinds of fish that are sold to restaurants and markets.

Fish breeders should enjoy working outdoors. A fish breeder should have a high school diploma. Courses in fish behavior, fish physiology, and business also are recommended.

For more information: Write to the Marine Resources Research Institute, South Carolina Wildlife and Marine Resources Department, PO Box 12559, Charleston, SC 29412.

Marine Conservationist

Several years ago, Alaska banned the commercial fishing of Alaskan King Crab. The reason? The population of Alaskan King Crab had become dangerously low, and marine conservationists feared that the species would become extinct.

Marine conservationists are scientists who work to see that the use of ocean resources does not cause undue harm to the environment. Overfishing and the pollution of ocean waters by industry and other sources are some of the concerns of marine conservationists. They also try to solve problems that are created when natural resources such as oil or minerals are taken from the ocean floor.

A marine conservationist should have a college degree with a major in biological or environmental science.

For more information: Write to the American Society of Limnology and Oceanography, Great Lakes Research Division, University of Michigan, Ann Arbor, MI 48109.

Chapter Review

CHAPTER SUMMARY

37-1 Natural Resources

- Renewable natural resources, such as air, water, soil, and living things are renewed or replaced on a regular basis.
- Nonrenewable natural resources, such as coal, oil, natural gas, and minerals, cannot be replaced once they are used up.

37-2 Renewable Resources

- Pollution consists of anything that can harm the environment.
- Air pollution includes both particulates, such as dust and soot, and gases, such as sulfur dioxide and carbon monoxide.
- Water pollution is caused by sewage from cities and towns, fertilizers and pesticides from farms, and toxic chemicals from industry.

37-3 Living Resources

- Wildlife, the plants and animals living in an area, are renewable natural resources.
- An endangered species is in danger of becoming extinct.
- A threatened species is close to becoming endangered.

37-4 Energy Resources

- Nuclear energy, solar energy, geothermal energy, and energy from wind and water are alternative energy sources.
- Several problems associated with the use of nuclear energy include the following: high cost of building nuclear power plants; danger of an accident releasing harmful radiation; dangerous radioactive wastes; and the fact that uranium fuel is a nonrenewable mineral.

VOCABULARY LIST

acid rain (635)	erosion (639)	nonrenewable resources (632)	recycling (633)
biomass fuels (643)	extinct (640)	nuclear energy (642)	renewable resources (632)
CFCs (635)	fossil fuels (642)	particulates (635)	solar energy (643)
conservation (632)	geothermal energy (644)	pollutants (633)	threatened (640)
endangered (640)	natural resources (632)	pollution (633)	wildlife (640)

VOCABULARY REVIEW

Matching Write the word or term from the Vocabulary List that best matches each description.

1. natural resource that can be reused or replaced
2. anything that damages the environment
3. rain polluted by gases in the air
4. tiny pieces of dust or soot
5. wearing away of the soil by wind or water
6. close to being endangered
7. energy from splitting atoms
8. energy from plants
9. close to being extinct
10. chemicals that are destroying the ozone layer

Identifying Relationships Identify the word or term in each group that does not belong. Explain why it does not belong with the group.

1. extinct, endangered, threatened
2. nonrenewable, fossil fuels, wildlife
3. geothermal, solar, fossil fuels
4. natural resource, pollutant, air
5. conservation, pollution, recycling

Completion Write the word or words that best complete each sentence.

1. Natural resources are materials and _____ that are used by people.
2. The part of the atmosphere that protects the earth from the sun's harmful rays is the _____ layer.
3. Most air pollution is caused by motor vehicles and _____.
4. The _____ Act is a federal law that protects water quality.
5. The two main causes of soil erosion are _____ and water.
6. In the United States, _____ is used as a fuel in nuclear power plants.
7. Wood and alcohol are _____ fuels.

Finding the Main Ideas Use the section number to find the sentence that answers each question. Then write the sentence.

1. What are three examples of nonrenewable resources? (37–1)
2. What are two ways to help conserve fuels? (37–1)
3. What are three pollutants in smog? (37–2)
4. How do towns and cities conserve water during a drought? (37–2)
5. How can farmers reduce soil erosion? (37–2)
6. How does wildlife benefit people? (37–3)
7. What is coal mainly used for? (37–4)
8. What is the most common biomass fuel? (37–4)

CONCEPT REVIEW

Writing for Understanding One way to find out if you understand something is to write a brief summary of the information in your own words. Reread Section 37–1, Natural Resources, on pages 632–633, and write a brief summary of the information.

Critical Thinking Answer each of the following in complete sentences.

1. How would an increase in the number of people in an area affect wildlife in that area?

2. Why is acid rain more of a problem in the northeastern United States than it is in Hawaii?
3. How can riding a bicycle help reduce air pollution?
4. Why is wind energy not practical in some parts of the United States?
5. Why can biomass fuels be considered a form of solar energy?
6. Would solar energy be a good energy source in your community? Why?

EXTENSIONS

1. Write to your state wildlife agency for a list of endangered and threatened species in your state. Draw a map of your state and indicate the areas where each species lives. Try to find out what conditions in those areas may have endangered the species that live there.

2. Choose an endangered species. Using the library for reference books, write a report on this species. Describe why and how the species became endangered and what is being done to save it.
3. Read *Silent Spring* by Rachel Carson and write a book report.

Safety is a very important part of science. You can avoid accidents in the science laboratory by handling materials carefully and by following directions. You should not perform activities without direction from your teacher. You also should never work in the science laboratory by yourself. Other people should always be present.

You will see safety symbols in some of the activities. Before beginning each activity, always read the activity, and note any safety symbols and caution statements.

SAFETY SYMBOLS

Disposal

- Clean up your work area after you are finished.
- Dispose of all materials properly. Follow the instructions for disposal given by your teacher.

Clothing Protection

- Wear your laboratory apron to protect your clothing from stains or burns.

Humane Treatment

- Animals are living things. Always treat all animals in as humane a way as possible.
- Make sure all animals receive the appropriate food, water, and shelter necessary for their survival.

Heating Safety

- Be careful when handling hot objects.
- Use the proper procedure for lighting a Bunsen burner.
- Turn off the Bunsen burner or other heat source when you are not using it.

Fire Safety

- Always tie back long hair when working near an open flame.
- Confine loose clothing.
- Do not reach across an open flame.

Sharp Objects

- Be careful when using scissors, scalpels, knives, or other cutting instruments. Cuts and puncture wounds may be caused by improper use of sharp objects.
- Always cut in the direction away from your body.

Caustic Substances

- Use extreme care when working with acids and bases. Both acids and bases can cause burns. If you spill an acid or a base on your skin, flush your skin with plenty of water. Notify your teacher immediately.
- Never pour water into an acid or a base. Always pour an acid or a base into water.

Cleanup

- Always wash your hands after an activity.

Eye Safety

- Wear your laboratory goggles, especially when working with open flames and chemicals.
- If chemicals get into your eyes, flush them with plenty of water. Notify your teacher immediately.
- Be sure you know how to use the emergency eyewash system.

Poison

- Never mix chemicals without directions from your teacher.
- Never put substances used in the laboratory into your mouth.
- Inform your teacher immediately if you spill chemicals or get any chemicals in your eyes or on your skin.
- Do not eat or drink in the laboratory.

APPENDIX B: *The Metric System and SI Units*

The metric system is an international system of measurement based on units of 10. More than 90 percent of the nations of the world use the metric system. In the United States, both the English or Imperial Measurement System and the metric system are used.

Systeme International, or SI, has been used as the international measurement system since 1960. SI is a modernized version of the metric system. Like the metric system, SI is a decimal system based on units of 10.

In both SI and the metric system, prefixes are added to base units to form larger or smaller units. Each unit is 10 times larger than the next smaller unit, and 10 times smaller than the next larger unit. For example, the meter is the basic unit of length. The next larger unit is a dekameter. A dekameter is 10 times larger than a meter. The next smaller unit is a decimeter. A decimeter is 10 times smaller than a meter. Ten decimeters is equal to one meter. How many meters equal one dekameter? 10

When you want to change from one unit in the metric system to another unit, you multiply or divide by a multiple of 10.

- When you change from a smaller unit to a larger unit, you divide.

- When you change from a larger unit to a smaller unit, you multiply.

SI Units

The basic unit is printed in capital letters.

Length	Symbol
kilometer	km
METER	m
centimeter	cm
millimeter	mm

Area	Symbol
square kilometer	km²
SQUARE METER	m²
square millimeter	mm²

Volume	Symbol
CUBIC METER	m³
cubic millimeter	mm³
liter	L
milliliter	mL

Mass	Symbol
KILOGRAM	kg
gram	g
tonne	t

Temperature	Symbol
KELVIN	K
degree Celsius	°C

Some Common Metric Prefixes

Prefix		Meaning
micro-	=	0.0000001, or 1/1,000,000
milli-	=	0.001, or 1/1000
centi-	=	0.01, or 1/100
deci-	=	0.1, or 1/10
deka-	=	10
hecto-	=	100
kilo-	=	1000
mega-	=	1,000,000

Some Metric Relationships

Unit	Relationship
kilometer	1 km = 1000 m
meter	1 m = 100 cm
centimeter	1 cm = 10 mm
millimeter	1 mm = 0.1 cm
liter	1 L = 1000 mL
milliliter	1 mL = 0.0001 L
tonne	1 t = 1000 kg
kilogram	1 kg = 1000 g
gram	1 g = 1000 mg
centigram	1 cg = 10 mg
milligram	1 mg = 0.001 g

One of the most important tools in biology is the microscope. A microscope enables scientists to view and study objects or structures not visible to the unaided eye. The compound microscope is used most often in biology classes.

A compound microscope has two or more lenses. One lens, called the ocular lens, is located in the eyepiece. The ocular lens usually has a magnification of 10X. An object viewed through this lens would appear 10 times larger than it would look with the unaided eye.

The second lens is called the objective lens. Compound microscopes may have many objective lenses. Most compound microscopes, however, have two objective lenses. Each objective lens has a different magnification. The magnification is printed on each objective lens.

To find the total magnification of a microscope, multiply the magnification of the ocular lens by the magnification of the objective lens that you are using. For example, the ocular lens magnification of 10X multiplied by the objective lens magnification of 10X equals 100X. The total magnification of the microscope is 100X. Looking at an object under this total magnification, you would be seeing the object 100 times larger than the object would look with the unaided eye.

A microscope is a delicate, but relatively uncomplicated, easy-to-use tool. Before you try to use a microscope, however, you should know the parts of a microscope and what each part does. Study the parts of the microscope and their functions. Then, read the procedures for working with a microscope. Use these procedures when you work with a microscope.

Parts of the Microscope

1. **Eyepiece:** holds the ocular lens
2. **Body tube:** keeps the ocular and objective lenses the proper distance apart
3. **Arm:** supports the body tube
4. **Stage:** platform that supports the slide
5. **Stage clips:** hold slide in position
6. **Diaphragm:** adjusts the amount of light entering the stage opening
7. **Base:** supports the microscope
8. **Illuminator:** mirror or electric light that is the light source of the microscope
9. **Revolving nosepiece:** holds the objectives and can be turned to change objectives
10. **Low-power objective:** shorter objective that contains a lens with a magnification of 10X
11. **High-power objective:** longer objective that contains a lens with a magnification of 40X
12. **Coarse adjustment knob:** moves the body tube up and down for bringing the object into view
13. **Fine adjustment knob:** moves the body tube up and down for focusing clearly

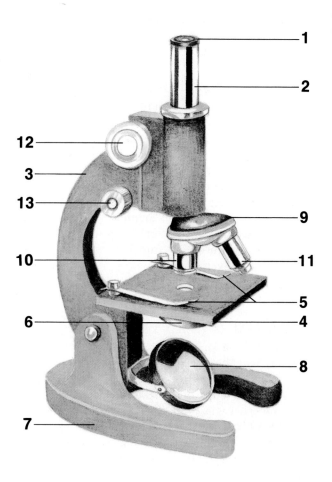

Procedures

1. A microscope should be held with two hands, one holding the arm of the microscope and the other supporting the base.

2. When adjusting a microscope, be careful that you do not place your fingers or other materials on the lenses, eyepiece, or illuminator. These parts should be touched or cleaned only with special lens paper.

3. Rotate the nosepiece so that the low-power objective (10X) is in line with the body tube. You will hear a click when the objective is directly over the stage opening.

4. Turn the coarse adjustment knob to find out which direction raises the objective and which direction lowers the objective.

5. Use the coarse adjustment knob to raise the low-power objective to about 2 cm above the stage.

6. Look through the eyepiece. Be sure to keep both eyes open.

7. Switch on the light or adjust the mirror. You should see a circle of light. This circle of light is the microscope's field of view.

8. Move the lever on the diaphragm to adjust the amount of light that you want to come through the opening of the stage.

9. Place a prepared slide on the stage. Use the stage clips to hold the slide in place.

10. Look at the side of the microscope. Use the coarse adjustment knob to lower the body tube carefully until the low-power objective almost touches the slide. **CAUTION: Do not touch the slide with the objective.**

11. Look through the eyepiece and turn the coarse adjustment knob slowly until the object comes into view.

12. Use the fine adjustment knob to focus clearly.

13. Use the lever on the diaphragm to adjust the amount of light entering the opening of the stage.

14. To view the object under high power, turn the nosepiece until the high-power objective clicks into place.

15. Look through the eyepiece and use the fine adjustment to focus under high power.

Preparing a Wet-Mount Slide

1. Obtain a clean microscope slide and a cover slip.

2. Place the specimen that you wish to view in the center of the microscope slide. Using a medicine dropper, place a drop of water on the specimen.

3. Place the edge of a cover slip so that it touches the water. Using a dissecting needle or sharpened pencil, gently lower the cover slip over the specimen.

4. Remove excess water by placing a piece of paper towel along the edge of the cover slip.

5. If the specimen begins to dry out, add a drop of water along the edge of the cover slip.

6. To stain a specimen, place a drop of the stain at the edge of the cover slip. Using forceps, hold a piece of paper towel at the opposite edge of the cover slip from where the stain was added. The towel will soak up water and the stain will be drawn under the cover slip. Some stains that you might use are iodine, methylene blue, and Wright's stain.

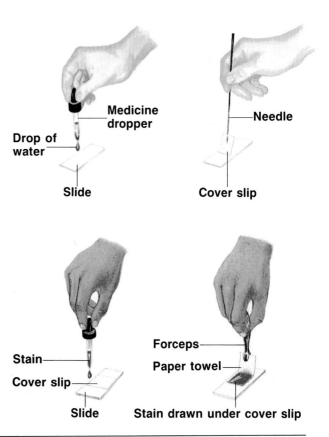

Medicine dropper

Drop of water

Slide

Needle

Cover slip

Stain

Cover slip

Slide

Forceps

Paper towel

Stain drawn under cover slip

You often can figure out the meaning of a new science word by studying the word parts. The prefixes and suffixes listed below will help you figure out the meaning of many new science words.

Word Part	Meaning	Example
a-	not; without	abiotic; asexual
anti-	against	antibiotic
bi-	two	bilateral symmetry
bio-	life	biology
cephalo-	head	cephalopod
chemo-	of, with, or by chemicals	chemosynthesis
chloro-	green	chlorophyll
cyto-	cell; cells	cytology
-derm	skin; covering	echinoderm
di-	twice; double; two	dicot
eco-	environment; habitat	ecology
ecto-	outer; outside	ectoderm
epi-	on; on the outside	epidermis
geo-	earth	geology
hemo-	blood	hemoglobin
hetero-	other; another	heterotroph
hydro-	water	hydrogen
-itis	disease of	bronchitis
leuco-	white	leucocyte
-logy	study of; science of	biology
mono-	one	monocot
-ose	carbohydrate	cellulose; glucose
-ped(e)	foot; feet	centipede
photo-	light	photosynthesis
-phyte	a plant; to grow in a certain way or place	sporophyte
syn-	together with; by means of	protein synthesis
thigmo-	touch	thigmotropism
tri-	three	triceps
trop-; tropo-	turn; respond to	phototropism
-trophic	having to do with nutrition	heterotrophic
uni-	one	univalve
-vore	to eat	herbivore
zoo-	animal	zoology

GLOSSARY

Pronunciation and syllabication have been derived from *Webster's New World Dictionary*, Second College Edition, Revised School Printing (Prentice-Hall, 1985). Syllables printed in capital letters are given primary stress. (Numbers in parentheses indicate the chapter, or chapters, in which the term is defined.)

PRONUNCIATION KEY

Symbol	Example	Respelling	Symbol	Example	Respelling
ah	mo**le**cule	(MAHL-uh-kyool)	ks	tho**rax**	(THOR-aks)
aw	ab**so**rption	(ab-SAWRP-shun)	oh	embry**o**	(EM-bree-oh)
ay	ad**ap**tation	(ad-uhp-TAY-shun)	oo	t**ua**tara	(too-uh-TA-ruh)
e	**e**lement	(EL-uh-munt)	or	Apato**sau**rus	(uh-pah-tuh-SOR-uhs)
ee	**e**cology	(ee-KOL-uh-jee)	oy	vir**oi**d	(VEER-oyd)
ew	n**u**cleic	(new-KLEE-ik)	uh	d**a**ta	(DAYT-uh)
f	**ph**loem	(FLOH-em)	y	m**i**gration	(my-GRAY-shuhn)
ih	cut**i**cle	(KYOOT-ih-kuhl)	yoo	alb**u**men	(al-BYOO-mun)
j	**g**emmules	(JEM-yoolz)	z	metaboli**s**m	(muh-TAB-uh-lizm)
k	addi**c**tion	(uh-DIK-shun)	zh	diffu**s**ion	(dih-FYOO-zhun)

A

abiotic: nonliving (35)

absorption (ab-SAWRP-shun): in digestion, the movement of nutrients into the bloodstream (21)

acid: solution that contains more hydrogen ions (H^+) than pure water (3)

acid rain: solution formed when sulfur dioxide and nitrogen oxides combine with water in the atmosphere to form acids (37)

adaptation (ad-uhp-TAY-shun): characteristic of an organism that helps it survive (2)

addiction (uh-DIK-shun): drug dependence (28)

air bladder: air-filled structure that helps brown algae float near the water surface (7)

air sac: air-filled sac of a bird that helps supply oxygen and regulate body temperature (18)

albumen (al-BYOO-mun): egg white (18)

algae: group of photosynthetic protists (7)

allergen (AL-ur-jun): any substance that causes an allergy (27)

alternation (ol-tuhr-NAY-shun) **of generations:** sexual and asexual generations of spore plants (9)

alveolus (al-VEE-uh-lus) [pl. **alveoli** (al-VEE-uh-ly)]: respiratory structure in which exchange of oxygen (O_2) and carbon dioxide (CO_2) takes place (23)

amnion (AM-nee-on): fluid-filled membrane that surrounds an embryo (25)

amoebocyte (uh-MEE-boh-syt): structure of a sponge that transports digested food to cells and helps the sponge reproduce (12)

anemia (uh-NEE-mee-uh): blood disorder in which the blood cannot carry normal amounts of oxygen to body cells (22)

angiosperm (AN-jee-uh-spurm): plant that produces covered seeds (10)

annual rings: difference in the appearance of springwood and summerwood of a woody stem (11)

antennae (an-TEN-ay): first two pairs of appendages on a crustacean (15)

anther: structure of a flower that produces pollen grains (11)

antibiotic (an-ti-by-AHT-ik): substance that kills harmful bacteria (6, 27)

antibody (AN-ti-bahd-ee): protein made by the body to fight off antigens (22, 27)

antigen (AN-tuh-jun): foreign substance that enters the body (22, 27)

anus: opening through which wastes leave the body (13)

aorta (ay-OWR-tuh): largest artery in the body (22)

aortic arches (ay-AWR-tic ARCH-es): tubes through which blood is pumped in earthworms (13)

appendage (uh-PEN-dij): movable extension of an animal's body (15)

artery (ART-uhr-ee): blood vessel that carries blood away from the heart (22)

asexual (ay-SEK-shoo-wuhl) **reproduction:** method of reproduction that requires only one parent organism (2)

atrium (AY-tree-uhm): upper chamber of the heart (22)

autosomes (AWT-uh-sohms): chromosomes in the body cells of an organism (30)

autotroph (AWT-uh-trohf): organism that can make its own food (5)

axon: long, thin fiber that carries messages away from the cell body of a neuron (24)

B

bacillus (buh-SIL-us) [pl. **bacilli** (buh-SIL-y)]: rod-shaped bacterium (6)

bacterium (bak-tir-EE-um) [pl. **bacteria** (bak-TIR-ee-uh)]: single-celled organism in the Kingdom Monera (6)

bark: outer covering of a woody stem (11)

base: solution that contains more hydroxide ions (OH⁻) than pure water (3)

behavior: response of an organism to its environment (19, 24)

bicuspid valve: valve between the left atrium and left ventricle of the heart (22)

bilateral symmetry (by-LAT-uhr-uhl SIM-uh-tree): having two identical halves (13)

bile: liquid made by the liver that breaks down fat (21)

binary fission: form of asexual reproduction in which one cell divides into two identical cells (6)

binomial nomenclature (by-NOH-mee-uhl NOH-muhn-klay-chuhr): system of naming living things by a two-part scientific name (5)

biology (by-OL-uh-jee): science that deals with the study of living things (1)

biome (BY-ohm): large region of the earth that has characteristic kinds of organisms (36)

biosphere (BY-uh-sfir): thin zone of the earth that supports all life (35)

biotechnology: applied biology (1)

biotic (by-OT-ik): living (35)

bivalve: mollusk with two shells (14)

blade: broad, flat part of a leaf (11)

blue-green bacterium: bacterium that makes its food by photosynthesis (6)

bronchioles (BRAHN-kee-ohls): smallest tubes of the respiratory system (23)

bronchus (BRAHN-kus) [pl. **bronchi** (BRAHN-kee)]: tube that extends from the bottom of the trachea into the lung (23)

budding: asexual reproduction in which a small part of a cell breaks off to form a new organism (8, 12)

C

cambium (KAM-bee-uhm): thin layer of living meristem tissue between the phloem and xylem of a woody stem (11)

camouflage (KAM-uh-flahj): ability of an organism to blend in with its surroundings (15)

canopy (CAN-uh-pee): "roof" of treetops (36)

cap: umbrella-shaped part of a mushroom (8)

capillary (KAP-uh-ler-ee): tiny blood vessel that connects arteries and veins (22)

capsid: coat of protein covering a virus (6)

carbohydrates (kar-buh-HY-drayts): compounds made from carbon, hydrogen, and oxygen (3, 26)

cardiac muscle: heart muscle (20)

carnivore (KAR-nuh-vawr): animal that feeds upon other animals (19, 35)

cartilage (KART-ul-ij): strong, flexible bonelike tissue (16, 20)

cell: basic unit of structure and function in living things (2, 4)

cell body: part of a neuron that contains the nucleus and most of the cytoplasm (2, 4)

cell membrane: living part of a cell made up mostly of lipids and proteins (4)

cellulose (SEL-yoo-lohs): nonliving substance that makes up the plant cell walls (8)

cell wall: nonliving, outer part of a plant cell or a fungal cell (4, 8)

centriole (SEN-tree-ohl): small organelle near the nucleus in an animal cell (4)

cephalopod (SEF-uh-loh-pahd): "head-foot" mollusk (14)

cerebellum (ser-uh-BEL-uhm): part of the brain that controls balance and coordination (18, 24)

cerebrum (suh-REE-bruhm): part of the brain that controls movement and speech (18, 24)

chemical change: change in the chemical properties of a substance resulting in new substances (3)

chemical digestion: process by which large food molecules are broken down into smaller molecules (21)

chemosynthesis (kee-moh-SIN-thuh-sis): process in which chemical energy is used to make food (2)

chitin (KYT-n): hard substance that makes up the exoskeleton of arthropods and the cell walls of most fungi (8, 15)

chlorophyll (KLAWR-uh-fil): green pigment that is used for photosynthesis (6, 9)

chloroplast (KLOR-uh-plast): round, green structure in a plant cell that contains chlorophyll (4)

chorion (KAWR-ee-ahn): membrane in an amniote egg that lines the inside of the shell (17)

chromosomes (KROH-muh-sohms): dark, threadlike particles in the nucleus of a cell that control heredity (4, 30)

cilia (SIL-ee-uh): tiny, hairlike structures (7, 23)

cirrhosis (suh-ROH-sis): liver disorder (28)

climate: average rainfall and temperature in an area (36)

climax community: balanced community that is the end product of ecological succession (35)

clitellum (kly-TEHL-uhm): part of an earthworm in which eggs are fertilized (13)

clone: organism that is genetically identical to its parent (31)

clutch: group of eggs laid by a female bird (18)

cnidocyte (NY-duh-syt): stinging cell (12)

coccus (KAK-sus) [pl. **cocci** (KAK-sy)]: spherical or egg-shaped bacterium (6)

cocoon: protective covering that surrounds an insect during its pupal stage (15)

cold-blooded: having a body temperature that stays about the same as the temperature of the surroundings (16)

collar cells: cells that line the body cavity of a sponge (12)

commensalism (kuh-MEN-sul-izm): relationship in which one organism benefits while the other organism is unaffected (35)

community: all the organisms living in a certain area (35)

compact bone: dense, hard part of a bone (20)

complete metamorphosis: four-stage process of metamorphosis including egg, larva, pupa, and adult stages (15)

compound: substance formed when atoms of different elements share electrons (3)

conifer: "cone-bearing" seed plant (10)

conjugation (kan-juh-GAY-shun): form of sexual reproduction in which two paramecia exchange nucleic acids (7)

conservation (kon-suhr-VAY-shun): wise use of natural resources (37)

consumers: organisms that obtain food by eating plants and other animals (35)

contour feathers: feathers that cover a bird's body and give the bird its shape (18)

control: experimental setup that is used to make comparisons (1)

controlled breeding: breeding organisms to produce offspring with certain traits (31)

cork: layer of dead cells below the bark (11)

cornea (KAWR-nee-uh): clear, curved layer of the eye (24)

cortex: layer of cells in which water and food are stored in a root (11)

cotyledon (kaht-LEED-on): first leaf, or "seed leaf," of an angiosperm (10)

crop: digestive organ that stores food (13, 18)

cross-pollination (PAL-uh-nay-shun): transfer of pollen from the stamen of one flower to the pistil of another flower (11, 29)

cubic centimeter: unit of volume (1)

cuticle (KYOOT-ih-kuhl): nonliving waxy substance that covers the surface of some leaves (11); nonliving layer of cells on a fluke (13)

cytoplasm (SYT-uh-plaz-um): all the living substance in a cell except the nucleus (4)

D

data (DAYT-uh): record of observations (1)

day-neutral plant: plant that does not depend on the length of the day to produce flowers (11)

decomposers (dee-kum-POHZ-ers): organisms that feed on dead organisms (6, 35)

dendrite (DEN-dryt): fiber that carries messages from other neurons to the cell body (24)

depressant (di-PRES-unt): drug that slows down the central nervous system (28)

dermis: layer of living skin cells (20)

dicot: angiosperm with seeds that have two cotyledons (10)

diffusion (dih-FYOO-zhun): movement of molecules from areas of greater concentration to areas of lesser concentration (4)

digestion (dy-JES-chun): process of breaking down food into usable forms (2, 21)

division (duh-VIZH-un): classification group used in botany instead of phylum (5, 9)

DNA: chemical that is the main substance in chromosomes (30)

dominant (DOM-uh-nuhnt) **gene:** stronger of two genes (29)

down feathers: small, fluffy feathers (18)

drug: chemical substance that causes a change in the mind or body (28)

E

ecological succession (suhk-SESH-uhn): process by which populations in an ecosystem are gradually replaced by new populations (35)

ecology (ee-KOL-uh-jee): study of the relationship between living things and their environments (1, 35)

ecosystems (EE-koh-sis-tums): all the living and nonliving parts of an environment (35)

ectoderm (EK-tuh-durm): outer cell layer (12)

egg: female sex cell (25)

element (EL-uh-munt): substance that is made up entirely of atoms of the same kind (3)

embryo (EM-bree-oh): developing plant (10); hollow ball of cells formed by cell division of the zygote (25)

endocrine (EN-duh-krin) **system:** group of glands that secrete hormones into the bloodstream (24)

endoderm (EN-duh-durm): inner cell layer (12)

endoplasmic reticulum (EN-duh-plaz-mic rih-TIK-yuh-lum): fine network of tubes or canals located within the cytoplasm of a cell (4)

endoskeleton (en-doh-SKEL-uh-tun): internal skeleton (14, 20)

enzyme (EN-zym): protein that controls chemical reactions in the body (21)

epidermis (ep-uh-DUR-mis): outer layer of cells of an organism (10, 20)

epiglottis (ep-uh-GLAT-is): flap of tissue covering the opening to the trachea (21, 23)

esophagus (i-SAF-uh-gus): muscular tube that connects the mouth to the stomach (13, 21)

estrogen (ES-truh-juhn): hormone produced by the ovaries (25)

evolution: process by which organisms change over time (5, 32)

excurrent (ek-SKUR-unt) **siphon:** tube by which water leaves a clam (14)

exoskeleton (ek-so-SKEL-uh-tun): external skeleton (15)

experiment: test of a hypothesis (1)

extensor: muscle that straightens a joint (20)

extinct: no longer exists on the earth (33, 37)

F

fat bodies: structures that help nourish a developing frog (17)

fats: compounds made up mostly of carbon and hydrogen (26)

fermentation (fur-mun-TAY-shun): process by which sugars and starches are broken down into alcohol and carbon dioxide gas (8)

fertilization (fur-tul-i-ZAY-shun): union of a sperm cell and an egg cell (9, 11, 25)

fibrous (FY-bruhs) **roots:** root system made up of thin, stringlike roots (11)

flagella (fluh-JEL-uh): whiplike structures on a cell that aid locomotion (7, 12)

flame cells: cells in a planarian that remove excess water and liquid wastes (13)

flexor: muscle that bends a joint (20)

flower: reproductive part of an angiosperm (10, 11)

food chain: model of the flow of energy through an ecosystem (35)

food web: combining and overlapping of many food chains (35)

fossils: remains or traces of organisms that lived in the past (5, 32, 33)

frond: leaf of a fern (9)

fruit: mature ovary containing seeds (10, 11)

fruiting body: mass of hyphae on which the sexual spores of fungi are made (8)

G

gallbladder: organ that stores bile (21)

gametes (GAM-eets): sex cells (4, 8, 29)

gametophyte (guh-MEET-uh-fyt): generation of a spore plant that produces eggs and sperm (9)

ganglia (GAN-glee-uh): mass of nerve cells (13)

gas: substance with no definite shape or volume (3)

gene pool: all the genes in a population (32)

genes: units of hereditary information (29)

genotype (JEE-nuh-typ): combination of genes for a particular trait (29)

genus: classification group of related species (5)

geographic isolation: separation of two populations by a physical barrier (32)

germination (jur-muh-NAY-shun): growth of an embryo plant from a seed (11)

gestation (jes-TAY-shun) **period:** length of time during which an embryo develops (19)

gills: organs that absorb dissolved oxygen from water (14, 16); structures lining the underside of a mushroom cap (8)

gizzard: muscular grinding organ (13, 18)

glottis: tube between the throat and the lungs of a frog (17)

gradualism (GRA-joo-uhl-iz-um): process of evolution through slow change (32)

ground tissue: plant tissue that stores food and provides support for the plant (10)

guard cells: bean-shaped cells that surround and control the size of the stoma (11)

gymnosperm (JIM-nuh-spurm): seed plant with uncovered seeds (10)

H

habitat (HAB-i-tat): place where an organism lives (35)

hair follicle: structure found in the dermis from which a hair grows (20)

half-life: time it takes for one-half of a radioactive substance to decay (33)

hallucinogen (hul-LOO-suh-nuh-jen): drug that distorts or alters the senses (28)

hemoglobin (HEE-moh-gloh-bin): iron-containing molecule in the blood that carries oxygen (22)

herbivore (HUR-buh-vawr): consumer that eats only plants (19, 35)

heterotroph (HET-uhr-uh-trohf): organism that cannot make its own food (5)

hibernation (HY-buhr-nay-shun): sleeplike state that helps animals survive the winter (19)

homeostasis (hoh-mee-oh-STAY-sis): ability of an organism to keep conditions inside its body constant (2)

hormone (HAWR-mohn): chemical messenger that regulates many bodily functions (24)

host: organism in which a parasite lives (6)

hybrid (HY-brid): organism with two different genes for a particular trait (29)

hyphae (HY-fay): filaments of fungi (8)

hypothesis (hy-PAHTH-uh-sis): suggested solution to a problem based upon known in formation (1)

I

immunity (im-MYOON-i-tee): resistance to disease (27)

inbreeding: crossing of closely related organisms (31)

incomplete dominance: blending of the traits carried by two genes (29)

incomplete metamorphosis: developmental process that includes egg, nymph, and adult stages (15)

incurrent siphon (in-KUR-unt SY-fuhn): tube by which water enters a clam (14)

index fossils: fossils always found in rock layers of only one age (33)

ingestion (in-JES-chun): process of taking food into the body (2)

insulin (IN-suh-lin): hormone that reduces the level of glucose in the blood (24)

interferon (in-tur-FEER-ahn): chemical made by the body that stops viruses from reproducing (27)

invertebrate (in-VUR-tuh-brayt): animal without a backbone (12)

involuntary muscles: muscles that you cannot control (20)

iris: colored part of the eye that controls the amount of light that enters the eye (24)

J, K

Jacobson's organ: organ on the roof of a snake's mouth that detects odors in the air (17)

joint: place where two or more bones meet (20)

kidney: excretory organ that removes waste products from the blood (23)

kilogram: basic unit of mass in SI (1)

kingdom: classification group made up of related phyla or divisions (5)

L

larva: wormlike stage in complete metamorphosis (15)

larynx (LAR-inks): organ located on top of the trachea that contains the vocal cords (23)

lateral (LAT-uhr-uhl) **bud:** bud that grows from the sides of the main stem and develops into branches and leaves (11)

lateral line: series of pits in a fish's side that are used to sense movement in the water (16)

lens: piece of glass that bends light (1)

lichen (LY-kuhn): a fungus and an alga living together (8)

ligament (LIG-uh-muhnt): band of tough tissue that connects bones (20)

lipid (LIP-ud): compound made up mostly of carbon and hydrogen (3)

liquid: substance with a definite volume, but no definite shape (3)

liter: SI unit of volume (1)

locomotion: movement of an organism from place to place (2)

long-day plant: plant that produces flowers in the summer as a result of long-term exposure to sunlight (11)

lymph (LIMF): tissue fluid in the lymphatic system (22)

M

mandibles (MAN-duh-bulz): jaw structures of a crustacean (15)

mantle (MAN-tul): thin membrane covering the visceral mass of a mollusk (14)

marrow: red or yellow soft tissue that fills the spaces in spongy bone (20)

mass: amount of matter an object contains (1)

mass selection: crossing plants with desired traits for many generations until offspring show the desired traits consistently (31)

matter: anything that has mass and volume (3)

mechanical digestion: physical breakdown of food into small pieces (21)

medulla (mi-DUL-uh): part of the brain stem that connects the brain and spinal cord (24)

medusa (muh-DOO-suh): free-swimming umbrellalike form of a cnidarian (12)

meiosis (my-OH-sis): separation of chromosomes during the formation of gametes (4)

menstruation (men-stroo-WAY-shun): process in which the tissue lining the uterine wall and excess blood leave the uterus (25)

meristem (MER-uh-stem): plant tissue that grows very rapidly (10)

mesoderm (MES-uh-durm): middle layer of body cells (13)

metabolism (muh-TAB-uh-lizm): total of all the chemical reactions that take place in the body cells (26)

meter: basic unit of length in SI (1)

migration (my-GRAY-shuhn): movement of members of a species into and out of a population (18, 32)

minerals: inorganic nutrients (26)

mitochondria (myt-uh-KAHN-dree-uh): organelle that produces energy (4)

mitosis (my-TOH-sis): process of distributing the chromosomes during cell division (4)

molecule (MAHL-uh-kyool): smallest particle of a substance that has all the chemical properties of that substance (3)

molting: shedding of an arthropod's exoskeleton (15); process by which a bird's contour feathers are replaced at least once a year (18)

monocot: angiosperm with seeds that have only one cotyledon (10)

monohybrid (mon-oh-HY-brid) **cross:** cross involving only one trait (29)

muscular dystrophy (DIS-truh-fee): disease of the skeletal muscles in which the muscles gradually are destroyed (20)

mutation (myoo-TAY-shun): change in the structure of a gene or chromosome (30, 32)

mutualism (MYOO-choo-wul-izm): relationship between two different kinds of organisms that benefits both organisms (35)

mycelium (my-SEE-lee-um): mass of hyphae (8)

N

nasal cavity: hollow opening between the nose and throat (23)

natural selection: process by which organisms with certain traits have a better chance of surviving and reproducing (32)

nematocysts (NEM-uh-toh-sists): coiled stingers inside cnidocytes of a cnidarian (12)

nephridia (ne-FRID-ee-uh): tubelike structures that are used for removal of liquid wastes in earthworms (13)

nephrons (NEF-ronz): filtering structures of the kidneys (23)

neuron (NOOR-ahn): nerve cell (24)

niche (NICH): an organism's job, or role, in its environment (35)

nicotine (NIK-uh-teen): stimulant drug in tobacco that causes physical and psychological addiction (28)

nictitating (NIK-tuh-tayt-ing) **membrane:** third eyelid of a frog (17)

nonvascular plant: plant that contains no vascular tissue (9)

notocord (NOT-uh-kord): strong, flexible support rod (16)

nuclear membrane: thin membrane that surrounds the nucleus (4)

nucleic (new-KLEE-ik) **acids:** organic compounds that make protein, control the cell, and determine heredity (3)

nucleolus (new-klee-OHL-uhs): small, round structures inside the nucleus (4)

nucleus (NEW-klee-us): part of the cell that controls all of the cell activities (4)

nutrients (NOO-tree-unts): materials needed for growth, energy, and the life processes (2, 26)

nutrition (noo-TRISH-uhn): complete process of ingestion and digestion (2); study of food and its effects on the body (26)

nymph (NIMF): young grasshopper with no wings or reproductive structures (15)

O

olfactory (ol-FAK-tuhr-ee) **cells:** smell receptors in the nose that respond to gas molecules (24)

omnivores (AHM-nuh-vawrs): animals that eat both plants and animals (19, 35)

operculum (oh-PUR-kyoo-luhm): protective gill cover of a fish (16)

organ: tissues that work together to do a specific job (4)

organelle: small structure in the cytoplasm that has a special job to do (4)

organism (AWR-guh-nizm): living thing (2)

organ system: group of organs that work together to do a certain job (4)

osculum (AS-kyuh-luhm): large opening on a sponge (12)

osmosis (ahs-MOH-sis): diffusion of water through a membrane (4)

ovary (OH-vuhr-ee): female reproductive organ (11, 25)

overdose: large dose of a drug that results in unconsciousness or death (28)

oviduct (OH-vuh-dukt): long tube between the ovary and the uterus (25)

ovules: small structures in which egg cells develop in a flower (11)

P

palisade (pal-uh-SAYD) **layer:** layer of cells located beneath the epidermis of a leaf (11)

pancreas (PAN-kree-us): small digestive organ located below the stomach (21)

parasite: organism that lives on or in the bodies of other living things (16)

parasitism (PAR-uh-syt-izm): relationship in which an organism lives on or in another living organism (35)

particulates (pahr-TIK-yuh-luts): pieces of dust or soot given off mainly in smoke (37)

pathogen (PATH-uh-juhn): substance that causes disease (27)

pellicle (PEL-i-kal): stiff, flexible membrane surrounding a paramecium (7)

penis: structure in males that surrounds and protects the urethra (25)

periosteum (per-i-AS-tee-um): thin, tough membrane covering a bone (20)

peristalsis (per-uh-STAWL-sis): wavelike movement that moves food through the digestive system (21)

permafrost: permanently frozen ground (36)

petals: colorful parts of a flower (10)

petiole (PET-ee-ohl): stalk that attaches the blade of a leaf to the stem of a plant (11)

phagocytes (FAG-uh-syts): white blood cells that destroy pathogens (22, 27)

pharynx (FAR-inks): in a worm, organ between the mouth and intestine (13); the throat (21)

phenotype (FEE-nuh-typ): visible traits of an organism (29)

phloem (FLOH-em): vascular tissue in seed plants that carries food made in the leaves to all other parts of the plant (10)

photosynthesis (foht-uh-SIN-thuh-sis): process by which light energy is used to make food (2, 6, 9, 35)

phylum (FY-luhm) (pl. **phyla**): classification group made up of related classes (5)

physical change: change in the physical properties of a substance (3)

pistil: female reproductive part of a flower (11)

pith: tissue in the center of a stem (11)

placenta (pluh-SEN-tuh): organ through which a developing mammal receives nourishment and gets rid of wastes (19, 25)

plankton: microscopic algae, protozoans, tiny animals, and plants that float near the surface of the water (7, 36)

plasma (PLAZ-muh): liquid part of the blood (22)

plasmid: ring of bacterial DNA (31)

platelets: cell parts that control blood clotting (22)

pollen: small grains that contain a plant's sperm cells (10)

pollen cone: male cone of a conifer (10)

pollination (pahl-uh-NAY-shun): transfer of a pollen grain from a stamen to a pistil (10)

pollution: anything that harms the environment (37)

polyp (PAL-ip): cuplike form of a cnidarian (12)

population: all the members of one species that live in the same area (32, 35)

pore: tiny opening at the surface of the skin (12, 23)

predation (pri-DAY-shun): relationship in which one organism kills and eats another (35)

predator (PRED-uh-tuhr): animal that eats other animals (16)

preening: activity of birds taking care of their feathers (18)

pregnancy (PREG-nun-see): period of development of an organism inside its mother's body (25)

prey: animals eaten by other animals (16)

producer: organism that makes its own food (35)

proglottids (proh-GLAHT-ids): body sections of a tapeworm (13)

protein (PRO-teen): compound made up of carbon, hydrogen, oxygen, and nitrogen (3); organic nutrient made up of amino acids (26)

protozoan: one-celled protist that cannot make its own food (7)

pseudopods (SOO-duh-pahds): fingerlike projections of cytoplasm used for movement and food-getting in sarcodines (7)

puberty (PYU-bur-tee): time at which a person becomes sexually mature (25)

pulmonary (PUL-muh-ner-ee) **circulation:** pathway of the blood between the heart and the lungs (22)

punctuated equilibrium (PUNK-choo-wayt-ed ee-kwuh-LIB-ree-um): theory that species remain the same for millions of years, then, within a short period of time, certain species suddenly die off while other species suddenly appear (32)

Punnett square: chart that shows possible gene combinations (29)

pupa: stage in which an insect does not eat and spins a protective covering around itself (15)

pure: organism with two of the same genes for a particular trait (29)

R

radial symmetry (RAY-dee-uhl SIM-uh-tree): arrangement of body parts like the spokes of a wheel around its hub (12)

radula (RAJ-oo-luh): rough, food-getting tongue of a snail (14)

recessive (ri-SES-iv) **gene:** the weaker of two genes (29)

recombinant DNA: pieces of DNA that contain DNA from a different organism (31)

rectum: lower part of the large intestine (21)

red blood cells: cells that give blood its red color and carry oxygen (22)

reflex: automatic response of the body (24)

regeneration (ri-jen-uh-RAY-shun): ability of an organism to replace lost body parts (17)

replication (rep-luh-KAY-shun): process by which DNA is duplicated (30)

resolution (rez-uh-LOO-shun): measure of how clear an object appears (1)

respiration (res-puh-RAY-shun): process by which organisms obtain energy from food (2, 23)

response: reaction to a change in the environment (2)

retina (RET-in-uh): part of the eye where light-sensitive receptor cells called rods and cones are located (24)

rhizoid (RY-zoid): rootlike structure (8, 9)

rhizome (RY-zohm): underground stem (9)

ribosome (RY-buh-sohm): round structure in cytoplasm that makes proteins (4)

RNA: ribonucleic (ry-boh-noo-KLEE-ik) acid; nucleic acid that acts as messenger for DNA (30)

S

saliva: digestive liquid made by three pairs of salivary glands (21)

saprophyte (SAP-ruh-fyt): organism that feeds upon dead organisms (8)

scavenger: organism that feeds on dead or dying animals (16)

scientific method: problem-solving model (1)

scolex: head of a tapeworm (13)

scrotum (SKROH-tum): pocket of skin that holds the testes (25)

scutes (SKYOOTS): modified scales covering the shell of a tortoise or turtle (17)

seed coat: outer covering of a seed (10)

seed cone: female cone of a conifer (10)

self-pollination (pahl-uh-NAY-shun): transfer of a pollen grain from the stamen of a flower to the pistil of the same flower (11, 29)

semilunar valves: valves between the ventricles and blood vessels (22)

sepals (SEE-puhls): structures that surround and protect the petals of a flower (11)

septum: thick wall separating the right and left sides of the heart (22)

setae (SEET-ee): hairlike bristles that help an earthworm move (13)

sex chromosomes: X and Y chromosomes that determine the sex of an organism (30)

sexual (SEK-shoo-wuhl) **reproduction:** method of reproduction in which cells from two parents join to form a new organism (2)

short-day plants: plants that can flower with less than 12 hours of sunlight (11)

skeletal muscle: muscle attached to a bone that makes movement possible (20)

smooth muscle: involuntary muscle found in the walls of blood vessels, the stomach, and other organs (20)

solid: substance that has a definite shape and a definite volume (3)

solute (SAHL-yoot): in a solution, the substance that dissolves in the solvent (3)

solvent: in a solution, the substance in which the solute dissolves (3)

species: group of organisms that look alike and can reproduce among themselves (5)

sperm: male sex cells (25)

spicules (SPIK-yools): solid structures that give a sponge its shape (12)

spiracles (SPIH-ruh-kuls): small openings near the bottom of each segment of an insect's abdomen (15); pair of openings through which rays and skates take in water (16)

spirilla (spy-RIL-uh): spiral-shaped bacteria (6)

spirochetes (SPY-ruh-keets): corkscrew shaped spirilla (6)

spongin (SPUN-jin): rubberlike substance that makes up some spicules (12)

spongy bone: spongelike material that makes up the ends of bones (20)

spongy layer: layer of cells in a leaf involved in gas exchange (11)

spontaneous (spahn-TAY-nee-us) **generation:** theory that organisms could come from non-living matter (2)

spore: reproductive cell (8, 9)

spore case: structure that contains spores (9)

sporophyte (SPAW-ruh-fyt): asexual generation of a moss or fern that produces spores (9)

sporozoan: parasitic protozoan that cannot move from place to place on its own (7)

stamen (STAY-muhn): male reproductive organ of a flower (11)

stimulant (STIM-yuh-lunt): drug that speeds up the activity of the central nervous system (28)

stimulus (STIM-yoo-lus): change in the environment that causes a response (2)

stomata (STOH-muh-tah): small openings in the underside of a leaf (11)

swim bladder: organ of a fish that allows the fish to remain at any level in the water (16)

symbiotic (sim-by-OT-ik) **relationship:** relationship in which two organisms help each other (8)

synapse (SIN-aps): gap between the dendrites of one neuron and the axon of another (24)

systemic circulation: pathway of blood between the heart and the body excluding the lungs (22)

T

taproot: root system in which one root grows larger than the other roots (11)

technology (tek-NAHL-uh-jee): applied science (1)

tendon: tough, elastic band of tissue that attaches muscles to bones at joints (20)

tendrils: wiry leaves of vines that are used by the plant to cling to objects (11)

terminal (TUR-muh-nul) **bud:** bud located at the tip of a stem (11)

testes (TES-teez): male reproductive organs (25)

testosterone (tes-TAWS-tuhr-ohn): hormone produced in the testes (25)

theory: statement of a principle that has been supported by data over a period of time (1)

tissue: groups of cells that look the same and do the same job (4)

trachea (TRAY-kee-uh): windpipe (23)

tracheophyte (TRAY-kee-uh-fyt): plant in which water and nutrients move through tubelike cells (9)

trait: characteristic of an organism (29)

transpiration (trans-puh-RAY-shun): process by which plants lose water through the stomata in their leaves (11)

transport: life process of moving nutrients and removing waste products (2)

tricuspid valve: valve between the right atrium and right ventricle (22)

trochophore (TRAHK-uh-fawr): larval stage of a mollusk (14)

tropism (TROH-pizm): plant response (2, 11)

tube feet: thin, hollow cylinders ending in suction disks that help a sea star move (14)

tympanum (TIM-puh-num): organ used for hearing by a grasshopper and a frog (15, 17)

U

umbilical (um-BIL-ih-kul) **cord:** structure that connects the embryo to the placenta (25)

univalve: mollusk with one shell (14)

urea (yoo-REE-uh): nitrogen waste filtered out of the blood (23)

ureter (YOUR-et-uhr): tube that carries urine from the kidneys to the urinary bladder (23)

urethra (you-REETH-ruh): tube that carries urine to the outside of the body (23)

urinary bladder: sac that stores urine (23)

urine (YOOR-in): liquid waste (23)

uterus (YOOT-ur-us): female reproductive organ in which the embryo develops (19, 25)

V

vaccines: substances made from dead or weakened bacteria that increase immunity against some diseases (27)

vacuole (VAK-yoo-wohl): storage area in the cytoplasm of a plant cell (4)

vagina (vuh-JY-num): the birth canal (25)

variable (VER-ee-uh-bul): something that can have more than one value (1)

variation: differences among organisms (32)

vascular plant: plant that has vascular tissue in its roots, stems, and leaves (9)

vascular (VAS-kyuh-luhr) **tissue:** tubelike cells of tracheophytes (9)

vas deferens (vas DEF-uh-renz): part of the male reproductive system (25)

vegetative propagation (vej-uh-TAYT-iv prahp-uh-GAY-shun): asexual reproduction in plants (31)

vein: vessel that carries blood to the heart (22)

ventricle (VEN-tri-kuhl): lower chamber of the heart (22)

vertebrates (VUR-tuh-brayts): animals with backbones (16)

villi: tiny, fingerlike projections on the folds of the small intestine (21)

viral replication (rep-luh-KAY-shun): process by which viruses reproduce other viruses (6)

virus: piece of nucleic acid covered with an outer coat of protein (6)

visceral (VIS-uhr-uhl) **mass:** part of a mollusk that contains the body systems and the heart (14)

vitamin: organic nutrient found naturally in many foods (26)

volume: amount of space an object occupies (1)

voluntary muscles: muscles that can be controlled (20)

W

warm-blooded: having a body temperature that remains fairly constant (18)

water-vascular (VAS-kyuh-luhr) **system:** organ system of a sea star used for movement and getting food (14)

white blood cells: cells that protect the body against disease (22)

wildlife: plants and animals in an area (37)

woody stems: thick, hard, nongreen stems (10)

X, Y, Z

X chromosomes: female sex chromosomes (30)

xylem (ZY-luhm): plant tissue that carries water from the roots to the leaves (10)

Y chromosome: male sex chromosome (30)

zygote (ZY-goht): fertilized egg (25)

INDEX

Illustration page numbers are printed in bold type.

A

spores, 120, 126, 128-129, 131
sporophyte, 147, **148**, 148, 150, 154
sporozoans, 112-113
stamen, 187
staphylococci, 96, 96, **98**
stems, 161, 171, **180**, 180-182, **182**
sternum, 309
stimulants, 492
stimulus, **26**, 26
stomach, 366-367
stomata, 184, 186
succession, ecological, 611-612, **612**
sugars, 49, 51
survival of the fit, **556**, 556, 558
Sutton, Walter, 523, 523 *table*
sweat glands, 356, 411
swim bladder, 279, 280
swimmerets, 256
symbiosis, 132
symmetry, 203, 204, **216**, 216, 241
synapse, **421**, 421, 492
syrinx, 312
systemic circulation, 385, 386-387
Systems International (SI), 12, 12 *table*, 649

T

tadpoles, **293**, 293, 294
taiga, 620
tapeworms, **218**, 218, 281, 608
taproot, **178**, 178
taste, sense of, 426-427, 428
taxonomy, 4 *table*, 76, 79-82
Tay-Sachs disease, 533
technology, biology and, 5-6, 540-542, **541**, 543,563
teeth, 315, 328, 329, 331, 364, **365**, **371**
tendons, 352
tentacles, 203-204, 208, 234, 240
terminal bud, 182
territoriality, **335**, 335, 336
testes, 438, 439
testosterone, 438
Theophrastus, 76
theory, 7
therapsid, **322**, 322
thigmotropism, 192
thyroid gland, 431
thyroxine, 431
ticks, 98, **254**, 254-255, 608
tissues, **63**, 63
    plant, 144, 145, 170-171, 172, **179**, 179, 180, 181, 182, 184
tobacco, 497-500

tongue, 364-365
tortoises, **297**, 297
touch, sense of, 426
toxic wastes, 125, 638
toxins, 475
trachea, 400-401
tracheophytes, 144, **145**, 145, 150-154, **151**, **152**, **153**
traits, 508, 509-510, **510**, 526-531, **528**, 538-540
transgenesis, 337
transpiration, 186
transport, 34-35, **35**, 402-403
triceps, **353**, 353
tricuspid valve, 379
trilobites, 562, **572**, 572
trochophore, **234**, 234, 235
tropical rain forests, **619**, 621-622, **640**, 640-641
tropisms, 26, **192**, 192
tubers, 180
tundra, 618-619
turbellarians, 219-221
turtles, **297**, 297
tympanum, 259, 289

U

umbilical cord, **443**, 443-444, 447, 451
United States Recommended Daily Allowances (U.S. RDA), 51, 463
univalves, 234-236, 244
urea, 409
ureter, 411
urethra, 411, **438**, 439
urinary system, **411**, 411
urine, 410-411
uterus, **326**, 326, 440, 441, 445

V

vaccine, **482**, 482-483, 541
vacuole, **62**, 62, 63
vagina, 440, 441, 447
valves, heart, **379**, 379
van Leeuwenhoek, Anton, 56
variables, 8
variations, 551, 556, 560, 561. *See also* adaptation; evolution
vascular bundles, **181**, 181
vascular tissue, 144, 145, 171, 172, 179, 180, 181, 182, 184
vas deferens, 439
vegetable-fruit food group, 177, 464, 464 *table*, 517

vegetative propagation, 542
veins, **381**, 381-382, 444
ventricle, 378-379, 386-387
vertebrae, 272, 420
vertebrates, 268, 272
vestigial structures, 577
villi, **369**, 369, 370
viral replication, 93-95, **95**
Virchow, Rudolph, 56
viroids, 95
viruses, 92-95, 94, 288, 474, 474 *table*, 481, **482**, 482-483, 484
    classification of, 92-93
    disease, caused by, 91, 95, 103, 406, 407, 475, 478
    spread of, 93
visceral mass, 234
vision, 424-425, 584
vitamins, 102, 362, 391, 459-461, 461 *table*
voluntary muscles, 352

W

Wallace, Alfred Russel, 555
warm-blooded animals, 306, 322
water cycle, 602, **603**, 603
water pollution, **638**, 638
water-vascular system, **242**, 242
Watson, James, 524
white blood cells, **388**, 388-389, **480**, 480
wildlife, 317, 640-641
windpipe, 399, 400
withdrawal sickness, 494
woody stems, 161, 171, 181-182
worms, 214-231
    flatworms, 217-221, 222, 245
    rotifers, **223**, 224, 224
    roundworms, **223**, 223, 223 *table*, 229
    segmented, 215, 224-228, **225**, **228**, 608

X, Y, Z

X chromosome, 523, 529, 531
X-rays, 19, 563
xylem, 171, 172, 179, 180, 181, 182

Y chromosome, 523, **529**, 529, 531
yeasts, 131
yellow marrow, 346
yolk sac, 296

zoology, 4
zygote, 443

PHOTO CREDITS

Arnold, (b) Cherseman/Peter Arnold; p. 298, (l) Kleiman/ Photo Researchers, (r) McHugh/Photo Researchers; p. 299, Photo Researchers; p. 301, Heron/Woodfin Camp. **Chapter 18:** p. 304, Sullivan, Rogers/Bruce Coleman; p. 306, McHugh/Photo Researchers; p. 314, Lei/Omni-Photo Communications, Inc. p. 315, (t) McHugh/Photo Researchers, (bl) Claudio/Peter Arnold, (br) Pfletschinger/Peter Arnold; p. 316, (t) Bova/Photo Researchers, (b) Florio/Photo Researchers; p. 317, Morgan/Peter Arnold. **Chapter 19:** p. 320, Pfletschinger/Peter Arnold; p. 323, (t) Bledsoe/Photo Researchers, (b) Maslowski/Visuals Unlimited; p. 324, (l, r) McHugh/Photo Researchers; p. 325, Cancalosi/Peter Arnold; p. 327, Rue III/Animals Animals; p. 328, (t) Cancalosi/Peter Arnold, (b) Cunningham/Visuals Unlimited; p. 330, (t) Kelley/Photo Researchers, (bl) Photo Researchers, (br) Faulkner/Photo Researchers; p. 331, Lindblad/Photo Researchers; p. 332, (t) Animals Animals, (b) McHugh/Photo Researchers; p. 333, Holton/Photo Researchers; p. 335, (tr) Rue III/Photo Researchers. (bl) Shan/Animals Animals; p. 336, Rue III/Photo Researchers; p. 337, Short/Bruce Coleman. **Unit 6:** p. 340, (l) Photo Researchers, (r) Mowbray/Photo Researchers; p. 341, (t) Haling/Photo Researchers, (bl) Hagen-/Griffiths/Omni-Photo Communications, Inc., (br) Anderson/Woodfin Camp & Associates. **Chapter 20:** p. 342, Langley/DPI; p. 346, Photo Researchers; p. 347, Lei/Omni-Photo Communications; p. 348, Photo Researchers; p. 349, Focus on Sports; p. 350, Photo Researchers; p. 352, (l, c) Photo Researchers, (r) Grave/Photo Researchers; p. 356, Eyden/Photo Researchers; p. 357, Migdale/Photo Researchers. **Chapter 21:** p. 360, Photo Researchers; p. 366, The Bettman Archive; p. 370, Rotker/Taurus Photos; p. 371, Weber/Peter Arnold; p. 372, Kage/Peter Arnold; p. 373, (l, r) Dr. Marc Lenchen. **Chapter 22:** p. 376, Kage/Peter Arnold; p. 381, Resche/Peter Arnold; p. 382, Knoll/Taurus Photos; p. 383, (tl, tr) Photo Researchers, (br) Moore/Taurus Photos; p. 385, The Granger Collection; p. 388, (tr) Sklav, Peiper/Photo Researchers, (bl) Oszarzak/Taurus Photos, (br) Dauget/Photo Researchers; p. 389, Kage/Peter Arnold; p. 390, Lei/Omni-Photo Communications, Inc.; p. 391, (t) Rotker/Taurus Photos, (b) Photo Researchers; p. 393, Stoecklein/The Stock Market. **Chapter 23:** p. 396, Bruce Coleman, Inc.; p. 399, Walker/Photo Researchers; p. 406, Rotker/Taurus Photos; p. 408, Lei/Omni-Photo Communications, Inc., p. 409, Rotker/Taurus Photos; p. 413, McIntyre/Photo Researchers. **Chapter 24:** p. 416, Photo Researchers; p. 419, (t) Photo Researchers, (b) Glaubermann/Photo Researchers; p. 420, Laffont/Sygma; p. 424, Eagle/Photo Researchers; p. 427, Photo Researchers; p. 431, Wide World Photos; p. 433, Bill Gallery/Stock Boston. **Chapter 25:** p. 436, Photo Researchers; p. 442, Scharf/Peter Arnold; p. 443, Photo Researchers; p. 444, Photo Researchers; p. 448, (l) Hagen-Griffiths/Omni-Photo Communications, Inc., (r) Szasz/Photo Researchers; p. 449, Kerasate/Photo Researchers; p. 450, Hahn/Taurus Photos; p. 451, Tsiaras/Photo Researchers. **Unit 7:** p. 454, Warren/Photo Researchers; p. 455, (l) The Granger Collection, (r) McIntyre, McIntyre/Sygma. **Chapter 26:** p. 456, Katchusky/Taurus Photos; p. 458, Vandystadt/Photo Researchers; p. 459, Porges/Peter Arnold; p. 463, Bucher/Photo Researchers; p. 464, (all 4) Lei/Omni-Photo Communications; p. 467, Carroll/Peter Arnold; p. 469, Uzzell/Woodfin Camp. **Chapter 27:** Kay/Peter Arnold; p. 475, (t) Richards/Photo Researchers, (b) Pfletschinger/Peter Arnold; p. 478, Maynor/Photo Researchers; p. 480, Kage/Peter Arnold; p. 482, Karp/Omni-Photo Communications, Inc.; p. 485, McCoy/Rainbow. **Chapter 28:** p. 488 DPI; p. 491, Lei/Omni-Photo Communi-

cations, Inc.; p. 492, (l) New York State Division of Substance Abuse Services, (r) Hodge/Peter Arnold; p. 493, Degginger/Earth Scenes; p. 496, (l, r) Rotker/Taurus Photos, (b) Murray/Photo Researchers; p. 498, (l) Lei/Omni-Photo Communications, Inc., (r) Karp/Omni-Photo Communications, Inc; p. 500, (l, r) Rotker/Taurus Photos; p. 501, Karp/Omni-Photo Communications, Inc. **Unit 8:** p. 504, (tl, tr) Pearcy/Animals Animals, (b) Chellman/Animals Animals; p. 505, (l) Peter Arnold, (r) Lesk/ Photo Researchers. **Chapter 29:** Frank/Bruce Coleman; p. 508, The Bettman Archive; p. 511, Dwight Kuhn; p. 517, (t) Smith/Earth Scenes, (b) Department of Agriculture. **Chapter 30:** p. 520, McHugh/Sygma; p. 522, Kage/Peter Arnold; p. 531, Hutchings/Photo Researchers; p. 532, Photo Researchers; p. 533, (tr) McIntyre/Photo Researchers, (bl) Cooper/Peter Arnold. **Chapter 31:** p. 536, Porterfield/Photo Researchers; p. 538, The Granger Collection; p. 539, (t, bl) Palek/Animals Animals, (br) Joyce/Photo Researchers; p. 543, Rotker/Taurus Photos; p. 544, Runk/Grant Heilman; p. 545, Photo Researchers. **Unit 9:** p. 548, (t) The Granger Collection; p. 549, (t) Kage/Peter Arnold, (b) Krasemann/Peter Arnold. **Chapter 32:** p. 550, Zeisler/Peter Arnold; p. 552, (l) Schaefer/Peter Arnold, (r) Leeson, Leeson/Photo Researchers; p. 554, (t) The Granger Collection, (b) Lanting/Photo Researchers; p. 556, (t) DPI, (b) Kent/Animals Animals; p. 557, Cortsinger/Photo Researchers; p. 559, Aushier/Animals Animals; p. 560, McDonald, McDonald/Bruce Coleman; p. 561, Leeson, Leeson/Photo Researchers; p. 563, Susan D'Auria. **Chapter 33:** p. 566, Degginger/Animals Animals; p. 568, (l) Kent/Earth Scenes, (r) Jangoux/Peter Arnold; p. 569, (t) Hodge/Peter Arnold, (b) Murray/Earth Scenes; p. 572, Call/Earth Scenes; p. 579, Morgan/Peter Arnold. **Chapter 34:** p. 582, Manzonowicz/Art Resource; p. 584, Williams/Bruce Coleman; p. 588, (t) American Museum of Natural History, (bl, br) Museum Trustees of Kenya/Photo by Richard Beatty; p. 589, (t) American Museum of Natural History, (r) Musee de l'Homme; p. 590, American Museum of Natural History; p. 591, (l) American Museum of Natural History, (r) McHugh/Photo Researchers; p. 593, Hodge/Peter Arnold. **Unit 10:** p. 596, (t) Weber/Taurus Photos, (b) Hodge/Peter Arnold; p. 597, (l) Reinhard/Photo Researchers, (r) Garradd/Photo Researchers. **Chapter 35:** p. 598, Krasemann/Peter Arnold; p. 602, Lockwood/Animals Animals; p. 605, (tl) Rowell/Peter Arnold, (tc) Kent/Animals Animals, (tr) Bertrand/Peter Arnold, (b) Rue III/Earth Scenes; p. 608, Gross/Peter Arnold; p. 609, D'Alessio/Taurus Photos; p. 610, (l) Schroeder/Animals Animals, (r) Morgan/Peter Arnold; p. 611, Thomas/Photo Researchers; p. 613, Neal/Photo Researchers. **Chapter 36:** p. 616, Krasemann/Peter Arnold; p. 620, (l) McHugh/Photo Researchers, (r) Calhoun, Calhoun/Bruce Coleman; p. 621, (t) Valenti, Valenti/Taurus Photos, (bl) Dick/Animals Animals; (bc) Bayer/Bruce Coleman, (br) Rotner/Omni-Photo Communications, Inc. p. 622, Williams/Taurus Photos; p. 623, Thomas/Taurus Photos; p. 626, Pfletschinger/Peter Arnold; p. 627, (l) Migdale/Photo Researchers, (r) Georgia/Photo Researchers. **Chapter 37:** p. 630, Bucher/Photo Researchers; p. 633, Conklin/Monkmeyer Press Photo Service; p. 634, Degginger/Earth Scenes; p. 635, (l) Kirk/Peter Arnold, (r) Cross/Peter Arnold; p. 636, Mellet/Taurus Photos; p. 638, Photo Researchers; p. 639, (l, c) Lefever/Grant Heilman; p. 640, Hernandez/Photo Researchers; p. 641, Florio/Photo Researchers; p. 642, Allen/Peter Arnold; p. 643, (l) Peter Arnold, (r) Beckwith/Taurus Photos; p. 644, Monroe/Photo Researchers; p. 645, (t) Welsch/Photo Researchers; p. 645 (b) Heron/Woodfin Camp.

PHOTO RESEARCH BY OMNI-PHOTO COMMUNICATIONS, INC.